The Facility Management Handbook

Third Edition

The Facility Management Handbook

Third Edition

David G. Cotts
Kathy O. Roper
Richard P. Payant

AMACOM

AMERICAN MANAGEMENT ASSOCIATION
New York • Atlanta • Brussels • Chicago • Mexico City • San Francisco
Shanghai • Tokyo • Toronto • Washington D.C.

Special discounts on bulk quantities of AMACOM books are available to corporations, professional associations, and other organizations. For details, contact Special Sales Department, AMACOM, a division of American Management Association, 1601 Broadway, New York, NY 10019. Tel: 800-250-5308. Fax: 518-891-2372.

E-mail: specialsls@amanet.org

Website: www.amacombooks.org/go/specialsales

To view all AMACOM titles go to: www.amacombooks.org

This publication is designed to provide accurate and authoritative information in regard to the subject matter covered. It is sold with the understanding that the publisher is not engaged in rendering legal, accounting, or other professional service. If legal advice or other expert assistance is required, the services of a competent professional person should be sought.

Library of Congress Cataloging-in-Publication Data

Cotts, David G.
  The facility management handbook / David G. Cotts, Kathy O. Roper, Richard P. Payant. — 3rd ed.
      p. cm.
  Includes bibliographical references and index.
  ISBN 978-0-8144-1380-7
  1. Real estate management. 2. Building management. I. Roper, Kathy O. II. Payant, Richard P. III. Title.
  HD1394.C68 2010
  658.2—dc22

                                                                    2009014402

Printing number

10 9 8 7 6 5 4 3 2 1

To my friends, mentors, colleagues, employees, and contractors who have shown me that facility management is an applied science and only as good as the results achieved . . . and we achieved much.

DGC

To my wife, Gayle, for her tolerance with me as I spend every available minute reading, writing, and revising. And for her review and positive recommendations.

RP

To my guys, Michael and Mitch, and to all the facility management students and practitioners who provide so much to their organizations.

KOR

Contents

Preface to the Third Edition

The Facility Management Handbook remains the best-selling facility management book ever, and it is about to be translated into its fourth language. It became evident, however, that there was a need for a third revision: The current edition is nine years old. That alone justified the new book, but we also recognized the importance of including the topics of sustainability and security/emergency planning in the rewrite. The catastrophic events of September 11, 2001 had a tremendous influence on the practice of facility management whether managers had security and emergency management in their dossiers or not.

You need only monitor the recent issues of facility management trade publications to recognize the importance of sustainability. We suspect that any FM who does not have the topic high on his agenda will have it placed there by customers. In the past year, most of the trade magazines have devoted entire issues to the topic with followup articles throughout the year.

To provide expertise on these subjects, the co-authors of the new edition are Rich Payant, the facility manager at Georgetown University, a FM author and educator, and Kathy Roper, a professor at Georgia Institute of Technology and acknowledged expert on sustainability.

We have tried to tap into the knowledge base of all of the professional organizations involved in facility management through personal contact and screening their pertinent surveys, research, and publications. In addition, we have contacted our personal network of experts for their opinions of the current status of facility management, its greatest challenges, and its best practices. We acknowledge these sources in the Acknowledgements and have woven their input into our work.

Throughout the *Facility Management Handbook, Third Edition,* we highlight the following:

- How to demonstrate the business value of facility to upper management.
- How to reverse the underfunding of our facility infrastructure which has been documented, in the public sector at least since 1990. This was when the National Research Council's study, *Committing to the Cost of Ownership,* was published.

These are the two great challenges of facility management here at the end of the first decade of the Twenty First century. Every university FM program, the professional associations, and the Federal Facilities Council should be focused on finding answers and prescribing solutions. This book is your authors' initial effort which we hope others will seize upon until the problems are solved.

While the question, "What's changed since the last edition?" is always subjective, we offer the following as major changes, which impact the way facility management is practiced and perceived.

- The profession and the job title are much more accepted and recognized than they were in 1999.
- There are better education programs available based on research and best practices.
- There is an unrelenting cost squeeze on facility departments.
- Some degree of outsourcing is inevitable even in areas that have traditionally resisted this trend, such as government and highly-unionized shops.
- Many of us are struggling with the issue of using illegal labor (or turning a blind eye as some contractors do) versus not having the labor to perform certain tasks.
- The predicted personnel crunch is upon us as "baby boomers" retire from management, supervisory, and technical positions. Economic difficulties notwithstanding, this dictates succession planning even for our own position.
- Areas in which we operate (the built environment, utilities, safety, etc.) are increasingly being regulated by all levels of government.
- Public sector FMs will increasingly accomplish major expansions using public-private partnerships.
- Energy to run our facilities has become a major cost and even greater public relations issue.
- The concept of facility management is expanding world-wide, rapidly driven by the globalization of business, increasing concern for international standards and the growth of professional organizations outside of North America.

- Facility managers are moving away from low-bid contracting in all but the simplest contracting situations.
- Analytical systems have been developed to assist in risk, resource, and financial management.
- A second (perhaps third) generation of facility management information technology is available to assist the facility manager in both managing and promoting his department and projects. In this regard, we will use the acronym IWMS, Integrated Workplace Management System, as a generic term for a system of any manufacturer that supports planning, design, work management, lease management, space management, maintenance management, and some degree of project management within facilities while meshing with the organization's financial and management reporting systems. We are not pushing anyone's product and have not included BIM, Building Information Management, under IWMS.

Regarding the last two items, it may be that the systems are just more accepted. While it is too lengthy to even synopsize here, readers should Google the IBM Center for the Business of Government's report, "Ten Challenges Facing Public Managers." Each of these challenges has a concurrent one for FMs, most of them fully as applicable for the private sector FM as for public sector colleagues and relevant today.

Unfortunately, as we and our experts look at the current and short-term status of the profession, we have some major concerns:

- The function and the facility manager still are not viewed as important within the company as, for example, Human Resources or Information Technology, and their managers.
- Facility managers generally do not have the knowledge or expertise of a business leader. We need to better link facilities with the organization's business strategy to improve our strategic position.
- Facility managers often fail to appreciate the budget as a principal management tool and to insist that it be structured as such. FM departments should "budget like we work."
- There are too many professional/trade organizations in the fields covered by the basic functions of facility management. The leadership of these organizations are starting to talk and even cooperate (IFMA's CEO is on SAME's board, for example) but facility and property managers are not well served by the disparate organizations.
- Facility managers have failed to make the point convincingly that maintenance and repair needs to be funded consistently. The National Science

Foundation has produced report after report on this subject. This situation is compounded by aging infrastructure.

- Customer service, a hot topic when the Second Edition was published, has been seriously ignored as recent cut-backs have forced new priorities.
- Because they are willing to provide resources, vendors have tended to dominate the publications, training, and research of the professional associations.
- Cost considerations have become so paramount in most organizations that it is difficult to obtain adequate funding for required programs.
- Globalization has had a profound effect on facility management. While the profession is becoming recognized internationally, many FM costs (construction, energy, etc.) are literally skyrocketing as the world modernizes.

Because we received positive feedback from those studying for professional designations and from educators, we have retained the basic structure of the book to include the popular "pulse points." While we have upgraded the glossary, we point the reader to an ever-growing one, FMpedia, being compiled at www.IFMAFoundation.org.

Finally, we retain some of the conventions used in the Second Edition which makes it much easier for both the reader and the authors. FM is used as an abbreviation for both facility manager and facility management. Second, when we use the word organization, we mean company, institution, or agency. In those cases where the subject is applicable only to the public or private sector, then we use agency or company. Also, we use *he* when referring to facility managers to avoid the awkward *he* or *she* construction.

Acknowledgments

Prior to writing this book, we actively sought out the professional and trade organizations involved in facility and property management. In addition, we contacted a number of very special experts who, over the years, had impressed us with both their interest in, and their vision for, facility management. In both cases we asked them to assess the current state of facility management and their thoughts on where the profession is going, what its best practices are, and what is holding it back. We are forever thankful for their insights and willingness to both challenge our biases and to provide us their insights. This panel consisted of:

- Dr. William Badger, Professor, Arizona State University, Tempe, AZ
- Ed Buonaccorsi, General Services Administrator, Santa Clara, CA
- Gerald Davis, Consultant and FM standards expert, International Centre for Facilities, Ottawa, Canada
- Stormy Friday, Consultant and author, The Friday Group, Annapolis, MD
- Chris Hodges and Jim Whittaker, Principals, Facility Engineering Associates, Fairfax, VA
- Lenny Jachimowicz, Vice President, Marriott International, Washington, DC
- Diane MacKnight, Consultant, MacKnight Associates, Alexandria, VA
- Trevor Neve, Independent consultant, Logistics Management Institute, McLean, VA
- Michael Schley, FM technology developer and consultant, Raleigh, NC
- John Standish, Maintenance management manager, Smithsonian Institution, Washington, DC
- Eric Teicholz, FM technology developer and consultant, Cambridge, MA

We also requested that the professional and trade organizations point us to pertinent research and literature to share with you, the reader. A hearty thanks to all who responded, particularly Shari Epstein, IFMA's Director of Research and David Neun, Director of Education for BOMI. Your considerations appear both generally and specifically throughout this book.

Over the years, facility management experts have striven to improve the profession in specific areas by serving on committees, by writing and speaking well, and, above all, by practicing what they preach. While all of them have broad knowledge to share in all aspects of facility management, we would like to recognize them, in alphabetical order, for their diligence in providing the best possible advice to the profession in their special area of expertise in many venues over a long period of time.

- Gerald Davis and Francoise Szigeti-standardization
- James Elledge-general knowledge
- Stormy Friday-organizational development and business skills/outlook
- Victoria Hardy-education
- Chris Hodges-sustainability
- Michael Hoots-financial and business management
- Dr. Dean Kashiwagi-innovative contracting
- Peter Kimmel-knowledge management
- Fred Klammt-research based practice
- Dr. Bernard Lewis (deceased)-operations and maintenance/authorship
- Edmond Rondeau-real estate
- Nancy Sanquist-information management
- Eric Teicholz-information management

You have been both a source of information and inspiration to us over the years.

Every book is a cooperative effort. We would like to recognize our editors at AMACOM, particularly Bob Shuman and Kate Rounds, who insisted that, while we dotted the i's and crossed the t's and stayed on schedule, we produce a book that is user-friendly and a step forward for our profession. We hope you find it as such.

SECTION

Background and Organization

This opening section deals with the nature of facility management, particularly its relationship to the business environment it supports. We emphasize the need for the facility manager to be a business leader and emphasize just what that means. We discuss what organizations and executives expect of facility managers and present a profile of success for facility managers. Finally, we look at organizations that can be adapted to meet the requirements of various organizations (but are too often ignored) and discuss the increasing difficult staffing issues to fill those organizations.

The Nature of Facility Management

Pulse Points

- *Both the organization and the facility manager should have a specific philosophy about facilities.*
- *Facility management is an essential business function; the facility manager is a business manager and should be placed at the same level as the managers of human relations and/or information technology.*
- *Different types of organizations require different approaches to facility management (and services may be provided in-house or contracted out), but there are a limited number of ways to organize depending upon the mission.*
- *Every FM organization will have some element contracted-out so contract negotiation and administration skills are essential for every facility manager. Facility managers need to be innovative in their contracting. Low-bid contracts are seldom appropriate, and we must partner with our contractors and consultants while insisting that they perform if they are to continue working for us.*
- *Good facility management is based on good leadership of a proper organization.*
- *Facility managers need to have the same level of business skills as their management colleagues.*
- *Facility managers must know their business—both the FM business and the business they support.*
- *While it is improving, facility management needs better basic research and better application of both existing research and best practices.*
- *Every facility manager should have a facility master plan as a priority. Included should be a recapitalization plan covering at least ten years. These two efforts not only will be key to your management, but will show that you know the language of business and are interested in the business planning of an organization.*

- *Facility managers are in a position where they can influence how substantial organizational resources are spent. Conduct your business with the highest degree of ethics and a sense of stewardship.*
- *Sustainability, security, and emergency management are functions with great management and customer interest, which every FM must accommodate.*
- *There has never been the emphasis on cost that there is now and facility managers, to be successful, must realize that fact.*
- *The FM professional associations should combine their efforts to constantly survey the attitudes of company and agency executives toward facility managers. The associations should encourage facility management being taught in business schools as well as supporting more FM degree programs.*
- *The FM professional associations should demonstrate and publicize that effective and efficient facility management has a payoff for organizations.*
- *The FM professional associations should participate in and coordinate their research efforts with the Federal Facilities Council.*

Facility management, commonly abbreviated as FM, is a fairly new business and management discipline to the private sector. In the public sector, however, it has been practiced as post engineering, public works, or plant administration for many years. In leased property, the profession is titled property management or building operating management though most of the required skills are the same as those needed in owned property. Outside of North America, until recently, facility management functions were often subsumed deep in the administrative structure of both private and public sector organizations.

The most recent definition of facility management is "a profession that encompasses multiple disciplines to ensure functionality of the built environment by integrating people, place, process, and technology."[1] It is interesting to note that this newest definition highlights the importance of technology, which was lacking previously. Exhibit 1-1 defines facility management in terms of commonly performed functions and sub-functions. This is more understandable to someone new to the profession. Every facility manager will be involved in managing the first fifteen of those functions either as the principal manager or as a major supporting manager. General Administrative Services (Function 16) tend to be managed by facility managers in very small organizations and by FMs, often Vice Presidents of Administration, in very large organizations.

In North America security and emergency management has become much more important to both the public and private sector since September 11, 2001. Companies and governments anywhere ignore these functions at their own peril.

When the first edition of *The Facility Management Handbook* was written, widespread office technology, networking, and wire management were just starting to have a major influence on the profession. By the second edition, the necessity to

Exhibit 1-1. Common functions of facility management

Management of the Organization
- Planning
- Organizing
  — By function, organization or location
  — Centralized versus user driven
- Staffing
  — Personnel management
  — Evaluation of mix of staff, consultants, and contractors
  — Training
- Directing
  — Work scheduling
  — Work coordination
  — Policy and procedure development
- Controlling
  — Work reception
  — Standards establishment (dollar range, quality, quantity, time to deliver)
  — Scheduling
  — Use of management information systems and new information technologies
  — Contract administration
  — Policy and procedure execution
- Evaluating
  — Design
  — Punch-list preparation and execution
  — Post occupancy evaluation
  — Program analysis
  — Contractor evaluation

Facility Planning and Forecasting
- Business unit knowledge gathering
- Strategic facility planning (three to ten year plans)
- Facility operational planning (twelve months to three years)
- Space forecasting (macro-level, organization-wide)
- Macro-level programming (organization-wide)
- Financial forecasting and macro-level estimating (organization-wide)
- Capital program development

(continued)

Exhibit 1-1. (continued)

Lease Administration
- Outleasing (as owner)
- Lease administration (as owner or lessee)
- Property management (as lessee)

Space Planning. Allocation, and Management
- Space allocation
- Space inventory
- Space forecasting (micro-level, one location)
- Space management

Architectural/Engineering Planning and Design
- Macro-level programming (one location)
- Building planning
- Architectural design
- Engineering design of major systems
- Macro-level estimating (one location)
- "As built" maintenance
- Disaster recovery planning
- Design document preparation and updating
- Code compliance
- Traffic engineering
- Zoning compliance

Workplace Planning, Allocation, and Management
- Workplace planning
- Workplace design
- Furniture specification
- Furnishings specification
- Estimating
- "As built" maintenance
- Code compliance

Budgeting, Accounting, and Economic Justification (Done concurrently with Planning and Design)
- Programming (same period covered as for space planning unless otherwise specified by the company)
- Work plan preparation

- Budget preparation (1-2 years)
  — Administrative
  — Capital
  — Operations and maintenance
  — Chargeback
- Economic justification
- Financial forecasting (1-2 years)
- Budget formulation
- Budget execution

Real Estate Acquisition and Disposal
- Site selection and acquisition
  — Environmental due diligence
  — Legal due diligence
- Building purchase
- Building lease
- Real estate disposal

Sustainability (these functions normally done concurrently with other functions)
- Site selection decisions to minimize environmental impacts
- Environmental policies to minimize waste and reduce resource usage
  — Recycling program management
  — Transportation management
  — Energy audits and retrofits
  — Building commissioning
  — Building systems audits and retrofits
  — Purchasing policies for reduced environmental impacts
  — Vendor relationship management for sustainability
  — Indoor air quality management
- Project management in compliance with environmental regulation
  — Federal, state, and local requirements
  — Sustainable guidelines adoption (LEED, Green Globes, Energy Star, etc.)
- Workplace improvements for productivity
  — Daylighting
  — Indoor air quality
  — Thermal comfort
- Aligning design with business functions
  — Sustainable maintenance and operations practices
  — Social responsibility reporting

(continued)

Exhibit 1-1. (continued)

Construction Project Management
- Project management
- Construction management
- Procurement management
- Preparation of "as builts"
- Project evaluation

Move, Add, Change (MAC) management
- Alteration management
- Renovation management
- Furniture installation
- ICT installation
- Provision of furnishings
- Art program management
- Equipping
- Relocations
- Procurement (to move, alter, change)
- Preparation of "as builts"
- Project management

Operations, Maintenance and Repair
- Exterior maintenance (roofs, shell, and window systems)
- Preventive maintenance
- Breakdown maintenance
- Cyclic maintenance
- Grounds maintenance
- Road maintenance
- Custodial maintenance
- Pest and rodent control
- Trash removal
- Hazardous waste management
- Energy management
- Inventory of systems and equipment
- Maintenance projects
- Repair projects
- Correction of hazards (asbestos, bad air quality, radon, underground leaks, PCBs, etc.)
- Disaster recovery
- Procurement (operations, maintenance, and repair supplies and services

---

Technology Management
- Operations
- Maintenance
- Central voice operations
- Data system operations and reconfiguration
- Network management
- "As built" maintenance
- Integrated Workplace Management System (IWMS)
  — Selection
  — Installation
  — Operation

Facility Emergency Management
- Emergency preparedness planning
- Threat assessment
- Command, control and communications
- Mitigation strategies
- Training, drill and exercise
- Disaster recovery planning

Security and Life-Safety Management
- Code compliance
- Operations
- Crime prevention through environmental design
- Access control
- Physical deterrents
- Electronic security
- Vulnerability assessment

General Administrative Services
- Food services
- Reprographics
- Mail and messenger management
- Fleet management
- Property disposal
- Moving services
- Procurement (as a function)
- Health and fitness program management
- Day care center management
- Concierge services and on-site vendors
- Landscaping and plant management
- Records management and storage
- Assembly management support and security

accommodate this technology actually drove building design in some cases. Now, we have adapted to the wide-spread use of office technology in our FM practice.

Sustainability, security, and emergency management have also edged to the front of the facility manager's plate. A recent IFMA Foundation-funded study showed that finance dominated facility manager's concerns.

Calling facility management "asset management," the National Research Council (NRC) in its 2008 report on "Core Competencies for Federal Facilities Asset Management through 2020, lists competencies for future managers that are highly coincident with those we list in Exhibit 1-1.[2] We personally feel that yet another change of terminology, from facility management to asset management, will only confuse our bosses and the business community and hope that the NRC might revisit that portion of their study.

Defining these functions becomes very important because they form the framework for professional development, research, and professional competency testing for the profession. The International Facility Management Association (IFMA), for example, has organized the functions into "competencies" around which it designs all of its professional programs. It is our opinion that one of the areas where the various professional organizations could first come together is in defining just what functions the facility managers should manage, and we offer Exhibit 1-1 as a starting point for that discussion.

Facility management embraces the concepts of cost-effectiveness, productivity, improvement, efficiency, and employee quality of life. In practice, these concepts often seem to be in conflict. For example, many facility managers find themselves sinking in the quicksand of diminishing white-collar productivity, placed at the precipice of office air-quality problems, or embroiled in waste management issues that pre-date their employments. Providing customer responsive services during these times of unrelenting cost cuts is a monumental challenge. Employee expectations and concerns almost always come before clear-cut technical or financial solutions. Often there are no set answers—only management decisions that must be made. It is this constant *ying* and *yang* of facility management; to balance the needs of the organization against the financial restrictions required to allow the operational units of the business to expand and grow.

Some say Murphy (of Murphy's law "If something can go wrong it will go wrong.") was a facility manager. Every good facility manager is a good *reactive* manager because reaction is a fact of life in delivering services. However, we cannot allow ourselves to be totally reactive managers. That approach can downplay planning, even though planning is the key to cost-effectiveness. You may not agree with all our facility management philosophy. However, a facility manager who does not have a philosophy regarding his position, his department, and the facilities managed cannot provide the leadership needed by the company.

The Development of Facility Management

The management of very large and complex facilities is not new to some people. Many municipal public works directors, facility managers of national or international corporations, or collegiate plant administrators first managed large facilities in the military. The Association of Facilities Engineering (AFE) and the Association of Higher Education Facilities Officers (APPA) were among the first to organize disparate professionals with diverse backgrounds into professional associations. Early in the 1980s the Facility Management Institute spun off the National Facility Management Association (NFMA). Canadian interest, however, soon led to the conversion of NFMA to the International Facility Management Association (IFMA).

Currently, the Building Owners and Managers Association (BOMA) and the BOMI Institute have similarly organized and served property and building managers. Professionals devoted to real estate acquisition, management, and disposal have similarly organized. In general, all of these organizations try to inform and educate their membership, provide professional designation(s), research their areas of expertise, and hold networking events bringing together their members and the vendors who service them. Some lobby politically, some don't.

Within the U.S. federal government there have been sporadic attempts to organize their facility managers. Uniformed services and their retirees have come together as part of the Society of American Military Engineers (SAME). Attempts have been made to organize federal facility managers in the Washington, D.C. area. The Federal Facilities Council, part of the NRC, is not truly a professional membership association, but serves as a focal point for federal FMs.

It is unrealistic to imagine that this panoply of organizations is instantaneously going to merge into a single international organization, or even one North American one. However, it is our sincere belief that cooperation in the areas of research, education, and professional designations is overdue. We see some encouraging signs (IFMA and SAME share a director on their boards, for example). There has been recent research cooperation among some of the organizations. But it will take enlightened management to move this effort toward better conformity and more consistent and enlightened memberships. Recent international efforts, mostly regional and national, have been encouraging.

Perceptions of the Profession and its Professionals

Often facility managers, in both the public and private sectors, either do not realize or fail to understand how they are perceived within their organizations—a major problem for the profession and for individual facility managers. Historically, facility managers and their departments have been viewed as:

- Caretakers
- Naysayers
- Advocates for employee welfare
- Controllers
- Employee efficiency multipliers
- Heavily reliant on the Purchasing Department
- Service providers
- Producers of voluminous policies and regulations
- Project handlers
- Major consumers of the administrative budget

Not all of these attributes are bad, but the business and government worlds are changing and so must we. Here are important business and cultural trends that have radically changed the private and public sectors:

Business Trends
- Focus on cost reduction and shareholder value
- Internationalization
- Rise of the chief financial officer
- Outsourcing
- Rising cost, particularly in the construction area
- The growth of E-commerce
- The integration of facility resource information into corporate business data
- Emphasis on speed of delivery
- Improved information technology particularly in the areas of architectural/engineering planning and work management
- Increased use of public/private partnerships
- The importance of the knowledge economy
- New sustainability initiatives and targets
- Concern about security and emergency preparedness

Cultural Trends
- Aging of the population
- Lack of skilled tradesmen
- An increasingly diverse workforce
- Environmental concerns
- Lack of loyalty and trust in institutions

- Generational perceptions of the value/use/importance of the workplace
- Concern for better ethics and stewardship

A new facility manager profile emerges based on these trends. The facility manager moves from a narrow technical focus where the language is "FMspeak" to the expanded viewpoint of a business leader who helps the company take a strategic view of its facilities and their impact on productivity. Here are the characteristics of a successful facility manager in today's business environment:

- Business leader
- Strategic business planner and implementer
- Resource obtainer
- Financial manager
- Spokesperson and advocate
- Agile purchaser, lessor, and contractor with a major regard for ethics
- Information manager
- Environmentalist
- Networker
- Mentor
- Innovator
- Risk taker
- Survivor

Having said this, a recent Aberdeen Group study of the industry states, "Although real estate and facilities life-cycle management has been viewed as playing a more strategic role within enterprises, the ultimate impact of these groups (facility and building management) is in question."[3] This should cause us all to pause. Are we really projecting the management image that we want? Why aren't facilities viewed as strategic as human resources and information technology, for instance?

Facility managers who thrive in the current environment have shed the role of technician and have adopted the characteristics shown in the above list. Unfortunately not everyone agrees (or has "gotten the word") and some facility managers think they can survive purely on their technical expertise. The professional organizations are trying to train their members to be better business-people and communicators. Clinging to the comfort zone of the boiler room and the work management center will relegate facility managers to a lesser role and reaction mode—if they are able to retain their positions at all.

Our bosses have not been queried on how they view our performance in over ten years (An IFMA survey of senior business and government managers, *View from the Top...Executives Evaluate the Facility Management Function* took place in 1997).

This might well be an effort worth pursuing again. A 2005 panel of distinguished industry experts (one of the book's authors participated) selected the following management traits as necessities for future success as a facility manager:

- Leadership and human relations skills
- The importance of overcoming "information silos," which keep healthy idea "cross-pollination" from occurring between facility managers and other groups such as IT and the corporate executive suite
- The ability of a facility manager to quantify contributions to the productivity of the organization
- The ability of a facility manager to quantify the impact of various facility initiatives on the productivity of the employees and the organization
- Understanding the financial metrics of the organization
- Comprehending value to the end user of the facility
- Communicating the strategic importance of the facility as a tool to support the organizational vision. This is best illustrated by the facility manager's role in supporting the daily mission of personnel.
- Perceiving the knowledge economy in terms of meeting the needs of the facility's end users
- Comprehending the use of technology for adding value
- Understanding the concept of branding a facility for purposes of meeting the strategic needs of a facility's end users[4]

A quick review of that list shows a dramatic shift of needed skills. The shift over the last ten years provides important clues to the education needed for those in professional organizations and college FM.

The Development of a Facility Management Philosophy

Considering both the trends and the expectations of facility managers, we have developed a philosophy for the professional practice of FM, and we recommend it to each facility manager.

- View facility management as a business function understanding the financial and organizational impact of our actions.
- Safety is always the first concern followed by legality, cost, and customer service.
- Someone should be directly responsible for every physical asset and function.
- There is a cost of ownership of facilities; it is the FM's task to ensure that management understands that cost.

- The facility manager's responsibility to management is well known; the FM should concentrate on responsibility to the employees.
- The facility manager should be cost-conscious in everything he does and capture all costs in his analyses.
- If something looks like a good idea, try it. If it doesn't work, change it.
- A good, commonsense decision beats "paralysis by analysis."
- The budget should be the chief management information tool. Put effort into its preparation and format, and then monitor its execution carefully.
- Every physical asset should be under appropriate life-cycle management.
- When an outside consultant is used, take care and time in defining requirements.
- Clarify life-cycle and sustainable design and operational intents before launching new projects.
- As the design-construct cycle proceeds, changes become costlier and less effective. The facility manager must retain control of the design-construct cycle.
- In the planning of major projects, engineering requirements are nearly always understated.
- Plan for flexibility and redundancy in building systems if the FM plans to occupy them permanently.
- Plan with care, and always retain the capability to react.
- Cultivate long-term relationships. Remember that the successful facility management organization is a team (staff, suppliers, contractors, consultants).
- Remember that the customer—and the customer alone—defines service. The facility manager's responsibility is to find out how his customer rates his services.
- The facility manager must regularly measure both the effectiveness and the efficiency of the department.
- The facility manager must be active in public relations outside the department. If he doesn't promote his department, who will?
- The best way to save money is to participate in facility business planning. A facility business plan should support the company business plan. Business plans should be the result of long-range facility master plans.
- The facility manager should prioritize the development of a facility management information system with the budget as the base document.
- Conduct oneself with a high regard for ethics.

When all facility managers adopt these elements of philosophy, or if they adopt their own, the practice of FM will improve immensely. Too often facility managers view themselves as victims or are so bogged down in their day-to-day work that they fail to grasp the truly important aspects of success. Not every point in the list is equally applicable to every organization, but facility managers who have a specific philosophy of leading are those who lead best.

There are twelve major actions that every facility manager should take in managing facilities and his department successfully. We call them the Big Twelve and they appear as Exhibit 1-2. When put into action, the facility manager has the tools to exhibit his leadership. Without them, there will be gaps in funding, staff, service assessment, or information. Some of the Big Twelve are duplicates of items in the philosophy we have already stated; actually, all of them are an outgrowth of it. If you have accomplished all of these tasks or are working on them, you probably have a good handle on your position and department. Your success will then depend on your ability as a leader because the basic building blocks of success are in place.

Exhibit 1-2. Big Twelve

1. Conduct and regularly update an assessment of both physical facilities and operations.
2. Measure! Measure! Measure!
3. Develop a Facilities Master Plan from which all mid-and annual planning derives. As part of the Master Plan, include a recapitalization plan covering at least ten years.
4. Get your organization right. Don't confuse staffing with organization.
5. In all but special cases, staffing will be a blend of staff, contractors, and consultants to minimize cost and maximize flexibility.
6. Institute a customer-based quality program that uses multiple means to obtain customer input.
7. Determine the information you need to manage and then develop automation to produce it for you. Your facility management information system should be budget-based.
8. Institute facility business planning which can feed into company business planning even if you are initially rebuffed by company planners. Use the company's criteria and system for making financial decisions.
9. Show results! Companies don't pay off for good intentions and plans. View your department as a business within your company.
10. Use innovative contracting. For other than simple contracting situations, low-bid contracting will result in unsatisfactory results. Partner with your contractors and consultants but demand that they perform if they are to continue to work with you.
11. Have a public relations plan each year that targets each of the constituencies that you have identified.
12. Get management commitment to good facility management. You, and you alone, can obtain it. It is worth the effort.

If we were a new facility manager, the Big Twelve is a roadmap for success within the organization!

Professional organizations should structure their research, training, and publishing efforts on this philosophy, particularly the Big Twelve. We do a good job of training the technical aspects of our jobs (O&M, project management, etc.) but need more education on the management aspects of being a success in the modern organization.

Facility Management as a Business Function

Although there has been improvement, the under-management of facilities found in Harvard and MIT studies twenty years ago[5] remains, often due to the fact that the CEO and CFO have been totally focused on current operating costs. An excellent example of this is the current condition of the Washington, DC Metro system, which increasingly finds itself unable to meet the demands of its customers.[6] This total concentration on annual costs with no view of long-term impacts, the necessity to uphold stock value quarterly, and the inability to raise taxes, have caused both the private and public sectors to be slow to realize the serious financial impact of facility management on long-term business health. For too long they have viewed their facilities with blinders on. For example:

- Facilities management is big business. For example, the U.S. Department of Defense has over 347,000 buildings accounting for over 2.3 billion square feet with a value of $838 billion in their last base structure report.[7]
- After payroll, facilities are usually the greatest component of an organization's administrative expense.
- Some facility departments have saved or avoided costs in the 30-35 percent range with no diminution of services. They've done this by applying sound principles of planning, lease management, and energy management.

Yet most facility managers are viewed narrowly as technical not business managers. Most MBA candidates are not even exposed to the subject. In fact, FM courses, other than real estate, are not even available to students in business school. No wonder facility managers first have to "sell" their program to upper management who are the product of these institutes.

Facility management is the quintessential business function, affecting not only revenues and costs but production, quality of life for employees, health and safety, the work environment and, increasingly, areas such as recruitment and employee retention. When facility management is practiced properly, the following benefits accrue to the organization:

- Facility plans match the organization's plans.
- Properly outfitted space is available when and where it is needed.
- Capital expenditures are planned and controlled.
- Employee productivity is maximized.
- Costs are minimized, sometimes avoided, and always predicted.

All experienced facility managers have "horror stories" of being kept out of the loop on some organizational strategic initiative. They then have to either make an unwise real estate decision at the last minute or spend premium construction dollars to ensure that facilities are ready to support the initiative.

One of our panel experts, Trev Neve, a consultant to a government think tank has a unique perspective on the business side of FM. He has managed facilities, consulted on improving the management of many others, and has been a founding instructor on a FM certification course (so he has seen FM from all sides). Trev has also been one of the principal advocates of better business practices and approaches within our FM organizations. He strongly advocates master facility planning as the basis for all other planning and operations. Trev is forceful when stating that part of that master plan should be a recapitalization plan covering at least ten years.

This allows us to do three crucial things:
- Replace worn-out and inefficient equipment,
- Meet sustainability goals through implementation of energy savings measures, and
- Be in synch with organizational business goals and show that we are capable of good business analysis.

In the recent *Facilities Industry Study,* all major FM organizations, FMLink, and *Building Operating Management* magazine asked their members and readers to list the skill sets they most needed to be successful. Not only was it encouraging to see the cooperation among the professional organizations, the results showed some progress toward a philosophy of FM in the selected skill sets. Those skills considered most important are:

- Customer service—40 percent
- Operations and maintenance—31 percent
- Communications—29 percent
- Project management—21 percent
- General management—19 percent
- Financial—17 percent

- Strategic planning—15 percent
- All other topics received—under 10 percent

Only two of those topics are technical in nature showing that FMs have "gotten the word." They need business skills.

When asked what they envision to be the issues of the future, we are encouraged to see that FMs recognize and envision the following as being challenges for themselves in the future:

- Outsourcing—43 percent
- Changing demographics of the workforce—38 percent
- Increased globalization—30 percent
- Mergers/acquisitions and their effect on facilities—30 percent
- Labor shortages—25 percent
- Resource scarcity (and its effect on prices)—23 percent
- Distributed work arrangements (like telework) and their impact on facilities—22 percent
- Shared services—21 percent
- The existence of facility management as a profession—20 percent
  (*Facilities Industry Study*, Association for Facilities Engineering, The Association of Higher Education Facilities Officers, Building Owners and Managers Association, International Facility Management Association, FMLink, and *Building Operating Management*, 2004.)

Except for the last item which is shocking in its insight, it is apparent that FMs are becoming business oriented. They understand that their world extends beyond the boiler room and the work reception center. So, we need to prepare for the future by having better education programs for FMs, by conducting more and better research, and by providing better literature and educational offerings for them from professional organizations. The bottom line of all of this is that the profession is changing and that FMs realize this (perhaps better than those of us who serve them do).

For those new to the profession or who are striving to achieve their certification, IFMA offers an excellent seminar, *The Business of FM,* to teach both the business of FM and FM as a business.

Profile of a Current Facility Manager

While it is more difficult to define the typical facility manager now than when IFMA conducted periodic FM profiles, it is interesting to note that, in the *Facilities Industry*

Study mentioned above, the plurality of those studied have the job title *manager* with 7 percent listed as vice president. 22 percent of FMs now have Masters degrees. More than half have sought and gained professional designation in the profession; 23 percent have an additional professional designation outside the profession (professional designations are gaining cachet). By far, the individuals surveyed were traditional FMs with the majority of their responsibilities being those normally associated with the profession. Not surprisingly, the responsibilities most frequently added to the FM portfolio in the past year are disaster planning/recovery (18 percent), managing more facilities (18 percent), and computer-aided facility management (16 percent). While the data is not exactly comparable to the old study mentioned, it would appear that FMs are, in general, managing more space than they did then. Interestingly, there is a substantial group managing under 500,000 square feet and an equally large group managing over 1,000,000 square feet. Disturbingly, 58 percent of the respondents are managing with the same budget or less from the previous year. The perceived major challenge of the FM position from 3–5 years ago, doing more with less, remains the same but intensified.

As we look both at this profile of FMs and the other results of the survey, we return to the Big Twelve. These elements are critical to the practice of better facility management, the better acceptance of the critical alignments of facility management to organizational success, and for better education, literature, and research in our profession.

Major Themes of Facility Management

Certain FM themes run through this book. We return to them again and again because they are derived from our philosophy, our reading of research and best practices, and our own experience.

- The cost of ownership. There are initial and ongoing costs to the ownership of facilities. These have been documented repeatedly by the National Academy of Sciences. Management must understand and provide for those costs, from planning through disposal.
- Life-cycle costing. As a general rule, all economic analyses and comparisons should be based on life-cycle costs. Bad decisions are often made when only capital or initial costs are considered.
- Integration of services. Good management means integrating different facility services (e.g., design and operations).
- Design for operations, maintenance, and sustainability. Operators and maintainers, even if they are contractors, must be actively involved in the design review process.

- Delegated responsibility. In large organizations, FM functions should be grouped into budget programs, with a manager responsible and accountable for each.
- Cost-effectiveness. The key is to identify and compare costs with meaningful benchmarking partners, and make those comparisons regularly over time.
- Efficiency improvement. Efficiency should be judged constantly through comparators, user feedback, and management-by-walking-around.
- Quality of life. The facility manager must actively promote and protect the employee quality of life. A safe workplace is the minimum; a workplace where the facility promotes individual and group productivity should be the goal.
- Integration of elements. The facility manager is the company's expert on facilities (the place), those factors which determine the success of work (the process), the documentation of those factors and systems (the technology), the employees (the people), and how they all come together.
- Redundancy and flexibility. Because the nature of this work is always partly reactive, the facility manager must build flexibility into the facilities, his organization, and departmental procedures.
- Facilities as assets. The facilities should be viewed as a valued asset (not just on the organization's books), that contribute in numerous ways to the company mission. *If this concept is sold to management, then the rest of the mission automatically becomes easier.* There is growing evidence that employees are judging employers on the quality of the facilities; this may make this argument easier.[8]
- FM as a business function. The facilities deserve to be managed in a businesslike manner. Facilities must be developed in parallel with the organization's business and planned to the same degree.
- FM as a continuum. FM is a continuum, from planning through disposal. It is not a series of discrete projects.
- Service. FM provides only one product, service. The nature of FM is likely to emphasize control and compliance, whereas he should demonstrate flexibility and service. This is particularly true in the public sector. A quality program is based on how service is perceived by the customer, and this must be sought in multiple ways. A successful service program depends on long-term relationships and commitment at all levels.
- Contracting. A facility manager must be an agile procurer of services. Traditional contracting methods are often subject to poor service, unsatisfactory performance, higher costs through change orders, and poor contractor-FM cooperation. Contracting should be ethical, performance-based, and stress partnership and equity for all parties.

The Facility Management Life Cycle

Exhibit 1-3 depicts the life cycle of any facility requirement. The only variables are space and complexity. For smaller facility departments, the landlord meets all or most of its space, build-out, operations, maintenance, and repair needs through terms agreed on in the lease. In owned facilities (normally associated with larger facility departments), functions like design, construction, or alterations may be done by outsiders, but control is resident in the facility manager.

Eventually a facility is occupied, operated, maintained, and repaired. Sometimes it is altered for use beyond its original intent. (Adaptive reuse has been popular in the revitalization of urban areas where, for example, old warehouses have been converted into trendy condos or apartments.)

A facility is probably evaluated several times during its lifetime. Does it fit its original intent? Is it worth renovating? Is an upgrade economical? Such evaluations may lead to renewed life through alteration or to a decision to dispose of the facility through sale or demolition. Gerald Davis at the International Centre for Facilities has been a pioneer in developing a rating scheme for comparing the serviceability of buildings. Serviceability is a system for rating the suitability of a facility for a particular organization.

Types of Organizations

Every organization has its unique personality, and the facility department is a reflection of that personality. All facility managers share some common characteristics in management style; however, the emphasis varies with the type of organization.

There is an almost infinite number of organizational cultures that we could examine. In the total universe of facility managers, there is a great deal of diversity (too much, in our opinion) of organization, policy, and procedures. Here we will discuss only the major cultures in which most facility managers operate. The technical environment in which the facility manager and the department must operate, together with its corporate climate, dictate the envelope in which the facility manager functions.

FM in the Public Sector

In general, no facility manager handles as diverse facilities, with as consistently inadequate resources, as a municipal, state, or federal manager.[9] Two of the authors have experience in this venue; one's entire career has been spent in this environment.

The public sector has a culture overwhelmingly shaped by bureaucracy. That is not a derogation; it is a fact. Nearly every action is governed by a regulation. Also,

Exhibit 1-3. Facility management life cycle.

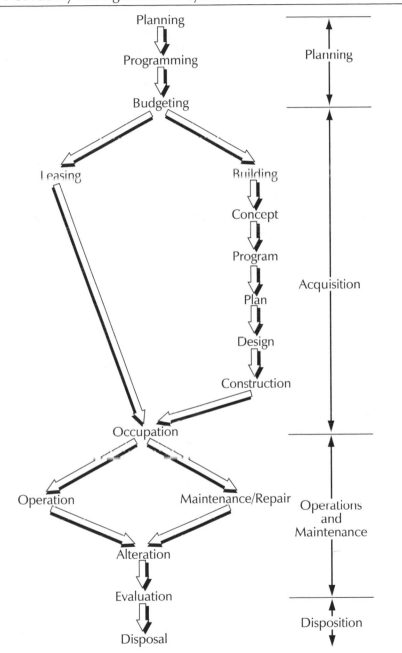

Note:
Operations and Maintenance is the longest phase, often 15–25 times
longer than all other phases for normal building use.

except for capital construction, public-sector programs are subject to the vagaries of short-term budgets. Change is difficult, particularly if it depends on another department, because there is little incentive for cooperation.

Two particularly difficult areas are procurement and personnel. Public-sector procurement policies are thick with detail and regulation. Thus, the facility manager often is at the mercy of a purchasing or contracting officer, whose priorities are not necessarily coincident with those of the FM. Other seemingly inevitable conflicts involve sole-sourcing vendors and products (often the most economical way to contract in terms of time and money from the procurement standpoint) and contract negotiations. Though directed (sole-source) procurements are at the heart of standardization programs, they are generally opposed or made bureaucratically difficult by public-sector purchasing departments. Similarly, many public-sector procurements, particularly extensions of existing contracts, are made more difficult because the purchasing department views negotiations as procurement with very limited applicability. They also think it should be avoided. Both of these situations arise because most public-sector purchasing departments (1) are overregulated by their legislative body, (2) are overworked and truly underpaid, and (3) have a low-bid mentality. (As explained later in this book, competitive bidding has its place, but its effectiveness is generally overstated. Also, it almost inevitably ratchets down the quality of service provided with each rebid.)[10] These inflexible procurement approaches greatly influence the climate in which the public sector facility manager must function.

There never seems to be enough money to accomplish the annual work plan in the public sector.[11] Almost all North American public-sector facility managers face an ever-increasing backlog of work. When this backlog is presented to the appropriate legislative body, the reaction has been to "shoot the messenger" by attacking the credibility of the facility manager. Capital projects, though, tend to have long planning cycles and fare better in legislatures because they bring "pork" to legislative districts. Thus, managing shortages of resources is a fact of life for the public-sector facility manager.

Maintaining a quality workforce is a particular problem in public life. The lack of managers and trained technical people could, in fact, be described as a human resource crisis.[12] Despite what people say, it is generally difficult to eliminate an unneeded position, especially if the position is filled, or to create a new position, particularly in a union environment. For this reason, public sector facility managers have increasingly contracted out many functions or turned to consultants to achieve management flexibility. Unfortunately, most public sector facility managers' actions are bound by the rigid human resources system endemic in government.

The public-sector facility manager must also be a particularly good reactor, since he may have been forced to backlog proactive programs to eliminate crises. And he must be cost-conscious, since funds in the public sector tend to come in specified "pipelines." It means knowing the system so that funds can be shifted from one account to another at the right time—legally. Also, it is a challenge to ensure that all funds are used on meaningful work items, even though some might not be top departmental priorities. Additionally, the facility manager must have *do-able* work that can soak up funds from other departments' excess funds in the last thirty days of a fiscal year.

Public-sector facility management is framed in regulation. No one will remember who upgraded the electrical system, but everyone will remember who misallocated funds, even if done unwittingly. A public-sector facility manager needs to be legally smart and conscious of the do's and don'ts of the bureaucracy.

Finally, the public-sector facility needs to maintain a special relationship with the mayor, county manager, governor, or other appropriate elected official. The facility department's budget is usually the second largest administrative cost in the government (only personnel costs are larger) so that the chief executive needs to know that the facility manager is doing the best he can with limited resources. For his part, the facility manager needs to know that he's on the administration's wavelength. If such a climate does not exist, it's time to do some active job searching.

Legislators have so overregulated the public sector that change is difficult. If this description sounds bleak, it is not intended to be. A public-sector facility department can be stable and dedicated with a great sense of mission. On the plus side, public-sector facility managers often have better organized departments, more effective standards, excellent written procedures, and a more philosophical approach to their jobs than do private-sector facility managers.

Educational Facilities

Whether public or private, educational institutions tend to follow the public-sector model due mostly to the size and diversity of their facilities. This is particularly true of resources. In fact, annual funding for college facilities in the United States has reached crisis proportions.[13]

The facility manager at a college or a university must not only be technically competent but might want to consider an advanced academic degree for credibility. This is because university staff expect decisions to be made in a collegial fashion which is not always conducive to efficient allocation and use of resources. Even such decisions as a setback of thermostats for energy management can become the subject of extended discussion. It can take years to get a policy approved. That is particularly true of decisions regarding aesthetics, the workplace, and historic preservation. And because there is so much consensus decision-making in educational institutions, it is important that the facility manager be somewhat politically savvy in order to sell his programs.

The facility manager faces other problems too. There are no more diverse facilities than those found on a large university campus. Many institutions cannot effectively maintain and operate their existing facilities even while building more.[14] One facility manager of a heavily endowed university when quoted on this situation said, "Yeah, but no one ever endowed an operations and maintenance contract." Also, a university's management climate has all the problems of large bureaucracies, plus the oversight of a board of regents or trustees. There will be more help than desired from the academic department heads of architecture, engineering, and design. On the positive side, facility management of collegiate facilities allows an FM to develop a unique experience in supporting the full spectrum of types and spaces and buildings. In short, this is not a job for a novice. A large educational facility needs someone who is experienced.

Private Sector

Although no two private companies are alike, and corporate cultures vary widely, it is still possible to draw some conclusions regarding facility management in the private sector. For example, private-sector organizations are much more flexible (and flatter) than those in the public sector and can be changed relatively easily. All administrative functions and personnel tend to be tied closely to the product or service they support. Because facilities costs tend to be the second highest administrative cost, there is often pressure on the facilities manager to reduce staff and cost.

Also, since most of the facility department's managers tend to be middle management, they are susceptible to downsizing. Thus, although the private sector offers greater flexibility, the manager is subject to more staffing instability.

Because organizations are driven by the need to provide service or product at a profit, private-sector managers are expected to make those changes necessary to manage their organization effectively and efficiently. Thus, procurement is less bureaucratic, with more emphasis on long-term relationships, negotiations, and rapid response, and leasing is done quickly. Private-sector facility departments place great emphasis on design, perhaps because their managers feel that they can increase productivity through better facility design. Perhaps economic justification for such changes has more influence in an environment controlled by profitability than by budget.

Costs are yet another difference. For example, the private-sector facility manager is less likely to expend funds on end-of-the-year, suboptimal projects. His emphasis is on reducing costs rather than staying within budget, yet it is still critical to avoid budget surprises.

A private-sector facility manager must be a particularly good communicator. Often his very existence depends on an ability to sell the value of the department to upper management; this is particularly true if he charges back his services.

Private-sector facility managers are ultimately judged on how service-oriented and cost-conscious they are. If they do not measure up, someone else will be found who will. They must be comfortable with quantitative measurements and evaluation, since they will be measured frequently as managers, and they must be capable of evaluating leases, capital project justifications, life-cycle analyses, and financial ratios.

Finally, they must have a business sense and an ability to speak in terms other managers in the company will understand. While it is an overstatement to say that private sector facility managers should run their departments like "a company within a company," that certainly is not a bad approach.

International Organizations

Increasingly many of us are being employed by companies that are truly international. That has accelerated recently and will continue to in the new "flat world." Because facilities are always, to some degree, a manifestation of the occupying company, managing facilities in an international or multicultural organization has unique characteristics.

For example, in some cultures, decision-making is often done by consensus and therefore takes longer. Also, once made, decisions are subject to constant review and accommodation. In many cultures, those who provide services are treated like servants; service-oriented facility managers may find that their managerial expertise is neither sought nor appreciated. The same cultural bias is sometimes reflected in the approach to user maintenance of facilities. Some cultures feel no obligation to keep their facilities clean or well maintained, or to participate in facility management by reporting deficiencies or problems.

In some cases, companies have opened facilities in less-developed countries. Logistics can be a significant problem due to the lack of the supply chain or the small vendors and contractors, which are taken for granted in North America. In some areas, you must pay extra to get even adequate service. Critical parts may need to be flown in while finding competent employees with technical or supervisory skills can be very difficult.

Contrarily, other cultures, especially northern European ones, have higher expectations for their facilities. Many items that North Americans normally regulate by organizational policy, procedure, or standards are fixed by law. Four common areas of contention are access to light, subterranean officing, locked windows, and workstation dimensions.

In each of these situations, the facility manager must be sensitive to multicultural concerns. Laws must be followed. Also, all employees are subject to the organization's policy. But with little effort and relatively few exceptions, everyone's needs can be met if the facility manager works at it.

Non-Profit and Not for Profit Organizations

The growth and professionalism of the FM industry has included the expansion of facility managers into the non-and not for profit organizations. The large national organizations operate much as other commercial organizations. However, the limited and frequently unknown budget situation of a not-for-profit requires additional skills for the facility manager responsible for these facilities. The ability to "sell" the facility needs to volunteers and donors is a key aspect that other facility managers do not face. This requires enhanced presentation and fund-raising skills as well as occasional innovative financing to keep operations and maintenance of the facilities in good order. A not-for-profit is the only case ever seen by us where an operating budget was included in the donation of a large capital project endowment.[15] This knowledgeable donor required the budget to maintain the capital project into perpetuity.

Advantages of non- and not for profit facility management include the ability to interact with local supporters (not always an advantage we must admit) and the opportunity to utilize professional and trade association donations of expertise, services, products, and labor that no other facility manager ever has donated.

Other Situations

A facility manager in an organization that is highly decentralized will find himself acting almost as an entrepreneur. That approach is much different from the facility manager in a highly centralized corporation. There is concern on control, documentation standards, and published policy and procedures.

Organizational attitudes toward facilities standards fall into three groups; controlling organizations that have published standards; flexible organizations that neither have nor see a need for standards; and organizations in the middle that have standards that are unpublished. The management style of the facility manager enforcing those standards must be generally congruent with the attitude of the organization, or he will find himself continually in conflict with both management and his customers. Standards can be changed over time or at moments of major physical change.

Conclusion

We end this chapter with a word of caution. We are optimistic about facility management, facility managers, and the professional associations that support them. We continue to be concerned that facility managers do not feel that they are respected and that decisions affecting facilities sometimes are made without FM input; facility managers are, too often, in a reactive mode. We need to realize that we are not core business and that we are a major resource consumer. That leaves us open to intense scrutiny. For that reason, we need to be innovative, entrepreneurial, good business people, and mold our *modus operandi* to the organization's culture. We need to articulate our success, be enthusiastic and customer-oriented, and look to align our department with organizational successes.

Finally, an answer to the professional associations that believe some practitioners see a time when there is no need for facility management. We renounce that concept in the strongest terms. A priority for professional associations should be to constantly monitor the attitudes of a broad spectrum of the government officials and CEOs observing their facility managers. This information should be made available to the profession. The associations should conduct and publicize studies aimed at proving the value of efficient and effective facility management, eliminating overlap and capitalizing on the research strengths of each association. The professional associations should be at the forefront of introducing facility management courses into MBA programs and in encouraging the development of even more facility management degree programs.

Notes

1. Definition of facility management. Website of the International Facility Management Association (IFMA) www.ifma.org, April 23, 2008.
2. *Core Competencies for Federal Facilities Asset Management,* (Washington, DC; National Research Council; 2008), p. 9.
3. *Real Estate and Facilities Management: A Collaborative Lifecycle,* (Boston, MA; Aberdeen Group) p. 2.
4. *Current Trends and Future Outlook for Facility Management;* (Houston, TX; IFMA; 2005), pp 5–16.
5. Peter R. Veale, *Managing Corporate Real Estate Assets* (Cambridge, MA; MIT Laboratory of Architecture and Planning, 1987), p. 1.
6. Sun, Lena H., "Catoe Outlines Service Goals," *Washington Post,* March 28, 2008, p. B-3.
7. *Department of Defense (DoD) Base Structure Report, FY 05,* September 30, 2004, p. 2.

 8. "Discontent Is in the Air," *The Examiner,* March 22, 2008, p. 27.
 9. Building Research Board, *Committing to the Cost of Ownership* (Washington, DC; National Academy Press; 1990), p. xi.
10. Dean Kashiwagi, *Best Value Procurement, 2d ed.,* (Tempe, AZ; Performance Based Studies Research Group; 2008).
11. *The Decaying American Campus; A Ticking Time Bomb* (Alexandria, VA; APPA; 1986).
12. Personal communications from Stormy Friday, President, The Friday Group; James Whitaker, President, and Chris Hodges, Principal, Facility Engineering Associates; and *Facility Industry Study,* (Houston, TX; Collaboration of professional organizations, FMLink and Building Operating Management magazine; 2004), items 16, 17, 18, and 20.
13. *The Decaying American Campus,* p. 2.
14. Building Research Board, *Committing to the Cost of Ownership,* p. 2.
15. Taylor, Robert L., "Standardized Design Process and Capital Planning for Salvation Army Corps Community Centers." A thesis submitted to the faculty of Georgia Institute of Technology, 2007, p. 50.

2

Organizing the Department

Pulse Points

- *Outsourcing is a staffing issue; not an organizational one.*
- *When contracting out, retain control of all functions.*
- *Someone should be directly responsible for every asset and function.*
- *The facility manager organizes his way out of 90 to 95% of FM problems. He centrally controls those functions with the greatest financial impact on the business.*
- *The facility manager is most effective when ranked not lower than two levels below the chief executive of the organization.*
- *Regardless of the job title, the facility manager should be placed organizationally at the same level as the manager of information technology and the manager of human resources.*
- *The basis of facility management organization is separate functions for 1) planning and design, and 2) operations and maintenance.*
- *Communications planning, design, engineering, operations and maintenance are facilities functions to the extent that they must be physically accommodated in the facility.*
- *Engineering should be given as much design attention as architectural and interior design. That is not the way many architectural-engineering firms approach design.*
- *Hiring, getting the right person in the right position, will become increasingly critical because of the shortage of educated, trained, and experienced personnel.*
- *The optimal organization is a mixture of staff, consultants, and contractors.*

It is not our intent to explore all the various theories of organization and organizational development. We offer here what we consider better ways to organize and the rationale thereof.

Considerations for Organizing a Department

The facility department must reflect the needs of the parent organization. Too often, facility departments reflect an organization's short-term resource limitations rather than its long-term needs. While we are aware that most FM departments develop along with the parent company[1], and that the organization of the department is always resource constrained, the facility manager should organize himself out of 90-95 percent of the department's problems. Good departmental organization is fundamental and is too often sub-optimized because facility managers (and, in fact, managerial gurus) have played down the importance of good organization.

There are many considerations in organizing for the facilities mission, such as the size of the department, whether there are single or multiple locations, local custom in international situations, and whether the business wants standardized versus user-driven services. You must consider how best to provide services, effectively and efficiently, before you can organize properly. Often how you have organized is not as important as **having thought through the known organizational considerations and problems.** There is no better time to re-organize properly than when a new facility manager comes on the job, but the facility manager who has a suboptimal organization should make it a priority to work on making corrections over time. We have done both.

The size of a facility management department varies from one staff member (backed by contract and consultant staff) to hundreds of staff members and contractors. Size and its corollary, span of control, certainly are major determinants in how the department is organized. But all facility managers must perform the same basic functions for their companies. Also, both very large and very small organizations typically have a lot in common in their approach to problem solving. For example, both tend to use consultants often. Small organizations use consultants owing to lack of staff; large organizations use them to assist in special projects, to limit the size of the worker pool and because they can afford them.

The facility manager's place in the corporate structure is important. Given the fact that corporate titles vary, if the FM's title is Director, then he will not have vice-presidential responsibilities. We recommend two general rules. First, the facility manager should be positioned at two managerial levels below the chief executive officer (CEO) in large organizations; it is unrealistic to think that the facility manager will report directly to the CEO. In a recent study of facility departments that supported primarily large organizations, only 10 percent of the department heads were titled Director and almost none appeared to manage the majority of FM functions.[2] While the study may not be very representative of the profession as a whole, it is disturbing. As a profession, we have some selling to do to get facility managers placed at a position in organizations that 1) allows them to have the political clout necessary to properly execute duties and 2) reflect the importance of facilities to the agency / company.

Secondly, the facility manager and the managers of information technology and human relations should be at the same level within the organization. Those two rules balance necessary access to the board room against organizational reality.

There is a vast difference between managing a corporate headquarters in one location and facilities in multiple locations worldwide. Multiple locations, even if in the same city, lead to yet a different organization. On the government side, there is more commonality between the structure of a city public works department and one in a small town than the public works organization of a state where most operations are conducted regionally.

An increasingly important factor in our field is the use of outsourcing. There is literally no function that cannot be outsourced from laborer, to equipment technician, to staff personnel, to management. It is truly amazing. Military public works functions contain almost no military personnel anymore except the boss and sometimes not even him.

For the past thirty years, it has been popular to downgrade organizational structure. At least two factors were at play. First, management consultants have been pushing downsizing because personnel are expensive, particularly their benefits and retirement costs. Secondly, there has been a tendency to downplay organization under the rubrics of "flattening the organization," "providing organizational flexibility," etc. Some of this has been accomplished by outsourcing with which we have no problem. As long as the facility manager controls essential functions, this need not be a concern. What can be done with staff can also be done with contractors and consultants *as long as the FM maintains the organization he needs to serve customers and he retains control of the overall organization.* There are appropriate organizational models for all organizations and they will solve most of the FM problems allowing the facility manager personally to concentrate on upper management, important customer issues, and directing the actions to solve the major problems.

Several of these organizational factors are control issues. One excellent rule in very large organizations is to control centrally those aspects that have the greatest impact financially (e.g., real estate, major construction) and control the rest through the development and oversight of policy.

In the mid-eighties, chargeback was introduced as a business concept. It would limit the amount of work required by customers to only that which was really needed because the customer paid for it. In facilities, total chargeback systems did not work because there are required facility services which customers simply will not pay for. But even partial chargeback often faltered because it made facility resource planning a guessing game. Actually, most facility managers found that, after about two budget cycles of chargebacks, rather than worrying about facility costs, the users simply paid whatever was charged because they had "bigger fish to fry." Chargebacks had two organizational aspects; the need to have a second accounting system and the uncertainty of which permanent functions to staff since the customer might not pay for them.

One of the most important organizational decisions is whether facility services will be on a centralized or decentralized basis. Often this decision is closely equated to the geographic considerations. For example, an organization with branch offices spread across a state has to give each some autonomy in facility matters or run the risk of paralysis through centralization, even though centralization generally is the most cost-effective way to organize. Another decision is whether facility services will be highly standardized, or if there will be effort to meet unique-user needs. Generally standardization and cost-effectiveness go hand-in-hand.

The difference between a line (management) and a staff function is an important one in organizing. In larger organizations, FM functions that would ordinarily be considered staff areas in smaller organization use line managers assigned to manage them. This occurs, for instance, in international design and real estate organizations.

Finally, there are substantial differences when organizations choose to own their facilities rather than lease them. The former have staff and managers; the latter emphasize contracts and lease administration. Most midsized to large organizations both own and lease property, and their staffing must reflect those requirements.

Little of this is new, yet we are often struck by the most elemental errors in organization caused by an apparent failure to understand the nature of facility management. Some organizations have grown like Topsy, with no view of how the department should be organized best to perform the facilities mission. The most common failures are these:

1. Treating all work as projects and trying to apply the principles and organizational structure of project management rather than facility management.
2. Failing to provide an organizational element to integrate and coordinate all work.
3. Mixing the planning and design functions with the operations, maintenance, and repair functions.
4. Forming an outside group to accomplish a major capital project, with no integration of that group into the facilities organization providing ongoing services.
5. Allowing technology installation to be accomplished by a work unit outside the department. Technology functions which affect the facility, including planning and design, should be accomplished in the facilities department.

6. Failing to provide engineering services to match the planning and design services in the department.

Because organizations are so complex, these problems never appear singly. There is always a long list of considerations. Because factors intertwine with politics and resource constraints to produce an almost infinite variety of facility organizations, there are many compromises. However, there are organizational models that serve as guides during the inevitable reorganizations.

Organizational Models

There could be many models—one to fit every situation—but our experience shows that about six models are sufficient. They can be named, generally in order of increased staffing:

1. Office manager model
2. One-location, one site model
3. One-location, multiple-sites model
4. Public works model
5. Multiple-locations, strong-regional, or divisional-headquarters model
6. Fully international model

In all, we display the facility department structure at the corporate headquarters. Also, we present the facility department as an institutionally funded, primarily centralized business function. In most models, the organization at a subordinate office is one of the other models shown. It is relatively unimportant, from a theoretical standpoint, whether one of the boxes on an organizational chart represents staff, consultant, or contractor.

In the models shown in Exhibits 2-1 to 2-6, the level immediately above the facility manager is included in order to illustrate to whom the facility manager typically reports. Note that there are sometimes different titles for the facility manager. The models also show the positions ordinarily at the same level of responsibility as the facility manager and any position with which he closely coordinates. In addition, we list the facility department functions typically performed by each organizational unit.

Office Manager Model

The office manager model (see Exhibit 2-1) is applicable to organizations that reside primarily in one leased building. It is heavily dependent on the landlord, consultants, and contractors, primarily because the organization does not want to devote human

Exhibit 2-1. Office manager model.

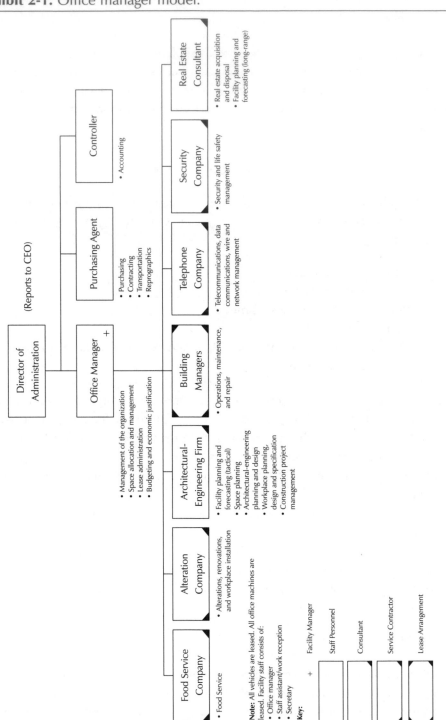

Director of
Administration

(Reports to CEO)

Office Manager +
- Management of the organization
- Space allocation and management
- Lease administration
- Budgeting and economic justification

Purchasing Agent
- Purchasing
- Contracting
- Transportation
- Reprographics

Controller
- Accounting

Food Service
Company
- Food Service

Alteration
Company
- Alterations, renovations, and workplace installation

Architectural-
Engineering Firm
- Facility planning and forecasting (tactical)
- Space planning
- Architectural-engineering planning and design
- Workplace planning, design and specification
- Construction project management

Building
Managers
- Operations, maintenance, and repair

Telephone
Company
- Telecommunications, data communications, wire and network management

Security
Company
- Security and life safety management

Real Estate
Consultant
- Real estate acquisition and disposal
- Facility planning and forecasting (long-range)

Note: All vehicles are leased. All office machines are leased. Facility staff consists of:
- Office manager
- Staff assistant/work reception
- Secretary

Key:

+   Facility Manager

[ ]   Staff Personnel

[ ]   Consultant

[ ]   Service Contractor

[ ]   Lease Arrangement

resources for facility management; it prefers to buy the service. Only the following functions are actually performed by organizational staff; management of the organization, lease administration, budgeting, accounting and economic justification, and some degree of security and emergency planning for its own staff.

Control of facility management is executed primarily though administration of leases (building, vehicles, and office equipment), service contracts, and consulting contracts. Management ultimately rests with the office manager (and perhaps an assistant and a secretary). The model displays the day-to-day mechanics of each function. Exhibit 2-1 shows a typical model. Some alternative placement of functions might be:

Function	From	To
Lease administration	Office manager	Purchasing agent
Space allocation and management	Office manager	Architectural/ engineering firm
Economic justification	Office manager	Controller
Transportation or re-prographics	Purchasing agent	Appropriate service companies
Food service	Food service company	Building manager/landlord
Security and life-safety management	Security company	Building manager/landlord
Real estate acquisition and disposal	Real estate consultant	Office manager/landlord
Facility planning and and forecasting (long range)	Real estate consultant	Office manager
Alterations, renovations, and workplace installation	Alterations company	Building manager

Of course, other contractors or consultants could be used—estimators, value engineers, brokers—but most essential services can be provided by those shown, or else they are highly specialized and infrequently used.

The extent to which a certain contractor or consultant is maintained largely depends on two factors: (1) the frequency of the function and (2) the magnitude of the function. A permanent arrangement for either staff or contract should be established for functions that occur frequently or have significant volume or financial impact.

Perhaps the most often used example of this model is for law offices.

Exhibit 2-2. One-location, one-site model.

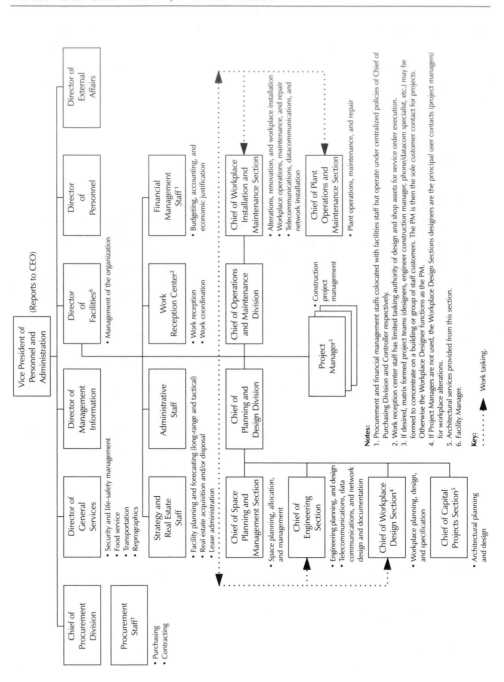

One-Location, One-Site Model

In many ways the one-location, one-site model, shown in Exhibit 2-2 is the simplest setup for a full-service facility department. It occurs in organizations that are large enough to have a facility division or department, but are located at one location and one major site in a major building or buildings that are owned. It illustrates several of the following principles:

1. Presence of an organizational unit to coordinate and integrate work
2. Management for both ongoing work and project work
3. Integration of communications
4. Adequate engineering
5. Balance between planning and design and operations and maintenance

This model is heavily weighted toward the use of in-house human resources, both as a contrast to the office manager model and because research has shown that such is likely to be the case.[3] It displays more organizational units than most companies will fund, but alternative functional placements or contractual arrangements are noted. Consultants, in particular, could be used or assist in staffing.

The figure is a typical model. Some logical alternatives for placement of functions might be:

Function	From	To
Life-safety management	Director of general services	Supervisor, engineering
Those listed under	Director of general services	Units under supervisor, operations and maintenance division
Tactical planning and forecasting	Strategy and real estate staff	Supervisor, space planning and management
Architectural planning and design	Manager, capital projects	Supervisor, workplace design
Construction project management	Project manager	Supervisor, workplace installation

In this model, contractors or consultants are most frequently used to provide a unique skill or to handle peak loads.

A large insurance company might be an example of this model.

Exhibit 2-3. One-location, multiple-sites model.

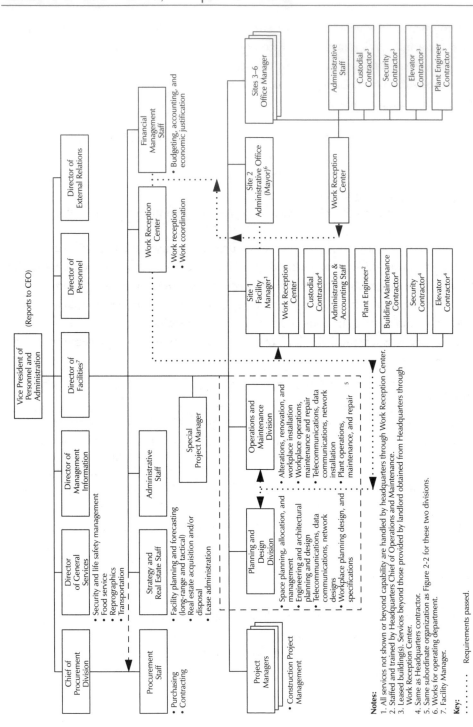

Notes:
1. All services not shown or beyond capability are handled by headquarters through Work Reception Center.
2. Staffed and trained by Headquarters Chief of Operations and Maintenance.
3. Leased building(s). Services beyond those provided by landlord obtained from Headquarters through Work Reception Center.
4. Same as Headquarters contractor.
5. Same subordinate organization as Figure 2-2 for these two divisions.
6. Works for operating department.
7. Facility Manager.

Key:
· · · · · · · ·   Requirements passed.

One-Location, Multiple Sites Model

The next model, shown in Exhibit 2-3, is typically a headquarters with major opera-tional elements (labs, branches, plants) located in the same county or metropolitan area. Homogeneous facilities at one location fit the model in Exhibit 2-2 better than this model.

One of the concepts developed here for the first time is the gathering, consolida-tion, and evaluation (and possible decentralized execution) of requirements. This can be done in one of two ways:

1. Decentralize certain operational elements to operate within set limitations. Larger, prescreened requirements are passed upward.
2. Have an administrator at each location aggregate and screen requirements.

Complete decentralization under this model is not economically justifiable. If complete decentralization appears to be a solution (one of the satellite sites is as complex as the headquarters, for example), the model in Exhibit 2-5 is probably more appropriate.

This model is between the first two in number of consultants and contractors used, acknowledging that additional resources are needed to compensate for time-distance factors. The more decentralized the organization is, the more probable it is that consultants and contractors will be used. Each of the remote sites is likely to be organized for facility management as shown in Exhibit 2-1 or 2-2 with ties back to the headquarters that are financial and reporting in nature, or for passing requirements. In all cases, the headquarters organization provides policy, oversight, budget control, and technical assistance. Many combinations of staff, consultants, leases, and contrac-tors can be used to provide services to remote sites, but generally only facility oper-ations and maintenance taskings are passed down for execution. In this model, design assets must be strengthened, as must the lease management, financial management, project management, and work reception and coordination functions.

This model is typical of a local firm soon to go regional or a new regional company.

Public Works Model

Exhibit 2-4 depicts the Public Works model, new in this edition, and adapted from the Department of Defense. The Directorate of Public Works at a military installation functions as the *City Engineer and the Department of Public Works (DPW)*. This organi-zation is responsible for a wide range of complex programs that require thorough coordination and planning. These are unique organizations which encompass

Exhibit 2-4. Public Works Model.[1,2]

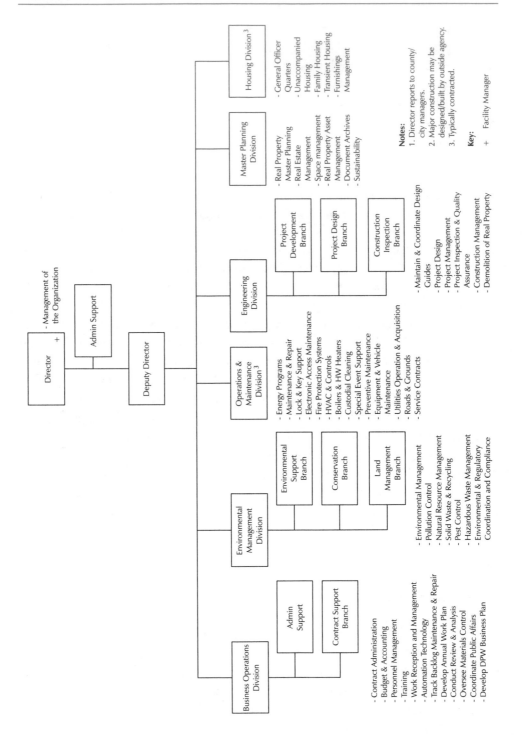

everything required to operate and maintain a small to medium sized city. Some of the functions include:

1. Receiving and processing work requirements, keeping a database current and tracking status of work
2. Contracting capability delegated to the DPW because of the uniqueness of what they do. Indefinite delivery type contracts are used extensively. Job Order Contracting (JOC) is another expedient contracting method that does not require a full solicitation process, customary in a normal sealed-bid contract award.
3. Environmental management which involves the protection of the environment and conserving natural resources for present and future generations.
4. Maintaining roads, grounds, utilities, and structures. This includes being responsible for providing continuous reliable water, sewer, electrical, and natural gas services.
5. Conducting condition assessments of all facilities and developing a list of Backlog Maintenance and Repair (BMAR) work. This is work that comprises those maintenance and repair projects that were scheduled to be started and had funds obligated, but remained unfinanced throughout the fiscal year. This is similar to Deferred Maintenance at a university.

These organizations parallel similar civilian DPW organizations around the world. For example, Canada, France, and Sweden use similar organizations. They all have one theme in common, which is to support existing and future citizens by ensuring that public works, infrastructure, and facilities are planned, funded, constructed, operated, and maintained in a cost effective manner and in the best interest of public health, safety, and welfare.

Perhaps it is because two of the authors have had extensive experience with this model but we recommend that, as all public and private FM organizations grow, they use this Exhibit 2-4 as their organizational template, with the addition of a real estate function, of course.

With the fifth model, shown in Exhibit 2-5, we start to discuss large organizations that operate in widely separated geographic regions, probably nationally. Subordinate regional or divisional headquarters have facility departments similar to those shown in Exhibit 2-2 or 2-3.

Operational issues are deemphasized except within the headquarters itself. The principal functions are allocating resources, tactical and strategic planning, real estate acquisition and disposal, policy and standards setting, technical assistance, macrolevel space planning and management, and oversight. In this, and the

Exhibit 2-5. Multiple-locations, strong regional or divisional headquarters model.

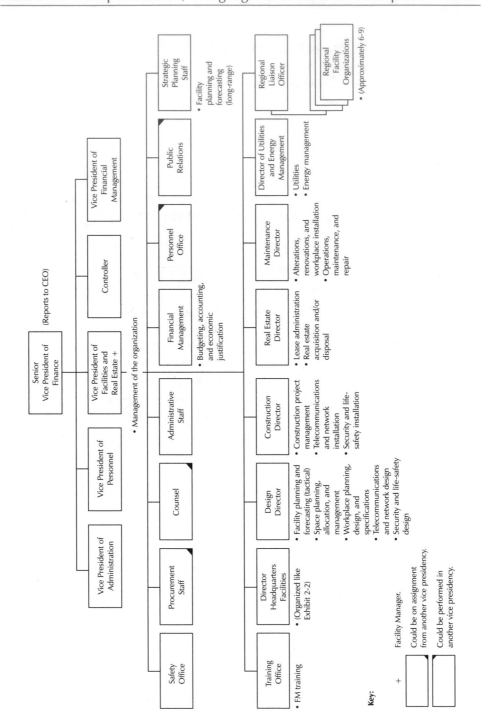

international model which follows, headquarters performs primarily policy and oversight functions.

Here the facility department is almost entirely staff. The facility manager has no direct responsibility for any of the general administrative services. It is not necessary that all the professional staff shown (counsel, for example) be directly assigned to the facility manager, but neither would it be unusual. The principal staff are directors with policy authority within their areas of functional expertise. The regions or groups have their direct line to the "boss" through their liaison officer at the headquarters.

Consultants and contractors, especially those who operate nationwide, are used extensively, particularly for real estate, planning, design and construction. Legal issues are a daily matter, and a law firm versed in facility matters is on retainer, or staff lawyers work directly within the vice presidency (similar to procurement specialists in earlier models). Both very small (office manager model) and very large (this model) organizations rely extensively on consultants.

This model might be typical for a national retail chain.

Fully International Model

The sixth model, shown in Exhibit 2-6, is another way to organize a very large facility department and could be used (totally or in part) interchangeably with the model in Exhibit 2-5. In both models, the headquarters functions as overseer, policymaker, problem solver, and resource allocator. The work of the organization is done by the regional or national offices or directorates.

These regional or national units can function primarily under their individual business unit with only technical FM direction from headquarters. We prefer this approach, but the field facility units could take their principal direction from headquarters, commonly called a *pipeline approach*. The organization depicted is large enough so that it has invested in a training academy to assist in standardizing policy and procedures. This is both extremely effective and extremely costly.

In both of the very large organizational models (Exhibits 2-5 and 2-6), the elements shown at the headquarters all serve primarily staff functions but at two levels. The true staff services the headquarters facility; the directorates are oriented on the field organizations. There is no magic formula, for example, to determine whether legal advice should be provided outside the department, from within the directorates, in the field units, or all of these. Counsel should be placed where needed. Whether it needs strong technical control, where they would remain in the legal "stovepipe," or whether they should be assigned within the facilities department depends on the philosophy of the organization regarding its legal resources.

Exhibit 2-6. Fully international model.

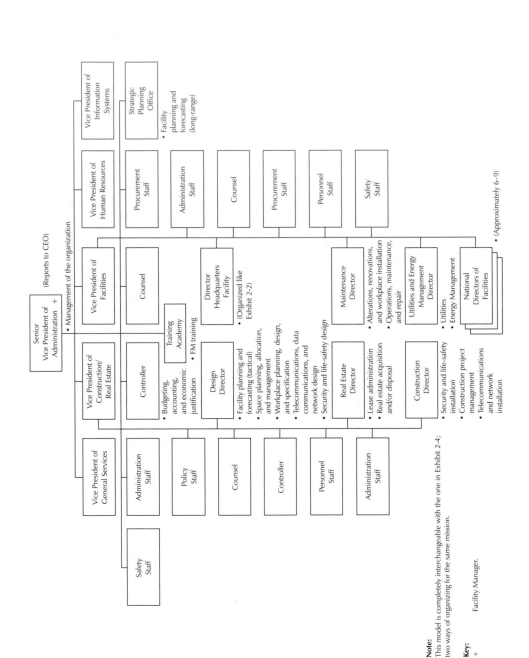

Note:
This model is completely interchangeable with the one in Exhibit 2-4; two ways of organizing for the same mission.

Key:
+   Facility Manager.

In this international situation, the legal system and language may impact this decision. As a rule, the first level of authority to buy or lease real estate needs direct access to counsel.

This model might be used by an international petroleum company, for example.

Model Wrap-Up

There is a tendency to look at these examples and conclude that, with so many blocks on a page, there is a need for a huge bureaucracy. Nothing could be less true. Nevertheless, the facility manager must be provided with a staff and line organization that allows him to manage efficiently and effectively. Contractors and consultants can be used in these ways. Corporate staff (human resources, procurement, controller, public relations) can often be shared effectively; co-locating corporate staff with the facility staff often works well. However, at some point, the facility staff must grow as the organization grows and will eventually reflect other business units with full line and staff organizations.

In a recent *Facilities Industry Study* conducted jointly by all of the professional FM organizations and focused primarily but not exclusively on North America, facility managers were asked which functions they handled and which they added in the past year.[4]

Current (above 60%)	Added in the Past Year (above 10%)
Contract administration-72%	Disaster planning/recovery-18%
Construction management-71 %	Managing additional facilities-18%
Energy management-68%	Managing CAFM-16%
Moves/relocations-63%	Records/document management-12%
Disaster planning/recovery-61 %	Strategic planning-11%
Space planning-61%	Lease management-10%
	Food service-10%

Except in colleges and universities (where APPA has done the research and a generalized model has been agreed upon and taught as a best practice), *organization remains the stepchild of good facility management and the least valued of the accepted functions of management.* A facility manager should solve 90-95 percent of his problems by organizing properly.

Staffing

As mentioned earlier, we think it is important to clearly delineate between organizational issues and staffing ones. There are unique staffing problems in facility departments, and it is helpful to understand their nature. Particularly in large corporations, the facility department's human resource needs are often both minor and unique compared to those of the main business elements. That means the facility manager's skilled human resource needs—quantitative and qualitative—are often not properly understood or given much priority. We have found this equally true in large government agencies. This situation is compounded by the general lack of skilled technicians and supervisory trade personnel which North American organizations will face for at least the next twenty years; its effect can only be lessened by the FM having direct access to personnel specialists knowledgeable with technical staffing needs. Only in very large organizations will the facility manager actually have an assigned personnel department. In medium-sized organizations, a human resources team, operating under the central human resources policies, is successfully co-located with the facility staff.

Most experienced facility managers are already employed, and only a few universities offer degrees in entry-level facility management. The pool of qualified facility managers is not large and those who are in place have been there a long time[5] and will retire soon. There are, however, some solutions to placement:

1. *Grow your own.* Large organizations, in particular, can develop a succession plan for functional managers to move through the organization.
2. *Hire retiring or resigning military personnel with facility management experience.* Two of your authors entered the civilian FM world in this manner. The Reserve Officers Association and Society of American Military Engineers are good sources of leads. The Non-Commissioned Officers Association is a superior source of senior technical and supervisory personnel.
3. *Use graduates of the universities.* Gain familiarity with existing FM programs by using their interns. (See Appendix C) Be particularly alert for the development of other programs; many universities worldwide are considering FM degrees or associate degrees or an area of concentration in facility management. Unfortunately, in the past ten years in North America, as many programs have failed as have started.
4. *Look to the professional associations.* The Association for Facilities Engineering (AFE), the International Facility Management Association (IFMA) and the Association of Higher Education Facilities Officers (APPA) assist in personnel placement.

5. *Hire from other organizations.* Some competent managers and technical specialists are dead-ended in their current organizations; they would be grateful for advancement.

6. *Hire a contractor or consultant already working for you.* This is our favorite method because the person hired already has a track record with you and your organization and has no learning curve. The downside is that you lose them as a contractor or consultant.

There are some staffing problems resulting from the imprecision of job titles. Facility managers, themselves, have different titles. What some people call an interior designer is a space planner in other agencies. When working with an organization unfamiliar with facility management, these inconsistencies make it very difficult to hire and properly grade people. A placement specialist once explained that he had to hire a research assistant when what he needed was a space planner because "that's the closest job title that we have in our inventory of titles." Textbooks and research material on facility management are less effective than they could be simply due to the proliferation of job titles. The professional associations should take the lead here to standardize job titles.

As is the case in many other administrative service areas, some competent people will find themselves dead-ended in facility management organizations long before their work life is over. The relatively small number of positions for full-fledged facility managers make this inevitable. For example, consider a director of construction, at age 45, working for a vice president three years her junior. These situations happen in organizations where FM skills are not the predominant skills of the business units of the company. Therefore, hiring from other organizations or hiring retired or resigned physical plant administrators and military personnel are practical solutions to the proper distribution of skilled personnel at one location. The professional associations, through their local chapters, can serve as a catalyst in this process.

A major current problem is the lack of skilled technicians (engineers, maintenance mechanics, supervisors) that prevails for many reasons (poor vocational education programs, lack of pay and prestige, the demise of apprenticeships, retirement of the baby boomers). The situation has, in fact, become critical. Elevator mechanics, for example, seem to be becoming extinct. Meanwhile, the systems (elevators, air conditioning, life-safety, security) are becoming more and more complex. By extensive use of manufacturers' training (to include paying for contractor or consultant training in some cases) facility managers are holding their own, but the base of trainable personnel has diminished noticeably in North America.

One of the greatest staffing issues concerns the use of consultants and contractors (sometimes humorously called the in-house versus out-house debate). However, the debate is largely over and almost all organizations are now a blend of staff, contractors, and consultants. The greatest impetus to farm out facility services came from a desire to flatten organizations by eliminating staff positions, to simply reduce the number of people on the books, and because it became increasingly difficult to hire staff due to organizational policies.

We believe in making maximum use of both consultants and contractors. In fact, we have a bias toward these blended organizations. The ideal organization is flexible, with a mix of in-house staff, consultants, and contractors as mentioned above. Consultants meet short-term, highly specialized needs; contractors provide the same flexibility for a longer term. Ideally, the solution is to use skill-oriented, body-shop contractors where the contractor provides personnel and first line supervision while the facility manager organizes, directs, and evaluates the contractor's performance. In all, the facility manager must retain the ability to set policy, maintain oversight, and develop requirements. Consultants can even suggest policy and help gather requirements, but in-house staff must approve both. A facility manager who abrogates those functions has lost control.

Also, before the facility manager enters into extensive consultant or contractual arrangements, he must have the right to select the appropriate contractor or properly skilled consultant. Fortunately, there have been great advances made in the area of these type of contracts, particularly job order contracting, large body-shop contracting, and best value contracting. If all a facility manager has to tie his contractor or consultant to him is a low-bid contract, he is in deep trouble. Fortunately, low-bid contracts seldom are appropriate for substantial staffing by contractors or consultants but it may take some convincing to make the Purchasing Department understand that.

Outsourcing

We are very suspicious of contracting out solely to reduce costs, especially because that has not been our experience. Too often studies that claim cost savings do not analyze all costs (looking only at one budget, for example) or fail to compare costs over time. There seems to be a general realization that you are going to get what you pay for and, unless your organizations are "fat" (and few of these exist anymore), contracting out is not going to be substantially cheaper. Service contract rates normally increase every time the contract is rebid if the same quality of services and service personnel are going to be maintained. So what appears to be a savings by contracting out may, by the second or third rebid, become more costly than if the service had remained in-house. Our general analysis is that contracting out to save money is fiction. If there are savings, it tends to be in the area of benefit costs.

A major factor in this area is the rise of extremely qualified facility management outsourcing companies. These companies literally can meet any need for any size facility organization across any function of facility management. In fact, facility managers need to carefully assess the lengths and depths to which they want to outsource. While most of these decisions seem to have been made to save money, the real advantages (provided you have the right contractor and relationship with that contractor) are in having flexibility of staffing and being able to quickly obtain needed expertise when called for.

A study which evaluates organizational structure and staffing levels within facility management organizations is overdue. This is important as we use contractors and consultants to perform an increasing number of core functions, and we bring the expertise of these organizations on board. The management (both onsite and offsite) of your contractor may be able to offer good organizational advice based on their experience from other clients. Yes, it could be to their advantage to recommend more staffing, but the final decision is yours. We discuss the necessary trust and relationships that should be developed between FM and contractor/consultant in the next section. It is the facility manager's job to minimize the divisions among staff, contractors, and consultants and to meld them into a facility team; an "us versus them" attitude within the FM department is fatal. Minimizing these divisions often starts by using some aspect of best value contracting[6] rather than low-bid contracting but it will not automatically happen. Procurement will say it cannot be done; human resources (and the union if involved) will say it should not be done. Before deciding to contract out, the facility manager must have upper management's support for his plan. This is much easier to obtain than it was ten years ago but is just the start of the outsourcing process.

Outsourcing can work—one of us has personally managed an organization where, over an extended period of time, all the supervisors and skilled workers were contractors. However because contractors change, we doubt that we ever saved much money. Nevertheless we had an organization that was the envy of others because it was extremely flexible and capable of meeting whatever challenges were thrown at us . . . and there were many. For instance, we completely gutted and renovated a major office building with our in-house forces (augmented substantially by our contractor) while the bureaucracy was trying to come up with a renovation contract. We delivered the project on-time and under budget. At another time, we moved over 8,000 staff in a nine month period with our in-house moving staff and contractor. At all times, if any contractor has a work or conduct problem, we simply ask the problem individual to move to a position outside our organization. Wholly secondary to this discussion but important to note, several of our supervisors became so valuable to their organization while on our staff that they were promoted to run their own contract operations outside our department. We always discussed the timing of their departure with our contractor but never held anyone back because, frankly, we were proud of them.

We prefer to use an outsourcing company that matches the size of our facility management task. It has been our experience that small to medium-size contractors are preferable, if appropriate, because they view our contract as a principal one, not just one of a string. We also believe strongly in body-shop contracting, where the contractor provides the skills and supervision and we provide the management. We partnered with our contractor before partnering was a common concept. In our contract documents and all discussions with the contractor's management, we are frank and honest and encourage them to be the same with us. This takes some time and some confidence building. We are often demanding, but we are fair and try to alert the contractor in advance of major increases or decreases of on-site staffing or the need for specialized skills not normally on site. In turn, we expect to be consulted before a key contractor person leaves our site. One point we learned early, money talks. Ensure that your contractor is getting paid within days of the submission of their invoice, particularly if they are a small business. This can be a problem in organizational bureaucracies.

Though it may not be for everyone because it requires multiple contracting actions, we prefer to contract with different firms for specific functions. To large firms, who provide everything from food service to mail service to construction and move management, you are just another contract. Secondly, firms who concentrate on specific functions probably can perform them better. The number of contracts must be balanced against your bureaucracy's ability to administer them. A full service facility department might, for example, have the following contracts:

Administrative Service	*Building Services*
• Food service	• Architecture, engineering, and
• Security	interior design
• Information technology services	• Operations and maintenance
• Mail, messenger, and	• Moving and asset management
reprographics	• Project management and
	estimating

One of the experts in outsourcing, Joe Incognito, lists the following questions that an organization should ask before it decides to outsource:

1. Has the organization successfully utilized the concept of outsourcing in the past?
2. Has the organization outsourced a business function in the past and realized less-than-expected results?

3. Does the culture of the organization allow for the outsourcing concept?
4. Does the need to rightsize the organization create a need to outsource?[7]

To these we would add the questions implied above regarding whether to go "big or small" and to outsource by function or to a single company. *It is our experience that the facility manager must control this decision and its implementation. As difficult as it is to fight the procurement bureaucracy at times, if you allow the outsourcing process to be dictated to you, outsourcing will be off on the wrong foot.*

Remember that you hired the contractor or consultant for his expertise and his initiative; you must allow him to display it. Get comfortable with your outsourcer before you sign the contract with him, and then trust him to help you improve your operation. That is one of the reasons that you hired him and he should understand that.

We would be reluctant to hire any outsourcing firm that did not have a quality management program that was compatible with ours or could not be adopted to our situation. This should be explored in the contracting phase. Second, outsourcing contracts are ideal for partnering arrangements. The facility manager should work with the purchasing department to build partnering into the contractual arrangement. The outsourcer needs to make the facility manager a hero; the facility manager wants to ensure that the contractor is successful. Any facility manager not skilled in contract administration needs to get training. Increasingly the job of the facility manager will be determined by the ability to contract for and manage services successfully rather than supervise them directly.

Personality and Skills of Facility Personnel

Perhaps too much can be made of the type of individuals who succeed in facility management. You look for the same characteristics in facility management candidates as all managers look for; managerial capability for managers and technical competence for specialists. Nevertheless, our experience does emphasize the following:

1. Academic degrees are given less weight than practical experience because currently academic programs, except for the university degree programs, do not produce managers or technicians skilled in facility management. This will change as more degree-granted experienced facility managers become available though this is occurring much slower than we would have believed ten years ago. Degree-granting programs in FM come and go too frequently.
2. A facility manager must be comfortable with a certain amount of reactive management.

3. Staff, consultants, and contractors must truly be committed to service.
4. Facility management is not brain surgery. Take a team player over a brilliant individualist if there is a choice. This, in addition to their technical expertise, is where ex-military personnel excel.
5. Facility managers should be comfortable about being measured quantitatively and should make their staff equally comfortable which is not always easy. People often resist being measured whereas we must promote just that.
6. Specialists who have not worked in a corporate environment should rarely be hired. For example, what would make an individual successful in a commercial design firm may not lead to success on an in-house staff.

There are a number of personality-typing tests which human resource departments are using to ensure that potential new hires are compatible with the company, their colleagues and their boss. One of the most common is the MBTI (Myers-Briggs Type Indicator). We are ambivalent about their use for hiring, but think it is an excellent idea for facility managers to have their personality typed by taking the MBTI. One of the first ever seminars given on facility management started everyone off with the MBTI as an ice-breaker (it was an enormous success) but it also caused most of those in the room who came from an engineering or business background to understand that personality counts . . . something that is still too often forgotten.

Customers' Top Ten Complaints to Facility Managers
*(Numbers in parentheses are ratings on the 1997 survey; NR means not rated)
1. It's too cold.(2)
2. It's too hot.(1)
3. Janitorial service is poor.(4)
4. Not enough conference rooms.(3)
5. Not enough storage/filing space in my workstation.(5)
6. Poor indoor air quality.(7)
7. No privacy in workstation/office.(9)
8. Inadequate parking.(8)
9. Computer problems.(6)
10. Noise level/too noisy.(NR)
Source: *IFMA Survey Ranks Top 10 Office Complaints*, IFMA website, June '03.

It is pretty amazing how consistent the first three complaints have been over time. Maybe we need a profession-wide conference on how to solve those three issues once and for all. Secondly, the items that have moved up on the list probably indicate more about the way we work than any failure in the facility department. Workers, by and large, do not like their small workstations and need more conference rooms for collegial work. Having said that, a new facility manager might well base his early initiatives on this list until he can get a handle on his specific problems.

Thorny Issues in Organization

The issue of line versus staff functions is always contentious. In very small organizations there is little need for staff support; if needed, it comes from consultants. In very large organizations almost all activities at headquarters are staff in nature; line functions are in the regions and lower. In midsize organizations, staff versus line becomes less clear. Planning and design are ordinarily staff functions, but in most midsize organizations, that kind of activity is so prevalent that often a line planning and design organization is formed.

The proper placement of the *real estate function* is often controversial. Frankly, because of historical situations, the real estate function is seldom under facility management. In small or midsize departments, the real estate and long-range planning functions are combined in one staff element, perhaps a real estate consultant, because, at that level, the functions are intertwined. Real estate becomes a line function when an organization occupies multiple, leased locations and is both a lessor and lessee. Facility management will have arrived when, in such a large organization, the Director of Real Estate reports to the Vice President of Facility Management, the management relationship we feel is proper.

Except in the smallest organizations where the facility manager does it, *strategic planning* is a function deserving special organizational consideration. In mid-size organizations, it can be placed in a staff office with real estate. In very large national and international organizations, strategic planning is a constant activity and should have its own staff office. Regardless of where the function is resident, there should be a facility plan for each organizational business plan.

It is puzzling that *engineering* should be an organizational problem, but it is. Time after time, organizations fail to staff properly to meet their engineering challenges. Engineering problems, in general, are costlier to correct than others and have the greatest potential for employer liability, yet many employers do not hire enough engineering consultants or staff to match their interior planning and design assets. Consultants can do the job well, but oversight, policy setting, and requirements framing must be done by knowledgeable staff.

Almost as a corollary to the engineering issue is the failure to ensure that facilities are properly documented clearly and uniformly. In our own practice we have observed a common failure to provide proper documentation in what are commonly called as-built drawings. We believe that this is a *design function* (though others certainly have a role). Organizations would never try to build a new building without detailed and correct drawings, yet they rebuild facilities piece by piece every three to six years without correct drawings because they have never provided for staff to update the original drawings properly. Once building information modeling (BIM) becomes standard, the problem will be lessened to the degree that we are willing to constantly keep our drawings updated. For those of us who have a large inventory of older buildings with building drawings of uncertain validity, it is worthwhile to systematically have those buildings surveyed, their systems categorized and their drawings brought up-to-date. BIM should be the standard for all new construction and for major renovations. The ability to conduct BIM and to receive the data may well determine which consultants we use and which building automation system we move forward with.

Where to place *project management* in an organization is a major issue. The area, within an existing framework, implies a matrix organization and is very appealing in midsize and large organizations in two cases: (1) special projects, like building a major new plant, or (2) providing operational managers a single facility's department contact to coordinate design, construction, moving, and communications for all work in that department. Theoretically, a project management unit should report directly to the facility manager. This works quite well for the first case, the special project. Such a case is displayed in the organizational model shown in Exhibit 2-3. For the day-to-day projects (typically 250 to 500 projects annually, ranging from $2,500 to $500,000 each, in an active mid-size facility department), the facility manager normally does not desire to be directly involved in each project (as shown in Exhibit 2-3) and often forms a project management unit under the planning and design manager.

A long-standing issue is where to assign responsibility for installed equipment. Kitchen equipment is a classic example. Generally we favor the facility department being organized and staffed to maintain all installed equipment, but we realize that often exceptions make sense (a credit union ATM machine or research equipment, for example).

Many of us who have been frustrated in our facility operations by "those guys in purchasing" have longed to have the *procurement function* placed under us. However, there are two good reasons not to do so: (1) Although the facility department tends to be a large customer of the procurement division by transaction, that office has other customers (and other problems); and (2) the facility department is better protected by having its procurements conducted and reviewed by another unit.

At the same time, the facility manager must make it clear, and the purchasing manager may well support it, that facility procurements are unique. In midsize

organizations, it has often been successful to co-locate two or three procurement officers (one contracting officer and one to two procurement specialists) into the facilities
department operating under the centralized procurement policies and procedures.
These officers must be treated as full members of the facilities' team. (We strongly feel
that contracts for consultant firms should be handled through the procurement
department; for individuals, through the human resources department.)

The issue of meeting *user requirements* has several organizational aspects:

- There are two ways for users to communicate their facility requirements to
  the appropriate individual in the facility department.
  1. Unlimited access
  2. Screening by the administrative officer of each business unit or by the
     "mayor" of each building
- Whether to provide service centrally according to a priority system or to
  ensure that everyone gets something every year by decentralizing funding
  expenditure early in the budget year.

We strongly support some screening of user requirements and a system—a priority
setting board for major requirements—that establishes the application of resources
against requirements, with some user input.

An FM organization on a *chargeback system* will be organized and staffed somewhat differently from one that is institutionally funded. A chargeback department
has more financial personnel devoted to calculating and collecting charges. The
department will probably be more contractor or consultant oriented to allow for the
peaks and valleys of a noninsured level of fund resources. There will also be an
emphasis on functions that can be defined as projects and therefore charged back.

If the facility manager does not have responsibility for *security*, several functions
can be troublesome if they are not thought out carefully; this is particularly true since
security and life-safety have become increasingly automated and part of the facility.
Typically security operates and tests the systems while facility management installs
and maintains them, often under contract, but neither department can function without the other. Familiar issues that need to be considered are proper placement of the
fire marshal, locksmithing and key control, testing of fire and life-safety systems, and
maintenance and repair of security, fire, and life-safety systems, particularly emergency repair. This short discussion indicates why security, life-safety, and emergency
management ought to be under the facility department.

No current, single, automated system, the Integrated Workplace Management
System IWMS), is going to be the answer to the facility manager's information
management needs though we believe this is technologically possible. In fact with

BIM we have an even more powerful management tool but one which must be integrated with other systems to provide information outside its original design intent. At least initially, in large organizations, IWMS should have a system manager (maybe a consultant) who should report to the facility manager. Other subsytems that may require separate, short-term system managers during their introduction are computer-aided design and planning, work management, financial management, and management information systems. Interestingly, where the problem has been and continues to be integrating multiple FM systems together, another issue is compartmentalizing the information so that the appropriate people have access to the appropriate information only.

Key Relationships for the Facility Manager

Functioning successfully in a bureaucracy requires establishing and maintaining relationships. Some of them are established in the organization chart for the company; all of them depend as much on the personality of the individual as on their position. However, experience indicates that you should be especially aware of your relationships with the following individuals ex officio.

- Information resources manager, particularly if this person is responsible for communications, networking, or a major computing facility which you must support.
- Procurement manager. Relationships need to be established at least one level deeper into this organization.
- Counsel
- Human resources manager
- General services manager (or food services manager and security manager, if these functions are separately managed)

Organizational Models

Because of numerous variables, no two facility management organizations are ever exactly alike. However, we have learned enough about facility departments that models have been developed and can be used for guiding specific company organizations. There *are* better ways to staff and organize; you should capitalize on them.

Unfortunately, too much organizational discussion for the past twenty years has concentrated on eliminating positions. Often *rightsizing* has been nothing more than a euphemism for reducing staff. This has clouded the matter of organizations.

A letter in the *Harvard Business Review,* from its editor, says it well: "Two great challenges lie increasingly ahead for the modern organization, to have the requisite typed and numbers of knowledge workers . . . and to have an organization in which they will thrive and with which they will want to remain."[8]

How to properly organize is a topic which has been inadequately researched but one that we feel is of such great importance that we want to give you three other approaches. The bible for organizational development in facility management organizations is Stormy Friday's *Organization Development for Facility Managers.* In APPA's *A Manual for Plant Administration* there are chapters on "Organization" by Jack Hug and "Evaluating Facilities Organizations" by Thomas Vacha. Also, in 2001, the IFMA Foundation funded a study and published *Designing the Facility Management Organization.* For middle and large-sized FM organizations, the federal government appears to have the best model. It is our opinion that better research on what works in FM organizations and organizational development needs to be done by professional associations. They would be ideal candidates, for a cooperative research effort.

Notes

1. Rondeau, Edmond P., Robert Kevin Brown, and Paul D. Lapides, *Facility Management,* (New York, NY; John Wiley & Sons, Inc., 1995, p. 2)
2. *Profiles 2007; Research Report #29,* (Houston, TX; IFMA, 2007), p. 10.
3. *Research Report #12,* (Houston, TX, IFMA, 1994), p. 13.
4. *Facilities Industry Study,* A Joint Study by IFMA, AFE, APPA, BOMA, FMLink, and Building Operating Management magazine (Houston, TX; International Facility Management Association, 2004), p. 4. Can be viewed at http://www.ifma.org/tools/research/surveys/industrysurveyreport2004.pdf
5. *Op. cit., Profiles 2007,* p. 12.
6. Kashiwagi, Dean, *Best Value Procurement,* (Tempe, AZ; Performance Based Studies Research Group, 2008, particularly Chapters 7 and 25).
7. *Conference Proceedings of the Fifteenth Annual Conference of the International Facility Management Association, 1994* (Houston; International Facility Management Association; 1994), pp. 3–6.
8. Theodore Levitt, "From the Editor: Management and Knowledge," *Harvard Business Review* (May–June 1989), p. 8.

Facility Management Leadership

3

Pulse Points

- *You alone must sell your department. Until we convince top management that facilities are equally important as human resources and information technology, we will never be as successful as we should be.*
- *Be a business leader within your company.*
- *The successful facility manager is a good communicator. Generally that means being able to speak and write well.*
- *Concentrate on your responsibility to your employees; your responsibility to management is known.*
- *Manage by facts but don't become paralyzed by lack of analysis; make timely, commonsense decisions.*
- *Hire well, keep a loose rein, and manage by walking around.*
- *Set the tone for quality and customer service.*
- *Manage to goals. Measure efficiency, effectiveness, and customer service by many and diverse ways.*
- *Develop a network of expert advice (being active in a professional association is an excellent place to start); learn how to use it effectively*
- *Facility managers will increasingly find themselves managing extremely diverse organizations of staff, contractors, and consultants . . . white, blue, and green collar.*
- *Leadership often involves selling and maintaining an evaluation system to employees who are, by nature, suspicious and resistant to such a system.*
- *Generational leadership will require both new approaches and new techniques.*
- *Stress honesty in all things.*

Leadership in a facility department is vital. Departments that run well and are well respected are managed by strong leaders. Although there is little research on the subject of FM leadership, six things are evident.

1. The skills and traits that traditionally have been characteristic of successful facility managers (technical knowledge, for example) are no longer enough. Both new and changed skills are needed today.
2. Those inside the department often have a different view of the role of a successful facility manager than those outside the department.
3. The requirements of a FM department are substantial—in most cases, meeting expanding requirements and customer expectations with decreasing resources. *Unless this is turned around, the FM organization will continue to spiral deeper into inefficiency and ineffectiveness and deferred maintenance will skyrocket.*
4. Business acumen and a sense of public relations are absolutely essential for facility managers.
5. Upper management must be convinced of the value of facility management to the point where facilities are given the same level of attention and importance as human resources and information technology.
6. By their nature and education, most facility managers do not fit the profile for business success.

Facility management is a contact sport and only dynamic leaders will ever be truly successful. In this chapter we discuss the implications of each of the Pulse Points and the six items listed above and try to profile a successful facility manager.

We are committed to the development of good leadership because no facilities team can function successfully without it. It is our observation that it is too often lacking. There are other leadership books available. In this chapter we concentrate on those aspects of leadership considered unique to facility management.

Leadership Philosophy

There is obviously no one way to lead, but there are principles applicable at all levels. Whether the facility manager is titled Office Manager or Vice President, the following apply.

The leader:

1. serves at least two constituencies; the external, which is business-oriented and normally political; and the internal, with a results-oriented, technical orientation. He or she must bridge these needs and demands.
2. is an activist if facilities are to be recognized as important, and if they are truly to be managed correctly.
   - Resources will never (or will never be perceived to) be adequate to accomplish all facility programs.

- The facilities, unlike personnel, cannot speak. They need an advocate.
- Facility management is not widely known as a profession. It needs to be explained and promoted.

3. integrates both diverse technical functions and a diverse workforce to work as a team to accomplish the mission.
4. hires well, uses the loose-rein technique, evaluates through agreed-upon metrics, and manages by walking around.
5. sets the tone for quality service.
6. simultaneously prepares for the future and reacts to today's crisis. There will always be a significant reactive component to the leader's job; a FM leader must be reactive without being a reactionary.

Too many facility managers simply try to be the best traditional facility manager, mimicking how their predecessor or their boss at the last job led. Unfortunately, and too few facility managers have realized this, the paradigm has changed. Today's workforce and marketplace require that we be seen as a business leader. It is no longer acceptable to be the best caretaker, maintainer, operator, and procedures writer. Instead, we must be that business leader, a superb service provider as defined by our customers, and an expert in public relations. Generational attitude shifts and expectations in both our customers and workforce require that we be tuned in to those changes. For those with primarily technical skills and training, acquiring those new skills can be a real challenge. It is somewhat discouraging to note that, in the last study conducted by IFMA, seven percent fewer facility managers had degrees in business and that fewer facility managers had either a bachelor's or master's degree than in 1994.[1] Though this data appears somewhat sensitive to which FM organizations are included in the sample and whether it is primarily a North American or international sample, these facts represent a challenge for our profession to promote college degree programs and to be prepared to "fill in the gaps" with high-level professional development courses.

This also serves to emphasize how important it is that facility management become a recognized profession and that colleges and universities offer degree programs in facility management. In the same context, it is discouraging that the same international study found that the preponderant function for facility managers was operations and maintenance. We need to ensure our upper management that we have skills that can take the facilities much further and demonstrate value for the organization. Two leaders in the area of leadership in facility management think we need to change the name of the profession to facilities asset management, which they advocate as a career.[2] While it is not officially stated anywhere, it is obvious that the U.S. military services are thinking along the same lines as they now use terms like installation management. Other organizations have recognized the inherent lack of understanding of the term "facility management" and have adopted a tag line, "managing the built environment," to relate our function and value.[3] We are not so sure that changing terminology does not just complicate the matter so will continue to use "facility management" in the remainder of the book.

Leaders and Leadership

There is no lack of excellent books on management and leadership and it is not our intent to advocate for one theory over another. Our approach is based on our long-service in the profession and in our observation of facility management over the past thirty years. At the same time, it is obvious that the composition, expectations, and quality of the facility management workforce have changed. Work itself has changed, the profession must change, and we must change as well.

Because facility management is still considered only an afterthought by the management team, facility managers today must become much more proactive business leaders. This point cannot be stressed strongly enough. It was brought home to us during the writing of this book when one of our contemporaries, concerned by the lack of business skills among fellow facility managers, started up her own FM business program at a local college.[4]

Facility managers must know the business they support, know their own business, run the department like a business, and be able to speak the language of business. How businesslike the facility manager is will largely determine how he is viewed outside the department, particularly by upper management. Each of our organizations has its own business language and we need to be able to speak in the same language of the decision-makers.

Because he is managing a technical staff, a facility manager must also be comfortable with the technical aspects of his job. Each of us also needs to be comfortable with quantitative analysis, specifically using numbers to measure operational effectiveness and efficiency. Unfortunately, too many facility managers, probably due to their education, tend to overemphasize their role as a technical manager. A quick review of Exhibit 1-1 indicates that no one person can expect to be expert in all FM functions. Therefore, it is important the facility manager manage from a customer service perspective and strengthen his job knowledge and skills as a business leader. The variety of required FM skills is another reason that we have always favored having a mixed workforce of staff, contractors, and consultants. You can hire the specialized expertise to perform the technical duties. Facility managers and key staff employees should be devoted to the leadership and management of the facilities function.

There is always a danger in stating that a certain type of leader of a particular management style will be successful in a given environment or position. However, there are certain leadership traits that are more likely to lead to success. For instance, successful facility managers should possess good management skills, be knowledgeable about facilities, and be comfortable managing experts in design, engineering, technology, finance, law, food service, security, etc.

This is basic. In addition, a good facility manager must be capable of simultaneously handling problems that require immediate resolution and those that are long range. He deals with questions for which there are no absolute answers and often that are emotionally charged. He understands his employee base (to include contractors) and their needs, as well as the advocates for building services. Some responses will require rapid reaction as well as strategic insight. He needs the ability to allocate shortages as well as resources.

The facility manager must be comfortable saying no diplomatically, be absolutely committed to providing service, be capable of allowing subordinates their independence within common objectives, and be readily available and recognizable within and outside the department. Be aware, however, that facility managers have a reputation as naysayers, not a characteristic valued in business leaders.

From the discussion above, leading the facility management organization may seem impossible because it is so diverse and the demands so great. The diversity of functions, the level of activity, the active interest of employees in their work environment (the social status inherent in the allocation of office space, for example), and the recurring lack of adequate resources make the facility manager highly visible. Systems and standards must handle 90-95 percent of the problems, but the facility manager must be personally available and visible to do the following:

- Tend to the other 5 to 10 per cent of the problems.
- Handle exceptions to standards and policies.
- Promote the department as a concerned, cost-conscious service provider and business advisor.
- Reinforce and motivate subordinates.

Because facility management is so diverse, the leader will never be knowledgeable in every aspect of FM. That means he must have a system to produce expert advice at an appropriate time and the wisdom and judgment to sort through often conflicting opinions to decide on a course of action. Developing a network of experts and knowing how to use the experts effectively are skills that must be developed. Unfortunately, the ability to hire the best person for the job is sometimes circumvented by the institutional requirement to hire the lowest bidder. This is why we urge facility managers to work with their Purchasing Department to embrace best value contracting. It is a trust-building exercise because the easiest and least controversial thing to do is to follow low-bid contracting . . . but it is so short-sighted in all but the simplest procurements.

One of the principles of management is to evaluate and we strongly favor measuring every function possible and holding someone responsible for meeting established goals in each functional area. Look particularly for functions that can add value to the organization. Some of our network of experts[5] and IFMA are committed to the Balanced Scorecard as an excellent method to set and track organizational goals. One great hint from those same experts is to be sure you are tracking outcomes and not processes.[6] At the same time, be wary of numbers and be somewhat of a skeptic. People may cheat on numbers but do so because the competition overwhelms their judgment. The leader creates an environment of healthy competition and, while pushing for progress, does not make a single failure to reach a goal a drastic event. Innovation and improvement must be encouraged, and the inherent risks can sometimes lead to mistakes, which can also be learning tools. Leaders who do not verify the validity of numbers against their personal experience often find that the numbers become their undoing. Those who lead honestly and promote that ethic within the department are most likely to have honesty in their reporting from subordinates. As President Reagan said, "Trust but verify."

There is a place for bureaucracy in any large organization. That is not a popular statement in modern organizational theory but, it is our experience that, facility management is best practiced in a structured organization, *especially* if that organization is a blend of staff, contractors, and consultants. Bureaucracy, properly structured, allows the day-to-day work of the department to proceed without crisis and to handle that 90-95 percent of the workload flawlessly. However, a bureaucracy is also the principal maintainer of the status quo and an enemy of creative change. At appropriate times, the leader must be willing to oppose the bureaucracy, promote change, or to seek exceptions to procedures.

Finally, management by walking around is essential and will probably be even more important in the future. It allows for frank, unstructured discussion and observation. Here, again, we raise the issue of honesty. If the facility manager has been up front with his workforce, they will discuss problems, issues, and solutions honestly with him. If nothing else, it verifies or denies the statistics in reports. For those who feel this technique is too unstructured, consider the fact that a study of managers shows that, "managers' activities" are characterized by brevity, variety, and discontinuity. . . They get their information almost randomly, favoring inefficient face-to-face meetings over a systematic paper flow."[7] It is doubtful that a management style stressing written communication, voluminous analysis, total reliance on quantitative factors, and a reclusive personal style will be successful in facility man-agement. *Yet it has been our experience that too many facility managers do, in fact, practice just such a reclusive management style.*

We have observed many good facility managers. They have the following characteristics:

1. Business-oriented
2. Technically competent
3. Capable of good oral and written communication
4. Comfortable with reaction
5. Customer service oriented
6. Cost conscious
7. Outgoing, even politically savvy
8. Decisive
9. Slightly legalistic
10. Capable of concurrent problem solving
11. Comfortable with and capable of quantitative measurement
12. Action-oriented
13. Able to deal well with people
14. Experienced
15. Honest

In general, this skill set is best developed through successful performance at a smaller or equal-sized facility. Human Relations and other managers should not expect that a lateral hire of another administrative manager into the facilities position will be successful.

As a facility manager, you must be a persuasive advocate for your department. You must know how to exercise the formal and informal chain of authority and communications lines, both internal and external. Your relationship with other key leaders and staff is particularly critical to the department. You must be not only an effective informal communicator but a skilled writer and presenter. You need to develop skills in presenting metrics and building information graphically since most of your audience does not have experience with things such as floor plans and building system metrics.

Since so many decisions involve major expenditure of funds, facility managers are expected to be able to make sophisticated economic arguments. While the number crunching can be done by staff, they must understand the context and methodology of net present value analyses, cost-benefit ratios, payback periods, return on investment, and other financial calculations. We call this speaking the language of business. It is essential that the facility manager be able to make arguments and departmental positions in the language that upper management uses and understands. In general, they do not understand technical arguments; they understand economic arguments, and we must be able to make them. Often you must convince a financial analyst, interested only in the economics, of the validity of your argument before you are even exposed to top management. One successful technique we have used is to actually solicit the analyst in developing the briefing for upper management.

There are as many situations demanding leadership as there are days of the year. We can't cover them all. We will explore two leadership scenarios of facility management; forming the facilities team and taking charge.

The Facilities Team

A major challenge for the facility manager is forming a facilities staff and getting it to function as a team. Unfortunately, many factors in a company work counter to a team approach, which is why a facility manager must be a leader, not simply a manager.

We have mentioned repeatedly the diverse nature of staffing in most facility departments; staff, contractors, and consultants. This allows for both maximization of skills and flexibility to meet peak workloads. Yet all members of the team, regardless of employment status, must feel that they are important and members of one team. This is true even for one-time contractors. In some organizations, even though it makes sense, a staff member is never to be placed in a position subordinate to a consultant. Bureaucratic personnel policies or traditions that preclude such assignments often run contrary to effective team building and require an aggressive leader to get them modified. In today's contractor and consultant-laden business world, this consultant may be the best (or only) person, to train, manage, and guide an employee, regardless of staffing status.

Unfortunately, some good management techniques often run contrary to good teamwork. Excessive dependence on quantitative measurement, particularly measuring one work unit against another, often leads to cutting corners, bickering, and even sabotage. Quantitative measurements always must be evaluated in context and used as indicators for discussion on ways to improve, not as the final word. Likewise, subordinate objectives must reinforce departmental goals. Successful teamwork and subordinates who stress an understanding and support of the entire organization must be rewarded.

A classic example of lack of teamwork is using a special team, responsible directly to top management, to construct a building. Typically the team has two goals: finish the construction on time (which can be at the expense of good workmanship) and within the capital budget (even if that often ensures that life-cycle cost for energy management and maintainability are sub-optimized). The operational side of the facilities team is excluded from design and review, almost ensuring later problems. Facility department leaders must integrate the FM team into the initial phases of the projects, so that this does not happen. Special-purpose groups have a place, at times they are essential, but their integration with the facility team is required for success. The facility manager should manage facilities throughout their life cycle (Exhibit 1-3).

Many typical procurement processes also run contrary to facility team building; probably none as consistently destructive as low-bid contacting. In one case, a custodial contractor who had been in place for years lost a low-bid contract by $13,000 on a $3 million base contract. The result was almost predictable. The new contractor was terminated for nonperformance after a year, and the disruption cost hundreds of thousands of dollars. What suffered most was the facilities team concept. Because the original custodial contractor covered nearly every square foot of the facility daily, he had been trained to be the eyes and ears of the facilities staff, reporting not only custodial problems but broken furniture, inoperable plumbing, malfunctioning elevators, and so on. The low-bid contractor never "joined" the team, and inadequately reported or failed to report these deficiencies. The leader needs to identify the procurement rules that detract from the facilities team, and work to change or modify them.

The requirement for a contractor to join the facilities team should be clearly spelled out in the contract. It should be a point of emphasis in all pre-contractual discussion. For example, an excellent renovation company got off to a woeful start on a new contract they had just won. The owner insisted on being involved in operations within the facility department rather than appointing an on-site superintendent who could manage the company's assets within the facility team. On a happy note, one meeting with the owner produced an on-site superintendent empowered to act for the company and that same superintendent is on site more than twenty years later spearheading the alterations portion of the facilities team.

There is no single professional experience more rewarding than forming the facilities team. Three general principles prevail. First, hire the best person or company to do the job over the long run whether staff, contractor, or consultant. Match the hire with the task. Second, ensure that control remains within the staff with a specific staff member being accountable to you for every major function. Due to funding and staffing limitations, that may not be immediately possible, but should be a priority of the new facility manager. Third, treat every member of the team as an equal team member. Work together, party together, be recognized together, and share the glory.

Once the team is up and functioning, the effort cannot end there. The leader must plan and direct that team for the long run as staff members retire, contracts terminate (by the third rebid, it is difficult for the incumbent to hold on to a lucrative contract), and new requirements surface. Managing a facility organization is managing a continuum of interrelated events. The team will change and must have both substitutes and built-in depth if it is to survive (yes, you might secretly groom a consultant or contractor to assume a supervisory staff position later on). No one, including the facility manager, should be irreplaceable. When all of these factors come together, a synergism is created, and the facility department functions in a manner that is truly greater than the sum of its parts.

A concept worth consideration for certain FM functions involves the use of self-managed teams, allowing workers to be responsible for organizing, regulating, and controlling the various aspects and conditions of their jobs in order to affect the outcome. Such teams exemplify some of the dynamics of the current workplace and workforce (total quality management, self-actuation, focus on independence, etc.) but we advise that you start out slowly after carefully selecting the proper functions to perform using the teams. Some team members find it hard to adapt and budget control can be difficult.[8]

Taking Charge

Few of us have an opportunity to form a department "from scratch." However, most of us have had or will have an opportunity to step into an existing organization and, using our leadership skills, make it better.

No other situation is as challenging for the facility manager as taking charge of a facility department. Most of the comments here apply to a midsize organization, but they are applicable to large or small organizations, as well as those staffed primarily with either in-house people or independent contractors. Anyone facing this challenge would do well to read Warren Bennis's and Burt Nanus's book, *Leaders: The Strategies for Taking Charge* particularly the section entitled "The Context of Leadership."

When taking charge of a facility department, the facility manager should gain perspective on what the parent organization desires. Some of this should have become apparent during the hiring process but there are always hidden agendas which need to be discovered. A reasonably detailed statement of both objectives and probable resourcing through the mid-term (3-5 years) should be requested from senior management. At the same time an indication of the true level of support to be expected and any major issues regarding facilities within the company or on the boss' agenda need to be well understood. Concurrently a quantitative assessment of the department is needed (some of the professional associations' surveys can help here), as well as in-depth discussions with the subordinate groups within their department. If he has a contracted organization in place, a get-acquainted meeting with each contractor and a meeting where they discuss how the contractor feels they are supporting the department, problems, if any, and how their support could improve may be helpful. Similar meetings with his colleagues in the company, particularly the managers of Procurement, Human Resources, Information Technology, and other support departments should be held to gain a complete understanding of the current view of the facilities team. At the conclusion of these meetings, a clear understanding should emerge of where FM stands in the bureaucracy, good and bad.

Finally, a review of the summary of customer comments on services for the past two years and talks to user groups for their perceptions of the timeliness and quality of services will provide insight. Senior administrative personnel or senior occupants form a good sample for these user groups. User groups may need a form or format (questionnaire, telephone survey) to remind them of the variety of services provided.

When the leader has a good overall picture of the present status of the department, he needs to establish a game plan to keep the organization operating while ensuring the needed improvements. Here are the steps taken from an actual situation where the initial organizational opinion of the facility department could not have been worse when the new facility manager arrived but, within three years, it became a top-flight provider of the full range of facility services.

1. Use the ink blot approach to implement physical change. Start small; use your FM organization's work areas as testing laboratories. Try a division or department trial on items like wall covering, furniture, and carpet before standardizing or distributing items companywide. Often vendors may give you samples to experiment with.
2. Unless satisfied, take action immediately (within the first year) in the following areas:
   • Concentrate on operational matters first. Establish policy, procedures, and standards. If possible, run a pilot on each or use focus groups to try them out. Insist that changes be implemented; set up feedback mechanisms on all changes.
   • Establish an efficient services reception and work coordination center with an automated work management system compatible with your other automation needs.
3. Establish, as soon as possible, organizational and procedural distinctions between planning and design and operations and maintenance.

4. Study the organizational chart. Sharpen lines of responsibility and authority. Ensure that someone, by job title, is responsible for each function in the department.
5. Make personnel moves while on your honeymoon. Be fair, but get the right team. (We do not agree with the philosophy of making wide-sweeping personnel changes, because that is seldom needed. At the same time, rid yourself of dead weight or those who cannot adapt to your approach). If Human Resources cannot support a position that you need, hire a contractor or consultant for all but management positions.
6. Expend the effort to explain all changes that affect your staff, the staff at large, your boss, and other service providers. This is a tremendously time-consuming, yet important task. Use multiple media and share this task with trusted subordinates once they are on board and knowledgeable.
7. Launch a public relations campaign. Put someone in charge of public relations, yourself if necessary.
   - Internal efforts within your organization: give awards, publicize your successes, keep the work force informed through a newsletter, and ensure you include "kudos."
   - External efforts: Sell to your boss. Promote your department by saying, "Here's what we can do for you."; use the current administrative network; send your newsletter to selected individuals outside your department; use the company newsletter or internal Web site—stress public interest stories featuring your department to include contractors; develop a professional departmental briefing and seek out opportunities to use it.
   - Develop an organizational Customer Service Manual, both hard copy and electronic, which explains departmental services, how to initiate each type of service, and explain what is chargeable work.
8. If something does not work, do not be afraid to change it, but ensure that it was properly implemented and supported, and understand why it went wrong. There is a fine line between strength of conviction and stubbornness.
9. Establish a system of collecting and analyzing user service evaluations with your automated information system. Make yourself visible and readily available to your customers to explain what you are trying to do, your constraints, how it fits into the company objectives, and to answer questions.
10. Develop and execute at least one project where tangible cost savings can be realized. Make it a "green" project and get double exposure. Publicize it!
11. Do several visible projects. A great deal of goodwill can be created with paint and carpet in office areas and cafeteria remodeling. Publicize these projects during work and upon completion!

12. Whether you can afford it immediately or not, plan to get every part of the facility, to include furniture, significant furnishings, and equipment under life-cycle management using your automated system. Implement what you can as fast as you can.

13. Initiate a preventive maintenance program in all interior areas that emphasizes furnishings, furniture, finishes, and general appearance. Priority should go to public areas, executive areas, general work space, and, finally, to garages, storage rooms, and closets.

14. Develop maintenance cycles consistent with need and political importance. This is very important because it determines one major portion of your budget. Implement a preventive maintenance program on all major equipment and areas listed in Appendix G-6. This will take some time, particularly for those items subject to predictive maintenance, because you may not have a maintenance history for those items. Your vendors can be very helpful in setting up preventive maintenance initially and you can then change cycles, costs, etc. based on actual experience.

15. Assess your design, planning, and consulting need—both quantitatively and qualitatively.

16. Inject yourself into the organization's business planning. For every organizational business plan, there should be a facility plan. Personally direct (if only for the first year) the preparation of the department's annual work plan, annual budget, and capital budget. You have to go through the cycle once to understand every aspect of these documents in order to direct their execution.

17. Learn, in detail, the paperwork flow from your submission of a request for goods or services until the vendor is paid. This bureaucratic chain is fraught with pitfalls. You cannot control this process until you understand it.

18. Personally review all existing service contracts and supply agreements.

19. Develop all comparators and management indicators that you want to use. Automate them with your management information system to automatically highlight where performance is out of standard or where it is excellent.

20. Write, or have written, an organization and functions manual for the department. Do not do this immediately to avoid excessive revisions. If you can write the functions clearly and sensibly, they probably are properly conceived and assigned.

21. Adopt programmatic budgeting. Working with your financial managers, reformat your budget so that it directly feeds your management information system. For example, if one of the management indicators that you

desire to track is maintenance and repair costs for a facility on a square footage basis, one line of your budget should be for maintenance and repair costs by facility without further complicated factoring, additions, or corrections.

22. Develop a system, perhaps individual business luncheons, with your operation colleagues to discuss how you might support the business units of your company better. Do not forget important administrative players like the heads of human relations, information systems, and purchasing. You should be meeting with these individuals quarterly—or at least semi-annually.

23. Start to develop an image for your department. Perhaps you want the department to be viewed as the environmental leader, or perhaps the risk mitigator. Perhaps you want to emphasize its contributions to company productivity—and hence the bottom line. Maybe accenting your ergonomic efforts will get the attention of top management. *It is not enough simply to do a good job; that is expected.* The challenge is to position the department so that it is viewed as an invaluable part of the business, not simply a cost center.

Of the twenty-three items above, some will be resisted internally, and many will have to be sold outside the department. That's why taking charge is such a leadership challenge. Founding a department or assuming leadership in a comatose one is a sixty-hour-a-week (maybe eighty at budget time) job for the first eighteen to twenty-four months. After that, it can be accomplished within normal hours-provided you have set up things correctly.

As the first year comes to an end, the new leader should be putting in place, or at least actively planning, the department audit. This major activity will set the tone and substance for the department for at least a decade. Although there is no standard format for this audit, there are firms capable of conducting one. Your local professional association chapter may be able to refer you to a local firm. An effective departmental audit consists of the following (in the process of organizing/reorganizing, you may have already done some of these items):

1. An organizational audit of mission, functions, organization, relationships, and position grading.
2. A physical facilities audit, to obtain a level of documentation needed for planning and design decisions, and a condition assessment that will allow for making knowledgeable decisions for maintenance, repair, and capital improvement. (This audit can be conducted at several levels and can be very costly. Our experience is that, eventually you will want a detailed

condition assessment of all facilities you intend to retain. If you can afford it, get the detailed audit as early as possible and ensure that the audit results are fed into your automated system in a way that both the manager and the maintainer can use. Building condition assessments are important to do on a continuous basis. Some organizations are on a five-year cycle, assessing 20 percent of their facilities annually.

3. A comprehensive energy audit.
4. A facility sustainability audit.
5. A way-finding and location audit.
6. A five year space requirements study for both leasing and capital improvements.
7. A standards audit.
8. A furniture, furnishings, and art audit that ensures standard, control, inventory, and security can be maintained over time.
9. A facility information system that ties all of the above together in a common database accessible to all managers.

This audit should be completed within eighteen to twenty-four months except for the automation aspects. During this time, the greatest leadership challenges are to retain management interest, support, and funding and to stay on schedule. However, by project's end, both the facility manager and all departmental managers should have the tools necessary to manage effectively and efficiently for the long term.

Leadership Style

Leadership style and personality are highly individualized (your co-authors have distinctly different approaches to leadership) so there is a temptation not to comment on it here. Unfortunately, not much research has been done in the facility management environment. What has been done determined that facility managers tend to be judgmental, i.e., decision-making came easy to them and that they focused on data and objects and had a short-term orientation.[9] It is important to understand personality types and a number of tools are available for this, one being the Myers-Briggs Type Indicator (MBTI).

Major changes in work itself, as well as social and environmental dictates are influencing leadership as a new generation of managers and the workforce have differing attitudes toward work, the environment, and the workplace.[10] Current facility managers look to a new generation of management gurus, writers, and speakers. As the workplace and its value dramatically change, organizations are forced to correct processes, allocation, and practices, but the management of the built environment is becoming more widely recognized and respected, providing increased importance for our profession.

We consulted a number of sources to see what the experts felt were the key to successful facility management leadership in the future. The National Research Council has, in fact, looked at the core competencies necessary to lead federal facilities asset management (their new term for FM) through 2020.[11] A member of the committee which produced that report and a very experienced facility manager and educator, Dr. Bill Badger, summarized the leadership skill set as follows:

- A smart owner's mindset
- A governing behavior of strategic decision-making
- A commitment to life-cycle management (Total Cost of Ownership)
- Competency in integrating, aligning, and innovating.
- Key business skills

To achieve these and to develop a depth of leadership and good succession planning, departments should commit 2 percent of their salary budget to education and training.[12] This was confirmed by our associate, Stormy Friday, who views staying current on technological advances and emerging key issues a major challenge for facility managers and for their associations to keep them "plugged in."[13]

In this chapter we hope we have explained techniques around which you can wrap your own particular leadership philosophy. We know these techniques work because we have implemented them in a variety of private and public settings. We hope this chapter will help you formulate or perhaps re-formulate your own approach to leadership. We close with the words of one management guru who has endured, Rosabeth Moss Kanter. "The individual may still be the ultimate actor, but the actions often stem from the context in which the individual operates. Leadership therefore consists increasingly of the design of settings which provide tools for and stimulate constructive, productive individual actions."[14] This truly describes what we feel is an effective facility management organization, knowledgeable and motivated individuals operating within a structure that has been well thought out and tested. Neal Angrisano, *TFM Magazine*'s Facility Executive of the Year 2008, perhaps stated it as well as anyone, ". . . because if there's one thing I'd like to tell all people out there in facilities management, it's that you've got a fantastic opportunity. You're the key person who can make so much happen. That's awesome."[15] As we mentioned at the end of Chapter 2, being properly organized can assure that you are the "key person" but it is up to you and your leadership to see the opportunity and to make things happen.

Notes

1. *Research Report 29, Profiles 2007*, (Houston: IFMA, 2007), p. 15.
2. Badger, William W. and Michael J. Garvin, *Facilities Asset Management; A New Career Field for Construction Management Graduates*, (Tempe, AZ: PBSRG: 2007). p. 1.
3. *Facilities Management Action Agenda; Second Year Implementation Report, 2007*, (Facility Management Association, Australia).
4. Meng, Phyllis in a personal correspondence with the author.
5. Whittaker, James and Chris Hodges in a personal correspondence with the author, April 23, 2008.
6. *Ibid.*
7. *Washington Post*, April 12, 1988, p. D4.
8. Kathy Roper and Deborah Phillips, "Integrating Self-Managed Work Teams into Project Management," *Journal of Facilities Management, Vol. 5, No. 1*, p. 23.
9. Martha Whitaker, in a personal correspondence with the author, August 14, 1989.
10. Personal communication from Stormy Friday, The Friday Group, Annapolis, MD, April 23, 2008 and Diane MacKnight, MacKnight Associates, Arlington, VA, May 24, 2008.
11. *Core Competencies for Federal Facility Asset Management Through 2020*, (Washington, DC: National Research Council: 2008.)
12. Personal communication from Dr. Badger, Performance Based Studies Research Group and formerly Head, Del Webb School of Construction, Arizona State University, March 4, 2008.
13. Personal communications from Stormy Friday, President, The Friday Group, Annapolis, MD, April 23, 2008.
14. *Facilities Management Leadership*, (Grand Rapids, MI; Steelcase, 1988), p. 4.
15. Schwartz, Heidi, "TFM Names Neal Angrisano Facility Executive of the Year," *TFM Magazine, January 2008*, p. 24.

Section

Planning, Programming, and Budgeting

In a recent discussion, one of our mentors, a person who cares greatly about the profession, said that the most sought-after course she was teaching these days was one on treating FM as a business. This is good because it remains our observation of the profession that too many of us still cling to our technical backgrounds whereas the successful department head needs to have business skills. In this section we introduce the first of those skills; planning, programming, and budgeting. Oftentimes, public sector facility managers, particularly federal employees, are already familiar with the system which starts with gathering requirements, then arranging them into programs, and ultimately finalizing them in a budget.

A good business manager plans so that actions are proactive, not always reactive. In this section we explore three aspects of planning from the facilities vantage point: strategic and annual planning to determine priorities and goals; space planning because space is the *lingua franca* of facility management; and financial planning to anticipate costs and expenditures to accomplish the organization's goals.

Too often facility management has been confused with operations and maintenance, project management or space management. Facility planning covers these and all functions of facility management (Exhibit 1-1). But that is not enough. Facility planning must be an integral part of the organization's business planning, not just an add-on. There is almost no organizational function that does not require facilities and they must be planned for concurrently with the development of the business plan. **For every organizational business plan (strategic, midterm, *ad hoc*, work, or other) there should be a corresponding facility plan.** These facility plans should be organized around the facility manager's selected programs and the budget should be organized by those programs. That enables us to track our efforts from concept through execution.

Within the facility department, there should be a logical sequence established from planning though budgeting. Not only should there be a horizontal flow from strategic planning though the work plan to the budget, but there should also be a vertical flow. Strategic plans feed subsequent iterations (e.g., this year's budget provides input for next year's).

Good facility planning offers the greatest single source of cost savings and avoidances for your department.

Strategic and Annual Planning

4

Pulse Points

- *Facility programs, the building blocks of planning and budgeting, should be consistent and trackable over time.*
- *The work plan is a specific manifestation of the programs in the strategic plan.*
- *There should be a facilities business plan to support every company business plan.*
- *Facility management functions should be grouped into budget programs with a manager responsible and accountable for each.*
- *Use life-cycle costing for all analysis of projects over $100,000.*
- *At least one person in the facility department should be focused on planning.*
- *Planning is the facility manager's entree into the business of the company.*
- *Prioritization panels, with user participation, can assist the facility manager in aligning oversubscribed programs.*
- *Prepare an annual work plan 5 to 15 percent in excess of the anticipated budget.*

The role of planning in facility management has special significance. First, it directly interfaces with the business aspects of the company. Second, it clearly exhibits how far from the boiler room the profession has come. Third, it substantially reduces costs and has a high relative return. Despite the emphasis on planning in modern management, it is astounding how few people and companies really buy into planning. "Our company is too dynamic [or complex or screwed up] to plan" is a common belief. That attitude is unfortunate, and probably derives from the fact that business writers have oversold the concept of planning and have failed to articulate exactly what it is.

Think of a plan as a map of an unexplored area into which you are moving. The nearest portion is reasonably detailed—the major obstacles are shown, and the map provides rough guidance for everyday activities. But as you get farther into the unknown, the map is vaguer and provides only general direction. Like Lewis and Clark, however, you should be updating as you go along, so that the next map is more detailed and more useful. This is why annual plan reviews and rolling planning are so necessary. Planning, particularly strategic planning, has come under criticism, some of that justified because U.S. businesses do not have a good record of planning strategically. However, failure to plan for facilities use is to be a prisoner of reaction.

Planning should be cost-effective. The military has the right idea. In most major headquarters, there is a staff devoted to operations and another devoted to planning. When the stakes are death or survival, there is a strong commitment to planning. Private businesses should learn from that. As our colleague Tom Kvan, who has done much to bring company business and facility planning together, says about strategic planning, "As much as anything, we plan [in order] to avoid disaster."[1]

In our experience, the problem is not planning but implementation. Here are some common mistakes:

- Plans are prepared entirely by consultants, without commitment from managers.
- Plans are prepared and then put on the shelf because (1) the goal is to *have* a plan, not to *use* the plan, and (2) the plan is not updated.
- Plans are 90 percent form and 10 percent substance.

Quite often a plan is nothing more than assurance that a consultant will get wealthier and the department has to start from scratch as each version is implemented. Likewise, many plans try to do too much too soon and thus lose credibility. Or they fail to tie strategic to annual planning, and annual planning to programming and budgeting. If this concept is alien, or if there is more than a 30 percent information void as you move step by step through these loops, then both the process and the planner deserve a hard look.

Facility planning, like most other business endeavors, is only as effective as a facility manager wants to make it. Good planning accelerates response time, improves coordination of major expenditures, and coordinates short-term activities with long-term goals.[2] Both the advantages of good planning and the risks of bad planning are apparent. It will be done well only if it is viewed as significant.

Types of Planning

There are two types of facility planning: strategic or long-range and short or mid-range (see Exhibit 4-1). A well-functioning facility department uses both.

Exhibit 4-1. Differences between short- and long-term facility planning.

Consideration	Short Term	Long Term
Time line	Less than three years	More than three years
Clarity of future	Reasonably clear	Not clear
Purpose of planning	To provide facilities	To provide infrastructure; to permit future short-range plans to be made more easily
Planning pressures	Lost business, laws and regulations, suddenly recognized need	Doubts and uncertainties, long-term savings, locating of highly fixed assets
Basis of projecting needs	Specific input information	Probable likelihoods
Techniques of planning	Space layout	Top down—bottom up
Nature of plans	Definite and specific	General and conceptual
Capital investment and budgets	Budget, cash-flow analysis	Investment analysis

Source: Richard S. Tryce, unpublished manuscript, June 14, 1988.

Planning should be done in the context of the company business plan. It is important to understand the relationship that exists among the company's business plan, the facility management plan, and the department's budgeting. It is also important to understand the concept of *facility programs*, the building blocks of each plan. These facility programs are the basic building blocks of facility management plans and budgets. They are those activities that you desire to plan, budget, resource, and manage directly. Exhibit 4-2 shows a list of suggested programs for a complete plan. These are appropriate programs for a midsize organization. A larger organization might use more categories, whereas a smaller company might use fewer. In general, the mid-range plan for an organization contains a consolidation of categories, the long-range plan fewer. Design and engineering can be absorbed in each project cost. You might choose other programs, but whichever ones make up your plan, they should be consistent and trackable from year to year.

The level of detail varies with both the plan and the size of the organization. Since there is no standardization of planning or planning cycles, the model in Exhibit 4-2 may require extensive modification to meet your particular needs. Nevertheless, the basic system here is workable.

Exhibit 4-2. Facility department annual work plan.

1. Capital Costs
   Construction
   Alteration
   Major repair
   Replacement
   Equipment purchase
   Furniture purchase
   Design and engineering
2. Annually Funded Costs
   (Nondiscretionary)
   Utilities
   Operations
   Maintenance and repair
   • Preventive maintenance
   • Corrective maintenance
   • Special maintenance
   • Minor repair
   • Major repair
   • Design and engineering
   Custodial
   Moving
3. Annually Funded Costs
   (Discretionary)
   Alterations
   Maintenance
   Repair

   Moving
   Design and engineering
4. Lease Costs
   Space
   Utilities
   Alterations
   Equipment
   Furniture
   Design and engineering
5. Lease Holding Income
6. Overhead Costs
   Personnel
   • Regular staff salaries and benefits (positions by category)
   • Supplementary staff (temporaries, nondesign consultants, etc., by category)
   • Training
   • Travel
   Office equipment
   Vehicles
   Design and engineering
7. Space Needs Projections
   Owned
   Leased

How often does a department prepare a plan? Both long- and short-range plans are linked to the department's budget. Budgets normally are prepared for one year (either fiscal or calendar), but multi-year budgeting is becoming more popular and has some distinct advantages. All managers are likely to be involved in three budgets in any one fiscal year; budget closeout, execution of the current budget, and development of the follow-up budget. Similarly, facility managers will be involved with two annual work plans—the one in execution and the one in preparation.

The department's budget should flow directly from an annual work plan, which is simply an orderly presentation of the amount of work, arranged by program, that the department can expect to accomplish in a year. The items are grouped by program to correspond to the programs in the plan. Unfortunately, too often one of two things sometimes happens: (1) the work plan is developed after the budget is approved, or (2) during the budget process the work plan is not updated, so there is a huge discrepancy between the approved budget and the approved work plan. To solve these problems, it is essential to manage the planning and budgeting processes, perhaps, in a midsize organization, with a full-time planner or consultant. Work plans prepared annually with a twelve-month term are adequate. However, some planners desire a fifteen- or even eighteen-month horizon, for the following two reasons:

1. They ensure that there is continuity of purpose during the end-of-year period.
2. They maximize the productive use of any excess funds that sometimes appear in the last days of a fiscal year.

Our purpose is to eliminate the sometimes exasperating funding of noncritical year-end projects simply because they require little time to design and execute. The longer-term work plan helps promote an important concept: the series of work plans as spaces on a continuum rather than discrete entities. Changes in priorities can be made by periodic reviews, not because something has already been designed or requires no approval from the corporate office.

We are committed to good midrange planning. We feel the ideal length is eighteen to thirty-six months, and that the first draft of each annual work plan derives from the mid-range plan. At least 70 percent of the mid-range plan should be translatable into an annual work plan once the planning process is mature. If facility planning is to be successful, it will reap its greatest rewards in mid-range planning. A sample format for both mid-range and strategic plans is given in Exhibit 4-3. The difference is only in the regard to specificity of assumptions and degree of detail.

If the department can plan in a truly meaningful way beyond five years, and the strategic planning document is actually used, great! But for purposes of this book, we consider strategic facility planning to be three to five years.

Tom Kvan provides interesting insight when he calls strategic planning descriptive and annual planning prescriptive. He feels that any company unable to plan beyond five years is blind in the area of facility management, particularly in an international environment. He says that each plan should describe not only what the facilities will look like but what facility department structure will be required to implement needed changes.[3]

Planning Techniques

While many books have been written on business planning, little has been done on the strategic or work planning of facilities. What is available tends to discuss how to plan strategically, for example, but not how to plan <u>facilities</u> strategically or

Exhibit 4-3. Mid- or long-range facility plan.

    I. Introduction

   II. Environment

  III. Assumptions[1]

  IV. Constraints[1]

   V. Discussion
     A. Presentation of scenarios
     B. Impact on/of programs for each scenario
        1. Capital
        2. Annually funded nondiscretionary
        3. Annually funded discretionary
        4. Lease costs
        5. Lease holding incomes
        6. Overhead costs
        7. Space need projections
     C. Discussion of most probable scenario (highlight critical deviations from other scenarios which could affect the facility department and/or business significantly; include risk and sensitivity analyses, if possible)

  VI. Conclusions

 VII. Recommendations

VIII. Appendixes
     A. Time-phased list of events to implement most probable scenario
     B. Capital[2]
        1. Environment[3]
        2. Assumptions[3]
        3. Constraints[3]
        4. Impacts on program
        5. New initiatives required[4]
     C. Annually funded nondiscretionary costs
     D. Annually funded discretionary costs
     E. Lease costs
     F. Lease holding income
     G. Overhead costs
     H. Personnel projection
     I. Space needs projection
     J. Organization chart for departmental structure

¹ Derived from business plan plus best input of facilities staff.
² Other program appendixes similarly organized.
³ Only those applicable from main plan.
⁴ Described up to one paragraph with programmatic estimates of start date, duration, and costs.

---

how to integrate our facility planning into the company planning. The single source that we found that addresses facility planning and organizational planning in the government ties facility planning only to capital budgeting not to annual budgeting.[4] This is like planning to buy a new car and considering only if we can afford the initial price. We try to address this deficiency. The exact planning system is organizationally dependent so we will confine ourselves here to a general discussion of planning in a mid- or large sized organization where a planning system is required to manage the process.

In the remainder of this chapter and book, we will talk about long-range planning (think beyond ten years), a mid-term plan (3-10 years) and a work plan (1-2 years) but our experience is that organizations are strategically planning for 3-5 years with an occasional organization planning out to eight. So, in most cases, our discussions of long-range and mid-term plans tend to be combined in practice.

When we queried our group of experts concerning major issues facing facility managers, Diane MacKnight raised the issue that the business environment is changing so rapidly that creating facility management plans is outmoded. She proposes instead that facility managers develop five strategy elements tied to their organizational business strategy.[5] We recognize the rapid pace of change, particularly in the private sector but still believe that, in the long run, facility managers should follow the planning and programming effort that produces annual budgets. We grant that, in the first two years of this effort if you start from scratch, there is a substantial workload and that there will need to be changes made on the fly. However, once you have a five-year program in place, for example, plans and budgets become simply a matter of making minor alterations of those programmed before submission.

Sometimes planning is done by a single person or small group. This maximizes the possibility that the resulting plan will be followed and best ensures continuity. On the downside, the input for the plan largely depends on the input of a small group, not necessarily reflecting the needs of the organization. This limited perspective is typical of a consultant-prepared plan; we call it OMOM, or one man on a mountain. Companies who turn their facility planning over to a consultant hired only for that task, or who use the OMOM approach, deserve what they get, a plan for which no one will take ownership and soon will be gathering dust on the shelf. The best way to get "buy-in" for a plan at any level is to involve all appropriate people in the preparation of that plan. Two of your authors have had experience with the planning methodology used at the U.S. Department of Defense and feel that the Planning, Programming, and Budgeting System (PPBS) employed there is a highly effective system which naturally includes the planning of facilities. It can be scaled down for use in smaller organizations and there are available examples of using PPBS in civilian organizations.[6]

Top down planning is similar to OMOM, but the one man or small group is the agency head or company president. It has the same advantages and drawbacks, but can be effective for an initial plan for a small organization. The problem comes as the organization grows. All planning, including facilities planning, wants and needs top-level input, but the CEO-level person cannot dominate planning for long. The old saw that "two heads [or three or five or seven] are better than one" is generally accurate for planning.

Another technique is AGIR—a gang in a room. Commonly known as brainstorming, this approach better ensures that various views and aspects are represented, particularly if the individuals are chosen well. The downside is too much input, some of it ego laden, which may yield inconsistent, even contradictory results. A good leader can control the process, maximizing the benefits.

Yet another technique is to bubble up information. By including managers from all echelons for input, you encourage them to buy in to the plan. The disadvantage is again the inconsistency of input unless there's guidance.

For midsize or larger organizations, the optimal planning cycle is depicted in Exhibit 4-4. Critical to this procedure is the need for top management to involve itself in framing and approving. (This procedure is applicable for budget and work plan preparation.)

The adequacy of planning is directly related to the availability of good data. Because of lack of data, it is often three annual planning cycles before the facility business plans are both accurate and useful. There are three major sources of facility data that are invaluable for facility business planning; site master plans, building audits, and serviceability evaluations.

As used in this book, and we wish in the profession, a *master plan* is the technical plan for an individual site; it shows all current and planned development on that site. A master plan is not a facility business plan, though people often confuse the terms. A company that expects to remain at an owned site should plan the future best use of that site through the master planning process. A twenty-year master plan is common.

A *building audit* both describes the current condition of all buildings and provides major projections of operational costs, maintenance costs, major repairs, and capital improvements. Most major architectural and engineering firms offer building audits as a service; some large FM departments have the capability in-house. Although the

Exhibit 4-4. Suggested planning cycle.

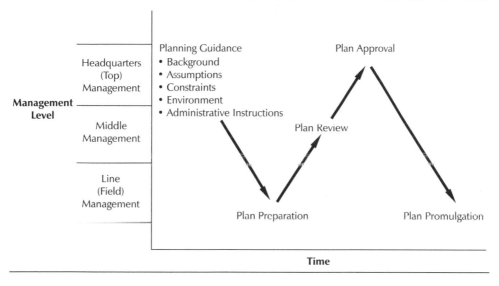

focus of this discussion is on planning, it's worth mentioning that a building audit can also be helpful after construction, to ensure that programming goals and/or contractual requirements were met.

The newest tool for good facility business planning is the *serviceability evaluation*. Gerald Davis and Francoise Szigeti of the International Centre for Facilities have been instrumental in refining serviceability tools and methods for buildings, which were recently recognized as an American Society for Testing and Materials standard. One major use of serviceability standards is to allow companies to evaluate current buildings or proposed leases or acquisitions against the needs of the organization. Those data can be invaluable for good facility business planning. Together with historical files, master plans, and building audits, a serviceability evaluation gives the facility manager good data for planning.

The Annual Work Plan

The annual work plan should flow from the mid-range plan. It should have the following qualities:

1. *Present a clear message.* The boss and facility employees should clearly understand the goals, objectives, and priorities when they read the facility work plan.
2. *Be clearly structured.* There should be direct parallelism between the format of long- and midrange plans, the work plan, and the budget.

3. *Be maintainable.* The work plan will probably need to be updated at least at midyear. It should be a tool, not an administrative burden. KISS—Keep It Simple, Stupid.

Gathering the requirements for the work plan is relatively simple. Up to 70 percent of the requirements will be specified in the midrange plan. The remainder of the work involves bringing in unplanned requirements and molding them into an effective document. Exhibit 4-5 is a matrix for gathering the final 30 percent of the requirements annually and integrating them into the plan.

One important planning consideration is timing. No item can be placed in the work plan unless a working cost estimate has been prepared. For work on a capital project, obtaining such an estimate can require a 10 to 30 percent design effort and at least gross estimating. That can take two to three months, even longer, so the procedure for gathering requirements must include this time.

Exhibit 4-5. Gathering work plan requirements.

Program	Responsible for Developing Requirement	Responsible for Prioritizing Requirement	How Cost Is Estimated
Capital	User/Facility management department	Facility management department	Estimated from conceptual design
Annually funded nondiscretionary	Facility management department	Facility management department	Extrapolated from historical data
Annually funded discretionary	User/Facility management department	Facility management department	Application of unit costs
Lease costs/income	Facility Management department	Higher management	Derived from existing leases
Overheads	Facility management department	Higher management	Application of planning factors and historical data
Space needs	User/Facility management department	Facility management department	N/A

It is recommended that capital project requirements be gathered separately from annual requirements. Because of the investment in capital projects and the need to develop them substantially before they can be estimated and analyzed for cost-effectiveness, the capital requirements and their justification should be in some detail. Normally a set of concept drawings is included with each submission. Gather the capital requirements annually, typically about a month before the capital budget is reviewed by management. Also consider forming a prioritization board to align the work plan requirements with the capital plan. Often, the work plan is a rolling one, with unfulfilled requirements rolled over to the next fiscal year, to be prioritized along with needs. In some companies, a midyear review of priorities may be appropriate.

The requirements for utilities, operations, service orders, preventive maintenance, leases, and most overhead costs should flow directly from the midrange plan or should be calculated in-house. These figures represent the nondiscretionary part of the work plan, so there is little need to prioritize: they are all priority 1. The facility department management information system should readily produce data that, with extrapolation, will allow highly accurate work estimates.

For alterations, minor (noncapital) construction, and maintenance and repair projects, gather and prioritize the requirements in much the same way as for capital projects. There may or may not be a need for an elaborate justification document. Costs are usually estimated using unit costs (e.g., dollars per square foot, dollars per people relocated). Because the requirements for this type of work often are double the funds available, a prioritization panel should both prepare the initial submission and conduct the midyear review.

In general, it is best to oversubscribe the work plan by 5 to 15 percent by category. This is because some projects will be unexecutable during the year and because a prudent facility manager always has substantive projects ready for execution in the final months of a fiscal year, should there be a windfall in the facility account.

The preferred format for a work plan is shown in Exhibit 4-2. Some items— preventive maintenance, for example—take no more than one line. Others require a prioritized list, and still others are a list with each item having a separate backup justification sheet.

There is some controversy about how widely the work plan should be distributed. One approach is to limit the document to the facility department, lest a user, seeing his project in print, will never be dissuaded should some problem arise. The other approach is full disclosure, particularly if users have participated in the prioritizing. Explaining why a project needs to be raised or lowered in its priority rank—or even cancelled—is one of the chores of management. If you cannot explain your action, maybe it was not correct.

Mid- and Long-Range Plans

A 1988 survey of real estate practices showed that although real estate accounts for one-fourth of the assets of U.S. companies, only 40 percent of those companies clearly and consistently evaluate the performance of their real estate.[7] We believe that this practice must be changed. Evaluating and utilizing a company's real property assets demands effective planning.

The format given in Exhibit 4-3 is applicable for both mid- and long-range facility plans. However, the relative importance of each program varies with time, as depicted in Exhibit 4-6. This graph is representative only; the actual weighting of each program is highly situation dependent. Nevertheless, several conclusions are apparent:

1. If good mid- and long-range planning can be done on space, leasing, and capital programs, there will be more effort left for planning annual programs when these peak in years 1 and 2.
2. In the long term, space forecasting and build-vs-lease planning are preeminent. If building is an option, considerable effort must be expended in midrange planning. However, some level of activity in those programs most closely associated with annual planning (operations, maintenance,

Exhibit 4-6. Relative importance of planning facility programs.

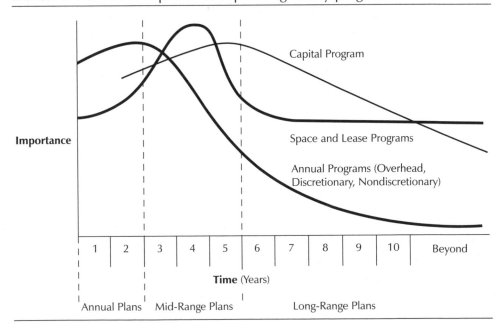

utilities, structure, position levels) is important even in the out-years of strategic planning.

3. In the near term (years 1 and 2), when the emphasis is on implementation, macrolevel planning of all programs continues.

It is important to realize that this is a snapshot of one ten-year period. As each year passes, the process rolls—that is, one year of the midrange plan becomes an annual plan for the next fiscal year. There is a rhythm and a continuity to this process.

Planning Input

The principle inputs for the mid- and long-range facility plans are the complementary company business plans. Particularly important are the sections regarding environment, assumptions, constraints, and conclusions. If the facility manager has been part of the business planning group or if the facility plan is developed concurrently with the business plan, little other input will be required. If, however, the facility plan is being developed in a vacuum, it is worthwhile reviewing the company plan with the principal managers, and perhaps even holding a brainstorming session among key persons. The facility manager can act as a facilitator for the session or hire a consultant to do so.

It is, of course, preferable for the facility plan to bubble up from the managers responsible for the programs. This means that they must be exposed to the business plan. Those managers will perform best if they are familiar with the business plan and are provided guidance on the facility plan, particularly if the facility manager feels strongly about one particular program. Planning, to be good, must be an iterative process. Particularly for a first effort, it could take three to five rewrites to get a plan correct. Remember that before any basic assumptions or constraints of the business plan can be changed, approval must come from the company planner. Ultimately, the facility manager is responsible that (1) the facility plan supports the business plan, and (2) that the facility plan is integrated and complete.

Planning Tools

The facility manager's ability to plan is in direct proportion to his staff's knowledge of its facilities and policies that allow for meaningful extrapolation and forecasting. There are many planning tools, but the following are the minimum an organization expects its facility manager to bring to the planning table.[8]

- Facility inventory
- Facility utilization information

- Facility costs (unit costs for every program element to include overhead and design)
- Cost indexes applicable to local labor, material, utility, and lease costs
- Agreed-on growth (or reduction) factors
- Standards, particularly for space and furniture
- Applicable utility information
- Input from the master plan, if available
- A typical cost slice for common types of services (for example, the typical design cost for a common alteration project as a percentage of total project cost)
- Personal needs and mix

One of the drawbacks of strategic planning, particularly the first time it is tried can be cost. The facility inventory, if it includes a condition assessment, can cost $1.50 per square foot and can consume huge amounts of staff time. Eric Teicholz and Gary Evans list alternative methods of assessing the condition of facilities through parametric estimating methods, inventory life-cycle analysis, and questionnaire-based modeling but suggest yet another, the theoretical condition index.[9] Actually, a mix of methods based on age, likelihood of retention, complexity of the facility and its system, and facility importance is probably best used for an initial condition assessment.

Since most new facility departments do not have these data, the facility manager's first efforts at planning may be less than successful. That is why planning must be viewed as an iterative process. It is extremely important to produce the first of each type of plan (annual, midrange, and long range) so that subsequent plans can adjust from those baselines, rather than be zero based. To this extent, the most valuable tools for preparing a facility plan are (1) last year's applicable facility plan and (2) the last two years' business plans.

Some facility managers who manage large, complex facilities whose companies own the properties and intend to retain them for an extended period (at least ten years) will prepare a master plan for such locations. This is common among U.S. colleges and universities and with the U.S. Department of Defense.

A master plan may have any format but commonly includes the following categories:

- Assumptions and constraints
- Summary of, or reference to, standards
- Facilities inventory by category, by condition
- Summary of applicable zoning and other restrictions, if any
- Visual depiction of fully developed facility (often various elements—housing, utilities, etc.—are shown separately and color-coded when combined)

- Time-phased schedule of facility changes
- Time-phased cost projections

If a master plan exists, it is valuable input for the facility plan.

Both the facilities plan and the master plan must comply with local codes and zoning. For national and international organizations, it is strongly recommended that a planning organization familiar with local codes be hired to assist. This allows the facility manager to evaluate a local company for possible implementation consulting, shows local authorities that the company is interested in their concerns, and provides expertise until a decision is made as to whether to staff locally.

Plan Format

From both research and personal experience, we have learned how little has been done to standardize facility planning. Each planner uses a different set of procedures and formats, and sometimes these change from plan to plan or year to year—an undesirable situation. If planning is to be effective, last year's plan should be comparable to this year's. (If there is more than a 30 percent deviation from year to year, you need to review the planning process.) A common format can be a major aid in this process of comparison.

In practice, there is commonality in annual planning. Most companies, if they prepare a work plan, construct it as a prioritized project listing by program. However, there is less commonality in formats for mid- and long-range plans. Exhibit 4-3 shows our suggested format. This format dictates some degree of uniformity in procedures also. But let's take a section-by-section look at the facility plan.

1. *Introduction.* The introduction sets the stage and tone. Commonly there is a purpose statement and some bridge material to the corresponding business plan, from which the facility plan has evolved or to other plans based on this document.

2. *Environment.* The planning team extracts from the business plan pertinent environmental considerations that will affect facilities. For example, construction material costs tend to remain much higher than the consumer price index. That fact is known by the facility department but probably not by the organization's business planners. On the other hand, factors here might be general comments regarding utility rate trends, local labor rate projections, or changing company attitudes toward administrative expenses.

It is unrealistic to expect company planners to supply all the environmental factors important to the facility plan. For example, in the late 1980s, construction material costs tended to remain higher than the consumer price index. That fact was known in facilities departments but probably not by company business planners.

These types of environmental considerations should be included here because it is important to help company planners and management put the facility plan in context. In fact, the facilities plan will concentrate more on internal company environment than does the business plan.

3. *Assumptions.* As you look further into the future, you must make certain assumptions in order to plan. These assumptions can be generated by knowledgeable individuals extrapolating current data, or consultants can be used. Sometimes it is helpful to ask the question, "What information do I need to prepare a facility plan for five or ten years hence?" Once answered, the response can be compared to the currently available facts. The information gap must be closed with assumptions—ideally, knowledgeable ones.

Assumptions can be so many and so varied that you must limit them to only those truly pertinent. Some assumptions applicable to the facility plan relate to standards, lease or build strategies, and in-house versus contracted services.

4. *Constraints.* Sometimes for emphasis, constraints on the plan's effectiveness are listed separately. However, often the environment, assumptions, and constraints are combined and handled as either introductory material or as assumptions. Our preference is that each appear separately. Constraints should be stated only to the extent that they exist. Here are two typical constraint statements:

> During years 5 through 7, the overhead budget is limited to zero absolute growth; growth in years 7 through 10 is limited to that determined by the consumer price index.

> No additional leased space will be allowed in Hartford for years 1 through 3.

Constraints, as applicable, can come from the company business plan. They are an effective way to shape the planning process, but should be used only when you are certain they are supported and supportable.

5. *Discussion.* Although preparation is more difficult, and the plan becomes more voluminous, you should include multiple scenarios. By showing a range of values, the plan more appropriately represents its degree of accuracy. Also, scenarios insulate you best from failure. Which scenarios to consider varies. Here are some common approaches:

- *Fiscal.* The budget or facilities department designates a high, low, and mid- or most probable budget value for each program for each year.
- *Projected.* Current budgets are projected into the out-years using a most favorable, least favorable, and average or most probable multiplier.

- *Rational.* Using assumptions and constraints specific to each year in the plan, three work plans are developed each year. If quantitative data are desired, the values for each work plan are calculated by program.

Once the method of selecting scenarios is determined, you can move to the heart of the plan—the impact of the programs. The principle function of this section is to present each program in each scenario, along with explanatory material and the impact of each scenario on the total plan. When you display all the programs in each of three scenarios, you can suggest modifications. This is the section that truly requires your input and attention, because judgment is crucial. The most probable scenario will undoubtedly be the most developed.

Explain major program highlights (e.g., bringing a new building on line) regardless of the scenario in which they occur. Put special emphasis on areas that could put the facility department at risk, since the principal role of a plan is to insulate against catastrophe.

Finally, designate and explain the most probable scenario. If the department has the ability to do so, perform sensitivity analyses on the scenario selected as most likely. What would happen, for example, if the funds available for leases in year 5 were reduced 5 percent? What would happen if space needs in year 3 exceed projections by 10 percent?

6. *Conclusions.* Present, in simple terms, your major conclusions for supporting the company business plan. In addition, address, in general terms, the impact of other scenarios and sensitivity analyses. In particular, your conclusions should highlight any situation where a facility issue could affect the company business plan.

7. *Recommendations.* In this section, you recommend the preferred course of action for the facilities of the corporation.

8. *Appendixes.* Include appendixes to the degree that they support the conclusions and recommendation. Typical appendixes include financial displays, list of events, personnel projections, space projections, and/or organizational charts.

Reviews and Updates

Once plans are in place, it is easier to adjust annually using the plan as a baseline, unless assumptions and constraints have changed radically. All facility plans should be reviewed annually by departmental managers. Each three to five years, the mid- and long-range plans should be zero based, under the direction of the department's planner.

It is extremely important that someone manage the total planning process. The output of long-range planning feeds and frames the midrange plan. The near-year portion of the plan, in turn, rolls over to become the basis of the annual work plan. Once developed, the process is logical and easy to administer.

At the same time, it is possible to concentrate on goals for six years hence or anticipate utility costs three years into the future.

There's often legitimate concern about the difficulty of dealing with uncertainty; however, uncertainty should not preclude planning—it only complicates it. Rather than develop point estimates for the future, develop scenarios. The company is best protected when a best-case, worst-case, and most-likely-case scenario are projected. Also, the envelope of certainty broadens as the horizon widens.

Formulating the initial facility plan will require great effort. It is quite likely that the first efforts will be suboptimal, even frustrating. It is not uncommon for it to take up to three years for you to feel really good about the final product. But don't get discouraged or stop the planning. The key is to get the initial plan published.[10]

There are synergistic effects from compiling and publishing your first facility plan. Managers in your department will have to become familiar with the company's business plan. Also, they will have to coordinate with each other to plan, and this will carry over to operations. By the time you are comfortable with your planning efforts, your department will be operating more effectively also.

Meredith Thatcher, an international facility management consultant, has an excellent summation of the quandary facing most facility managers who want to be actively involved in the strategic planning of their organizations. She spells out five elements necessary for successful strategic planning:

- Good access to the strategic direction of their organization.
- Clients and occupants who understand and allow for the various pressures on a facility manager.
- Sufficient funding to add value and respond to opportunities.
- A facility management plan that defines standards and performance expectations.
- A voice or champion within corporate management.

However, when she asked a group of FM's how many of them had all five elements, only one or two responded positively.[11] This, to us, says much about the status of strategic planning in our profession today. We hope that this chapter has both motivated you to improve in this area and has given you some of the tools to help you do so.

And, as they say, the music never stops. Meredith further emphasizes that, in order to plan strategically, you need to be knowledgeable of trends in economics, society, and technology.[12] Who would have thought, for instance, the impact of the microchip back in 1950? Or the impact of Generation Y attitudes on our workforce and customer attitudes? Or the influx of immigrants into our workforce in the numbers which have occurred? This is one of the great challenges of our profession; to be the harbinger to upper management of those trends which affect the built environment.

Notes

1. Thomas Kvan, personal interview, March 16, 1989.
2. William Joseph, *Facilities Strategic Planning*, Occasional paper, 1989, p. 2.
3. Kvan interview.
4. Alan Walter Steiss, *Strategic Facilities Planning*, Lexington Books, May 2004.
5. Personal communication from Diane MacKnight, MacKnight Associates, May 24, 2008.
6. Marvin W. Peterson, "The Potential Impact of PPBS on Colleges and Universities," *Journal of Higher Education, Vol. 42, No. 1*, January 1971.
7. "Real Estate Industry Study," Harvard Business School, in Richard S. Tryce, manuscript.
8. For some of these suggestions, we credit William Adams, *Developing a Long Range Facilities Forecast*, occasional paper (Houston: International Facility Management Association, 1986).
9. Eric Teicholz and Gary Evans, "Condition Indices and Strategic Planning," *FMJ, July/August 2007*, pp. 58–62.
10. Charles J. Bodenstab, "Directional Signals," *Inc.* (March 1989): p. 141.
11. Meredith Thatcher, "Risk and Resilience: Strategic Thinking in Your World," *FMJ, July August 2007*, p. 10.
12. *Ibid*, p. 14.

Financial Management

Pulse Points

- *In order to manage finances properly, the facility manager must have adequate funding for operations and maintenance and repair (to include deferred maintenance), the areas most often underfunded.*
- *The most successful facility managers view themselves as business managers.*
- *All economic analyses and comparisons should be based on life-cycle costs and should consider the cost of ownership.*
- *Know your company's rules for capitalization, and follow them carefully. Don't cheat.*
- *Manage carefully the depreciation charges for your capital program in your annual budget.*
- *The facility manager must have a working knowledge of capital evaluation tools.*
- *Vendor-supplied cost analyses are not dependable.*
- *Use a landlord mentality when developing and implementing allocations and rules for chargeback.*

In order to discuss managing finances properly, the facility manager must have adequate resources. This does not mean that there will not be times when the belt must be tightened but, in the long run, physical assets deteriorate if not properly maintained. No business strategy or technique can reverse it. In the private sector, deteriorating facilities probably can be sold, though there is a high cost for relocation and the ability to sell is dependent upon market forces. In the public sector, however, most facilities, once built become a part of a constantly increasing inventory of assets which must be operated, maintained, and occasionally renovated. This is particularly true for complexes like university main campuses. For this reason, the National Research Council has recommended that 2-4 percent of the replacement value of a facility be spent on maintaining it annually.[1] One of your authors was on the committee that made that recommendation and actually used it successfully in his practice. As a profession, we have not made this point on the cost of ownership well and it is at the core of why facility managers are not appreciated more. Harvey Kaiser calls this 2-4 percent budget amount "the less glamorous commitment."[2] Everyone in the profession should read Scott Carlson's excellent article on money and management, "As Campuses Crumble, Budgets Are Crunched,"[3] and then should ensure that it is in the "Must Read" portfolio of every member of upper management. Until we solve this problem of lack of organizational commitment to their facilities (and solutions are offered in the article), our results will always be sub-optimized.

In small organizations, financial forecasting and macrolevel estimating are used sporadically, primarily in planning and budget preparation. In large organizations, specialists work full time preparing financial forecasts and cost estimates in support of various programs or projects. The importance of financial forecasting and macrolevel forecasting can best be appreciated by the facility manager who finds a capital project approved but is unable to start because of an inadequate budget made many years before. Another example is the facility manager who leaves $5 million on the table at the end of a fiscal year because the staff misforecast the department's ability to commit funds. These horrors occur because the skills required for macrolevel estimates are not normally those required for construction estimates, and financial analysts normally are ill equipped to provide facility financial forecasts.

Life-Cycle Costing

One of the most important economic concepts for a facility manager to understand is *life-cycle costing*. Properly conducted, life-cycle costing allows a comparison of two different options of different expected lives or the total cost of one option over its expected life. It can be used to compare the benefits of retaining a service in-house or outsourcing that service, or to compare two different choices for a piece of equipment to accomplish the same task, or to determine whether to replace or repair existing equipment.

Unfortunately, life-cycle costing is more often mentioned than practiced. Applied to facility management, life-cycle costing acknowledges that the company buys into a chain of costs when it buys a building—the cost of ownership. The life cycle of costs (in constant-year dollars) could be used to evaluate two options for meeting the same requirement—to build in the suburbs versus lease in the city, for example. At the project level, life-cycle costing would determine the wisdom of installing a rub-rail on conference room walls versus the expenditures required in the future to repair and paint those same walls.

Proper life-cycle costing allows a comparison of actions having different life expectancies to account for the time value of money. Savings for proposed projects or products can be hard to recognize, harder to quantify, and hardest yet to document. It often takes a joint effort between an experienced facility department staff person and a financial analyst or economist to quantify future costs or savings. These skills can be hired outside, but a facility department with an ongoing capital program should develop an in-house capability to do life-cycle costing. *Major FM decisions made solely on first costs are never good decisions and are more likely wrong than right.* Life-cycle costing is one of those best practices that the profession should embrace as a standard.

Financial Forecasting

Financial forecasts are one of the bridges that allow the financial resources of a plan to be assessed and plans to be converted to budgets. The primary purpose of a financial forecast is financial planning. The forecast may lead to a budget or a project estimate, but it is primarily concerned with planning. When preparing a budget, the facility manager uses a variety of forecasting techniques to obtain a total budget figure. It is very important to understand whether the budget is to be in "constant" or "then year" dollars, particularly in a time of inflation. Failure to account for an increase or decrease in value over time can seriously affect your budget estimates.

A number of sophisticated forecasting techniques have been developed and are in common use:

- Regression analysis
- Moving averages
- Econometric modeling
- Exponential smoothing
- Delphi method
- Simple projection

Each company has its own method of forecasting. Since a capital budget consists of discrete projects, it is the sum of individual estimates. On the other hand, the budget for operations and maintenance requires different forecasting techniques for each program. The different techniques are summarized in Exhibit 5-1. In a dynamic organization, the financial forecast is a combination of historical extrapolation plus increments for increases or decreases caused by new requirements times a unit cost, which itself may be subject to inflation.

Macrolevel Estimating

Forecasts, as they apply to projects, are called *estimates*. Early in any large project, it is necessary to determine what it will cost. Often some estimate is needed soon after the project is conceived, in order to line up board or executive approval. This occurs before there's an architect—before there's a conceptual design, in some cases.

Later, other macrolevel estimates may be necessary to secure administrative approval or to complete a project budget based on a design. This kind of macrolevel estimating normally is possible only after the design is approximately 30 percent developed. Similarly, facility managers often have so many small projects on their agenda that making a detailed construction estimate for each is impractical and unnecessary. What's really needed is a budget figure to control each project so that the sum of all projects does not exceed the overall budget. Those project budget figures are often best arrived at by macrolevel estimating.

There are three different types of macrolevel estimates. The *informal estimate* may well be called "intuitive" or "experiential." It's most often done from the barest of information, which means it can be done quickly. Such words or phrases as *blue sky, ballpark, guesstimate, seat of the pants,* and *approximate* come to mind.

The purpose of the informal estimate is to determine whether to allocate resources to research or study the feasibility of a project. The reliability of informal estimates is questionable and depends on the experience and skill of the estimator. Unfortunately, the informal estimate often is remembered by top management as if it were a more sophisticated and reliable estimate, especially when expectations are high. Qualifying footnotes always seem to get separated from the estimate at the earliest opportunity, so don't count on them. Most facility managers avoid being judged on the basis of informal estimates.

The *generic estimate* is formulated by consulting a database that offers standardized costs and duration for detailed aspects of a project or function. This budget is prepared by specifying each item and tabulating a total for all items. Indexes may be available to adjust for specific variances, such as between organizational types or geographic locations. Most macrolevel estimates are informal or generic.

The *comprehensive estimate* is the most reliable primary estimate. This type provides information on materials as well as processes or procedures. It is more effective in that there is attention to variations in how projects are to be completed under specific conditions, not just simple costs and durations from generic standards.

Considerations in Making Estimates

Most construction estimators will tell you that their skill is equal parts art and science. Macrolevel estimating is perhaps more of an art. A skilled construction estimator is not necessarily good at macrolevel estimating.

(text continued on pg. 107)

Exhibit 5-1. Forecasting operations, maintenance, and administrative programs.

Program	Forecasting Method
Personnel	Determine by extrapolation or the addition of increments/decrements the number of authorized personnel in each personnel category. Multiply each category times an average salary plus benefits increment for each category.
Utilities	Extrapolate historical usage based on square footage or cost per staff member. Increase or decrease if a known facility is added to the inventory or released. Utility companies now have extremely sophisticated analyses; if you are metered properly, they will produce highly accurate forecasts to account for anticipated weather abnormalities, rate increases, and other changes.
Breakdown maintenance	The number of service orders by category can best be extrapolated in a straight-line manner plus an increment/decrement if major facilities are to be acquired/released. The budget figure is then calculated by multiplying by the unit cost per category.
Preventive maintenance	The cost of preventive maintenance is nearly always driven by the labor cost. Determine the crew size for each preventive maintenance function. Multiply by the annual rate per craft, and add a historically derived cost of materials.
Repair projects	Obtain an estimate, in-house or based on a proposal for each project planned. Keep a 15 to 25 percent contingency for emergencies.
Alteration projects	If these projects are funded from the operations and maintenance budget and not capitalized or charged back, they can be estimated based on the number of staff to be moved or the number of feet to be altered multiplied by the appropriate unit cost. We try to retain a 25 to 33 percent contingency in this account but seldom succeed.

Program	Forecasting Method
Furniture (noncapital)	If you know the exact pieces to be purchased, your vendors can help you do your forecast. Our experience is that noncapital furniture purchases are consistent (at least in dollar volume) from year to year, so extrapolation from historical data should be adequate for your forecast.

Note: All extrapolated forecasts should be increased or decreased incrementally for known requirement increases or decreases. All funding forecasts should be adjusted for anticipated inflation or deflation if then-year dollars are to be used. These two concepts are commonly known as *volume increases* (decreases) and *price increases* (decreases).

Organizations that operate internationally but macroestimate centrally almost always use indexes to fine-tune their figures for local application. The *Engineering News Record* index, for example, is often used for construction.* In fact, many organizations have found it worthwhile to publish their data for estimating other programs.

Whereas construction estimators have reference books (e.g., Means and Richardson) to refer to, macrolevel estimators are most successful when using local data.† You should collect the following data for forecasting and estimating purposes:

Personnel costs:
- Costs by category
- Benefits costs
- Personnel positions

Utilities:
- Utilities rates by utility
- Degree days
- Usage data by utility

Maintenance costs:
- Costs per square feet or staff member (by location or facility)
  —Preventive maintenance
  —Custodial
- Shop costs

ENR Index, published by *Engineering News Record*, is an internationally accepted index for "moving" known construction estimates from one locale and applying them to another.
†Means and Richardson are common sources of construction, renovation, and facility costs. These references are used in the absence of company-unique data and are updated annually.

(continued next page)

Exhibit 5-1. (continued)

	—Unit cost per product
	—Annual cost
	• Annual cost of repair projects
Space:	• Amount (by category, by location or facility, by occupant)
	—Owned
	—Leased
	• Leasing rate
Alteration projects:	• Number of projects
	• Unit costs (by location or facility)
	—Per square feet
	—Per linear foot of wall
	—Per employee
Furniture:	• Items purchased by type
	• Prices
Indexes (for organizations at multiple locations):	• Construction
	• Maintenance
Grounds:	• Unit cost per acre
Roads:	• Amount by category
	• Unit costs by category
	—Repair
	—Replace

This is a representive list. Needs vary greatly, depending on the true requirements of the organization.

Macrolevel estimates are by their nature imprecise. Normally managers are comfortable with and expect an accuracy of +5 percent, but will accept +10 percent or –5 percent. Updating estimates at least annually is a problem for facility managers who have broad responsibilities, however. For example, the U.S. Army often has such a backlog of major construction projects that some take more than ten years from concept to approval. If the macrolevel estimate is not kept up to date, you'll find that approved funds are grossly inadequate. In periods of even moderate inflation, the absolute value of funds requested can depreciate by 20 percent in three years—a significant amount on a large project. Thus, at the conclusion of a project or at the end of a fiscal year, one of the principal purposes of evaluation should be to update the estimating database.

Capital Programs

Capitalization is an orderly and intelligent way to meet major new facility needs. The facility manager should actively participate in developing the requirements, prioritizing the competing needs, and managing the execution of a capital development program. To do this, he must not only understand the rules but follow them closely.

The costs associated with long-lived assets are sometimes referred to as *capitalized costs*.[4] These costs are often met by capital expenditures, which can be used to expand or modernize a company. The amounts spent annually are substantial. Total non-residential investment in structures in 2007 exceeded $303 billion in the United States in constant year dollars.[5] Thus it is important that you know the basics of capital budgeting.

Capital Budgeting

Capital needs flow from a business analysis. With regard to facility management, total space needs must be assessed first. Then the company must determine whether it is in its best interest to lease, build, or make more efficient use of existing space through renovation. If the decision is to renovate or construct, capital funds are normally used.

Determining what can or cannot be capitalized is normally the province of the controller. Often the rules are a combination of two factors: the existing tax code, which determines what can be depreciated over what period, and company rules, which usually set a floor below which a single purchase cannot be capitalized. Some fees associated with a capital project obviously can be capitalized; others cannot. Renovations and replacement projects both raise questions as to proper allocation of costs. There can be a temptation to "play" with the capital budgeting rules, particularly in those times when operations and maintenance is often underfunded. Hopefully the facility manager has helped develop the organization's capital budgeting rules. Then it is important to follow them diligently.

New Capital Projects

As most experienced facility managers realize, capital projects are extremely popular because of the following beliefs:

- They are the first material evidence of a new company initiative.
- They often help project the company image.

- They are sometimes the solution to company problems.
- They involve high expenditure over a short period of time, and therefore they are highly visible.

Some of these perceptions are only marginally correct, yet a facility manager must learn to deal with their results. For example, often there is substantial competition for limited capital dollars in any one budget year.

There are several ways to prepare a capital budget:

1. Based on a funding target from the budget department, gather your requirements.
2. Analyze the requirements, justifications, and numbers using some form of quantification to determine rank order.
3. Conduct a screening and prioritization session using a board that will then make a recommendation.

In smaller firms, capital funding may be extremely limited and expenditures may be dictated by the chief executive officer (CEO) or board. For larger organizations, these steps ensure a well-received submission for capital funds.

Step 1: Gathering the Requirements

Because there can be substantial expense in preparing a capital submission, a good facility manager limits submissions to a probable funding target plus 20 to 30 percent. Requirements should be submitted in a standardized format and forwarded over the signature of an appropriate line manager. Suggested information for such a submission includes the following:

- Fiscal year
- Location
- Project title
- Program and category code (if applicable)
- Project number
- Project cost
- Cost estimate (by major project phases): phase, unit measure, quantity, unit cost, and total cost of phase
- Project description
- Project justification
- Decision device (net present value, for example)
- Concept drawing or rendering

An excellent example of a capital project requirements document is DD Form 1391, available from the Government Printing Office.

Usually several members of the facility department assist in generating this information. Some designs are often needed so that at least a working cost estimate can be initiated, defining the project enough so that it can be considered. Be sure you have annual funds to do this type of preparatory work.

Step 2: Rank-Order the Projects

One of the most difficult tasks is to rank-order the projects based on criteria that are rational, discriminating, and meaningful to the company. Many such devices exist, but the most common ones are annual return on investment (ROI), cash payback system, discounted cash flow, net present value (NPV), internal rate of return (IRR), and benefit-cost ratios (BCR). An excellent discussion of the first five of these devices is contained in *Accounting Principles* by Weygandt, Kieso, and Kell. Whole books have been written on assessing costs and benefits for the BCR. NPV analyses or IRR are the current favorites for this type of analysis.

Some of these analyses can become quite sophisticated and difficult. Seek help, normally from the budget analyst or controller but a word of advice from an experienced real estate manager, Bill Agnello, is appropriate: "The facility planner and manager must take *personal* and *professional* responsibility for understanding and accepting the numbers game because your clients (internal or external) will be better served."[6]*

Step 3: Present to the Capital Project Board

The purpose of the board is to review all submissions, rank-order them using the appropriate decision device, and develop the department's capital budget request. If you are on the board, the board's recommendation should be final. In some cases, however, policy or politics may require capital project approval at the chief financial officer (CFO) or CEO level. If the board merely prepares a recommendation, normally the facility manager is at most a nonvoting chairperson or secretary.

Depreciation Expense

Some companies use a braking device called a *depreciation expense* to ensure that capitalization is not overused. The depreciation expense in your annual operating budget is the sum of the annual depreciation for that year for each outstanding capital project. Because most annual operating budgets are relatively fixed, if the

---

*For an excellent commonsense description of the use of basic financial management in FM and the use of spreadsheets, see Mike Hoots, "Dr. Spreadsheet or How I Learned to Stop Worrying and Love Financial Analysis," *Facility Management Journal*, January–February 1998, pp. 10–17.

depreciation expense reaches 8 to 10 percent of the total budget, you may be robbing Peter to pay Paul.

Controlling Capital Projects

Because capital projects have a classic peak-and-valley nature, many facility managers form a special team to manage them. Unfortunately, commonly the company project manager (particularly for the new headquarters) is a retiring executive or someone else who just happens to be available. But managing a major capital project is a challenging task. You should control the appointment of each capital project manager. In addition, the facility manager needs to ensure that, in addition to the design and construction team, each project manager has access to the following, either in-house or from a consultant:

- Legal counsel, preferably someone knowledgeable in construction contracting
- Construction accountant
- Value engineer
- Budget expert

Initial costs are always a major concern. However, you need to put those costs in perspective when considering a building design. Over the life of any building, 92 percent of the life-cycle costs of that facility will be the salaries of the occupants. The cost of operating and maintaining that building will be 6 percent, while the original design and construction is but 2 percent. Thus, prudent initial investments for operational efficiency and maintainability will leverage themselves over the life of the building.

Cost Justification

The ability to justify projects economically is an important skill. Companies set requirements for funds use far in excess of what is available in any one year. Two basic approaches have been developed to quantify the economic benefits of particular projects and to prioritize them. For instance, with the *accept-reject approach*, everything over a certain benchmark (benefit-cost ratio = 3.5, for example) is selected, and anything under it is rejected. Or the highest-ranking projects (rank-ordered by IRR, for example) up to the funds available are included in the budget; this is the *ranking approach*. Facility managers should be familiar with these analytical tools and should be aware of their strengths and limitations.

   Cost justification is the term used for making decisions between competing proposed projects or go/no-go choices on specific proposed projects. Although the technique is most applicable to capital projects, it can be used whenever there is some degree of freedom to select among competing projects and the analytical time can be cost-justified.

Cost justification has these objectives:

1. Selecting the project with the highest potential for reward
2. Selecting the project that limits or minimizes financial risk
3. Prioritizing the projects competing for limited resources

The factors brought together to evaluate investment alternatives include the net amount of the investment required for a project, the returns or cash flows expected from an investment in the project, and the company's lowest acceptable rate of return on investment, or its cost of capital. The actual cost-evaluation tools we consider here are these:

- Average payback period
- Actual payback period
- Net present value
- Internal rate of return
- Benefit-cost ratio

The first two methods of evaluating investment alternatives are listed to provide a concept only—the idea that an investment must pay back over a period of time to be justified. Payback, however, is overly simplistic, and we do not recommend that anyone use it for making capital decisions.

Average Payback Period

Calculating an average payback period is a method for making an accept/reject decision or to select one project against a standard set by management:

$$\text{Average payback period (years)} = \frac{\text{Net investment}}{\text{Average annual cash inflow}}$$

Advantages
- Simple to use
- Considers cash flows
- A measure of risk

Disadvantages
- Does not fully consider time value of money
- Does not consider subsequent cash flow
- Cash inflows can be subjective

To use this device, select the project that meets or beats the predetermined maximum average payback period or best average payback period of alternative projects. See Exhibit 5-2 for an example.

Actual Payback Period

This method uses the same data as the average payback period analysis but calculates an actual payback time. Actual payback is when the sum of prior cash inflow exactly equals the initial investment. The payback period is the time it takes to recover the cost of the investment through the net cash flow. The net cash flow consists of the after-tax value of savings generated by the project, and the tax write-off resulting from depreciation expense. To calculate the payback period, divide the annual net cash flow into the cost of the investment. A shorter payback period will be the investment alternative of choice with this method. A major drawback of the payback method is that ongoing long-term profitability is not included in evaluating the investment alternatives.

Advantages	*Disadvantages*
• Measures risk	• Does not fully consider time value of money
• Simple to use	
• Considers timing of cash flows	• Does not consider subsequent cash flow

To use the device, select the project that meets or beats the predetermined maximum payback period, or the shortest actual payback period among the alternatives.

Net Present Value

This analytic tool determines the dollar value, at time zero, of some future series of cash flows, discounted at the company's cost of capital. It measures expected future benefits (cash flows) against initial investment. The NPV method recognizes the time value of money. All the cash flows over the life of the investment are converted to

Exhibit 5-2. Payback period.

	Investment A	Investment B
Cost	$3,000	$7,000
Net annual cash flow	1,000	2,000
Payback period	3 years	3.5 years
Preferred investment:	Investment A	

present value. The present values of both cash inflows and the outflows are netted. If the NPV is positive, the investment alternative is not good. If comparing two investment alternatives, choose the alternative with the higher NPV or lower negative NPV.

NPV = Present value of future cash flows – net investment

To calculate an NPV, you must know the initial net investment, the company's cost of capital, and future cash flows

Advantages	*Disadvantages*
• Gives consideration to the time value of money	• Makes assumptions as to the cost of capital
• Considers all relevant cash flows	• More difficult to calculate; needs table of discount factors
• Commonly used and understood	

To use the device, select the project that has the highest positive NPV, or the smallest negative NPV from alternative projects. See Exhibit 5-3 for an example. The discounted cash flow can be complicated when you must take into consideration any salvage value of the investment and the annual depreciation amounts. Salvage value should be included as a cash inflow and converted to present value. Depreciation is not a cash expense; however, it does affect the tax expense by reducing the tax owed. So depreciation times the tax rate is a "cash inflow" to be converted to present value for each year depreciation is taken.

Internal Rate of Return

The IRR is the discount rate assuming an NPV of zero:

IRR = NPV = 0

To calculate the IRR of a project, you must know the initial net investment and future cash inflows. To make an accept/reject decision, you must know the company's cost of capital.

Advantages	*Disadvantages*
• Gives consideration to the time value of money	• Difficult to calculate without a good financial calculator
• Considers all relevant cash flows	• Less understood by nonfinancial managers
	• Assumes that all intermediate cash flows are reinvested at company's IRR

Exhibit 5-3. Net present value.

Example:

	Investment A	Investment B
Cost	$10,000	$11,000
Savings each year	$ 2,000	$ 4,000
Number of years with savings	4 years	4 years

(The discount rate is 10%.)

	Cost	Present Value Factor— P.V. of Inflow	Net Cash
Investment A	$10,000	$2,000 × 3.1699* = $ 6,340	($3,660)
Investment B	11,000	4,000 × 3.1699* = 12,680	1,680

Preferred Investment: Investment B

Present Value of $1 at Compound Interest

Period Hence	4½%	5%	6%	7%	8%	9%	10%	12%	14%	16%
1	0.9569	0.9524	0.9434	0.9346	0.9259	0.9174	0.9091	0.8929	0.8772	0.8621
2	0.9157	0.9070	0.8900	0.8734	0.8573	0.8417	0.8265	0.7972	0.7695	0.7432
3	0.8763	0.8638	0.8396	0.8163	0.7938	0.7722	0.7513	0.7118	0.6750	0.6407
4	0.8386	0.8227	0.7921	0.7629	0.7350	0.7084	0.6830	0.6355	0.5921	0.5523
5	0.8025	0.7835	0.7473	0.7130	0.6806	0.6499	0.6209	0.5675	0.5194	0.4761
6	0.7679	0.7462	0.7050	0.6663	0.6302	0.5963	0.5645	0.5066	0.4556	0.4104
7	0.7348	0.7107	0.6651	0.6228	0.5835	0.5470	0.5132	0.4524	0.3996	0.3538
8	0.7032	0.6768	0.6274	0.5820	0.5403	0.5019	0.4665	0.4039	0.3506	0.3050
9	0.6729	0.6446	0.5919	0.5439	0.5003	0.4604	0.4241	0.3606	0.3075	0.2630
10	0.6439	0.6139	0.5584	0.5084	0.4632	0.4224	0.3855	0.3220	0.2697	0.2267
11	0.6162	0.5847	0.5268	0.4751	0.4289	0.3875	0.3505	0.2875	0.2366	0.1954
12	0.5897	0.5568	0.4970	0.4440	0.3971	0.3555	0.3186	0.2567	0.2076	0.1685
13	0.5643	0.5303	0.4688	0.4150	0.3677	0.3262	0.2897	0.2292	0.1821	0.1452
14	0.5100	0.5051	0.4423	0.3878	0.3405	0.2993	0.2633	0.2046	0.1597	0.1252
15	0.5167	0.4810	0.4173	0.3625	0.3152	0.2745	0.2394	0.1827	0.1401	0.1079
16	0.4945	0.4581	0.3937	0.3387	0.2919	0.2519	0.2176	0.1631	0.1229	0.0930
17	0.4732	0.4363	0.3714	0.3166	0.2703	0.2311	0.1978	0.1456	0.1078	0.0802
18	0.4528	0.4155	0.3503	0.2959	0.2503	0.2120	0.1799	0.1300	0.0946	0.0691
19	0.4333	0.3957	0.3305	0.2765	0.2317	0.1945	0.1635	0.1161	0.0830	0.0596
20	0.4146	0.3769	0.3118	0.2584	0.2146	0.1784	0.1486	0.1037	0.0728	0.0514

* The sum of the first four entries in the 10 percent interest column.

Once the IRR has been calculated for all competing projects, select the project that has an IRR greater than or equal to the company's cost of capital.

Benefit-Cost Ratio

For very large projects, one way to reach an accept/reject decision is to calculate the BCR.

$$BCR = \frac{\text{Value of benefits of the project}}{\text{Costs of the project}}$$

Both benefits and costs are stated in constant-year dollars.

Implicit in such an analysis is that a wide variety of costs and benefits can be calculated. Ordinarily, calculating costs is much more straightforward than calculating benefits. As a minimum, a sophisticated economics staff is required to calculate benefits and costs. Which benefits and costs can be included is often stated in law or policy.

After the BCR for the project in question is calculated, the project is accepted based on whether the BCR exceeds a certain value fixed by policy. Seldom is a project with a BCR lower than 1.0 undertaken.[7]

Preparing Financial Analyses

As noted in the descriptions of the cost-justification tools, there is considerable room for interpretation in obtaining or calculating costs, benefits, inflows, and incomes, compounded by the fact that the data are often incomplete. Because so much judgment is involved, you need to control the process carefully. If the calculations are done by an accountant or budget department analyst, then you must be prepared to live with the results. The issue is not one of honesty; it is one of balanced judgment. For example, carpet *can* last twelve to fifteen years, but our experience is that tolerance for it wears out after six years. No matter which analytical tool you use, the results will be dramatically different when six rather than twelve years is estimated for new carpet.

In their enthusiasm to purchase a new product, some facility managers rely on the vendor to furnish economic justification or perform the analysis in the company's format. This is frequently done to justify the higher initial cost of carpet tile over broadloom, for example. But there are a couple of risks to that action. First, it may not be possible to support those numbers to management when they are challenged. Second, the calculations might not be supportable at a specific location and situation.

Chargebacks

Charging business units back for services provided has become so commonplace that we considered leaving it out of this section but a few comments are in order. First, because so many services that we provide are provided by a contractor, we tend to more readily know what the actual costs of that service are . . . a problem when most services were provided by organization staff. Three chargeback systems are in place:

- Charge the actual cost of services plus perhaps an overhead charge.
- Charge an allocated cost based on factors like space occupied or the number of employees.
- A combination of the first two systems.

The rationale for chargeback is the belief that, if the line managers have to pay the cost of facility services, they will be more cost conscious in ordering them. In practice, however, many of those line managers have accommodated those costs as "just a cost of doing business," while others are confused by the allocation rules and don't have the time to understand them so they endure them. So, if chargeback is used, in the interest of the organization, it behooves us to administer them effectively and efficiently.

Two methods of charging back seem to be most successful and are best practices. In the first, common facility services are contained in a *base rent,* which is calculated using gross square footage occupied. Services over and above the base package are charged at actual cost plus a markup for overhead. In the second method, the facility department develops a detailed model for all space and all services and the organization requesting the service is charged according to its impact on facility costs. Alan D. Wilson developed an excellent example of such a model for allocating costs at the Thomas J. Watson Research Center of IBM[8]. No matter which method is used, it is important for facility managers to determine the actual costs of every service that they provide (normally different for owned and leased space) and to understand their overhead cost structure and keep it updated at least quarterly. Our experience is that facility managers have never really calculated their costs of doing business by service to the extent needed for good chargebacks despite the fact that most services are now contracted. The key here is capturing your costs by the cost categories that are meaningful and having an IWMS which can provide you that cost information readily.

If an organization chooses to use chargebacks, it should use them properly and as a management tool. Otherwise they simply are a nonproductive administrative burden.

Tax Considerations

In the United States, the Congress has used depreciation and tax law as incentives to businesses to invest in depreciable property. All facility managers need to understand depreciation and its effect on the company and on their department. Facility departments tend to be the managers of the majority of depreciable assets for the company. At a minimum, the facility manager should understand the basis for each asset class managed, depreciation methods applicable to each class, when property was put in service and its appreciable life, and the difference between appreciable and nondepreciable property. Because there are value judgments and tax court precedents in many of these areas, the facility manager should not place himself in the role of rule maker for depreciation. He should seek the counsel of the legal and finance departments. Once the rules are set, he should follow them scrupulously. There are consultants, normally called tax engineers, who will assess property and recommend construction procedures to allow achievement of a more favorable tax status for buildings.

Notes

1. *Committing to the Cost of Ownership,* (Washington, DC: National Research Council, 1990), pp. 18–19.
2. Scott Carlson, "As Campuses Crumble, Budgets Are Crunched," *The Chronicle of Higher Education,* p. A 1.
3. *Ibid.*
4. Jerry J. Weygandt, Donald E. Keiso, and Walter G. Kell, *Accounting Principles,* (New York: Wiley, 1987), p. 504. Copyright 1987 John Wiley & Sons, Inc. Reprinted by permission of John Wiley & Sons, Inc.
5. Personal phone call from the Bureau of Economic Analysis, Department of Commerce, May 27, 2008.
6. William Agnello, "Capital Budgeting," Occasional paper presented at IFMA meeting, Houston, 1986.
7. "Cost Justification Tools for Managers," seminar notes prepared by the Minneapolis/St. Paul Chapter, IFMA, March 5, 1986, p. iii–1.
8. Alan D. Wilson, *Proceedings, IFMA Best Practices Forum, February 22–23, 1995,* (Houston: International Facility Management Association, 1995), pp. 193–211.

6

Space Planning and Management

Pulse Points

- *Management must have a space strategy that supports the organization's objectives and reflects its culture.*
- *Good space planning proceeds from a good business plan.*
- *Space use must be managed.*
- *Space standards are needed for good space management.*
- *Ownership of space should be established, or you will never be able to manage it.*
- *The space inventory should be managed by function, organization, and architectural use.*
- *Space planning and management are important but are not the totality of facility management.*
- *Modern IWMS and BIM give the facility manager the ability to manage space efficiently and effectively.*

According to Stephen Binder, former vice president of facility planning for Citibank, space is the frontier of facilities management.[1] Each facility manager is responsible for at least one facility with definite dimensions within which at least one productive activity takes place. The physical dimensions of a facility (the space) is the special context within which the manager executes his responsibilities. Therefore, the forecasting, planning, allocation, and management of space are important components of the facility manager's degree of success.

Planning in this context usually relates to growth, or the need for more space. Space growth has at least four potential components. First, there is growth in the industry or field—for example, retirement facilities are growing in size. Company growth, the second component, often reflects growth in the field but occurs on a schedule that might be different from industry growth—for example, a company in a growing field that has made a technological breakthrough. Third, internal programs or social trends (flextime, work at home) can result in employee growth different from the company's growth. Fourth, an organization's desire to accommodate individual needs translates into increased space needs. The complexity of these issues and the nonsequential nature of the requirements complicate the forecasting of space requirements and highlight the need for a good forecasting method.

Forecasting is predicting something as a result of rational study and analysis of pertinent data. It is the link between planning and programming. Space forecasting involves both identifying new space requirements and projecting the need for reallocation or disposal of unneeded space. This is the method most applicable to large international companies; it doesn't really exist in small companies.

Methods of Forecasting Space Needs

A company must have a space strategy that frames the way it handles space needs. This strategy should both support the business objectives of the company and reflect the culture of the organization. There are two basic strategies possible:

1. Occupy owned space, which permits maximum control
2. Occupy leased space, which permits maximum flexibility

Most companies operate somewhere between these two extremes, with substrategies such as overleasing or overbuilding in order to have space for future growth. We are often asked whether it is best to own or lease space. In fact, there is no right answer because the situation depends on the company. In almost all cases, a mix is desirable, determined by whether control or flexibility is more important. We discuss this matter further in Chapter 7.

Because the cost of space is so great, a company's strategy must be clear. For example, shortly after deregulation of the telecommunications industry, an employee of one of the emerging long-distance companies was sent on the road to rent space for business centers in every U.S. city with a population greater than 500,000, plus certain other selected cities. After over six months of site selection and negotiation, he returned to his headquarters, where he was told to cancel most of those leases because the new strategy was to operate through nine regional centers. Many leases were canceled at substantial financial cost because the company's strategy for space forecasting was not well developed before taking action. One objective of downsizing is to free up expensive space for disposal.

As we are writing this, the real estate market is undergoing a major adjustment and facility managers must be aware as the market changes. An in-house or consultant real estate expert should keep the facility manager informed so that disasters are avoided and opportunities are seized when presented. This requires good business planning internally as well. Bad examples abound. We are aware of a major organization which made a major high-value real estate purchase and renovation only to be faced with a major organizational downsizing which meant the building was only partially needed. Obviously the left hand of real estate and the right hand of human relations failed to communicate. We are amazed at the frequency with which that type of situation is happening. Perhaps, if facility impact had been considered, some savings could have occurred by releasing leased space actually reducing the number of personnel downsized.

At the current time your authors and their panel of experts note factors against building (high construction costs, extreme cost consciousness within organizations, higher costs of funds, greater scrutiny of credit-worthiness). Organizations are combining functions where they can and eliminating space, particularly in rental properties. In North America and Europe, few organizations are even thinking of building grand new corporate facilities, for example.

At the same time, some owners are willing to sign long-term leases to hold on to good lessees, being willing to forego the increase in profit margin from "flipping" properties for the security of having a good solid tenant committed for an extended time. The same market is quite different for a public sector facility manager. Public agencies would often like to own their own property (it will be cheaper long-term) but know that Congress simply is not funding the currently-owned inventory adequately so they are going with long-term leasing instead.

At the same time, in the public and private sector, LEED buildings are extremely popular both for solid reasons and for public relations purposes.[2] So there are many factors other than pure economics in a real estate strategy.

Once the company's space strategy is clear, there are two principal ways to forecast space needs. The first is to have space needs be an output of the business planning of the company. In the long run, this method is the only acceptable one. But if the company does not have an adequate business planning process, then space forecasting must be done periodically, using some survey technique. For either situation, you must have analytic tools in order to analyze the projected needs against the current inventory.

Macrolevel space forecasts are company- or corporate-wide forecasts (e.g., a new plant in Madrid, the expansion of a regional headquarters in Denver, or the closing of an R&D lab). These are best derived from the company's business plan and must be done with enough time to implement buy or lease decisions. Since the facility manager identifies the major space needs, a strategic or midrange facility plan almost ensures that this macrolevel space forecasting is accomplished adequately. However, on at least two occasions that we know about, midsize companies that had no midrange facility plan used a survey of top executives followed up by in-depth interviews to forecast their major space needs. These executives had an amazingly realistic and accurate view of their organization's space needs. A side benefit was that the interviews helped gather political support for upcoming changes. Having said that, we cannot overemphasize the importance of having space planning flow from facility business planning.

Facility managers tend to arrive at space forecasts by expedient estimating techniques. In practice, standard allocations (square feet per staff) are multiplied by the appropriate unit (number of staff) to produce a planning figure. The more details you know about the prospective occupants, the more accurate the macrolevel estimate can be. The Department of Defense has excellent tools for macrolevel forecasting. Each facility category has a category code; each category code has a space standard. Once these data are automated, the facility planner can determine whether a particular location can accommodate a particular unit, or whether more or less space is needed at a specific location. "Best-fit" exercises can easily be run. Crucial to success, however, are agreed-on standards that allow projections to be made quickly and accurately. In almost all cases, the feasibility portion is completed and the options narrowed purely on a space-available versus space-needs basis.

A trend we see emerging is that companies are basing fewer decisions on the initial cost of space. The American Society for Testing and Materials (ASTM) standard on serviceability will allow proposed new space for its ability to meet business needs. This approach, comparing the characteristics of a facility to the needs of an organization, is a step beyond macrolevel forecasting and, when it is developed, will permit more knowledgeable buy-lease decisions.

Often a location is not "saleable" within the company, even though the facility department might think it suitable or even desirable. Preparing a forecast for a suburban headquarters when only an urban location is politically feasible is a waste of time and effort. Location is not truly a space issue, but it does create a context for space forecasts. In a similar manner, preparing a forecast for a location where rental costs are beyond what the company will tolerate is unwise. While costing moves you into the area of budgeting, a prudent space forecast requires that costs be kept in the ballpark.

Although the entire subject of space forecasting is replete with policy implications, several issues stand out. For example, the organization needs to decide how to handle *swing space*—the space available to house units during renovation, alterations, and realignments—and *growth space*—space contiguous to operational units to allow for their planned growth. In some organizations, growth space is released to the unit manager; in others, the facility manager controls the space and releases it periodically.

It is our experience that annual swing space required is 2 to 3 percent in large organizations and 5 to 7 percent in small organizations. Growth space should be based on planned growth. A work unit—departmental or higher—should be provided three to five years' growth space. If the rate of growth is unknown but the organization is growing, as a general rule, give units 10 percent excess for growth upon relocation or renovation. If the extra space is properly managed, it is almost always more economical to provide for growth up front. When using these simple rules, however, do not forget that such growth is compounded (i.e., 121 percent at the end of two years, not 120 percent). In very large companies, compounded growth is significant.

Growth is also compounded in patterns of communication and interfacing. Whenever more employees are added to an activity, each potential interface also multiplies. For example, if an activity requires networking among twenty employees, the addition of a single employee changes the potential number of interfaces from 400 to 441, or a factor of 10 percent. A highly dynamic department may experience a growth rate of 30 to 50 percent per year. In that situation, the twenty-person activity would grow at least to twenty-six and increase the complexity of communication possibilities by a factor of 69 percent. (These figures do not take into account the potential that each new employee may also interface with individuals in other activity units.)

Space is not the only commodity that grows when a company is expanding. Activities that occur within that space, and must be planned for, grow also, but at differing rates. Some activities seem to grow phenomenally fast; others, more slowly. Whenever there are highly dynamic activities, there is usually a high churn rate. The emerging pattern ultimately usurps space designed for other activities and concurrently reduces the productivity of those activities. Whenever a significant imbalance might occur, you must anticipate expansion needs for the most dynamic activity, even at the expense of nondesignated space or a poor initial employee-to-space utilization ratio.

Some activities carry weighted factors in their growth. For example, activities that require exceptional support furniture or equipment for each employee require larger amounts of expansion potential, even when growing at the same rate as other activities.

Flexibility is different from growth. Growth requires additional space; flexibility requires that each space be constructed so as to permit and support a variety of different activities effectively, with minimal loss of productivity for any specific activity. Flexibility may include provision for intermediate stages of activity growth; an example is when a dynamic activity requires additional space contiguous to its current occupied space, and moving the entire activity to a more desirable location is planned for the distant future. The activity would grow into the flexible space and utilize that space until the move occurred; then it would relinquish the flexible space to some other prioritized activity. The 1990s have accentuated the need for flexible space planning. Companies and agencies radically changed the way they work, and who has a need for space.

Many of these considerations are difficult to quantify, though experienced facility managers know they exist. That's why in a growth environment you should err on the side of a high forecast if there is a judgment to be made.

Programming Your Space Requirements

Programming is the analysis of a specific function that contributes to the improved execution of that function. According to William Pena it is "the problem-seeking process that precedes problem-solving."[3] It varies from forecasting in that programming is focused on a particular problem.

Programming and design are distinct functions. Good programming must precede good design.

At least initially, the program is an unconstrained statement of space requirements. (The constraints are added during the budget process.) We have already mentioned that it is unwise to develop a space program that is not affordable, or politically saleable, or at the wrong location.

Space programming is applicable only to companies that have large space needs and holdings. When we speak of macrolevel space programming, we mean programming of whole facilities, or even complexes or locations. For small companies, this programming is done normally at the project level. Customarily there are several steps.

Establishing Goals

Perhaps the most important step of the space programming process is to determine the goal—what is to be accomplished. It is also important that the reason for the goal is understood, even if not stated. A possible goal statement might be: "We desire to acquire sufficient production and administrative space in Spain to meet our European production needs through the year 2015."

A clearly stated goal frames the space programming process. Therefore, it is important that the goal be developed with and approved by the applicable line managers and by top management.

In hindsight, it is obvious that some companies, anxious to imprint their corporate image on facilities, trapped themselves into buildings that no one really wanted after downsizing made them expendable.

Gathering Facts and Input

In some ways, gathering facts is the easiest part of the programming process. Two major facts can be obtained by answering these questions: What is desired? and When is it needed? The former is normally quantifiable; the latter can be tough to ascertain unless there is an existing plan or forecast. Other important facts are gained by answering other pertinent questions: What people and functions must be accommodated? When will the space become available and at what price? When is occupancy available? Throughout, consider how your facts are to be analyzed, coordinated with concepts, and compiled to produce a well-rounded, well-stated requirement.

Gathering input for the space program is similar to that required for the space forecast. As with the forecast, the quality of program will be much higher if it flows from the business plan. Also, the facility manager can determine needs much more quickly if the company has already set standards. If a survey technique must be used, he should place emphasis on input from line managers and workers.

Developing Basic Concepts and Determining Needs

Real estate, leased or owned, represents a substantial expense. Therefore companies are developing sophisticated systems to minimize the expense. (Imagine the facility manager making a presentation to the Executive Committee, which reduces real estate operating cost by up to 40 percent in four years.)[4]

These strategies have many forms (telecommuting, shared workplaces, hotelling, unlinked) but require an integrated effort of the facilities department, information technology department, and human resources department in order to be successful.[5] Some predictions in this area are startling. CoreNet Global feels that the pressure for cost reduction will be so profound that up to 50 percent of employees will regularly work in unassigned workspace in the very near future.[6] In our experience, unless these strategies are well thought-out, endorsed by the employees and supported with, for example, additional information technology, the tendency of employees to want to be part of a social organization eventually result in the organization moving back to conventional officing. We are not critical of these space strategies, only in most implementation efforts to date.

How a company wants to operate at a particular location will influence the amount, cost, and quality of space required. Will robotics alter substantially the space requirement for a new manufacturing plant? If an office building is involved, will it be planned to utilize open-space planning? What are the administration and logistics schema?

Using goals, facts, and concepts, the facility manager can produce a comprehensive needs statement. He can determine how much space of what quality is required, where, and by when. When determining needs, he should look at scenarios so that he has considered what's needed in a negative future as well as in an upside scenario.

Presenting the Program

Before an ambitious space program is presented, the facility manager of a rapidly growing company must be sure that he either has in hand or has programmed for adequate resources to turn the programmed space into usable space. Increases in facility staff tend to trail the expansion in a company. And failure to manage facility growth properly can be a major problem, seriously damaging your credibility.

The result of space programming should outline the clearly defined space requirements, measured against the available resources. The facility manager needs to assess the cost of the space, the time to obtain the space, and the quality of the space obtained. Thus, through programming, the space forecast is converted to specific requirements, to which costs can be assigned.

Space Accounting and Management

This chapter has already stressed the importance of space forecasting and programming. But in many instances the space problems are not a matter of forecasting so much as management of existing space. Part of the problem is that space is not well accounted for.

Accounting for space depends on good definitions. Although there is an ASTM standard definition, it is not as widely used as it should be.

Facility management will never be successful unless it is clear who controls the space. There are basically two possibilities: ownership by the line manager or ownership by the facility department. The extensive use of chargebacks strengthens the concept of line management's responsibility for its space.

When line managers own the space, the company holds that manager responsible, and charging back for space can be an effective control mechanism. The downside of this approach is that the facility manager has little or no control over the asset that most determines how he is viewed and evaluated.

When the facility manager controls the space, the common good is best served. The facility manager can adjudicate space disputes and assign space to the extent of his political clout. The disadvantage is that line units, as "renters," feel less responsible for the care and appearance of the facilities.

Some organizations have worked out a compromise. The approach we favor has space accounting the responsibility of the facility manager, who also recommends space standards as company policy. When business purposes or other reasons necessitate assignment or reallocation of space, the facility manager, as the technical expert, plans the action and "sells" it to the line managers involved. If that is impossible, the dispute is adjudicated one management level above the facility manager, as are exceptions to space standards.

Space Planning for Management Accountability

There are certain procedures related to management accountability of all space owned or leased. The first step to ensure proper management accountability is to obtain floor plans that reflect the current structure. Some method of differentiating among departments is advisable; shading is one method to accomplish this. In addition, core and common areas can be treated as company overhead or allocated to departments by predetermined rules. Operational costs of support areas can then be charged back to individual departments as a percentage of employee utilization to total employee base, or as a percentage of departmental space to total space. Unless departments are about the same size (in space and employees), do not suggest an equal division of operational costs among departments.

The second step is to seek departmental approval of the space for which each is accountable. Official drawings, sometimes called *key plans,* can indicate occupancy by each department. Some companies require that departmental managers sign off in agreement that they are actually using the space for which they are accountable. Any subsequent changes in departmental utilization must be reflected in an updated key plan. All circulation space is normally charged back to a specific department for purposes of accounting. Unassigned or unassignable space is either carried by the facility department or allocated to user departments on a pro rata basis.

A facility manager of a large company usually has blocks of unoccupied space that must be charged to some account in order to satisfy 100 percent of operating costs. At the same time, that space must be controlled, or it will disappear. Large blocks of unused space should be controlled, even to the point of locking them up. Small blocks should be assigned to local managers for growth space, if possible, before going under central control. If all space is charged back, all departments will have to share in costs for unallocated space, just as they do for unassignable space.

Proper allocation of space is important because facility expenses are often apportioned according to space allocation. Inequitable allocation among departments may be deliberate or an obvious error by the facility manager. Regardless, it is a fiscal and political problem. Allocation is an extremely complex process that requires excellent cost accounting, a good allocation process, and constant reevaluation. For an example of an excellent but extremely complex space allocation system see Alan D. Wilson's description of his best practice at IBM's Watson Research Center.[7]

Space Management Planning

There are basic planning elements that contribute to the facility manager's ability to manage space effectively within existing parameters and to forecast efficient utilization. The basic considerations are:

1. The amount of space available and the time frame for the availability.
2. The type of space available and the general condition and limitations of the architecture or construction.
3. Configurations of the space (dimensions, square footage, volume, shape and/or location).
4. Utilization of the space, including specific activities and necessary support functions. The utilization section discusses techniques of organizational analysis and adequate adjacencies.

How much space. Perhaps the least difficult of all considerations is that of how much space is needed. There are only two alternatives: Either there is existing space to which the scope of activities must conform, or the scope of activities will dictate the type, configuration, and utilization of a space yet defined. Allocating space to work units on a gross basis is extremely dangerous, whereas using gross space for companywide allocations can be quite acceptable.

Type of space. The utilization of space dictates the alterations, construction, and renovations necessary to existing conditions. Extensive demolition and new construction may be required to accommodate the specified utilization criteria, or alterations may suffice. In almost every situation where construction and renovation of existing facilities is compared with new construction, the costs of renovation are less.

There may be hidden liabilities to the renovation. For example, renovations may require relocation of employees, expose employees to dust and airborne contaminants, or cause excessive noise and distractions. Renovation projects usually include major compromises on efficient arrangements of activities or employees (adjacencies), and frequently offer fewer alternatives or less flexibility than new construction. The age of a structure may require that structural elements and the roof be evaluated carefully. Often the power supply and telecommunication support are inadequate and inefficient as well.

Configuration of space. Without launching the actual design process, the facility manager must often determine that certain space is more appropriate for one department than for another. Existing structures usually conform to a normative sizing according to the time when the structure was built and its location; that affects the space available for allocation. For example, ceiling heights have changed from higher to lower in recent years. Column placements are getting wider, and columns are growing large again. Many modern designs are based on an assumption of infinite open areas, and they suffer greatly when applied to older buildings. While there may be a certain charm in dealing with older structures, that charm may not be a suitable substitute for organizational needs.

New office planning concepts introduced in the early 1980s provided for increased functional density of workers in an open environment. By the mid-1980s, many departments downsized to individual workstations. And, according to the Steelcase Office Environment Index, there was a tendency toward larger individual workstations by the end of the decade.[8] Many older office buildings have construction features that will not facilitate larger workstations, especially closely spaced columns.

Changes in the workforce and the way that we work in the 1990s affect not only how we plan and program for space but how we provide workplaces themselves. Alternative office solutions have become so prevalent that lines of furniture and equipment have been designed solely to meet those needs.

Other employees are working from home or in satellite offices, and those who are working in a central location are more often doing so in a team mode. The programming and planning response to each of these alternatives is different and puts an unprecedented emphasis on space planning, programming, and management. Also, due to outsourcing and downsizing, many facility managers are becoming much more expert in consolidating space and planning for space disposal.

Obviously, the utilization criteria determine how efficiently a specific activity may be accomplished within a given space. Some sizes, shapes, or volumes of space lend themselves to certain kinds of activities. In general, the more dynamic an organization, the more important is flexibility; thus, large expanses of uninterrupted space are preferred. Existing architectural and design features prove most appropriate for companies with a less dynamic character. Older structures usually exhibit the least favorable square-foot occupancy ratios.

Locations of activities within specific spaces are important for greater productivity. Many times adjacencies may not be available on the same floor. Under those circumstances, you must determine whether connectivity with another floor in the same building is appropriate, or if the same floor in an adjacent building is better.

Utilization of space. Several techniques can be applied to specific activities programmed into a space. Sophisticated space planning systems are now accomplished by computer. In fact, computers have been instrumental in applying programming techniques to unaffected space without resorting to the "intuitive" process that Jean Cousin alludes to in his book.[9] Cousin refers to a "topological" approach for special organizations. *Topology* is primarily a mathematical term but relates to special organization in the sense of statistical relativity. Cousin thinks that we will ultimately arrive at a time when it will be possible to program activities and requirements into a computer, and the computer will arrange the activities within a special context effectively and efficiently. Cousin concedes that technology has not arrived at that point yet. It is interesting, however, that visionaries have been considering the possibility since the 1970s.[10]

There is no lack of literature on theoretical approaches to space planning. Several authors come to mind. Richard Muther offers a recipe for layout planning. He provides forms that can be used to gather data on flow of materials, activity relationships, and space relationships. Muther refers to his process as Systematic Layout Planning, and applies it also to the white-collar workplace, even though much of his book deals with manufacturing facilities.[11]

A third method for utilizing space is proposed by Roger Brauer, in his book *Facilities Planning*. Brauer's primary agenda is to define and manage "user requirements," offering programming techniques that prioritize individuals performing activities within a space. Conformities of space and construction are an extension of user needs, according to Brauer. His book also provides standard forms and examples of matrix development activities.[12]

Space planners Michael Saphier and Lila Shoshkes orient their thoughts toward equipment and the special displacement requirements of office workers. Their space planner model involves interviewing each employee and identifying the furniture support items. By the simple process of inventory application and activity adjacency, a place is found for all items—thus space is planned.[13] The space planner is likely to place less importance on overall productivity than is the facility manager utilizing either the Muther or Brauer models.

Other Planning Considerations

Universal planning is the response by Gensler & Associates, a giant among interior design firms, to the high costs of relocation in response to churn. Most conventional planning responses consider furniture configuration and communications matrices in relation to employee needs. The universal planning concept provides for a percentage of effectiveness (or ineffectiveness) by placing furniture permanently and moving employees.[14]

Universal planning provides an apparent savings in relocation expenses when there are high churn rates. There may be few overall advantages, however, when employee productivity figures are included in a long-term model or when strong communications links are essential. It is also likely that there will be some employee resistance, owing to the impersonal nature of the process.

We have always emphasized the need for flexibility in space planning. Flexibility, universality of design, and an allowance for growth can materially reduce the nearly constant renovation of space caused by churn in most modern corporations. In addition, most companies need to optimize their modern communications technology, for which they have paid a premium, to reduce the price of churn. Fellow workers no longer need to be seated contiguously for good internal communications.

Prioritizing the Space

Space is prioritized only when there is an intrinsic value to the space. Status is sometimes implied in a space or is seen so in its relationship to other space. Many times proximity to top management receives high priority. Value is often placed on nearness of windows, or panoramic vistas, or closeness to the top of a building. Mostly you will have little to do with the valuing process, although you can help establish policies that may determine the priority of activities taking place within the space.

Be aware that most middle managers who identify their responsibility with a specific activity will be on constant vigil to protect and expand their area. There is constant debate concerning the value of certain activities and their existing resources.

Space Accounting Systems and Inventories

One of the authors once noted that his organization's space for office workers seemed to be disappearing. Since his organization was already rapidly growing, the space loss (estimated at 6 percent of the inventory annually) soon became a matter of great concern. We confirmed that the company's space needed to be managed and that good space management depended on good space accounting. The specific problem was an overload of paper storage—in a supposedly "paperless" office with a computer on every desk. The local paper storage ate up office space. The solution was to implement a space accounting system. This system defines all space, assigns it to a responsible manager, and carefully tracks additions, deletions, and conversions. We recommend three different space accounting systems. In all but the largest companies, you can account for the three systems both by building and in the aggregate.

The first system accounts for space for architectural and design purposes. The best categories are based on area measurement terms, which are most valuable to the design team.

The second system is based on functional categories (e.g., warehousing, shops, office space). The size of holdings obviously dictates the degree of detail to which category codes are assigned and the space is accounted. International organizations may have eighty to a hundred category codes, a corporate headquarters eight to ten.

The third system accounts for space by occupant (user). Some facility managers prefer to account by occupant and category code. This system has broad application but is the information most often shared with users.

The facility space inventory should be reviewed annually. For inventories under 10 million square feet, we favor a formal review twice a year: once at annual planning time and once six months later. The review should concentrate on trends, standards compliance, and equitableness between occupants. One question that might be asked, for example, is, Do we really want to devote 76,000 square feet of downtown office space to paper storage? Another might be, Are we really making the best use of our conference space?

In the last few years, a combination of technologies has produced true facility management systems. For years we have been highly critical of many technology vendors who advertised space management systems as Computer-Assisted Facility Management (CAFM) systems. Now, however, we truly have Integrated Workplace Management Systems (IWMS) and soon Building Information Modeling (BIM) to assist in managing our space. These systems are now computer based and affordable to all facility managers who manage over 100,000 square feet. Using bar coding, a relational database, a geographic information system, and a good computer-assisted design and drawing system, the manager of a large facility can manage workplace information that will make him a powerful player in the business. Space management systems now have capabilities and information that business managers need in their work. Facility managers should leverage that capability for a seat in the inner circle of their companies.

Once you have your system in place, each time you allocate or reallocate space, be sure to capture that information. Too often space management is hampered by an out-of-date inventory or is based on crash inventories. Keep your database current.

Diane Stegmeier, a change consultant, who has researched space and move management widely and deeply, has developed the key issues for facility managers contained in Exhibit 6-1 which should be considered, together with other key players, before any major construction or renovation project affecting employees is undertaken.[15] Stegmeier is emphatic that projects must meet business goals and that business managers must be involved in the planning phase of any construction or major renovation.[16]

And just before the company planning cycle begins we suggest producing a three- to five-year space plan. That plan should consist of a detailed move schema and revised space inventory for year 1. The year 1 components should have management concurrence prior to their use in the company annual business planning cycle. For small to medium companies, include a block diagram. Years 2 to 5 should be represented by revised space inventory projections and block diagrams, if appropriate.

Conclusion

A recent *Fortune* survey of facility executives concluded that many facility executives feel that their companies are doing a good job of optimizing the use of their space, and they have an intuitive feeling that the workplace is important to employee productivity. At the same time, they are more reticent in agreeing that there is a link between the physical environment and significant productivity gains.[17] Until facility managers develop better research, they will remain at a disadvantage in managing space as well as in proving their business worth to their companies.

Exhibit 6-1. Key Space Issues for Facility Managers

- How much space should we allow in our facility to accommodate teleworkers when they work on-site rather than at home?
- What would happen if all of the teleworkers showed up at the office to work on a given day, rather than working remotely?
- Is there a "paint-by-the-number" plan to make this work (a step-by-step process proven to be successful)?
- What type of furniture is best suited for a home office? Can we provide a lesser quality, since it will be used only by one person?
- How much does the company need to provide versus what employees may already have in their homes (second phone line, high-speed internet service, suitable lighting, etc.)?
- Do I need to grow my facilities staff to respond to the needs of teleworkers?
- Does the company need to invest in fleet vehicles for facilities and information technology specialists to make "house calls" to teleworkers' homes?
- What if the organization finds it necessary to return to the current way of working after excess real estate has been sold off?

Notes

1. Stephen Binder, *Corporate Facility Planning* (New York: McGraw-Hill, 1989).
2. Personal responses from the authors and a panel of experts when queried on the general state of the real estate market, May 2008.
3. Jo Heinz, "Space Planning/Programming and Building Analysis," *IFMA Conference Proceedings* (Houston: IFMA, 1988), p. 326.
4. Bill Conley, "Make Yourself at Home with an Alternative Workplace Strategy," *FMJ September/October 2007*, p. 68.
5. Kevin Foley, "Information Systems and the Management of Flexible Workplaces," *FMJ September/October 2007*, pp. 30–34.
6. Don Durfee, "Take My Desk . . . Please," *CFO, October 2006*, pp. 99.
7. Alan D. Wilson, "Distribution and Measurement of Laboratory and Office Space Costs," *IFMA Best Practices Proceedings, Winter 1995* (Houston: IFMA, 1995), pp. 193–211.
8. Louis Harris and Associates, *Office Environment Index, 1980* (Grand Rapids, MI: Steelcase, Inc., 1981).
9. Jean Cousin, *Organisation topologique de l'espace architectural/Topological Organizaton of Architectural Space* (Montreal: University of Montreal Press, 1970), pp. 9–10.
10. *Ibid.*, p. 10.
11. Richard Muther, *Systematic Layout Planning* (Boston: Cahners Books, 1974), pp. 1–1 to 2–8.
12. Roger L. Brauer, *Facilities Planning, 2d ed.* (New York: AMACOM, 1992), pp. 1–10.
13. Michael Saphier, *Office Planning and Design* (New York: McGraw-Hill, 1968), pp. 68–72, and Lila Shoshkes, *Space Planning,* (New York; Architectural Record Books, 1976), pp. 44–48.
14. William Joseph, "The Need to Design for Change," *IFMA Conference Proceedings* (Houston: IFMA, 1988), pp. 7–22.
15. Diane Stegmeier, *Innovations in Office Design,* (New York: John Wiley & Sons, 2008), p. 114.
16. *Ibid.*, pp. 31–57.
17. *Facilities and Real Estate Strategies,* (New York: Fortune Marketing, 1996), pp. 3–4.

Real Estate

All facility managers are in the real estate business. Unfortunately, not all manage real estate: in fact few do as confirmed by the latest study of the international profession, *The Facility Industry Study,* by the combined professional associations. This fact is one of the greatest weaknesses in the practice of the profession today and, unfortunately, does not seem to be improving.

Real estate managers historically have come from the business management or legal tracks; facility managers still come from primarily a technical background. It is not, however, that facility managers cannot manage real estate. It is that upper management does not look to them to do so and has shown little tendency to move organizational real estate under the facility manager except in smaller organizations. Image is the problem here and one that the profession should work hard to overcome because, as we point out in Chapter 6, failure to do so can be disastrous.

In this section, we assume, unless noted, that the facility manager is managing real estate. We look at standard options for a growing organization: buying or leasing and site considerations. Also, we look at the considerations of becoming a lessor. Since some facility managers are also property managers by title, we also discuss that function.

Real Estate Options

7

Pulse Points

- *The facility manager should manage real estate.*
- *The facility manager must coordinate the user, legal, and financial requirements for good purchase-lease decisions.*
- *The facility manager should actively participate in site evaluation and acquisition.*
- *The facility manager should have an active plan to manage the inevitable politics of site selection.*
- *The facility manager should learn as much as possible about any site to be acquired, but enter all negotiations knowing that he probably knows less than the current owner.*
- *When considering a real estate acquisition, the facility manager must also think about an exit strategy.*

The decision to purchase or lease real estate goes to the very heart of a company—its culture, investment strategy, and desire for control. It is important for decision makers to identify the opportunity costs for each option, in present value terms, but the final decision may just as likely be made for subjective reasons. Nevertheless, in this chapter we discuss the factors that go into this decision as they relate to facility management, including the consequent responsibility of site selection, should that be within the manager's realm.

One of the better articles we have read on the strategic role of real estate in an organization points out that real estate alone is big business, that it has not always been managed well, that there is nearly always a real estate component to business plans, and that real estate is the arena where the facility manager is most likely 1) to get CEO-level exposure and 2) elevate the importance of the FM department in the eyes of management.[1] We have personally seen this happen in our own practice. Facility managers tend to feel that we do not get enough high-level executive interest in or support for facility management. Well . . . a major real estate transaction can give that to us so we must handle it well.

Purchase or Lease?

Although there are two major applications of the lease versus purchase process—the acquisition of major properties and sites, or major equipment—this chapter deals with the lease or purchase of real estate. The lease versus purchase analysis is a capital budgeting analysis that compares the pertinent costs of each method on an equal basis. Most facility managers need help in making these decisions.

Joseph Horowitz, director of administration for CBS, Inc., discussed user requirements and provides a predecision checklist for real estate decisions.[2]

Help can come in many forms but most facility managers need help if we do not have real estate expertise and legal support within our organizations. Even though organizational legal support is sometimes available, unless they are familiar with local real estate/zoning law, we recommend some level of consultant assistance. It tends to be expensive but can open doors and avoid pitfalls for any facility manager handling a major real estate or development project for the first time. While the following pages provide you tools to make real estate decisions, this is not an arena for first time players to venture without assistance.

A more detailed description and explanation of the varied forms and considerations for real estate decisions, whether you use a consultant or not, is the book *Managing Corporate Real Estate; Forms and Procedures* by Ed Rondeau, Robert Kevin Brown, and Paul Lapides.

In addition, building assessment is a technique that helps managers match an organization's needs to a proper building. For the financial aspects of this decision, there are accepted accounting principles regulated by the Financial Accounting Standards Board.[3] But to begin, let's look at the factors to be considered in the lease versus purchase question.

The Buy-Lease Analysis

In theory, the analysis is quite simple. The net present value (NPV) of the cash outflow associated with the lease option is compared to that for the buy option. The lesser value is the preferred option.

Most companies have a financial analyst or accounting firm capable of computing cash outlays and NPVs for each option. You'll need the following information:

- The company's cost of capital
- All lease terms having a financial impact, especially the lease payment

- The purchase price of the real estate or equipment plus any other financial terms related to the purchase
- The company's incremental cost of borrowing

Answers to the following questions must be obtained, compared, and analyzed to make an appropriate decision:

1. Has there been an appropriate in-house evaluation?
2. Has there been an independent evaluation?
3. Is the primary issue least-cost financing?
4. Is the purchase or lease decision to be treated as an independent project?
5. Is the lease to be considered a financial or an operating lease?
6. Have options been maximized?
7. Will the value of the property decline at least 75 percent over the term of the lease?
8. Have Internal Revenue Service (IRS) guidelines been checked?
9. Will the lessor absorb operating or maintenance charges?
10. Who will receive the investment tax credits?
11. How much equity is available from expendable property?
12. Will additional property be required to make this project operational?
13. What is the estimated productive life of the property?
14. What is the inflation trend?
15. What is the trend of interest rates?
16. Have state and federal legislative agendas been checked for pending legislation?
17. What are the additional expenses chargeable to this project?
18. What is the marginal tax rate?
19. If the real estate is purchased, how will the project be financed? (term and rate)
20. If the property is leased, how will the project be paid? (term, rate, options, and taxes)

Risk is a major criterion in a number of lease versus purchase decisions. Ideally, there should be no significant difference between the risk of owning and of leasing the same property. However, management's perception of the company's strengths and weaknesses, the economic climate, sustainability rating, if any, and governmental constraints may drive the decision.

Based on cash flow, each project should be evaluated independently. Items such as investment tax credits, other accrual items, return on assets, effect on working capital ratios, and effect on debt-equity ratios must be considered when analyzing a buy situation.

The asset will definitely become part of the business, but it must be determined how that will happen. Should the business pay rent, or should the business purchase the asset? There are benefits to both situations. Therefore, a financial analysis will be a present value comparison of cash flows resulting from purchasing an asset on the one hand or leasing the same asset on the other hand. The objective is to select the particular action that minimizes the present value of cash outflows.

A buy/lease analysis requires finding the cash outflows associated with the lease option, determining the cash outflows associated with the purchase option, and computing and then comparing the net present values of the cash flows. For an example, see Exhibit 7-1.

Whether purchase or leasing is preferred varies also according to the investment capability and philosophy of the company. For instance, certain government agencies are regularly either owners or lessors. Manufacturing companies are more likely than service companies to choose ownership, due to the heavy capital investments for equipment and infrastructure.

Advantages of Purchasing

Although it is seldom stated, most arguments for buying are emotional, political ones. Companies like the control inherent in purchasing, particularly real estate. For organizations that want to convey a high standard or a unique look, the purchase option greatly enhances that. In fact, the desire for control is so strong—particularly in large, well-established companies or smaller companies greatly concerned about their image—that "doing the numbers" is often a waste of time.

Other advantages of purchasing are that property appreciates in value over its life; in fact, some view purchase as a good hedge against inflation. Also, life-cycle costs are normally less, property has a disposal value at the end of its use, property can be a source of later financing, and annual depreciation can be written off. Finally, expansion and alterations at an existing site can usually be accomplished more rapidly.

Advantages of Leasing

Leasing certainly has its advocates. For a young company, leasing its space may be the only real option. If a company cannot resource at least a minimal facility department, leasing may be the only solution. Even some major companies have policies that expansion, at least initially, is accomplished through leasing. Almost all companies lease some property for unexpected new requirements, to meet temporary needs, or for initial expansion. In the current business environment, companies use a balance of owned and leased space to provide them business flexibility.

Exhibit 7-1. Buy versus lease.

Your company's lease is coming due next year and you need to decide whether you will remain at your current address and sign a new lease or move to a building that your company would then purchase. The cost of capital is 10 percent. The tax rate is 40 percent. The building would be depreciated using straight line with a $800,000 salvage value. Current IRS law requires a building to be depreciated 31½ years, but for purposes of this example, the building will be depreciated only 5 years.

Alternative A: Sign a five-year lease with annual lease payments of $700,000. Your company is currently in this building and will not need any major modifications to the building.

Alternative B: Purchase a building for $2,000,000 and spend another $600,000 in renovations for your company's needs.

Alternative A

Years	0	1	2	3	4	5
Lease payments	(700)	(700)	(700)	(700)	(700)	
Tax shield	280	280	280	280	280	
Net cash flow	(420)	(420)	(420)	(420)	(420)	
Discounted cash	(420)	(382)	(347)	(316)	(287)	
Cumulative	(420)	(802)	(1,149)	(1,465)	(1,752)	(1,752)

Alternative B

Years	0	1	2	3	4	5
Buy building	(2,000)					
Renovation cost	(600)					
Depreciation		(360)	(360)	(360)	(360)	(360)
tax shield		144	144	144	144	144
Salvage value						800
Net cash flow	(2,600)	144	144	144	144	944
Discounted cash	(2,600)	131	119	108	98	586
cumulative	(2,600)	(2,469)	(2,350)	(2,242)	(2,144)	(1,558)

Preferred Alternative: Alternative B. Your company should move into the new building and make the purchase.

Source: Heidi Lord Butler, notes from IFMA "Facility Accounting" seminar, Seattle, November 1989.

The other advantages of leasing are the tax deductibility of lease payments, accelerated if not immediate delivery, the opportunity to have state-of-the-art buildings and less risk of obsolescence, a predictable cash flow during the initial term of the lease, the lack of a large initial capital outlay, and maintenance with the lease.

Perhaps the most negative characteristic of leases is the inability to predict and control costs. Even a tightly negotiated lease leaves option year costs contingent on some type of index. At renewal, the company can face substantial increased costs or the option of moving elsewhere.

Sale-Leaseback

A method that combines the features of real estate ownership and leasing is sale-leaseback. If applied correctly, this maximizes the value of the company's real estate assets by reducing occupancy costs while permitting the company to maintain long-term control.

In a sale-leaseback, the corporation sells one or more of its properties to a limited partnership and simultaneously leases back the real estate for long-term use. The typical transaction has three participants: the seller or lessee, the purchaser or lessor, and the lenders. Sale-leasebacks offer many benefits, including:[4]

- Raising funds for 100 percent of the property's value
- Long-term, fixed-rate capital
- Long-term control
- Off-balance-sheet treatment
- Earnings improvements
- Cash flow

The Negotiating Process

When negotiating a lease, an entirely different set of considerations must be made. The extent to which the lessee may be favorably accommodated is strongly affected by both financial considerations and other factors. For example:

- *Size of organization.* Large organizations always ask for and receive more favorable lease terms than smaller organizations. If your size or the nature of your organization makes you a prestigious tenant, strengthen your position during lease negotiation.
- *Stage of building construction.* During the early stages of building construction, a lessee can get the most favorable lease considerations.

- *Part of building occupied.* Generally the highest floors with the best views afford the fewest leasing concessions. Accepting lower-status space offers the greatest opportunity for other concessions.
- *Availability of space in the area.* In overbuilt cities (vacancy rates of 10 percent or more) leasing organizations are much more likely to be accommodating. In cities where the vacancy rate exceeds 15 percent, it is not uncommon to ask for and receive up to one-third of the term of the lease in free rent, in addition to special furnishings and other concessions. It is reasonably common for a lease to be written at "net zero" or just for the lessor's operating expenses under these conditions.
- *Term length.* Most leases for commercial spaces are for five or seven years. The facility manager in search of space should remember that lease terms may be written to accommodate the lessee, and different lengths may be better for the organization. A lease with a term of five years will leave the organization that is growing rapidly with a burden of inflexibility years before the lease expires. It might be better to negotiate an original lease of three years with options to absorb additional space at a fixed rate at the end of the three years. Options to expand into suitable space (which may afford, for example, a better view, more status, or greater accessibility to interfacing departments) are also possible.
- *Operating expenses.* Operating expenses and parking are issues of some importance and may also be negotiated according to the relative strength of the market, position of the lessor, and priorities of the lessee.

The advantage of a lease decision over purchase may depend greatly on specific negotiable items in the agreement. For instance, cash benefits may accrue to the lessee if terms require little or no down payment and balloon payments after one or more years. The organization is then able to apply 100 percent of its income to operating expenses and keep its cash flow liquid.

It is important to negotiate the proper kind of lease (e.g., operating, financial, maintenance, leveraged) and be certain that the IRS recognizes the agreement as a true lease, not a rental-purchase agreement. (The rental-purchase agreement is treated as ownership by the IRS.) It may be an advantage to ensure that the lease does not affect the debt-equity ratio of the organization, since the IRS requires that most bank loans have debt accounted against equity.

It may be advisable to negotiate a varying cash flow. For instance, balloon payments can be scheduled to coincide with cash-rich periods within the fiscal year and avoid periods of cash drought.

In negotiating, understand the position of the lessor. Often the lessor is willing to offer lower rates if he retains investment tax credits and rights to depreciation tax credits. A fluctuating taxable income may affect the lessor's willingness to grant advantageous fixed-rate terms, or he may be willing to offer variable-rate terms that are satisfactory.

Site Selection and Acquisition

Facility managers in companies that acquire and dispose of facilities routinely have a real estate division and financial, legal, architectural, and engineering experts well equipped to handle the acquisition and disposal of real estate. For most facility managers, however, site selection and acquisition can be the initial step on a major capital project that could be the highlight of their career. For that reason, it should be done with care, discretion, and prudent use of expertise to obtain the best deal for the best dollar on the schedule expected.

For the majority of facility managers, site selection and acquisition is so infrequent that it takes on a life of its own. There are always political aspects to site selection, for example. A common saying in the corporate world is that the headquarters relocation will always reduce the CEO's commute. It is not possible to eliminate politics totally, but you can take several steps to make site selection as objective as possible.

1. Establish a confidentiality policy and restrict access to those having a need to know, including administrative personnel.
2. Ensure that in-house personnel are objective and have broad-based knowledge of the company's requirements. Often a consultant is needed for focus and to do the legwork and analysis.
3. The criteria for selection must be credible and truly the most important factors. They must be developed within the corporation, and used to judge all sites. This is a substantial effort, and a consultant can be used here well.
4. The acquisition team should identify those individuals and groups who will be winners or losers in the various options or who will try to influence the decision. An internal relations campaign should be launched both to strengthen the voice of supporters and to minimize the detractors. Make sure everyone supports what the team decides because it is best for the company.

Given the importance of site selection, internal politics are inevitable. Fortunately in large firms, site selection is almost routine, thus less politically charged.[5]

Site Selection Team

The first task in selecting a site is to put together a team or committee to determine who the decision maker is and to set the criteria for selection. But if the decision is political, or if the chief executive officer (CEO) or chairman has predetermined the location, admit it up front and do not waste time on a search. That sounds simple, but when the matter isn't viewed realistically, there's often much wasted time and energy.

In either case, prepare detailed cost comparisons for all sites or locations. Be sure that no single individual or department analyzes all the information, so that you obtain an adequate range of options and negate personal bias. It may be the final responsibility of one individual or department to propose the site or property; however, the team should offer its combined expertise.

Whether the team is all in-house personnel or includes an outside consultant depends on your personnel and their familiarity with the local market. A consultant is often used because most companies acquire sites so seldom that the staff cannot provide adequate advice, and large companies that operate internationally are not versed in local market conditions.

The consultant to use is a matter of personal preference. There are relocation advisers in all major U.S. cities to provide a technical and free alternative to brokers.

While we do not have any data, it appears that some organizations, for a variety of reasons, want to be in a sustainable building. We know of no situation where LEED has been the major reason for relocation or new construction, but better energy management has been a strong supporting factor for a specific location or design factor for renovation or new construction.[6] But your relationship with the consultant is more important than the type of consultant hired, particularly since brokers' fees can be negotiated. Also, it is not unusual for a company to augment the site selection team with an architect, a builder, legal counsel, and a financial analyst.

Decision Making

The factors or decision matrix used to organize the decision making may be simple or complex. Typical factors are given in Exhibit 7-2. However, each acquisition is unique and depends on the type of facility to be located and the work to be performed there. The more sophisticated decision models weigh factors according to their predetermined importance.

Undoubtedly cost is a factor in site selection, so the cost factors must be quantified. Typical cost factors are presented in Exhibit 7-3. Most facility managers prefer a rule of thumb approach to solving problems whenever possible. But facility managers

Exhibit 7-2. Major factors in location searches.

Access to Markets/Distribution Centers
   Cost of serving markets
   Trends in sales by areas
   Ability to penetrate local market by plant presence
Access to Supplies/Resources
   Cost of transporting supplies
   Trends in supplier by area
Community/Government Aspects
   Ambience
   Cost of living
   Cooperation with established local industry
   Community pride (appearance, activity, citizen views)
   Housing (availability, pricing)
   Schools, cultural, and recreation programs
   Colleges, graduate programs
   Churches, civic groups
Competitive Considerations
   Location of competitors
   Likely reaction to this new site
Environmental Considerations
   Sustainability Guideline Regulations
Interaction With the Remainder of the Corporation
   Is this supposed to be a satellite plant?
   Supplied by or supplier to other company plants?
   Extent of engineering/management assistance from headquarters
Labor
   Prevailing wage rates
   Extent and militancy of unions in the area
   Productivity
   Availability
   Skill levels available
Site Itself
   Area of site—layout of structure
   Price of site structures
   Construction/remodeling costs—insurance
   Condition
Taxes and Financing
   State income tax
   Local property and income taxes
   Unemployment and workman's compensation premiums

Tax incentive/concessions
Industrial/pollution control revenue bonds

Transportation
Trucking services
Rail services
Air freight services
Availability of mass transit

Utilities/Serviced
Availability, quality, price of water, sewage, electric, and natural gas services
Quality of roads, police, fire, medical, and similar services

Source: Bruce N. Wardrep, "Factors Which Play Major Roles in Location Decision," in McKinley Conway and Linda L. Liston, eds., *Facility Planning Technology* (Norcross, Ga.: Conway Data, 1987), p. 322. The authors have updated this listing to reflect factors which have developed since 1987.

Exhibit 7-3. Quantifiable location factors.

Site and preparation costs
Construction (renovation) costs
Equipment costs
Labor and fringe benefit costs
Start-up costs (e.g., training)
Working capital requirements (e.g., inventories)
Freight (in and/or out) expense
Property taxes
Workman's compensation premiums
Unemployment compensation premiums
Relocation expenses
Revenue forecast

Source: Bruce N. Wardrep, "Factors Which Play Major Roles in Location Decision," in McKinley Conway and Linda L. Liston, eds., *Facility Planning Technology* (Norcross, Ga.: Conway Data, 1987), p. 322.

with strong mathematical backgrounds might prefer to use mathematical modeling. *Facilities Locations, Models and Methods,* by Robert F. Love, James G. Morris, and George O. Wesolosky, discusses mathematical modeling for facility location.

The list of sites to be considered can be generated by the consultant, based on confidential general criteria set by the company. If no consultant is used, ascertain site availability from in-house data or a local guide to locations, available in most localities without charge and without unnecessarily exciting the real estate market.

The site search and evaluation should be as confidential as possible, but relocation searches are about as hush-hush as the Super Bowl and often take on characteristics of that event. Despite these limiting aspects of the process, the company and the facility manager must ensure that the final decision is credible, transparent, equitable, and comprehensive.

Acquisition

The line between site selection and acquisition is a fuzzy one. The acquisition process starts when the requirements and criteria for the site have been developed. Acquisition without a real estate professional, particularly one familiar with the local area and its political jurisdiction, is not recommended. If a real estate professional is not on staff, then hire a consultant because acquisition can be a snake pit without one. The seller will always know the property better than you. Consequently, try to learn as much about the site as possible. Don't overlook critical sources of information. Exhibit 7-4 is a listing of possible sources. The time spent finding this information translates into a firmer position during acquisition and can help avoid embarrassment.

If time and finances permit, use a team composed of yourself; an operations person; structural, mechanical, and electrical engineers; a communications specialist; and a security, fire, and life safety expert to prepare a property assessment. This assessment will focus on hard costs for the final acquisition decision and highlight factors that might block acquisition.

One of the best practical discussions of real estate strategies is the HOK consulting report, *Exit Strategies*. An exit strategy is a methodology for explicitly addressing factors that affect real estate risk and for accommodating the many changes that confront facility managers every day. Here are some of the considerations for exit strategies:[7]

- You have fewer options when downsizing. Downsizing companies should concentrate on leasing versus buying.
- A rapidly growing company should refrain from owning real estate until it has the cash that can be diverted to building ownership. Once cash is committed to bricks and mortar, it becomes nonliquid.
- High-volatility companies need to spend the most time in planning their real estate strategy and any individual real estate action.
- Alternative work strategies may assist or alleviate the impacts of exit strategies. Some of these alternative work strategies have implementation costs.
- The facility manager can provide the most value by giving good advice on controllable risk. A market-based partner may help in reaching good decisions.

Exhibit 7-4. Sources of site information.

Federal and State Agencies
    U.S. Geological Survey maps
    Army Corps of Engineers' or state floodplain studies
    Soil conservation maps
    Regional land planning studies
    Environmental and sustainability requirements or certifications

City and County Authorities
    City and county records
    Zoning ordinances and maps
    Property tax assessment records
    Planning abstracts or surveys

Documents of Public Record
    Mortgage history
    Liens or other financial encumbrances
    Long-term leases
    Easements, covenants, equitable servitudes
    Reversionary and remainder interests, rights of entry, power of termination (rare)

Other Local Informational Sources
    Previous or comparable sales
    Accessibility consideration; rights-of-way and availability of required modes of transportation

Site-Specific Data
    Building permits
    Building blueprints and specifications

Interviews
    Planning consultants or other counselors
    Real estate appraisers
    Economic development agencies
    Present and prior owner

Source: Bruce N. Wardrep, "Factors Which Play Major Roles in Location Decision," in McKinley Conway and Linda L. Liston, eds., *Facility Planning Technology* (Norcross, Ga.: Conway Data, 1987), p. 322. The authors have updated this listing to reflect factors which have developed since 1987.

- Before building or leasing, particularly the former, evaluate the market attractiveness for future sale, lease, or sublease. This is particularly important when considering building or renovating unique facilities with substantial mechanical or electrical infrastructure. Single-purpose facilities can be very difficult to dispose of.

- International acquisitions emphasize the need for thoughtful exit strategies.
- We can't always change our mind later; our decisions to build are, in fact, cast in stone.
- Orderly acquisition and disposition tends to be the most cost-effective.
- When negotiating a lease, ask for all of the rights that you can get that won't cost anything to obtain.
- Facility managers should prepare multiple scenarios for business units so that their managers can choose among options. Never underestimate the time for decision making. Cost estimates need to consider both this deliberation time and that, once a decision is made, implementation will take time, particularly if leases have not expired.
- Never neglect the impact of business interruption.
- Downsizing often frees up small pockets of space. That space often can't be marketed until consolidated. There is a cost to that consolidation.
- Make sure that costs for an acquisition are in line with other speculative space in the area.

The company counsel and a real estate professional can guide you around the potential pitfalls in negotiating the sale and closure. With their guidance approach the acquisition with three rules in mind:

1. Create the time envelope for the acquisition process and control it.
2. Negotiate with the principal owner.
3. Maximize leverage with the initial offer.[8]

The process of selecting a new site or property is only one phase of the strategic process of managing assets of the organization. You can attempt to influence top management to include relevant facility data in the formal decision making by offering specific information that significantly skews the financial projects, derived from your site-selection process.

The site and property selection process, when combined with the strategic planning process, offers greater visibility and credibility to the facility manager within the organization than most other functions do. Therefore, upper management will tend to judge the facility manager disproportionately on the quality of the site selection process.

Notes

1. Jim Blaschke, "Transforming Corporate Real Estate into a Strategic Function," *FMJ January/February 2008,* pp. 70–73.

2. Joseph Horowitz, "A Facility Manager Look at Office Leases," *IFMA Conference Proceedings,* (Houston: IFMA, 1988), pp. 125–138.

3. Bruce N. Wardrep, "GAAP Consideration of Lease versus Purchase Analysis," in McKinley Conway and Linda L. Liston, eds., *Facility Planning Technology,* (Norcross, GA: Conway Data, 1987), p. 266.

4. John E. Jamerson, Michael J. Leahy, Peter M. Bradley, and Andrea D. Terzi, "The Sale-Leaseback," *Facility Planning Technology* (Norcross, GA: Conway Data, 1987), p. 176.

5. Based on Charles F. Harding, "Company Politics in Plant Locations," *Facility Planning Technology,* (Norcross, GA: Conway Data, 1987), p. 354.

6. Tom Ramstack, "Property Lines; Energy Savings Seen in Retrofits," *The Washington Times,* April 29, 2008, p. C8.

7. *Exit Strategies* (St. Louis: HOK Consulting, 1996), pp. 2–19.

8. H. Basil Hallquist, "The Fundamentals of Acquiring Corporate Real Estate," *Facility Planning Technology* (Norcross, GA: Conway Data, 1987), p. 202.

8

Lease Administration and Property Management

Pulse Points

- *A company with multiple facilities requires careful lease management.*
- *The facility manager needs to be familiar with the principles of property management.*
- *When real estate development is the organization's goal, the facility manager should be part of the corporate development team.*
- *Properties should be disposed of when they are no longer of value to the organization.*
- *Development projects that are designed specifically for investment or resale purposes may severely inhibit the flexibility of the facility to respond to the productivity support needs of the workforce.*
- *Public sector facility managers must be politically astute in disposing of major public facilities.*

Regardless of an organization's preference, at some time it may become a lessor. For that reason, it is desirable to have at least a rudimentary knowledge of lease administration. And since many corporations choose purchase over leasing, it behooves facility managers to understand property management, including when to develop and when to dispose of real estate.

The tenant-landlord relationship often is affected by the national economy and the commercial real estate market. We noted that in Chapter 7 and the recent history is chronicled by Roy Hirshland who feels that, overall, tenants and landlords are collaborating more closely, particularly in the areas of flexibility of terms, increased flexibility in the review of tenant's financials, keeping energy costs in line, and in the types of build-outs allowed.[1]

Lease Administration

When an organization, for whatever reason, decides to lease space, certain changes in management and attitude are necessary. Someone must be in charge of administering the lease (lease management) and in meeting tenant needs and ensuring they comply with the lease (property management). Additionally, at least part of the facility department must reorient itself from a tenant to a landlord perspective, while taking on both different types of legal and financial obligations.

The joint BOMA-BOMI* document entitled "Leasing Concepts" is a guide to leasing from the lessor's point of view, presenting a "know your enemy" strategy. Another approach is Michael Stack's "Lease Negotiations," available from IFMA. Our personal favorite is *Managing Corporate Real Estate* by Robert Kevin Brown, Paul D. Lapides, and Edmond P. Rondeau. Lease administration is a critical function for any organization leasing space. The facility manager who misses a lease renewal date or other lease option will be in jeopardy. So record keeping in this area, or the use of experienced consultants can make or break you.

The Corporate Owner as Landlord

We have two disturbing observations on corporate real estate and lease management. First, too many large organizations separate their real estate function from the other facility management functions. (The same companies mistakenly isolate design and construction also). The result is disjointed, suboptimal management of facilities. Second, too many companies turn the management of leases over to unqualified people, often as a secondary assignment. Real estate transactions are highly complex and require specialized financial, legal, and market knowledge. When there is no real estate professional on staff, get a partner to help. A knowledgeable professional is a hedge against a bad deal with long-term consequences.

In general, corporate owners are not good landlords unless they maintain a real estate staff, either in-house or a consultant. This is perhaps even truer in the public sector. There certainly are marvelous success stories of universities financing their expansion by leveraging their endowment in the real estate market, particularly if some of the endowment consisted of real estate.[2] That is commendable, but the

---

*BOMI is the Building Owners and Managers Institute: BOMA, the Building Owners and Managers Association.

portfolio must be managed toward a set objective, the organization must be willing to accept a new level of liability, and the function must be properly resourced.

In Chapter 7, we discussed strategies for determining the proper mix of owned and leased facilities. In general, companies are using leasing much more extensively than in the past because leases provide the flexibility needed until rapid, short-term growth can be consolidated into assured cash flow or during periods of downsizing.

For most public agencies and corporations, the better policy is to own or lease only that space required for planned growth—that is, three years if planning is for three years, five years for five-year planning. There are some who disagree however. Alfred Behrens of Volkswagen, one of the first companies to manage real estate for other than corporate needs, states, "By the nature of our . . . industry we are also in the real estate business, and we might just as well make the best of it."[3] However, since facility management is already a daunting prospect, we recommend only those challenges of your own choosing.

Organization and Documentation

In medium and large companies, a small staff office is assigned the responsibility of lease administration. This staff reports directly to the facility manager (see Exhibits 2-2 and 2-3). Since leased space is often a short-term solution for space problems, this same staff often is also charged with strategic planning. If the company cannot spare an individual exclusively for lease administration, then this function is best given to the individual with planning responsibility. Because it requires contact with people outside the company, one individual should be the lease manager. In its most recent survey, the International Facility Management Association (IFMA) found that over 70 percent of facility managers serve in the role of lessee, fewer than 30 percent as lessor.[4] But whoever is responsible for leasing operations must rely on counsel— either a staff attorney or outside counsel specializing in lease law.

A systematic process organizing the company leases is essential. Some modules of computer-aided facility management systems (CAFM) may provide for this documentation, but your automated system, Integrated Workplace Management System (IWMS) should provide pertinent information (options, termination dates, lease increases, etc.) at the time when it should be acted on. Ed Rondeau lists the following benefits of a tracking system:[5]

1. Saves time.
2. Identifies opportunities to reduce real estate expenses.
3. Increases accuracy and reduces records duplication.
4. Provides reports and real estate analyses.

5. Efficiently transfers correct information to appropriate levels of the corporation.
6. Aids real estate strategy formulation.

The Lease Agreement

The lessor writes the lease and thus controls the leasing situation. Assuming that you have competent legal counsel, there should be few problems, but some areas require special attention if you are the lessor:

- Increasing use of technology requires that leases address the hours of operation and the cost of substantial electrical and HVAC (heating, ventilation, and air conditioning) systems.
- The lease should specify proper installation and apportioning of costs for supplemental HVAC.
- The lease should certify that the space is free of PCBs, asbestos, lead in the drinking water, and common air pollutants.
- The agreement should be clear about special-purpose space, which varies substantially from common use, of the facilities. An example could be file rooms (high floor loads) and computer rooms (high HVAC, fire safety, and electrical loads).
- There must be adequate access and egress for material and debris, particularly for facilities that do not have freight elevators or loading docks.
- The lease must specify the use of tenant material handling devices inside the facilities.

Lacking a standardized lease for facility managers as lessors, anyone entering into a lease should be particularly concerned with the following:

- Escalation clauses
- The building standard or "work letter"
- Tenant allowance and their applicability against extra work
- Signage
- Approval of tenant's extra work
- Access by lessee's contractor
- Weekend HVAC
- Division of costs for:
  —Operations
  —Major building alteration
  —Landlord repairs
  —Building services

- Subleases
- Appurtenances (parking, toilets, storage space, etc.)
- Rules
- Renewal options

Leasing can be mystifying, frustrating, and worrisome because it is fraught with legalism and seemingly biased toward the landlord. Nevertheless, if you are willing to learn the basics of lease negotiations, you will more effectively employ your counsel, broker, or consultant.

Trends in Lease Management

The nature of work is changing, and the real estate market shifts constantly. So you need to be aware of developments in lease management and anticipate changes. For example, tenants are seeking different kinds of buildings. This has produced the following trends.[6]

- Companies seek flexible buildings capable of housing research, laboratories, office space, warehousing, and support space—all in an attractive setting with increased amenities.
- Lessors are shifting as much risk as possible to tenants.
- Tenants are becoming more sophisticated in stating their requirements and in selecting buildings to fit their needs.
- More tenants are considering becoming developers and/or owners.

It has been said that capital costs come and go but rent is forever. However, the financial impact (cost or income) is only one aspect of lease administration. Equally important are issues of liability and legalities. This is an area requiring both expertise and management. Whether you function as a lessor, a lessee, or both, you must bring those skills to the table.

Property Management

Property management is managing a facility to maximize profit. There is no negative connotation to the word *profit*. In fact, several large property management companies could give management lessons to facility managers. With a certain type and class of property, customer-oriented property management makes good business sense. Nevertheless, the bottom line is maximizing profit from those properties. Since many corporate facility managers also serve as property managers, it is worthwhile to discuss good property management. While there are many similarities, the facility manager should keep in mind the basic difference between himself and the property manager. The approach to a common problem may, in fact, be quite different.

With increasing outsourcing and the reduction of staff, there is an inclination for an in-house organization to adopt a "Property Management Model" for facility management, the heart of which is having an experienced engineer supervisor assigned to each building to handle all O&M problems.

If planned carefully and implemented properly, this may work. But if planners ignored O&M functions which building engineers control and normally are provided centrally by a property management company, the consequence is that facility management organization is reduced to marginal performance.

Organization and Documentation

Normally the on-premises property management staff is smaller than for a corporate facility manager. Service and response are spelled out in the lease. Services over and above those are provided only if specially funded and in good time. This is because building services are primarily contracted out, with instantaneous reaction only for emergencies or life-threatening situations. Exhibit 8-1 represents a typical property management organization of a midtown, midrise office building.

Exhibit 8-1. On-premises property management organization.

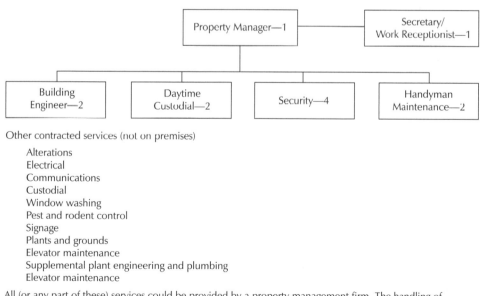

Other contracted services (not on premises)

Alterations
Electrical
Communications
Custodial
Window washing
Pest and rodent control
Signage
Plants and grounds
Elevator maintenance
Supplemental plant engineering and plumbing
Elevator maintenance

All (or any part of these) services could be provided by a property management firm. The handling of communications is dependent upon who owns the switch.

The property manager is an exceptionally important individual to the tenants. Increasingly, it is the custom not to have a resident manager and, in some cases, not even an engineer or handyman on the premises. The property is serviced on an as-needed basis by on-call or roving personnel, with one manager managing four or five properties.

Certainly there is a break-even point for the size property that justifies a resident property manager. However, the following benefits to the tenants accrue when a property manager is resident:

1. Rules and regulations are enforced, and violations are discovered before they become serious.
2. Contractual services are performed to a higher standard.
3. Small problems are solved before they become crises.
4. There is less physical abuse of the facility.
5. Tenants have a visible presence for complaints, suggestions, and praise.

All of these result in a better-run building and a happier tenant. That should be reflected in higher renewals and the ability to charge top dollar for well-run space. We cannot recommend rental of properties that do not have a resident manager, particularly in metropolitan office settings.

The same arguments for a managerial-level person on-site apply to a resident engineer or handyman. There is no greater insurance policy. A flood because no one knew where to find the shut-off valve, or the closest handyman was thirty minutes away when the main broke, will more than offset several years salary saved for an on-site handyman. However, it is important that this technical person have a sense of proprietorship in the building and be customer oriented. A lead engineer, skilled in the building's systems and in customer service, can serve the building and the tenants well.

Since profit maximization is the raison d'être for leasing a building, it is important that leases be systematically controlled. A proper lease management system has four characteristics:[7]

1. It is a real property database.
2. It is an action-reporting system.
3. It is a management-reporting mechanism.
4. It is a tool for real estate planning.

Services

Property managers should be interested in how their services are being rendered and how they are perceived by the tenants. There are many inexpensive ways to gain this knowledge—for example, by:

- Monitoring work requests for timeliness and completeness—by trade and by building location
- Quizzing the work receptionist or having him keep statistics or conduct short surveys
- Following up all or a percentage of service requests for satisfaction, with phone calls or with a brief questionnaire
- Having a tenant advisory council meeting, perhaps quarterly

It is extremely important that once this information is gathered, you take action and communicate your response back to the tenants.

Trends in Property Management

The changes in lessor-lessee relationships that were noted for lease management earlier in this chapter apply to property management as well. It is recommended that facility managers who also serve as property managers keep current with these trends and anticipate change.

Property Development

We admit a certain ambivalence toward facility managers' becoming property developers. Some argue that it shows how far facility managers have come; others say that the facility manager already has enough on his plate without taking on another major task; yet others are concerned that even before facility management is defined, it is merging into property management, where there's a different philosophy. The considerations are similar to those regarding ownership or leasing of property: Stay out of the development business but also realize that some of your colleagues will become developers by default. So if development is to be done, it deserves to be done well. And by "doing well," we mean that the shareholders receive a competitive return on their investment.

The Development Process

The process of development usually connotes a transition of function and improvement of a property. In Chapter 7 we urged the facility management department to work closely with finance, counsel, and top management in the lease versus purchase decision. We also suggested developing a comprehensive real-property database. Those suggestions are even more appropriate when considering property development.

The major difference between developmental activities and site selection or acquisition is that site selection is part of a process, the results of which are concerned with greater productivity. Development implies that improvement of a property will return a profit outside the organization. In other words, in site selection the facility manager offers advice that can optimize profits from internal activities; in development, the advice is tempered with considerations affecting the future leasing and resale of the property. The significant criteria for maximizing internal activities were considered in the previous section. Here we focus on the factors affecting return on investment as it relates to property acquisition and improvement planning for the leasing and eventual resale of the property. As implied in a quote from Alfred Behrens earlier in this chapter, a site selected to meet a corporate need may well offer opportunities for development as well.

Development Constraints and Considerations

A facility manager may be able to control most of the factors related to internal activities, but a developer develops sites to meet the needs of potential clients as well.

In property selection, attempt to persuade top management to consider properties in terms of employee and vendor access, or for their transportation capabilities. Investment properties may be better suited at locations that will service other clients. A facility manager is concerned that stacking plans (how departments relate to each other in a multifloor building) are consistent with communications needs and work flow. That same building, viewed as an investment property, should be developed according to the needs of potential clients.

A dynamic organization planning a building program may wish to construct a number of buildings that afford a panoramic vista. But when vistas are not available, lakes, rivers, or fountains can be constructed instead; this makes the total site desirable to others and promotes further development.

When developed for a particular company, the architecture for a building is integrated, and access to amenities is universal. However, when a building is constructed for outside clients, the architecture may be varied, and each will demand amenities not to be shared by others. Heterogeneous architecture presents considerable problems with regard to grounds keeping, traffic control, security, and features such as walking paths, jogging trails, food service, and emergency preparedness.

One concern of great interest to investors is the potential for efficient expansion. By their nature, some investment properties may not have the flexibility to respond to certain renters' specific needs. For example, an urban site, despite a favorable location, may not be appealing to a think tank desiring tranquility and a scenic view for its headquarters.

Among the factors inhibiting development flexibility are the following:

- Specific state regulations, zoning, or community demands
- Limited access to major streets
- Limited air rights
- Wildlife preserves and permanent open space
- Quiet zones
- Limits on land reclamation
- Inadequate public transportation
- Limited-capacity sewage and waste disposal
- Limited water and power access
- Historic preservation covenants
- Public housing dictums
- Public amenities dictums

If a facility manager becomes a developer, he must be equally concerned about his ability to dispose of the property to meet company business plans. Many of the factors listed above are equally applicable in a disposal scenario. Two other considerations are the extent that there might be regulatory time bombs on the property (e.g., submerged, leaking tanks or contaminated waste) or that the facilities are so uniquely engineered or so closely identified with a single company that no other organization wants to occupy them. Both factors can be deal breakers and make properties difficult, if not impossible, to sell.

The Development Team

From the facility manager's perspective, there is little to recommend the acquisition of a property for investment purposes. There are few advantages and many potential headaches. Nonetheless, the property may be acquired. The chief financial officer (CFO) will have a major interest in the development project, but it is the facility manager who must control the development team.

Although each development project is a unique challenge, the makeup of the team is fairly standard:

1. The facility manager
2. A land-use consultant
3. A concept designer
4. Counsel with local land-use expertise
5. An internal client representative (if one is involved)

The sole purpose of this team is to develop a project that will best meet company needs within available resources. They must sell the project to the necessary board or other decision-making body.

Your CFO can assist in determining what an adequate return is. The primary determinant is the cost of capital. However, the question then becomes one of choosing among potential investments. John Dues, of Mead Land Services, suggests the following:[8]

1. Manage the allocation of capital or cash resources to business units selectively.
2. Ascertain or confirm the long-term viability of each investment in its business.
3. Determine the overall performance objectives of the units.
4. Facilitate identifying critical threats and opportunities facing the business units.
5. Provide a baseline for measurement and control of performance during the planning horizon.

These criteria help the team judge whether an investment fits the strategic planning objectives of the business. If it is compatible, then it is probably a proper investment, and the project can be assessed further, using primarily capital investment evaluation techniques.

The facility manager contributes information to the team effort regarding probable operating expenses, leasing information, engineering and architectural attri-butes of the project, maintenance programs, and costs for office building or industrial property developments.

By its composition, the development team should have the proper technical, financial, and political expertise to prepare whatever decision-making document is used by the company or agency. When that is done, the necessary groundwork should already be in place to ensure that board approval will be achieved, and the team can disband.

Ownership and Financing

The form of ownership a company chooses for its development project depends on both its financial commitment and development philosophy. The advantages and disadvantages of the three major types of ownership are shown in Exhibit 8-2.

Having chosen an ownership form, the company then often wants to select a development partner. Five criteria are important for selecting that partner:[9]

1. *Integrity.* Choose a firm with which you are comfortable.
2. *Financial strength.* Have the resources to fund the project without constant concern.

3. *Experience.* Have completed a similar project.
4. *Appropriateness to the scope.* Select a firm appropriate to the type of financing you are envisioning.
5. *Familiarity with the location.* Both partners will feel more comfortable if the development partner knows local conditions.

To structure the financing of the development project, the facility manager, in conjunction with the CFO, must be aware of the aspects of real estate that translate into assets and that can be traded for cash. They must both also be aware of the possible objectives of lenders, equity investors, and developers. And they must realize the actual financing means peculiar to real estate, which reconcile the inherent attributes of property with the objectives of money suppliers.[10]

Furthermore, the financial plan for the company should identify the cheapest sources of money, create investment incentives to replace high cash returns, and use devices that defer to the greatest extent the need for cash. Some options that meet these criteria are (1) structuring the development as a tax shelter, (2) using tax-exempt financing, (3) choosing land leaseback, and (4) engaging in joint ventures with institutions.[11] The facility manager will have internal financial and legal advice

Exhibit 8-2. Forms of development ownership.

	Advantages	*Disadvantages*
Leasehold control	• No building management • Less administrative cost • Minimum front-end investment • Cost expensed immediately for taxes	• Lowest appreciation potential • Generates no leverage
Fee simple	• Fullest range of financial options • Considerable tax benefits	• "In-house" management attention needed • Up-front investment high • High administrative costs
Joint venture	• "Off-balance sheet" financing • Minimum contribution • Risk minimization • Flexibility	• Can be complicated

Source: Peter Haverkampf and Gary Salton, "Real Estate as a Corporate Reservoir," in McKinley Conway and Linda L. Liston, eds., *Facility Planning Technology* (Norcross, Ga.: Conway Data, 1987), pp. 18–19.

during the development of the financial plan to support a development project. However, it is necessary at this point to reflect on responsibility. If midway through the project the finances (or any other aspect) goes sour, it is the facility manager who is on the line. For that reason, the facility manager should rightly challenge every aspect of the project development as it proceeds. Internal experts and consultants need to make the facility manager comfortable, or no aspect should proceed.

One last note of caution: Most companies that lost a lot of money in development ventures did not understand the true extent of their risks.[12] One of the principal roles of the facility manager is to ensure that company management is aware of not only the opportunities of development, but the downside risk. Admittedly, in the enthusiasm of a major development project, those risks are not popular, but they must be presented.

Successful development requires both a company devoted to that business and also a change of philosophy of the facility manager toward at least a portion of the facilities for which he is responsible. That cannot be done without careful thought and planning and complete commitment.

Cash-strapped public sector organizations in both the US and the UK are increasingly turning to public/private partnerships. Sometimes these partnerships are also used to bypass some of the bureaucratic steps required to develop property in the public sector. Two of your authors marvel at the effectiveness and efficiency of the public/private partnership construction of family housing on military installations as the armed forces struggle to meet the needs of an increasingly married force structure. Other successes have been in sport stadiums, mixed-use technology parks, and even schools.[13] These initiatives are extremely complex, usually involve a good portion of political input, and are often controversial.

Property Disposal

Property disposal has become a much more complicated process than when decisions were made simply on market factors like price and location. No one will buy a property without conducting extensive due diligence investigations to ensure that no legal and environmental problems exist. Sometimes the mere whiff of an environmental problem can scare off a potential buyer, because whoever is holding the environmental problem at the time that it is discovered tends to be liable for the solution to that problem.

A facility manager must be as sensitive to excess real property as to purchase and development. Often, however, timely disposal seems almost an afterthought. And as important as disposal can be, the literature is noticeably silent on this topic. The ultimate horror story in this regard is the company paying rent on a facility it already owned. That facility should obviously have been a candidate for disposal.

How does real estate become excess to the needs of an organization? It can be obsolete. The company can be downsizing or changing products or services. An example can be found in the public sector, where changing demographics have closed many schools. Also, the organization may have relocated.

Leland Smith, a senior vice president at Grubb and Ellis' Commercial Accounts, in his inimitable style, lists the five traditional ways to dispose of excess facilities:[14]

1. Unload this turkey on another operating division as an internal transfer of assets at full book value.
2. Put your widget plant on the market as a widget plant and try to get its full replacement value as a ready-to-operate facility. Hire a broker and tell your boss it is his fault if you can't sell it.
3. Redeploy or auction the equipment, then put the land and buildings on the market as an ideal facility for any conceivable use.
4. Sell it to whoever will take it off your hands and hope to get its depreciated value. Tell your treasurer you've done the company a favor by minimizing the tax consequences of the sale.
5. Donate it to charity, take the tax write-off, and give yourself a plaque for being a good corporate citizen.

Unfortunately, this is typical of the standard approach to property disposal. However, there is another view: The excess property might represent planned excess capacity, obtained at a favorable market rate for future expansion. Surplus real estate is not, in and of itself, good or bad. It is part of the life of a facility, and it deserves to be managed like all real property assets. Most often the problems occur when property becomes excess unexpectedly and it remains excess and becomes a burden, normally financial.

As a general rule, there can be hidden costs in excess property, so only property that has been planned as excess to an organization's need should be retained. There is the old saying, "Hang on to land; it is under all and they are not going to make any more of it." The reciprocal is, "Value is generated by earning power." Vacant, non-productive land is not a liquid asset; at current interest rates, and considering the cost of management and taxes, land must double in value every four to five years to be an outstanding investment.[15]

Methods of Disposal

The best discussion we've seen of disposal options for facility managers with excess property is by Robert E. Baird. He cites the following as alternative disposal methods:[16]

1. Sale and partial lease-back
2. Subdivision
3. Raze and redevelop
4. Tax-free exchange
5. Short-term financing
6. Short-term lease with purchase option
7. Donations

An alternative to disposal is adaptive reuse. Two of your authors have several excellent examples in our Northern Virginia neighborhoods: An excess school has been converted to administrative space for the school district. A former but inadequate police station is now a full-service, one-stop human services center. For adaptive reuse to work, the company must be comfortable with the function for the new use.

Disposal Process

Disposal of real estate requires the same close coordination as purchase or leasing. Imagine the embarrassment of the facility manager who has just sold the headquarters of a subsidiary in Chicago, only to find that the headquarters for a new service product in another subsidiary will be needed there in six months. Hard as it is to believe, some organizations lack a real-property information system to identify property as excess to their needs. And of three corporate real estate databases that we reviewed, only one had the capability of identifying upcoming excess property or cataloging surplus property.

The facility manager should follow a detailed procedure for shopping around excess property for an appropriate period in all parts of the company. Most public sector agencies have such procedures. Once they are cleared through operations, the facility manager must develop a game plan with the finance department to maximize the profit or minimize the loss. With the plan in hand, he can then go forward with that popular partner, the company counsel, and a broker if one is appropriate. Each potential disposal property should be carefully evaluated, inspected thoroughly, and its features categorized according to potential buyer types and needs.

Each disposal situation requires an understanding of equity in the property. Many times equity exists in the property, but often it may be enhanced by unused or deferred tax deductions or allowances. There may also be taxes that are due at the time of disposal of a property. Potential buyers will be interested in the property's present cash value as well as its capitalization rate. They will also want to know the amortization rate and how much depreciation they can expect, at what rate, and the financial leverage possible.[17]

Prospective buyers should also be informed regarding the property valuations and assessments for similar properties in the region.[18] They will ask about any special exemptions or tax relief inherent in the property. For instance, sometimes prior agreements with state or local authorities include tax abatements or special considerations that can be passed on to new owners.

In the Public Sector

One of the more interesting aspects of the public service life of one of your authors was his involvement in military base closures. Several of these facilities were declared in excess of the military's needs or were proposed for new missions or funding cuts. An elaborate bureaucratic system had been agreed upon with Congress, and it included the following for each site:

- A mission analysis
- A financial analysis
- An environmental impact statement to include the impact on the local economy
- An assessment of national historic significance
- A public hearing

The system was so elaborate, the analysis so detailed, and the environment so political that no bases were ever closed if the closure was contested. The analyses were so complex and contained so much subjective data that they could easily be challenged or returned for further analysis. Public-sector facility managers in particular must be politically astute if they plan to dispose of major facilities.

Congress and the president realized these problems were serious and nearly impossible to overcome if politics was to be the principal driver for base closures. Therefore, to determine the bases to be closed to match the 1990s downsizing of the Department of Defense, they established a commission of experts who prepared an impartial list of base closures based on the analyses listed above. Congress then had to pass or not pass the recommended package in toto. Politics was not completely eliminated from this process, but the country was able to close most of the necessary bases.

Notes

1. Roy Hirshland, "Once Only Bound by a Lease: Landlord and Tenant Relationships Evolve to True Partnerships," *FMJ July/August 2007,* pp. 24–26.
2. Jane H. Lehman, "Many Universities Getting Real Estate Lessons," *Washington Post,* June 3, 1989, pp. E1, E19.

3. Alfred H. Behrens, "Managing Corporate Real Estate as a Profit Center," in McKinley Conway and Linda L. Liston, eds., *Facility Planning Technology* (Norcross, GA: Conway Data, 1987), p. 118.

4. *Benchmarks II,* 1994, (Houston: IFMA, 1994), p. 10.

5. Edmond P. Rondeau, "Contel Finds Great Way to Manage Real Estate," *IFMA Journal April 1989,* p. 28.

6. Arthur M. Delmhorst, "Why Tenant-Landlord Relations Are Changing," in *Facility Planning Technology,* p. 150.

7. John D. MacEachron, "Managing Real Property Assets," in *Facility Planning Technology,* p. 291.

8. John J. Dues, "Real Estate Management and the Corporate Planning Process," in *Facility Planning Technology,* p. 11.

9. Peter Haverkampf and Gary Salton, "Real Estate as a Corporate Reservoir," in *Facility Planning Technology,* pp. 18–19.

10. Howard T. Slayen, "Financing Corporate Real Estate Acquisitions," in *Facility Planning Technology,* p. 82.

11. *Ibid.,* pp. 83–84.

12. *Current Trends and Future Outlook for Facility Management* (Houston: IFMA, 2005), pp. 6–7.

13. Robert A. Sigafoos, *Corporate Real Estate Development* (Lexington, MA: Lexington Books, 1976), pp. 157–158.

14. Leland F. Smith, "Turning Obsolete Buildings into Income," in *Facility Planning Technology,* p. 254.

15. H. Basil Hallquist, "The Fundamentals of Acquiring Corporate Real Estate," in *Facility Planning Technology,* p. 203.

16. Robert E. Baird, "More Innovative Approaches for Surplus Properties," in *Facility Planning Technology,* pp. 250–253.

17. Charles F. Floyd, *Real Estate Principles,* (Chicago: Longman Financial Services Publishing, 1990), p. 2.

18. *Ibid.,* pp. 272–275.

SECTION IV

Sustainability

Rapid change in the interest and acceptance of green or sustainable buildings and building operations has occurred over the last decade. The perceived ability to reduce costs, improve employee satisfaction, and help to "save the earth" has given facility managers a dramatic new area of focus.

This section provides an overview of the green movement, applications of sustainability to facility management, the financial case and models for justifying sustainable products and services, as well as some suggestions and resources for gaining acceptance as you bring more sustainable practices to your organization.

It is a natural fit for facility managers to understand and embrace the concepts of sustainability and lead the effort to create long-range savings and implement sustainable practices for their organizations. Since facility managers have always been required to operate with constrained budgets, the value of energy savings is not a new concept. Similarly, the need to reduce resources and provide materials in our buildings that help decrease occupant health issues always has been a challenge facing most facility managers. What is new is the acknowledgment that life cycle analysis—looking further out for impacts and savings—is recently accepted in most for-profit corporations. Not only is it accepted, but life cycle analysis is quickly gaining momentum as organizations compete to be the most sustainable companies. The facility management contribution to the sustainability effort is substantial (many organizations will look to us for leadership in this area). It also provides an avenue for increased visibility to the value facility management provides in supporting the organization.

Facility managers cannot ignore sustainability because it is a management "twofer." First, it meets an internal and external public relations movement which, in and of itself, is fast becoming an imperative. Second, the short and long-term savings from a properly justified and organized sustainability program are in synch with organizational goals and show the facility manager to be a business-oriented manager.

> *"We do not inherit the earth from our ancestors; we borrow it from our children."*
> Native American Proverb

9

Definitions, Background, and Applications of Sustainability

Pulse Points

- *Sustainability is not a new concept, but is recently becoming a new marketing, management, and operational tool in business and society.*
- *There are multiple sustainability guidelines worldwide. LEED is one popular U.S. based rating system for designing, building, and operating buildings.*
- *Facility management is a natural initiator of sustainable practices since facility management has long promoted the use of life cycle assessment for decision-making.*
- *Sustainable practices apply not only to design and construction of new buildings, but to ongoing operations of buildings. These are all within the purview of the facility manager.*
- *Regardless of the sustainability guideline chosen for adoption, the use of sustainable practices is increasing and rapid regulation is anticipated in this area over the next decades, requiring facility managers to understand, adopt, and disseminate green practices.*

A short history of sustainability

Sustainability is not a recent creation. The modern sustainability movement began in the U.S. in the 1960s and 1970s when pollution problems and the rapidly rising cost of oil, coupled with oil embargo, caused many organizations to reassess their energy usage and methods of obtaining energy, and reconsider their impact on our lands. Huge toxic waste dumps were creating havoc; the days of cheap, easily provided energy were fading. A shift was beginning. In 1962, Rachel Carson published *Silent Spring,* bringing environmental awareness to the public. After discovery of the harm created by numerous toxic disasters, the U.S. Environmental Protection Agency (EPA) was created by the U.S. Congress in 1968. And at the very end of that year, astronauts shared with the entire world the very first view of our entire earth as they travelled around the moon. They also provided, via satellite link, the first "earth rise" from the moon, visible to humans. This unique view gave inspiration for many additional efforts to understand our earth as an integrated whole, rather than as countries divided arbitrarily by political and social borders.

In 1972, the Club of Rome published the astounding *Limits of Growth* paper, which revealed the exponential growth of human populations. Later in 1987, The World Commission on Environmental Development released the Bruntland Report, *Our Common Future,* named after its chair, Gro Harlem Bruntland. This created the first "global agenda for change." Since that time, governmental, business, and general public awareness of the need for more sustainable practices has grown. As more and more "green" products came into the marketplace, with no regulation nor restriction on what was called "green" or how to classify sustainable products, the U.S. Green Building Council was formed in 1993. This consensus non-profit organization is composed of leaders from across the building industry working to advance construction that is environmentally responsible, profitable, and healthy.[1]

Around the same time, numerous other international organizations were releasing sustainability guidelines for their countries. Exhibit 9-1 outlines some of the major international sustainability guidelines sources. While each country has some specific details in the regulations and guides, the overall movement is aligned to help developers, builders, and those who operate buildings decrease their uses of materials and resources, while providing more efficiency and savings over the life of the building.

Definitions

So how do we define sustainability for buildings? The Bruntland Report defines sustainable development as, "ensur(ing) that it meets the needs of the present without compromising the ability of future generations to meet their needs."[2] This definition, which we think is also appropriate for facility management, is taken from the Native American Iroquois Nation proverb "We do not inherit the earth from our ancestors; we borrow it from our children." This concept of concern for future generations

Exhibit 9-1. International Sustainability Guideline Sources

Guideline/Standard	Country	National or International
U.S. Green Building Council's Leadership in Energy & Environmental Design – LEED	United States	41 international countries
Building Research Establishment's Environmental Assessment Model – BREEAM	United Kingdom	15 + international countries
Green Building – GB Tool from International Initiative for a Sustainable Built Environment – iiSBE	Housed in Canada	International focus
Green Globes	Canada	North America
Comprehensive Assessment System for Building Environmental Efficiency – CASBEE	Japan	National
Green Building Council of Australia's Green Star Rating Tools	Australia	National
Deutschen Gesellschaft für nachhaltiges Bauen	Germany	National
Other national/local standards and guidelines		Country specific

guides many of the sustainability principles we discuss here as well as those for green building design and operations.

As facility managers we have long requested improvements and innovations to save energy, provide better workspaces for employees, and improve the operation of our buildings. Too often, due to short timeframe stakeholders' demands, we were denied these improvements because of the need to increase shareholder value within the next quarter or year. So it is natural for facility managers to be beneficiaries of the new wave of sustainability, as we now have senior business leaders recognizing the long-range, whole life cycle viewpoint that the sustainability movement brings to the marketplace. After years of requests for energy retrofits that could yield tremendous paybacks in three to five years, the short 18-24 month return on investment is no longer *always* required in a marketplace that looks for everything green, including green offices, operations, and maintenance standards. The new acceptance of sustainability allows facility managers the ability to realize tremendous benefits in energy, waste reduction, water, and other material and resource reductions, as well as benefits such as employee satisfaction increases, productivity increases, and other "soft" benefits that are difficult to define with precise financial values.

Other terms that may need clarification are the financial tools used to calculate the costs and benefits of any project or installation. One key component of the impact of sustainability is the focus on whole life-cycle costs. Frequently referred to as Life Cycle Analysis or Assessment (LCA), (the total costs to design, construct, operate, maintain, and dispose of buildings) it has changed the way we look at these measures. In a short-term environment, return on investment or payback periods are typically very short, around two years or less. This short-term requirement restricts facility departments, but keeps company capital available for appropriate investments such as research, development, marketing, and other capital intensive pursuits, which an organization may value more highly than long-term savings. LCA is comprised of three components: inventory, assessment, and analysis. Exhibit 9-2 shows the interrelated nature of these three components of LCA. A baseline or inventory is the first step toward understanding the total LCA.

More information on how to calculate LCA and other financial tools are available in chapter 11 – Financials of Sustainability.

Design and Operational Sustainability

The initial focus of most industry sustainability guidelines began with construction of new buildings. The ability to influence sustainable outcomes is most easily identified by contrasting a traditional building, or one built without consideration of

Exhibit 9-2. Life Cycle Assessment Relationships

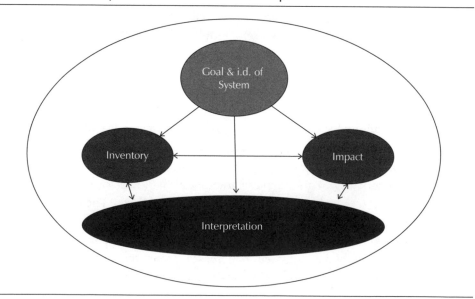

integrated systems and savings, with a new, highly integrated, high-performance structure. The design and commissioning provides great momentum for the sustainability movement as more and more organizations become familiar with the U.S. Green Building Council's Leadership in Energy and Environmental Design (LEED) guidelines and the need to improve our total life cycle costs through design, construction, the long operational period, and final disposal. Acceptance of new building improvements has been well embraced.

However, the existing stock of buildings throughout our country and the world provide a much larger opportunity for impacts, especially in the areas of maintenance, operations, and disposition of materials. In 2004, the Existing Buildings category of LEED (LEED – EB) was established and rolled out to provide guidelines specific to greening our existing structure stock. While new building projects are exciting, they are infrequent for most organizations; therefore, the existing building guidelines are the primary focus of facility managers operating in their current facilities. Changes to update this guideline in 2008, now the LEED – EB: Operations & Maintenance guidelines, provide a more balanced approach, avoiding site and design specifications irrelevant to existing buildings.

Sustainability Applied to Existing Buildings Operations

Of primary interest to facility managers is the ability to support the organization and provide high performance spaces for accomplishing organizational objectives. Reduction of energy usage is the most visible, and most easily documented, feature of sustainable building systems. With energy costs soaring, mandates to dramatically reduce energy usage are widespread throughout the world. Facility managers are ordered to keep cost escalations within sometimes unrealistic ranges, and are also charged with continuing to keep the organization and its workers comfortable and productive in their workspaces.

With climate changes seemingly impacting many areas of the U.S., water usage is a new consideration for areas that formerly had no water shortages. Droughts in various areas of the country force organizations and individuals to reconsider how they waste water and mandate cutbacks. A dramatic example is provided in the Southeastern U.S. where, after three years of severe drought, major cities initiated water restrictions not only for home watering. Limits were imposed for major corporations to reduce water usage by at least 10 percent. Companies with high water usage such as bottling companies and landscaping firms were dramatically impacted and forced to deviate from standard business practices to meet these new limits. Atlanta, Georgia, home of Coca-Cola, is one city that has required major cutbacks in water usage. Coca-Cola Enterprises, the bottling company for Coke, has been forced to dramatically reduce water usage as businesses were regulated to cut at least 25 percent of commercial water use in 2007. Creative innovations are needed to make these rapid and dramatic reductions possible for most organizations.

Resource conservation is another area with major potential for savings within existing buildings. Recycling programs from as far back as the 1970s have been in place for paper, glass, and some metals. But today facility managers have opportunities for other savings as well. Even minor reconfigurations of space often require interior renovations that create huge trash waste with sheetrock, aluminum or wood framing, cabling, carpet, and other old materials potentially going into a landfill. But all of these products are now recyclable, with some even paying high premiums, a better concept than facility management paying to dispose of these waste items. With metal prices skyrocketing, new small, niche businesses are springing up to capture unused cables and strip out the metals for reuse. Instead of paying landfill fees, enterprising facility managers are requesting that renovation companies recycle all waste to capture savings or provide payments back to the project budgets. Innovative ideas are springing up in all areas of recycling, even selling waste fiberboards to dairy farmers for use as cattle bedding instead of sending it to the landfill! The fiberboard breaks down eventually and provides warmth for the cattle in the process.

Recycling efforts in office areas often inspire tremendous employee loyalty, especially with the newer employee generation just coming into our organizations. With all things being equal, youth is looking for the environmentally conscious organizations to employ them. This is a surprising and suddenly more important area for facility management focus—attracting top talent. As more middle-aged baby boomers retire and leave the workforce, finding replacements and experienced workers becomes more difficult. Facility managers are now expected to provide an "exciting" workplace to entice these new employees. In his new book, *Saving the World at Work,* Tim Sanders estimates that almost two-thirds of recent college graduates say they will not take jobs at companies with poor social values. He also notes that customers are important since 65 percent of American consumers say they would change to brands associated with a good cause, considering quality and price remain equal.[3] Sustainable initiatives often contribute to this effort and make the organization more attractive.

An important area of sustainability is the procurement process. Although not always the direct responsibility of the facility manager, our policies and attention to detail here can create major waste or contribute major savings, especially in the area of transport costs. Attention to detail is needed to ensure that we are purchasing local, or as close to local as possible, avoiding high fuel costs in transporting materials and products to the organization. Many consumers, whether personally or commercially, are unaware of where their products originate. Are the paper towels in your restrooms shipped from the Pacific Northwest to your Florida facility or do you purchase from local Florida manufacturers? Are the finishes specified for your executive office renovations exotic imports or locally, sustainably harvested products? These small details can have huge impacts on the environment and often save an organization in shipping and production costs. While there has been a perception that green products carry a higher cost, as more enter the market, and users ask for them, the costs go down. In many cases, due to reduced transport costs, these green items can be procured locally for less than ones traditionally purchased. This trend will continue as more organizations and individuals demand sustainable products and more manufacturers fulfill the demand. The area of sustainable purchasing policies should also extend to our vendors and service providers. Again, attention to detail should include clauses in outsourcing contracts requiring that providers also implement these procurement policies when they buy products for our organizations. Documentation and verification requirements for these practices should also be included in our contracts to assure compliance. Most responsive vendors will provide what is necessary to meet their customers' demands, and the progressive vendors are already offering these options to their clients.

Sustainability Guidelines

The recent increased interest in and applications of sustainability measures point to the need for standardization of "green" products and services. In the U.S. there are a number of sustainability guidelines, including the U.S. Department of Energy's *Energy Star* program, which rates electronics and appliances regarding energy usage. There are also the popular U.S. Green Building Council's Leadership in Energy and Environmental Design (LEED) guidelines for all stages and phases of buildings. Originally introduced in 1993, the LEED New Construction guidelines first provided standardization and a third-party rating system to demonstrate adherence to sustainable practices in designing and building commercial buildings. These rules have expanded to include Existing Buildings, Residential, and separate guides for developers and tenants in the Core & Shell and Commercial Interiors categories of ratings. The LEED ratings for buildings range from Certification at the basic level, to Silver, Gold, and Platinum for increasing levels of adoption and use of sustainable measures. Each of the areas have specific prerequisites and points that can be gained in five areas: sustainable sites; water efficiency; energy and atmosphere; materials and resources; and indoor environmental quality. An additional innovation category provides opportunity for points that may not be covered in other areas or those that exceed those guidelines outlined in the five categories.

The volunteer efforts of experts and users have provided the U.S. Green Building Council (USGBC) with rapidly expanding offerings on their website to reduce paper and mailing impacts. We recommend frequent review of the latest offerings and updates at *www.USGBC.org/LEED*.

The LEED guidelines for existing buildings are less well defined. Operations and maintenance proposals are not as well documented since they are newer and have fewer certified buildings accumulating data. Over the last eight years, however, Adobe Systems Inc., in San Jose, California, has invested more than $1.4 million in energy-related facility projects and received close to $400,000 in rebates from local energy suppliers. These green initiatives have helped the technology company to save more than $1.2 million annually, which translates into a 121 percent return on investment with an average payback period of 9.5-months.[4]

Other guidelines in various countries mentioned earlier in Exhibit 9-1 reflect some, but not nearly all, of the global guidelines being utilized throughout the world. This list is growing as countries adopt new parameters each year. Especially for those facility managers operating in a global environment with responsibilities in multiple countries, consideration of the local guidelines and rating systems may be one option. Another option might be the analysis of their strengths versus the USGBC LEED rating system or the International Standards Organization (ISO) 14001 series of sustainability standards. These criteria, which are utilized by many organizations, especially those in manufacturing industries already utilize many of the other ISO measures.

The big task for facility managers is rapid adoption of sustainability as a concept influencing every aspect of operation. The result can lead to cost savings but needs to be pursued because sustainability will most likely be regulated and mandated in the near future. Rapid change in the field is ongoing, so be alert to news, watch facility management newsletters, and blogs and association updates for these important changes. In the U.S. many cities and several states have already mandated that all government buildings meet specific LEED standards. This is expected to expand to most cities and states within the next few years, so familiarity with LEED is urgent for U.S. facility managers or those managing offices within the U.S. Landlords and tenants alike will be required to meet minimum levels and reduce carbon emissions regarding global international benchmarks.

Carbon Reduction

An additional measure that many organizations are adopting is the "carbon footprint" metric. Efforts to reduce carbon emissions and measurements of existing and reduced carbon impacts are a new management metric utilized in many organizations. The carbon footprint is the measure of the total amount of carbon dioxide (CO_2), and other greenhouse gases, emitted through the burning of fossil fuels. This metric should include the direct as well as indirect emissions required to deliver, manufacture, transport, and support modern human life. This includes transportation, energy to run HVAC systems, lighting, and other electronic energy consumption, as well as the costs to have raw materials delivered, and even the costs to manufacture the boxes or packaging our products go into before sale. The calculation also includes the shipping and distribution costs to get these products into stores or deliver them to consumers. So the entire production cycle is included, no matter whether the organization provides a product or service. Travel for executives, sales and marketing personnel, and employee travel to and from an office location are also included. When we try to calculate all of these impacts it can become overwhelming, especially if we include the imbedded carbon impact of products we take for granted in the workplace, such as our computers, office supplies, and everything we use on a daily basis. To simplify the measurement, somewhat, the embedded energy and carbon effects are normally attributable to the originating organization and are often not included in the direct carbon impact measurement.

Like so many other facility metrics, the key to greenhouse gas reductions and carbon reductions is the establishment of a baseline that can be reduced over a specified period of time. Most organizations will have targeted energy reductions of between 20-60 percent within the next decade. For more information on how to measure and reduce carbon and other greenhouse gases, we recommend the World Building Council for Sustainable Development website at www.wbcsd.org. Case studies on large organizations are available and provide tips and techniques that are updated frequently. Another good source is California Green Solutions website at www.californiagreensolutions.org.

The field of sustainability is rapidly expanding with new products, services, and regulations constantly being unveiled. The best advice is probably to think like your parents, and always try to conserve ("turn off the water when you brush your teeth"), avoid waste ("eat everything on your plate"), and be considerate of other generations who will have to deal with the legacy we leave behind ("clean up your toys when you finish playing"). Resources are also expanding rapidly to provide help in learning about new regulations and guidelines, so stay alert and look to facility management associations to keep you aware of the latest developments.

Notes

1. U.S. Green Building Council website, http://www.usgbc.org/ShowFile.aspx?DocumentID=3338, retrieved March 31, 2008.

2. United Nations, 1987, "Report of the World Commission on Environment and Development," General Assembly Resolution 42/187, 11 December 1987.
3. Cone, Inc., "2008 Green Gap Survey Fact Sheet," as quoted in *Saving the World at Work* by Tim Sanders, Doubleday Business, 2008.
4. Cammell, Amy, 2008, "Adobe System's Green Initiatives Generate Huge Savings," *Tradeline, Inc.,* [Electronic version] retrieved July 30, 2008 at http://www.tradelineinc.com/reports/EAB5E3A6-2B3B-B525-8D330EE0D9E6A531.

10

Sustainability in Practice

Pulse Points

- *Sustainable buildings are not just designed and constructed, but also operated in sustainable ways. This may be the largest contribution facility managers bring to sustainability—the sustainable operation of existing buildings, whether sustainably designed or not.*
- *Green products are more readily available and continue to grow in number and quality as more users demand green products. Pricing is also falling as more products create competitive pricing in the marketplace.*
- *Growth of green office initiatives and sustainability will continue to impact the practice of facility management. This is not a trend but a major societal shift.*

In chapter 9 we provided an overview of the sustainability movement, but facility managers need to know how to build and/or operate buildings in a sustainable manner to successfully adopt green initiatives. The design is obviously a first step, but we also include information to take an existing building that might have no sustainable factors and move it into the 21st Century without razing and starting from scratch. Many facility managers are faced with operating marginally designed buildings, attempting to improve the indoor environment for more satisfied and productive employee performance, and reducing operating costs overall. All these abilities are needed in today's facility manager. The job is not becoming more specialized, but broadening to include management of these new initiatives within organizations.

Sustainable Design

The design of a new facility provides the best opportunity to have a sustainable impact. Orienting the building to maximize or minimize the sun's energy absorption, depending on climate, is a first step. The design, selection, integration, and commissioning of building systems, such as energy management and automation, security automation, piping, ventilation, and other integrated systems can all be synergistically planned if a green building is the intent. Participation of knowledgeable design and construction team members in the design stage can enable green building design without adding to the cost of the final structure. Thoughtful planning provides opportunities for trade-offs and upgrades that are difficult to retrofit. It is therefore incumbent on the facility manager to bring together these players when planning new construction.

Even before the site is selected, the discussion of the needs, purposes, uses, and intent of the building can provide guiding principles that will bring together everyone's best ideas, provide true value engineering, and result in a maximized design. We have seen projects that did not accomplish this well, causing budget overruns and dissent among project team members, and frequently resulting in less-than-expected delivery to the occupants. Facility managers' careers can be ruined if the one-time new construction has these results. That is why it is critical to first have clear agreement among the customers/users, management, and the design/construction team on the goals for the building, including sustainability goals.

Many public sector organizations in the U.S. are now required to build to specific LEED standards, so that makes their process more easily defined. Similar requirements for other international locations mandate sustainability standards, especially for public or government owned buildings. For those facility managers in public and non-regulated organizations or locations, as well as private organization facility managers, the choices made in the initial process impact the final product. The relationship between timing of decisions and costs is shown in chapter 12 in Exhibit 12-2. Sustainability decisions make this relationship even more important by potentially impacting costs, as well as the final users of the building. It may be worthwhile to consider hiring architects familiar with LEED guidelines or those who have previously worked on projects with sustainability certifications. The process of documenting the decisions, materials, and performances is not inconsequential, and the use of a LEED accredited professional on the project provides one additional innovation credit point.

We recommend that facility managers who have no prior experience with sustainable design be sure to hire an experienced green building architectural firm, one with LEED accredited professionals, who have designed buildings that have gone through the LEED or other certification process successfully.

The best, though hardest, way to learn about sustainable methods and guidelines is by participating in a sustainable project design as the facility manager.

Sustainable Construction

The next step following design is the construction of the building. Multiple products and materials are becoming available to support more environmentally friendly construction. Low or no-volatile organic compound (VOC) emitting adhesives, paints, and other finishes are now available at little or no additional cost compared to traditional products. The recent demand for them has increased production and availability and keeps the costs down as competitors vie for your business. Higher efficiency windows, specialized building cladding, and new integrated building automation systems provide substantial savings over the life of the building and often require little or no change to building design, only specification of the newer, more sustainable materials.

Commissioning is another effort that pays back in ongoing savings through assurance that systems are operating as designed and meeting the efficiencies expected. With little added effort, commissioning and sustainability reviews can often be combined and performed by the same individuals. Construction companies experienced with sustainable projects will often have reduced costs over those who need to learn about the installation and handling of new sustainable materials. Be sure to require appropriate experience from the contractor and sub-contractors, as well as the documentation on sustainable products that will be needed for a certification submission such as LEED.

The construction phase of a new building is also a critical time for reduction of materials and wastes. Many companies have found that they can reduce costs of waste disposal through various recycling methods. Rather than sending the damaged and leftover materials to a landfill and paying disposal fees, these materials can be recycled and businesses may pay to obtain these materials. Even if payment is not possible, sorting and recycling of waste materials is possible and costs little to manage on the construction site.

The use of new technologies such as building information modeling (BIM) also provides opportunities for savings during construction. Clearly pre-defined deliveries can avoid scheduling interruptions, so that deliveries can be scheduled for the most appropriate time and often reduce storage problems on site. Material conflicts or non-compatibility can be identified prior to ordering to save time, money, and disruptions. Later availability of complete specification information from BIM data can be invaluable to facility managers after construction is completed, when replacement or additional stock is needed for future alterations after occupancy. The ability to have easily available records is a tremendous saving in time and effort following construction. Becoming more sustainable in our materials selections and processes we use to operate the building provides the incentive for many of these BIM initiatives.

Sustainable Operations

The ongoing green operation of a building provides the biggest impact facility managers can bring to sustainability. The life cycle of a building reflects the largest investment of time and resources during the occupancy and operations and maintenance phases. Figure 10-1 shows the relative timeline for each phase of a typical building life cycle, and sustainable operations should be thought of over the entire operational phase.

Occupancy and operation of a green building is still a new experience for many employees. The time used to educate employees moving into a sustainable building or spent training facility operational staff on highly integrated equipment is essential to maximize the benefits that can be obtained with proper usage and operation. Employees unfamiliar with automated sensor controls that turn off lighting may need to be educated to plan periodic movement to avoid having the lights go out on them as they become engrossed in reading reports, or other detailed work habits that require little movement. While it might be a brief distraction, reoriented habits can result in tremendous savings for organizations that have longer, more flexible working hours for employees. There is no need to keep a room or area lit if no one is on site and sensors enable facility managers to do this without manual set backs or specifically programmed hours which could limit some employees flexibility.

Retraining facility management staff for new automated or integrated systems is also required, especially if this is the first major change that your organization has experienced. It may be difficult for some "wrench-turners" to learn the new electronic or wireless relay setups and configurations. Manufacturers often provide the needed training with or supplemental to the purchase of these systems. Be sure to

FIGURE 10-1. Building Life Cycle Phases

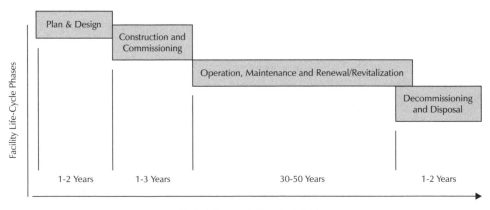

plan training time for employees just prior to move-in. The changes that automation and integrated systems provide can sometimes require reorganization within the facility staff. If they previously adjusted temperature controls throughout the office manually, either as planned or when called by occupants, the staff will need new duties when the self-regulating systems are online. Retraining in how to address the occupants may also be needed in these cases, so that technicians can inform employees that "the system takes approximately 10 minutes to readjust" (instead of employees hearing chillers turn on when the technician manually adjusted the thermostat). Consider all the stakeholders who will need re-education at some level regarding sustainable buildings; each needs different information in order to help facility management operate building(s) at maximum efficiency:

- Customers / Users
- Facility management staff
- Financial accountants
- Service and product providers / suppliers / vendors
- Procurement / contracting officers
- Senior management
- Landlords or tenants
- Public officials regulating the building (permit officers, tax assessors, etc.)
- Visitors or customers

Additional areas of change in operations for sustainable buildings cover the entire spectrum of managing the facility. Obvious recycling programs for office products, reductions in energy and other resource usage, and one particularly challenging area, procurement processes, are all areas which are seeing change.

Attention to details that traditionally have not been important may include requests or requirements for providers to document their raw material sources, their sustainability efforts, and documentation of the distribution and transport impacts of the purchased materials. These efforts and attention to detail deal primarily with carbon emissions and greenhouse gases. However, they give insight into the total procurement impacts which can be ignored as, "Not our responsibility"; they provide potentially nine of the 14 LEED credit points in the Materials and Resources section of LEED – Existing Buildings certification. Procurement is a large area of responsibility for facility managers since we purchase goods and services for the entire organization. This makes the facility managers' role in sustainability another area for increased recognition and value for the organization if done well.

Indoor air quality, energy, water, and other resource management, as well as site issues are the primary areas where facility management can dramatically improve sustainable operations. Energy usage has been on the FM radar for many years since it provides substantial cost savings, especially with recent dramatic increases in energy costs. Some of the areas of greatest impact include lighting retrofits, which fairly inexpensively replace older fixtures or bulbs with more energy efficient replacements. With quick pay-back periods, these retrofits have been popular over the last 20 years and are continuously reducing the amount of energy to light our buildings, parking lots, and other spaces.

Similar savings through improvements in water efficiency are possible and provide not only green impacts, but ongoing savings each time water bills are due. With changes in weather patterns in many areas, new attention to reduced water usage is now required in commercial buildings. Simple and inexpensive to install aerators for sinks and showers provide immediate reductions. Other more dramatic improvements can be seen in programs to collect rainwater and run-off for irrigation systems and even systems that utilize recycled or grey water, for air handling units.

Reductions in all sorts of material usage and recycling programs remain popular and provide more "soft" improvements like improved employee loyalty and ability to attract new, young employees. The financial returns are often not seen in recycling programs. However, increased need for resources in developing economies such as China and India may improve the financial value of many recyclables such as metals and plastics. As discussed stripping copper and other metals from abandoned cabling has become a niche industry and new enterprises are springing up to fill other material needs, so look for the opportunities to recycle these previously trashed materials.

Improvements in indoor air quality (IAQ) are a major issue for facility management. Any facility manager who has dealt with "funny smells" in the office or employee reactions after television news shows relating "sick building syndrome" information, knows how important employee comfort and safety can be in the workplace. The U.S. Environmental Protection Agency (EPA) estimates that indoor air quality averages two to five times worse than outdoor air, and can cause negative productivity impacts in commercial buildings.[1] Smells are usually associated with volatile organic compounds (VOC's) in many products such as carpet or wall covering adhesives, paints, cleaning products, and copier emissions. New green standards for these materials have been established and are validated by third parties in the Green Seal Standard and Environmental Choice Program.

Other IAQ impacts can be managed through appropriate thermal and humidity levels and these are set by the American Society of Heating, Refrigerating, and Air Conditioning Engineers (ASHRAE). The correct elimination of carbon dioxide is also important to avoid sleepiness and inability to concentrate in office settings. This is usually handled if the air intakes are balanced, but slight increases in indoor carbon dioxide can negatively impact workers. Finally, the perception that facility management is providing a "safe," comfortable indoor environment is key for improving worker productivity as the U.S. Department of Energy (DOE) notes in their study with the Rocky Mountain Institute showing a 6 percent increase in productivity with improved IAQ.[2]

Site issues are also important and provide opportunities for reduced transportation usage as well as direct facility impacting options such as telecommuting and compressed work schedule schemes which generally allow for less overall real estate provisioning. With less land needed, reduced rent, less utility usages, and increased employee satisfaction can result. This is the synergistic effect resulting from creative use of workspaces and distributed workplace options (See more information in chapter 6 – Space Planning and Management). The newest LEED – Existing Building Maintenance & Operation guideline – from USGBC in 2009 provides additional scoring opportunities for these types of synergistic options. The recent changes acknowledge the move from a design and construction viewpoint to the ongoing operational view to which facility management devotes so much of their focus.

Facility managers who take buildings through LEED-EB certification will not only demonstrate dedication to the environment and community, but will reduce operating costs and at the same time improve working conditions for staff and occupants.

Green Products and Services

Since the mid-1990s sustainable or green products and services have been on the rise. One of the primary reasons for creation of the USGBC LEED program was to deal with "green washing," which involves companies touting sustainable products that may or may not meet normally accepted standards and could just be marketing hype. There are a number of certification groups that provide third-party verification of the sustainability of products. The Forest Stewardship Council (FSC) certifies lumber products, which are grown and harvested sustainably, and were one of the first industries to set up this type of self-regulating certification. Other industries have been slow to provide meaningful self regulation or adopt third-party verification outside the building standards mentions earlier. There are new providers of lists of verified products and services scrutinized by outside panels, such as McGraw-Hill's *Green Source* publication, or the Environmental Protection Agency (EPA)'s Energy Star program which provides lists of approved products on their web site at www.energystar.gov, and the USGBC set up the LEED Accredited Professional examination to provide consultants with a validation that they are familiar with LEED processes and understand the integration required for sustainable buildings.

Interestingly, as we were preparing this chapter, we came upon a website marketing consulting services to evaluate a broad range of facility initiatives to increase shareholder value, achieve sustainability, and reduce costs. That indicates to us that at least one firm is interested in pursuing sustainability as good business.

In addition to a larger number of products, simple economic forces have caused the cost of sustainable products to become more competitive and, in many cases, they are no more expensive than traditional counterparts. This helps to make selection of sustainable products more cost effective, since first costs as well as the ongoing savings can be tremendous. As more buildings are built and operated in sustainable ways, a broader understanding of sustainable products grows so that supply and delivery of green products and buildings will impact the way facility management is practiced. The Green Building Alliance in 2008 predicted that the green building products market would be worth $30–40 billion per year by 2010.[3] We anticipate that additional regulations in the near future will require that reduced carbon, energy, water, and waste will quickly require modifications to the way facility managers and senior organizational management view sustainability.

Currently, many organizations embrace sustainability primarily for their marketing and sales impacts. If competitors provide sustainable products we will, too, is the attitude. But regardless of the initial motivation, the savings and attitude of conservation and awareness of use permeate the organization and in short order, the organization is a truly green organization, with employees providing suggestions for savings, suppliers bringing new services and materials to light, and senior managers embracing the concepts of life-cycle costing and funding. This is where facility management can provide a major impact and value for the organization. With the focus on resource reduction and the concepts of life-cycle analysis well understood, many of the initiatives to provide appropriate preventive maintenance for building systems, proposals to retrofit systems that are not energy or water efficient, and the creation of new distributed workplace arrangements for workers utilizing technological solutions, will all soon be possible and enable the facility manager to better support his organization. Efficient facility solutions to organization's needs rather than provision of more of the same old, now outdated 20th century solutions, are needed from FM working in organizations with knowledge workers as the dominant employee. Even industrial manufacturing facilities have updated technologies to allow for increased efficiency, savings, and better operational use of the buildings facility managers provide. Large manufacturing facilities operate with building automation that allows for peak load shedding, maximization of efficiencies, and cost savings measures that streamline the facility and manufacturing processes.

Internal Initiatives

Within many innovative organizations, there already exist pockets of innovation and adoption of sustainable practices. In the early 2000s, British Petroleum (BP) saw an innovative employee initiative to launch a formal recycling and conservation program, *Global Green Office Initiative,* in which employees from Melbourne, Australia began an education and action program which provided guidelines, later adopted by senior management and distributed to employees worldwide, to get the program underway. Their robust measurement system allowed employees to begin reductions and the reporting allowed the facility management group to receive recognition and support for the green initiative as it was rolled out internationally to all BP offices. Focused on areas of energy and water reductions, waste and recycling, paper and office supplies management, these guides were developed at the grassroots level. Therefore, they were well adopted and utilized by employees throughout BP.[4]

Another more recent innovative effort is the launch of new Sustainability Officer, or Sustainability Director, positions to oversee an organization's entire span of green programs, from marketing, to employee recycling, improving employee health, to changes in how office space is allocated and utilized, and of course, compliance with changing regulations and local dictates. The U.S. government has agencies with Chief Sustainability Officer positions in place now but we envision this to be necessary only for very large organizations, totally committed to the program, with a widely dispersed facility portfolio. The position, if needed, should be a staff position at the organizational headquarters. Within one agency, the Acting Chief Sustainability Officer described a creative new internal web site for employees called "Go Green Get Health," which recognizes the "interconnectedness between public health and the health of our environment."[5] With the clever use of acronyms their site ties concepts of the new program to easily remembered initiatives bringing employees on board and providing ways to enhance and grow sustainability programs.

With growing awareness of climate change, we expect that more facility managers will soon be responsible for new programs that expand the environmental responsibility of their organizations. Many will be employee-driven measures, others will come from marketing efforts to increase the green perception of customers, but regardless of their source, these green programs are quickly becoming standard within facility management responsibilities worldwide.

Sustainable office procedures within the workplace can begin a domino effect that soon impacts families, schools, communities, and eventually the entire world. Some of the now, almost standard processes for sustainably operated facilities include a number of fairly simple concepts of office management and facility management that may have an initial small impact but grow when shared:

- Eliminate unnecessary photocopying—encourage email or use double-sided printing only when necessary
- Reuse packaging for shipping
- Reduce energy usage—turn off equipment and lights when not in use or install sensing mechanisms; use energy efficient appliances and electronics

- Reduce transportation costs—provide options for employees like ride-sharing and reduced costs mass transit passes
- Buy close by—Avoiding transportation is an easy carbon reduction tool
- Save money and materials by reusing, refurbishing, conserving, and sharing resources—reduce, reuse, recycle, and buy back
- Use low maintenance, less disposable, more natural products
- Buy sustainable business products
- Remove office toxic substances and require non-toxic cleaning practices
- Form employee teams to lead eco-efforts within the organization
- Communicate efforts to suppliers, vendors, and customers and require their participation
- Remember seven generations forward

While many efforts may seem small and insignificant, the sustainability process needs to start somewhere. Office programs can be an excellent education on the topic, provide savings for the organization, and bring green credibility to the organization. Whether your organization has a sustainable new building, or facility management launches new recycling programs, as Edmund Burke, the famous 18th century British statesman said, "Nobody made a greater mistake than he who did nothing because he could only do a little."

Notes

1. U.S. Environmental Protection Agency, "The Inside Story: A Guide to Indoor Air Quality," online at: http://www.epa.gov/iaq/pubs/insidest.html, retrieved May 2008.
2. Browning, William D., Romm, Joseph J., US Department of Energy, and the Rocky Mountain Institute, 1994, "Greening the Building and the Bottom Line, Increasing Productivity Through Energy Efficient Design."
3. The Green Building Alliance, quoted in the U.S. Green Building Council's Green Building Facts, available at www.usgbc.org/ShowFile.aspx?DocumentID=3340, retrieved June 2008.
4. BP booklet, "Green Office Initiative: a practical guide," internal employee publication, 2004.
5. E-mail correspondence with Liz York, A.I.A, LEED AP, Acting Chief Sustainability Officer, Centers for Disease Control and Prevention, Atlanta, Georgia, July 2008.

11

Sustainability Financials, Acceptance, and Implementation

Pulse Points

- *Life cycle cost analysis is the primary tool to analyze green buildings versus the traditional design, construction, and operation of buildings.*
- *Savings are not the only benefit of sustainable practices—environmental improvements and social impacts also factor into sustainable decisions for most organizations.*
- *It does not have to cost more to build a sustainable building if green intent is established properly and early.*
- *Facility managers can document tremendous savings when sustainable operational practices are adopted.*
- *Various management tools can be used for sustainability projects.*

One of the excuses most frequently heard about building or operating sustainable buildings is that it costs more. With current technology, experienced planners, architects, engineers, constructors, and facility managers, green building can be cost neutral and provide enormous savings over their operational life cycles. The financial case for sustainability is being improved daily as we learn of new products, new guidelines, and new ways of managing the built environment. Your authors have found that if agreement is reached early enough in the planning process by all parties, some buildings can actually cost less than traditional buildings, since synergistic savings and value engineering provide up-front coordination and reduced wastes.

Then the energy, water, and other savings that result during occupancy are gravy for the owners and occupants.

Life-Cycle Costing

The use of life-cycle cost analysis (LCA) is the primary way to demonstrate savings and also justify the benefits of sustainable buildings and operational practices. LCA provides the total cost of facility ownership, rather than simply the initial cost to design and construct a building, system, or operation. We advocate it when considering all major fund expenditures as mentioned in Chapter 5. LCA provides a holistic view of financial and non-monetary impacts of a decision which include benefits that are often difficult to calculate in strict financial terms. LCA is also useful for system analysis, and brings the full useful life costs to bear on the decision. Exhibit 11-1 shows the input/output relationships that need to be considered in any LCA. All the materials that go into any building or system must be included. This includes both raw materials, as well as external methods, to get the raw materials into your building or system. These external methods are often overlooked, but can provide a key ingredient toward efficiency. For example, if we consider the cost to not only buy, but to transport and get drywall to our construction site, we may find that a greener alternative may not be the least expensive product from a purchase price standpoint. If shipping charges to transport the product across the nation or globe are added, this might be the more costly and less green option. The inclusion of dispo-

Exhibit 11-1. Life Cycle and Systems Analysis Model

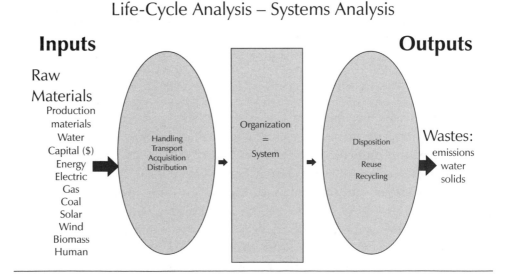

sition costs are also a part of LCA and can also tip the scale to different products and options if we consider these costs along with the initial acquisition costs. A chair that costs $30 less to purchase, with equal transportation costs, may not have recyclable components, and, therefore, would incur a $40 landfill fee at disposition, offsetting the initial cost difference. Most buying decisions do not include this eco-critical disposition consideration unless LCA is utilized.

To begin a LCA, the initial step is to set the analysis period. For a building owner, the useful life of the building may be the selected period for analysis, or the allowable depreciation period may be used. For other service or product decisions, the contract period is normally used for the analysis period.

In the next step, a number of costs must be gathered to analyze the entire acquisition, operation, maintenance, and disposition of any facility or system. These cost fall into the following areas:

- Purchase, acquisition, design, and construction costs (first costs)
- Energy and resource costs
- Operation, maintenance, and repair costs
- Replacement costs
- Alteration/Improvement costs
- Residual value – resale/salvage value or disposition costs
- Carrying charges – interest payments on loans, taxes, and other regulated costs
- Non-monetary costs/benefits such as improved safety or aesthetics

Sources for these costs for sustainable buildings may come from internal data for items such as interest rate charges or historical energy costs; or they may come from other external sources such as RS Means or BOMA benchmarks for expected construction costs and typical maintenance charges. The Whole Building Design Guide website (www.wbdg.org/resources) also provides helpful links to many sources for costs needed to complete a LCA.

After these costs are summarized, a decision on the discount rate to be utilized is required. Most corporations have an internal rate they are charged to borrow funds and use this as their hurdle rate. Other organizations utilize present value analysis since inflation may be unknown (See Chapter 5 for an explanation of these techniques). Consistency is the key to maintaining analytical accuracy. A statement of the assumptions used for the analysis also provides reviewers the needed information in case new or different assumptions are required during approvals. With an established analysis period, cost information, and discount rate determined, LCA is easily performed by using the basic formula:

LCC = First Costs + Present Value of recurring costs – Present Value of residual value

With this calculation, understanding the total of all costs is possible and can be further analyzed for payback or other expected results. Many organizations currently operate with only financial analysis, the economic information, used for building decisions. New impacts of Corporate Social Responsibility (CSR) and environmental concerns are creating new interest in expanded accounting procedures.

Triple Bottom Line Accounting

Social accounting remains a controversial subject but we present it here because, in the experience of at least two of your authors, there could be pressure on top executives (and thus on the facility and financial departments) to quantify environmental and social impacts in decisionmaking on all major organizational commitments of funds.

Often debated, but still used in some organizations is the concept of *Triple Bottom Line Accounting,* (3BL) which refers to analysis of not only economic factors, but also environmental and social impacts to decision making. Criticized for its lack of objective metrics, the business world is increasingly relying on subjective, intuitive, common sense measures that cannot be strictly converted to dollars, pounds, yen, or Euros. In line with many organizations' attempts to bring Corporate Social Responsibility (CSR) to the forefront, 3BL is one methodology that has gained acceptance. Accountancy has even developed social and ethical accounting, auditing, and reporting (SEAAR). This new financial movement has been accepted by the accounting firms, as well as their customer organizations and the guidelines are included in the Global Reporting Initiative (GRI), and parts of various ISO standards.[1] The general dissatisfaction with 3BL results from its subjectivity and lack of financial tieback. However, many organizations are expanding their concepts of metrics and including SEAAR or 3BL reports with metrics such as:

- Employee satisfaction ratings increases
- Percentage of senior management in recognized minorities
- Number of incidents/fines for various environmental restriction noncompliance
- Energy usage reduction organization-wide
- Recycled paper, aluminum, copper, glass and plastics reporting
- Reductions of landfill space and charges from prior year
- Charitable donations of excess FM materials in percentage of profits to local and national charities

Applying these types of metrics to facility management can bring increased understanding of the broad role FM performs for the organization, especially in the areas of resource reductions, employee satisfaction and comfort, and recycling efforts.

Economic Studies

The research is beginning to reflect the growing use of sustainable methods of managing facilities. After several years of operations with sustainable buildings, many of the promised savings are finally demonstrated and documented. However, most current documentation involves the beginning phase, new construction analysis. In his breakthrough study, "The Costs and Financial Benefits of Green Buildings," for the state of California, Gregory Katz was one of the first to demonstrate the long-term value of sustainably built buildings. Using conservative numbers, the study found the range of costs to build green from zero to nine percent in 2002 and 2003. In ensuing years, through market competition and more informed participation and value engineering, the cost premium for a sustainable building has declined to approximately 1.7 percent, most of which includes LEED application and administration fees, rather than actual project costs.[2] If projected out over the entire life of a building, 20–50 years, these up-front costs are overshadowed by the potential resource savings, estimated to be 20 times that of the initial cost, over the same timeframe. Strict financial payback was used in these calculations. Added on top of the financial savings are improved satisfaction, productivity (reported as increased test scores in the 2006 report), health, attendance, and an increase in the ability to attract and retain staff. All of these "soft" factors have importance in today's facilities and provide additional ways for facility management to provide value to the organization.

Another important study of the economic impact of sustainable buildings is the report provided to the U.S. General Services Administration (GSA) "GSA LEED Cost Study" by Steven Winter Associates, Inc. in 2004. This study found that for minimally certified buildings (Certified level of LEED) there is a premium of –0.4 percent to 1 percent and for Silver certified buildings, –0.03 percent to +4.4 percent.[3] These validations of low or no-cost premiums need to be shared with senior management since a persistent barrier to acceptance of sustainability costs comes from the initial, early cost premiums that have now been mostly overcome.

These economic studies are based on new construction of LEED buildings. There may be even higher pay-offs with adoption of LEED – Existing Buildings: Operations and Maintenance category guidelines since these impact ongoing operational issues which always take funding away from organizations' financial bottom line. It is important to recognize the widely accepted figures of between 65 and 90 percent of a company's budget for employee salaries and benefits, such that even a small increase in overall worker productivity would be more beneficial than dramatic savings in energy usage. The increased productivity documented in sustainable buildings provides a dramatic motivator for improving the competitive advantage of an organization through a highly productive workforce. Some improvements found in sustainably built/operated facilities include:

- Reduced absenteeism
- Increased productivity
- Increased occupant satisfaction
- Advantageous recruiting and retention

External incentives can also contribute to the feasibility of sustainable projects, and it is possible to gain direct credits and paybacks from instituting sustainable initiatives. Many municipalities offer tax incentives for energy efficient systems. Products and other tax credits may be available for various sustainable decisions, such as employment training incentives in exchange for certain site location decisions, tax deductions for meeting sustainability guidelines in some cities, as well as other potential savings that can be factored into a life-cycle analysis. The Building Owners and Managers Association (BOMA) and the Clinton Climate Initiative recently announced that five U.S. banks will each make $1 billion in loans available to retrofit buildings with such amenities as energy-efficient chillers, computerized energy management systems, and solar and wind power systems.[4] These and other opportunities can make the small difference that will push a financial decision into the low or no-cost range and provide the last detail for approval.

Most organizations will use a Net Present Value determination of life-cycle costs over their specified timeframe for decisions on sustainable buildings. (See chapter 5 – Financial Management for details on NPV calculations). Adoption of sustainable practices often requires an analysis of functional processes in order to determine how savings will impact staffing and internal processes. These can usually be accomplished with little impact on staffing beyond training in the new methods and procedures. Pay-back periods are typically short and adoption of new green practices is welcomed by most employees. As long as appropriate planning and communication occur.

Strategies for Gaining Enterprise Endorsement of Sustainability

Often the most difficult step is the first step. For organizations that have never used green practices or built or operated in a sustainable building, the first step is fraught with controversy, discussion, rumor-making, and rumor-bashing, as well as some excitement. Once the agreement that "it's the right thing to do" is made, the facility manager can launch the team to begin the project. Whether it involves a new building or changes to existing building operations, sustainability is still unproven for many organizations.

A key component of sustainability adoption in any organization involves change. To aid in change management, understanding provides important insights that allow workers at all levels of the organization to grasp the need for and impacts of the change. An integrated approach is important to convey. The Exhibit 11-2 Sustainable Facility Management Framework is one useful tool to help managers and facility staff relate to the many levels of integration required to succeed with change toward more sustainable facilities and facility management.

Each component in the framework exerts influence on the others, so that once understanding of sustainable expectations reaches the desired level in some areas, the influence impacts other areas and exponentially expands the understanding and acceptance of sustainability. These people, processes, and the places are integrated and must work together to maintain momentum.

Another change management strategy is the use of ADKAR—an acronym for Awareness, Desire, Knowledge, Ability and Reinforcement. This five step process is used to introduce the new concept along with new ideas and practices (Awareness); stimulate interest and participation in the change (Desire); provide needed information, directions, and guidelines for participation (Knowledge); include new equipment, tools, training, and updates to enable participation (Ability); and finally provide incentives and rewards for acceptance of and participation in the change (Reinforcement).[5] This change management strategy is similar to any project that requires approval, planning, implementation, and feedback for success.

Exhibit 11-2. Sustainable Facility Management Framework

Sustainable FM Integration Framework

Along with risk assessments, contingency, communications plans, and stake-holder buy-in, similar project management methods can be used in implementing sustainability changes. Preparation is the important key and appropriate planning for sustainability changes makes for smoother adoption throughout the organization.

Notes

1. David Owen and Tracey Swift, 2001, "Introduction: Social accounting, reporting and auditing: Beyond the rhetoric?" *Business Ethics, A European Review,* vol. 10/1.
2. Katz, Gregory, 2006, *Greening America's Schools: Costs and Benefits,* [Electronic version] Retrieved June 30, 2008 from http://www.cap-e.com/ewebeditpro/items/O59F12807.pdf.
3. Steven Winter Associates, Inc., 2004, Retrieved June 28, 2008 from http://www.swinter.com/services/documents/GSALEEDCostStudy_casestudy.pdf
4. Rebchook, John, "BOMA and Clinton Climate Initiative unveil program," *Rocky Mountain News,* June 23, 2008.
5. Hiatt, Jeffrey, 2006, *ADKAR: A model for change in business, government and our community,* Prosci Publishing.

The Design-Build Cycle

How many facility managers understand how a large architectural-engineering firm designs a major project? How many understand, from a builder's perspective, how a manufacturing facility is constructed? How has the need for sustainability and the desire to follow green building guidelines affected how we plan and design buildings? Without a good working knowledge of these dynamics, suboptimum projects will result, even using the most reputable of firms because user input, through the facility manager, is an absolute requirement in good project planning.

As the industry has become increasingly specialized, the facility manager is slowly being recognized as the one to ensure a satisfactory final product, coordinating the multiple parties involved in new construction or major renovation projects. In the industrialized world, where there are an abundance of high-quality design firms, competent constructors, and building standards, the project will be optimized when the expertise of the owner's representative, hopefully the facility manager, matches that of the design and construction services providers.

Perhaps more than any other facility management function, the design-build cycle has been studied, codified, and automated. Facility projects are planned, programmed, designed, codified, reviewed, constructed, and evaluated similarly, whether they involve a new manufacturing site or merely an alteration of existing space. Even the contract forms have been largely standardized by the applicable professional organizations, and these standards are being spread to the developing world by these same organizations. At the same time, new contracting devices and methods such as best value procurement and public/private partnerships, as well as new sustainability targets and guidelines both solve problems and add complexity to the profession and to the design-build function.

We feel a note of caution is necessary here. It has been our experience that this aspect of our jobs is the most susceptible to bribery and other corruption. While we do not address this issue in the following chapters, it is extremely important that facility managers conduct themselves with a high sense of ethics and be watchful that others do the same. Our actions from selecting an architect, to agreeing on what kind of boilers will be used, to managing the selection of the builder impact huge organizational resources, and we must always be concerned about our actual actions as well as their appearance in the process.

In our personal experience, we have witnessed internationally-known architect-engineer and construction firms try to use political influence by contacting social contacts among upper management to obtain either the design or construction contract non-competitively on major projects. Often executives truly do not realize that they are bypassing the proper design-build processes, so they must be warned that a good business practice, managed by the facility manager, is in place and that bypassing that practice is not good business.

We start this section with a discussion of project management, then proceed sequentially through the life of a project, including evaluation.

12

Project Management

Pulse Points

- *Project management is not facility management.*
- *The facility manager must control, if not manage, all large capital projects for which he will become responsible.*
- *Life-cycle costing should be used for project decisions.*
- *Partnering provides an opportunity to avoid litigation during major projects.*

In general terms, *project management* means managing a distinct piece of work to be completed on time and within budget. For the facility manager, project management means taking a project through the design-build schedule to ensure that operational requirements are met within the budget and on schedule.

Often projects are defined by a dollar value (work of value above $6,000 being a project, for example), by the level of effort required (one man-day per trade not to exceed two man-days total, for example), or whether they require planning or design effort. In those ways, projects are differentiated from routine work and preventive maintenance. In fact, the management of projects is but one function of facility management. Yet one common failing is a tendency to view all facility management activities as separate projects, each justified at set costs with discrete start and end dates. This is the situation that causes walls to be demolished for alterations only a week after they were painted for maintenance. This mind-set builds a facility at the least capital cost that makes the project manager look good, but has increased operating and maintenance costs over the life of the facility. As we say many times in this book, the essence of facility management is cost-effectiveness, quality of service, and operational efficiency for the life of the facility. Project management, improperly applied and with the wrong incentive and evaluation system, can be extremely harmful to good facility management.

Unfortunately, because capital projects are so visible, there is always great pressure to minimize initial costs and bring the project in at the earliest possible date.

Often this ensures suboptimizing the life-cycle costs, which typically are three times the capital costs. Annual budget pressures ("The money disappears on September 30 or end of the fiscal year") cause the same type of costly thinking on smaller projects. Many governmental facility managers have their favorite story of poor-quality projects funded in an end-of-the-year spending binge.

There certainly is a place for project management in facility management. Capital projects, discretionary annual projects, and repair projects are programs best managed in a project mode. (Project management is inappropriate for utilities, custodial work, leasing, preventive maintenance, and administration.) As a general rule, nonroutine services, those that require high user contact or discretion, and those that coordinate multiple functions are candidates for project management.

Definition and Organization

In most organizations, capital expenditures—with the exception of furniture and furnishings—are developed, justified, and executed as projects. Within the annual budget, however, only certain work, with these characteristics, is handled as a project:

- Largely discretionary (or could be delayed)
- Design is involved
- Cost exceeds a floor cost ($5,000, for example)
- Multidisciplinary
- Requires high user involvement

As a facility department moves to midsize, it is essential to define (normally in coordination with the budget department) what work will be handled as projects.

Large capital projects, particularly if they are rarely done, are often handled by a separate project team whose manager reports to the facility manager. When the capital project is run out of the chief executive officer's (CEO) or chairman's office, there is a built-in propensity for long-term disaster. (See reference to this situation in the Introduction to Section V.) Unfortunately it is also common to appoint a retiring or "spare" vice president as manager. The project manager for a major capital project must not only be competent. He must also have the trust of and be compatible with the facility manager. The facility manager must control, if not manage, all capital projects.

When faced with managing a major project, the facility department can manage the project itself, hire its own project team, or hire a development team. If a department manages the project itself, at least in theory, it controls the project. This approach probably has the lowest overhead. However, most organizations do not have the depth or breadth of skills to manage a large project. Even when both design and construction services are contracted, a large project is incredibly time-consuming. Someone must be a full-time project manager. In addition, it will probably be necessary to dedicate one full-time contracting officer, one architect, one engineer, one interior designer, and one project accountant to the project for its duration. Few facility managers can spare these people from their normal departmental duties. Specialized support, like legal support during permitting, will have to be sought from an outside source. Finally, this approach represents the greatest technical risk if the department is not used to managing major projects.

If individuals are hired to form a project team, it should be possible to get a team that is both technically proficient and loyal to the department. The extent to which individuals feel that they are a member of the facility department team is directly proportional to the degree to which they are welcomed and trained. Initially, the team will not be used to working with one another or with the department, and there may well be difficulty assessing how this situation is developing until it is too late. The success of this approach is highly dependent on the project manager's being able to pull the team together. Finally, the cost of the project team has to be funded out of project costs.

Hiring an already assembled project team should make it possible to have a team with all of the skills and with team members who are used to working with one another. They may even have worked on a similar project. This team should be able to hit the ground running. Although this approach presents the least technical risk of the approaches mentioned, it is also the most expensive because the department is paying a management fee to the employer. Choosing the development firm can get political; everyone has a favorite developer. It is still probably desirable to have an internal project manager to work with the team since the facility manager tends to be the most distant from daily happenings on the project under this approach.

Most organizations accept the need for using a design-build team (architect, engineers, interior architects, consultants, and builder), but companies commencing large capital projects should also consider augmenting their internal facilities, legal, accounting, and purchasing staffs with the following:

- Construction accountant
- Estimator
- Construction procurement specialist
- Inspectors
- Scheduler

Before contacting consultants, however, the facility manager should organize the internal staff so it can control the design-build team. Especially critical are procedures to establish requirements and formal reviews by in-house experts.

The Design Phase

Crucial to completing any project on time and within budget are the proper program, plan, and design. These are developed during the design process (see Chapter 14). These aspects of a project set the tone and fix the available resources as well as its form and function. Too often facility managers neglect design. It's unclear whether this is out of deference to architects or because they are unaware of the design cycle or how design firms work. Perhaps it's because large projects are often handled outside the department, and by the time the facility manager takes control, the project has been designed.

Devote special attention to the project management organization—both the project management team and the committees for user and technical input or communication with users and management.

Chapter 14 discusses the selection of an outside design team and the proper relationship between the facility manager and the design team. The team should not only bring technical competence to the project but also mesh well with the facility department.

During the design phase, look not just at the architect's work but also the work of major consultants. Participate in major design decisions.

Experienced facility managers soon learn the importance of good estimators to the design process. Without a reliable estimate at every step of design, the project cannot be properly controlled.

Also, extensively and rigorously review the schedule at each stage of design.

The Construction Phase

The contracting and construction of a building can be managed in many ways. This is perhaps why, of all portions of the design-build cycle, construction is the most studied and the aspect about which we know the most. Exhibit 12-1 shows the advantages and disadvantages of four common ways of contracting for construction.

If possible, the design firm and the project manager should help select the builder. However, if the contracting method is construction management, then select the construction manager first and have him assist in selecting the design firm. (Caution: In some markets, architectural-engineering (A-E) firms and builders are so tightly linked that impartiality may not be possible.) Also, though certainly not required, it is preferable to use local builders, particularly in areas with complicated codes and permit processes. In some ways, the developer is a captive of the system, but fighting local codes, permit offices, and customs with a "foreign" builder is likely to cause both grief and delay.

Exhibit 12-1. Construction contracting methods.

Lump Sum—Sequential Design and Construction	Construction Management or Cost-Plus-Fixed-Fee	Guaranteed Maximum Price	Turnkey
Advantages			
Complete plans for bidding available.	Impact of escalation reduced.	Complete plans not necessary.	Complete plans not necessary.
	Foundations and structure can be bid in advance.	Foundations and structure can be bid in advance.	Foundations and structure can be bid in advance.
Fixed price at start of construction.	Impact of escalation reduced.	Maximum price known during design process.	Price fixed at start of project
		Escalation impact reduced.	Impact of escalation reduced.
Single responsibility of contractor.	Construction manager working as owner's agent, not in adversary position with owner, designer.		
Quality and O&M aspects of design under control of owner.	Quality and O&M aspects of design under control of owner.	Quality and O&M aspects of design under control of owner.	
	Advice of contractor available during design period.	Advice of contractor available during design period.	
	Design-construct period reduced.	Design-construct period reduced.	Design-construct period reduced.
	Changes to plans discouraged due to telescoped design period	Changes to plans discouraged due to telescoped design period.	Changes to plans discouraged owing to telescoped design period.
Disadvantages			
Lengthiest process.			
Length of design period encourages modifications.	Total cost of job not known until after foundations and frame underway and plans complete and bid.	Any owner changes affect guaranteed price.	Ability of owner to make changes severely restricted.
Advice of contractor for affecting economies not available during design.			
Impact of escalation most severe.			
Contractor placed in adversary position with respect to owner and designer.		Contractor placed in adversary position with respect to owner and designer.	Contractor placed in adversary position with respect to owner.

(continued)

Exhibit 12-1. (continued)

Lump Sum—Sequential Design and Construction	Construction Management or Cost-Plus-Fixed-Fee	Guaranteed Maximum Price	Turnkey
Contractor may seek change orders and loopholes.	Extra costs may arise from modifications needed after plans are completed.		Aesthetic and O&M quality of design may be questionable because they are not directly under control of owner.
Contingency and profit factors higher than CM/cost-plus-fixed-fee method.		Contingency and profit factors much higher than for lump-sum and CM/cost-plus-fixed-fee methods due to great risk involved.	Contingency and profit factors higher than CM/cost-plus-fixed-fee and guaranteed maximum price. Total cost may be highest of all methods.

Some construction contracting methods have become extremely complex particularly on large public/private projects or in efforts to reduce costs or speed up the project. Design-build is an increasingly popular alternative to the traditional design-bid-build.[1] An excellent discussion of the pros and cons of these construction contracting methods is contained in Christopher M. Gordon's 1994 article, "Choosing Appropriate Construction Contracting Methods" in the *Journal of Construction Engineering and Management*.[2]

Anyone who has been involved with the project approval process appreciates the complexity of issues and frequent frustration involved in obtaining the necessary permits and approvals from local government. This is such a prevalent problem in some jurisdictions that some law firms have developed a reputation as expediters to ensure relatively fast permit approvals. Silicon Valley facility managers, many of whom were faced with fast-track projects to meet the business needs of booming technology companies, met with local government officials to develop permit streamlining practices, programs, and policies. The result is a set of guidelines that should be emulated across the profession.[3]

Direction and control of major projects is best exercised on two different levels. Policy issues are decided by a *policy committee* composed of a responsible vice president or chairman, a facility manager, a project manager, a design team project manager (or construction manager), legal counsel, and a controller representative. This committee normally meets monthly but may meet as often as weekly. In addition to policy, the committee considers and approves all major changes, communicates to the CEO and board, and takes under advisement issues forwarded by the experts committee.

The *experts committee* closely approximates the design-build team and makes the day-to-day decisions that keep the project on time and within budget. Committee members typically are the project manager, the design team project manager, the builder's project manager, an in-house design chief, in-house engineering chief, in-house operations chief, project accountant, legal counsel, chief inspector, a staff representative or line manager, and a security or safety representative. Of these, the project accountant, legal counsel, chief inspector, and design team project manager are nonvoting. This committee usually meets weekly with an agenda approved by the chairman. Members of the design-build team make presentations, the team reviews the progress, they resolve the problems, and the team recommends issues for the policy committee.

In large projects, the project manager spends an inordinate amount of time in meetings. This must be both realized and appreciated. The team builds the project while the project manager is concerned with these issues:

- Managing the team
- Keeping management informed and transmitting policy to the design-build team
- Keeping the design-build experts "tuned in and turned on" to organizational requirements and perceptions
- Handling public relations

This seems as if we are advocating management by committee, and to a certain extent we are. Large construction projects are, by their nature, collaborative. The project manager must be skilled in guiding the project through these committees.

These two committees should not steamroll issues, but majority membership should ensure that the project manager controls the truly critical issues. Particularly on the policy committee, he should have done his homework so that there are no surprises at meetings.

The project manager prepares an agenda and distributes it for each meeting. A good format has these items:

1. Update
2. Comparison to budget and schedule
3. "Get back to ya's" from the project manager
4. Old business
5. Other problems
6. New business
7. Review of tasks assigned

There is a different emphasis on these items in each committee.

The agenda should be circulated at least twenty-four hours in advance, and it should be reviewed by the project manager personally. Meeting minutes should be circulated within forty-eight hours of the meeting, with corrections required within an additional forty-eight hours.

Preparing for and going to meetings is the single greatest demand on a project manager's time. The successful project manager knows how to manage these activities.

Common Pitfalls

Major construction projects are, by their nature, complex. However, there are truly outstanding designers, architects, engineers, and builders to assist. Thousands of things can go wrong; some problems will crop up despite your best efforts. That is why it is important to have a strong team. Once the mistake is found, the team can correct it quickly and cheaply.

The number of problems can be lessened or minimized by avoiding the following pitfalls:

- Not contracting with an experienced A-E firm; using the chairman's favorite architect.
- Failing to provide the design team with important requirements.
- Not determining sustainable intent prior to design.
- Allowing the A-E firm to pick its own consultants without your review or approval.
- Hiring a builder who has never built in the market.
- Failing to have work inspected or operational tests performed.
- Failing to establish a budget, fiscal controls, or proper construction accounting.
- Approving changes before they are designed and costed.
- Failing to schedule fixed reviews or progress meetings.
- Not observing the work of the builder's subcontractors.
- Failing to agree on procedures for punch list, operational tests, beneficial occupancy, training, warranties, and project turnover.
- Failing to define documentation (type, quantity, and format) required at turnover.
- Failing to budget for contingencies.

Partnering

There are many definitions for partnering, and, in practice, it tends to vary from project to project. Partnering is a structured process that obligates the partners (hopefully all members of the design-build team) to foster innovation, teamwork, continuous quality improvement, and team problem solving. The following characteristics of a partnering agreement are common:

- Clarifying the role of each partner in the process.
- A commitment to information sharing with the establishment and a procedure to do so consistently.
- The sharing of lessons learned and formalized postmortems of major or repeating events.
- Formalized trust building and training.
- Establishing common goals, objectives, and priorities for the project.
- Defining risks and establishing procedures to manage them.
- Fostering innovation.
- Establishing ways to measure success.
- Developing mechanisms to resolve differences quickly.

These elements are often placed into a single document, called the *partnering charter*, which all major decision makers on the project sign.

Does partnering work? In one study, the U.S. Army Corps of Engineers Kansas City District, found that partnering reduced modifications by 39 percent, time growth by 55 percent, and cost growth by 38 percent.[4] Not everyone is enthralled with partnering. The breaking down of some of the "firewalls" in normal contracting by which adversarial relationships kept the various parties honest disturbs some traditionalists. However, it appears that partnering can offer savings to all concerned where there is a genuine desire to cooperate and all parties are roughly equal in experience and political power. Traditional project management has been so rancorous and litigious that any process that goes counter to that tradition is welcome.

Studies abound documenting the effectiveness of project partnering, and researchers are now documenting the critical factors needed for successful partnering and risk reduction, such as a collaborative approach, resource sharing, and a quality focus.[5]

Best value contracting attempts to establish a win-win situation for both the owner and the contractor. This kind of procurement is an extension of the concept of performance-based contracting developed by Dr. Dean Kashiwagi and the Performance Based Studies Research Group at Arizona State University. It has been tested over 13 years with 98 percent customer satisfaction and no contractor-generated change orders.[6] Because it was first used in the areas of job order and indefinite demand, indefinite quantity contracting, it also has high applicability for outsourcing of FM services. However, any facility manager wanting to implement best value contracting should take himself and his procurement officer through one of the seminars at Arizona State first. This is necessary because 1) performance based contracting is not intuitively workable and 2) it is often opposed by procurement personnel just because it emphasizes techniques that often conflict with the "hands off" approach of low-bid contracting. Others oppose it just because it is not conventional.[7]

Large and Small Projects

Most facility departments handle work over a certain dollar value (such as $5,000 each requirement), or which requires substantial design input but is small and is part of an annual project program. Often projects are broken down into move projects, maintenance and repair projects, or other alterations.

Some large organizations accomplish 200 to 250 of these projects annually, averaging one start-up and one close-out each working day. The scale of work projects can be daunting. Requirements, therefore, are gathered by project managers assigned regularly to work with certain customers or in particular geographic areas. In smaller organizations, project designers gather the requirements and manage the process from beginning to end.

After the requirements are costed, they are prioritized and met according to priority. Often the priority list is reviewed semiannually. Because these projects are so popular, there is almost never enough funds to do all the work. Large organizations often institute steps to control and prioritize the funds. There are three ways to do this:

1. Establish administrative approval levels for varying levels of projects (e.g., $10K, manager; $50K, director, $250K, VP).
2. Delineate between new work (construction, alterations) and maintenance and repair, and put a ceiling on the amount that can be used for new construction.
3. Establish a joint user-facility department review committee to set priorities for project accomplishment and then review those priorities at midyear.

In small organizations, definitions and approval levels are less of an issue because the volume of work is much smaller. Even fairly small projects (less than $10,000) are well known to company management before even planning is set in motion.

The difficulty in managing small projects is gathering requirements and costing the projects early enough so that the facility manager can submit his estimated budget. This can best be accomplished by having an annual requirements-gathering process with a midyear review to pick up changes. Management then approves this list, in aggregate, for design and construction.

Highly sophisticated project management systems have been developed, many of them within the U.S. Department of Defense. And now computers have automated almost all of these systems. Using software such as Microsoft Project, the facility manager has a project management tool formerly available only to project management firms. There are systems for mainframes as well as PCs. There are systems for handling multiple small projects. No other function of facility management has been as well developed as project management.

Some of the more common project management methods are:

1. Critical path method (CPM)
2. Program Evaluation Review Technique (PERT)
3. GANTT charts
4. Precedence method (PM)
5. Resource constrained scheduling

Critical to all these methods is the ability to estimate time and resource use accurately. A quality estimator or estimating team is extremely important because these estimates must be made initially, when only a project estimate exists. Both CPM and PERT use "not more than and not later than" estimates to help set realistic budgets and schedules.

Because a change in one project—especially the need for additional resources—can affect other department resources and programs, the facility manager must carefully assess these changes before they are made. It is not enough to view how the changes will affect the particular program budget or schedule, but how they will influence leasing needs, maintenance and repair programs, and the like. This is one of the major factors that separates facility management from project management. The facility manager must understand the total picture. Any failure to do so puts both the project and the department in jeopardy. In conclusion, we recommend two books on project management: Steve Binder's *Corporate Facility Planning,* which places project management in a corporate context, and Carole Farren's *Planning and Managing Interior Projects,* which discusses in detail the kind of project management performed by most facility managers.

Notes

1. Warren Michelson, "Design-Build," *TFM, November 2007,* p. 14.
2. Christopher M. Gordon, "Choosing Appropriate Construction Contracting Methods," *Journal of Construction Engineering and Management,"* Vol. 120, Issue 1; pp. 196–210.
3. *Permit Streamlining* (San Clara, CA: Santa Clara County Manufacturing Group Facility Managers Committee, 1994), pp. 1–13.

4. Jeffrey W. Hills, "Partnering: Does It Work?" *The Military Engineer* (December 1995), p. 45.

5. Wei Tong Chen and Tung-Tsan Chen, "Critical Success Factors for Construction Partnering in Taiwan," *International Journal of Project Management,* Vol 25, Issue 5, July 2007, p. 475.

6. Dean Kashiwagi, *Best Value Procurement, Third Edition* (Tempe, AZ: Performance Based Studies Research Group, 2008), p. 8–1.

7. *Ibid.,* p. 8–5.

13

Programming and Project Development

Pulse Points

- *Planning for major projects nearly always understates engineering requirements.*
- *The facility manager should program for maintainability as well as functionality, and place special emphasis on support areas.*
- *Project planning integrates information from the facility plan with requirements gathered through programming.*
- *The facility manager plans with care but always retains flexibility.*

Anyone who has dealt with real estate, even as a homeowner, knows the importance of location, location, location. Because most facility managers do not control real estate, normally they will not be asked to select which country, state, or city an organization should locate to. He can do his organization and himself a great favor, however, by examining the following micro-level locational factors listed below during the selection process.[1] (We have slightly modified Carpenter's list.) This factor alone shows why the facility manager should manage real estate. Remember, we will be living with the site a long time once selected!

- ADA compliance
- Branding and image
- Codes and limitations
- Cleanliness
- Costs of doing business
- Cost of living expenses
- Non-operating costs
- Demographic information

- Distance to airports, harbors, and freeways
- Environmental considerations
- Ability to exit if needed
- Expansion space
- Ability to support sustainability
- Floodplain status
- Historic designations or locations
- Local hazards
- Mass transit
- Property and business taxes
- Property owner and manager reputation, if leased
- Standardization
- Utilities
- Weather and susceptibility to natural disaster
- Zoning

Project programming, planning, and design are well-established procedures within the design community. The facility manager will be responsible for deciding whether he wants to develop the project using in-house, contracted, or consulting designers. The project programming process involves gathering the requirements for a specific project and examining the relationships of individual tasks. The program is a tool for managing the project and a guide to anticipated results. Its essence is (1) an understanding of what is needed and expected by the user and (2) the establishment of performance expectations at specific time intervals.

It is not possible to develop an aesthetically pleasing or functional work environment without first defining the overall objective for the space to be used. Many textbooks regard the establishment of project objectives as the first stage in the design-build cycle. For example, Manuel Marti, a prominent theoretical space planner, indicates that the overall organizational framework shapes the entire process.[2] We interpret this more literally to mean that the structure, culture, and philosophy of the parent organization establish the parameters within which any project is identified, prioritized, and executed. The organization's philosophy may be modified by circumstances that develop during the design-build cycle; however, the initial assumptions and resource allocations are always determined by corporate philosophy.

Often, the only stated objective is the number of individuals to occupy a specific space (with perhaps some type of financial limitation). The planner then is asked to offer solutions within the constraints of that space and budget. In such circumstances planning activities are likely to be suboptimal. The project can be accomplished, but not necessarily as effectively or efficiently as it could have been. But if complete requirements are collected and analyzed, the results can be more than satisfactory. This is what programming can and should do.

The project programming process involves gathering the requirements for a specific project and examining the relationships of individual tasks. The program is a tool for managing the project and a guide to anticipated results. Its essence is (1) an understanding of what is needed and expected by the user and (2) the establishment of performance expectations at specific time intervals. We discussed macrolevel space programming in Chapter 6. In this chapter, we apply the programming process to define and gather the requirements for a specific project.

Aspects of Programming

The task definition stage of programming defines the project expectations. It is a statement of what should be able to happen as a direct result of successful completion. One of our favorite sayings describes the results when this step is not properly performed: "If you always do what you've always done, you will always get what you've always got." Don't validate obsolescence.

The feasibility analysis stage of any project is conceptual. In general, programming means that the company has determined that the overall project is feasible. However, as requirements are gathered, solutions will come to mind, and the feasibility needs to be verified. Feasibility analysis should go deeply enough to ensure reliability of expenditure and profitability projections. A fully developed program permits the facility manager to plan effectively and eliminate unwanted surprises. The following specifics should be included in the feasibility analysis.

1. *Technological feasibility,* including employee training and organizational resources such as machinery, equipment, computers. In planning major projects, don't understate engineering requirements; later deficiencies are costly to correct.
2. *Operational aspects,* such as employee morale, adaptability, organizational policy changes, modifications to facility, and anticipated success.
3. *Economic aspects,* to determine whether the completed project will return a greater dollar benefit than the expenditure in staff and resources.
4. *Communications aspects,* which give insight into both needed communications links and contiguity of location for various units. The Quickborner organization, pioneers in the concept of the office landscape, is normally credited with looking at organizations as dynamic entities, particularly at how units within the organization communicate with each other.

5. *A maintainability program* should be developed. By carrying out good maintenance programming, not only can the life-cycle costs of a building be reduced substantially, but maintenance can be accomplished easier.
6. *Sustainability goals* should be stated.

Political considerations are an important part of any program. Senior executives should be consulted early to determine their "hot buttons," those program aspects that either must be in the project or that can't be in the project. Identify those issues early on. They often form the performance envelope within which all other programming is done.

In a most successful application of this concept, a vice president and the project manager of a firm hired to manage the planning, design, and construction of a major urban project, personally interviewed the top-level executives of the affected organization. After discussing their findings with the facility manager and key members of the project team, they conducted feedback sessions with the top-level executives so that most of the political aspects of the project were either solved, or at least highlighted, before detailed programming even started. This proved of great value in an organization renowned for its politics, and paved the way for a smooth major design-build effort.

Sources and Methods

The depth and breadth of the programming effort varies somewhat. Exhibit 13-1 is a list of possible areas. It goes beyond the normal areas of programming investigation but may be a good model as companies concern themselves not only with adequate and safe workplaces but ones that allow for individual expression and a sense of control. It is important to realize that some requirements will be in direct conflict with other requirements. For example, the organization may want to maximize productivity by expecting specific behaviors from its workers, but workers may not perceive that behavior to be in their best interest. Under such circumstances, you may find yourself having to advocate a specific strategy to management. Concerning sustainability, the reverse situation could be true. Employees may want to pursue a sustainability program that is not in current management thinking.

A program is likely to establish expectations on the part of top management and might be used, at least, in part, to judge the effectiveness of the facility manager. It is in your best interest to use the most reliable information possible. If there's faulty information, disastrous results may follow. If top management's expectations are overly ambitious, that may be equally damaging. A program may also be expected to assist in the planning for contingencies as well as in the normal management of a project.

Exhibit 13-1. Possible areas for programming.

Natural Compliances
- Site
- Surroundings
- Region
- Urban location
- Functional placement
- Accessibility
- Natural conditions
- Elements
- Weather
- Seasons
- Energy and resources

Environmental Compliances
- Temperature
- Light
- Sonic conditions
- Shelter
- Environmental impact
- Preservation
- Pollution

Functional Compliances
- Purpose
- Activities
- Movement
- Flexibility
- Scale
- Use
- Manpower

Physical Compliances
- Measurement and scale
- Gender
- Health
- Hygiene
- Security
- Hazards
- Disability
- Comfort

Psychological Compliances
- Ego
- Privacy
- Authority
- Aesthetics
- Style
- Scale
- Habits
- Phobias
- Status
- Image
- Character
- Individuality
- Impact
- Isolation
- Behavior
- Territory
- Personalization

Sociological Compliances
- Culture
- Creed
- Race
- Demography
- Economic status
- Class
- Impact

Regulatory Compliances
- Government
- Private policies and systems
- Legal and contractual conditions
- Codes
- Related agencies
- Commissions
- Associations
- Special interest groups
- Violations
- Variances

Economic Compliances
- Quality
- Cost
- Purpose (function)
- Investment
- Return
- Interest
- Depreciation

(continued)

Exhibit 13-1. (continued)

• Capital plan	• Land acquisition
• Economic trends	• Taxation
• Projection	**Temporal Compliances**
• Operating costs	• Historic value
• Maintenance	• Preservation
• Marketing	• Schedules
• Sales	• Change
• Budget	• Growth

Source: Manuel Marti, Jr., *Space Operational Analysis* (West Lafayette, Ind.: PDA Publishers, 1981).

There are at least four sources to query for requirements for a major renovation or new facility:

1. Top management
2. Operating staff
3. Support staff
4. Regulations and codes

The requirements of top management often need to be gathered before a decision can be made to go ahead on a project, so this step may already be complete before you start programming. For example, a 1997 National Construction and Development Survey by the National Association of Corporate Real Estate Executives (NACORE) states that 46 percent of building decisions are made by CEOs.[3] These are the most political of requirements; thus, this initial level of programming is extremely important and cannot be assigned to an inexperienced architectural programmer. We favor the facility manager's either doing the interviews personally or controlling the participating consultant. In either case, there should be agreement on the questions to be asked.

Typically interviewed are the chief executive officer (CEO), chairman of the board, all senior vice presidents, the budget director, and the vice presidents of affected units. Their comments must be treated individually, no matter who gathers them. If those interviewed express concerns or state strong positions, the issues must be addressed (not necessarily validated) and the results conveyed to the individuals. When you ask questions of this group, you must deal with the answers.

Gathering requirements from operating staff depends on two basic issues. If standards are in place, less programming needs to be done. Normally, interviewing every employee is unnecessary. In large companies a 10 percent sample, assuming that you get a representative cross section of staff, is more than adequate. Also, if management will not fund workplace functionality, there is no sense expending the effort to accommodate it. In that case, the degree of employee involvement becomes an FM judgment usually driven by resources.

Usually the requirements of support departments are not systematically and uniformly well gathered. Exhibit 13-2 is a list of functional areas that should be investigated. In developer-originated buildings, there may be a rationale for skimping on support facilities. In corporate or public buildings, this skimping is an invitation to both higher operating and higher maintenance costs. Most design firms are unable to program for support facilities, and too often the support managers cannot realistically state their requirements. Frequently the use of an industrial design consultant can prove helpful in getting this information into your programming.

Programming implies a series of projects within a time frame.[4] All the information gathering and problem identification in the world will not make a program. Thus the programming must also establish schedules. Completion schedules, along with project criteria and quality controls, will differ from project to project, but you should not lose sight of the fact that they are essential to the success of the project.

When the information gathering is completed, the results of all surveys and data should be combined, interpreted, and approved before they are passed on to the design team. The gathered data can also be used to start a facility database. Data definitely should be retained as the base document for a postoccupancy evaluation.

For the overall facilities program, annually one program should be the subject of an intense review by the facility manager. The questions asked are:

1. What is the mission of this program? The goals? The objectives? How well are they being met? Is change needed?
2. Is the program adequately resourced? If not, how can this requirement be accomplished?
3. How effective is the program? How cost-effective? How did the units produced measure against historical production figures?
4. How is the program perceived? By the manager? By the facility manager? By the users?

It is readily apparent that data are needed in order to perform an adequate evaluation. The facility manager should be conscious of future program evaluation requirements and structure the program-monitoring systems so that they will provide those data.

Benefits of Programming

Since programming is an orderly and systematic process, it would appear logical that facility managers would embrace it enthusiastically. That's not always true. The reluctance seems to stem from the following:

1. Lack of familiarity with the programming process.
2. A view of programming as a luxury or an unneeded design cost.
3. Impatience to get to a design solution.
4. Time pressure to complete the project.

Every manager probably has his favorite programming horror story, but Doug Lowe of 3D International has a great one: A dramatic, award-winning headquarters for a new business segment of an international corporation was ineffective almost immediately because there was no programming to detect the flexibility necessary for this new, rapidly expanding business. Therefore, a unique floor plan suitable for a mature company with little growth and few moves was designed. The building was obsolescent when built.[5]

Some interesting results come out of programming. An organization found that its population did not fit the anthropometric model (a model of the average office worker, used to design commercial furniture). To meet specific needs, furniture was designed for greater adjustability.[6]

Doug Lowe offers this argument regarding the value of programming:[7]

1. Programming is a logical process that works.
2. Programming is separate from other services offered by architectural-engineering (A-E) firms.
3. The FM can use a good programmer to lead the A-E and wind up with a project that meets his needs.
4. A good program will cause a building to be designed from inside out.
5. The FM can use a good programmer to take control of the decision-making process.
6. The FM and programmer will probably become allies, further strengthening the FM's position in the information chain.
7. A good programmer can help the FM set up procedures to deal with repetitive or other types of data that are better processed in-house.
8. A good programmer will produce a program that will be truly usable by all of its targeted audience.
9. A good programmer will develop a procedure to update the program, thus incorporating future changes.
10. Programming has many uses, and a facility manager has many uses for programming.

Upon completion of programming you will know the "what" that the project needs to accomplish; planning will explore the "how" the project will be implemented.

Exhibit 13-2. Support activities to be considered in programming.

Shipping and Receiving
- Loading dock space
- Temporary storage
- Secure storage
- Berthing space
- Access to dumpster
- Centrality
- Proximity to freight elevators
- Proximity to primary users

Security
- Operations center location
- Guard posts
- Personnel access system
- Vehicular access system
- Executive access system
- Access by visitors and nonsecure personnel

Mail and Distribution
- Access to national mail system
- Distribution/collection schema
- Secure storage
- Access by external messengers

Motor Vehicle Pool
- Overnight storage
- Daytime parking
- Pick-up/drop-off points

Shops
- Access to materials
- Sizing
- Access to freight elevators
- Locker room
- Security

Food Service
- Layout
- Access to staff
- Centralized or decentralized coffee bar
- Access for foodstuffs
- Egress for garbage
- Locker room
- Vending locations

Conference Services
- Stage
- Audiovisual requirements
- Acoustics
- Lighting and lighting controls
- Recording capability
- Seating (fixed or movable)

Vertical and Horizontal transportation
- Personnel elevators
- Freight or service elevators
- Escalators
- People movers
- Robots
- Access by people and goods
- Access to garages and roofs
- Security

Miscellaneous
- On-site furniture storage
- Custodial closets

Communications
- Closets
- Duct systems
- Location of file servers and network command elements

Establish Purpose and Scope

Like most other human endeavors, and certainly most all facility department efforts, a project is best achieved when there is focus on purpose and scope. The first step in planning is reviewing the project's purpose. The *purpose* clearly states the goal of the project and perhaps the problem it will solve. The *scope* describes the limits (financial, spatial, functional, and time) of the project. Spend time and effort now to ensure that you share an understanding of the scope and purpose with management. After all, it will be your task to transmit that understanding to the project team.

Project Planning

Project planning is the next step in the seamless progression that turns a set of requirements into a useful, productive facility. It is the bridge between the program and the design. Like the other steps in the design-build cycle, there is some spillover during planning. Some requirements will become modified or sharpened during planning; some elements of design may even need to be predetermined. The result of planning, however it is done, is a project schedule and budget that the project team, particularly the project manager, can accept so that design can proceed with confidence.

The planning process for facility projects requires identifying a problem and then applying the resources necessary to solve it. In his book *Problem Finding and Problem Solving,* Alfred Schoennauer outlines techniques for two kinds of problem solving: after-the-fact and before-the-fact.[8] Many problems fall into that after-the-fact category, and these must be attended to daily.

A facility manager must plan effectively so that the operations of the company can proceed with few interruptions regardless of any emergency. The planning must consider available resources, specific aspects of a potential disaster, and corporate culture. Alas, the average facility manager reacts to things rather than anticipates them because it is not possible to make FM a continuum of before-the-fact processes. The balance of this chapter deals with aspects of the interior planning process, which represents a nearly perfect example of before-the-fact problem solving.

Most projects should evolve from the midrange facility plan, or at least from the annual work plan. That implies that some planning—perhaps a concept and a preliminary cost estimate—has already been done. Realistically, however, probably one third of even major projects will arise ad hoc. With luck, there will still be enough time for project programming and planning so that design and construction can proceed with a solid base.

Once the company commits to a project, the programming will have defined the company's needs and identified the physical and resource requirements to meet those needs. Now the company will expect the facility manager to meet those stated requirements (the program) with available resources and according to schedule. This is where the planning process comes in.

Planning involves determining the general design-and-build solutions and general sequence of the design-build cycle so that the following is possible:

1. It can be determined that the project is feasible.
2. A schedule can be developed.
3. A not-to-exceed budget can be developed.

Although it can be very detailed, planning is generally that last low-cost (staff) step before costly design, purchasing, and construction processes begin. As such, good planning has great potential for cost savings.

Organizing the Plan

The single common element when planning a white-collar work environment is the space to be occupied by the workers. That space may be owned by the company or leased. It may be divided, decorated, pierced, shared, filled with objects, heated, cooled, powered, illuminated. Stephen Binder calls space "the first frontier" for facility managers.[9]

In our business, planning most often is driven by space and funds, so an assessment of each is necessary. Planning is frequently formatted in terms of space, with the costs an output of the plan.

Resources and Methods

In facilities projects, the planner normally does not lack for information resources. Many projects have had a former life, and information should be available. At a minimum, the following should be available:

- The midrange facility plan
- The annual work plan
- Facility standards
- Sustainability plan or target sustainable certification level
- The program
- Information on like projects done recently
- For capital projects, the project evaluation calculations
- Information on how space needs will be met—for example, by leasing, building, altering, or renovating

- Concept design
- Concept budget
- Concept schedule
- Serviceability study

Depending on the size of the project, the last three items may be provided or you may be asked to proceed without them. Most planners do better-quality work if they are not totally unconstrained. Conversely, the best planner in the world cannot do well if necessary information is not forthcoming.

In Chapter 12, we listed several planning methods (e.g., critical path method, GANTT charts). All of these methods are good planning tools, so it is a matter of picking the proper tool for the project. For example, one organization did so many small interior alteration projects in a year, most of which had a life of from one to four weeks, they used a manual management system that tracked only four events per project. For large projects, we favor automated systems that calculate minimum and maximum values for completion dates and can budget for each event.

Turner Construction and ARAMARK have developed a proprietary approach to the design and construction process, called Concurrent Facilities Engineering, which they feel can save the owner both immediate and long-term costs. It is based on the following four tools:

- The Facility Forecasting and Planning Study
- The Facility Preparation Service (focus on proper operations and maintenance)
- The Transition Tool (focus on initial occupancy)
- The Operations and Management Program (develops staff training and benchmarks)

This is an approach to a project which involves design-build-operate and maintain.[10] For the contractors, this is a foot-in-the-door to providing operations and maintenance services; for many owners, it offers a simple solution to both a building and an operating problem.

It is important to have an organizational database that can produce design and construction unit costs for planning (see Chapter 6). Any organization altering over 50,000 square feet, doing over ten projects, or moving over 100 staff annually should have a database of unit costs that is constantly being updated. If a small to medium facility department cannot invest in a planning or estimating staff, it should consider hiring a cost or estimating consultant to keep applicable unit costs updated. Initially the consultant can provide typical costs for the work the department plans, designs, and executes. Eventually, this will build a unique database for the facility manager.

At the risk of beating a dead horse, we reiterate the importance of standards to cost-effective planning and design. By using standards, and assuming that the design team will use them, the facility manager can reduce planning complexity and time by 50 to 70 percent. We suspect that this is why many facility departments have standards even though they are not officially accepted. Allow the facility designer to plan and design the vast majority of any project quickly (this is accelerated when standards for space and furniture can be fed into a computer-assisted design and drawing system) so that design time and effort can concentrate on unique spaces.

Fiscal Matters

It is very difficult to state hard and fast rules for the fiscal portion of project planning, but if possible, have a finance representative participate in the project planning. If, during the planning process, you exceed the budget used to calculate the project's net present value or internal rate of return, you should report that to the chief financial officer (CFO). Other than that, it is difficult to provide specific guidance. While a not-to-exceed figure arrived at too early or too arbitrarily may preclude planning and design options, it's unrealistic to think there will be no fiscal constraints.

While there is always concern that overstating the front-end costs will kill the project, be conservative in your estimates until at least 70 percent of the design is complete. Provide a range for the project estimates at the planning stage and state clearly a contingency based on the final probable cost. As always, use life-cycle costing when making decisions about various aspects of the project.

Approval

Within the department, three staff functions must buy in to the plan: the planner, the project manager, and the facility manager. In some cases, all of these functions may be performed by the same individual. A CFO representative should be a party to all major project planning, as should an appropriate business unit representative and the design manager. Ultimately, you must either approve the plan or recommend it to the level having the proper approval authority so that design can commence.

Notes

1. Charles C. Carpenter, "What Makes the Best Location," *FMJ*, January/February 2008, pp. 14–15.
2. Manuel Marti, Jr., *Space Operational Analysis* (West Lafayette, Ind.: PDA Publishers, 1981).

3. National Construction and Development Survey 2000 as quoted in "Survey Shows Growth in Building, Outsourcing, and the Dakotas," *Facilities Design and Management*, December 1997, p. 10.

4. Douglas H. Lowe, "Why You Should Find a Good Architectural Programmer," in *Facility Management—Meeting the Need of Tomorrow* (Houston: IFMA, 1988), p. 204.

5. Ibid., pp. 211–212.

6. Maree Simmons-Forbes, "J" building mockup and staff demographic results for The World Bank, undated.

7. Lowe, "Why You Should Find," pp. 211–212.

8. Alfred Schoennauer, *Problem Finding and Problem Solving* (Chicago: Nelson Hall, 1981).

9. Stephen Binder, *Corporate Facility Planning* (New York: McGraw-Hill, 1989).

10. Michael Murdock and Chris Lehmann, "Bringing FM into the Design and Construction Process," *FMJ*, March/April 2008, pp. 14–18.

The Design Process

Pulse Points

- *Even when design is outsourced, the facility manager must control the design process.*
- *Good design starts with a good concept and a good program.*
- *Complex projects are best designed by a team.*
- *Use elevations, models, and Building Information Modeling (BIM) to sell your project.*

In this chapter we progress to the point where others in the company see drawings, renderings, perhaps even a model. Because these are the first tangible portions of their project, it is commonly believed that a project begins with design. Nothing is further from the truth; good design must be based on good programming and project planning (Chapter 13). However, those functions remain either hidden or are misunderstood by others in the company, so the expectation level at the design stage is high.

Fortunately, design expertise is common, in North America at least. Local licensing and membership in major professional organizations (e.g., American Institute of Architects, multiple engineering associations and societies, American Society of Interior Designers) ensure a high standard among design professionals. The metropolitan Washington, D.C., Yellow Pages alone has over 300 architectural and 250 interior design listings. That means that any facility manager, whether or not his department has an interior design capability, has access to competent design. It's merely a matter of finding the correct fit among the facility manager, the company, and the design team. There is growing awareness that the best designs are a collaborative effort,[1] but the facility manager and project manager must remain firmly in charge.

The Design Scene

Design firms of all types have accepted facility managers as their principal contacts with companies and agencies to a much greater degree than was true ten years ago. We think that is a sign of the maturity of the FM profession and that the relationships among designers, builders, and facility managers are becoming better defined. The instances where the chief executive officer's (CEO's) golfing buddy becomes the architect for the new headquarters facility seem to be occurring less and less.

First, a word to people on both sides of the user-designer equation. Certain business restrictions and contracts define the envelope within which both parties can operate. There must, however, be more than a contractual relationship. We strongly advocate a team approach with open and frank discussion. Time is better spent discussing design options than maneuvering for a better position. We rarely enter into a contract with a firm that we cannot treat as part of a team. If the fit is not good, both parties are probably better off not doing business together.

Facility managers need design firms (architects, interior architects and designers, engineers, and special consultants). No facility manager does 100 percent of the design in-house, 100 percent of the time. Design, in fact, is the most frequently outsourced FM service.[2] Facility managers at small organizations in particular need the skills of contracting with and managing design firms. Therefore, the designer must demonstrate that his firm is unique and best suited to a company's needs. We admit to a bias for full-service firms, in that the design project manager manages all design elements on his side of the table while all user requirements and owner input are funneled through the facility manager. That way the facility manager can use a design firm to its best advantage.

The good facility manager knows the capability of local design firms and tries to match the design resources to the project. He maintains a file of potential firms for small, medium, and large projects. Unfortunately, some companies with strong, centralized purchasing departments take a dim view of negotiated or directed procurement of design services, and therefore make matching difficult.

The design firm's project manager must realize that the facility manager has internal clients who must be satisfied. This is particularly true for some types of projects, those for religious institutions, for example. The facility manager is responsible to his management, to see that the project is completed on time and within budget. The company's employees look to the facility manager to safeguard their health, provide a productive environment, and maintain facilities that are efficient and economical. This has become even more critical for facility managers as the organization struggles to attract and retain the highest quality employees. Often the deciding factor in potential employees' decision may be the design and appeal of the facility. In essence, the facility manager must live with and operate the building long after the design firm has moved on. A good design firm understands that environment and helps the facility manager with those internal considerations.

Selecting a Firm

In medium and large companies, design teams are selected by an evaluation committee of knowledgeable, in-house experts. The committee should be structured—or packed, if you will—so that the facility manager controls final selection; but committee experts in security, telecommunications, networking, life and safety, and building operations add significantly to the facility manager's ability to select the right design firm for the project. A typical evaluation schema (two-step) is shown in Exhibit 14-1. Other desirable members on the evaluation panel are:

- The corporation's project manager (chairman)
- In-house design representative
- Individuals with in-house sustainability experience and qualifications, such as LEED accredited professionals
- In-house engineering representative
- In-house security or safety representative
- In-house communications representative
- User representative
- Purchasing agent (nonvoting secretary)

Exhibit 14-1. Design firm selection criteria.

Phase I (Determining Short List)

	Percentage Allotted
Project management qualifications	25
Qualifications of key staff	20
Like project experience	25
Approach to request for proposal	15
Financial and insurance capability	15

Phase II (Evaluating Short List)

	Percentage Allotted
Project manager qualifications	25
Qualifications of key staff	20
Like project experience	25
Approach to request for proposal	10
Presentation	20

Although there are drawbacks to the beauty-contest aspects of evaluation panels, there is a great advantage in having a wide range of expertise and corporate political views. For projects that intend to meet specific sustainability guidelines, such as LEED certification, an experienced LEED accredited professional is a must for the selected firm. Further, there is a balance to be struck between objectivity of selection and the need for a firm that is a good team player. One of the tenets of the quality management movement is that corporations establish long-term relationships with organizations like design firms.

Perhaps the most difficult factor to evaluate in a design firm is its cooperativeness. Experience and technical capability are readily verifiable, but the fit on the project team is difficult to assess. In an ongoing relationship, of course, this is a known quality.

Some facility managers may be restricted by corporate procurement regulations in their selection of the design team. This is most often to the detriment of good team selection because it bureaucratizes what should be a personal process. A facility manager should work hard in the organization to establish rapport with in-house experts so that the experts will give their technical evaluation without insisting on hiring only "name" firms.

While there may be disincentives, it is essential that the design firm attempt to assess corporate decision-making procedures of potential clients before submitting a proposal. Also, designers should talk in depth to the operators of current buildings where the client resides and to the operators of similar buildings. These investigations contribute greatly to a firm's ability to submit a knowledgeable proposal. Some firms flounder because they fail to understand the politics in an organization. While a good project manager can and should expedite decision making, he is no guarantor for all corporate decisions—or their timeliness. A wise design firm reinforces the information capability of the project manager and helps him solve internal decision-making problems.

If possible, and if the project is large enough to justify it, the facility manager should visit a similar project that the proposed design project manager has managed or that the design firm has done. He should talk to the project manager and facility manager alone, asking what the design firm considers good design and seeking examples.

The facility manager should also require designers to prove that they understand designing to maintain, asking them to show examples. No other concept has had so much lip-service (except perhaps life-cycle costing). Finally, the facility manager should pay special attention to engineering. For many reasons, poor engineering design causes great problems, many of which can be mitigated only after the fact. In golf, you drive for show and putt for dough. In design, engineering is like putting; the inadequacies can be extremely costly in both operational and corrective costs.

Select the design firm for its expertise, experience, and demonstrated coopera-tiveness. Creativity and awards are not necessarily criteria for selection unless those are objectives of the project. Facility projects usually go much smoother when creative egos are not present and when the project objectives are the moti-vation for *all* participants.

If these suggestions are followed, project execution will be both productive and well controlled. As the design firm commences the design process, the facility man-ager must ensure that the personnel he was promised are actually on the job. The design firm should design and the project manager should control the management of the total project. The facility manager must ensure that user decisions are avail-able to the design team at the proper time. This, of course, can be a problem in mul-tilayered bureaucracies or when decision making is fragmented.

Design Reviews and Presentations

Early on, formal design reviews should be established. Normally, these reviews are conducted:

1. The feasibility study, if conducted
2. The concept, if done by the design firm
3. The program (if done by the design firm), with user sign-off
4. At 25 to 35 percent developed design (last chance for substantive revision)
5. At 80 to 85 percent developed design (still time for those finishing touches)
6. The final design (before the release for procurement)

On fast-track projects these reviews may be combined, but each time the process is fragmented, the facility manager assumes greater risk for the workability of the total product.

Never underestimate the value of elevations and models. Because we are expe-rienced, we understand two-dimensional drawings but our customers and manage-ment may be seeing the project for the first time. BIM (Building Information Modeling) can be invaluable here; it is possible to give our users an actual walk-through of the new facility once design is advanced. BIM is the virtual representa-tion of the physical and functional characteristics of a facility. It provides not only a visual for our users but technical, logistical, cost, and change order estimates for our design and management team, if used correctly. In a recent industry survey, more than a third of the construction project and program planners say they use BIM and the use has increased 3 percent in 2003, 6 percent in 2005, and 11 percent in 2006. Of the users, 74 percent said they would recommend it to others.[3] The Open Standard

Consortium for Real Estate (OSCRE) is attempting to establish international standards for BIM so that it works hand-in-hand with existing FM technology and retains its usefulness to the FM for the full life cycle of the building.[4]

A presentation to senior management is a must, even if not requested. If possible, include the CEO, the senior occupant of the newly designed space, and your boss. It is best if the facility manager or project manager does the presentation, but whoever does so must be well rehearsed. The presentation sells the project.

For projects introducing new concepts or technology, use a mockup. They are expensive, but they can be invaluable for design evaluation and for selling new systems and technologies—or, for that matter, to discover that great ideas won't fly. Vendors do an outstanding job of supplying mockups, which should help reduce costs.

Building Commissioning has become such a popular procedure that a trade association, the Building Commissioning Association (BCA), has formed. If you desire to write building commissioning into your construction documents, the BCA can provide samples.

Documentation and Follow-Through

The key to good facility management is documentation. The design firm should be more than willing to update all documentation into a common format at a reasonable price.

It's a good idea to write several important end-of-project procedures into contracts and specifications. They vary from organization to organization, so you must guide the design firm in what should be included. At a minimum, include the following:

- Recommendation on amount and storage of attic stock
- Punch list procedures
- Operational testing procedures
- Documentation
- Furnishing and finish boards
- Training on equipment
- Warranty turnover
- Instruction book turnover along with all other facility intelligence

It is now possible for the facility manager to obtain drawings, warranties, and instructions in automated form.

During construction, you will have to ensure that the design team stays involved. How involved the designer will remain is not only a contractual matter but varies widely among design firms. It is likely you will frequently need interpretations of design intent, best given by the designer. How well the firm will support you during construction and how well it will provide pertinent information to make project decisions is a major factor in determining further work with the firm.

Finally, both you and the design team should assess how well the project works three to six months after occupancy. The postoccupancy evaluation should address only those items you are willing and able to correct on-site or as part of downstream projects. Also, the evaluation is not done for academic purposes; the study should fit the size and complexity of the project (see Chapter 12).

Design Practices and Considerations

We do not attempt to provide a design manual. For excellent treatment of the details of interior design projects, we recommend Carol Farren's *Planning and Managing Interior Projects*.[5] However, facility managers need to understand the design process so they can control the process.

Design Outputs

Until good design is put in a form and format useful to contractors, it remains simply a good idea. Historically, a hierarchy of plans for transmitting design into construction has been developed. Each project has unique needs, but some plans are common to most projects.

The *base plan* is a scaled drawing of a specific floor of a building that indicates all permanent and/or structural aspects of that floor. Usually found on the base plan are such items as the building core, lavatories, exits, fenestrations (doors and windows), and support columns. Almost all subsequent plans may be overlaid on the base plan to provide adequate information for each floor without replicating the structural information on each plan. When used in a computer-assisted design and drawing (CADD) situation, all plan-view drawings can be viewed as layers stacked on top of each other. Hard-copy prints (blue line, black line, etc.) may be plotted individually or as a single overlayed plan.

The *demolition plan* is a scaled drawing of a specific floor of a building that indicates the removal of particular walls or partitions, plumbing, telephone and electrical units, and custom fabrications (cabinets, etc.). Demolition plans are used only when remodeling or renovating.

The *installation plan* is in plan view and also in scale with other drawings. This plan identifies the location of modular panels, and indicates the location of sources of power for each series of connected panels (panel runs). Also indicated are individual panels that offer electrical outlets and power, which are not powered and which require power to be passed through to other panels. Individual power circuits are located and noted on this plan too. The plan is used to coordinate the work of furniture manufacturers and installers to ensure proper specification and installation at a later date.

The *component plan* is a scaled drawing related to a specific floor of a building and is a second overlay to the installation plan. On this plan, the components are noted that will be "hung" on the panels shown on the installation plan. Locations of hinges and cabinet door swings are also on this plan, as are indications of lighting specific for each workstation (task lighting).

The *floor plan* (furniture plan) indicates the remaining furniture to be placed on a specific floor. It is completed in the same scale as the drawings of panels and components. Noteworthy in this plan are the files, shared equipment, and seating.

This drawing is often a single sheet, but may be a third overlay, merely adding to the installation and component plans.

The *reflected ceiling plan* (lighting) is a scaled drawing produced from the perspective of looking down on the ceiling from above. This view is the opposite of the view from the floor looking upward in the actual space—thus, the term *reflected ceiling*. The lighting depicted on this plan generally is suspended in a ceiling of acoustic panels (tile) with access openings noted. The lighting is intended to supply an overall lighting condition in the space, sometimes called ambient lighting.

The *information and communication technology plan* is a scaled drawing of a specific floor, often combining a diagram of placement of data and telephone sources and wires when they utilize structural aspects of the building as avenues of supply. Specific notes are required to identify sources or wiring when plenum or surface supply conditions exist.

The *floor covering plan* is another scaled drawing of a specific floor that indicates the kinds and extent of floor covering to be used in each space. Often this plan is simply a schedule or note.

The *wall covering/finish plan* is a scaled drawing of a specific floor drawn in plan view, indicating the extent of coverage of a specific paint or wall covering in the space. Often this plan does not completely represent an intended coverage and will require additional information in the form of elevations of specific spaces located on the floor. (The information often is covered by a schedule rather than a drawing.)

Each of these plans requires notations *(schedules)* that refer to additional information found elsewhere in the plans. The schedules may represent a specific piece of information such as color, size, or performance or may be a specific set of instructions or specifications. Common types of schedules found in plan sets include panel size, finish and power capability, lighting, materials and finishes, floor covering, acoustical material, and furniture.

Details and *joinery plans* represent specific, unique circumstances. These plans vary in scale and in information presented. Some common conditions that require special instructions include cabinetry; custom details in ceiling, walls, and windows; or unusual conditions that occur when two dissimilar plans connect or converge.

Perspectives and/or *renderings* are not necessarily to scale. They are not intended to present exact instructions to installers or builders. Rather, these drawings provide an opportunity to view an enclosed space in three dimensions. The view captures all furniture and architectural elements in relationship to each other, something that cannot be accomplished in two-dimensional representation. Perspective drawings show space as the user will view it and represent all color and textural aspects that further describe the relationships within the space. Renderings are more expensive to produce than scaled drawings and normally are used to help top management and users understand the intended final product.

Before the design process can begin, it is essential that a facility manager understand the rules of design. Those rules may be divided into three categories:

1. Identification of systems and subsystems
2. Development of standards
3. Regulations and constraints

Systems and Standards

Every project that is interior-related must address one or more systems. These systems for interior projects include:

- Building systems
- Floor systems
- Wall systems
- Ceiling systems
- Fenestration systems
- Furniture systems

The systems, to varying degrees, dictate to the designer what can be designed in a particular space. The degree to which these are written standards for various design factors is shown in Exhibit 14-2. Interestingly the data indicate an across-the-board increase in policy writing.

Managers whose major function is to lease space usually develop a set of building standard allowances. That is, each prospective tenant is automatically provided with materials to satisfy wall, floor, and ceiling system needs. If a prospective tenant desires to upgrade from the systems offered by the landlord, he may elect to receive

Exhibit 14-2. Design factors covered by policy or standards (percentage of respondents).

	Percentage Written	Percentage Unwritten	Percentage None
Office types	54	30	16
Space allotments	55	29	16
Artwork/plants	26	41	33
Furniture arrangement	46	33	21
Office locations	31	37	32

Source: *Facility Management Practices, 1996* (Houston: IFMA), p. 25.

an allowance in dollars toward the purchase of different materials or systems. Nevertheless, the manager or landlord determines a prescribed system for each surface in his building before the leasing process can begin. He must also coordinate all systems beforehand.

A facility manager must also determine standards and coordination guidelines for the systems in the space to be occupied. The ceiling and flooring systems present the best potential variation and therefore have the simplest solutions. For instance, large, open areas are normally capped with a suspended ceiling that universally covers the space. Housed within the suspension skeleton is a configuration of lighting fixtures that collectively produce adequate ambient light. (A review of fixture placement should be made later to determine a minimum amount of glare and general quality of the light.) The amount of light required varies according to work performed and whether light sources are also located at the task. Sprinkler systems (when required) utilize either the suspension skeleton or plenum produced by the suspension of the acoustical or reflective panels. Plenums also house air-handling systems (heating, ventilation, and air-conditioning—HVAC) and often serve as air return ducts for the HVAC system. The light reflectance quality of the ceiling is important in calculating the overall performance of the space and is usually presumed to be at least 80 percent reflective. The suspension skeleton is also used to support speakers when sound masking systems are deployed.

Materials placed on the floor offer the potential for sound absorption and aesthetics but do little to complement the acoustical or illuminated environment. Carpeting or soft floor covering may absorb the sounds of impact (walking) but not represent efficient noise reduction. Hard-surface flooring may contribute to sound reflectance, however. The color and texture of floor covering are often below the presumed 20 percent reflectance formula used to predict illumination levels in a space. Lower performance may require more illumination. The ceiling presents few physical hazards for occupants, while the floor must present adequate footing (nonslip) under all conditions. Several different materials must be used to ease the transition of walking from hostile outside environment into the workplace. Perhaps the most significant aspect of coordinating floor covering systems is understanding the required maintenance for each material or condition. Traffic patterns and intensity may also determine the floor covering.

Walls are often overlooked when considering both illumination and acoustical performance. The illumination predictability formula is 80/50/20: an 80 percent reflectance is expected from a ceiling system, 50 percent from the walls, and 20 percent from the flooring system. Most wall surfaces have assumed a decorative role in the interior design of a space. When dark colors or heavy textures are used, the 50 percent reflectance may be diminished. As with floor coverings, diminished reflectance requires additional illumination in the ceiling.

Footprints of space (potential variations) may be somewhat determined by accessibility standards. A barrier-free environment will have noticeably wider circulation space than is required by standard regulations and codes. Be aware of the philosophy of your organization in regard to accessibility when developing standards of space utilization. Insist on isometric drawings of each workstation to ensure performance needs. Also test on site at least one configuration of the various standards, using employees under conditions similar to those that will actually be encountered.

Furniture systems are usually limited to partitions and componentry of a workstation. In reality, seating must be considered part of the system. Most seating today has adjustable features touted by manufacturers as productivity enhancing and ergonomic. While it is true that the technology of office seating has improved greatly, no significant findings support increased productivity as a result of the new seating technology. You should ensure that testing of seating be completed under work conditions before making the final selection. Exercise care to analyze manufacturers' claims.

Effective and Efficient Space Allocation

After the decisions have been made regarding furniture systems, a facility manager begins the task of dividing up the space for employee use. Effectiveness and efficiency of space are not synonymous. Effective use of space implies that the space function is maximized—that is, each worker at a workstation is provided with maximum functional support for each task at hand. Space efficiency is the ability to achieve maximum density per square foot. The ultimate objective is to provide maximum support in as small a space as possible without constricting the workers.

A second efficiency may be achieved through design of multiple workstation modules. CADD programs use the principles of space planning to help you design a single workstation, then reproduce it as many times as necessary for a single drawing of a multiple workstation module, thus simplifying the planning process.

Office support furniture and equipment continue to change. The most futuristic innovation, developed to meet the need for quiet and privacy within a team environment, is the individual workstation that resembles an airplane cockpit. The cockpit is outfitted with the individual's computer, screen, and ergonomic seating. This workstation can be independently controlled for air quality, lighting, temperature, and plug in/plug out of existing building systems as well. Further it provides concentration and privacy for the worker so as to avoid unnecessary distractions from co-workers.

Conventional Panel-Hung Systems

Conventional panel-hung systems require that panels of standard module width be used (most common are two-foot widths and four-foot widths). The most common workstation standards are then expressed in extensions of those modules.

Aesthetics are enhanced with partition strings on 45-degree angles with the horizontal walls in the space, and with radius panels at the termination of panel runs or as entrances to individual workstations. An efficient arrangement is small squares with replicated panel widths in the same side of each workstation. Aisles should be minimized (within code compliance) and circulation space kept to a minimum. To minimize design time on the project, use CADD to design multiple workstations.

Circular Radiating Clusters

The most efficient use is maximum-density clusters (six workstations) as close together as possible. The visual arrangement is similar to "spots" when viewed in plan and will define a truly aesthetic appearance. While these clustered workstations increase density significantly over conventional panel-hung systems, workstation function may be significantly reduced. It's a trade-off between density and functionality.

Clustered Panel Systems

Providing the modularity of conventional panel systems, clustered panels may even be reconfigured into or interfaced with conventional arrangements. These systems provide maximum function at minimal per-workstation costs with indicated flexibility.

When using CADD, select from a variety of footprints that range from two to eight workstations in a single grouping. Different from other systems, clustered panels can further group up to sixty-four or more workstations for the most efficient design. They maximize circulation space and the efficiency difference between a circle and a square ($3.1416/4$) to demonstrate the greatest possible functional density.

The aesthetic appeal of this system is unique. Linking patterns of groups form soft organic shapes in a space conducive to departmental communication and interaction. It also provides a significantly greater capability for lateral filing than does any other system.

In a 1994 national survey, nearly 75 percent of senior business executives, government officials, facility executives, and building association leaders queried felt that the government should fund research and development studies of office productivity. Over 93 percent of that same group felt that high-quality work environments can increase worker productivity.[6]

Productivity Information

A number of furniture manufacturers have made claims that their specific product increases productivity. Some studies support the claim that appropriate furniture and other work-support tools also contribute to increased productivity, although those studies do not claim product specificity. Perhaps more important than furnishings in determining productivity are how people view their jobs. According to Robert Nolan, who writes on issues of office productivity, there are five basic expectations of people with respect to their workplace:[7]

1. Job security
2. Sense of community
3. Well-defined job expectations by employer
4. Feedback on performance
5. Opportunity

Sometimes a facility manager or space planner will project productivity increases under certain conditions or using a specific product or technology. Yet it appears that employee perceptions, not specific pieces of furniture, are most important to productivity. New trends in collaborative working require, however, that furniture meet multiple needs for the workers and often this challenges existing standards within many organizations. You are well advised to discount the productivity claims of manufacturers and establish productivity projections based on established figures.

Product Specifications and Contracts

Many products appear to be similar, but do not take advertised claims at face value. Test a product that appears to approximate the purpose and scope desired, and be sure such testing is done under controlled conditions and as close to actual working conditions as possible.

Guarantees for products should be for at least as long as their tax depreciation schedule. Manufacturers' suggested maintenance programs should be included in every purchase. Each specification package should contain provisions for warehousing the product if the space is not available for occupancy on the projected date. In addition, penalty clauses will be a deterrent for late delivery or faulty merchandise. Finally, all specifications should ensure product replacement availability at a specific future date, to ensure aesthetic and maintenance continuity.

All furniture manufacturers offer dealers standard discounts on their products. When a major company makes purchases over a period of years, the total may be much more than a dealer purchases in a year. Your contract with the manufacturer can be written to cover future furniture needs as well as current ones, thereby including a discount that may significantly exceed the normal wholesale price available to dealers.

Refining the Budget

An economic model is essential to the birth and life of any project. An economic model is a budget, a guide, or sometimes an educated guess. All models presume certain conditions and may achieve a high degree of accuracy if those conditions hold true. It is essential for a facility manager to minimize the variance from the presumed conditions. In other words, a successful project results from well-defined project parameters.

Assuming that attention was given to the data-gathering stage and that the data were thoroughly analyzed, budgetary parameters should be fully understood by this point. The workstation standards will be helpful in establishing the cost figures for purchasing furnishings, warehousing needs, maintenance programs, churn factors, and installation or construction costs. Assuming that the architectural and design fees are hard numbers (not open ended), those numbers may also be safely projected into the budget.

The most difficult numbers to project are costs of internal time to complete the project (estimates of supervision, employee downtime, survey involvement). Those numbers are estimates and come from a number of different sources. Ask for documentation supporting the estimates that come from outside sources.

As the design progresses, the budget should become more specific. Ordinarily, the project budget should be locked in by the time that design is 30 percent complete.

Notes

1. Vivian Loftness, "Research: Fundamentals for Design Professionals," *Construction Specifier* (May 1989): p. 112.

2. *Facility Management Practices* (Houston: IFMA, 1996), p. 15.

3. "BIM Adoption Accelerating, CMAA/FMI Owners Survey Finds," *Government & Industry e-News, December 2007,* Society of American Military Engineers, p. 1.

4. Noreen Seebacher, "Accelerated Development Could Benefit the Environment," *GlobeSt.com, February 15, 2008,* pp. 1–2.

5. Carol Farren, *Planning and Managing Interior Projects,* Second Edition, (Kingston, Mass.: R. S. Means Company, 1999).

6. *On-Site Research Findings; National Summit on Building Performance* (Washington, D.C.: Cramer-Krasselt, 1996), pp. 5, 15.

7. Robert E. Nolan, Richard T. Young, and Ben C. DiSylvester, *Improving Productivity Through Advanced Office Controls* (New York: AMACOM, 1980).

15

The Construction Phase

Pulse Points

- *Both design-build and fast-tracking offer opportunities for cost savings but place greater pressure on the design team.*
- *Costs can be minimized by selecting the correct method of contracting and construction process for major projects.*
- *Prequalify design firms and builders.*
- *Award good performers; drop nonperformers.*

Construction costs have never been so volatile in your authors' memories as they are right now. Steel and concrete prices are increasing at 1.3 percent per month at a time when the demand for construction in North America is being cut back.[1] Fuel costs on horizontal construction are at historic highs. This is causing some bizarre situations. Private sector projects are being pushed through to completion even when they do not have an occupant. This is being done simply to reduce costs with hopes that one will be found. Simultaneously, for projects not underway, financing is difficult to obtain and lending institutions are not willing to expose themselves to much risk. All in all, it is a very tricky business situation and one which facility managers must be aware of. In the public sector, projects, once approved, continue but project managers are finding it very difficult to do the amount of work planned with the allocated resources. Ultimately this means that less programmed work will be accomplished in a given period. Public agencies, strapped for cash because they cannot raise taxes, are turning to public-private partnerships for specific projects or even for entire developments such as recent sports stadiums or tollways. Never in our lifetimes has the business climate had such an effect on construction . . . and there is no end in sight.

One of the difficulties of trying to break an integrated subject like facility management into its component parts is that the reader loses the sense of concurrency and integration necessary to manage facilities well. For example, construction cannot be divorced from either planning or design (Chapters 6 and 14) or project management (Chapter 12). In fact, partnering and the trend toward design-build have blurred what distinctions existed between these functions. For projects managed internally or using design-bid-build, it is neither desirable nor financially wise to skip any steps in the project planning and development cycle.

Public agencies, watching how public-private partnerships expedite construction by not depending on design-bid-build construction, are themselves looking to streamline construction procedures (and reduce costs in this environment). They do this by accomplishing as much construction per unit time as possible. Time is money even in the construction industry, which has been criticized as notoriously inefficient. The loss absorbed by construction inefficiency is silently absorbed by society as a whole.[2] Therefore, there is a necessary emphasis on streamlining project and construction costs, which facility managers (and their management and procurement partners) must be aware of and implement.

Particularly in the private sector, once a decision has been made to commit to a construction project, all parties try to compress the schedule as much as possible so that the business purpose of that project can begin as early as possible. One builder said, "All of our projects are now fast-track!" Since construction is often started before design is complete, there is great pressure on getting all of the "front-end things" right. Business issues drive construction also. For example, for some companies, a scenario where a developer builds a building to their specification and then leases it to them might best meet both of their technical and financing needs.

Construction of new facilities always brings particular attention to the facilities department. At times construction has been called the glory function of facility management, since the programming, planning, and design come to fruition.

Construction is often defined as the installation or assembly of a facility. For practical purposes, most large facility departments handle two kinds of construction, often using a dollar value ($100,000, for example) to differentiate between major and minor construction.

Major construction normally is funded with capital funds, as part of a multiyear capital construction program. Minor construction is similar to alterations, and although it can change the very nature of the facility, it often is funded out of the annual budget.

Minor Construction and Alterations

Almost all organizations fund some level of work that could be capitalized but comes from the annual operating budget. The most common reasons are that there must be funds available to meet reactive needs, and the size of the projects is below the company cutoff for capitalization. Thus, funds for minor construction often are mixed with maintenance and repair moneys, and they compete for priority. In fact, that can become such a problem that the U.S. military has put a ceiling on the total annual dollars that can be used for new work, minor construction, and alterations versus maintenance and repair.

For most companies, a typical minor construction project is related to moves or expansion to accommodate new space or equipment needs. It is typically $10,000 to $50,000 in scope, and can be designed and constructed with in-house resources. This type of job is best managed by a project manager focused on the user. An alternative is the interior designer or space planner who also coordinates design, construction, moving, communications, installation, furniture and furnishing installation, and project turnover.

In general, specialized construction management systems are not cost-effective on such small jobs, though Program Evaluation Review Technique (PERT) and GANTT charts may be used to report to management. Often, off-the-shelf project management systems such as Microsoft Project or a variety of specialized software for estimating, project tracking, and cost control are used. In medium-size organizations, it is not uncommon to have 150 to 200 such projects going annually, mostly to implement churn. With so many small projects occurring in such a brief time frame, the facility manager is unable to oversee most individual projects and must devote most or all of his time to managing the program as a whole.

Minor construction is fairly easy to reduce to a routine that is highly efficient, providing there are standards and available design and construction capability. The management challenge is to keep this work from absorbing maintenance and repair funds.

Major Construction or Renovation

Some facility managers never manage a major construction or renovation project, while others construct new facilities on almost a routine basis. Most, however, have at least one experience with a major capital project. Because these projects have high visibility in the boardroom, every facility manager should be comfortable with this type project. In fact, because these projects have historically been given to a retiring vice president, seizing the initiative may be one of the biggest challenges for a facility manager.

Initially, the key to managing a major construction or renovation is organizing the design-build team; this is explained in Chapters 12 and 14. Early on, a decision needs to be made regarding the contractual arrangements needed to manage and build the facility. For example, if a structure already exists on the site, you may have to bid the asbestos removal and facility demolition separately from the construction services. The extent to which the in-house staff manages the construction depends on the form of contract employed. The choice is usually between construction management and general contracting.

Construction management (CM) is one popular method of contracting. It is the inevitable result of building more complex buildings and the need for better continuity, at least from design through turnover. In a recessionary period, CM also offers substantial reductions in project cost. CM is different from general contracting:

Construction Management

1. Places a premium on the ability of the construction manager.
2. Requires significant participation by the facilities department.
3. Needs better coordination between design and construction.
4. Better for phased construction.

General Contracting

1. May be the only option for a small facility department.
2. Commits the facility manager to lump-sum contracting.
3. One contractor performs most trade work.
4. The project is not so large that it requires phasing.
5. There is little need for close coordination between the architectural-engineering firm (A-E) and the contractor.

Hiring a construction manager should reduce the total project cost or the time to design and construct. Sometimes the company can fill the construction management function without hiring additional people.

Although the term *construction management* has been used for several years, actually there are three generally accepted CM practices. In one form, the construction manager is retained by the facility manager early in the design stage, then assists in managing the design process, offering his expertise to ensure that the facility manager's interests are represented.

In another form, the construction manager is hired following completion of the design. He then is responsible for the construction process, helping the owner obtain contractors for the various segments of the project, providing project coordination, and expediting the work.

In the third form, the construction manager may actually perform portions of the work with his own crews or contract for the work with other companies if that is less expensive. We have seldom seen this used, for obvious reasons. (See Exhibit 12-1.)

The Construction Process

The most common method for major construction is the conventional construction process. When the design work is completed, the bidding process leads to selection of one or more contractors to handle the construction. There are many alternatives to this process that may be useful under certain circumstances. In the public sector, law often requires that construction projects be awarded by competitive bid.

Following are explanations and definitions of some alternatives to the standard competitive-bid process, based on completed designs for large projects. These alternatives are intended to save time and money but usually increase owner involvement. Thus, the success of these alternative processes depends on the owner's knowledge, ability, and expertise in construction management. Those are only some of the alternatives. Variants seem to appear regularly.

Design-Build Alternative

Under this process, one firm usually has responsibility for both the design and the construction of the facility. The design-build format can be used in a competitive-bid process, but it requires extensive planning and a method of analyzing the proposals submitted by the candidate firms. This method gets the construction underway as the plans for each segment are completed, rather than waiting for the total project design. It saves time and therefore money. It also controls cost in that a price for the project is established early on in the design process. If executed properly, design-build promotes the team concept and encourages integrated problem solving, two other major advantages.

This alternative may, however, be limited by a strong desire for design compatibility among various buildings to be constructed at different times. Thus, heavy programming responsibility falls on the facility manager.

Fast-Track Alternative

Fast-tracking compresses the time between the start of design and completion of construction. This works well on relatively large projects and can be adapted to either competitive bid or negotiated contracts. Many facility managers feel that, given the cost of capital, all major projects should be fast-tracked to some degree.

As with design-build, fast-tracking saves time by starting construction on selected parts of the project prior to completion of designs. The designer must complete segments of the construction documents in a sequence that follows the proposed sequence of construction. Once the design for a phase is finished, work is contracted. Then other portions of the design are completed. This pressures the design team and tests the competency of the designers. The process requires careful cost-estimating allocation to ensure that funds are sufficient for the entire project. Fast-tracking also restricts the designer's ability to incorporate desired changes into the project after the initial construction contracts are awarded.

Turnkey Alternative

A turnkey process has great appeal to small facility departments facing a unique, one-time project. The contractor or developer arranges for and obtains all necessary construction financing and may, in fact, manage the project from concept through construction. Once the project is complete, the contractor exchanges the title of the building for either full payment or future payments.

Selecting a Builder

The developed world is blessed with many companies that can design and build large, complex facilities. In fact, excellent builders can mobilize at almost any site, some of them elsewhere in the world. Nevertheless, a builder must be chosen carefully, using these criteria:

1. Successful completion of multiple projects at the location selected
2. Successful completion of similar multiple projects
3. Financial stability
4. A qualified and compatible manager
5. Current project load

We admit to a certain discomfort with some methods for analyzing the technical capabilities of a builder. The selection often takes on aspects of a beauty contest, compounded by the fact that the references given seldom provide either an "encouragin' or discouragin' word." Most selection processes encourage bureaucratic procedure rather than commonsense evaluation. We favor a two-step evaluation procedure, the second phase involving an interview with the manager of each company.

Perhaps even more than selecting a design firm, we favor Best Value Contracting in the selection of the builder or design-build contractor. For too long, our relationship with our contractor has been one of confrontation and bickering whereas we should be partnering to minimize risk, increase performance, and achieve a win-win situation. In today's construction environment, we must stay on time and on budget and be committed to settling the inevitable construction problems in a way that is fair and equitable to all. The facility manager must be comfortable with the selected construction contractor from the beginning of the project. It is necessary that a professional distance be maintained in any contractual arrangement, but we must view that relationship as a partnership.

Construction Contracts

The traditional construction contract is a fixed sum, reached through competitive bidding or negotiation. In recent years, however, other types of contracts have been used to meet both market and management needs. The advent of construction management, with fast-track and design-build alternatives, may help companies gain some of the benefits of these innovative construction contracts. Following is a brief explanation of some of the common contract alternatives.

Guaranteed Maximum Price

The guaranteed maximum price (G-max) establishes a maximum project cost. It then provides incentives to the contractor to reduce this cost. The maximum cost can be obtained through competitive bid or negotiation, and the contract provides the means of apportioning the financial savings that are established.

By its nature, this contract shifts considerable design responsibility to the contractor, so the designer and owner must review all cost-saving measures proposed by the contractor. The major difference between design-build and G-max is that in the latter the owner controls the proposed design deviations. In design-build, the contract is for the design, with owner review and approval.

Since the G-max form shifts most of the responsibility for design omissions to the contractor, it is necessary that the company have a strong, detailed design at the beginning of the process. If the design is poor or incomplete, the contractor is likely to inflate the G-max price to cover the ambiguity.

Cost Plus Percentage

In the cost plus percentage contract, the facility manager pays the actual cost of the project but allows a fixed percentage for overhead and profit. There is no incentive on the part of the contractor to control costs.

Cost Plus Fixed Fee

The cost plus a fixed fee contract is structured to remedy the problems associated with cost plus percentage by limiting the cost ceiling. It eliminates any incentive for the contractor to drive the cost upward, since the profit margin is set.

Cost Plus Fixed Fee With Upset Figure

The fixed fee with upset figure contract is a compromise. It establishes a fixed cost ceiling for the completed project, and the contractor realizes a profit as long as costs remain below the fixed ceiling.

Multiple Prime Contracts

Most facilities are constructed with a single prime contract that covers the entire project. An alternative is to award multiple prime contracts, preferred by some large facility management organizations. In these contracts, each of the prime contractors has a direct contractual relationship with the owner. The company must hire a construction manager or must have one of the multiple prime contractors provide coordination.[3]

Miscellaneous

There are methods and nuances other than those listed above. There is even some movement toward design-build-operate and maintain, a concept used formerly in combat zones by the military. For an excellent discussion of the most appropriate and applicable method for your needs and experience, go to http://cmaanet.org/selecting_the_best_method.php.

Construction Documentation

Many companies suboptimize their ability to execute construction projects—and later, alteration and renovation—because they fail to obtain complete documentation. Exhibit 15-1 presents documents that should be considered as deliverables for every project.

The items most often forgotten or issued too late are move lists, demolition plans (including cable removal), and communications plans. Because all trades must be coordinated, it is necessary for all plans to be issued and viewed by the construction manager in toto; piecemeal issuance can only cause delays or confusion.

For experienced alteration or renovation crews who regularly work with the same design team and buildings, the volume of construction documentation can be reduced substantially. This is also true when the company uses demountable partitions, standard furniture, standard office layout, and good office and space standards. Document everything that is needed—but *only* what is needed.

Exhibit 15-1. Construction documentation for experienced in-house renovators.

Item	Always Needed	Remarks
Demolition plan (includes art relocation)	No	Can be overlay or notes.
Architectural plan	Yes	
Signage schedule	Yes	
Finish plan	No	Can be notes.
Telephone plan	Yes	
Electrical plan	Yes	
Electrical schedule	Yes	
Wire plan	Yes	
Wire labels	Yes	If used.
Cable removal plan	Yes	If cable moving required.
Fire/life safety plan	Yes	
Fire/life safety schedule	Yes	
Cable labels	Yes	If cabling involved.
Furniture plan	Yes	Or reference to a standard.
Furniture schedule	No	Can be notes.
Reflected ceiling plan	No	Only if major ceiling alterations.
Mechanical plan	Yes	Only if major mechanical work.
Specifications	No	Notes normally suffice unless major build out or major construction.
Details	No	Normally needed for millwork only.
Move (from-to) lists	Yes	

Facility Management Concerns During Construction

Building Information Modeling (BIM) is still an unknown factor in construction management. Large savings can result from employing the predictive capabilities of BIM through

- Using cost attributing features of the model to assess alternative design and construction schemes.
- Virtually coordinating contract documents and shop drawings to identify and resolve geometric conflicts in advance of construction.
- Creating a 4D schedule to optimize the sequence of construction, manage project logistics, and communicate the project plan to subcontractors in coordination meetings (and proactively make adjustments based on their feedback.)
- Using the 3D and 4D models to demonstrate the scope of work to subcontractors during the bidding process, eliminate ambiguities, and reduce cost contingencies in subcontractor bids through increased clarity.
- Quickly assessing and quantifying the impact or scope of changes on all trades and overall project plan.[4]

As amazing as BIM is, and as promising as it seems, facility managers may still be slow to accept it for a number of legitimate reasons. First of all, it is a relatively new technology (the advantages listed above are still being considered by the construction management community). Second, it has an initial cost that probably has not been planned on in either the construction project or the facility management budget. Finally, adoption of BIM usually means completely converting all other forms of project management, work management, and FM accounting which is not only costly, but time consuming. BIM will undoubtedly work its way into facility management in the same way that CAFM did as soon as standards are established, slowly and probably precipitated by a single large project for any single organization.

Besides ensuring that the project will be constructed on time and within budget, the facility manager must concern himself with these factors during construction:

1. Building systems
2. Maintainability
3. Operating costs, particularly energy management
4. Staffing and organizing
5. Turnover procedures and training
6. As-built drawings, warranties, and sample books

Paying attention to these issues during construction will help ensure that the company will assume an operable building at turnover and that initial operating problems will be minimized.

In an informal survey of facility managers, several of whom are heavily involved in construction, the following were found to be typical of cost savings or avoidances that could be expected from good facility management related to construction:

1. *Good programming (5 to 20 percent).* You will save money if you carefully define your requirements up front.
2. *Value engineering (10 to 30 percent).* Your design-construction experts can often recommend different products or methods that will reduce costs and improve quality.
3. *Fast-track construction (5 to 10 percent).* Savings here are in both the cost of capital and the earlier productive use of the site.
4. *Design-build construction (5 to 10 percent).* Design-build saves time and thus costs, and it allows for effective cost control.
5. *Innovative procurement (5 to 20 percent).* Savings here vary from the use of such things as national sales contracts and multiple prime contractors.

Cost Control

We want stress again the need to do life-cycle costing for all major components of significant construction projects. One of the places where the facility manager should inject himself into the process is to ensure that he sells life-cycle costing to his management. Someone on his team will be able to crunch the numbers (although the facility manager should review and challenge them), but only he is in a position to sell the results of life-cycle costing to management. It is often a hard sell, but an incentive to do so is the fact that the facility manager and his budget will be living with the result for the life of the building.

New sustainability initiatives and the desire for green buildings is helping to advance life-cycle costing; the facility manager is the primary promoter and beneficiary of these initiatives and should understand these concepts thoroughly.

Because of the high cost of major construction or renovation projects, cost control is always an issue. Unfortunately, it is often misunderstood. Too often, it is viewed simply as driving the initial capital cost down. Also, nonfacilities managers do not realize the cost of late operational decisions that affect design or construction. Exhibit 15-2 is a graphic representation of the effect that timely decision making can have on project costs.[5] Early in the project, the project manager should develop an expenditure profile and should track expenditures against it closely.

In construction, there are great advantages to the proper use of computer-assisted facility management. Technology can be especially useful in three areas: payments, schedules, and change orders. The use of BIM will enhance the FM's capability in all three.

Payments. Automated payments to A-E firms and to contractors are almost mandatory to administer construction contracts on large projects. This is especially true when using CM techniques or multiple prime contractors. You could have as many as twenty or thirty contracts for a single project. This way, payments are triggered by completion of schedule items.

Scheduling. Monitoring schedules is an area that benefits from automation. Most contractors prepare detailed schedules in order to mesh the work of subcontractors and the delivery of material. Commonly, both construction documents and schedules use the Construction Specification Institute classifications of work as a basis for the computer network, and that information is often shared with the design-build

Exhibit 15-2. Relation between timing of decisions and cost savings.

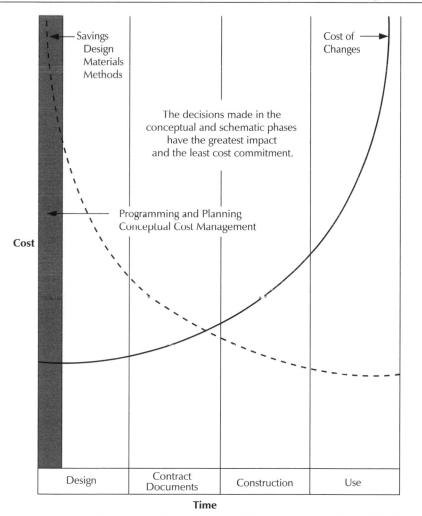

Source: Larry Gleason, "Modeling Facility Construction Alternatives," *IFMA Conference, 1987 Proceedings* (Houston: IFMA, 1988), p. 317.

team. By comparing schedules to completion dates, you can spot bottlenecks in the process quickly enough to correct them.

Change orders. Change orders are of two types: *pending change orders* (suggested changes not yet approved by all parties) and *approved change orders* (changes that have been approved). Normally there are more pending change orders than approved change orders. The automation can ensure that all parties have a record of these changes and a method to resolve change issues quickly.

Quality Control

We recommend a qualified construction inspector for projects over $250,000. This is in addition to the inspection services normally performed by the A-E firm. Although we are unaware of any major policy change from the American Institute of Architects, our observation is that architects tend to shy away from providing inspection services for clients. We are sure that this is driven by the litigious nature of the construction business. At one time, architects used to be so actively involved that they often were project managers for small owners. Now they provide only the necessary on-site presence to ensure that their design is being generally followed. This is not intended as a criticism but as a situation to which the facility manager of a major project needs to respond by providing inspection and work validation services beyond those provided by the architect. Other services that should be provided on large projects, either with in-house or contracted personnel, are cost estimating and schedule review; construction accounting and auditing; and legal, code, and permit advice.

Control of construction is exercised through the review and change approval process. Major reviews should coincide with major events, but team reviews should be held at least weekly. We favor a two-tiered review approach, with a technical review always preceding a management review.

One quality-control item often ignored, but which can preclude many problems, is operational testing prior to acceptance. If a mechanical system is designed to perform in a certain way, the mechanical engineer should design a test to ensure compliance, and the system should be tested. No manufacturing facility would ever be acceptable without such tests, yet office building systems are frequently accepted without significant testing.

Involvement of In-House Personnel

It is extremely important to keep in-house personnel involved in the construction process. The builder should feel comfortable with them on the construction site, and they should be actively involved in reviews and testing. The facility being constructed is unique, a one-time effort, which in-house personnel will have to operate, maintain, and repair. The best time for these employees to become familiar with the building is as it is built. Some A-E firms, construction managers, and general contractors view involvement of in-house staff as threatening. You can dispel that attitude, making it clear that in-house personnel will be involved.

Turnover Procedures

Too often the turnover of a facility seems almost an afterthought. Here are some considerations for the end of a project:

1. Beneficial occupancy
2. Punch lists
3. Preparation: completion of work, sign-off
4. Operating tests: composition, scheduling
5. As-built drawings: shop drawings, cable management schema, medium (CADD, reproducibles, copies), distribution, completion date
6. Warranties
7. Finish and sample boards
8. Attic stock: inventory, storage method
9. Training

The use of BIM will help the facility manager manage many of these considerations, but until you are fully integrated into BIM, these considerations are frequently handled through well-supported documents and procedures at the time of turnover. Attention to these details will add inestimable value to a project. If the facility manager is prepared to handle it, the information contained in items 5 and 6 (as-built drawing and warranties) can be supplied in automated format along with pictures and schematics, maintenance schedules, and instruction books for all major equipment. A major project's completion, if properly managed, can provide major impetus toward a complete computer-assisted facility management system. Sometimes the cost of automating can be funded in the project cost.

For all major projects, we attempt to perform a postoccupancy evaluation (POE) six to eighteen months after occupancy. There are now consulting firms that specialize in POEs, but whether you use an outside consultant or your own staff, you should accomplish these objectives:

1. Determine whether there was a correct program for the project.
2. Measure whether the goals of that program were met.
3. Gather input from the staff on overall effect of the program.

4. Determine corrective action for the next similar project.

POEs raise expectations. If you are not willing to make corrections or adjustments, do not bother to conduct them.

Potential Problems With Construction Projects

In recent years, there has been concern about inefficiency and low productivity in the construction industry. While all of these problems may not be applicable to an individual project, being aware of them may help you avoid them:

1. Failure of both parties to understand the project's scope
2. Irrelevant contract requirements
3. Too generous decisions on contract appeals
4. Reliance on negative incentives
5. Excluding the builder from planning and design
6. Inadequate claims processes

There are some suggested fixes, most hinging on a new relationship among the user, A-E, and contractor, whereby teamwork rather than confrontation is emphasized and awarded:[6]

1. Invite the builder aboard early.
2. Use the design-construct approach more often.
3. Read the contract.
4. Seek realism in pricing; do not go blindly for a lump sum.
5. Use value engineering constructively and cooperatively with incentives for active participation.
6. Unless absolutely unavoidable, eliminate sequential procurement.
7. Eliminate cut-and-paste contracts.
8. Use incentives for really good work.

For facility managers who manage large, multiyear construction programs, there are other suggested remedies:

1. Use design standards and standard designs that can be site adapted.
2. Benchmark and document the performance of designers and builders. Award the good performers, and stop doing business with the nonperformers.
3. Prequalify design firms and builders whenever possible.
4. Whenever possible, build flexible facilities that are not unique to your

organization. The future is unpredictable, so hedge your company's bets through flexibility. One of your authors' better management decisions was to insist on access flooring and "overdesigned" electrical systems in new buildings in the early 1980s.

5. Keep the operations and maintenance staff on the project team from concept through turnover. Their input will often save the company from major errors and operational problems that will cost the company annually well into the future.

Some of these measures are probably considered anticompetitive by the public sector, which is a shame. Public-sector facility managers have been given more flexibility to get away from firm, fixed-bid contracts, but there still is a long way to go to give public-sector facility and project managers the tools needed to optimize quality while minimizing resources. As we appeal for flexibility in design, we feel just as strongly that facility managers need flexibility in contracting and then need to be held rigorously to producing results that are acceptable to their customers.

Disputes

We have long been bothered by the litigious nature of construction in the United States. It often seems that everyone on a major project sues everyone else on the project. And ironically, opponents in a lawsuit on one job often are working together on the next. Is this really a system that serves anyone but the lawyers?

We recommend that anyone doing a large amount of construction contracting seriously consider alternative dispute resolution (ADR) both to settle protests and to resolve disputes. Partnering, arbitration, mediation, and minitrials are all examples of ADR methods.

Notes

1. "Reed Construction Data," *Reed Business Information,* at www.reedconstructiondata. com, March 2008.
2. Engy Serag, Amr Aloufa, and Linda Malone, "Reconciliation of Owner and Contractor Views," *Journal of Professional Issues in Engineering Education and Practice,* January 2008.
3. Richard A. Eustis, "Construction Phase," in *Facilities Management* (Washington, DC: APPA, 1984), p. v–71.

4. "Building Information Modeling and the Construction Management Practice: How to Deliver Value Today?" White Paper authored by the CMAA Emerging Technologies Committee, Construction Management Association of America, p. 2.

5. Larry Gleason, "Modeling Facility Construction Alternatives," *IFMA Conference Proceedings*, (Houston, IFMA, 1988), p. 317.

6. "Contract Construction Procurement," *The Military Engineer, November/December 1988*, pp. 590–593.

SECTION VI

Facility Emergency Preparedness

This is a topic which we felt had to be covered in the Handbook because facility managers, to one degree or another, have always been and will always be involved in emergencies and disasters which occur in their facilities. Some organizations have actually created the position most commonly called Emergency Manager. In such an organization, the facility manager must be involved in both the planning for and the reaction to emergencies. In some organizations, the facility manager is the emergency manager.

In North America, the world theoretically changed on 9/11/2001. However, an informal IFMA study of four distinctly different association chapters in late 2007 was disturbing. Too many organizations did not have either emergency evacuation procedures (13%) or disaster recovery plans (30%) in place and the results on realistic drills were similarly shocking and disturbing. Not surprisingly the facility department was highly involved in all aspects of emergency planning.[1] One of your authors believes it has always been a part of our DNA.

In general, our perspective in this section is as a facility manager as part of the organizational team in dealing with emergencies not as the Emergency Manager.

The International Association of Emergency Managers and their website, www.IAEM.com, has some excellent and timely material on dealing with emergencies and we recommend that site to all facility managers, particularly for the emergency management definition and principles listed here[2]:

DEFINITION: Emergency management is the managerial function charged with creating the framework within which communities reduce vulnerability to hazards and cope with disasters.

PRINCIPLES: Emergency management must be

Comprehensive	Progressive
Risk-driven	Integrated
Collaborative	Coordinated
Flexible	Professional

The chapters which follow adhere to this definition and to these principles.

Notes

1. Victoria Hardy, "Emergency Measures in a Post 9/11 World," *TFM, January 2008*, pp. 32–33.
2. *Principles of Emergency Management,* (International Association of Emergency Managers: Falls Church, VA: 2007), pp. 4–10.

16

Planning, Definitions, and Threat Assessment

Pulse Points

- *Facility managers must constantly "think outside the box" to develop solutions to challenges. Solicit comments and ideas from facility employees, organizational employees, tenants, long term contractors, and consultants.*
- *The facility manager's FIRST PRIORITY IS LIFE SAFETY!*
- *Stay informed of the latest techniques in emergency preparedness. Read trade publications and speak with colleagues.*
- *Share your facility emergency plan with your insurance provider.*
- *Always prepare for the worst case. What can go wrong, will go wrong!*
- *Expect the unexpected to happen. If it has not already happened, it will.*
- *You must provide emergency communications.*

Emergencies can happen anytime and anywhere. They can be large or small, depending on a person's relative situation. These emergencies can range from devastating regional disaster situations such as Hurricane Katrina or the tsunami in Indonesia, to local snow and ice storm power outages, to floods in a facility, to violent shootings such as those that have occurred on university campuses. In every case the facility manager is involved. Many organizations continue to maintain the attitude that "it will never happen here." This is cavalier thinking that can result in loss of life, loss of income, and even loss of business. But when it does happen, rest assured that the facility manager will be deeply involved in the recovery.

Threat Assessment

A good plan is thorough, carefully prepared, exercised, and drilled. It addresses the various types of potential emergencies, and identifies where assistance can be obtained. It also evokes comfort and confidence that the facility organization is competent in its abilities to react accordingly. As a facility manager, it is incumbent on you to educate yourself and train your staff on how to respond to emergencies and understand the impacts and threats.

Numerous publications exist which discuss risk management and threat assessment processes. The National Oceanic and Atmospheric Administration (NOAA) offers a good example of such an assessment.[1] It could be modified to suit your needs. Also, the Building Security Council (BSC) has developed a system for facility managers to assess the risks to their facilities consisting of a building classification system, countermeasure evaluation system, and rating and point system.[2]

The threat assessment should be prepared for and focus on two broad areas. First, prevention and, failing that, mitigating the effects of an emergency event. Second, maintaining emergency preparedness and crisis response. Threat assessment provides the leadership of the organization with a tool to assess the weaknesses of the organization, and more specifically, the facility. It is not a substitute for common sense and sound judgment. We recommend that the assessment be prepared in a spread sheet format for ease of data posting and review. An example is shown in Exhibit 16-1.

Exhibit 16-1. Example of a Threat Assessment

Threat Assessment

Emergencies	Probability of Occurrence	Human Impact	Property Impact	Business Impact	Internal/External Resources	Total
Fire	9	9	9	9	Functional Fire Protection system	36
Flood • Internal • External	 5 2	 4 4	 6 6	 5 7	 Alarm System Pumps	 20 19
Tornado	4	9	9	9	Alarm System	31
Hurricane	5	9	9	9	Trained Employees, Contractors	32
High Winds	7	5	6	5	Trained Employees, Notification System	23
Power outage	5	7	5	9	Emergency Power	26

List Potential Emergencies

List in separate columns, on a spreadsheet, all potential emergencies that might occur at the facility. Examples would be: fire, flood, electrical outage, civil disturbance, etc.

Estimate Probability of Occurrence

For each potential emergency, assign a probability of occurrence on the basis of a number from 1 to 10; 1 being the least likely to occur and 10 being the most likely to occur.

Assess the Potential Human Impact

Assign a human impact rating on the basis of a number from 1 to 10. A 1 would have no potential impact and 10 would have a great deal of human impact.

Assess the Potential Property Impact

Use the numerical technique above.

Assess the Potential Business Impact

Use the numerical technique above. The higher the probability the greater the impact on the business. With the Hurricane Katrina disaster many smaller businesses never recovered.

Assess Potential Internal and External Resources

Use the numerical technique, above. Consider any resource which would mitigate the impacts.

Add the Assigned Numerical Scores for Each Column and Place the Totals on the Spread Sheet

To use these numbers, we suggest that you consider 20% of the largest numerical column total to represent 80 percent of the maximum total required for rescue and recovery. Draft your plan accordingly. Finally, the remaining 20% of the numerical column to be used should be considered as having minimal need for rescue and recovery. Using this approach should provide maximum use of available resources and optimum facility protection.[3]

Emergency Planning

Emergency planning is a continuous process. It involves a detailed and systematic examination of all aspects of a contemplated emergency. Effective plans provide a methodology to respond to any emergency. They are based on well-thought-out assumptions and are not static. They are modified, refined, and updated as a result of new information or as situations change. The essential characteristics of a plan include the following.

Mission

The objective of all planning is to accomplish the mission. The mission should be a clear, concise statement.

Assumptions

All plans must be based on factual information or valid assumptions. Any assumption that is made must be as accurate as possible and kept to a minimum.

Resources

All resources must be considered and their availability validated. If the facility manager intends to obtain support from a contractor, there should be an agreement in writing which is reconfirmed periodically. Community resources must also be coordinated regularly. In-house assets must be inventoried and kept updated; this includes personnel, material, and equipment. Mutual aid agreements and partnering should be implemented wherever possible. For example, colleges and universities can have mutual aid agreements between themselves to share residential housing wherever possible. Utility companies have agreements to share electric power repair teams to restore electrical power during power outages. In every case, these agreements should be in writing with specific responsibilities designated and cost arrangements agreed to beforehand.

Organization

Delineation of decision-making authority, responsibilities, and clearly defined relationships is imperative. It is best to keep employees doing what they normally do in non-emergency situations in order to lessen the potential for confusion and redundancy. Contract, as mentioned above, for specialized skills but be as reasonably sure as you can that those individuals will be available in an emergency because often they perform critical tasks. If this is a municipal or county plan, query the local National Guard for specialized services.

Decentralization

Facility managers cannot be expected to do everything themselves; therefore, decentralize to the maximum extent possible. Train your subordinates so they have confidence in their abilities.

Simplicity

The plan should be kept as simple as possible in order to eliminate confusion and misunderstanding. Use simple, direct language that is easily understood and is not ambiguous.

Flexibility

The plan is just that, a plan. This means there has to be the element of flexibility which allows for adjustment and corrections based on the site conditions at the time.

Coordinated

All elements of the plan must fit together, like a puzzle. This means that all aspects of the plan have been synchronized so that everyone knows his or her role and also what others are doing.

Categorizing Emergencies

Risk Concerns

Anybody in the FM business knows that emergencies can happen at any time. An overflowing toilet is an emergency. If detected immediately as it begins to overflow, the damage can be minimized to only a few gallons of water on the floor which can then be absorbed by a few towels. That same overflowing toilet can become a disaster if it continues to overflow. Undetected for many hours, it can result in several thousand gallons of water seeping its way to floors below, damaging property, and possibly even impacting the mission of the organization. Likewise, a smoldering or defective wire caught early is a relatively easy problem to correct. However, a small flame can readily ignite surrounding materials resulting in an explosion or fire that could destroy a facility. Quick and correct response to an immediate emergency can mean the difference between a minor and major emergency.

In another example, IFMA has studied violence in the workplace among its members and found that organizations reported that 43 percent of them had a violent incident in the three years prior to the study. The study recommends post-incident actions and measures to react better to such incidents in the future.[4]

The above examples mean that most of our emergency planning will be based on risk management, prioritizing what is most likely to happen and, if it happens, what will be the impact and cost to the organization.

Emergency Categories

Emergencies can essentially be categorized into: *man-made, natural, and technological.*

1. **Man-made Emergencies.** These include workplace violence, labor strikes, civil disorder, economic degradation, arson, hostage situations, indoor air quality issues, hazardous material spills (e.g., include: broken natural gas lines, improper mixing of chemicals, solid, liquid or gas infectious agents which include medical and human waste, refrigerants for HVAC, etc.) and terrorism acts such as: environmental, cyber-terrorism, agro-terrorism, bomb threats, conventional bombing, and nuclear, biological, and chemical attacks.

2. **Natural Emergencies.** These include any emergency resultant from weather or environmental conditions (e.g., drought, fires, flooding, earthquakes, tornadoes, hurricanes, high winds, snow, ice, hail, extreme heat, lightning, tsunamis, volcanic eruptions, etc.)

3. **Technological Emergencies.** These include: telecommunications failures and interruptions (e.g. electrical power loss and malfunction, fuel shortage due to technical interruptions, and heating, ventilation, and air conditioning [HVAC] failures.)

Development of an Emergency Plan

Steps in Development

Realizing you need a plan or that an existing plan needs to be revised or updated is a good beginning. Plans should be developed to fit the organization. It is not the number of pages in the plan that is important. It is the quality of what is in those pages. A good plan is not measured by quantity, but by the quality of the information it contains. There are some basic strategies which can be used in the beginning to get started. Below are some initial steps to take.

1. Appoint a leader to lead the Emergency Preparedness Team.
2. Organize the team and include representation from various functional parts of the organization. For example: Human Resources, Legal Counsel,

        Purchasing, Financial Affairs, Information Technology, Public Affairs, Manufacturing, Engineering, Production, Security, Risk Management, Environmental Health and Safety, etc.

3. Develop the purpose (mission) of the team (with everyone's input) and final desired outcome.
4. Outline the areas/functions to be addressed.
5. Establish a timeframe with milestones (schedule).
6. Identify mission essential services, products, and operations.
7. Conduct reviews of existing plans, interviews of "experts" including outside agencies and organizations (including community), and hold brainstorming sessions. These sessions should focus on the type of emergencies which occurred in the past, the type of emergencies expected, and technological and equipment emergencies that could impact the organization's mission. Analyze each type of emergency from a scenario perspective.
8. Conduct a risk assessment (internally or contracted) using the types of emergencies brainstormed previously.
9. Identify available internal resources.
10. Identify needed external resources.
11. Establish financial recommendations and a budget.
12. Identify and review insurance requirements.
13. Modify plan as needed.

Organization

Emergency preparedness plans establish the organizational structure in order to respond to any type of emergency or disaster situation. Organizational structure is designed to facilitate command and control. It takes into account the physical aspects needed to accomplish the task at hand. Consideration must be given to the type and magnitude of the emergency or disaster, the communications systems required to support the mission, how the situation will be managed, the control center, information gathering systems, analysis, the administration of the information (record keeping, filing, reporting, and tracking), and the staff, equipment, and facilities required to support, plan, and execute. The facility manager has the responsibility to ensure that his organization has an emergency response plan and employees are trained to respond to specific emergency situations.

Organizational Considerations

Most emergencies relate directly or indirectly to facilities or infrastructure. Consequently, facilities organizations are uniquely organized, staffed, and equipped for handling emergencies. Experience has proven that it is best to keep emergency response operations as close to normal day-to-day operations as possible. After all, facility organizations have the communications tools and management systems already in place, and have contractors with whom they interface daily, available to respond. The organization structure should be flexible enough to allow for expansion and extension of duties. Expansion of duties could include liaising with local government, community groups, emergency relief agencies, and/or contractors, and providing for emergency shelter. Specialized skills can be contracted; there are companies devoted to disaster/emergency recovery.

Concept of Operation

The concept of operation is a statement of how an emergency is handled from start to finish. It is stated in sufficient detail to ensure appropriate action. After normal work hours, the security office will be the first to receive notification of an emergency. This is due to several reasons: officers patrol buildings and can physically detect a problem, alarm systems (fire and environmental) terminate at the security office, or individuals detecting an emergency situation call the security office. Once notified the security office initiates the Emergency Response Plan.

1. At the implementation of the emergency preparedness plan, the facility manager should convene a meeting of the entire facilities emergency response team. At this meeting he should summarize the issues, provide guidance, set priorities, make resources available, and begin the coordinating process to respond to the emergency.
2. Facility management personnel will implement the emergency response process by: conducting damage assessment surveys of property; documenting injuries and fatalities; detailing the various steps and processes taken during the emergency; coordinating for equipment, supplies, and material; executing contracts; assisting with facility evacuation; and supporting any mass care requirements.
3. The facility manager will ascertain the type and extent of the emergency and inform the organization's Command Operations Center. Depending on the situation the facility manager would activate the Damage Assessment Team and direct the team to initiate a preliminary assessment of key facilities and utility systems. This information will be quickly collected, analyzed, and passed to the facility manager who will inform the organization's Command Operations Center (see pp. 270–271). More detailed assessments will be conducted once the emergency is under control.

Communications

One last but most important issue is the subject of communications. Assume that your normal communications systems will be inoperable. This needs to be a consideration in the location and equipping of your Command Operations Center and your Facility Emergency Operations Center (FEOC) (see Exhibit 17-1). Also consider that, when local but widespread disasters occur, cell phone systems are overloaded and of little use. Examine which portions of your plan are contingent upon communications and ensure that those functions are able to communicate. This is critical and often overlooked.

Notes

1. National Oceanic and Atmospheric Administration, See Website www. csc.noaa.gov/rvat/hazid.html
2. Schmidt, J. A., *Measuring and Managing Risk,* The Military Engineer Magazine, March–April 2008, p. 45–46. See Website www.buildingsecuritycouncil.org
3. Lewis, B. T., Payant, R.P., *The Facility Manager's Emergency Preparedness Handbook.* New York: AMACOM, 2003, p. 10.
4. *Violence in the Workplace,* Houston, TX: International Facility Management Association, 1995. See Website: www.ifma.org/tools/research/violence_workplace.cfm

17

Command, Control, and Communications

Pulse Points

- *Reliable and accurate communication is critical to the organization's emergency plan.*
- *Facility Managers must understand there is internal and external communication. They must do both well. The plan must include how communication will be made with organization employees, tenants, local authorities, other agencies, and the media.*
- *Documentation is always an investment in the future. It will greatly assist with obtaining funding after the emergency.*
- *Standard Operating Procedures (SOP) should always be followed. Essentially, what FM's do day-to-day is what they would do in an emergency.*

Response during an emergency is dependent on several factors. One key factor is consistency. Organization policies and procedures will provide the consistency to support the organization's overall emergency plan. There should be seamless transition from the normal day-to-day activity to the emergency response. In some large organizations there are separate positions for a facility manager, emergency manager, and security manager. In smaller organizations, these roles are filled by the same person, who is usually the facility manager. This chapter will focus on a large organization where the roles are performed by separate individuals.

Emergency preparedness is a function of planning wherein life safety and property protection are the main goals. Without planning, direction, and control there would be chaos. Below are important facility management functions that must be considered and carried out when developing the organization's Emergency Preparedness Plan.

Command

The word *command* signifies authority and influence over others. Whoever is in command is responsible for what the organization does or fails to do. The leader discharges his responsibilities through an established protocol and delegates appropriate authority to subordinates. When this is done, there is a chain established linking each level of the organization. This is known as *chain of command.*

Chain Of Command

When an emergency involves the facility or physical infrastructure of an organization, then the facility manager is normally the individual with onsite responsibility for life safety and property protection (either by virtue of the position or by designation from the emergency manager). This is normally true until a local government executive (i.e., AHJ, or the authority having jurisdiction) arrives on the scene and assumes the authority. This can also be delegated by the AHJ to the facility manager or emergency manager. Whatever the case, there should be a written protocol established. It should outline the broad, overall responsibilities of the facility manager and the organization's relationship with the AHJ. In most cases, the local jurisdiction is responsible for this step but it is an important one and should be pressed for if not forthcoming. Government to government or private to government coordination during crises is both difficult and critical. This is because there are issues such as police powers and condemnation involved and the more issues that can be resolved in advance, the better. Components which should be covered include:

- Access to facilities (e.g., keys)
- Available resources and services that can be provided (e.g., facility plans)
- Annual facility tours and joint training (e.g., drills)
- Individual and organization actions (i.e. who assumes control and when?)
- Protocol signatures by the AHJ and organization facility manager

Establish Authority

The organization should issue a corporate policy statement establishing the need for the organization's Emergency Preparedness Plan. This policy statement should include: the general policy, purpose and scope, procedures, establishment of the emergency operating center, emergency preparedness committee members, responsibilities, and command and control.

Control

The responsibility for control at the scene of an emergency rests with the security manager, with support provided by facilities management. Within a hospital environment the same responsibility exists (i.e., the security manager has the responsibility for initial control of emergency scenes). Generally, the authority having jurisdiction (AHJ) takes control upon arriving at the site.

In the United States, emergency management is a cooperative effort among federal, state, and local governments, and the private sector. This charge is in accordance with the 1979 creation of the Federal Emergency Management Agency. Federal, state, and local agencies have the responsibility to protect the public. Correspondingly, private sector organizations have the responsibility to protect employees and the general public from possible hazards by ensuring safety in manufacturing and industrial practices. Also they must comply with all pertinent safety requirements and laws. Governments in each country have different philosophies and capabilities, and organizational plans must reflect this. In some cases, the local facility manager may well find himself pretty much on his own.

Succession Responsibility

In the absence of responsible top management, there exists a need to define a successive line of responsibility for decision making. There must be a well-defined chain of succession. The facility manager must clearly inform the organization's Command Operations Center of the line of succession within his own organization.

Command Operations Center

Generally, the organization will have a command center or emergency operations center if the emergency is large enough and impacts the entire organization. This is a central location where various departments (e.g., human resources, legal counsel, information technology, risk management, financial affairs, public affairs, security, production management, and facility management) will station representatives who will staff the center on a 24-hour basis. In large facility organizations, the facility department should have its own emergency operations center where all related activities can be coordinated. Ideally, the command operations center will have:

- Space for several work stations to receive and coordinate various activities concerning casualty information, damage assessment, and business continuity
- Reliable communications with support agencies and internally within FM
- A computer system to enter information into a central database
- Facility "as built" drawings (in CADD form) and in hard copy
- Contact lists for emergency personnel, vendors, and contractors
- List of personnel having disabilities
- Catalogs and other resources
- Standard Operating Procedures (SOPs)
- A conference room with map board and grease boards to conduct periodic situation meetings; and facility intelligence information concerning each facility

Facility Emergency Operations Center (FEOC)

The facility department should have its own emergency operations center where all facility related activities can be coordinated. The FEOC mirrors the FM department's Work Management Center (WMC). Exhibit 17-1 provides an example of a structure of the Facility Emergency Operations Center for a large facility department.

At the initiation of an emergency situation, the organization will activate its emergency response plan and the Command Operations Center. The facility manager

Exhibit 17-1. Structure of a Facility Emergency Operations Center (FEOC).

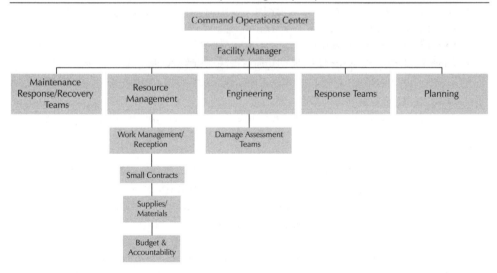

Source: The Facility Manager's Emergency Preparedness Handbook, 2003, AMACOM.

should do likewise by activating the FEOC. The main difference between the normal work management function and the FEOC is that it now operates on a 24-hour basis, and it receives missions and taskings from the organization's Command Operations Center. Exhibit 17-3 on the next page illustrates typical flow of information when responding to an emergency.

Functions of the FEOC

The FEOC is a dynamic organization. During an emergency it has many important functions. Exhibit 17-2 below depicts these functions.

FEOC Physical Configuration

The FEOC will occupy the same space as the regular WMC. It requires the following configuration, equipment, and information.

- At least two work stations with computers linked to a central computer server hosting the CMMS
- Flash lights or some type of emergency lighting

Exhibit 17-2. Functions of the FEOC

- Receive and process all facilities emergency related information.
- Maintain the log of all FEOC emergency information.
- Coordinate all utility service information.
- Maintain communication with the Command Operating Center.
- Coordinate small contract work.
- Develop work estimates.
- Conduct planning and scheduling of project work.
- Track all work and enter into the computer maintenance management system (CMMS) database.
- Maintain the emergency work budget and accounting systems.
- Collect information concerning key buildings and post that information to existing drawings.
- Maintain contact information for employees, vendors and suppliers, contractors, and consultants, including home telephone numbers, pager numbers, after hours contact numbers, mail and e-mail addresses.
- Maintain an emergency information log and maintain organization utility and energy account data files, including energy contracts, account numbers, telephone and e-mail contact information, and names of key points of contact. This data should also be stored at an offsite protected location.

Source: Facility Manager's Emergency Preparedness Handbook, 2003.

- Copies of all emergency plans and SOPs
- Facility utility plans and "as built" drawings
- Communications equipment: telephones, FM radio system, cellular phones, satellite phone, e-mail capability
- Conference room with a facility wall map, cable television, and dry erase or chalk boards

Start Up of FEOC

The FEOC begins operating at the start of an emergency. At that time there are specific actions that should be taken. Exhibit 17-4 lists most of these actions.

Budget and Accounting

The FM work control center is responsible for:

- Developing the emergency preparedness budget (in larger FM organizations it would be the Budget and Accounting Section)

Exhibit 17-3. Information Flow Chart

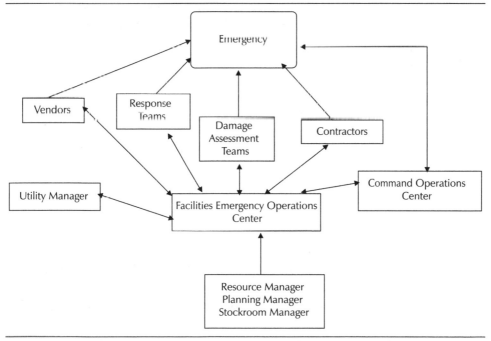

Source: Facility Manager's Emergency Preparedness Handbook, 2003.

Exhibit 17-4. Start Up of FEOC

- The senior person at the time of an emergency is the FEOC manager until relieved by a trained, qualified FEOC manager.
- The FEOC should be prepared to relocate from the primary site to the alternate site.
- Open the Emergency Information Log.
- Begin developing a list of all facility management personnel on site.
- Check all communications equipment, including computers since e-mail is now a major means of communicating with managers and the organization's Command Operations Center.
- Conduct a radio check with personnel on site.
- Begin the notification process of all managers.
- Coordinate with Safety and Environmental Health Staff.
- Conduct check of all utilities.
- Begin listing emergency tasks and other information on a display board.
- Begin notification of the Damage Assessment Team leader and its members.
- Conduct update briefing for Damage Assessment Team members.
- Verify that radios and radio chargers are working.
- Coordinate food and drink support.
- Begin coordination with contractors for any support required.
- Obtain updated inventory status on equipment and materials.

Source: Facility Manager's Emergency Preparedness Handbook, 2003.

- Perform the cost accounting and funds control of expenditures
- Implement procedures which document emergency expenditures separately from the normal facility operating funds
- Coordinate the annual emergency budget with the various members of the organization's emergency operations center for review and concurrence, prior to submission to top management for final approval. Once approved, the budget estimate should become a corporate budget line item for future years. When constructing an Emergency Preparedness Plan, the accepted rule as developed from numerous surveys conducted by the International Facilities Management Association (IFMA) and the Federal Emergency Management Agency (FEMA)[1], is:
  - An initial cost of $1.00/SF, is the minimum cost to develop and implement a plan, and
  - An annual maintenance cost of 20–25 percent of the basic initial cost.

The above rules are fine for North American facility managers. However, facility managers in other parts of the world must consider location, country, currency, exchange rate, and inflation.

Engineering Services

In emergency situations, engineering services play an important role for the facility manager. Assessing damage, estimating, and developing the scope of work for necessary repairs is critical to stabilizing and recovering from emergencies. Architect-engineer firms can be used effectively in this situation, but there should be a pre-crisis agreement with the firm.

Materials Control

Facility management stockrooms must be ready to provide support with needed materials, contact and leverage vendors, and maintain accurate records and material costs relating to emergencies.

Work Control

The work control function is as important during an emergency as it is during normal operations. Processing of work orders, scheduling, and dispatching are essential to tracking work done in response to emergencies. Personnel in the work control center must be very familiar with emergency plans.

Support Services

These are services that can be provided to control or mitigate emergency situations. Information which should be incorporated include:

- Resources available
- Temporary housing support, if required. Agreements will be required with various housing entities.
- Updated list of telephone numbers, e-mail addresses, and points of contact, including federal, state, city disaster assistance contacts
- Local building codes and regulatory requirements
- Insurance information
- Flow chart of the chain of command
- Reporting procedures and required documentation
- Information on how to track costs and submit applications for federal, state and local emergency funds.

Responsibilities

Responsibility is usually depicted as a bureaucratic term. When "defined in writing [it] lets managers know what is expected of them and what limits are set to their authority."[2]

Facility Manager Responsibilities

The facility manager, if not the emergency manager, because of his position within an organization, has the responsibility for coordinating resources, implementing evacuation plans (when necessary), providing shelter (when necessary), and directing the facilities portion of emergency response. All of the above is summarized in the organization's emergency preparedness plan. *However, the number one responsibility is always safety of individuals and the number two is protection of property!* Keep in mind that the corporate chief executive has the legal responsibility and will delegate that job to you.

As the individual responsible for facility emergency preparedness, the facility manager is the advisor to emergency manager, a senior vice president and in some cases, the CEO or president of the organization. In this position, the facility manager has to be astute and tactful enough to make recommendations in such a way that they are not perceived as threatening. In other words . . . know how to interact with a superior, especially in a crisis situation. Do the background research, develop the options and, finally, make the recommendations in such a way that the supervisor still feels in control. This technique will develop a bond of trust between the "boss" and the facility manager; his credibility will skyrocket. Always keep in mind the welfare of the organization and the employees, and through caring and competence cultivate trust![3] Following are the minimum responsibilities of the facility manager:

- Demonstrate competence!
- Always keep safety and property protection as the number one and two objectives.
- Coordinate closely with local support agencies: police, fire, other emergency service departments, planning department, and public works. Initiate annual meetings or luncheons where information and plans can be exchanged and discussed.
- Coordinate with private sector organizations such as utility companies, Red Cross, and major industries.
- Coordinate with the local FEMA office.
- Know the organization's emergency plan inside and out.
- Make training a foundation of the emergency plan.

- Become familiar with pertinent codes and regulations. Research, identify, and collect all pertinent federal, state, county, and local laws, codes, and regulations that pertain to facility rescue and recovery operations (i.e. fire protection, communications, physical security, life safety, shelter, evacuation, property protection, media relations, and community mutual aid agreements.)
- Identify critical products, services, and operations that must be available for use in emergency or disaster situations.
- Identify existing internal resources and capabilities that could be used in emergency or disaster situations.
- Identify and lock in, if possible, external resources that would be of assistance during an emergency or disaster.
- Conduct an insurance review with legal coordination. If not already done, recommend to the Command Operations Center coordinator that current insurance policies should be assembled and reviewed for suitability in emergency and disaster recovery situations. Where coverage is found to be lacking, immediate steps should be taken to increase fiscal coverage of the policies.
- Designate an energy contracts manager and backup.
- Prepare for damage assessment and survey mission. Specific responsibilities include the items shown below:
  - Develop notification procedures of team members.
  - Coordinate information and prepare for update briefings.
  - Gather supplies/materials required for use.
  - Ensure damage assessment training is scheduled and conducted.
  - Develop inspection/survey checklists for each facility with focus on structural, mechanical, and electrical systems for use by team members.
- In an emergency situation involving fuel energy, the incident could be such that the individual who allocates energy would have to relocate. This was the case on 9/11/01 when the World Trade Center was destroyed, and again on 8/28/05 during Hurricane Katrina. In the worst cases, the entire energy source may disappear and need to be provided from a different source/location. This type of occurrence could have major impacts on an organization's billing and payment cycle, especially if it happened when payment or usage data were due. Therefore, to keep the continuity of operations flowing, it makes sense to have duplicate information located at another site. The following should be done:
  - Coordinate with suppliers and work out emergency delivery service during emergency situations.
  - Request that contractors and suppliers review the organization's emergency response plan.

- Reproduce duplicate information concerning the energy delivery contracts and account data.
- Keep emergency contact information for vendors and suppliers updated.
- Establish alternative means of paying fuel bills should an emergency occur.
- If boilers do not have electronic ignition capability, then propane or bottled gas should be stored onsite in order to maintain gas fired ignition.
- Keep the Utilities Management Plan updated.
- Develop an energy/utility contract's implementation letter with "force majeure" language which could be invoked within 24 hours. (Note: Force majeure is defined as anything that could be an "act of God," such as weather events, or unpredictable events such as a labor strike or war).[4]
- Develop and maintain an emergency contact list consisting of, at a minimum, home telephone numbers, pager numbers, mail and e-mail addresses for: employees, vendors/suppliers, contractors, and consultants.
- Finally, demonstrate confidence in everything you do!

Emergency and Security Manager Responsibilities

During an emergency, security of the facility or the site is probably one of the most difficult undertakings. Security is the responsibility of the security manager, but in a crisis, his resources will be stretched and he may need our assistance to provide physical barriers (where he cannot place security officers). In many organizations, physical security is part of the responsibilities of the facility manager.[5]

Communications

In today's world, people want information immediately. They have become accustomed to technology providing them with instant capability to speak or text with whomever they want in a matter of seconds, almost anyplace in the world. Consequently, it is increasingly important to develop a communications plan as part of the overall emergency preparedness plan but it is equally important to understand that normal communications will probably be disrupted, and cell phones will be overloaded. According to Amir Moussavian, CEO of MIR3, "instant, two-way communication with employees and administration can be the difference between success and failure when it comes to execution of a . . . disaster recovery plan."[6]

The communications plan should cover both internal and external communications. Before any information is passed out, however, it must be first vetted through the leadership of the organization. In general, the facility manager and his organization wants to cooperate and maximize internal communication but minimize it externally. The facility manager should make a special point of this to his organization. External communications should be handled by those authorized to speak for the organization by the chief executive. There must be agreement on what information will be dispersed. Information should be disseminated from one central organization spokesperson in order to minimize confusion, and it should be done according to an internally established priority. A good communications plan will go a long way to stifle rumors and incorrect information, minimize negative media exposure, and maintain the organization's positive image.

Internal Communications

Employees, students, and tenants want to know what is happening and what is being done to protect them. Early information should be provided by numerous means, depending on the severity and situation at hand. Text messaging is now becoming an important tool to disperse information quickly to targeted groups. Internet pages and e-mail are other tools that can be used. Provide as much factual information as possible and include who was involved, what happened, what caused the situation, and what is being done to correct or respond to it, as well as when and where the incident happened. As information becomes clearer, updates should be provided.

External Communications

Vendors, suppliers, contractors, and government agencies will also want information and updates. The same tack should be taken with internal communicants. We need to stress this to our vendors.

News Media Communications

As soon as an incident occurs, the news media will flock to the site and begin collecting information for broadcast. While any communication must be open and factual, the facility department does not speak for the organization and should refer all media to the proper contact individual, insisting that they follow all appropriate access rules.

Summary

Information is critical. Obtaining, analyzing, and disseminating it is a major issue for command and control of any organization. Software which links various databases and enables emergency situations and actions to be taken and tracked is now available. This software is so sophisticated that it allows users to know what is happening and be able to stay in touch from anywhere on this planet. The Virtual Emergency Operations Center (VEOC) is here. Your organization Command Operations Center may be using it. If so, then this is something you, as the FM, need to get involved with. Note that unless someone is very familiar with and uses this software on a daily basis, it will be clumsy and in some cases take time to re-learn efficiently. So, our recommendation is to have someone in the organization use it frequently. By this we mean using it when you experience smaller emergencies so when a true disaster is impending the use of this software will be *second nature*.

Notes

1. IFMA, Presentation on Emergency Preparedness in the Built Environment, November 2001.
2. DuBrin, A. J., *Essentials of Management, (7th ed.),* Cincinnati, OH: South-Western, 2006. p. 263.
3. Lewis, B. T., Payant, R.P., *The Facility Manager's Emergency Preparedness Handbook,* New York: AMACOM, 2003, p. 28.
4. *Ibid.,* p. 47.
5. *Ibid.,* p. 29.
6. Zalud, B., *Carrying On After a Disaster, Security Magazine,* July 2008, p. 12.

18

Emergency Preparation and Training

Pulse Points

- *Facility managers must ensure their personnel are cross-trained on every facet of the organization's emergency plan. This develops self confidence and ensures they can step in when needed.*
- *Ensure that personnel and their families know evacuation routes, where community shelters are located, and sheltering-in procedures.*
- *Establish out-of-region telecommuting work sites where employees can work remotely.*
- *Develop scenarios and conduct periodic drills and exercises to ensure facility personnel know what to expect and what to do in an emergency. Instruct and drill organization facility occupants and tenants in evacuation and sheltering-in procedures.*
- *Quality is what counts; not quantity. In other words, a short plan that has quality content is better than a thick, massive plan that no one will read.*

Emergency Preparedness

Preparedness is insurance! Just as insurance companies depend on risk assessment, so should the facility manager consider the risk vulnerabilities when developing an emergency preparedness plan. Obviously, not all facilities should be prepared in the same way to combat a risk which may have negligible impact. For example, a warehouse may not require the same preparations as the corporate headquarters building. Additionally, geographic location would make some risks more obvious. Hawaii would be susceptible to tropical storms, whereas Canada would not be. Kansas has a high probability of tornadoes, whereas Florida is more prone to hurricanes.

The risk factor also is driven by cost. If the probability of a particular emergency is low, then does it make financial sense to spend money preparing for an eventuality that may not occur? This is a question that the organization will have to answer for itself. Exhibit 18-1 defines what makes an effective emergency plan.

Lack of preparation leads to chaos and panic. You can have the best plan in the world; however, if no one knows it and if it cannot be implemented, then it will be a total failure. Information has to be communicated to both the workforce and the facility occupants. The more they know, the more workable the plan.

Steps of Emergency Preparation

Preparing for emergencies is a continuous process. It involves a detailed and systematic examination of every aspect of a possible emergency. This is followed by a sequence of logical steps which ultimately results in an emergency plan of action. Each plan is tailored to the needs of the organization and should be flexible enough to adapt to changing situations.

Determine Requirements

The first step in this sequence is to determine assumptions, bearing on the problem, and the requirements that are associated with those assumptions. Identify conditions that must exist if a specific plan is implemented. The potential threats that could occur are also considered. Finally, there are several additional elements that also must be included/considered.

1. **Human element.** Internal organizational employees, visitors, vendors, and contractors;
2. **Facility element.** The physical plant and building systems;
3. **Regulatory element.** Regulatory agencies who enforce codes and laws, and respond to emergencies;
4. **Business Continuity element.** The continuation of the organization's mission following an emergency.

Exhibit 18-1. An Effective Emergency Plan Is...

SIMPLE, hard to read thick plans with small print are not read
PARTICIPATIVE, individuals as well as managers have to be involved
BELIEVABLE, confidence comes from knowledge and experience; therefore, the plan must be publicized and exercised.

Evaluate Requirements

Evaluation of requirements is done by conferring with other organization staff members and outside agencies to ensure that all factors have been considered. This information is then assembled and should be reviewed for any implications and interrelationships. The evaluation phase results in conclusions and recommendations which identify possible courses of action that should be addressed with the senior leadership of the organization.

Prepare the Plan

1. **Before. ...*Preparation Phase.*** Consider the process of preparations and include the need for documentation and review of existing plans and procedures. Examine mitigation possibilities by identifying: pertinent codes and regulations; required products, services, resources, contracts and operations; critical products and services; internal and external resources and capabilities; and temporary housing support (if necessary). Perform an insurance review. Determine detection techniques and preventive actions. Develop an emergency response training program and include training on: specific life safety equipment, emergency preparedness requirements, responsibilities, and procedures. Finally, conduct drills and exercises to enable all employees to become familiar with how to respond to emergencies.

2. **During. ...*Response Phase.*** The concept of response during the emergency would involve activating the emergency preparedness plan; documenting event situations and response actions taken; ensuring that managers understand their responsibilities; coordinating for any external support which has been previously agreed to; and implementing the public relations communications plan.

3. **After. ...*Recovery Phase.*** Once the emergency situation is stabilized, the recovery process will begin. Again, documentation is critical; especially, if funding is being sought from FEMA or other government agencies. It is at this point that damage assessment teams are deployed and salvage operations begin.

Analyze and Modify the Plan

This is the "debugging" phase. The plan is examined in detail and coordinated with various staff elements and outside agencies to flush out any issues that need resolution. This would be a good time to conduct various drills to fine tune what is in the plan and where necessary work out details to clarify and simplify.

Implement the Plan

Once the analysis is completed and you are satisfied with the plan as it is, then proceed with its publication. Distribution of the plan is important since you want all concerned to receive a copy. Additionally, you should determine which organizations outside the facilities department should receive a copy. Publish sufficient copies so that you don't run out. It never hurts to have more since there is always someone or another agency that wants a copy. Make sure you **date stamp the plan** because if you modify and then reprint, you'll need to know which iteration is being used. Establish a timeline to review, revise, and re-publish the plan annually.

Rehearse the Plan

Once the plan is prepared, it needs to be rehearsed. The more familiar personnel are with the plan, the easier it is to implement and respond to emergencies. It's like exercising a muscle . . . the more you exercise it, the more flexible and stronger it becomes. At the conclusion of each rehearsal, there should be a lessons learned session wherein everyone involved is responsible for listing at least one item concerning the following: what went well?; what did not go so well?; what needs to be improved or modified?

Mitigation Measures

Mitigation is the reduction of potential emergency situations. Its goal is to avoid hazardous circumstances and reduce risk. Essentially, it is the review process to determine what actions can be taken beforehand to minimize emergencies from occurring. The facility manager has the most responsibility to mitigate hazards within the organization. He is responsible for complying with and following existing laws which include such areas as: building codes, fire regulations, zoning ordinances, public health ordinances, and hazardous materials ordinances.

Strategies for Hazard Mitigation

Mitigation strategies include actions that require financing as well as those that involve innovative idea implementation. Sometimes helpful information can be obtained from product manufacturers or from utilities. These strategies are based on the risk assessment and identification of hazards. Below are several strategies for applying mitigation actions.

Prevent the Hazard from Occurring

This is the most basic strategy since it involves ensuring conformance with local ordinances, such as the requirement to sprinkler all public buildings. An example is the implementation of building inspections to ensure conformance with building codes.

Limit the Amount or Size of the Hazard

Establish a limit on various types of hazardous materials that can be stored for any amount of time. This reduces the possibility of a hazardous spill. Another example is to improve building codes so that potential hazards can be eliminated.

Separate the Hazard from What is Intended to be Protected

Limit the locations where hazardous materials can be used or stored. This can be done through zoning ordinances. Locations where hazardous material is stored openly, such as gasoline tank farms, should have a containment facility surrounding the possible hazard.

Prevent the Release of Existing Hazards

Ensure hazardous material containers are properly marked and in good operating condition.

Modify the Basic Components of the Hazard

Ensure a neutralizing agent is available in case the hazardous material container is breached.

Disseminate Information

Make information concerning hazardous materials available to the public. Ensure a good hazard communication program is in place.

Facility Management Initiatives to Reduce Risk

In addition to reducing potential hazards, the facility manager must act to reduce risk. There's never enough funding to do everything the facility manager plans to do. Therefore, there is a certain amount of risk which must be accepted. The leadership of the organization and legal department should address this and provide guidance concerning the amount of risk the organization is willing to accept. There are some actions which the facility manager can implement that will reduce the risk factor and ultimately help the organization. Below is a listing of actions that can be taken.

1. Implement a preventive maintenance program.
2. In conjunction with the security department, implement an access control system to manage the physical access to the organization's space.
3. Install emergency power systems such as generators, inverter batteries, and uninterruptible power supplies (UPS).
4. Inspect and test fire protection systems in accordance with NFPA standards and local codes.
5. Install Closed Circuit Television (CCTV), in coordination with the security department, to improve security.
6. Develop contracts or agreements that can be immediately implemented when an emergency occurs.
7. Estimate downtime and notify occupants and customers as to what to expect and situations for which they should plan.
8. Locate potential offsite storage locations and initiate pre-emergency contracts or agreements.
9. Identify critical equipment and materials needed in an emergency. Have them on hand and easily accessible. Exhibit 18-2 lists the typical equipment and materials that should be available.

Exhibit 18-2. Critical Emergency Equipment

- Tarps to cover openings (e.g. doorways, windows, equipment)
- Plastic sheeting to cover expensive equipment such as computers
- Wet vacuums and water extractors
- Sump pumps, with hoses
- Mops, buckets, squeegees
- Sandbags and sand
- Portable barriers and barricades
- Small emergency generators and light sets
- Rope, chains, and cables
- Lumber (e.g. studs, plywood, etc.)
- Hand tools

Source: Facility Manager's Emergency Preparedness Handbook, 2003 AMACOM.

Evacuation

The organization's emergency preparedness plan should cover evacuation of all personnel, employees, tenants, customers and patrons, visitors, persons with disabilities, and patients in the case of hospitals and medical clinics. The plan should address how and when an evacuation should occur, assembly area locations away from the facility, crowd management and traffic control, and it should define the role of facility management's support. Consideration of panic must be part of the decision process. This means that facility fire codes must be strictly adhered to and enforced. Finally, evacuation planning should involve a review of the National Fire Protection Association life safety code (NFPA 101).[1]

Facility management personnel should be trained in evacuation procedures for the facility. Past practice had been to not use elevators for evacuation. A lesson learned from the 9/11 tragedy is that elevators may be a viable evacuation alternative and this life safety issue is now being reevaluated.[2] Specific evacuation procedures will be followed for hospital buildings. Elevator keys should be immediately available to expedite the relocation process for patients.

Information concerning facilities and special requirements for evacuation should be provided to outside agencies and should be updated annually. Consideration should also be given to providing this information electronically via digital mapping. This capability allows for information on facility layout and various systems to be shared quickly and with many individuals concurrently. It can even be sent to first responders as they travel to an emergency site.

Single Building Facility Evacuation Support

In the event of an emergency that may require evacuation, security personnel, in concert with local police and fire department personnel, will evaluate the level of threat. Based on their determination, a recommendation may be made to evacuate the facility immediately or in a staged manner. A staged evacuation is more complicated and is usually used for high-rise buildings. Of course in the event of a fire, the fire alarm would be activated and building occupants would evacuate immediately.

Large Area or Multiple Building Evacuation Support

Facility management staff should assist security personnel as required. This may mean placing barricades at specific locations; directing evacuees to assembly areas (or safe areas if in the hospital); assisting with the movement of non-ambulatory patients; knowing the safe refuge locations within the buildings and checking those locations for any disabled individuals; having a locksmith available to unlock doors during the sweep of the buildings; and having an electrician or fire alarm technician available standing by the fire alarm panels. Multiple evacuation routes should be established to prevent bunching and to avoid possible hazards such as shards of glass from windows, resulting from explosions.

Evacuation Assembly Areas

Evacuation assembly areas should be pre-selected and located at least 500 feet (160 meters) away from the buildings. Ideally, assembly areas will be located in an open space, away from the possibility of improvised explosive devices (IED). Alternate assembly areas should also be identified and planned for in the unlikely event of small arms fire or ambush. All personnel must be accounted for in accordance with established procedures. This information must be provided to the Command Operating Center.

Accounting for Personnel

When evacuating multiple buildings extra caution must be taken to account for all personnel in the organization after a facility evacuation has been ordered based on an existing emergency / disaster condition that has been observed. This is information that is required in order to start "rescue" operations for individuals who remain unaccounted for. To accomplish this task requires both planning and action procedures such as:

1. The Human Resources Manager should prepare personnel listings for each unit, section, branch, division, and department and distribute these to appropriate supervisors and managers. Information should include any physically challenged individuals (employees or students), work location, residential information (if student), and designated place of safe refuge. These listings should be so printed that they are small enough to be encased in cellophane holders that will fit into a pocket or handbag. These listings should be revised, updated, and redistributed quarterly.

2. If the decision is to evacuate, then information will be transmitted throughout the organization and evacuations should commence. Safe refuge areas should be checked by facility management personnel (and in some cases *Floor Marshals,* where they exist), assigned to that building or floor. All personnel should proceed along predetermined evacuation routes to established assembly areas. Once there, the senior person will call the roll and take a "head" count. The list of those present at the assembly area will be called to the organization's Command Operations Center.

Shelter-In (sometimes known as Defend-In-Place)

There may be circumstances requiring personnel in a facility to remain inside. This could be due to a man-made or natural emergency event. In the case of a hospital, some patients are confined to their beds and possibly attached to life sustaining equipment and cannot evacuate. As a result, hospitals are designed to accommodate these situations. When people remain inside the building, the term commonly used is *shelter-in*. It can also be referred to as *defend-in-place*. This strategy enables occupants, or patients in the case of a hospital, to be relocated to safe areas within the building. Safe areas can be internal, isolated rooms having no windows, or designated floors and stairwells which are specially designed and constructed to limit the transfer of smoke and minimize the spread of fire.[3]

Leased Facilities

Leased facilities should be coordinated no differently than owned facilities. Standard conditions and services, which the owner must provide, are carefully defined in each lease. The owner of the facility should have an emergency preparedness plan covering his responsibilities during an emergency situation. The tenant organization should also have its own emergency preparedness plan for the facility and it should be coordinated with the owner. At a minimum, tenants should ensure their employees know locations of the nearest fire extinguisher and how to use it and conduct periodic evacuation drills. Specific types of emergencies that have a higher probability of occurring should be addressed in the emergency plan. These emergency situations would include bomb threats, workplace violence, what to do for hurricanes and tornadoes, and hazardous materials. All employees should be familiar with the emergency evacuation and security plans. The lease, itself, should address emergencies and responsibilities on the part of the owner and the tenant.

Supplies, Services, and Contracts

In large organizations, the facilities management department relies on its in-house abilities. During an emergency however, these capabilities may be over-committed. As a result, the department needs an alternative, a quick response ability. A good, dependable source of contractors and vendors is necessary to provide immediate response, supplies, and materials. In emergency situations, depending on the magnitude of the event, a region's stock of supplies and materials will vanish quickly unless there is an agreement in place for those supplies, materials, and services to be provided.

Supplies

Managers are responsible for identifying the supplies and materials they feel are necessary, and critical, to have in stock at all times; either in the FM stockroom or at a vendor's storage site.

Services

To ensure that service is continued and that the organization's mission is not impacted, the facility manager must ensure that agreements are in place with supporting vendors and contractors. Essentially, these support agreements are based on relationships cultivated over time. These agreements ensure that needed material, supplies, and parts are made available when needed.

Contracts

Generally, contracting requires full and open competition. In emergency situations, however, this can be avoided but it requires justification and approval. A Letter of Intent to contract for a service in an emergency situation is sometimes used. Its purpose is to provide interim authorization to a contractor to order long lead time equipment in support of emergency project work and to begin mobilizing. Job Order Contracting (JOC) is another tool that can be used by facility managers when quick response and fast execution of emergency work is required. Having a "JOC" contract in place allows the facility manager to get the work done quickly, reduces in-house supervisory and administration requirements, and minimizes price gouging from contractors during emergency situations. Job Order Contracting is promoted by the *Center for Job Order Contracting Excellence*.[4]

Training

Having a good emergency response plan is commendable. Keeping personnel trained in various emergency response skills is a totally different and challenging issue. Adequately trained personnel will ensure a positive response to any emergency situation. Effective training is imperative if facility management response teams are to respond safely, quickly, and effectively during emergency situations. Stated another way . . . emergency response teams are only as effective as their training.

Training Objectives

Below is a list of training objectives established to support the facilities emergency response program.

1. Periodically conduct drills to exercise the Facilities Emergency Response Plan.
2. Exercise the "startup" of the Facilities Emergency Operations Center.
3. Train Damage Assessment Teams in assessment techniques.
4. Exercise various response scenarios.
5. Ensure trade mechanics are familiar with all equipment, locations, and shut down procedures.

Team Training

The facility manager is the individual who drives the training program. This individual establishes the requirements, allocates resources, sets priorities, and ensures that all personnel are competent to perform their required emergency response functions. Specific basic training subjects are shown in Exhibit 18-3.

First Responder Training

Not all emergency situations occur during the normal workday. Many emergencies occur when only a few night trade mechanics and engineers are on shift. Additionally, if an emergency occurs during the workday it may take some time for outside agencies to respond. The Emergency Response Teams may be the first on site, and they must be trained on what to do. These individuals are the "first responders on the scene" and as such require the training shown in Exhibit 18-4.

Exhibit 18-3. Team Training

A. Documentation of training requirements completed
B. Understanding established emergency protocols
C. Emergency reporting requirements
D. Organization emergency responsibilities
E. Damage assessment training
F. Basic first aid
G. Hazardous materials communications
H. Knowledge of confined space requirements
I. Knowledge of basic fire protection systems and response requirements
J. Lockout-tagout procedures
K. How to fit, test, and use personal protective equipment
L. How to use equipment: radio, cell phone, digital camera, video camera, etc.

Source: Facility Manager's Emergency Preparedness Handbook, 2003, AMACOM.

Exhibit 18-4. First Responder Training

A. Location of all utility shut off valves and disconnect switches
B. Hydraulic pressure safety precautions
C. Use of facility emergency showers and eye wash stations for expedient decontamination
D. Essential information concerning critical systems (e.g. pressures, temperatures, RPM's, etc.)
E. Proper inspection/survey procedures
F. Danger signs and signals (what to look for and how to respond)
G. Fire extinguisher training
H. Evacuation procedures
I. Annual light search and rescue training

Source: Facility Manager's Emergency Preparedness Handbook, 2003, AMACOM.

Training Exercises and Drills

Exercises and drills should be conducted periodically to enhance emergency response. Drills should be conducted as often as needed (monthly, quarterly or semi-annually) to ensure that personnel are competent and comfortable with their response requirement. Exercises should be conducted at least annually to evaluate the training and the overall state of readiness.

1. **Exercises.** These are generally unannounced. The intent is to allow participants to believe an actual emergency is occurring. Exercises can be used to evaluate the state of readiness.

2. **Drills.** These are preplanned simulations of an emergency. The participants know that it is a drill and they will be required to respond based on their training. These can be "by the number" event situations wherein participants respond and discuss/critique their emergency response to the situation.

Facility Intelligence

Facilities today are very complex. For example, on a college campus consisting of approximately 4 million square feet, there are thousands of shutoff valves and circuit breakers/disconnects which support the various utilities. It is impossible for any trade mechanic or engineer (especially if they are not a full time employee, but a consultant hired to conduct an assessment) to know the exact location of each valve and disconnect. The facility plans are useful, but often they are not updated with the latest changes to the facility. Additionally, many of these utility shutoffs are hidden or inaccessible . . . they could be covered or buried. Having a "facility smart" book with all of this information, along with a set of "as built drawings," makes locating these shutoffs during an emergency much easier. It also makes sense to coordinate this "facility smart" book with outside agencies, such as the fire department.

Developing such a book will not happen overnight. It will take years! It's an ongoing process. This information can be as extensive and as detailed as you are willing to invest time, effort, and funding, but in an emergency **it will pay for itself!** A recent trend in the design of new construction is the use of a technique called Building Information Modeling (BIM).

BIM is a repository for digital, three-dimensional information and data generated by the design process and simulations—it's the design, fabrication information, erection instructions, and project management logistics in one database. The data model will exist for the life of a building and can be used to manage the client's assets.[5]

Incorporating this information into the Facility Intelligence "smart book" will greatly improve the information available to operators and responders during an emergency situation. Exhibit 18-5 lists some topics that should be considered for inclusion in such a "smart" book.

Exhibit 18-5. Facility Intelligence

- Alarm system information, including location of annunciator panels and sprinkler shutoffs
- High voltage feeder locations and the building these feeders support
- Underground storage tank locations and sizes
- Emergency generator locations, sizes, and areas supported
- Life safety systems
- Elevator summary and reset procedures
- Chiller inventory including sizes and areas supported
- Main fire valve locations
- Main domestic water valve locations
- Main natural gas valve locations
- Potential potable water sources
- Access control information
- Equipment shutdown procedures

Source: Facility Manager's Emergency Preparedness Handbook, 2003, AMACOM.

Notes

1. National Fire Protection Association, NFPA, 101, Life Safety Code. See NFPA Website www.nfpa.org/aboutthecodes/aboutthecodes.asp?docnum=101
2. Page, D., "Elevator Evacuation", *Homeland1.com News*, March 1, 2008. See Website www.homeland1.com/columnists/doug-page/articles/390291
3. Harrington, G., "Emergency Preparedness: Evacuation vs. Defend in Place Strategies," *Building Operating Management Magazine*, April 2005. See Website www.facilitiesnet.com/bom/article.asp?id=2743
4. Center for Job Order Contracting Excellence. See Website www.jocexcellence.org
5. *Preparing for Building Information Modeling*, American Institute of Architects, 2005, See Website www.aia.org?print_template.cfm?pagename=pm_a_20050722_bim

19

Emergency Response and Recovery

Pulse Points

- *During recovery, logistics is the most critical function on which the facility manager depends. Develop a dependable list of out of region vendors and contractors who can respond with labor, equipment, and materials.*
- *Emergency plans must include internal intermediate logistical support for one week. Following a catastrophe, it may take several days for support from out of region providers to arrive.*
- *Ensure the organization's Human Resources department has a policy for how leave and salaries are handled during an emergency. This is important if facility personnel are incapacitated and cannot report to work. It is also a morale issue.*

Response

Responding to an emergency means implementation of the emergency response plan. It is the application of everything that was discussed, trained, and drilled in preparation for an emergency. Hopefully, when the time comes to execute the organization's emergency response plan, all teams know what to do, where to assemble, where equipment is located, and what information is needed immediately.

Stages of Emergency Response

According to the Federal Emergency Management Agency (FEMA) there are five stages of emergency response.[1]

Notification and Warning

Depending on the nature of the emergency, there may or may not be sufficient notice prior to its onset. If the emergency is one that will impact the region and there is time to plan, then the public would be notified through the news media (radio, television, internet). If the emergency is imminent, then some type of early warning, such as a siren or public address system will be used. Emergency employees will be notified similarly and also probably through an organization "call tree," as stated in the Emergency Preparedness Plan.

Immediate Public Safety

This stage is concerned with providing emergency medical services, search and rescue, and evacuation assistance. The security manager and the facility manager will be involved, within the organization, to ensure these services are made available immediately to the employees of the organization. Outside agencies, such as local police, fire department, and hazardous material teams may also be called in, depending on the situation.

Property Security

Again, depending on the type of emergency, the security manager and the facility manager will work closely to ensure that property is protected. Assistance from the local police, fire department, and Public Works department may be required.

Public Welfare

This stage is divided into caring for people and assessing damage. Again, the security manager and the facility manager must work together closely. Outside agency support such as the Red Cross, National Guard, and Relief Services may be called in depending on the gravity of the situation. These agencies are organized to provide temporary shelter and food, and can establish communications to notify distant family members and friends of the status of their loved ones.

Restoration

These are the actions taken to restore necessities of life. They include such things as snow removal to keep roads open, utility restoration, hazardous material cleanup, and radiological decontamination.

Facility Management Response

Facility management response to emergency situations must be deliberate, coordinated, and professional. The FM organization must be flexible and able to transition quickly from normal day-to-day activity to an emergency response posture. All actions in response to an emergency must be coordinated through the Facilities Emergency Operations Center.

Information for First Responders

First responders can be in-house facilities personnel in a large organization, or they can also be local police, firefighters, emergency medical technicians, etc. In any event, before these individuals rush in to an emergency situation, they should be given some information which will assist them in their response and also provide them with life safety information. When possible, answers to the questions shown in Exhibit 19-1 must be provided.

Damage Assessment

The purpose of damage assessment is to evaluate facilities, buildings, grounds, and utilities to determine the impact on the organization's mission. When there is an emergency and damage has occurred, one of the first issues is to determine whether personal injury (or even worse, death) was sustained and the extent of any property damage. The CEO of the organization will be interested in immediately knowing if there was loss of life and what the impact will be on the organization's mission. The organization's Command Operations Center will also demand information. Consequently, the facility manager will be attempting to assess the severity of the emergency as quickly as possible in order to give an initial status report.[2]

Damage Assessment Team Composition and Responsibilities

In some facilities organizations, it may be possible to assemble the Damage Assessment Team using in-house personnel. In smaller facilities organizations, this function would most likely be contracted. The main objective, however, is to ultimately obtain good, accurate information. At the initial stage of an emergency this may not be possible. If damage is severe, it may be necessary to use qualified members of the team to stabilize and recommend immediate emergency engineered repairs so that rescue operations can be conducted safely. As the emergency situation becomes more stable, then the team can efficiently conduct the

Exhibit 19-1. Emergency Response Information Needs

- What type of emergency is it?
- Where is the emergency?
- Is the area locked or unlocked?
- Who has the keys?
- Who has knowledge of the area?
- Is the area accessible by more than one way?
- Are facility plans available?
- How many personnel could be involved in this emergency?
- Who is available who understands the utility situation?
- Are there any hazardous materials in the area? If so, what materials and where are they stored?
- Who is in charge?

Source: Facility Manager's Emergency Preparedness Handbook, 2003, AMACOM.

detailed assessment. The team should have the ability to expand and contract based on the severity of the damage. It should be made up of qualified, trained and experienced personnel and headed by a competent, experienced individual who serves as the team leader. The team leader is responsible for activating the team when requested to do so. Composition of the team is decided by the team leader and is based on the immediate situation at hand. Once the team is assembled, the team leader conducts the initial briefing, for example covering such issues as shown in Exhibit 19-2.

Upon completion of the assessment, the team leader will review the assessments with each individual team member and summarize the information into a Damage Assessment Report which is then sent to the facilities emergency operations center. Preliminary assessment information can be compiled and called into the emergency operations center over the FM radio or cellular telephone. This preliminary information will give the facility manager, along with the Command Operating Center, immediate information which can then be used to begin planning the next phase. It can also be furnished to the CEO and to the Public Relations staff, who will be trying to prepare responses to an aggressive media.

Responsibilities of Damage Assessment Team Leader

The team leader has a major responsibility to ensure he understands the situation at hand, has the right mix of engineering specialties, and has the ability to balance many priorities. Specific responsibilities are depicted in Exhibit 19-3.

Exhibit 19-2. Damage Assessment Team Briefing

Date/Time: _____

Subjects Covered	Issues	Notes / Comments
Extent and nature of the assessment about to be covered	Utilities are still on	Need to shut down
Checklists to be used	Specialty checklists	Need more copies
Define priorities	Priority 1: injured/ victims?	
Ensure all team members have proper protective and communications equipment		
Assign team members to specific tasks		
Questions		

Exhibit 19-3. Damage Assessment Team Leader Responsibilities

   A. Providing timely, accurate assessments of any emergency related damage
   B. Assisting emergency responders by recommending physical stabilization actions to protect individuals and property during rescue operations
   C. Coordinating all damage assessment functions
   D. Providing advice to local emergency response organizations (fire, police, ambulance, etc.) concerning stability and immediate safety
   E. Providing safety advice to construction contractors, maintenance personnel, material suppliers, utility suppliers, etc., and recommending corrective repairs
   F. Surveying facilities and infrastructure, submitting reports, and recommending priorities of work and restoration
   G. Coordinating utility information
   H. Ensuring that unsafe facilities are cordoned off

Source: Facility Manager's Emergency Preparedness Handbook, 2003, AMACOM

Damage Assessment Information Sources

In preparing to conduct damage assessment inventories, general facility information can initially be obtained from several sources. This information includes:

1. Manufacturer's recommendations, which are usually annotated in operational and all internal equipment manuals
2. Building construction and renovation specifications of former renovation or new construction contracts, which are kept in the engineering archives
3. "As built" drawings, which are the final project plans, annotated with changes made in the field
4. Preventive and predictive maintenance databases
5. Warranty information
6. Known deficiencies

Damage Assessment Logistics Considerations

Available equipment and resources, for use by damage assessment teams, must be identified well before it is needed. This equipment should be specified in an equipment database and the location of that equipment should be known and continuously updated. Any cost for the purchase of equipment or material should be tracked and this information should be provided to the budget and accounting department. In addition to equipment, the facilities organization should also have standing contracts which can be initiated immediately. Exhibit 19-4 depicts the equipment that Damage Assessment Teams should carry with them. Exhibit 19-5 lists the service contracts which may have to be called for support.

Damage Assessment Documentation

The Damage Assessment Team is required to complete assessment reports. These are critical to the assessment because they document problems and sometimes, solutions. Eventually, these reports will have costs placed on the recommended corrective work and this information will be included in the overall cost to support the emergency. Excellent computer programs do exist to assist with customizing these reports. What is critical is that a database of this information must be preserved and constantly kept updated.

Recovery

The final phase of Emergency Preparedness is recovery. It starts when the emergency is under control and stabilized. Recovery, essentially, has two phases: short term and long term.

Exhibit 19-4. Damage Assessment Team Equipment

- Vehicles (if needed)
- Measuring tapes
- Notebooks
- Flashlights with extra batteries
- Tape recorders
- Cameras (digital is preferable in order to scan photos into a computer)
- Video cameras
- Laptop computers
- Hand tools
- Key access
- Rags
- Safety equipment (e.g. hard hats, luminescent vests, etc.)
- Radios or cellular telephones
- Security/crowd control barricades

Source: Facility Manager's Emergency Preparedness Handbook, 2003, AMACOM

Exhibit 19-5. Damage Assessment and Recovery Contracts

- Fuel
- Temporary shelters
- Elevator/escalator maintenance
- Pest control
- Utility distribution repair/cleaning
- Snow/ice removal
- Tree services
- Roofing
- Paving
- Concrete repair and installation
- Crushed rock/stone
- Refuse collection and trash disposal
- Construction (open top) dumpsters
- Portable structures
- Moisture control and document freeze drying capability in the event of extensive water damage
- Additional equipment (e.g. emergency generators, portable chillers, snow plows, portable boilers)
- Temporary labor force

Source: Facility Manager's Emergency Preparedness Handbook, 2003, AMACOM.

Short Term Recovery

This is the first priority of recovery and consists of restoring vital systems to operational capability.

Long Term Recovery

This is the continuation of the recovery. It can take months and even years to restore the area to original, pre-emergency conditions.

Recovery Planning

The immediate priority is to move as quickly as possible to some state of normalcy and stability. The organization Business Continuity Plan will help in meeting the critical business functions by answering many questions. Facilities management will enter all information into the automation system and schedule work based on priorities established by the facilities manager, in concert with the Command Operations Center. There are several issues/questions, shown in Exhibit 19-6 that should be considered. Answers to these questions will help with developing a viable recovery plan. Having a recovery plan in place cannot be stressed enough. According to Deborah Keller, Director of Port Development for the Port of New Orleans, "preparation for a worst-case scenario must include the formulation of a long-term recovery plan." She explains that "the Port of New Orleans was excellent at preparing for storms. However, there was never the time, never the interest, [and] never the commitment of the money or the resources to prepare for recovery."[3]

Recovery - General Concept

At this point, the emergency is being controlled and the situation is stable. As a result, facilities personnel will most likely revert to normal work management procedures of scheduling and prioritizing work. All facilities personnel should participate in recovery operations and should be briefed on details prior to commencement of the recovery phase.

Recovery operations must be documented in the Facilities Emergency Operations Center computer maintenance management system. Emergency related computer codes should be established for the purchase of materials, repair work, and contracts. This will help when applying for federal assistance. Below are some items that should be collected and archived.

1. Photographs, videos, and newspaper articles
2. Damage assessment records
3. All costs expended on recovery operations

Lessons learned and recommendations should be documented in order to develop mitigating plans for the future. For example, the British developed standards to avoid progressive collapse in buildings as a result of the 1968 Ronan Point apartment collapse in London's East End.[4] These standards have now been adapted by many countries. Another example occurred as a result of Hurricane Ivan in September 2004. According to executives for the Emerald Coast Utilities Authority (ECUA), in Pensacola, Florida, "the ECUA's insurance firm recommended that a third-party consultant be engaged to help document the costs of recovery. Having a consultant come in and provide assistance in pulling that stuff together is a major godsend to your staff. They can focus on getting your utility system back in operation."[5]

Recovery – Facilities Restoration

Depending on the size of the emergency situation, the majority of the work will be contracted because most of it requires restoration expertise. "Disaster restoration experts can provide recovery solutions ranging from restoration and mold remediation to reconstruction. Forming a partnership with a provider that has the skills

Exhibit 19-6. Recovery Planning Issues

1. What is the mission or core business of the organization?
2. How long can the facility be down without causing a major disruption to the core mission?
3. What are the core business functions?
4. What is the priority for critical functions?
5. Are alternate sites needed?
6. Are seasons of the year important? If so, what and why?
7. Has a business impact analysis been conducted?
8. What are the critical inter-relationships that must be understood by the FM?
9. What are reasonable timelines for recovery?
10. Is there a list of vendors and contractors that can be called to respond to the situation?
11. Have pre-arranged agreements been put in place?

Source: Facility Manager's Emergency Preparedness Handbook, 2003, AMACOM.

and expertise to clean up a disaster and restore the building is crucial to resume *business-as-normal* operations.[6] Exhibit 19-7 is a partial checklist of items that must be checked.

Recovery – Administration and Logistics

Vital records will be recovered and restored. Employee assistance and support programs will be coordinated, if necessary. Consideration should be given to conducting crisis counseling. The cost for all related emergency issues must be compiled.

Exhibit 19-7. Restoration Actions

- Structural integrity of facilities should be verified. Undamaged property should be reported and protected.
- Cleanup operations will involve removal of smoke, water, and debris.
- Environmental regulations and compliance must be followed.
- Hazardous waste must be disposed of properly.
- Life safety systems (e.g. fire protection, sprinklers) will be restored to normal operation.
- Building automation systems including environmental, security, and panic alarm systems will be restored.
- Electric power systems will be inspected and tested.
- Sanitation systems, especially in kitchens and cooking areas, will be inspected.
- Medical gases will be restored.
- Boilers will be restored to normal operation in order to produce steam.
- Information Technology will be provided support to restore communications.
- Mechanical and electrical rooms will be cleaned and equipment inspected and tested.
- Preventive maintenance on emergency generators will be initiated.
- Air quality assessment to ensure there are no residual toxic gases will be conducted.
- Salvage operations will be initiated and include:
  - Segregating damaged from undamaged property;
  - Determining holding sites where damaged material/equipment can be stored until viewed by the insurance company;
  - Turning over damaged goods for salvage once the goods are released.
  - Ensuring everything is DOCUMENTED properly.

Source: Facility Manager's Emergency Preparedness Handbook, 2003, AMACOM

Coordination with outside agencies will continue. Inventory of equipment, materials, and parts will be conducted. All ongoing actions which could have insurance impacts must be provided to the organization's risk manager.

Recovery – Facility Manager Responsibilities

The FM must account for all personnel. All accidents and injuries must be tracked and employee health and safety departments informed. Financial expenditures must be tracked and documentation maintained. Coordination with vendors for additional support, labor, equipment, food, and medical support will be ongoing. All work being conducted will be coordinated and tracked. Facility plans will be provided to contractors as needed. All work that is completed will have an "as built" drawing associated with it. Finally, contact will be made with government agencies for approval to resume building occupancy.

Notes

1. Federal Emergency Management Agency, FEMA. See www.fema.org
2. Lewis, B. T. and Payant. R. P., *The Facility Manager's Emergency Preparedness Handbook*, New York: AMACOM, 2003, p. 30–34.
3. American Society of Civil Engineers (ASCE), *Workshop focuses on Lessons Learned in Disaster Preparation, Response, and Recovery*, December 2007. See Website: http://pubs.asce.org/magazines/ascenews/2007/Issue_12-07/news3.ht
4. Page, D., *The Last Line of Defense*, Homeland Protection Professional, July 15, 2006. See Website www.homeland1.com/columnists/doug-page/articles/350127
5. American Society of Civil Engineers (ASCE), *Workshop focuses on Lessons Learned in Disaster Preparation, Response, and Recovery*, December 2007. See Website: http://pubs.asce.org/magazines/ascenews/2007/Issue_12-07/news3.ht
6. Monroe, L. K., "Disaster Recovery: Confidence in Crisis," *Buildings Magazine*, April 2006, p. 40.

SECTION  VII

Facility Security Management

Emergency preparedness and security management go *hand in glove*. Today facility managers have to think, plan, and manage in both realms. Tragic examples of threats becoming reality have proven the need for increased security. Within the United States this is a relatively new way of thinking because we have felt insulated for years. For European and Asian countries this has been a way of life, and they have developed good systems through the many lessons they have learned.

This section focuses on security management from the facility manager's point of view. Although there is some detail on specific types of security, the intent of this section is to emphasize the importance of facility management in support of security requirements. Terrence Gillick, a security consultant in New York City, states it this way "... years after the attacks on the World Trade Center, facility executives find themselves increasingly focused on the safety of tenants and employees when assessing physical risks and vulnerabilities, and other pressing concerns about security."[1] That said, we believe that all facility managers must have some background in physical security. We not only operate a facility and provide service to tenants, we are also responsible for their safety and security. Some facility organizations manage security directly as part of their mission. Other facility organizations provide support to an established public safety organization. In either case we, as facility managers, have a responsibility to understand the concepts of physical security and be able to relate these concepts to our own service support organization. We must be knowledgeable enough to provide competent advice to security staff and the organization's leadership. Finally, we must understand the most appropriate security countermeasures that should be employed.

Physical security is not just a North American issue. It's a worldwide issue for every organization, be it governmental, private, commercial, or institutional.

Facility managers of these global organizations need to have a strong understanding of physical security since any organization could be faced with security issues requiring immediate and appropriate support. Remember . . . any facility in any location on the planet is subject to the power of nature's forces, technological failures, or man-made destruction. Therefore, with protection of people and property as primary concerns, the *hand in glove* operation of facilities and security should be a perfect match.

Notes

1. Gillick, T., *Assessment and Mitigation of Risks to Physical Security, Information Security, and Operational Security*, Building Operating Management Magazine, February 2005. See Website: http://facilitiesnet.com/bom/article.asp?id=2566

20

Facility Security Goals and Responsibilities

Pulse Points

- *Every facility manager has a responsibility for security within the organization.*
- *The first goal of a facility manager is protecting people. The second is to protect property.*
- *Security involves four principal groups: facility management, public safety, information technology, and employees. All must cooperate and collaborate.*
- *The key to staffing is not quantity, but quality.*
- *Quality employees are well trained.*
- *The installation of high tech equipment is useless if you do not have the appropriate staffing and training to monitor, analyze, understand, and maintain it.*
- *A good security plan includes screening and background checks of new employees, training, preventing unauthorized entry, safeguarding sensitive information, inspections, controlling disposal efforts, and good policies and procedures.*

Introduction

Physical security has always been a major consideration for most organizations. It has taken on more importance in the last ten years because of terrorist incidents like the attacks on civilian targets in Europe, the Middle East, Asia, and the shootings at various business establishments, universities, and schools. In addition, theft of information is on the upswing. The continuous thefts of laptops and hard drive computer information have resulted in compromising the private information of thousands of individuals.

Today's global business environment requires organizations, including higher education, to take security seriously by developing a security plan. This means that facility managers have greater responsibility and are being asked for their recommendations concerning security.

Every facility manager must think about physical security and assist with developing a security plan in conjunction with their security counterparts. The result of a facilities security plan is the protection of employees, assets, and products of an organization from threats, without and within.

Facility Physical Security Goals

The general goals of physical security are to control access, prevent the interruption of the organization's mission, and eliminate or reduce theft and losses. Regardless of the size of a facility in total acreage, number of buildings—whether one-story or multi-story—the security planner must first conduct an in-depth study of the entire facility and determine the needs when approaching and planning a security program. This effort should take into account the goals of the organization as they relate to security, geographic issues or constraints, and the type of general and specific protection that is desired, within budgetary limitations. These goals are accomplished using tangible countermeasures ranging from fencing and lighting to electronic surveillance equipment, with carefully defined policies and procedures and event reporting systems. Security programs, because they cost money, must be judiciously planned in order that the greatest return may be obtained for the money spent. While facility managers are concerned with the general organization goals, they also have immediate specific goals which are discussed below.

Protect People and Property

As a result of the World Trade Center attacks, new and more stringent high-rise building codes and safety requirements are being proposed. These include such special security precautions as:

- hardening buildings against structural damage,
- building wider stairwells for evacuation,
- pressurizing stairwells to eliminate smoke,
- improving fireproofing,
- building air intakes which are inaccessible from street level,
- detailing building evacuation plans,
- reinforcing elevator shafts so that they could be used for evacuation,

- providing backup emergency lighting,
- using photoluminescent paint and electroluminescent light strips in stairwells, and
- coordinating access control requirements.

Some cities are requiring that multi-story buildings have fire safety directors, building evacuation supervisors, floor wardens, and evacuation teams. These positions would coordinate safety drills and maintain lists of occupants and tenants who require evacuation assistance.

When it comes to physical security, managers must understand the key role that perception plays with the people being protected, as well as potential criminals who may be attempting to intrude. Effective security protection includes the perception of security as well as the actual measures taken. Surveillance warning signs and dummy cameras help to give the illusion of security.

Protect Organizational Mission

If an organization's mission is interrupted, the result can have a serious negative impact on its employees, customers or clients, shareholders, and the community of which it is a part. Missions can be impacted by sabotage, vandalism, natural disasters, environmental disasters, and industrial accidents. As a result, a well designed security plan must be comprehensive and supported by detailed policies and procedures. At a minimum, it must include evacuation protocols and routes, assembly locations, procedures for maintaining order on site, and requirements for assembling resources to cope with the emergency event. As the facility manager whose organization is providing support for security, remember that a *thinking outside the box mentality* is employed by those intending harm to the facility and its people. Therefore, when implementing countermeasures try thinking like the intruder.

Protect Information

Information resources contain data that facility managers and the organization use to efficiently complete a job. Electronic information requirements and usage have multiplied exponentially in the last ten years. The major security threat facing companies today is electronic in nature. This includes faulty software, decaying and antiquated infrastructure, viruses, hackers, and worms.

As a result, the risk of data being lost, compromised, or stolen has become a main focus for all organizations. This is especially true since information technology has zoomed ahead faster than development of ways to protect it. Today, e-commerce is the way business is conducted. A firm that loses its server has its business processes and revenue stream at risk, and could even experience financial destruction. Facility managers along with their information technology counterparts must understand how dependent their organizations are on e-mail, e-commerce, and business process disruptions.

Today, information is everywhere. It can be found on laptops, desktop computers, personal digital assistants (PDA), at work, at home, while traveling, from customers, vendors, and contractors. Compare today to twenty years ago when information resided only on company mainframe computers. The security challenge in the future is to determine how to protect it no matter where it is located or how it is used.

Facilities Security Responsibilities

Facility managers and security managers share responsibilities for protecting an organization's people and assets. It remains unclear which manager has the overall responsibility (it varies from organization to organization and often depends on individual personalities). The distinction is hazy when compounded with new electronic technologies and leads to the question: who should lead the physical security effort for an organization or a facility?

The future of physical security involves the information technology manager, security manager, and the facility manager. There will have to be collaboration and cooperation between all three if the organization's physical security program is to work efficiently and effectively. The intertwined nature of operating facility systems such as access control, life safety systems, heating, ventilation and air-conditioning (HVAC), lighting, and environmental monitoring illustrates the importance of communication and collaboration when planning facility renovations. Emergency preparedness, damage assessment, structural integrity of facilities, and evacuation plans are areas in which facility managers must have greater knowledge of functional needs because of the daily involvement and interaction. The responsibilities of facility managers, security managers, and the information technology manager are shown in Exhibits 20-1, 20-2, and 20-3. Additionally, employees play an important role in safeguarding and securing the organization's assets, especially those assets that are sensitive and critical. Whether understood or not, the responsibilities of employees must be considered.

Employees

Employees should be considered a *force multiplier*, as the military would call them, since they understand the day-to-day operation and recognize when something is

Exhibit 20-1. Facility Manager Responsibilities

- Create a facility management program which helps reduce security risks
- Develop an understanding of current physical security trends
- Assist with developing cost effective security solutions to meet upcoming facility and organization requirements
- Ensure proper planning, evaluation, application, design, installation, and construction of facility enhancements for all aspects of physical security
- Provide criteria and guidance to ensure the proper design, installation, and acceptance testing of all organization projects related to physical security
- Identify problem areas that impact security design
- Coordinate physical security surveys with public safety offices
- Coordinate with the security manager during the planning, design, and construction phases of all construction projects to identify physical security requirements
- Provide equipment and manpower to support security measures
- Ensure that backup power systems will function when needed
- Obtain computer training on integrated systems beyond the basic skills

Exhibit 20-2. Security/Safety Manager Responsibilities

The organization public safety officer will:

- Recommend physical security considerations according to the organization's mission and vulnerability to terrorist acts, criminal acts, or other disruptive influences
- Conduct physical security surveys and inspections in conjunction with the facility manager
- Coordinate with local law enforcement offices
- Monitor the resource management of the organization's physical security program
- Coordinate the organization's physical security requirements with the facility manager including immediate requirements as well as planning, design, and construction projects
- Review all planning documents and construction plans and specifications for construction and renovation projects at all stages of development
- Establish and enforce uniform security standards and procedures
- Have a thorough understanding of the organization's business plan

Exhibit 20-3. Information Technology Manager Responsibilities

- Integrate information security procedures into all business processes
- Create and implement a Computer Emergency Response Team (CERT)[1]
- Determine existing information security capabilities (e.g. firewalls, password protection, and network security)
- Establish the need and verify the functionality of emergency power backup systems
- Determine and verify offsite data storage
- Conduct an information technology gap analysis to determine shortcomings and what measures should be implemented to mitigate exposure
- Develop information security plans to contain a security breach and the restoration of critical data
- Plan and conduct mock information security exercises

askew. All employees must understand that security is a responsibility not to be taken lightly. Employers can influence how their employees respond by taking some simple steps.

1. Educate employees on their roles and responsibilities, the link between security and preparedness, and the cost of providing security which ultimately impacts them.
2. Invite employee participation and suggestions in developing security plans. People who participate in planning are more likely to cooperate. One suggestion is to ask them to develop scenarios for how they would attack, penetrate, or compromise their facility.
3. Cultivate and continue nurturing employee awareness of security. Employers can do this through the use of newsletters, sending information through the organization intranet, staff meetings, and other communications tools.
4. Empower employees by providing them with knowledge of the security plan and the resources they have available. This will diminish their fear and anxiety and encourage their contribution to the security of the organization.
5. Promote personal and family security as part of the organization's security plan. This will encourage employees to be observant and report unusual activity.
6. Integrate information concerning the security plan with other organization initiatives such as employee safety and accident reporting. This will soften the emphasis on security and allay fears and anxiety by making safety in the workplace the primary concern.

7. Conduct security drills and exercises. Including employees provides them with a sense that they are contributing to the organization's security plan, building their confidence, and developing the perception they are part of the plan.

The Future

The growth of the security industry will continue to explode with new technologies in the next few years. This means that physical security will become more integrated with the information technology industry.

Internet

The uses for the Internet will continue to evolve. Its capabilities will expand in the future because it eliminates the need for cable and wiring installation and reduces maintenance, all of which reduce cost. Internet applications provide more flexibility for operators, again reducing operating costs. A variety of systems can now be monitored and operated from one central location and do not require someone to physically travel to a site to check and make adjustments. The hub can be remotely controlled from a few miles away or from a different continent. Imagine the capabilities, the challenges, the potential in monitoring the physical, technological, and manpower security of a facility located on another continent. This serves as a further reminder of the importance of facilities management, public safety, information technology, and employees cooperating and collaborating for the benefit of the organization.

Smart Cards

Smart cards store personal information in an imbedded microprocessor. This is unlike magnetic strip or proximity cards, which have no personal information stored. Smart cards can be used for financial transactions much like credit and ATM cards, subscriber identity modules (SIM) for cellular phones, pay television, paying for utilities, as an electronic wallet in place of cash, or feeding parking meters and vending machines. They can also be used for identification purposes, including authentication of identity, driver licenses, and medical information such as blood type and allergies.

Biometrics

According to Sapna Capoor, industry analyst with Frost and Sullivan, a global growth consulting firm, the biometric "market earned revenues of $186 million in

2005 and is likely to grow at a compound annual growth rate (CAGR) of 27.5 percent to reach $1,021.1 million in 2012."[2] Biometrics are now seen more often in organization security. It functions by identifying individuals from their fingerprint, hand geometry, or iris or retina scan. It is considered a more secure technology than magnetic card swipes or proximity cards. One drawback in a large organization however, could be the time it takes to compare fingerprints or iris/retina scans with database information. A card reader or proximity card takes only a second to scan whereas a biometric scan, using current technology, could take several seconds. In a large organization many people could be queued in line to be scanned, resulting in delays. These holdups will decrease as technology improves.

Intelligent Video (also known as Video Analytics)

Intelligent video was initially developed for military use and surveillance activities. It has since been modified for use by civilian security organizations. Its power rests with its programming. Sensors are programmed to visualize objects in three dimensions and match behavior against pre-established patterns. Any activity that falls outside the pre-established patterns will trigger an alarm to a computer desk top, PDA, cell phone, pager, or any other compatible technology. These systems, which are real time, proactive, and preemptive, can result in a cost savings since fewer patrol guards are needed. For example, the perimeter of the facility can be easily covered by a few sensors. Instead of needing several patrol officers per shift, the organization is sufficiently covered by one or two. The intelligent video would take the place of the other officers.

Today, closed circuit television cameras can be adapted with video analytic sensors which greatly enhance their capability, especially when motion detectors are added. This technology is evolving quickly and is being used for other applications such as monitoring for vandalism, theft, pipeline damage, and general monitoring of various infrastructures, utility plants, corporate and industrial properties, schools and university campuses, financial centers, transportation facilities, large sporting events, and home security functions. Future applications are limited only by the human mind.[3]

Three Step Identification

In the future, organizations will use a three step process of individual identification. First, individuals will be identified by a biometric, fingerprint, or iris retina scan. Second, individuals will have to scan their smart cards. Finally, individuals will have to cite a password.

Interoperability

Future automation systems, including the Integrated Workplace Management Systems (IWMS), will be able to link access control, fire protection monitoring, physical security systems, and other systems so the facility manager and chief security officer will have real time information.

Summary

In summary, facility managers more than ever before play a key role in the security of their organizations. It is extremely important that they ensure security support training is incorporated into their procedures and that good working relations are cultivated with their counterparts in public safety and information technology.

Notes

1. Carnegie Mellon University, *Computer Emergency Response Team Coordination Center (CERT/CC)*. See Website: *http://www.cert.org/certcc.html*
2. Capoor, S., "Face Recognition Biometrics Industry Gears Up for Immense Growth," Find Biometrics, October 19, 2006. See http://www.findbiometrics.comarticle/300
3. Doron, D. "Video Analytics." *Today's Facility Manager Magazine.* January 2008, p. 16.

21

Facility Security and Planning

Pulse Points

- *Planning always has a purpose.*
- *Planning is the organization's bridge from the present to the future.*
- *Plans must be customized to fit the organization.*
- *Security plans focus on physical and technological security in support of the organization.*
- *Plan implementation is driven by cost.*
- *Planning does pay dividends.*
- *There is no perfect plan.*
- *Perception is reality when it comes to security.*

Security Planning Considerations

Today, security is everyone's business. Because cost is always a governing factor, however, security plans must be balanced against the potential risk faced by the organization. Plans need to be flexible and customized to fit the need. A 2003 issue of a facility trade publication, *Today's Facility Manager*, researched how the facility management profession is evolving. The report titled "The Changing Role of the Facility Executive," cited security as one of the most important issues that impact facility executives today. Over 50 percent of executives interviewed stated they are more involved with security issues than ever before.[1]

Facility managers are responsible for operating and maintaining every aspect of a facility. As a result, they must be involved in the security planning from the outset. They know the day-to-day quirks and workings in a facility better than anyone else and can provide insight and verification of what security measures should be taken.

Review of Security

Every organization should review its overall physical security needs with regard to the facility location, layout, design, and construction. This includes assessing the effectiveness of external and internal controls, and how they pertain to deterrents, control points, authorization levels, hardware, and security devices. Effective security plans include the need for personnel screening prior to employment, and for continued evaluation, monitoring, and assessment. This is extremely important, especially, in high risk areas.

Control and enforcement of a facility must be exercised concerning authorization levels, key usage, access restrictions, sign-in, and sign-out procedures, opening and closing procedures, and surveillance. All security violations *must be documented*. Written policies must be developed defining classifications and restrictions on handling this sensitive information. Finally, an education and training program should be established emphasizing the need for continuous security.

Planning Process

All of the above is important when it comes to security, but how does the facility manager make it all happen effectively? It starts with planning, and the facility manager and chief security officer are the catalysts responsible for developing the blueprint of a security plan. They initiate the planning process which includes: organizing and leading the security planning team, developing the security plan, implementing the plan, and measuring the results. Since no two organizations are exactly alike, each security plan must be developed to fit each situation.

The plan serves three important functions. First, it clarifies, focuses, and matches security requirements to the organization's mission. Second, it provides a logical and systematic methodology for implementing those requirements. Finally, it provides a point of reference against which achievement of established goals can be measured and analyzed.

Planning Team

At a minimum, the planning team must include the following: facility manager, chief security officer, information technology manager, safety manager, and any stakeholder who would be impacted by or required to support the plan. Clear guidelines must be established with the initiation of the team and include such considerations as meeting times and duration, agendas, individual responsibilities, timelines, plan expectations, and the final deliverable.

Security Planning Approach

When developing a security plan, the planning team must focus on four areas: assessing the organization's security need (the risk); addressing those needs through the security plan; implementing the plan; and continuous review, adjustment, and testing of the plan. The final plan must be realistic, supportable, and affordable.

1. **Assessment.** Judge the current state of security within the organization. This could be done using internal organization resources or by outsourcing to a security consultant. The assessment should match the current state of security against the desired state. A good technique to use is to conduct a strengths, weaknesses, opportunities, and threat (SWOT) analysis. Determine the current *strengths* of organization security, the current *weaknesses, opportunities* to improve the current state of security, and identification of *threats* that need to be considered. Another term for this would be vulnerability assessment.

2. **Developing the Plan.** The planning team will have to answer questions concerning the what, when, where, and how of planning for security. Some of these answers will have to come from interviews with senior organization executives. The military refers to this as obtaining the commander's guidance.
   - <u>What</u>: What are the goals and vision of the organization over the next five to ten years? What changes does the organization see coming that will impact security? What security issues and risks exist currently? What assets have to be protected? What will be the short and long term costs of the security requirements?
   - <u>When</u>: What period of time is being considered? What is the timeline if the organization is planning to grow in size?
   - <u>Where:</u> Will the organization remain in the same geographic location, or expand into new markets? Is it planning to purchase or lease new space?
   - <u>How</u>: How will security support the current mission and future vision? How will the sense of ownership of the plan be inculcated in all employees? How will progress be measured?

3. **Plan Implementation.** Implementation of the plan is driven by answers to the above questions and its associated costs. Consider organizing the procedures into smaller prioritized action plans which will make them more palatable and achievable. Finally, develop training for the staff, implement technology that matches the risk, and initiate policies and procedures to administer the plan.

- <u>Components of the Plan</u>. Security plans can be divided into three components: physical security, operational security, and technological security. See Exhibit 21-1.
- <u>Priority.</u> Depending on what is involved and the cost to implement, the plan may be phased in over time. Trying to implement a complete plan at one time may be overwhelming and too costly for the organization. Some parts may be simple and easy to implement the first year. The more

Exhibit 21-1. Components of Security

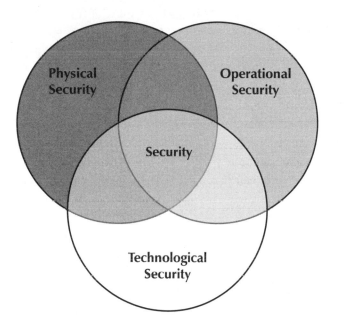

The *physical security* component is focused on the obstacles and barriers. This is the application of barricades, fencing, gates, walls, outside perimeter lighting, signage, and locks. *Operational security* involves people. Specific issues include the provision of staff to support the security protocol, the education and training of employees, and procedures for managing contractors, vendors, and visitors. The third component is *technological security*. This involves the management of technical data and systems. It includes the integration of video surveillance monitoring systems, alarm systems for intrusion detection, building automation systems that control HVAC and lighting, fire alarm systems, communications systems such as FM radios and emergency call boxes, and access control of space.

complex and costly parts of the plan may be prioritized for implementation in the future.

- Security Training. Training will elevate security awareness among all employees. It should include employee familiarity with the plan and use of the installed security equipment for conducting data and information analyses. Security and facilities personnel should be trained in how to diagnose and respond to facility threats. Responding to a threat must be practiced. If it is not, then the plan is just another document sitting on the shelf, gathering dust.

- Use of Technology. Determine which technology is best to support the requirement at hand. Doing this requires an understanding of the risk. Consideration must be given to the organization's mission, crime in various geographic and demographic locations, previous security issues, and current conditions.

- Policies and Procedures. Good policies and procedures must be understood by everyone and interpreted in the same manner. All employees, building occupants, vendors and contractors, and visitors should be provided with a copy of detailed procedures to follow in the event of a security or emergency situation.

4. **Review and Revise.** Emphasize the chief executive's support for the plan, schedule regular reviews, and solicit feedback. It is important that this be done within the first ninety days of implementation. If employees know that support exists at the highest level of the organization and that plans will be reviewed regularly, then those individuals and groups responsible for implementation will take greater interest in ensuring that details are well coordinated. Consider having a performance measure for security compliance included in employee reviews. Feedback and recommendations from employees are also important in order to assure their cooperation.

Communications

Communication with employees, security and facilities staff, and occupants and visitors is the most important action that can be taken. Everyone wants to know what is happening and unless they are told, their anxiety will increase. Listed below are a variety of simple methods to achieve this.

1. **Scheduled Training.** All new occupants and new employees must be scheduled to attend emergency/security training within the first two weeks of employment.

2. **Newsletters.** Distribute periodic newsletters to inform people of any revisions to the security plan and to update them on technology.

3. **Use Available Technology.** Text messaging is now common and being used by many organizations. This technology allows for hundreds, or even thousands, of people to be notified within minutes of the need to shelter-in. Another simple but effective tool for mass notification is the use of a siren, horn or whistle. When an organization uses this method of mass notification, people recognize the alert and prepare to shelter-in.

4. **Conduct Periodic Drills and Exercises.** Develop realistic scenarios that the organization could face, based on the threat assessment and associated risks. Plan periodic drills and occasional exercises for all organization employees.

5. **Public Address Systems.** Public address systems provide a means of notifying many individuals of dangerous situations and giving them instructions as to what they should do.

6. **Alarms.** Duress alarms are important in specific situations. Individuals in key and sensitive positions, such as bank managers, school principals, business executives, teachers, etc. can be threatened and accosted. Duress alarms provide them with the ability to silently notify authorities that an emergency situation is occurring.

Crime Prevention Through Environmental Design (CPTED)

There is more to security than locks, keys, alarms, and cameras. When planning to renovate or construct a new facility, security should be a major consideration. Crime prevention through environmental design (CPTED) was originally conceived in the late 1960s and has evolved over the last forty years into an approach which has gained international acceptance with law enforcement entities. The theory of CPTED is based on the concept that design, using information from the *built environment,* can have a positive impact on reducing crime and improving quality of life. According to CPTED security consultants, a private consulting firm specializing in security, there are four built environment strategies which should be used in design guidelines when preparing a facility security assessment.[2]

Natural Surveillance

In theory, if someone knows they are under surveillance, that person is less likely to commit a crime. Integrating this definition with design guidelines to maximize visibility would tend to dissuade criminal activity. Examples would include the following:

- Have windows overlooking open areas such as parking lots, sidewalks, and entry gates.
- Keep window shades and blinds open.
- Landscape areas near buildings and other key locations in such a way that monitoring and surveillance are maximized.
- Use outside lighting to reduce shadows and blind spots

Natural Access Control

The intent of access control is to channel personnel and vehicles to specific locations where access is controlled. Examples include:

- Having one main entrance to a building or parking facility where everyone who enters can be checked.
- Elevating vegetation located near buildings at least six feet to eliminate locations where someone can hide.
- Ensuring storefront entries are kept clear, allowing easy visibility for security officers.
- Closing off access to stairwells and ladders to prevent perpetrators from gaining entrance to roof tops.
- Using fencing, locked gates, and masonry walls to direct people toward specific entrances.

Territorial Reinforcement

Territorial reinforcement makes use of design features to discourage criminal activity by making the intruder stand out. This is done by defining the property boundaries using fencing and gates, landscaping, signage, and sidewalk and roadway pavement. The intent is for security officers and employees to more easily identify individuals who do not belong. This strategy tends to make authorized personnel feel more protected whereas unauthorized individuals feel uncomfortable.

Maintenance

Maintenance of a facility provides a glimpse into how well a facility is managed. It can give a positive impression, or a negative one. Deterioration of surroundings is seen as a weakness and, therefore, criminal activity is more apt to occur. Examples of conditions that convey a perception of weak security and encourage crime include the following:

- Insufficient lighting resulting from broken and un-repaired lights.

- Inoperable emergency call boxes.
- Fencing in a state of disrepair, or with gaps and holes in the fence fabric.
- The *broken window theory* underscores the need for maintenance. Broken windows, if left unattended for a long period of time, generate a perception that the organization is deficient and could devaluate property into a blight condition.

The concept of *crime prevention through public art* helps clarify the need for a good maintenance program to support the organization security plan. Public art is a means of re-instilling pride in all the inhabitants of a specific neighborhood. When a neighborhood or community experiences severe blight, resulting in decline, there is a feeling of anxiety and depression. A public art program helps to project a positive image in which residents, tenants, and owners can take pride.[3] This is not a new idea. For centuries, many European and some Asian countries have used colorfully painted building exteriors and art murals reflecting local culture and religious scenes on their buildings. The pride generated by these frescoes has had a positive impact on minimizing graffiti and re-instilling respect for property.

Vulnerability Assessment

Understanding the potential vulnerabilities of a building design helps with making decisions concerning structural integrity, building envelope, architectural design, facility perimeter security, and safety requirements. Today, vulnerability simulations and modeling allow building owners, facility managers, and security managers the opportunity to visualize where potential problems may occur and the impacts those problems will have on the facility, occupants, and the mission of the organization. This capability enables decision makers to better understand the issues associated with various security scenarios, how they impact new construction and renovations, and how they can mitigate risks faster and more effectively.

1. **What is a Vulnerability Assessment?** Once known, potential threats to an organization can be mitigated by taking specific corrective actions to reduce or eliminate the threat. These vulnerability assessments are used in developing and prioritizing security plans, modifying existing operational procedures, and making policy changes where necessary to protect critical assets.
2. **Why Assess?** Organizations need to understand the impact of the threat they could face. Vulnerability assessments provide the understanding of the risks and threats. This information can then be used to develop options to combat the risks and threats. Periodic reviews and updates of

the assessment should be conducted to identify changes in threats and risks and how these changes impact the security plan.

3. **Who Assesses?** The conduct of a thorough vulnerability assessment involves an understanding of people, culture, science, and engineering. Therefore, several individuals having expertise in each of these areas should be consulted.

4. **Techniques Used?** The vulnerability assessment process varies in complexity based on the organization's mission. The process is founded on various factors which include: size, population impacted, evaluation of existing countermeasures, analysis of current risk, state of infrastructure, knowledge of and types of potential threats, available security technology, applicable local, state, and federal regulations, and other factors germane to the organization. Elements of a vulnerability assessment are depicted in Exhibit 21-2 and described below.

   A. Provide a description of organization mission and goals. Consider the following:
      1) Priority of services provided?
      2) Who are the customers?
      3) What are the assets and processes most important to achieve the organization mission and goals?
      4) What are the organization's contractual obligations?
   B. Identify and prioritize detrimental situations and conditions to avoid. Consider the following consequences:
      1) Economic impact to the organization.

Exhibit 21-2. Elements of Vulnerability

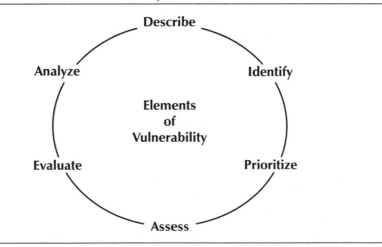

2) The lack of employee confidence in the organization's ability to provide protection.

3) Problems arising from specific events.

C. Identify critical organization assets which would be impacted by some type of attack or intruder. Consider the following:

   1) What could an attacker do to disrupt the operation of critical facilities, assets, or processes?

   2) Has a vulnerability assessment been conducted concerning the operation and maintenance of physical barriers, facility infrastructure, and electronic, computer, or other automated systems?

D. Conduct a probability assessment of the potential that such an attack or criminal action could occur. Consider the following:

   1) What modes of attack would impact critical assets?

   2) Is there a specific scenario that is more likely?

E. Evaluate existing countermeasures. Consider the following:

   1) What physical security capabilities are currently used for detection, delay, and response?

   2) What cyber security capabilities (firewalls, security protocols, wireless data, and voice) are currently used?

   3) What security policies (personnel security, physical security, lock and key control, credentialing, security drill and exercise records) and procedures exist?

F. Review and analyze risks, and make recommendations to reduce those risks. Consider the following:

   1) What are the current risks?

   2) Will recommended risk reduction actions reduce vulnerability?

   3) What strategies should be considered to reduce vulnerability?

      a. Examine current business practices. Do current policies, procedures, and training support the need for improved security?

      b. Examine system upgrades. Will changes in operations, equipment processes, or infrastructure make the organization safer?

      c. Examine security upgrades. Will improved detection and response capabilities make the organization safer?

New Facility

The importance of prior planning for security in a new facility cannot be overstressed. Incorporating the amount of security desired at the time of preliminary architectural planning will result in cost savings and will provide senior management an early look at the overall security plan and its cost. Management will then have an opportunity to make positive security-oriented decisions that otherwise might be brushed aside if they have to be added as an afterthought. Planning should not be totally confined to the facility under construction but should be done with an eye to expansion possibilities five and ten years in the future.

Personnel entrances, parking facilities, and guard control points should be carefully planned as well. The security of docks and a central location for shipping and receiving should be considered. Vehicular and pedestrian traffic should not be routed through areas of this nature.

Utility security should be designed into the overall site plan. This includes electrical switchgears, HVAC equipment, emergency power generation equipment, emergency water sources, standby fuel supplies, and transformer banks. It is at this time that fencing and outside lighting, entrance gates, lobby security, guard posts, alarm systems, vaults, docks, warehousing requirements, and internal security requirements are considered. The utilization of industrial hardware and lock and key requirements are discussed, reviewed, and implemented at this time as well.

Leased Facility

Prior to leasing or purchasing an existing building or facility, a physical security survey should be conducted to assess security needs commensurate with facility use. All door locks should be changed prior to occupying the facility. This could be a problem if inferior hardware has been used in the original construction; however, the expense of converting to a heavy duty system is worth the cost. Consideration must also be given to crash-out doors, windows, roof hatches, outside ladders, utilities, skylights, ventilators, manholes, subterranean ducts, storm drains, lighting, fencing, and parking garages. The security of most of these items should be covered in the lease agreement.

Construction Site

Construction, when it directly involves security, should be carefully planned and monitored. Security of sensitive rooms such as telephone closets, control lighting booths, and mechanical spaces must not be overlooked. Tool cribs and similar storage areas should be constructed using solid walls and a roof covering whenever possible. Facilities housing organizations handling large sums of money, such as banks and credit unions, should have adequate safes and well planned work areas fitted with alarm systems, including duress alarms, when applicable.

Summary

In today's world security plays a very important role throughout an organization. Planners have to consider security when planning projects. This is a cost and a requirement that now has to be considered with every new construction project, major renovation, and even some O&M projects. Planning for security will pay dividends if the result is making the organization safer.

Notes

1. Parkinson, J., "The Changing Role of the Facility Executive," *Today's Facility Manager.* December 2003. See Website www.todaysfacilitymanager.com/tfm_03_12_news3.asp
2. "Crime Prevention Through Environmental Design," *CPTED Security,* See www.cptedsecurity.com/index.htm
3. "Crime Prevention Through Environmental Design," *Crime Prevention Through Public Art: From Blight to Bright,* 2005. See www.cptedsecurity.com/public_art.htm

22

Facility Security Implementation

Pulse Points

- *Planning is the starting point for security implementation.*
- *The purpose of an access control plan is to measure risk.*
- *The fewer entry points to a facility, the better.*
- *The best security preventive measure is to control access.*
- *Technology continues to be the wave of the future.*
- *Personnel must be qualified and trained.*

Technology Today

Prior to the Internet revolution, security systems were operated via cable and telephone lines. Surveillance was limited to local coaxial cable and by today's standards, considered relatively slow. The internet has enabled systems to operate at the speed of light from anywhere in the world and with wireless capability. Remote monitoring is commonplace. Security systems such as closed circuit television images (CCTV) and access control functions can be monitored from handheld personal digital devices.

There is disagreement concerning which tools, systems, or technologies are best for running security programs. Some facility managers are opting for security audits to help resolve this uncertainty. Additionally, technology has far surpassed the evolution of trade association-approved-and-accepted written security standards and guidelines. This has greatly complicated the issue and resulted in individual standards being developed.

The issue for facility managers is to balance security requirements against facility operational needs and budgetary concerns. All three conditions are achievable by integrating current security technology with core building services systems. The synergy gained by this integration will help provide better security, make more efficient use of facility operational systems by improving the diagnoses of everyday situations, and ultimately reduce cost through efficiency and conservation. Using integrated systems, facility managers can secure a facility and at the same time detect heat loads, adjust the heating and cooling accordingly, synchronize elevator usage to peak employee arrival and departure times, adjust vendor delivery times to minimize impacts which can cause parking congestion, and adjust maintenance support schedules such as cleaning. The same can be done with lighting. Not only is the facility physically secure, its core building systems are adjusted to meet the need. This helps to fine tune the operation of the facility and maximize building automation systems to support occupants while concurrently decreasing operating expenses.

Integration of facilities, safety, and security systems is advantageous and timely. With careful planning, integration of systems can result in greatly enhanced security and safety. For example, pedestrian door control can be integrated with the CCTV surveillance system, the elevator system, the fire protection system, automatic door opening hardware, emergency call boxes, parking gate arms, etc. The integration continues when the alarm is transmitted to pagers, cell phones, Personal Digital Assistants (PDA), or any other wireless device.[1] At its most basic foundation, integration means that one system can influence an action in other systems. Exhibit 22-1 depicts a potential integration of security, facility, and emergency systems. The integration of systems improves efficiency, effectiveness, fosters synergy and results in cost savings.

Access Control

Every organization should clearly define its access control measures and tailor them to the local conditions in order to ensure accomplishment of its mission. Facility and security managers are focusing on controlling who is allowed entry, when they are allowed, and where they have access. This control is the foundation of the organization's security program.

1. Credentialing. This is an administrative process used to validate the qualifications and legitimacy of employees, organizational members, vendors, and contractors by assessing their background. Many organizations conduct their own credentialing by using a credentialing specialist or electronic service. This is especially true in the health care industry. Personnel credentialing typically is undertaken at commencement of employment (initial application) and at regular intervals thereafter (reappointment). Credentialing of vendors or other organizations may begin prior to the

Exhibit 22-1. Integrated Control Systems.

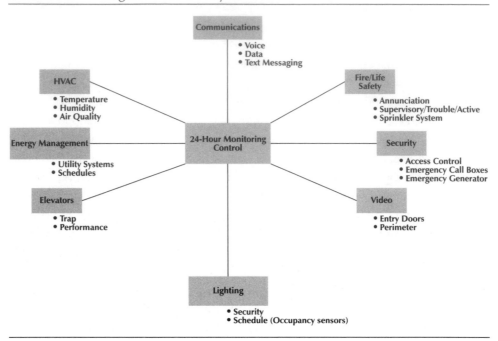

purchasing process, and repeated regularly. The process is generally an objective evaluation of an individual's current training or experience, competence, and ability to provide particular services or perform particular procedures. Credentialing devices are used to identify a person having legitimate authority to enter a controlled area. A coded credential (card or key) contains coded information which is machine readable. An electric signal unlocks the door if the prerecorded code matches the code stored in the system when the card is read. Typical types of cards used include:

   A. Magnetic stripe cards which require that the card be swiped through a card reader;

   B. Proximity cards which must be passed within several inches of a reader, but not swiped;

   C. Smart cards which have a microprocessor and memory, containing personal information embedded into it and must touch the reader in order for the information to be communicated; and

   D. Bar codes which are cards, tape, or papers that have coded black bars printed on them. These are read by an optical scanner which is passed over the coded bars and are seldom used for entry control.[2]

2. Visitor Control. Most organizations find it beneficial, if not essential, to institute some form of visitor control. From a safety and liability standpoint, control of visitors is important for protecting proprietary information, preventing theft, and as a general good business practice. Visitors should be directed to a receptionist and escorted by an employee inside the organization proper. For obvious reasons, visitors should not be allowed to roam a facility on their own, unescorted. Distinctive visitor control badges, color-coded and dated to be automatically voided at the end of the visit period should be used. Integrated systems are now available wherein occupants can use Web-based wireless technology to communicate and authorize visitor access. A temporary access card can then be issued to the visitor, allowing access to the space. The visitor is then tracked throughout the building.[3]

3. Property Control. Property, whether tools used to manufacture a product, office equipment, raw stock, various supplies, or the product itself, must be controlled. Controlling the use and movement of property is difficult without an established process, security measures, and guard force. Strict control over information, inventory, shipping and receiving docks, and stockrooms is necessary. Receiving dock personnel should have locked areas for high theft risk goods and a proper accountability procedure to assure that goods ordered are those received. Shipping docks should be protected by internal fences, locked hold areas, and alert employees who are required to maintain proper accounting procedures.

Strict control over the issuance of organization owned tools is a necessity. Whenever possible, tools should bear a distinctive organization marking and be signed out to individuals with a bar code tag, or other appropriate identification system. Bar coding is today's technology for recording the tool, its condition, the user, and the date signed out in a database for easy information retrieval and archiving.

4. Utility Control. Protection of a facility's utility systems should be given high priority. Main transformer distribution areas, fuel storage tanks, and critical HVAC equipment should be protected by eight foot chain-link security fencing, with minimum clear area of 50 feet. Gas valves and meters, risers, electrical panels, and communications equipment rooms should be locked and protected. Manholes, air and water intakes and exhausts, and other utility openings that pass through perimeter barriers should have security measures equivalent to that of the perimeter. For detailed information on specifications concerning security standards see the Websites of the American National Standards Institute, Builders Hardware Manufacturers Association, and publications of the U. S. Army Corps of Engineers (USACE).

Physical Deterrents

Physically barring access to the facility is the first line of defense. Physical security provides a deterrent to intruders and it forces those interested in committing a security violation to think twice. A good physical security plan incorporates a multi-level security system, also called a layered approach. See Exhibit 22-2. These layers are arranged so that the highest security area is located at the core and the lowest level of security is located at the outermost layer. The objective of each layer is to increasingly impede or discourage intrusion. Layering of security is an old concept. "In the era of castles, security was sought from rings of protection: cleared fields, a moat, outer walls, inner walls, and towers."[4]

1. Outer Layer. This layer consists primarily of barriers and deterrents such as fences, bollards, angled steel plates called wedge barriers that can be hydraulically raised, anti-ram gates, lighting, signage, security guards, intrusion alarms, mechanical locks, biometric locks, and credentialing. The purpose of this layer is to discourage trespassing.

2. Middle Layer. This layer includes such areas as: doors and glazed and film coated windows, ventilation ductwork, roofs, and ceilings. The purpose of this layer is to provide prevention of access and early warning of facility penetrations.

Exhibit 22-2. Security Layers

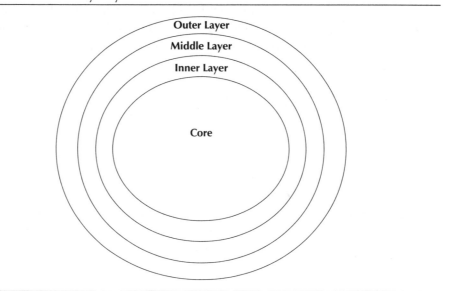

3. Inner Layer. The inner layer controls movement and secures interior space within the facility by reinforcing door and window access control, security guards, signage identifying unauthorized areas, lock systems, closed circuit television (CCTV), safes, and vaults.

Ideally, the security plan will integrate natural, man-made and human deterrents and enable the organization to achieve a layering of security as previously mentioned. This integration will keep the security plan flexible and easily adaptable to the current situation. Examine the security of your facility from an intruder's viewpoint.

A. **Natural Deterrents.** Natural protective deterrents are ditches, water obstacles, or other terrain features that are difficult to traverse. Good security planning makes use of these features to help dissuade unwanted intrusion.

B. **Man Made Deterrents.** Security of a facility requires that access into it be controlled. This can be achieved by the use of structural barriers and other forms of deterrence.

1) **Structural Barriers.** Structural protective barriers are man-made devices such as fences, bollards, walls, floors, roofs, grills, bars, roadblocks, or other construction that are used to restrict, channel, or impede access. Protective barriers form the perimeter of controlled, limited, and exclusion areas. Utility areas such as water sources, transformer banks, commercial power and fuel connections, heating and power plants, and air-conditioning units may require these barriers for safety. Barriers create a psychological deterrent for anyone thinking of unauthorized entry. They may delay or even prevent passage. This is especially true of barriers against vehicles and forced entry.

2) **Turnstiles.** Turnstiles have been used for many years as a means of controlling entry into a facility. They are simple and often overlooked or not considered for access control. Today, with improved technology, turnstiles can be either mechanical, optical, or video.

   a. Mechanical turnstiles control entry by restricting the direction in which someone can transit the entry point. They can be designed to operate with card readers, coins or tokens, electronic keypads, etc. The advantage of these functions is that they do away with guard control. A suitable barrier must be installed above the top of the turnstile to prevent persons from using it as a step ladder for access over a fence.

   b. Optical turnstiles channel pedestrian traffic into lanes where infrared beams create an invisible electronic field. As pedestrians move through the field they are monitored and information is stored in micro-processors. These electronic fields have the ability to distinguish human beings from objects. This security monitoring equipment is best suited for high volume pedestrian locations such as building lobbies.

   c. Video turnstiles are used extensively in Europe. These are primarily tools used for counting the number of people entering and departing a specific location such as a store or shop, bank, library, restaurant, etc. These turnstiles function by having a closed circuit television camera, which is connected to a computer, located at the entrance to the facility. When someone crosses its path, a count is logged into the computer. Video turnstiles are used when there is a large volume of people and it is important to determine the number of people entering and leaving an establishment.

3) **Lighting.** Security lighting should be used as a psychological deterrent and should also be used along perimeter fences when the situation dictates that the fence be under continuous or periodic observation. Lighting is relatively inexpensive to maintain and reduces the advantages of concealment and surprise for a determined intruder.

   a. Security lighting is desirable for those sensitive areas or facilities within the perimeter that are under observation. Such areas or facilities include loading dock areas, vital buildings, storage areas, parking areas, and vulnerable control points in communication and power- and water-distribution systems. Security lighting has considerable value as a deterrent to thieves and vandals and may make the job of the saboteur more difficult. It is an essential element of an integrated physical-security program.

   b. A secure auxiliary power source and power-distribution system at the facility should be installed to provide redundancy to critical security lighting and other security equipment.

   c. When planning for security lighting, the facility manager should consider the following.[5]

- Cost of replacing lamps and cleaning fixtures, as well as the cost of providing the required equipment (such as ladders and lifts) to perform this maintenance
- Provision of manual-override capability during a blackout, including photoelectric controls
- Effects of local weather conditions on lighting systems
- Fluctuating or erratic voltages in the primary power source
- Grounding requirements
- Provisions for rapid lamp replacement
- Use of lighting to support a CCTV system

- Re-strike time (the time required before the light will function properly after a brief power interruption)
- Illumination and color. Metal halide, white light, is now the preferred light for security
d. CCTV-Camera lighting requirements. The following considerations apply when lighting systems are intended to support CCTV assessment or surveillance.[6]
- Camera's field of view
- Lighting intensity levels
- Maximum light-to-dark ratio
- Scene reflectance
- Daylight-to-darkness transitions
- Camera mounting systems relative to lighting
- Camera's spectral response
- Cold-start time
- Re-strike time

Human Deterrents

Screening job applicants is important to eliminate potential acts of espionage, sabotage, and other security risks. Personnel screening should be incorporated into standard personnel policies. An applicant should be required to complete a personnel security questionnaire, which should then be screened for completeness and used to eliminate undesirable applicants. A careful investigation should be conducted to ensure that the applicant's character, associations, and suitability for employment are satisfactory.

1. Medical screening should be considered (based on an applicant's position) to evaluate physical and mental stamina. Once an applicant has been identified for employment, he is placed on an access-control roster.
2. An identification (ID) system is established at a facility to provide a method of identifying personnel. The system provides for personal recognition and the use of security ID cards or badges to aid in the control and movement of personnel activities.
3. Standard ID cards are generally acceptable for access into areas that are unrestricted and have no security interest. Personnel requiring access to restricted areas should be issued a security ID card or badge.
4. Employees are familiar with those who should be in the work area. Once trained, they will become more observant and will report suspicious activity. In today's environment, this is an accepted fact in the business world.

Psychological Deterrents

1. Perception. An effective component of any physical security plan is the perception of the security measures being taken. In many instances, *perception is reality*.

2. Perceived Impediments. Even an organization with the best security available is a failure if its employees, customers, vendors, and contractors do not feel safe. Organizations that communicate with employees regularly and consider the impact of perception when developing their security plans are more apt to have the plan accepted. These organizations ensure that specific guidelines are included in the design of their physical security systems which address perception. Using the concept of CPTED reduces anxiety and changes the way employees feel about their work environment.

Lock Security

1. Lock Systems. Every organization should establish minimum lock and key control measures. Key security is a low-tech security solution, but it remains the prevalent means of protection for people and property. However, electronic access control is quickly becoming a preferred security solution for exterior doors and high risk areas. Cost for electronic access remains the driving factor; therefore, most organizations today opt for a combination of electronic access and traditional lock and key access. Electronic access control is most effective when installed at entrances used by a high volume of people. Traditional locks and keys are better suited for low trafficked areas such as individual offices, residential, or student rooms.[7]

There are positives and negatives to using traditional keys. On the positive side, keys are familiar to most people. They are accustomed to hearing them jingle in their pockets and purses. The negatives include: they are easily misplaced and lost, they can be broken off in the lock core, and locks can be easily disabled by vandalism.

When master and sub-master individual keys are lost, obviously all locks accessible by the lost key must be changed. Heavy duty industrial hardware should always be used because it is heavier construction and usually offers a wider range of locking operations. Pin-tumbler locks are considered the best alternative. Locks having six and seven pin tumblers are among the most secure and versatile today and allow for easy expansion of the master system. The advantage of using six and seven pin tumbler locks is that a master and sub-master key system can be used. This means that a complex of offices can have each office on a different key with all offices openable by one key which remains in possession of a security or management official.

Should a key be lost, it becomes a relatively simple matter to change the lock core and make a new and different key. For specific information on lock hardware and exit device standards see the American National Standards Institute and Builders Hardware Manufacturers Association (ANSI/BHMA) standards A156 and A156.30, which is available on the Internet.

2. Lock Bumping. Lock bumping is a technique used to open door locks. This technique was formally publicized in the early 1970s when Danish locksmiths announced they could override lock cylinders by *bumping* or *knocking* a lock. This became public knowledge in Europe in 2002–2003 and spread to the United States around 2006. The technique involves the use of a hammer to tap the back of a lock bumping key which causes the tumbler pins inside the cylinder to jump and slide out, freely allowing the tumbler to turn.

Today, the internet offers information on lock bumping and how to purchase bumping keys. This is becoming the new security threat for conventional mechanical locks. Using a *bumping key,* intruders can disable a conventional mechanical lock in seconds and gain entry to a space with no sign of forced entry. Using high security locks will prevent bumping.[8]

3. Keyless Locks. Keyless locks are becoming more prevalent. One simple reason is they cannot be bumped as discussed previously. Some are hard wired, others operate wirelessly. When selecting these types of locks, it is advisable to include a key override to gain access in the event the keyless portion of the lock ceases to operate.

Magnetic stripe and proximity cards are being used more and more frequently. The major advantage to using these cards is their convenience and controllability. They can be easily programmed or de-programmed from one central computer. Installation cost is still high, but wireless technology will be a major factor in reducing the cost.

Information Security

In the last ten years, information security has taken on new and important meaning. Information security breaches have exposed millions of individual records and operating systems to criminals and terrorists. Facility managers should work closely with their information technology counterparts to develop training programs for educating organization personnel on the need for data security.

Facility Electronic Security

1. Duress Alarms. Duress alarms are used to signal a life-threatening emergency. They often are identified by terms such as: panic alarm system, personal alarm system, man down system, emergency nurse call system, and employee security system. These alarm systems have a myriad of applications but are most commonly used as senior citizen personal alarms, correction facility officer personal alarms, epilepsy alarms, environmental hazardous emergency alarms, and personal security alarms. They can be fixed or portable and are usually manually operated.[9]

 A. Fixed duress devices are mechanical switches mounted at inconspicuous locations such as under a desk top or on the floor. They can be easily activated by a push button, or foot operated if located on the floor.
 B. Portable duress devices are wireless and consist of a transmitter and receiver. The transmitter is usually small enough that it can be worn or carried. The receiver is positioned in a fixed location within the facility and transmits a signal or is hardwired to an alarm monitoring station.

2. Electronic Entry Alarms.

 A. **Electronic detection systems.** These should be capable of detecting individuals crossing a detection zone by walking, crawling, jumping, running, rolling, or climbing a fence. Current technology includes active infrared, microwave, buried line (e.g. fiber optic and coaxial cable), fence-mounted sensors, video motion detection, linear beam (e.g. electronic fence), and glass-break sensors (e.g. acoustic and shock).[10]
 B. **Door and hatch contact alarm switches.** Electric strike locks should be used for interior doors. Magnetic door contact switches should be installed at all building exterior doors to monitor doors which are propped or forced open. Care must be exercised in designing for the use of these locks on doors used for egress to ensure egress is permitted at all times, especially with fire alarm activations. Exterior facility locations such as entry hatches or equipment vaults should be equipped with high security magnetic switches. Industrial doors and roll-up doors should have high security wide gap magnetic switches.[11]

3. Biometrics. Biometric devices are used to control entry based on the measurement of one or more physical or personal characteristics of an individual. They consist of a reader and scanning device, software which converts the collected information into digital form, and a storage database for future retrieval. This technology is spreading and is currently used for time and attendance reporting, facility access, and signature verification. Some organizations are now combining biometrics with smart card usage to raise the level of security and minimize breaches. Various types of usage of biometrics are depicted below.[12]

A. **Fingerprint Scan.** An individual's fingerprint is scanned and matched against what is stored in the organization's database. It is used for positive verification of the individual for access to a space, verification of time and attendance, permission of access to equipment and sensitive records, desktop usage, and transportation. Its use is limited only by our capacity to find ways to use it.

B. **Iris Recognition.** This is the most accurate of all biometric technologies. It's used primarily in high security locations such as government and private research centers, correctional facilities, and financial institutions.

C. **Hand Geometry.** This technology is used in high security facilities where there is an expectation of a harsh environment such as extremely cold or hot temperatures. Examples include nuclear facilities, construction sites, or maximum security correctional facilities.

D. **Facial Recognition.** This biometric technology is continuing to evolve. It is not used extensively today, but that will change with time and improvements. Currently, three dimensional technology (3-D) is being developed, it will be integrated with improved lighting capacity, and will have the ability to rotate an image. This technology appears to be the future of biometrics as far as application and acceptance. It is discreet and passive.

E. **Other Biometric Technology.** There are many variations of biometric technology, including voice biometrics, signature biometrics, and DNA biometrics.

4. Closed Circuit Television (CCTV).

A. Technological improvements in CCTV now provide for network integration. This means that millions of camera video images can either be hosted on a computer server or, in newer systems, stored internally in the camera. These systems also can access live or recorded video.

B. These digital systems now enable quick and easy locating of images in the database based on the time of the incident. Other capabilities include the triggering of cameras based on motion detection or alarm activations. Some jurisdictions, for example large cities such as Los Angeles or Las Vegas, are now requiring visual confirmation of an activated alarm prior to responding.

C. Real time visual camera images can also be sent to Personal Digital Assistants (PDAs), cell phones, and e-mail, any place in the world.

D. Command centers where camera images are centralized now use intelligent video technology to help with monitoring. It is impossible for individuals to monitor hundreds and even thousands of camera images. Therefore, integration software techniques being used today include camera activation based on specific criteria such as unusual individual behavior, known as behavior recognition, which tracks pedestrians, intruders, and vehicles. This sophisticated software activates cameras when an activity falls outside established parameters. It can be used to create electronic fences that would activate a camera when someone crosses an electronic boundary. Because the fence is electronic, a chain link fence is not needed, thus maintaining the aesthetics of the grounds.

Employee Protective Measures

1. Insider Threat.

Security intrusions or thefts by employees amount to several billion dollars annually. Many companies prefer to believe such security breaches or thefts are really not happening or would not happen to them. Often, employers will not take action against offenders, and they are even reluctant to impose additional security measures to lessen losses. Measures that will improve security and lessen theft should always be considered. Exhibit 22-3 lists the actions that employers should take.

Exhibit 22-3. Employer Protective Actions

- Conduct careful pre-employment screening.
- Consider implementing a company sales program for surplus equipment. Ensure computer equipment is wiped clean of data before being sold or given to charitable organizations.
- Apply well-publicized disciplinary action for those caught stealing.
- Control employee and visitor pedestrian traffic through entrances.
- Maintain tight inventory control.
- Utilize an organization property pass system for removal of all organization property from the premises.
- Install signage at all entrances stating that packages, and vehicles entering the area inside the organization's perimeter, are subject to periodic searches.
- Shipping and receiving areas should be off limits to unauthorized employees.

---

2. Emergency Phones.

Emergency phones (also known as emergency call boxes) can be installed anywhere because of technology today. Wireless cellular capabilities enable these emergency communications systems to be located in remote locations such as elevators, parking garages, parking lots, sidewalks, and along isolated roads. These phones must be clearly identifiable from a distance because they are to be used for true emergencies. They should be easily activated by simply pressing a button or removing the receiver from its cradle.

Notes

1. Freidenfelds, L., "Real Needs Must Drive Security Integration," *Building Operating Management Magazine,* October 2004, p. 51.
2. U.S. Army Field Manual 3-19.30, *Physical Security,* January 8, 2001, p. 6–40.
3. Freidenfelds, L., "Real Needs Must Drive Security Integration," *Building Operating Management Magazine,* October 2004, p. 51.
4. Page, D., "The Last Line of Defense," *Homeland Protection Professional,* July 15, 2006. See Website www.homeland1.com/columnists/doug_page/articles/350127
5. U.S. Army Field Manual 3-19.30, *Physical Security,* January 8, 2001, p. 5–1.
6. Ibid., p. 5–4.
7. Kennedy, M., "The Key to Security," *American School and University Magazine,* September 2001, p. 34C.
8. Lock Bumping. See www.lockbumping.org
9. U.S. Army Field Manual 3-19.30, *Physical Security,* January 8, 2001, p. 6–28.
10. Ibid., Chapter 6
11. Ibid., Chapter 6.
12. Freschi, C., "Biometrics technology Touches the Future," *Security Magazine,* November 2007, p. 94.

References

American National Standards Institute (ANSI). See www.ansi.org

American Society for Testing and Materials (ASTM). See www.astm.org

Builders Hardware Manufacturers Association. See www.buildershardware.com

National Fire Protection Association (NFPA) 101, "Life Safety Code"; NFPA 101B, "Code for Means for Egress for Buildings and Structures".

U.S. Army Corps of Engineers (USACE) Publications. See www.hnd.usace.army.mil/TECHINFO/engpubs.htm

Operations and Maintenance

Some facility managers look at existing space as merely something to be tolerated until the next alteration. Some even shun operations and maintenance, perhaps because they think those functions tie them too closely to the boiler room. One of our themes, in fact, is that facility managers need to be more business oriented. The fact is we deal with the built environment and facilities need to be operated and maintained. Space is in play at all times; it is being maintained, repaired, altered, or renovated constantly. Furniture is moved, exchanged, or replaced. New signage replaces old. Light fixtures are relamped.

Operations and maintenance is the high volume part of our business. A medium-sized, major headquarters can have 50,000 requests for service annually and four times that number of preventive maintenance items corrected. Not only is it high volume but each of those service requests has a customer depending upon us to respond effectively and we hope to do it efficiently.

This is a major effort that needs to be organized well and made to run like clockwork while avoiding bureacracy and poor customer service. Operations and maintenance are big business and important business. There is no greater challenge than to provide quality services at minimal cost around the clock which seems to be the standard against which operators and maintainers are judged.

Two issues have dominated operations and maintenance throughout our professional lives. One is that maintenance and repair is consistently underfunded, often while organizations are expanding their capital expenditures. A university facility manager supposedly said, "Everyone is anxious to endow a new building, but no one ever endowed a maintenance and repair contract." Studies that document the under-funding of maintenance and repair abound, particularly in the public sector, yet the situation continues to worsen. This is an area of crisis for the profession. There are glimmers of hope, but so far, no widespread realization that our facility infrastructure needs the level of funding for proper operations and maintenance.

Second, because we have not consistently used life-cycle costing or solicited the advice of operators and maintainers during design and construction of facilities, we are faced with larger operations and maintenance challenges than need be. This is an area where there is widespread agreement on the desirability of using good sustainability principles to produce the most economic and functional design.

In recent years, as facility managers have downsized and outsourced, it appears to us that they have both outsourced and downsized the operations and maintenance function to a greater degree than the other functions of facility management.

This downward spiral must be reversed.

23

Contracting and Types of Contracts

Pulse Points

- *Contractor evaluation criteria should reflect what is truly important to the facility staff and their customers.*
- *Partnering requires a well developed system and procedures to be successful. Above all, it takes a commitment to make it work.*
- *Contracts applicable to construction and major alteration are probably not best suited to contracting for operations and maintenance.*

The ability to effectively and efficiently contract has always been a required skill of the facility manager. Before the term "contracting out," now called outsourcing, had ever been heard, facility managers contracted for specialized needs and for large renovation and construction. No facility department had every capability and the capacity for surges of work within its internal workforce so these services had to be contracted.

One of the major topics of the past twenty years within facility management has been outsourcing. When companies are willing to contract out their accounting department, for example, it is not surprising that the facility department is a candidate for outsourcing. If you are not core business, you had better perform your own analysis of the costs and benefits of contracting out because if you don't, someone else will do it for you.

We are unabashed advocates of outsourcing. The reasons most often given for outsourcing are:

- Outsourcing saves money, particularly if the in-house staff have high benefits.
- A contracted workforce can better adjust to fluctuations in work. They have a surge capability.

- Contractor personnel provide better access to higher-quality skills.
- With the decline of both quality and quantity in the technical labor pool, outsourcing reduces the time that the facility manager must spend on personnel matters.
- Large contractors can use their size to get price breaks on supplies and services.
- Outsourcing allows the organization to concentrate on its core business.
- The number of organizational employees is reduced, a desirable feature for organizations who want to appear "lean and mean."
- Particularly in the public sector, you save authorized personnel spaces.
- With outsourcing, the company can provide services or a level of service that in-house personnel cannot.
- Outstanding contractors exist nearly everywhere. In fact, certain companies have grown to meet the outsourcing trend in our industry.

Having said that, we should add that there are good reasons *not* to outsource some functions. For instance, no contractor should do strategic facility business planning. Also, many companies have facilities whose operations are so sensitive that the facility staff serving them needs to be company employees (although that type of facility does not occur as often as you might think). You must not, as our friend Martha Whitaker says, "outsource your soul."

Most of the objections to outsourcing concern the loss of control or the fact that the workforce will be less loyal to management if contracted. Certainly a judgment needs to be made by every organization when considering outsourcing, but our observation is that facility managers tend to be too conservative when outsourcing. Pressed to cut costs and personnel spaces, we should use our limited resources for top-flight in-house contract managers and planners who have technical supervisory experience while outsourcing the technical work and on-site supervision. Another absolutely essential staff member is an accountant who specializes in facility accounts. Preferably this individual works for you but, at a minimum, should be located with you. Thankfully, certain types of contracts and contractors have developed to provide the facility manager with exactly the workforce needed, provided he can properly define what is needed. In fact, some contract forms give the facility manager great flexibility in staffing provided that he and the contractor will partner to ensure mutual success.

In almost all of the services offered by the facility department (discussed in Chapters 24–27) contracting to a third party is a viable option. The trend has consistently been to go in this direction. Most organizations end up doing what they feel comfortable with or what they are forced into by upper management. Regardless of the motivation for outsourcing, the organization must decide three issues: (1) what level of control is desired, (2) what level of service is required, and (3) what response level is required. If these can be met by a contract, the organization is probably better off contracting out as long as specifications ensure the services. In most cases, three- to five-year service contracts are best. Contracting annually to exclusively low bidders tends, over several rebids, to ratchet quality down to an unacceptable point.

We have never been advocates of selling outsourcing for its large cost savings. Cost savings from contracting out can be illusory. Make sure the contracts minimize the facility manager's administrative time, allow for more flexibility in matching resources and workload, and produce the efficiencies and economies of scale on large contacts. If you are satisfied with the effectiveness of an in-house service, try to capture those procedures in your outsourcing contract. Unless you have no alternative, be reluctant to adopt a sample contract that your outsourcing contractor may hand you as a "good model contract that is working well with my last client."

According to the Outsourcing Institute, the following are the most important factors in contracting out:

- Understanding company goals and objectives
- A strategic vision and plan
- Selecting the right vendor
- Ongoing management of relationships
- A properly structured contract
- Open communications with affected individuals and groups
- Senior executive support and involvement
- Careful attention to personnel issues
- Near-term financial justification
- Use of outside experts[1]

Each of those factors has it's own applicability to a particular situation, but we would like to mention several key aspects. Traditional low-bid, adversarial contracting will not work. Perhaps formal partnering is not necessary, but when you are widely outsourced, your contractor is now your staff. We are convinced that a facility manager can get as much loyalty from a contract staff as from in-house staff. It all depends upon establishing a work relationship. It is our experience that each principal contractor should have a superintendent—or foreman-level individual on-site with the authority to speak for the contractor on 90 percent of the contractual and staffing issues and 100 percent of the operational issues that will arise. The facility manager and the contractor should, early in the contract, meet frequently to iron out the kinks. These meetings should soon need to be less and less frequent . . . or you have the wrong contractor. It is our experience that many contractors are not used to being treated as contributing partners to accomplish the mission and initially may need assurances from you that that is your intention.

If possible, facility managers should go slow in outsourcing, and use fact-based decision making. You are so much better off if you know your true costs of doing the services that you want to contract, to include distributed overheads. That sounds elemental, but too many outsourcing decisions have not been made when they should have or have failed to produce promised savings solely because the cost figures for current operations were fallacious.

Once the decision is made to outsource, the facility manager should work with the procurement staff to outsource one function at a time rather than the whole department at once. One of the most important things to do, and one of the most difficult, is to be honest with staff and to keep them informed as the outsourcing analysis proceeds. No facility manager should ever get in the position of promising staff continued employment, but he should be sensitive to their concerns.

In the last publicly published Annual Outsourcing Index, the Outsourcing Institute found that price was the top criteria for selecting a contractor followed by commitment to quality, flexibility in contract terms, the contractor's reputation and/or references, and its scope of resources.[2] This survey was taken during a slow economic period similar to what we are experiencing today. Interestingly, medium-sized organizations were less concerned about cost than very large ones or small ones; their principal concern was quality.

Just as you wouldn't send your child to a school without first checking its credentials and talking with the teachers, don't pick a service provider out of the phone book. Do some research, talk to their management, and get a list of previous customers (who match your contracting needs as closely as possible) from the potential contractors. And check out their employees, who may be working for you soon.

Types of contracts-We have already discussed in Chapter 15, the types of contracts suitable for major alterations and construction. Soon after companies started to consider outsourcing, the military actually developed a contract form which fit the model for small construction and alterations jobs, operations, and maintenance. It was called IDIQ, indefinite demand, indefinite quantity, contracting and seemed ideal for facility management. Facility managers, and finally their procurement counterparts, realized that the traditional forms of contracting often did not work when contracting for continuing or for unique services the demand for which ebbed and flowed. In other words, the facility manager knew he was going to want service X, or sometimes supply item Y, during the next three years but did not know exactly when or in what quantity. Other FMs, wanted a form of contract for services or supplies that they could call for in an emergency or crisis. IDIQ contracts are for a fixed period (the base) usually with optional extensions if service is performed well. The contract defines what services are desired during the base period and specifies how services can be obtained through the issuance of a task order and who is authorized to issue such a task order. Payment is at a fixed rate with, perhaps, an escalator clause for inflation.

The exact origin of IDIQ contracting is uncertain but it was first widely used within the U.S. Department of Defense and finally through the entire U.S. federal government before it became popular in the private sector.[3] Interestingly, its growth parallels the growth of facility management probably as facility managers realized the inherent advantages of the IDIQ contracts. This accelerated as FM services were increasingly contracted out because of the ease of use of the IDIQ for those services where the type of service was well known but quantity over the next year, for example, was not. Interestingly, several companies, influenced often by retiring military officers who joined their ranks, developed business units specifically focused on IDIQ contracting.

After a number of years, entrepreneurs started to fine tune IDIQ contracting and developed the job order contract, JOC. Again, most of the development of JOC occurred in the public sector but soon private industry began to use JOC and JOC contractors appeared. A JOC contract follows certain procedures leading to an agreement focusing on achieving good work performance and reasonable costs. It consists of the following elements:

- Standard specifications established in the master contract with a summary of work, also including any specific or client-driven conditions.
- Construction item costs specified in a Unit Price Book.
- Facility manager issues a Request for Qualifications (RFQ), evaluating firms using best-value, performance-based criteria, or an Invitation to Bid awarded to the lowest responsive and responsible bidder. (More about this later).
- A minimum amount of work is guaranteed for the contractor. This is usually a small amount for consideration—a requirement in most states for contracts. (This might, for instance be $25,000 in a total JOC contract of $5,000,000 which is a real incentive to the contractor to perform well because if the FM is unhappy with your work, he may issue another JOC contract for the same services and give the first contractor just the minimum).
- Issuance of contractor's work orders based on owner's requirements.
- Cost for work orders based on standard specifications, unit costs, and the contractor's co-efficient. (This co-efficient is critical for the contractor because it must cover overhead, profit, and unexpected costs, yet be low enough to make him competitive)

- Open communications between the facilities team and JOC contracting team, including a kick-off partnering session between everyone utilizing he contract.[4]

It is our experience that, in a satisfactory JOC or IDIQ contract, the contractor stands to gain a substantial amount of work not covered in the master contract because 1) he is on the ground and 2) he has a proven record of performance.

The major advantages of job order contacting are:

- Fast and timely delivery of projects and services and occasional supplies.
- Low overhead cost of service procurement and delivery.
- Development of a partner relationship based on work performance.
- Reduced legal fees.
- ELIMINATION OF CHANGE ORDERS!!!!!
- Standard pricing and specification familiar to both parties resulting in efficient and effective estimating, design, and fixed price service contracting.[5]

JOC contracting, rather than IDIQ, is normally used when there is a higher mix of minor construction and alterations rather than routine operations and maintenance. However, both are as flexible as the procurement gurus will allow. One of your authors, because of time restraints, gutted and refurbished an urban office building using an IDIQ contract and saved an estimated one-third of the build-out design and construction costs because his procurement officer allowed him to triple the estimated three year amount of the contract in one year. So, good IDIQ and JOC contracting requires not only good FM-contractor cooperation but good cooperation between the organization's FM, legal, and procurement personnel.

Best Value Procurement-As JOC spread and developed, a professor at Arizona State University, Dr. Dean Kashiwagi, (and later his compatriot, Dr. Bill Badger) took an interest in developing JOC to its fullest. During their work, Dr. Dean focused on the relationship between the facility manager and the contractor and later expanded it to all contracting. His research revealed the following (among other similar conclusions):

- Performance has no proven relationship to price.
- The source of the majority of problems is the "low bid" award process.
- Tests have shown that best value construction provides 98 percent performance in terms of meeting the schedule, budget, and quality expectations of the client.

Based on these conclusions (and considering the input of the major management minds of the last twenty years and the leadership concepts of Dr. Badger),

Dr. Kashiwagi founded the Performance Based Studies Research Group at Arizona State University in the late 80s and developed the Performance Information Procurement System (PIPS), a best value delivery process in 1991. He has tested it in 530 contracts (the first was on a roofing system contract) and it has proven successful in new construction, design and consulting services, major construction, operations and maintenance, systems replacement, dining services, and even marketing and consulting in both the private and public sectors.[6] Interestingly, and as was found with IDIQ and JOC, some contractors now advertise that they are PIPS-qualified. Because you must be committed to best value procurement (and trained in it if you do not understand it), we are reluctant to unqualifiedly recommend it but we absolutely agree with its approach to contracting and that, in order to operate a primarily contracted organization (and that is the trend), we must work cooperatively in a win-win relationship with our contractor while always ensuring the sanctity of the contract.

IDIQ, JOC, and best-value contracts are the principal examples of systems designed to solve 90–95 percent of the FM's problems by good organization so that the FM can concentrate on the remaining problems which really need personal intervention. Another result of performance-based contracting is that good contractors love it and find that it produces steady work, more work than expected, and high profit because we squeeze the inefficiencies out of the system.[7]

Methods of Contracting Services-If the facility manager decides to contract for services, there are multiple ways to do it. One is to contract for a specific project based on a given set of specifications. This is the way that we contract for major construction and alterations. The alternative is to sign for services or supplies for a given period based on a listing of unit costs for those services as discussed in IDIQ and JOC above. Particularly the first time you contract this way, select two to five contractors as qualified (don't offer them a contract) so that, if your choice does not work out, you can easily contract with an alternate source. Remember, all you agreed to with your original selectee was a minimal dollar amount that you can expend over the base period of the contract. We have experienced high volume periods when we actually needed two different contractors performing the same type of work.

Our preference is to gather services into broad groups like custodial, or electrical services, or building maintenance for contracting. Our experience is that, though there are efficiencies of scale, asking one contractor to provide all services lowers performance. We require the contractor to provide an on-site superintendent (foreman for smaller contracts) and all first line supervision but the facility management staff assumes responsibility for work assignments, quality control, and therefore, cost control but this is our preference, not necessarily inherent in either IDIQ or JOC.

One note of caution for those who employ contractors. The Internal Revenue Service investigates cases in which companies convert staff into contract positions or hire new staff as private contractors to avoid paying the employer portion of the social security tax. Sometimes in a unionized shop, such situations will be reported by the union. Be careful to observe the "duck rule" "If it looks like a duck and quacks like a duck, then it's probably a duck." Contract employees normally (1) work for a contractor's supervisor, and (2) are subject to be moved to other job sites. If the only reason to convert a staff position is to avoid taxation and the person continues to function like an employee, the company could be liable. We have, however, hired contractor management and additional supervisory personnel for short periods when we had a peak workload.

It is worthwhile to discuss the need for the facility manager to define both his requirements and the quality of the contractor needed to meet those requirements. Often when there is unhappiness with the procurement process or with a contractor's performance, the root problem is in inadequate specification or selection criteria.

The evaluation criteria and their comparative weights must reflect what is truly important to the facility manager (references, bonding capability, financial stability, stability of the workforce, ability to perform a specialized task), particularly if pre-qualification is used. Then the facility manager must set the cutoff score low enough so he will retain competition yet high enough to eliminate those with whom he cannot live. This sensitive process, of which the facility manager is only one participant, explains why procurement is an art, not a science. Time spent on properly defining a requirement, and on properly stating and weighting selection criteria, will not only lead to much smoother bidder evaluation process, but will probably secure a better contractor.

Some purchasing departments and facility managers burden themselves with one-year term service contracts. Our experience is that a three-year term contract with two one-year options and pricing tied to a local pricing index is almost ideal because it provides continuity of service, yet ensures the continuation of competitive pricing.

Too many facility managers abrogate their responsibilities and rights in service contracting. Like all other functions, service contracting needs to be managed, and the facility manager must understand that clearly and exercise his responsibilities.

Placement of the Procurement Officer-Most facility management organizations do not have a procurement officer and/or purchasing agent assigned. These individuals are so important to the facility managers, increasingly so as we outsource. If assignment is impossible, consider co-location of the procurement personnel. If co-location is not possible, then the facility manager must spend time training the procurement staff in our unique contracting needs.

Contractor and Consultant Evaluation-Service contractors and consultants should be competitively evaluated as part of the procurement process. When negotiation or directed procurement (sole sourcing) is not allowed, use a two step procedure when the dollar cost of the procurement (say $250,000) justifies it. The first step is an evaluation of technical ability, references, insurability, and financial capability of your contractor or consultant. The second step is to evaluate four to six short-listed candidates using the results of an interview, previously submitted material, and costing information.

How are these evaluations to be scored? Many public agencies unfortunately are tied to selecting the contractor or consultant submitting the lowest bid (and that is fine for well-defined, non-controversial requirements). Except for those simply defined tasks, it is preferable to use the "most qualified" method and allocate 30–45 percent of the total score to price. In this way, the number of points allocated to the pricing of each contractor is calculated as follows:

$$\text{Score of contractor} = \text{Max score (points)} - \text{max score} \times (.5)(TS - LC)/LC$$

where: TS = Price on contractor being evaluated

LC = Price of lowest contractor

If you are interested in best value contracting, the evaluation system is more complex. Actually, you have some ability to pick and choose among the procedures, but at least for the first time, it is somewhat more time consuming and complex because all of the players need to get educated. An excellent step-by-step procedure is spelled out in Dr. Dean Kashiwagi's *Best Value Procurement, Second Edition,* pp. 8–12 through 8–64.

Partnering-A facility manager who tries to manage a fully contracted department through a low-bid contract that emphasizes the adversarial relationship with the contractor is doomed to fail. In a largely contracted-out organization, the facility manager needs to consider contractor personnel, at least from an operational point of view as "his," members of the FM team. He has no real alternative but to do so. The facility manager must work with the contractor's on-site management or supervision to provide customers seamless, customer-oriented service. Anything in the contract or his relationship with the contractor that gets in the way of serving customers has to be changed. Mutual focus on customers is the essence of partnering. This is not mere rhetoric. We have managed a completely outsourced situation and we practiced what we preach here . . . and it works to the advantage of customers.

That philosophy deemphasizes the importance of the form of the contract and emphasizes results. Initially, this may be difficult. First, if the organization has a centralized procurement function, the contact there may be reluctant to deviate from the strict wording of the contract to allow mutual give and take which inevitably must occur. Second, no contract is perfect the first time. The facility manager needs to understand that and act accordingly, working with the contractor to create winwin situations. Regularly scheduled operational reviews with the contractor are very helpful. In some cases, the facility manager must be willing to give, expecting the contractor to do so in the future. If that doesn't occur, this may be the wrong contractor.

For every major contract, you should have the contractor provide a manager, supervisor, or established foreman on site (your choice since you pay). That individual must have the ability to speak for the contractor on all operational matters. After about six months, the contractor's front office becomes not much more than a pay and personnel office for our contracts. You should meet with the contractor's front office personnel only when you have a problem, or quarterly, to ensure they understand where you are going as a department and how it affects their contract.

The facility manager must be confident in his ability to administer contracts so that he can manage the fine line between cooperation with the contractor and keeping that contractor at arms length. When faced with conflicts (and they will come up), he can resolve it by determining what is best for his customers. Partnering can so easily become conflict of interest, inch by inch. We constantly stress cooperation with our contractors but the facility manager must be ever alert to conflicts of interest be they a lunch, baseball tickets, or a weekend at a posh resort.

This concept works as well for supplies as it does for services. One very large facility management organization turned all of its supply activities over to the local supply house. After a few initial problems, they were amazed to find that they got their materials faster, with less paperwork, and at a lower price because of the contractor's expertise and muscle in the local marketplace. Others, of course, have their contractors supply their own materials and, in special situations, supplies which the facilities staff need.

Some organizations like to have formal partnering agreements with their contractors. Often these agreements address open and effective communications, how problems and disagreements will be resolved, use of the team approach, trust in both the experience and commitment of all team members, and the goal to which all are committed.

Successful partnering is dependent on a team approach to common goals, with both partners able to talk frankly and as equals. We have always been the most successful by motivating the contractor toward exceptional behavior and performance. To most contractors, the greatest incentive is a contract extension with a suitable price adjustment. For a contractor who is performing exceptionally, that is a major plus. For us, department stability is a major payoff.

On the other side of the ledger, not all contractors are capable of being good partners. In our experience, one very fine performing company had to be dropped because its president would not let go and let his on-site supervisor meet our customers' needs. There are as many challenges for the contractor in partnering as for the facility manager.

Outsourcing and partnering are inextricably tied to one another. The modern facility manager needs to be a contract manager extraordinaire. In all but the exceptional case, his success will depend on how well he orchestrates a primarily outsourced workforce to meet organizational goals. It is a different management model, but one that can work exceptionally well as long as the transition to it is slow, thoughtful, and uses facts, not opinion.

Automation-An issue which is hard to address in specifications is the degree to which the facility management team will use automation and whose automation will be used. Large, full service contractors tend to want to use their own automation system when they move into a new organization, the system which they are used to but then they have none of your building data in their system. Also, once building data is in the contractor's automated system, they have a powerful bargaining chip which gives them a leg up at the next re-bid. If the owner's system is outdated or overtaxed, the decision becomes somewhat easier but we recommend using the owner's system until the decision is made whether to change out the system and then who is to purchase the system. This scenario needs to be thought out carefully and provided for in the pre-bid analysis.

Notes

1. Outsourcing Institute, www.outsourcing.com.
2. *Seventh Annual Outsourcing Index, 2002,* Outsourcing Institute, www.outsourcing.com.
3. Wilkinson, Kevin J., "More Effective Federal Procurement Response to Disasters: Maximizing the Extraordinary Flexibilities of IDIQ Contracting," Air Force Law Review, Spring 2007.

4. Greenhouse, Bunnatine H., "IDIQ Contracts," June 2000, from Department of Defense Acquisition Community Connection website at https:// acc.dau.mil/CommunityBrowser.aspx?id=44463, accessed May 23, 2009.

5. Ibid.

6. Dean Kashiwagi, *Best Value Procurement, Second Edition*, (Tempe, AZ; Performance Based Studies Research Group; 2008), p. 8–1.

7. Charlie Serakawa, "A Review of the University of Hawaii's Best Value Projects," *Performance Based Newsletter*, Performance Based Studies Research Group, December 2, 2007, p. 1.

24

Work Coordination

Pulse Points

- *The Work Reception Center (WRC) is the facility department's eyes and ears, receiving requests and prioritizing work.*
- *The Work Reception Center can be the means to control and manage a charge-back system.*
- *Because of the volume of work already handled there, the Work Reception Center, "the heartbeat of facility management," is an ideal place to locate the department's service evaluation function.*
- *Work reception personnel should be trained and procedures should be developed so that 90–97 percent of the workflow can be handled routinely without managerial input.*
- *One of the greatest challenges to the facility manager is to ensure that the Work Reception Center remains customer service friendly and does not become bureaucratized.*
- *The Work Reception Center, if properly located and protected and with augmented communications, is an ideal Emergency Management Center.*

As vice president of Facilities West, the late Art Hahn promoted good facility management through what he called pulse points, or critical operations. One of these pulse points is the *work reception and coordination center* (WRC), the eyes and ears of the facility department. It is the single point where all, or nearly all, facility services are received, prioritized, tasked, coordinated, and evaluated. One of your authors refers to the WRC as the "heartbeat of FM."

No matter the size of the organization, the WRC can provide a full complement of services. In the smallest organizations, the WRC is often the assistant to the facility manager. In large organizations, the WRC may be a separate work unit (see Exhibit 24-1). Managing the WRC is a high-stress job requiring frequent breaks and probably rotation after a period of time. One way to relieve battle fatigue is to hire

Exhibit 24-1. Work reception and coordination center.

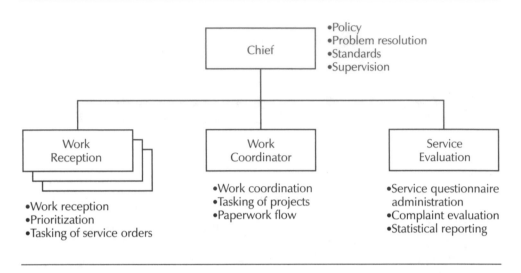

service receptionists from a temporary agency and rotate them after about six months. Another approach is to rotate a mix of nonmanagerial technical staff through the WRC on three-to six-month details. The latter builds widespread mission appreciation within the entire organization.

Under one operating concept, employees trained in telephone techniques operate within a rigid framework, normally a checklist. The stress here is on accurately gathering and passing on information to the appropriate service provider. The second approach is to employ service receptionists who understand completely the operations and nuances of the facility department. On the surface this would appear to be preferable, but it tends to reduce the volume of requests that can be handled and occasionally causes conflicts because the service receptionists start to make judgments beyond their knowledge.

Excellent WRCs can operate under both concepts; whichever is used, training and quality control are essential. If the work receptionists are not controlled, management decisions will be usurped, with the facility manager unaware.

Equipped with the proper automated system, the WRC can also be the center for the invoicing of all chargebacks. Some facility managers have made their WRC the chargeback enforcers. By its nature, it is at the core of the gathering of information for calculating unit costs and benchmarks. If the department is so equipped, the service orders for all preventive and cyclic maintenance can be both generated and closed at the WRC. Finally, it should be the hub of the department's service evaluation.

Work Prioritization and Flow

The premise of a WRC is that the receptionists have the authority to task the routine work of the department. Priorities vary from organization to organization and from time to time; however, most WRCs prioritize work by importance, dollar value, and complexity.

Prioritization by criticality involves determining whether work requested is needed to protect life or property (priority 1), is detrimental to operations (priority 2), or is routine (priority 3). Typically, priority 1 requests are handled immediately by telephone. Priority 2 requests are tasked on a written service order and the work accomplished within one workday. Routine service orders (priority 3) are also tasked by a written request, with the work accomplished in three to five workdays.

Prioritization by dollar value is purely a policy matter, and recognizes that, above a certain level of funding (say, $1,500 to $2,000), management and/or the design team scrutinizes the assignment before it is tasked. Another somewhat more complicated alternative is to limit the effort (one to two workdays, typically) that can go into a service order.

Prioritization by complexity is also a matter of policy. Typically, any task that changes the form or function of the facilities is not immediately tasked for implementation, even though the dollar cost may be small. It is first sent to the planning and design division. For instance, frequently all electrical service orders are passed through planning and design regardless of implementation cost, since outlet installation can have far-reaching effects.

An effective method of screening requirements before they reach the WRC is to appoint a mayor for each building or a facilities point of contact (POC) for each major element; some large organizations use a combination. For instance, the POC in each department screens requirements and passes them on to the mayor of the building. There are advantages to this system, but it can add an unnecessary level of bureaucracy if the POCs and mayors are not empowered to reject frivolous requests and are required to prioritize the requirements.

It is also extremely important that work flow be properly established. Proper work flow ensures that 90 to 97 percent (by volume) of the work of the facilities department is handled routinely. That allows the facility manager to concentrate on the 3 to 10 percent of the work requiring managerial intervention. One of the signs of a facility department in trouble is that staff members call the facility manager directly to resolve routine work requests. Another sign is more than one point of entry for work coming into the facilities department. One of the greatest challenges to the facility manager is to ensure that the Work Reception Center remains customer service friendly and does not become bureaucratized.

Exhibit 24-2 shows the entry and distribution of work within a typical facility department. Exhibit 24-3 is a detailed work flowchart for routine service orders.

Procedures

The WRC is the driving force behind all routine work in the facilities department. Since this work constitutes such a high percentage of the department's mission, it is important that it be done well. While each organization has its own unique requirements, there are common procedures. For example, the WRC should have the capability of receiving work requests twenty-four hours daily and be staffed one half hour before and after normal duty hours. Stagger the work hours of the receptionists or use other operational personnel in addition to the regular receptionists.

Also, it is counterproductive to spend great effort confirming whether those requesting routine work are authorized to do so. One organization required almost all requests be in writing and signed by an officer of the organization; only a few services could be requested by phone or email. The WRC had a book of authorized signatures against which to check. The system literally buried itself in paper. Faced with either increasing the staffing of the WRC or falling further behind in processing requests, the organization eliminated the paperwork and went to requesting almost

Exhibit 24-2. Work flow within a typical facility department.

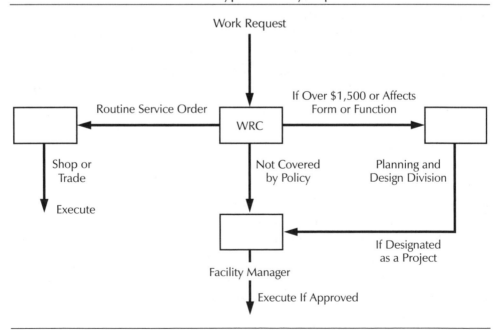

Exhibit 24-3. Simplified current work flow in call to work reception center.

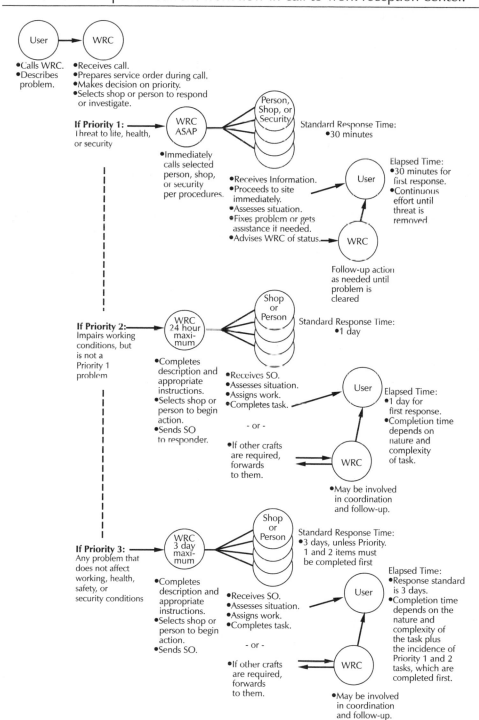

all work by phone. Modern systems not only allow the complete tracking of work requests but should be able to:

- Regularly produce management reports showing, by trade, the volume and costs of requests completed per time period,
- Highlight both long-standing or sensitive work requests not accomplished, and
- Produce reports allowing customer service follow-up on work requests which, for some reason, cannot be done in a timely manner.

Although we could find no data, we suspect that most WRCs now receive work request by email.

Also, it is counterproductive to spend great effort confirming whether those requesting work are authorized to do so. At one time one of your authors required almost all requests be in writing and signed by an officer of the company; only a few services could be requested by phone. The service reception center had a book of authorized signatures against which to check. We were literally buried in paper. Faced with the prospect of either increasing WRC staffing or falling further behind in processing the requests, we eliminated the paperwork and converted to almost 100 percent phone requests. The only requests now requiring paperwork are signage, so that the name is spelled correctly, and furniture, because we cannot meet the requests for six to eight weeks and it is easier to file paper.

If, however, you have a telephone-based Work Reception an answering system is a must, because a good WRC frequently has a queue for service. The answering system should be capable of tracking the following items:

- Total number of calls
- Number of calls answered within a specified number of rings
- Average waiting time
- Number of calls not completed (the caller hung up)

All incoming calls should be answered within two rings or get a recording informing the person that the call is on hold and offering an option to call back at a less busy time. If the WRC requires certain information, the caller should be so reminded at that time. Callers on hold should also be reminded every twenty to thirty seconds that the next available work receptionist will take the call. Some WRCs tape all incoming calls; check with the legal department before doing so to ensure compliance with company policy and local law.

Decisions concerning seemingly small matters can sometimes make a real difference in the quality of a WRC. For example, what is an appropriate background sound for callers on hold? Our preference is for easy listening music, but others have had success with all-news radio or company information bits. We have found it most efficient for work receptionists to use telephone headsets, freeing both hands. That becomes even more important with increasingly automated workstations.

If you do not operate your WRC 24/7, you must decide how calls during non-working hours will be handled. Some organizations collect them on the answering system but, if available, many organizations have non-working-hour calls go to the Security Operations Center. We dislike the impersonal nature of having calls to the WRC shifted to an answering system under any circumstances but realize that staffing and operational situations may require that this occur. When this happens, ensure that some type of call-back standard (within one hour of reopening, for example) is in place and adhered to.

Staffing the WRC is subject to many variables. Even if there is only one work receptionist, that person needs breaks—extended ones. Otherwise fatigue and stress make the job unappealing. The justification for additional staffing is often documented in the log of the telephone answering machine. If the average wait time, the number of calls dropped, or the response time exceeds management's standard, more staffing is probably justified.

Work Coordination

The WRC must coordinate all work: preventive maintenance, cyclical maintenance, maintenance and repair projects, service orders, alteration projects, and capital projects. It is a facility manager's nightmare, for example, for a wall to be painted under cyclic maintenance two days before it is demolished as part of an alteration project. Not only is this wasteful, but it destroys the department's credibility. Work should be coordinated with other service organizations. The WRC should be aware of all conferences, parties, facility projects, and after-hours activities so that proper support and no conflicting activities will be scheduled. In a large organization, one person should coordinate work, control the flow of paperwork through the facilities department, and task all nonroutine work. In a medium-size organization, this individual can also handle service evaluation. In a small organization, the amount of work can be small enough so that the facility manager or work receptionist can also function as work coordinator. (For additional guidance on aspects of work control, see David R. Howard, *Critical Issues in Facilities Management;* Work Control.)[1]

Work reception and coordination is one of the facility management functions most often automated (56 percent) but its rate of automation seems to have slowed.[2] There are many excellent systems that allow the work receptionist to task the appropriate shop directly using an automated service order. Once the work is completed, the shop enters the time and materials expended, and the service order is closed. Preventive maintenance and project work can be similarly automated. The system can print out expenditures to date by shop, by service-order number, by budget code, by building, or by organization. In modern organizations, there is a separate printer and PC in each shop so that service orders can be processed there.

Service Evaluation

The WRC is in a unique position to evaluate service, both quantitatively and qualitatively. For service orders, we recommend the following quantitative evaluation each month:

1. By shop, evaluate
   - Service orders carried over
   - Service orders received
   - Service orders completed monthly and year-to-date
2. By shop, by priority category, evaluate
   - Number completed within time standard
   - Number not completed within time standard

To measure service-order performance qualitatively, send questionnaires to approximately 30 percent of the service recipients. Another approach is to target one to two buildings or organizations each month. The results of these questionnaires can be compiled and reviewed monthly, quarterly, and annually along with quantitative results.

Custodial services and other service not obtained by submitting a service request are measured qualitatively by questionnaire—similar to service orders.

Projects normally are evaluated using a postoccupancy evaluation or with a special questionnaire. Quantitatively, projects are evaluated on whether budget was met, schedule was adhered to, and the program was met. The WRC can administer project evaluation as a matter of administrative convenience, but it is probably best evaluated by the planning and design division or directly by the facility manager.

The importance of the WRC in customer relations cannot be overemphasized. Since 90 to 97 percent of the department's work flows through the WRC, its image is largely determined by how courteously, effectively, and efficiently work requests are treated. The work receptionists must be courteous and diplomatic, even when staff calling in work requests are not. They must be able both to give the status of requested work (automation helps immensely here) and understand the implications of even the most innocent request. Your local phone company (and some communications consultants) can provide in-house training to help work receptionists both maximize their use of time and improve their telephone etiquette. The training is well worth the cost.

The Work Reception Center, because of the training and capabilities of its personnel and its equipment, can be an ideal Emergency Management Center (See Chapter 17) although it may need to be augmented with additional communications for the Emergency Management team. In case the WRC has to be relocated, the alternative site for the Emergency Management Center is an ideal site for WRC to re-commence operations until the initial facility can be restored. If for no other reason, this symbiosis thrusts the facility manager into emergency planning and management.

Notes

1. David R. Howard, ed., *Critical Issues in Facilities Management,* vol. 2 (Alexandria, Va.: APPA, 1988).
2. "Facility Management Practices," *IFMA Report 16* (Houston: IFMA, 1996), p. 24.

25

Facility Operations

Pulse Points

- *Facilities operations is a multidimensional function, requiring solid management skills.*
- *Disaster recovery has major facility complications and the facility manager will be intimately involved.*
- *Managing the company's environmental program can provide visibility to the facility manager.*
- *Indoor air quality may become a major environmental issue.*

Most facility management literature gives either of two impressions of facility operations: it does not exist, or it is a big machine that is turned on daily and operates smoothly with little or no funding, problems, or management attention. Neither could be further from the truth. Facility operations is a multidimensional function of facility management. It's often the forgotten function, but good management and organization ensure that 90 to 97 percent of problems are solved so that management can focus on the 3 to 10 percent of problems that truly need their attention. The truth is that facilities operations account for 50 to 75 percent of the facilities budget.

Facility operations includes these areas:

- Plant operations
- Energy management
- Hazardous waste management
- Recycling
- Inventory management
- Communications and wire management
- Alterations management
- Relocation and move management
- Furniture installation

- Disaster recovery (See Chapter 19)
- Maintenance and repair
- Security (See Chapter 20–22)
- Fire and life safety

Maintenance and repair are discussed in Chapter 26; fire and life safety are covered in Chapter 27.

Plant Operations

Of all facility operations, the one function most commonly relegated to the back burner is plant operations. That is unfortunate because there is nothing back burner about modern plant operations. A bright, highly proficient operating engineer bemoaned recently that plant equipment had evolved much more rapidly than had the education and licensing requirements for operating engineers. The skills he *really* needed were in electronics with some basic computer skills, whereas he had been trained in the traditional steam fitting, sheet metal, and plumbing skills.

There is no absolute definition of *plant,* but for the purpose of this book, consider the plant to be made up of the following systems:

1. Heating, ventilation, and air-conditioning (HVAC)
2. Mechanical and electrical vertical and horizontal transportation
3. Major electrical
4. Emergency power
5. Plumbing

In North America, the energy crisis of the early 1970s precipitated a revolution in building systems. Concurrently, computer-controlled building systems were just reaching the market. Together they made it possible, for a relatively modest capital cost, to provide individualized environments to a degree never before possible, at a substantial savings in both cost and size of the plant. Today it is not uncommon to see the HVAC system of large complexes controlled by a personal computer that also troubleshoots the system and provides a historical record of its operations. Such systems are commonly co-located with fully integrated fire and life-safety or security systems.

Historically, buildings have had their own engineer, be it a jack-of-all-trades. Some have even had a second maintenance mechanic. During the late 1970s and early 1980s, however, it became increasingly popular to gather all building operations staff under central control and dispatch them where and when needed. As a result, little preventive maintenance was done, the occupants felt deserted, maintenance was ignored to accomplish project work, and intimate knowledge of the building was lost.

Today, it is felt that some type of resident facility management technical staff is best for all occupied buildings over 250,000 square feet. For large complexes, there is controversy over how to organize the plant operations staff. Many departments have their own operating engineers, but increasingly this function is being contracted out. One possible way to organize a plant operations unit is shown in Exhibit 25-1. Note that elevators are part of the operating plant. It is a good match since elevators are electromechanical equipment.

The plant operations function has perhaps the most routine tasks, but that does not mean they are not important, even critical, to facility operation. Unsatisfactory heating and cooling is the most common building complaint in office buildings. If the chief executive officer (CEO) is trapped in an elevator or Legionnaire's disease breaks out among the staff, the critical nature of plant operations immediately becomes evident.

The key to cost-effective plant operations is a solid, continuing energy management program and centralized building management. The former is discussed in the next section of this chapter. As for the latter, it is possible to operate an automated building maintenance system (BMS) under two different philosophies. The most cost-effective system has one individual (not necessarily even a knowledgeable one) monitoring all building systems from a central location manned twenty-four hours a day. That individual recognizes problems as displayed on a computer screen and notifies the appropriate operations personnel for corrective action.

Exhibit 25-1. Organizing for plant operations.

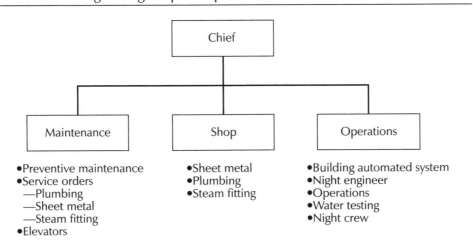

The second approach has building functions monitored separately. In the most common arrangement, there are both a security operation center (also covering fire and life safety) and a building operation center, with these functions monitored by technical experts. This latter allows a higher degree of initial technical input but also is more costly.

Most new building designs incorporate an automated building maintenance system. It is also possible to retrofit these systems into existing buildings. Control points, detectors, and computer capacity can be increased incrementally as funding and installation capability become available. Several companies make total building systems, and each year more features are added, especially with the move to individually controlled environments.

Energy Management

Energy management is not a separate function but rather an activity that spans every facility system. Modern energy management had its genesis in the oil crisis of the early 1970s. Two results came from that crisis: remarkably more efficient (and smaller) energy-consuming equipment and an understanding that energy is a major cost element and needs to be contained. The sudden appreciation for energy undoubtedly was a factor in the rise of facility management as a profession. The person who paid the light bill suddenly became an important corporate player.

The sustainability movement re-invigorated the interest in energy management when, in 2007 the costs of fuels and natural gas sky-rocketed and utility costs went out of sight. Even before this happened, a good energy management program could save and avoid costs averaging 30 to 33 percent conservatively. Energy represents about 30 percent of a building's operating costs. A 30 percent reduction in energy consumption (in California, for example) can lower building operating costs by $25,000 per year for every 50,000 square feet managed. For every $1 invested in energy efficiency, building asset value increases by an estimated $3.[1] What had been desirable in 2005 is now an imperative.

There are many techniques and devices for energy management that have proved effective. The following are elements of a good energy management program:

1. The organization of the program is based on responsible committees to set policy and sell the program.
   - Appoint an energy manager responsible to the facility manager.
   - Have two levels of committees: a steering committee chaired by a senior manager with membership of the budget director, the facility manager,

and two or three line managers, and a technical committee chaired by the facility manager.

- Appoint the senior administrative person in each department responsible for user-dependent energy management matters (for example, turning off the lights) in that department.

2. All policy is developed by the technical committee, approved by the steering committee, and signed by the CEO. To be effective, energy management must be perceived as a management program, not a facilities program.

3. A detailed energy consumption baseline is established for each utility. Consumption against this baseline should be calculated at least annually to track progress. Utility companies will assist in these analyses.

4. A hierarchy of energy management measures is implemented:
   - Capital intensive (payback less than seven years suggested).
   - Moderate cost (can be budgeted in annual budgets with no significant effect).
   - Low cost or no cost.

5. Energy management is incorporated into all designs, and all new designs are reviewed from an energy management perspective.

Increasingly, companies will be developing an energy strategy with particular emphasis on leveraging whatever volume advantage a firm has to obtain more favorable terms from privatized suppliers. This development is not without drawbacks. Caveat emptor now becomes the cardinal rule when purchasing energy, just as it is with any other commodity in a free market. Although there may be a price advantage to large users, facility managers must now worry about the quality of electricity provided, guarantee of source, and price stability. There are also concerns that small users will get left behind and that the cost of an inefficient plant will have to be absorbed by someone (hopefully not your company).

Depending on the sophistication of a company's current energy management and its ability to exercise some muscle in the market, facility managers and their companies stand to reap some real benefits. Already, utilities are downsizing and cutting costs so that they will be competitive in a deregulated market; industry consolidation, if controlled, should have the same effect.

Increased competition and marketing should work to facility managers' advantage. Cost savings may not be the only fallout of energy deregulation. In addition, value-added services (maybe the utility will actually own and maintain a company's chillers and boilers) may be intriguing to certain facility managers. Finally, a nearby co-generator may be willing to sell energy at below-market rates to absorb excess capacity. All of this can be confusing, if not outright scary. In order to manage this process, Wayne Robertson, director of energy consulting at Heery International, suggests the following actions.[2]

- Build a team; at first you may need to depend on a consultant.
- Evaluate facility requirements using an energy audit.
- Actively seek out your utility to ensure that they notice you.
- Seek package discounts and rate incentives.
- Form or be involved in a users' group.
- Aggressively seek rate options.
- Perform a co-generation study and design.
- Evaluate peak shaving generation and gas cooling opportunities.
- Look for local co-generation projects.

Another highly effective procedure is to join an energy management benchmarking group. A simplified procedure for benchmarking is contained in Derek Greenauer's paper "Adding Value to Energy Management by Benchmarking" which can be obtained off the internet. Your local professional association may already have an energy management benchmarking group set up. By moving aggressively now, the facility manager may establish a structure to permanently reduce energy operating costs.

Energy services companies (ESCOs), most of which are former electric utilities repackaged to provide an array of energy services, offer the facility manager new products and services. ESCOs now provide resource planning software, energy conservation products and services, on-site energy systems, and retail-wheeling advice. The extent to which ESCOs give truly independent advice is yet to be determined, but they certainly provide expertise to facility managers that was not generally available before deregulation.

Hazardous Waste Management

This topic includes a variety of management challenges, from abating asbestos to disposing of contaminated medical waste. The recommendations alone could fill a book.

Asbestos

By far the most common hazardous waste is asbestos. Hopefully, due to extensive removal efforts and the limitations on asbestos' use, abatement efforts have declined substantially. After much nervousness, even panic, facility departments have learned to cope with asbestos and approach its abatement in a commonsense manner. It is possible to abate asbestos and to continue operations in the same building. The following are trademarks of a good asbestos abatement program:

1. Appointment of an abatement operations and maintenance manager.
2. Training of an in-house abatement crew or hiring of a reputable contractor. (We strongly favor the latter.)
3. Securing the services of an environmental hygiene firm to do independent testing. This firm preferably does not work for the facility manager (suggest the health or human resources department), which ensures its independence.
4. Establishment of abatement files as follows:
   - Historical record of all abatement efforts.
   - Air quality reports following each abatement effort provided by the hygienist hired by the contractor to do testing.
   - Record of procedures on each abatement site.
   - Disposal record from the disposal contractor.
5. Enactment of an internal relations program for staff that is both general and site specific. The independent environmental hygienist can be an excellent instructor.

The best arrangement has the contractor mobilize within a certain time to abate asbestos against previously approved rates. Some facility managers have one such contract (this ensures uniformity of abatement); others use two or three contractors so that one is always available when the need arises.

Some facility managers hire a contractor, often using the lowest bid, and then adopt a "see no evil, hear no evil" philosophy about the handling of asbestos waste. It is a managerially unsound approach and can place the company in legal jeopardy should improperly disposed asbestos be traced. On the other hand, there are both good contractors and good consultants. It is unnecessary to hire someone who tries to bully or frighten you with horror stories. Hire a contractor (or consultant) who will be responsive and will work both to protect the health of the staff and minimize disruption.

Do not fear asbestos; manage it!

Other Waste

Many facility managers are faced with handling either hazardous manufacturing or medical waste. Fortunately a company that handles medical waste normally also has the knowledge and experience for proper storage and disposal. Perhaps in no other area is the old saw, "If in doubt, do it right," so applicable. In the past some organizations have simply turned over their waste to a disposal contractor and washed their hands of it, without concern for proper disposal or interim storage. That is not only bad management but runs counter to public concerns and legal trends. Protestations that the contractor erred will not even be heard. To protect the company:

1. Have competent legal advice for dealing with hazardous waste issues.
2. Hire a waste management contractor with a proven track record.
3. Use an environmental hygienist, preferably hired by your medical department, to monitor your in-house and contractor's handling, storage, and disposal of hazardous materials.

For a discussion of the relatively new regulations facing so-called small (waste) quantity generators, see "Complying with Hazardous Waste Regulations," in the AFE's *Guide to Better Facilities Management.*

Recycling

Recycling remains one of the functions most affecting facility management and is expected to have a high priority in the future.[3] While markets will always fluctuate somewhat, what can be efficiently recycled has become much better defined, not always with a reduction in the volume of waste unfortunately. However, several facility managers have made a name for themselves within their companies by actively pursuing, normally with employee input, an aggressive recycling program.

Initially, you may need a half- to full-time person to establish a proper recycling program and oversee implementation. (The recovery of valuable by-products from industrial processes is not what is being discussed here. Normally their capture and reuse is under the purview of the vice president for manufacturing.)

Most recycling consists of segregation and either resale or disposal of the segregated products. Commonly, waste is segregated as follows:

1. Paper (newspaper, white paper, all other)
2. Aluminum cans
3. Glass bottles and jars (clear, green, brown)
4. Scrap metal
5. Styrofoam
6. Computers and electronic equipment
7. Paint cartridges
8. Clothing
9. Waste oil
10. All other

Most current programs segregate only three to five of these products at the facility level, with all other waste going in the "all other" category for disposal.

Recycling is not cheap ($5 to $20 per employee for initial containers). Often in urban areas, interim storage space or extra segregated dumpster space simply is not available. Personnel to segregate waste is an additional expense. But some companies have worked with local agencies to employ the disabled for this chore.

Unfortunately, many facility managers who have tried to be out front on recycling have experienced frustration. For example, some who funded the additional costs of recycling from the sale of paper have seen the bottom drop out of the paper market as more and more companies turned to recycling. Large organizations should consider cogeneration of waste materials if it can be cost justified and if the facility is in an area where the stack effluent will meet Environmental Protection Agency (EPA) standards.

Some degree of segregation is needed at the workbench, production line, and desk level. Generally the facility manager is expected to provide the three Ps: policy, proper containers, and pickup. However, the program will be suboptimized if viewed as solely a facility department's program and responsibility. Company management must support the recycling effort for it to be successful.

Despite the cost, the often confusing nature of the legislation, the lack of markets for many recycled products, and the additional space requirements, most companies realize the need for recycling and are making an honest attempt to implement a program.

Indoor Air Quality

Indoor air quality could be the Achilles' heel of facility managers. Many buildings have been constructed so that air quality cannot be adequately controlled. In the traditional office building, for example, temperature can often be controlled only by zone. In order to reduce operating costs, the amount of fresh air (and humidity) brought into the building with each change of air has been severely limited. Often ducts are filled with fungi, dirt, and dust (which is stirred up each time the ductwork is modified), and filters are often ineffective for the type of dust and pollen to which employees are allergic.

A new announcement of federal indoor air quality standards has seemed imminent for the past several years but appears to be hung up politically at the EPA. Nevertheless, indoor air quality problems will only increase, regardless of more stringent regulation. Facility managers need to adopt a program that emphasizes good operational practices (better space layout, for example), improved maintenance practices (better custodial cleaning, for example), as well as capital investment to correct past problems.

Employees will continue to insist on more control over their indoor environment and better air quality. In the long run, providing better air quality can lead to better employee efficiency. This is an area where facility management can contribute to the bottom line.

Inventory Management

An accurate inventory of facility property has two purposes. First, managers like to have an accurate count of what they manage. Second, for tax purposes it is necessary to know what furnishings and equipment of what vintage are on the books so that they can be depreciated properly.

In general, the rules for inventory management are not made in the facility department. Inventory management is much like purchasing or procurement—vitally important but dependent on policies and procedures most often set by others. By far the facility manager's greatest involvement is with furniture inventory (74 percent), with 62 percent responsible for furniture disposal and 35 percent responsible for the disposal of other property.[4] The inventories to manage these functions can be maintained through a number of methods, the most promising of which is bar coding.

Bar coding is a technique to affix a number to a piece of property in order to track its physical location and create a file on that piece of property. A handheld scanner can download information into a computer and track individual pieces of furniture, certain types or components of furniture, furniture from a certain manufacturer, or even standard furniture sets. Bar coding the locations also makes it possible to maintain inventories easily; some manufacturers even offer their products bar coded.

While bar coding is moderately expensive, it is efficient and effective for inventory management in mid- and large-size organizations. Implementing a bar code system requires a well-thought-out inventory schema and a good bar coding system.

The principal considerations for implementing a bar coded inventory system are:

1. What is the degree of detailing desired in tracking? Units? Assemblies? Parts? Once the numbering system is set, stick to it.
2. Will color, fabric, or condition be described? That may dictate the system.
3. How will locations be defined? Are those locations understandable to designers? To users? Others may want to tap in to the inventory for their needs.
4. Will the inventory be differentiated regarding depreciated value, owned versus leased, and other factors? If so, a smart code may be needed in the bar code.

5. How will the initial tagging objectives and strategy be done? Some staff object to having their furniture tagged unless they are present, yet waiting for their presence slows the process. Placement of the bar code on any single piece of furniture must be consistent and accessible yet aesthetically acceptable.

6. How will the information be updated? Establish an update procedure.

Properly managed bar coding can allow management of property from acquisition through disposal.

Of course technology may be changing this. The high costs of manual inventory procedures will eventually make way for laser bar-code reading and direct input into a computer database. This will allow an up-to-date inventory of furniture in use and available for distribution. Then reliable inventory printouts will be more important. Also, fallout from unfriendly takeovers will force company financial officers to change the way furniture is accounted for and inventoried (from a depreciation schedule inventory to an assets listing inventory). In this way, a current, accurate valuation of total assets is possible.

Communications and Wire Management

Slightly more than half of most facility managers manage telecommunications.[5] That may present a problem because no other function in this information age has such a profound influence on facilities as data and telecommunications work.

For years the communications function consisted of paying the telephone bill to the local phone company. Suddenly this function has become one of the most dynamic, largely owing to deregulation of the phone system, increasing computerization of business functions, and interconnections of computers through hardwiring or the telephone system.

Communications is where the information systems department and the facility department come together. The communications function is as likely managed in the information systems department or as a separate division than in the facility department. This is because, to the information services department, the communications system is the electronic highway over which information flows. To the facility department, the communications system is a major user of space (antennas, risers, file servers, modems, closets, and wire trays), requiring additional trades on projects, and a set of wires and outlets that must be accommodated and that restricts layout flexibility. But no matter where the communications function is placed, there must be close and continuous coordination, starting with planning and design. Generally communications engineers, particularly those with a voice communications background, have not been trained to design and document their wire installations to the degree other building elements are planned and designed.

There is a legitimate debate within facility management concerning the degree to which communications should be documented. Should communications wiring and devices be drawn, or should they be documented by alphanumeric schedules? Should all communication runs be depicted, or should only termini be shown? Or is the best system some combination or permutation of the above?

Our preference is for documentation in the form of drawings of the following:

1. All communications risers
2. The type and location of outlets unless standardized
3. The location of all equipment (multiplexors, net commanders, file servers, etc.)
4. The location of any communications element for which space planning is necessary
5. The location of all frame rooms, closets, and cabinets
6. All fiber-optic runs
7. The entry point of outside services
8. All antennas
9. All communication ducts
10. All cable trays

This is the minimum for effective wire management. Room-type information should be recorded on a communications overlay; information on the cable plant and risers should have separate sheets, just as mechanical and electrical systems do. Although it is not specifically a part of wire management, we like to record on key plans the basic power requirements and heat output data for each piece of office technology equipment in place. This information can be maintained on the overlay of room information, as an equipment schedule, or in a separate alphanumeric database. It should be capable of being manipulated so as to assess the effect of moving office technology on the HVAC and electrical systems.

It is our experience that the average (even the better-than-average) architectural-engineering (A-E) firm does an inadequate job of planning and designing telecommunications and data communication systems. Perhaps the reason is that they did not have to do so when Ma Bell existed. Consequently, design services must often be obtained from a specialized communications consultant. When the facility is large enough to justify such a firm, a design-build company can design, build, and maintain all low-voltage systems, not just data and telecommunications.

Communications management is a function of the nature of the company or business. It is quite a different task to rely on the local telephone company than to run one's own telephone switch. Exhibit 25-2 is one possible organization for a communications division in a facility department of a large corporation with a broad range of communications needs. Note especially the need for the electronic communications specialist. Using this model, applicable organizations can be scoped up or down. One rule of thumb for communications organizations is that there be one professional for each $750,000 in annual communications expense.[6]

With the arrival of data communications, premises-based switching, private satellite communications, local area networks, and facsimile transmission, the communications function suddenly is a full plate. Several principles are in order:

1. Various technologies must be understood because functionability increasingly is user driven.
2. A wide variety of solutions from multiple vendors exists for every communications problem. Don't be the first to buy in; try to protect against obsolescence.
3. Communications is a business function. Conduct an economic analysis before choosing among options.
4. Look for opportunities to maximize technology by expanding existing systems. For example, voice, data, mail, fax, e-mail, and messenger service probably would benefit from single management.
5. Multiple options and vendors should increase the leverage of the facility manager.

John Richardson describes the communications revolution this way:

> Some day when you leave your office for the day, a sensor in your building will note your departure. Automatically the lights will be turned off and the heat turned down. You will ride home content in the knowledge that your organization has put new ideas to work to control spiraling communications cost and improve worker efficiency. You will, in effect, have taken advantage of the revolution in semiconductor technology.[7]

As Richardson's description shows, communications is becoming more entwined with facilities. Even now the telephone can be used to control both individual HVAC and lighting. Therefore, companies and facility managers need to reexamine who should manage communications. Companies continue to put the two disciplines under separate management, at their ever increasing risk. Whether communications is managed independently or in the information services department, the facility manager must ensure that planning, design, installation, and even

Exhibit 25-2. Possible organization for communications division of a facility department.

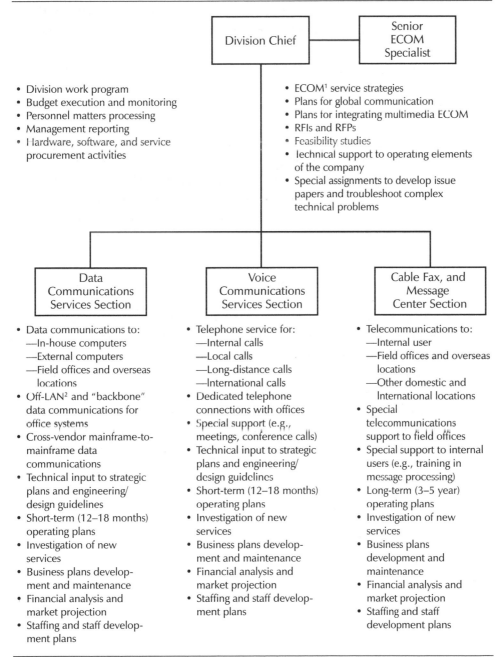

1. ECOM = electronic communications.
2. LAN = local area network.

maintenance are coordinated, since no single other function has such a pervasive and encompassing effect on facilities.

Increasingly companies are going to wireless communications (WiFi). WiFi not only decreases the cost and intensive labor of wired communications, but it fits the working habits of our increasingly mobile employees, with no fixed office space, each equipped with a laptop computer. We are, in fact, in the midst of a communications revolution which will allow us to communicate most anywhere with multiple devices, none of which is hard-wired. Hard-wired applications are fast becoming the exception. One of your authors has thought wistfully that he wishes he had the copper recovery rights for just one of the buildings that he hardwired during the automation explosion of the 1980s.

WiFi brings with it a separate set of problems, particularly security and signal strength. Unfortunately, laptops with secure information on them and with employees who handle secure information also work in coffee shops, fast food restaurants, and homes where signal bandits troll for unprotected WiFi transmissions.

Alterations Management

There is probably no other function so popular as altering space; 55 percent of facility managers say that they do it continually.[8] Everyone enjoys a renovated cafeteria, an upgraded workplace, or a facelift on the assembly line. Since alterations are so popular, they must be carefully controlled or they will hemorrhage the facility budget. This is a particular problem where funds for alterations are mingled with funds for maintenance. Unless alterations are well managed, maintenance funds will be diverted into alterations, to the detriment of the department. This has grown to such a problem that the U.S. Army, for example, restricts the amount of maintenance and repair funding that could be diverted to alterations.

In corporate North America, where churn rates of 20 to 30 percent are the norm, alterations are a way of life. In fact, downsizing often accelerated the necessity to alter space. Alterations can become the preponderant function of the facilities department—the yardstick by which the facility manager is measured. This creates a project mentality in the department, whereas the proper approach views alterations as one function, albeit an important one, in a facility's life cycle.

There are a number of standards that allow alterations to be managed well and to the advantage of the organization:

1. Space, so you don't move walls six inches to suit someone's ego.
2. Materials, so you don't use mahogany paneling where drywall will do.

3. Construction practice, so that you don't build in bookshelves where a free-standing bookshelf will suffice.
4. Layout, so you're not reconfiguring an office because someone wants his back to the door.
5. Engineering, so that you are not providing eight electrical outlets in a room but are providing proper access to electrical and data outlets.

If adhered to, these standards allow minimal guidelines for construction, particularly if the workforce is stable. That leads to a 30 to 40 percent savings in design costs.

A second major means of control is proper document flow between the design division and the alterations division, within the alterations division, and through the work reception center to ensure that alterations work is coordinated with maintenance work.

Someone should be tracking the flow of a project from inception through close-out. In large organizations (those handling more than one hundred projects annually), both the design division and the alterations division need to establish single points of contact through which all projects enter and leave the division, formalized routing documents, and an automated system for tracking project progress through the system. In large organizations, this tracking is often done for the department by a work coordinator in the work reception center. The issuance and pass-off between divisions should be formally noted, probably as critical events in the project management system.

Computer-assisted design and drawing systems make the upkeep of accurate drawings relatively simple, provided later alteration drawings use official construction drawings as a base and later changes in the field are incorporated. Too often, partial drawings or schematics (cut sheets) are used to do small alterations or renovations. That practically guarantees that the information will not be updated in the database. Given that 30 percent of all space is renovated annually in the average corporation, costly as-builts will be completely out of date within four years. Actually, drawings that are 10 to 20 percent out of date tend to be viewed as obsolete, so less than a year's failure to update can ruin a good set of facility drawings. The facility drawings listed in Exhibit 25-3 should be on hand for alterations.

As important as they are, few alteration programs have good estimating support. Proper estimates of alteration costs require specialized skills. The estimator must be familiar with construction costs in general and, more important, with the costs of altering space at that site. He must be capable of both gross (for working and conceptual estimates) and detailed estimating and must work on many small estimates but have a database unique to the site. Above all, the estimator must work rapidly and accurately. Since the estimator needs site-specific knowledge to work properly, an

Exhibit 25-3. Facility drawings required for alterations.

Essential	*Optional Layers* [2]	*Schedules*	*Others*
Base building	Reflected ceiling	Electrical panels	Typical
Key plans[1]	Electrical	Floor design loads	perspectives
Site survey	Mechanical	Security devices	Renderings
	Fire	Communications	
	Life and safety	conductivity	
	Plumbing	Historical	
	Mechanical room	information (e.g.,	
	layout	architect, when	
	Parking	constructed)	
	Communications	Finishes	
	Data	Masonry	
	Communications	Space by floor (e.g.,	
	Security	gross, core,	
		circulation,	
		occupiable)	
		Ceiling heights	

1. Key plans are base building drawings with single-line room drawings. For each room and room occupant, some information is provided (e.g., phone number, name, organization, grade, and applicable standards).
2. Some of these layers may have sublayers. For example, the plumbing overlay could be divided into water supply and sewage.

outside estimator is of little value. Therefore, the facility manager should employ a staff estimator or use someone hired as part of the A-E package. There is no effective cost control without proper estimating. BIM probably will radically change the way we plan alteration projects with our clients and document them after we complete them. If anything, it will be more important that we take time in planning and design and alteration and major construction to document the work done because, under any system, manual or highly automated, "garbage in; garbage out."

We have found it helpful to categorize work by size. Except for projects that require design, we allow the work reception center to assign work under $2,000 (best estimate) directly. For larger projects, we feel specific authority is needed. Here are some helpful rules for assigning large projects:

1. Placement in the work plan is authority for the design division to begin conceptual design and obtain a working cost estimate.

2. Projects under $100,000 can proceed for design and execution if the working estimate is within allocated funds (unless the facility manager desires to allocate funds quarterly or semiannually).
3. Projects over $100,000 can proceed beyond concept only after specific approval by the facility manager.
4. Projects whose conceptual estimates exceed the funds allotted may proceed only if authorized by the facility manager.

This system is workable, and though seemingly bureaucratic, dampens the tendency to overspend on the alterations budget or to expend all alterations funds in the first quarter of the fiscal year.

If too many projects are chasing too few funds, there should possibly be an alterations prioritization committee. This committee is most effective if it is a user group, with the facility manager as secretary. The committee establishes priorities for the alterations budget and reviews progress and reprioritizes at midyear. If the committee members are chosen properly, consensus is not difficult; however, it must be certain that committee policy allows some deviation to meet health, safety, and operational emergencies.

The manager of alterations must insist that workers are doers, not thinkers or designers. All changes other than small field changes need to be referred back to the design division for redesign, approval, and additional funding. If this rule is not strictly enforced, expect leakage of 15 to 25 percent of the alterations budget.

The alterations program is implemented in many ways. Increasingly, the work is contracted out, often to a term service contractor responsible for operations, maintenance, and alterations or minor construction. Some large companies even provide design services to ensure that all aspects of the facilities mission are integrated at the contractor level (i.e., they see the big picture). A very successful variant is to have a body-shop contract whereby skills are ordered by the number of tradespeople to meet the peaks and valleys in a work program. Often in such a program tradespeople stay in the facilities even though the contractor changes upon rebidding; they are a de facto in-house crew.

We prefer to use the designer as project manager during alterations. That fixes responsibility, allows for rapid decisions on changes, and means a single contact from concept through project completion. Some large design firms have separate project managers oriented toward client organizations who coordinate both the design and execution phase of all alterations.

Most project management systems are too sophisticated for alterations. For the vast majority of such projects, data entry efforts exceed the benefits since projects are simple, relatively low cost, and of short duration. A weekly report is often of more value. There are successful automated systems that track annual alterations work rather than individual projects.

Relocation and Move Management

With 20 to 30 percent churn rates, corporate America must accept relocation as a fact of life. Even manufacturing facilities are subject to relocation.

Actually there are two levels of relocating. The first is strategic and involves a major acquisition or disposal of space; this is increasingly cost-driven.[9] That is not the type of relocation we discuss here.

Relocation management in facility operations is management of departmental staff relocations caused by adding or losing staff, loss or gain of leases, or movement to a more suitable space. In many organizations, these moves are funded from the same budget as building maintenance.

We prefer to separate alterations from relocations for two reasons:

1. Management frequently likes to focus on the annual or unit costs of relocations. Alteration projects tend to have higher unit costs than relocations, which distorts record keeping when the functions are combined.
2. Often relocations are mandatory; there is some degree of choice in whether alteration projects will be done.

The controls and procedures for alteration management equally apply to relocation management. Two interesting phenomena have arisen:

1. Relocations have become so prevalent that large international developers and real estate companies have developed relocation networks. Those networks promise to handle all aspects of personal and corporate relocations.
2. Moving companies in major metropolitan areas now often have specialty units to relocate libraries, computing facilities, medical facilities, etc.

Organization

Almost all companies employ a moving company (some have staff movers) to move furniture, equipment, and supplies within their facilities. Often this function is managed by the facility manager; if not, it still has a major impact upon the facilities and their operation.

Move management entails the following:

1. Major inter- and intrabuilding moves

2. Moves to support the alterations program
3. Moves to relocate facilities stock
4. Service-order moves
5. Delivery of supplies within the institution
6. Fixed moving commitments (e.g., two movers to the loading dock, one mover delivering copy paper)

The first four of these functions are directly controlled by the facilities staff; the last two tend to be managed by others, and they work relatively unsupervised. Consequently it is often necessary to send the most dependable movers on fixed commitments and supply delivery. Though these movers are not always working for the facilities department, they are viewed by staff as facilities people, so they must be at their best.

Service-order moves are handled through the work reception center. There also should be close coordination with the food service staff, the conference services staff, and the security staff to ensure that setups and takedowns for major events are systematically provided. Keeping lobbies, cafeterias, and conference rooms set up properly at all times is a major challenge.

For construction or alteration projects, movers are just another trade that needs to be scheduled—this time to clear for construction, install or reinstall furniture, and deliver personal goods. The project manager is responsible for seeing that moving crews are scheduled.

Often, when a division's staff evacuates an area prior to construction, they leave behind files, office supplies, even obsolete office technology. The custodial staff normally is trained not to touch such items, yet they must be cleared out before construction can begin. The move manager or a responsible mover can go through the space, then contact the office supply room, the administrative officer of the evacuating staff department, and the appropriate file room to set a suspend date for removal. All items left after that date are treated as trash.

All move coordinators need both short- and long-term storage. Long-term storage can be at a location off site. As a rule of thumb, the long-term storage site should be able to service the facility within two workdays. The short-term facility requires immediate access to the loading dock, should be sized to meet all demands with lead times less than two workdays, and should contain items that experience has shown need to be available on a short response time. A portion of short-term storage facility should be secure storage.

Once construction is complete, the offices need to be set up and the staff's personal belongings moved in. That is the normal sequence of events, but be alert for special conditions. It is embarrassing to have to remove a newly installed and stained mahogany door frame because a senior executive's sofa will not go through the door.

Move supervisors and lead movers should be expert in the organization's entitlement and layout standards. Once the staff occupies an office, and it is discovered that it was laid out incorrectly, it is difficult to change. To avoid this, have the move coordinator review the final punch list from the staff's perspective. They are on-site at the appropriate time and all other crafts should be essentially complete, so it should be crystal clear to them exactly what needs to be done to complete the project and turn it over to the users in A-1 condition. One creative facility manager photographs each desk prior to a move and tries to recreate that setup after the move.

Procedures

Our preference for providing moving support is through a term contract with a local firm for movers and equipment. We normally include provisions for local storage. If possible, a core crew with at least one supervisor stays in the facility, supplemented by additional movers as needs demand. For large evening or weekend moves, the moving contractor can hire off-duty military personnel complete with first-line supervision (a sergeant or petty officer), if possible, to work with the company's crew.

Moving requests are handled just like other facility work requests: through the work reception center. However, provide a separate dispatcher for all move-related work, because the number of inquiries and amount of required handholding is very high.

Prior to a move, distribute packing boxes. It should be department policy (1) what is user packed, (2) what is mover packed, and (3) what is not to be moved. Everyone should be in agreement, and items should be clearly labeled, normally with a color code. Also, company policy should clearly state to what degree items are to be designated on a manifest. There is a trade-off between the cost of documentation and the chance of an item's being lost. (For example, we think it is a waste of time to manifest interoffice moves.) We have found it helpful to provide pre-move instructions. Even with such instructions there is a certain amount of customer interface to ease the trauma and increase the efficiency of the move. Give special thought to items requiring special moving (e.g., a safe or artwork).

The movers must control the freight or service elevators, either through dedication or an elevator key system. Also, there should be staging areas for temporary storage of goods. Access to loading docks at both origin and destination must be arranged. If traffic will be disrupted, make special arrangements with local police. Ordinarily, the moving company makes these arrangements.

Some degree of tender loving care is required for customers in the two or three days after a move. Assign a crew of movers, working with the move coordinator, to make post-move adjustments. On day 2, the handymen, again coordinated by the move coordinator, can assist in hanging pictures, replacing doors, and the like. On day 3, the handymen can go systematically through the area, correcting nicks and dings and spot painting. On all three days, day porters make a midday trash pickup, and movers remove packing boxes and excess furniture. Each of the first three nights after a move, there should be heavy cleaning, with carpet spot cleaning on the third night.

Move management must always be mindful of three principles:

1. Security is at its weakest during the chaos of a move. Take extra security precautions.
2. People are under stress during a move. Try to plan and execute the move calmly and efficiently.
3. Always have an alternative plan for critical parts of the move, like another freight elevator, or a single moving truck, or a security system requiring special access.

Experienced movers, a well-informed staff, and plenty of supervision can ensure a smooth move.

Furniture Installation

Our experience has been that furniture attic, or back-up, stock should be 4 to 10 percent of total inventory, with a minimum of at least one backup item for each component or set and two for all common components. Bookcases and lateral files seem to disappear because they are easily defended as exceptions or special cases, so additional attic stock may be required.

With gradual conversion from case goods to systems furniture, the skills necessary to install furniture are not necessarily best provided by movers. In fact, in some areas union work rules preclude this. We prefer initial installation by the company providing the furniture, but finding the best installation crew is a matter of economics and personal preference. Some in-house capability is desirable to satisfy any urgent needs to reconfigure, install, or remove furniture. In large organizations frequently there are special installation needs—special shelving comes to mind. It is best to have these items installed initially by the manufacturer but reconfigured or reinstalled by the department's alterations crews or maintenance personnel.

Once furniture is installed, treat it like all other building elements. Inspect and repair it under a preventive maintenance program. Respond to service orders and conduct cyclic maintenance, particularly refinishing and upholstery cleaning.

Finally, plan for replacement. It is best to have a minimal repair capability for jobs like spot cleaning and caster replacement during work hours, with heavy repair (reupholstery, refinishing, major cleaning) done on a scheduled or off-hours basis.

Notes

1. "Best Practices Guides; Commercial Office Buildings," Flex Your Power, www.fypower.org, p. 1.
2. "Power Buying." *Facilities Manager* (January–February 1997): 24–25.
3. "Facility Management Practices," *IFMA Report 16* (Houston: IFMA, 1996), p. 28.
4. "Demographics and Trends," *IFMA Report 2* (Houston: IFMA, 1986), p. 34.
5. "Facility Management Practices," *IFMA Report 2* p. 14.
6. John R. Richardson, "Telecommunications; Changes in Management, Regulation and Technology," in *Facility Planning Technology,* McKinley Conway and Linday L. Liston, eds. (Norcross, Ga.: Conway Data, 1987), p. 919.
7. Ibid.
8. "1989 Modernization Survey," *Buildings* (June 1989): 120.
9. Eileen Carstairs, "The Corporate Relocation Game," *Corporate Design and Realty* (January–February 1987): 35.

26

Maintenance and Repair

Pulse Points

- *The facility manager needs to educate management in the cost of ownership. Until this is done and upper management understands the importance of maintenance and repair funding, the facility manager will always be in a reactive mode.*
- *A company should budget 2 to 4 percent of the replacement value of its facilities for annual maintenance and repair.*

In 1989–1990 the National Research Council conducted a study of the maintenance of public buildings in North America. The resulting report, which emphasized our failure to maintain and repair our inventory of public buildings, made these recommendations:

1. Agencies should make qualified staff and managers specifically responsible for maintenance and repair (M&R) and should ensure that they are trained and recognized. M&R funds should not be diverted to minor alterations and improvements.
2. M&R programs should be built on formal condition assessments.
3. The annual M&R budget should be 2 to 4 percent of the current replacement value of the facilities, excluding land. This amount is over and above the amount to overcome a backlog of maintenance and repair.[1]

Although the explanation does not appear anywhere in the published study, the brevity of the recommendations was driven by the committee's desire to recommend some simple rules that could be understood and sold to legislators who appropriate the money for maintenance and repair of public buildings.

This report was enthusiastically accepted and is often quoted. But the bottom line is that the report has been ignored by the persons who really matter, legislators in the public sector and upper management in the private sector. Or perhaps we have never been able to effectively make the argument concerning the importance of maintenance and repair (M&R) . . . or facility management itself. Why else would legislatures and upper management allow an organizational asset to crumble before their eyes? A new report by the Association of Higher Education Facilities Officers and the National Association of College and University Business Officers indicates that for institutions of higher learning, deferred maintenance levels have risen $5.5 billion since 1988, and the gap between institutional capacity to fund capital needs and the funds available continues to increase.[2] Observation and anecdotal information from other parts of the public sector confirm that the situation continues to deteriorate.

The National Research Council, noting that it had not achieved the desired results published another report, "Pay Now or Pay Later"[3] hoping that the catchy name might attract some attention among Congress, local legislators, and the upper management of private companies. However, with the emphasis on cost cutting in the last fifteen years, the situation has, in fact, become worse. We continue to add to our inventory but don't maintain what we have. We probably have built more in the public sector than we can afford, but most assuredly we have built more than we are willing to maintain. It is our opinion that the situation has reached crisis proportions and that the lack of operations and maintenance funding is a major theme of this book. Until we convince the decision-makers of the need for better M&R funding, the facility manager will always be in a reactive mode. As this book is being written, most of the world is in a major financial crisis with management in both the private and public sector having to reduce costs. Because maintenance and repair was neglected in good financial times, it will be even more difficult to properly fund M&R in the current economic climate.

M&R in the private sector has been equally ignored. The reasons range from a concentration on short-term goals, to a lack of penalty for underfunding M&R in any specific year, to the tenuous and ill-perceived connection between building maintenance and the corporate bottom line. During this period of emphasis on cost cutting, facility managers were lucky to maintain level funding of M&R, to say nothing of reducing backlog.

Public authorities face the dilemma of shrinking budgets with public resistance to tax increases, while responding to increased calls for services. Decisions to underfund the M&R of public buildings are often made because the officials do not understand the implications of underfunding, nor, in many cases, do they even have the criteria to alert them that they are underfunding.

It is often difficult to discern the consequences of a reduction in M&R. The physical evidence is usually not immediately visible; several years may pass before the effects can be observed. And facility managers do not themselves usually have evidence that they can use to defend their requests, nor can they describe in specific terms the consequences of underfunding. Yet the costs to correct the effects of long-term underfunding often exceed the cost of the M&R that would have precluded those deficiencies. No single M&R program model can fill every need at every corporate level, yet there are principles and concepts that ensure a cohesive approach to M&R. Before discussing the elements of such an M&R model, let's agree on some basic terms.

Key Terms

• *Maintenance*—the work necessary to maintain the original anticipated useful life of a fixed asset. It is the upkeep of property and equipment. Maintenance includes periodic or occasional inspection, adjustment, lubrication, cleaning (non janitorial), painting, replacement of parts, minor repairs, and other actions to prolong service and prevent unscheduled breakdown, but it does not prolong the life of the property or equipment or add to its value.

• *Repair*—work to restore damaged or worn-out property to a normal operating condition. As a basic distinction, repairs are curative, and maintenance is preventive. Repair can be classified as minor or major. Minor repairs are those associated with maintenance activities that do not exceed one to two workdays per task. Minor repairs do not appreciably prolong the life of the property or equipment or add to its value. Major repairs are those that exceed two workdays per tasks, or are beyond the capability of existing maintenance personnel. Major repairs often are defined as those that can prolong the life of property or equipment, but should not increase its value. They usually require contracting for repair service.

• *Replacement* of building-related components or systems—the act of replacing an item of permanent investment or plant equipment. It is the exchange or substitution of one fixed asset for another having the capacity to perform the same function. The replacement may arise from obsolescence, wear and tear, or destruction. In general, as distinguished from repair, replacement involves a complete identifiable item.

The Cost of Ownership

When a corporation or public authority decides to acquire a new building, it commits itself to a stream of costs that will be realized throughout the life of the building. (See Exhibit 26-1.) The total cost may be identified as the cost of ownership of the building. This cost of ownership concept is useful in developing budgets for

Exhibit 26-1. Typical costs of ownership.

Acquisition
- Site costs
- Design
- Construction or purchase

Operations
- Utilities
- Custodial

Maintenance and repair

Replacement of components

Alterations and improvements

Rehabilitation and replacement

Disposal

M&R. If authorities recognize that the costs of M&R are informally committed at the time of acquisition, then understanding the annual M&R budget is easier.

The stream of costs includes the cost of the acquisition itself—that is, the cost of acquiring the site, the costs of design and construction, or the cost of purchasing an existing building. These costs are visible and, unfortunately, are frequently considered to be the only costs worthy of immediate attention during acquisition. But several other costs accompany the acquisition decision. Operations costs must be accounted for throughout the useful life of the building. The building's functional costs, such as the cost of personnel to maintain, repair, and replace major building elements, are also part. Included are the costs of utilities and of cleaning the building. In addition, routine and recurring maintenance of the building is realized as a stream of costs, as are costs of repair and replacement of major building components such as boilers and air-conditioning systems.

The stream of costs also includes the ultimate replacement of the building or its rehabilitation, assuming the function continues longer than the economic life of the structure. Ultimately, the stream of costs includes the cost of disposal. This may be demolition or the cost of sale to another party. The authority planning to acquire a new building should acknowledge these costs and view them as inherent in the ownership of the building.

Another cost component should also be recognized: alterations and improvements. If alterations and improvements permit a change in the use of the facility, then the accompanying costs are associated with the cost of ownership relative to the new function. If alterations and improvements are incurred without a change in function, then they must be justified in terms of increased efficiency or effectiveness. Too often alterations and improvements are funded from the operations and maintenance (O&M) budget, where they often eat up the funds that should go to M&R.

Organizations typically fund maintenance using procedures that inhibit effective M&R. Budgets are prepared and funds for building operations and maintenance are combined, usually resulting in a relatively large outlay. Inevitably, the operations component of O&M is significantly larger than the maintenance component. When management must reduce a budget, they then look at O&M as a whole. However, those responsible for managing the buildings can exercise very little control over the operations component. As a result, operations is typically fully funded and maintenance is reduced. There are specific effects associated with underfunding M&R (see Exhibit 26-2). Unfortunately it is possible to underfund routine and recurring M&R for a period of time without immediately visible results.

Corporations should recognize the cost-of-ownership concept. All elements in the stream of costs should be funded at an appropriate level. Although the M&R component varies from building to building, it is possible to develop a relationship between this and an inventory of buildings. For instance, different relationships have been developed to express average levels of M&R. Cost per square foot is frequently the yardstick for determining an appropriate level of M&R budgeting.

A simple method of stating M&R needs is in the annual percentage of replacement value of the building. In order to understand this relationship, consider the

Exhibit 26-2. Effects of underfunding.

Code failures	Service failures
Structural failures	• Power
Safety failures	• Heating, ventilation, and air-conditioning (HVAC)
Health failures	• Leakage and intrusion
Excessive costs	Premature loss
• Excessive replacement	Loss of contents
• Minor failures lead to major failures	Social costs
• Treating symptoms, not the cause	• Poor aesthetics
• Increased consumption of utilities	• Poor morale
	• Inability to attract best employees
	• Increased pollution
	• Loss of readiness
Lower productivity	Absenteeism and turnover

elements of an M&R budget: routine and recurring maintenance plus the cost of annual repairs (including the costs of the replacement of major components, such as boilers and air-conditioning units). The long-term, average relationship between the replacement value of an inventory of buildings and annual M&R requirements is in the range of 2 to 4 percent. The specific percentage for any inventory depends on several factors, including the age of the buildings, the type of construction (permanent vs. temporary), the loading of the buildings, and the climate. One of your author's observations and discussions with facility management experts indicate that M&R funding at 2 percent of replacement value is minimum; less results in a degradation of inventory over time. Of course, this recommended range may not be as relevant to a small inventory of buildings in a local community as it is to a large inventory at a state or federal agency. However, even with small inventories, the 2 to 4 percent range of M&R funding is valid over time.

Following the publication of the 2–4 percent funding range, one of the authors, in fact, confirmed the validity of that range in his own practice.

Repair or replacement of major deficiencies in building components that have evolved as a result of long-term M&R underfunding is an implicit part of the stream of costs. When funding is not available for all repair projects in a given year, a backlog of repair projects is created, and the condition of the property and the significance of that condition must be assessed in order to reduce this repair backlog. Cost of ownership implicitly recognizes the need to correct high-priority deficiencies with a structured program to reduce repair backlog, but such corrections are outside the 2 to 4 percent funding range for any one year.

On the other hand, fully funded M&R results in an equilibrium point of funding that maintains the inventory and backlog of repairs. At this point, routine maintenance is fully funded, as are routine repairs. In an era of fluctuating budgets, good management dictates that maintenance be funded first, with repairs variable. Alas, repairs continually postponed also escalate into disasters. At a minimum, authorities should strive to reach this funding equilibrium; otherwise, the buildings are consumed through lack of maintenance and repair.

An organization can determine replacement value in several ways. The controller, in fact, will probably dictate how it is to be done. The simplest approach estimates what it would cost in any given year to replace a building to perform the same function as the original. Another approach applies escalation factors to the acquisition cost of the building. Some companies have developed computer programs to perform this calculation and to provide a replacement value or current plan value for the total inventory each year. A number of indexes are available, including those published by the U.S. Office of Management and Budget for the U.S. federal government and those published by *Engineering News Record*. There is the potential for inaccuracy in any of these estimates, particularly since some public buildings are over a hundred years old. It is necessary for each company to evaluate its inventory and develop the best approach for determining its replacement value.

The company is bound by the procedures established by its reviewing authorities for the formulation and presentation of its budgets. We are not recommending a single approach appropriate for all levels of detail and budget formats. The cost-of-ownership concept, however, does provide a framework for indicating the funding level for M&R. Management can then take a long-term look at funding levels and develop a strategic plan for appropriate M&R funding.

Maintenance and Repair Management System

To be effective, an M&R program must operate in the context of a complete facility management system. Maintenance, like all other functions, needs to be goal oriented. Exhibit 26-3 shows one approach to establishing goals and objectives for an M&R program.

It is difficult to present one M&R management system equally applicable to all organizations; no two building maintenance organizations are organized identically. However, the model in Appendix F-5 is as comprehensive and applicable as possible. It starts as a classic management model: planning, organizing, staffing, directing, controlling, and evaluating. However, the next level of detail is a checklist for good M&R management. Automated facility management (such as computer-assisted facility management, or CAFM) is often a possibility. While priority should be on systematizing maintenance management, whether automated or manual, the database for facility holdings in excess of 100,000 square feet should be automated for efficient management.

Computerized Maintenance Management Systems (CMMS) are available to automate the repair request system and align it with condition assessment modules and lifecycle costing programs. The Society for Maintenance and Reliability Professionals (SMRP) provides guidance for setting up such systems. For additional information, see www.smrp.org.

The elements in the M&R model are interrelated. There are, however, a number of feedback loops:

- Planning-programming-budget-execution-evaluation
- Budget-accounting-work plan-management information system (MIS)
- Capital budget-maintenance and repair budget
- Condition assessment-level of annual funding
- Work management-staffing-work standards-output

Exhibit 26-3. Universal maintenance objectives.

Overall maintenance goal: Provide economical maintenance and housekeeping services to allow the facility to be used for its intended purpose.

Specific maintenance objectives:

- Perform daily housekeeping and cleaning to maintain a properly presentable facility.
- Promptly respond to and repair minor problems in the facility.
- Develop and execute a system of regularly scheduled maintenance procedures to prevent premature failure of the facility and its systems and components.
- Complete major repairs based upon lowest life-cycle cost.
- Identify, design, and complete improvement projects to reduce and minimize total operating and maintenance costs.
- Operate the facility utilities in the most economical manner while providing necessary reliability.
- Provide for easy and complete reporting and identification of necessary repair and maintenance work.
- Perform accurate cost estimating to ensure lowest-cost solutions to maintenance problems.
- Maintain a proper level of material and spare parts to support timely repairs.
- Accurately track the costs of all maintenance work.
- Schedule all planned work in advance, and allocate and anticipate staff requirements to meet planned and unplanned events.
- Monitor the progress of all maintenance work.
- Maintain complete historical data concerning the facility in general and equipment and components in particular.
- Continually seek workable engineering solutions to maintenance problems.

Source: Gregory H. Magee, *Facilities Maintenance Management* (Kingston, Mass.: R. S. Means Co., 1988), p. 14.

Managers should establish policies and procedures to monitor each of these periodically.

The following are the elements of an effective M&R management program, roughly corresponding to the model; where an item is contained under several management functions, it appears where first noted.

Planning and Programming

A good M&R management system starts with the basic data, plans, policies, procedures, and standards to set proper priorities, describe the facilities and their condition, define the work, establish standards, and organize the work into a plan that is both responsive and doable. (In many cases, however, because of years of underfunding, the database has deteriorated.) The inventory of facilities describes the category of facility, states its condition (whether by ongoing inspection or a condition assessment), then assesses the critical nature of any deficiency. New elements, whether capital additions or correction of errors, are entered at least annually.

Exact categories, priorities, and definitions of work are developed. Preventive maintenance, for example, is differentiated from repair. Facility managers select definitions and categories of work that fit their needs and then stay within those definitions to determine the elements of their work plan. Other common ways to categorize work are by priority for accomplishment (e.g., emergency vs. routine) or by approval level required to implement (e.g., $1,500 or less, $1,500–$20,000, $20,000–$100,000, or over $100,000).

The annual departmental M&R work plan contains major M&R projects in priority order, a lump sum to fund preventive maintenance, and a lump sum to fund routine service-order M&R work. A prioritized list of underfunded requirements, in priority order, is also attached.

Generally M&R is planned and funded annually; however, it should operate with a midterm plan that sets priorities on major and cyclical M&R and that provides three- to five-year guidance on the thrust of the M&R program.

Budgeting

Of all the functions of a good M&R program, budgeting usually requires the most management attention; it is, after all, the lifeblood of M&R, an annually controlled function with multiple review points. Each company identifies its requirements in its own unique way (e.g., bubble up or top down), but often all sources of requirements are not considered (What impact will more carry-out fast food in the cafeteria have on carpet maintenance?). There needs to be a comprehensive scheme to collect requirements.

In the model, requirements are examined and prioritized before being submitted in the budget. If funds are likely to be available beyond the critical requirements, they are rank-ordered by priorities established in the midyear plan. Alteration and minor construction funds are not mingled with M&R funds. There are strict rules governing the leakage of M&R dollars into alterations funds.

When the budget is assembled, the manager conducts several analyses, including historical comparisons, unit cost comparisons, comparison to a target percentage of current replacement value, comparisons to the current year's budget, and trend analyses. Variances then become a principal part of the narrative of the budget along with new issues. If the funding guidance is lower than the accumulated requirements, statements of the impact of the funding constraint, by category, are submitted.

The cost accounting and MIS are responsive to proper M&R management requirements. A proper system is able to produce current cost data to assess requirements for preventive maintenance, minor maintenance and repair (service orders), cyclic maintenance projects (by project), and repair projects (by project). It is capable of doing so by time period and by facility. If cost comparators are used, the MIS is able to calculate them.

Each large company decides whether to track expense or commitment data, or a hybrid of both, during budget execution; smaller companies, particularly those with an inventory principally of buildings, track the unit cost (recommended dollar per square foot) of preventive maintenance and service orders. (Some larger organizations prefer to track total M&R dollars by activity code, with special emphasis on critical trends.)

The effect of the capital budget on the M&R budget is worth mentioning for at least three reasons: (1) additions to the capital inventory add to the base for M&R, (2) decisions based on life-cycle costing, rather than more capital costs, have positive, major downstream effects on future M&R budgets, and (3) designing to maintain is a principal concept in all design policies.

Organizing

Organizing an M&R management program at the national or international level (usually a staff function) or at the local level (usually both a staff and a line management function) can be very different. However, certain common features should be in place.

1. A manager is clearly in charge of M&R, from policy through evaluation.
2. The M&R program is placed where it is not subjected to competition for new construction funds.
3. A clearly defined channel for gathering, categorizing, and executing M&R is in place to ensure coordination with operations, alterations, and capital construction.

The M&R manager has an analysis capability and a good information system. In medium and small companies, buildings are metered (data collection systems put in place) to collect comparative data by individual building or within a facility category. Finally, well-developed material management and purchasing functions—knowledgeable of and responsive to the M&R manager—are essential for a well-run program.

Staffing

Staffing for good M&R management varies significantly according to the size of the company, yet a number of principles are common:

1. The M&R program staff is as technically competent as the capital program staff. The M&R staff is involved in reviewing all capital projects.
2. Only when necessary (because of the small size of the building inventory, for example) is M&R a part-time staff function.
3. The M&R program is staffed to inspect for deficiencies, as well as to inspect the M&R work.
4. Training is available to improve management and technical skills.
5. Leadership qualities in a manager are emphasized, so the M&R program is proactive.

The correct mix of contract and in-house staff is an important item for consideration, particularly during the program execution phase. We do not have specific guidance, but the best situation is what the manager is comfortable with and can afford in terms of salaries and staff positions. Tasks related to policy, standards, budgeting, work plan development, and quality control and evaluation should be retained in-house.

The brain drain has seriously hindered our ability to operate, maintain, and repair our facilities because older supervisors and technicians are retiring and the trades and our training programs simply have been unable to fill the gap. One solution is a smart asset management program where experienced technicians are treated like the valued resource that they are. Using the IWMS, these technicians are assigned and tracked just like important parts and equipment and the less-experienced technicians are assigned to less critical tasks and projects.[4] This does not, however, solve the problem in the developed world as less and less young people enter technical apprentice programs compared to the increasing demand.

Directing

The function of directing is almost synonymous with implementing. The common threads at any level are:

1. An appropriate level of design and documentation
2. The ability to respond rapidly to a crisis
3. A recognition that a substantial portion of the workload is reactive

Over time, experienced managers can predict the last two items reasonably accurately despite their apparent unpredictable nature.

The quality of direction in an M&R program normally reflects the information available to the manager. For example, how can limited funds be properly prioritized unless the manager has determined the most critical needs? Proper direction is based on a number of factors, including established priorities, condition assessment, need, and the work plan.

In many large companies, a major function is allocating M&R funds among executing activities. This allocation often dictates how the activities will execute their work plan. Factors to be considered include:

1. Budget guidance
2. Priorities
3. The ability to execute the work plan
4. Criticality of facilities
5. Quality of the submitted requirements
6. Past performance history
7. Condition assessment

Particularly at medium to small facilities, a strong work management and coordination center, automated diagnostics, and commissioning procedures for new buildings can be directed and have strong influences on a good M&R program.

Controlling

The principles of M&R control are consistent for all types and sizes of companies. Control devices include policy, procedures, standards, work plan, budget, approval levels, management information systems, and documentation. The manager, given whatever level of resources, balances and manipulates the following:

1. Control of the budget
2. Control of expenditures
3. New crises
4. New priorities
5. Possible windfalls

To do so, it is absolutely essential that a real-time management information system be available. Above all, someone should be accountable for all aspects of the M&R program.

Evaluating

With the emphasis on benchmarking, M&R evaluation has taken on an entirely new character. Traditionally, facility managers evaluated their M&R programs according to factors such as:

- Comparison of the year completed with the prior year or an average year
- Whether priorities were met
- What critical facilities were accommodated
- Trends such as total backlog or against a target percentage of the replacement value
- Leakage of M&R dollars
- Comparison by activities: category or building, leakage, and percentage of work plan executed
- Whether the right skills were employed

Benchmarking of M&R has become prevalent. That has been driven by the quality management movement and is largely concerned with matters of efficiency. The benchmarking process involves identifying specific areas for study, measuring performance in these areas, identifying other companies against which to benchmark, comparing the department's performance against its benchmarking partners, and then figuring out who has the best practices and how to incorporate those best practices into the department. The professional associations have assisted in this regard. The Building Owners and Managers Association (BOMA) publishes the *Experience Report* annually. The International Facility Management Association (IFMA) publishes *Benchmark Report* triannually. APPA has developed and published a benchmarking model called the Strategic Assessment Model, which, among other things, assesses M&R. The model includes fifteen benchmarks by which colleges and universities can assess their maintenance programs against others and a recommended standard. Possible M&R benchmarks are contained in Exhibit 26-4.

If the benchmarks generated by the professional associations are inadequate, the facility manager can hire a benchmarking consultant to help gather the data and find data against which to compare. Once the benchmarks have been established and implementation procedures are in place and functioning (my experience is that it takes two to three cycles to get the bugs out), then the manager should set goals and objectives to improve M&R. This process involves allocating resources. However, once the facility manager has decided to emphasize a certain area—improved customer satisfaction, for example—and has implemented procedures to do so, the

Exhibit 26-4. Typical benchmarks for maintenance and repair.

Efficiency Benchmarks	Effectiveness Benchmarks
Total and work time per work order	Percentage of customer services for which customer satisfaction is measured
Cost per work order—total and by category	Percentage of positive comments received—total and by category
Total maintenance and repair costs—total and by category	Backlog of deferred maintenance
Costs as a percentage of replacement costs	Hours available vs. hours worked
Number of work orders completed on time for preventive and routine work	Ratio of preventive maintenance hours to routine maintenance hours
Funding of maintenance and repair as a percentage of the total facilities and capital budget by time period	Equipment failures
	Number of work orders by time period by category
	Number of positive comments received per time period

benchmarking process should be able to track progress so that responsibility can be fixed, success can be reinforced, and failure can be recognized early.

Putting Maintenance and Repair in Context

We have already mentioned the serious problems of underfunding of M&R in North America. Since this condition has existed throughout our professional lives, we doubt that top management and legislative bodies will suddenly change and adequately fund M&R. Therefore, it is essential for facility managers to ensure that they are using allocated funds wisely. Often they are simply spending money without making any rational decision as to where they get the biggest payoff from our limited funds. Central to good decision making in this area is *condition assessment* (CA).

In its simplest terms, CA is a total audit of the facilities with a detailed list of discrepancies, including code violations. Most contain a funding profile for the next five to ten years for M&R and a projected replacement date for building elements and equipment. A benefit that we discovered during a CA is that we learned which design firms truly designed for maintainability and durability and which manufacturers produce equipment with the longest service lives. Another benefit is to observe outside experts and their technology and techniques to assess the condition of the company's facilities. Some of those same technologies are applicable to the department's M&R program.

Almost all large architectural-engineering (A-E) firms have CA capability. In most cases, they can do their work with minimal destructive testing. We strongly advise against trying to do CA with in-house staff. They can guide and oversee the operation, but they don't have time for the in-depth analysis required by a good CA, and they may unconsciously bias the results. Although the cost is admittedly high, the CA can be the heart of a reasonable M&R plan and program. Another benefit of using an outside consultant is that management will listen (where they may not listen to their internal experts). A CA, if properly constructed, can also benefit you by determining your energy needs and possibilities for conservation and efficiencies. Although it was costly, the CA that one of your authors did on his facility complex formed the basis for strategic facility decisions for at least ten years, the absolute maximum time that large facility departments should allow between CAs. Another approach for very large organizations is to conduct a CA of a sampling of facilities— 10 to 20 percent—each year so that all facilities are audited within a time frame of five to ten years.

The Maintenance Plan

We have found that public-sector agencies are far ahead of their private brethren in organizing comprehensive maintenance programs. However, in implementation there is less variation because everyone invariably underfunds M&R. Every building element should be covered by an appropriate level of maintenance, determined by management and considering (1) the cost-effectiveness of maintenance through increased serviceability and extension of service life and (2) the desired appearance of the facility elements.

There are almost an infinite number of approaches to maintenance and repair, but they tend to fall into one of six categories:

1. Inspect and repair only as necessary (IROAN).
2. Cyclical repair—repair performed on a specific cycle (e.g., replace roofs every seventeen years).
3. Preventive maintenance—maintain equipment according to a preestablished checklist and cycle (e.g., change generator oil every 100 hours or semiannually, whichever occurs first).
4. Predictive maintenance (the use of sophisticated nondestructive testing to avert the breakdown of critical equipment).
5. Breakdown maintenance most of which can be repaired on a service order (e.g., a burned-out light bulb)
6. Repair projects (e.g., replace all window assemblies in a factory).

A comprehensive maintenance program uses each of these techniques to ensure that every facility component is maintained and repaired in a cost-effective manner consistent with facility standards.

From our observations, plant systems have the most thorough and sophisticated maintenance plans, particularly for preventive maintenance.

Historically, custodial service (janitorial service, carpet and floor cleaning, window washing, and insect and rodent control) has not been considered part of maintenance, but that is incorrect thinking. These services are an integral part of comprehensive maintenance. For example, carpet repairs are minimized if carpet cleaning is done effectively. Maintainability should not be an afterthought. Designing for maintainability should be a priority for every architect, engineer, interior designer, and facility manager.[5] This is also true for designing for sustainability.

The maintenance plan should include user input. Users can play both active and passive roles. For example, they can:

- Use trash receptacles.
- Report spills quickly.
- Use equipment, particularly elevators, properly.
- Report deficiencies.
- Place signs only on authorized bulletin boards.
- Refrain from using water fountains as slop sinks.
- Turn off lights when not in use.
- Turn off water faucets.
- Use mats to clean feet.
- Report unsafe conditions.

It is estimated that this level of staff involvement can reduce building maintenance costs by 10 percent. The actions can occur through a number of stimuli, such as managerial emphasis, pride in the organization and its facilities, and an education or internal relations program.

Through Presidential Executive Order 13327, all U.S. federal agencies are required to develop and implement Asset Management Plans (AMP). The most essential element of a successful AMP is the establishment of service levels which typically cover reliability (manual water valves are exercised annually), quality (total complaints are not to exceed 25 per month), customer service (hold time on calls will be less than 2 minutes for 95 percent of the calls), and regulatory compliance (residual chlorine meets EPA standards). These service levels, if properly selected, then translate into the funding necessary to make informed decisions on the best way to apply all available resources to optimize maintenance of the facilities.[6] While we agree with development of AMPs we believe this order missed its mark. Despite the documented deficiencies in funding federal public buildings, facility managers are now asked to adjust M&R to the funding level, rather than being given the 2–4 percent of the replacement cost of the facilities needed to properly maintain and repair the facilities.

Another approach to "getting a handle on the M&R problem" is to calculate BMAR (or BMR), the Backlog of Maintenance and Repair, also called deferred maintenance. The basis for calculating BMAR is a condition assessment which then allows deferred maintenance costs to be calculated to bring the facility inventory (normally done or led by an outside contractor or consultant) up to whatever standard the facility manager and his management desires. The critical component is to openly agree on and assess for the desired outcomes so that all concerned are "operating off the same sheet of music." Calculation of BMAR does not produce details of specific projects but does provide sound information for capital planning for alterations, major repair, and even construction which can bring the facilities up to established studies.

Preventive Maintenance

We have been most successful operating a preventive maintenance (PM) program with three teams:

1. Plant
2. Exteriors, interiors, furniture, security, fire and life safety systems, and furnishings
3. Electrical switchboards, floor panels, and devices

Preventive maintenance of specialty items (elevators, building controls) is best contracted through the manufacturer. All told, these teams report all items beyond their capability to the work reception center so that a service order can be processed.

All three PM teams, particularly the second, need to understand the limits of their maintenance work and when a service order must be written. Painting is always an issue. The PM team should paint, but only spot painting; the PM foreman must be sensitive to when excessive spot painting will produce a leopard look and when the painters should be called in.

The PM team cycle is largely determined by each manufacturer's recommended maintenance frequencies. We try to have all public and executive areas inspected weekly. We inspect thoroughly the building exteriors annually and examine the garages and back hallways at least semiannually. The second PM team is concerned primarily with occupied areas of the building. It should try to visit these areas quarterly. Each building occupant, particularly the administrative staff, should know the particular handyman on the PM team. For this reason, the team members must be capable of interaction with the staff. If this program is managed well, it is the best public relations program for the facilities department as well as its eyes and ears.

Increasingly facility departments, but particularly their vendors, are using sophisticated, nondestructive methods to predict equipment failure before it happens, among them, thermography, wear-particle analysis, ultrasound, oil analysis, and vibrations analysis. Often these technologies are used in tandem or as a second opinion before a critical piece of equipment is pulled off-line. These technologies can also be used to identify sources of energy inefficiencies. Some of these technologies require expensive equipment and extensive training; others can be brought in-house at a reasonable cost if the demand for predictive maintenance exists. Predictive maintenance, not surprisingly, is most often used in maintaining industrial facilities because the technology and expertise already exist to maintain the production equipment.

Several organizations have implemented reliability-centered maintenance (RCM) which can be an effective cost avoidance strategy. RCM is both logical and fact-based and, some would say, is the only rational maintenance system because there should be 1) a reduction in maintenance hours and 2) maintenance performed when and where needed. Actually, the situation is much more complex. Not only does implementation of RCM require substantial upfront analysis but also needs to have a knowledgeable leader to make that analysis. Consequently, RCM has not been as widely used as might be assumed. Gradually, however, as more and more facility managers become familiar with RCM techniques, we see them being more widely adopted. Even then there are levels of RCM based on dispersion of the facilties, age and condition of the facilities, and whether the facilities are newly constructed or existing. The level chosen will depend on your return on investment based on both time and cost and the possibility that you can truly mitigate risk.

New technology like thermography is helpful in solving complex repair problems and new techniques are being developed especially as facility managers are being asked to do more with less. Predictive maintenance, condition-based maintenance and reliability-centered maintenance are similar systems which gravitated into facility management.[7] Reliability-centered maintenance, for example, came from the equipment-rich environments like NASA. We admit to less experience than is needed to make judgments on these systems but it is our observation followed up by discussion with colleagues that these systems work well on equipment, less well when tried in a more general application.

Cyclical Maintenance

This topic does not appear in most books on maintenance management because it is not a pure category of work. Rather, it is a concept—a convenient way of thinking about maintenance. Experience shows that certain items need to be maintained on a certain basis. For instance, battery-powered clocks need new batteries semiannually. The team can use the weekends to set the clocks forward and back for daylight savings time and also change the batteries. If not done sooner, all interiors should be repainted every three years. Though carpeting will often last ten to twelve years, for a number of reasons, we replace it every six years. Cyclical maintenance is actually replacement, but of a nature that expedites planning and budgeting. Ensure that cyclical maintenance practices are in agreement with the life expectancy of the products. For instance, you may have convinced your boss to switch from broadloom to carpet tile because the latter's greater life expectancy justified the higher initial cost.

The Work Reception Center

We discussed the role and operation of the work reception center (WRC) in Chapter 24. The WRC is key to a successful M&R program. It is the one place where anyone can report a facilities problem and get action, without fuss or long bureaucratic review. A typical history of problem solving in the M&R program is as follows.

	By Number of Problems	By Cost
Preventive maintenance	75%	50%
Service orders	24	30
Projects	1	20

Several conclusions can be drawn from these data, but one that is inescapable is that M&R projects can often be solved through a good PM program and a work reception center. If the WRC functions properly, the facility manager and the maintenance manager (if there is one) can spend their time managing major repair projects.

For the WRC to function properly, the staff must:

1. Be given authority to task shops directly to accomplish all but exceptional work.
2. Have clear guidance on what work is an exception.
3. Be equipped with a maintenance management system that allows them to develop, track, and close work orders and to develop work and cost history by shop, user, and facility.

Realistically, all but exceptional service orders should be completed within seventy-two hours. Whenever this cannot be achieved, the WRC should notify the individual with a brief explanation and a probable completion date.

Repair Projects

Despite all best efforts, some repair projects will arise each year. In addition, the value and complexity of some work may make it necessary to develop and control it as a project (a major roof repair is a good example). Some companies allow certain major repairs to be capitalized, but normally that is not possible. Because these projects tend to be large and often require design, they need to be planned and programmed. They also need to be spread over a number of years so that they do not have too severe an impact on any single annual budget.

Migration of Funds

Most organizations fund all their alteration and renovation projects from the same account as maintenance and repair. That is an invitation to long-term neglect of the latter. There are nearly always alteration and renovation requirements far in excess of the funds available. Unless controls are established, it is almost inevitable that alterations will consume a greater and greater portion of the annual O&M budget. Two controls have been used effectively.

1. Setting a dollar amount or percentage ceiling on the annual amount of alterations work
2. Allocating the funds, using a user's priority board chaired by the facility manager

We are disappointed with what we consider to be the continuing degradation of the maintenance and repair of our facilities. It is well documented as pointed out earlier in this chapter. For all facility managers who want to be on the cutting edge, we offer the following techniques:

- Wider use of building diagnostics and condition assessment, particularly technology-based, continuous-read systems.
- Increased application of preventive maintenance to all aspects of facilities and their furnishings, not just the plant.
- Formulaic funding for normal maintenance and repair—for example, 2 to 4 percent of replacement value.
- Better use of M&R funds through CA and the use of computerized maintenance management.

There are two outstanding books on maintenance management that should be part of every facility department library: John E. Heintzelman's *The Complete*

Handbook of Maintenance Management and Gregory Magee's *Facilities Maintenance Management.* These books provide both solid maintenance philosophy and cost-effective techniques for implementing and maintaining a quality maintenance program.

One final sobering note, since it involves two of your authors directly, is most, but not exclusively, applicable to colleges and universities. *We are building ourselves into a problem, not out of one!*

One approach to solving the M&R backlog problem is unique to colleges and universities and non-profits where building programs are primarily funded through contributions. Under this approach, an endowment is established to fund M&R simultaneously with the funding of construction. Another strategy is to stop building until you catch up on maintenance.[8] Yet a third approach is controlled construction and major renovations.[9] As mentioned in the section concerning BMAR, they can be used to wipe out large chunks of the backlog. However, everyone needs to be aware that, the minute the ribbon is cut, the new or renovated facility starts to deteriorate and needs to be maintained.

Notes

1. *Committing to the Cost of Ownership* (Washington, D.C.: Building Research Board, 1990), pp. xi–xii.
2. Harvey Kaiser and Jeremy S. Davis, *A Foundation to Uphold* (Washington, D.C.: APPA, NACUBO, Sallie Mae, 1997), p. 2.
3. *Pay Now or Pay Later; Controlling Cost of Ownership from Design Throughout the Service Life of Public Buildings* (Washington, D.C.: Building Research Board, 1991).
4. Jerry D. Cederstrom, "The Brain Drain," *TFM*, February 2008, p. 16.
5. Edwin B. Feldman, *Building Design for Maintainability*, (Atlanta, GA: Service Engineering Associates, 1982).
6. Cynthia Nielsen, "Asset Management Plans," *The Military Engineer*, September–October 2007, pp. 47–48.
7. John Kuchler, "Predictive Maintenance," *TFM*, February 2008, p. 18.
8. Nancy Thomson and James P. Whittaker, "The BMAR Approach to Asset Management," *The Military Engineer*, January–February 2008, pp. 61–62.
9. Scott Carlson, "As Campuses Crumble, Budgets are Crunched," *The Chronicle of Higher Education*, May 23, 2008, p. 3.

Facility Services

Pulse Points

- *Most administrative services should be considered for contracting out. They require expertise that is not likely to be on staff.*
- *Facility managers should anticipate the expanded or new services that their customers will demand.*
- *When faced with managing a new administrative service, benchmark with and learn from the best-in-class.*

In this chapter we discuss the general administrative services that facility managers have traditionally managed, as well as some emerging services. As middle management has been reduced in companies and agencies, facility managers have taken on more services, to the point that many are questioning again whether *facility manager* is really a descriptive term for the position. In fact, a major study of federal facilities suggests the term "facilities asset manager."[1]

According to a survey, the general administrative services managed by facility managers were as follows:[1]

Service	Percentage	Change in Eight Years
Security	71	+ 13%
Mail services	54	+ 10%
Communications	53	+ 10%
Copying services	44	+ 2%
Records management	50	+ 10%
Moving and shipping	50	+ 11%

We discussed Security in detail in Chapters 20–22. Clearly there has been an increase in the role of facility managers as organizations have flattened.

Certain facility managers, of course, manage functions not even surveyed. Each service mentioned here is a major management function. However, we discuss only some managerial considerations plus how each of these services affects and is influenced by traditional facility services. We refer to the manager of each specific service by that job title (for example, security manager). Large organizations may have a technical manager to handle these specialties for the facility manager, but often that individual is the facility manager in smaller organizations.

Traditional Services

Food Service

Food and facility services are inextricably intertwined. Capital costs for food service facilities are high. Food products soil carpets and furniture. Food preparation areas have high maintenance costs. Because of the fear of spoilage, food service equipment must be kept functioning continually.

Food service is often performed at five levels:

1. Coffee service
2. Carry-out and fast food
3. Full-service cafeteria
4. Private dining rooms with table service
5. Banquet and party service

Increasingly, companies are placing coffee services in the workplace. First, it reduces the time away from the desk. Second, it provides a meeting place for employees to mingle informally. It is interesting to observe these coffee bars. Some are austere and communicate the message, "Get your coffee and don't dawdle." Others are more elaborate, with tables and chairs encouraging communication. Neither approach is right or wrong; each simply reflects the company's approach to work.

These coffee bars require day-porter service to keep them operating and clean. Some companies hire the replenishment of the coffee bars; some use in-house personnel; in others, volunteers make the coffee. Cleanup of the equipment and the immediate area, however, is best done by a day porter. Also, decentralized coffee bars cause an increase in carpet staining, probably because staff often get their coffee in open cups rather than in the covered cups normally sold in a cafeteria. Recycling is changing the face of coffee service (ceramic cups are making a comeback), but it is not making it less complicated.

Whether the company should subsidize food service is an often-debated issue. The consensus is that there is an advantage to have staff eat on the premises so a subsidy is justified. This subsidy most likely consists of paying the rent, utility costs, and repair and maintenance costs rather than defraying the actual costs of food and service.

When food service is provided, the issue is whether to contract out or provide in-house service. During this era of staff reductions, most companies are using food service contractors. There are numerous competent contractors available, with some specializing in cafeteria, fast food, or coffee. Others provide the full spectrum (table service dining and banquets as well), but at a higher cost owing to increased overhead.

Another concern is whether to hire a national contractor or a local one. A national company centers on the resources available, allowing the client a wide range of talent to support the food service operation. But local companies involve their management or ownership in the operation. The parameters of profit for a regional company are less than for a national contractor.[2]

The company needs to set the tone for the quality of its food service. It is difficult to make the banquet and private dining rooms profitable at a price competitive with local restaurants unless some of that overhead is borne by a high-volume cafeteria. That is particularly true if the food service operation is required to "eat" a large amount of official entertainment costs. The company needs to decide whether food service is to be a profit center, a break-even operation, or a subsidized service. The contractor can then recommend options to meet the company's objectives.

Maintenance of the food service equipment is somewhat vexing. One approach is to hire a maintenance package from the food service contractor; another treats food service equipment the same as other installed equipment. The amount of equipment often is the determinant. When justifiable, our preference is to have the maintenance mechanics assigned to the facility department but under the operational control of the food service manager, who also determines their working hours. The security force, all engineers, and all electricians must be extremely sensitive to the specialized needs of the food service facilities, particularly for uninterrupted gas, electricity, and refrigeration. Many facility managers tell sad tales of failing to reactivate power to a food service walk-in refrigerator following weekend maintenance and finding spoiled food on Monday morning. Remember that food storage and preparation occurs at other than normal hours.

Reprographics

One of the catch terms of the early 1980s was the "paperless office." Anyone who has managed the paper copying function for a large organization knows the term is a myth. Paper enters a facility and is copied in volumes unthought of even ten years ago. It is not unusual for a large company to produce hundreds of thousands of copies annually.

It used to be necessary to hire outside art and design people and a commercial printer, or to establish an internal print plant, if the company needed high-volume, high-quality printing. But with the advent of high-speed copiers, volume no longer was an issue. Then desktop publishing began providing sophisticated graphics and layout. With PC-based desktop publishing and color laser printing, highly sophisticated color reprographics will be almost completely decentralized to the work units. Most departments can now produce documents at desks that only five years ago we would have sent to art and design and then to a printer.

Because the technology (and also the philosophy) of reprographics is changing so rapidly, it is difficult to assess the impact of reprographics on facilities. Generally, the cost and ease of installation and maintenance of desktop copiers permit wide dissemination of equipment down to the lowest work units. It is reasonable to require users to "eat" the space to support a desktop copier, but most companies place high-speed, high-volume copiers at designated central locations. Quite often they are stacked vertically so that an employee always knows what location to go to on a floor to find the copy machine.

The location of these copy machines should be chosen carefully. They require large volumes of paper. That paper needs to be moved to the copier in bulk and replenished often. Moving paper in bulk can be extremely damaging. Storage and movement of completed products poses a similar problem. In some exceptional cases, the storage of paper or documents actually can exceed normal floor-load criteria. Also, these machines require a dedicated electrical circuit, substantial space, and special ventilation, particularly if they are used full-time.

Most companies prefer to lease their equipment, although various options are available for buy-lease, maintenance, and copy paper supply. Another decision is whether to have permanent attendants man the high-volume copy centers or to allow staff to operate them. The choice depends on the complexity of the equipment and the expected volume of use. In addition, there is a trend toward decentralizing the support and leasing of desktop copiers directly to work units.

Digital technology is playing an increasing role as the technology is simplified and as consumers become more familiar with applications. Digitization allows different pieces of office equipment to communicate with one another, thus enabling workers to accomplish many tasks while seated at their desks. For example, a letter can be scanned into a computer and attached to an e-mail with just a few keystrokes. In addition, the full-color copier is coming into its own. PC-based color copies are now available to everyone at a relatively low cost.

In some cases, the volume and complexity of printed material still require a printing facility. The first option, particularly in urban areas where pricing is competitive, is to contract out. Normally at least two rates are established: one for normal printing and one for immediate turnaround. Ensure that requirements for expedited printing are spelled out in all contracts with printers.

The second option, housing a print plant in the facility, presents unique challenges. Newsprint comes into a facility on large rolls, which are difficult to handle without damaging the facility. Both newsprint and the completed product require some degree of humidity control and storage space. Also, a print plant places a major demand on freight elevators.

Mail and Messenger Services

One of the legends of the corporate world is the chief executive officer (CEO) who began his career in the mailroom. Surprisingly, there are many examples of people who have risen through the ranks from the mailroom. One theory is that if you understand how mail is distributed, you understand how the organization works.

Managing the mailroom requires concentrating on essentials and details. Since mail is one means of communication, there is merit in common management for all communications means in the company. The five factors critical for success are personnel, facilities and equipment, technology, adherence to postal regulations, and emphasis on users.

Staffing is the most challenging area for the mailroom manager. There is a diversity of personnel and of products, particularly when the staff is a mix of in-house and contractors or vendors. Products may include first-, second-, third-, and fourth-class mail; parcels; overnight express mail; registered and certified mail; facsimile and messenger center products; and messenger services. During a recent consulting contract, one of your authors was observing the mailroom in the late morning. At the same time, the company's mail clerk was trying to service a U.S. Postal Service mailman, three parcel service delivery men, and two messengers.

Good human resources management in the mailroom does not differ from management in other areas of the company. People must be challenged. Everyone must understand the mission of the mailroom and must realize that they contribute to that mission. Motivation is essential, as is participation in establishing goals and decentralization of responsibility.

Many mailrooms resemble a sweatshop. To avoid this, the facility manager should seize every opportunity to (1) use industrial design to make working conditions more efficient and more pleasant and (2) improve production and reduce boredom. The location of the mailroom (access to the loading dock, controlled access of outside vendors, central location) is critical for effective operation and security. The following points should be considered in design:

1. Work flow should be from left to right, owing to traditional mail equipment design.
2. The layout should be flexible.
3. L- or V-shaped mail-sorting areas are best.
4. Since many tasks are repetitive, study the ergonomics of all workstations.
5. Minimize interruptions through proper layout.
6. In midsize and large companies, use a mail conveyor system.
7. Involve security in determining the mailroom's location.

The availability of entry-level personnel, a traditional source for the mailroom, is becoming tenuous. This means the mailroom manager may have to resort to non-traditional approaches or replace people or functions with technology. Part-time employees such as retired employees or high school students may be hired to supplement the full-time staff. Mailroom jobs can also be enhanced through cross-training.

Ultimately, users will determine the success or failure of the mailroom. Constantly evaluate and seek user feedback.

- How do users feel about the mailroom's performance in general?
- How do users measure the mailroom's operation?
- What can the mailroom do to serve users better?

Never underestimate the value of public relations. Consider an open house in the mailroom. Participate in the company briefing for new administrative assistants. Consider promoting a mailroom user group.

A real challenge is staying current with postal service and other vendor rules and incentive programs. To do so, keep a library, obtain vendor briefings, and join the local Postal Customer Council.

Smooth work flow, minimum interruptions, and intelligent selection of carriers cut mailroom costs.

Lee Yeaton, vice president of Pitney Bowes Management Services, recognizes the challenges of managing a cost-effective mail center. Mailrooms traditionally are low on the priority list of corporate concerns even though, according to a Pitney Bowes study, mail accounts for over 9 percent of operating costs at Fortune 500 companies. He recommends examining the entire process, not just the mail center:

- Focus on the areas that will affect the business the most.

- Ensure that you are communicating by the most economical method. It often costs less to send a fax than a first-class piece of mail. And 17 percent of third-class mail is never opened, much less read.
- Are duplicates eliminated from the mail stream?
- Is all mail properly classed?
- Does mail conform to postal automation standards?
- Is your business mail reaching the right customers? Should the recipient be paying postage instead of you?
- Do you stay in touch with postal and technology changes that can reduce costs while increasing customer service?[3]

The proper application of technology is one more area for cost-cutting— for example:

- An integrated system connecting scales, meters, a security system, and a PC
- An electronic scale with a memory capable of accounting against a budget, of calculating chargebacks, and that is adjustable for postal rate changes
- Postal meters

The mail must go through, so ensure all equipment has responsive maintenance and repair backup.

More than $10 billion was spent in 1989 on overnight delivery service.[4] Since then, overnight delivery has absolutely exploded; some would say unnecessarily. Often our customers think only of speed and ease of transmission of their delivery, not cost. The accounts payable manager can determine how much the company spent on this service. The reality is that 30 percent of these costs probably can be cut. Express mail and overnight delivery have become almost routine in modern business. To manage express mail costs, focus on three major areas: use, rates, and bills. Consider the following as mailroom procedure:

1. Select the proper mode such as same-day service via air, ground or fax; overnight service via air or ground; two-day service and three- to five-day service. Many services do "best way" calculations if asked.
2. Express delivery is a highly competitive industry. Vendors readily offer discounts to their large customers, but discounts are inconsistently applied.
3. Specify when the material is needed. Sometimes express has become a habit, not a necessity. Log and publish the use of express if there is an appearance of abuse.
4. Certified mail-return receipt can be a less costly alternative to express when urgency is not an issue.

5. Check for errors. Billing errors and overcharges are frequent. Often discounts are not given.
6. Consolidate packages going to the same destination, which is less expensive than sending multiple packages.
7. Obtain a one-time external audit targeted on cost-effectiveness.

Finally, if priority or express mail has become a major expense, which it has in most companies, appoint an express mail manager to lower the costs.

Increasingly, companies are seeking more rapid ways than mail to communicate. However, we believe that the mail and mailroom will be with us for the foreseeable future. Trends in mail are:

- More user-oriented postal services and interconnection of public and private technologies or systems for the advantage of each and discounts for participants
- More work-share programs between the postal service and private companies
- More electronic postage transfer
- Bar-coded addressing and sorting
- PC-based addressing systems
- Robotics in high-volume user mailrooms

Just how rapidly this field is changing is exemplified by the facsimile machine. The fax greatly reduces the workload on central mail services. Companies that grew to operate worldwide providing priority mail service suddenly found their existence threatened. The use of e-mail should have a great effect on both "snail mail" and fax, but most companies find that the expected trade-off does not occur. The volume of all three seems to increase. Conventional mail and priority mail are likely to remain necessary for heavy freight and printed matter like books and brochures. But the mail service manager will have an even greater array of price and technological options in the future. The department's success will depend on how quickly new cost-effective methods are instituted for receiving, processing, distributing, collecting, and disseminating information (not mail).

Transportation and Fleet Management

Normally the facility manager is not the fleet manager in a company with a primary role in transportation (e.g., a newspaper, retail, or wholesale marketing company). Often, however, the facility manager finds himself the manager of a small fleet of executive sedans, service vehicles for facilities staff, and shuttle buses.

Executive sedans present special problems not only because they have high visibility and sensitivity but because of security concerns. Often the drivers perform a security function also. Chauffeur service, of course, can be maintained in-house, but it can also be contracted as part of a security contract or with a chauffeur service. The provision of sedan service for the company is similar to that of chauffeur service. Sedans can be owned, provided as an unique package, or be part of a fleet package.

Whether to own or lease vehicles is very much a function of the facility manager's willingness and resources to operate and maintain a fleet. The primary reason for maintaining in-house fleet management is control. Leasing arrangements now largely negate that reason. A leased fleet can be responsive and well controlled, so the trend is to lease. We suspect that is prompted by resource, legal, and liability considerations as much as anything else.

Regardless of how the fleet is managed, certain principles should be observed:

1. Vehicles should be centrally dispatched and controlled.
2. Parking, whether on-site or off-site, should be provided for all vehicles. We hold that vehicles should not be garaged at an individual's home or be allowed to be taken home except as an infrequent exception. It becomes viewed as a perk and can create unnecessary morale problems, as well as serious liability exposure.
3. Maintenance can normally be provided best through outside sources (the lessor or the dealer). Extended warranties available on most vehicles actually make maintenance relatively cost effective. Fleet rates for maintenance services can be negotiated.
4. If you provide gas and oil (or use a credit card), someone should check consumption per vehicle monthly. Another easy-to-implement control is to insist that the normal provider of gas and oil dispense only into an authorized vehicle (license number clearly indicated on the credit card invoice), not a separate container, without a separate approval document.
5. Assign licensed drivers or operators to each vehicle and allow operation by someone other than the driver or operator only as a management exception.

In medium to large facilities, other vehicles can often improve the efficiency of the facilities department:

- A self-propelled or towed extendable personnel lift
- Golf carts
- Small pickups
- A self-propelled material lift
- Street or sidewalk sweepers
- A four-wheel drive vehicle (with a bull-blade for snow, where appropriate)

Many large companies find that a shuttle bus system is necessary in large urban areas. The shuttle can improve normal distribution of mail as well as move people, but it must run on a consistent schedule. Early or late operating hours are some of the most important times for shuttle service; whether employees can use the shuttle as a primary commuting means is a policy issue.

It is important that shuttle pickup points be easily accessible (sometimes special security arrangements must be established). Drop-off locations should be out of traffic so that riders can be discharged or taken on in safety. Pickup points should also be selected and illuminated so that persons waiting for the shuttle feel safe and are not exposed to accumulated exhaust. If possible, panic phones should be available at all pickup points.

Shuttle drivers can be one of the most valuable tools for internal public relations for the department (or one of its most serious PR problems). The drivers should know not only their routes but the location of common facilities (cafeterias, lobbies, etc.), the schedule of daily and special events, and the identity of principal company officers and their office locations.

Records Management

Unless a company's core business is closely tied to records management (an insurance company, a library), properly managing records has been underemphasized. This is likely to change in the near future as companies are increasingly dependent on accessing more information faster yet buried by the increased volume of information. Typically records were maintained at two or three locations (office, central file, historical file) with no uniform policy on records retention or archiving. But the inability to share information, shrinking facilities, and increased computer-generated paper have brought records management to the forefront. It is now estimated that 95 percent of business records are still stored on paper.[5]

Records management at the work-unit level is important to both the records manager and the facility manager, but it is difficult to control. Companies try to control pack rats by limiting the number of files issued, but there are so many exceptions granted that the approach is ineffective. The most effective controls are well-developed records management policies and standards for review, retention, disposal, retention, and archiving. If the pack rats are ever to turn in their files to a central location, they must be assured that their information needs will be met responsively (most seem to require twenty-four-hour response) and without effort. Central files and archives must be located, equipped, and managed to provide that level of service.

Some of the more common media to store files are tape, disk, microfiche, optical disks, flash or thumb drives, and CD-ROM. These new media, while they store information more efficiently, still offer substantial file management challenges. Some of the popular file management techniques are:

- Numbering systems
- Color coding
- Automated indexes to paper-based filing systems for active records
- Automated file change-out and control system
- Automated records center for inactive records
- Computer-assisted microfilm retrieval systems
- Automated vital records or disaster recovery plans on databases
- Development and application of networking or communication technology to provide multiuser configurations

Applying that philosophy to records management, look to the companies for which records are their lifeblood and have either major government oversight or fiduciary responsibility (insurance and mortgage companies come to mind) for best practices in record management. USAA, for example, is recognized for its excellent records management procedures.

Communications

IFMA reported in 2004 that only 16 percent of facility managers were the principal managers for information technology (IT)/telecommunications in their facilities. However, any facility manager is going to be intensively involved in the physical aspects of those responsibilities whether it involves having to install raised floors to accommodate wiring, having to build separate or to share wiring closets, having to build and service a clean room, having to provide additional power, or having to redesign office space to accommodate the IT workstations. Your authors have been practitioners during the IT revolution and have seen this aspect of their responsibilities require both better planning and design, extensive rework, and some degree of operations support to meet the IT needs of the organization.

Automation of the workplace has placed unprecedented demands on a company's communications network. In the 1980s, there was no bigger headache for facility managers than cable management. At the same time, deregulation of the telephone industry meant that a company could own its own telephone system, and unparalleled options of equipment and services were suddenly available. Not surprisingly, many communications managers found themselves ill prepared to handle the technical, policy, and operational issues that surfaced. The facility impacts alone were monumental and, in buildings thirty to fifty years old, at times seemed overwhelming—thus, the rise of the communications manager and the consultant for smaller companies.

Communications needs are unique to each company, often to departments within the company. Nevertheless, some extremely sophisticated assessment techniques are available. When assessing communication needs, look for the following at a minimum:

- Number of incoming and outgoing calls
- How many people use the lines
- Growth: location, personnel, businesses, profit

For a number of years following telephone deregulation, many companies chose to own their own, premises-based phone system. Some of that ardor seems to have subsided. Leasing again seems to be the financing option of choice. Still, there is increased sensitivity to communications and greater expectations for these in-house systems. For service-providing, instant communications has become a necessity. So, don't forget the following:

- Customers want choices.
- Poor systems give a poor impression of the company.
- Systems are expected to save time, energy, and money.
- Systems are often used as input and switching devices for other building systems.

Common features of modern systems include automatic call-back, message waiting, speed dialing, call waiting, call forwarding, teleconferencing, "Do Not Disturb" memos, intercom, toll restrictions, least-cost routing, station message detail recording, voice and data switching, and interface with voice mail. When buying a communications system, consider the following:

- What is included in the contract price
- Costs avoided by using new features
- Operating costs
- Maintenance costs
- Flexibility, particularly the ability and cost to expand
- Ability to switch equipment among company locations

It is increasingly evident that the telephone and telephone infrastructure will be used for a broad range of fax, videotext, and data transfer or retrieval services. These capabilities will be enhanced as fiber optics becomes more prevalent. A study of telecommunications, based on telephone interviews and mail surveys of 167 companies, found the following:

- *Corporate telecom networks.* The typical company surveyed had 808 domestic and 27 international network nodes. Typically, more than 20 large computers and 5,000 terminals and PCs were linked into these corporate networks on either a dedicated or dial-up basis.
- *Key issues facing telecom management.* Almost all of the communications executives interviewed named two or three "key" issues that they planned to address during the next twenty-four to thirty-six months. Named in order of importance, the issues included central site network management; LAN/ WAN connectivity and LAN integration; consolidation/network integration; and integrated services (ISDN).
- *Telecom operations.* More than $20 million was the typical budget for voice and data communications among the respondents. Nearly $6 million was being allocated for data communications equipment and service alone. These executives reported an average of 38 people assigned to their telecom groups.
- *Other key issues.* Also mentioned as central issues were cost-effectiveness, network availability, international expansion, and network capacity/band width.[6]

In many organizations employees, or at least key personnel, are issued wireless devices which act as phones, internet devices, and other communications aids. Facility managers find themselves in a position of being between the two worlds of hard-wired communication, which still must be maintained, and wireless which places yet other demands on facilities in terms of flexibility.

Consultation with our experts in the IT area produced mixed results regarding the widespread use of a wireless network. Anyone directly or indirectly involved in installing a wireless LAN or WAN would do well to read the 2005 study, "Wireless Systems in the Facility," available from the IFMA Foundation. The study foresees wireless as a fantastic business asset but limited and cautions that there will be a role for wired infrastructure for some time.

Electronic and Information Security

Electronic and information security is a corollary to records management, communications, and security. It applies to information security for electronic tools, particularly software, and for the company's informational data bank. Partly, information security is a victim of the information explosion. Administrative personnel, archivists, and librarians are overwhelmed by the volume of information to be managed and sometimes fail to protect it to the degree they should.

The mobility of employees among companies, some of whom are competitors, makes information security even more difficult. Also, systems themselves tend to aggregate data. They are designed to meet operational needs, and security is often an afterthought. In addition, security of reports is threatened by each new wave of equipment, such as color copiers and printers, that makes counterfeiting easier, along with unauthorized copies. To counteract this, distribute updated reports only if prior ones are handed back for shredding.

WiFi adds a whole new universe of communications security issues. In centralized facilities, with the proper consultant help, WiFi security can be effectively managed. However, when employees leave the premises and work from home, the train, coffee shops, or clients' facilities, communications security can be accomplished only with good training.

Shredders too are taking on additional importance. Some machines are so advanced that they can shred entire cartons of data, still in the carton. As another tactic, security specialists are using encryption to transmit reports. Encryption, however, has operational problems, and its lack of acceptance limits its use. In sum, our best hope for better information security may be better employee training and a campaign that emphasizes the importance of information and intellectual property.

Emerging Services

In this chapter we have discussed general administrative services commonly managed by facility managers. There are also some emerging services that will have an impact on the traditional functions when introduced.

Art Program

It has become fairly common for some capital costs to be set aside for purchase and installation of works of art; 0.5 percent of a major project is a common figure. Quite often those funds are used to buy a few major pieces for the entrance or lobby plus a large number of relatively inexpensive pieces to adorn corridors and office walls.

We prefer to consider all but major pieces of art as furnishings and include them in the planning and design of space. Limited funds are best used for prints rather than originals because it allows a broader distribution of art with limited funds, and it decreases inventory and security concerns. One successful program has been to box-frame 15-by-18-inch photographs of company operations and hang them in appropriate areas. This can be a valuable supplement to the art program and improve the quality of the workplace.

The degree to which art should be appraised, curated, accounted for, and secured can be a problem. Major pieces obviously should be secured. Large sculpture requires few security precautions beyond protection from weather and graffiti. Smaller pieces may require a pedestal, enclosure, and alarms. How extensive the inventory is must be carefully assessed for cost-effectiveness. We suggest any inventory be kept at two levels:

1. A PC-based management-level list that allows call up of a piece by property number, title, artist, location, assigned unit, value range, and place of purchase.
2. A card-based list that contains the following: photograph, property number, title, artist, gallery, and initial purchase price, medium, appraised value, and date of appraisal. (With a CADCAM, this file, too, can be PC-based.)

What degree of inventory to maintain is also extremely complex. For example, it probably costs up to $50 per entry to prepare either of the inventories. Obviously it is not cost-effective to inventory $25 to $75 prints. However, if ten of those prints are lost in a year, which is a good possibility, documentation is necessary to make an insurance claim. If the insurance deductible is relatively low ($500 per incident, for example), an inventory helps recovery of part of the loss. The collection should be reappraised every three to five years.

Large organizations should consider having an in-house frame shop, preferably contractor operated. Besides supporting the art program, a frame shop can be a superior service provider by:

- Supporting in-house exhibitions and photo or art displays
- Framing items like official maps, photos, and certificates
- Maintaining and relocating the company's art, when necessary, for alterations or painting
- Updating the location portion of the art inventory
- Maintaining the art locker—the storage room for all pieces not currently exhibited

Art selection, when there is a capital expenditure, is best handled by a volunteer employee committee, possibly chaired by the design manager. The committee should understand its budget, how much space it is expected to furnish, whether it be permitted to select a major piece and where it will be sited, any procurement rules, and the time schedule. While volunteer committees are sometimes difficult to deal with, art affects employee morale, so employee input is desired from the beginning.

Even with a professional design staff and a dedicated art advisory committee, it is probable that at least a part-time art consultant will be necessary. That consultant will probably be hired on an hourly basis and can assist with appraisal, maintenance, security, and purchasing advice. However, the consultant should not be allowed to sell art to the company. Whether the consultant is allowed to sell art to individuals in the organization is a policy decision.

Shared Services

Shared services are not really a "service," but a way of delivering services; it is ordinarily associated with property management rather than facility management. The landlord of a building with multiple tenants establishes service centers for services such as fax, high-speed copying, parcel mailing, cables, conferences, and exercise facilities, and charges the tenants for usage. This relieves any one tenant of high initial costs to establish the service. Much of the early publicity for smart buildings promoted this concept.

However, these shared services have generally not been well-accepted in property management settings. In some corporate settings, however, we are finding that some organizations have adopted the Shared Services name to better explain the multiple services that the facility management department provides. Shared Services, as a title, also provides an informative reminder to the user departments that the many services are to be coordinated and made mutually efficient through single management whether the oversight organization is called facility management or shared services. Perhaps tenants wanted more flexibility than the service centers could provide. Perhaps billing was a problem. Perhaps developers had difficulty recovering their capital costs in a reasonable time while charging a bearable rate. Perhaps demand for services was too erratic and fluctuated too widely to permit effective and efficient management.

Laptops, WiFi, and wireless communications devices have caused many companies to assign temporary workspace in their fixed facilities to a substantial portion of their workforce. An example is the salesforce where any one individual needs a desk space only once a week, or once every two weeks. Some companies have developed sophisticated manned or electronic systems for reserving this space often called hotelling. A variant is to use small conference facilities with easily relocatable partitions as hot-body offices, although the viability of this latter concept is not yet established. While local area networks and flexible telecommunications permit adequate communication among geographically separate members of the same work unit, employees still want turf with recognizable boundaries and social interaction with fellow workers.

Child Care

Of all benefits possible in the workplace, none has captured management's support so quickly as child care. While the human resources chief ordinarily has staff responsibility for child care, the facility manager has major responsibility for space, construction, maintenance, and repair of in-house day care facilities. The importance of a safe, clean facility cannot be overemphasized. Just let any trace of asbestos be found or the water in the drinking fountain be out of tolerance for lead, and concerns will be loudly voiced.

Child care developed from a single-parent, low-income issue into a major domestic policy issue. Corporate decision makers raise child care as a boardroom agenda as they face recruitment competition for a shrinking labor pool. Real estate developers view child care as a valuable marketing tool in an age of empty office buildings. A brief glance at corporate demographics reveals a 45 percent increase in the number of working mothers since 1950. By 1990, 60 percent of new entrants into the workforce were women. Eighty percent of women in the workplace will have a child at some point during their careers.[7] Child care is rapidly being recognized as a means to broaden recruitment, reduce absenteeism, lower turnover rates, improve public image, and increase morale. Some employers are even using the availability of day care as a factor in choosing relocation sites.

Some employers are exploring on-site child care options, but many find the realities daunting. Operating a child care center can incur significant risk—and just opening one can easily cost $250,000. Although the corporate staff can help with zoning and permits, offering a child care center requires hiring people with necessary skills. Consequently, the company must make sure that the apparent need is both broad-based and continuing before consent is given.

The most common form of day care management is contracted out, with policy set by a board of employee parents. If the facility manager supports a day care center, he must ensure that service is nearly instantaneous and extensive. Any problem in the day care center must be given a high priority.

Health and Fitness Facilities

Many facility managers who offer health and fitness centers exhibit frustration over their inability to control costs, particularly capital costs. Often that signifies that the facilities are driving the health and fitness program. The facility manager never gets ahead; this year the employees need an aerobics room, and next year there'll be a demand for a track. When the weight room is still in construction, someone will lobby for a swimming pool.

The health and fitness facilities offered to employees should reflect the program the company has established. Once management decides on a program, the facilities for that program can be planned and constructed.

We feel that the best fitness programs are designed by a professional, guided by an in-house board of directors. Whether the consultant simply helps establish the program, policies, and procedures, or also operates the facility with his own attendants, instructors, and safety personnel, is a corporate decision based largely on the risk manager's willingness to allow employees to use facilities without supervision. We have seen extremely successful programs run without supervision and without legal or insurance problems, while other companies insist on a full-time, CPR-rated professional staff.

Some of the facilities in common use are:

- Urban walking and running courses
- Par course (suburban areas)
- Aerobics rooms
- Weight rooms
- Exercise equipment rooms
- Saunas
- Handball, squash, and/or racquetball courts
- Multipurpose courts
- Massage rooms
- Tennis facilities
- Running tracks
- Swimming pool

The last three require large space and considerable capital outlay. In general, they are prohibitively costly in an urban environment. A swimming pool brings with it a whole set of engineering, construction, operations, and safety problems beyond what most companies want to tackle.

Whether the company has an institutional health and fitness program or not, changing lifestyles almost dictate that employees have access to showers and locker space. There is a particular demand for lockers and showers at the end or beginning of the workday, as well as at noon.

Company fitness programs tend to draw the most competitive employees. In turn, employees become advocates for their personal preference in equipment and operating hours. For this reason, an employee board of directors should develop and promulgate policy for the fitness center; the facility manager alone cannot and should not try to sort through each proposed addition or change.

Fitness centers have a major impact on facility management. They tend to have high capital costs, particularly if retrofitted into existing space. Athletic facilities are not by their nature more costly to operate and maintain, but because they often reuse existing space, their design may be suboptimized and therefore more costly to operate than a new facility designed specifically for fitness. Finally, fitness buffs are often zealots; as such, they expect superior services, and their expectations can bring pressures that result in increased operating costs.

Concierge Services

Having an on-site concierge became a major selling point for companies managing Class A office space. It was so popular that many organizations now offer it in their owned facilities.

This concept has worked well in fine hotels for years. With married couples both employed, the need for a concierge at work to handle the mundane but necessary, and sometimes extraordinary, chores becomes more and more viable.

The concierge service is run by an independent contractor who normally offers a menu of services. Some offer to take on almost any task. Most concierges perform for cost plus tips by getting a fee from the vendors to whom they take their business. Others charge a fixed, advertised fee per service. They are normally provided a lobby location, and often are provided heat, light, and electricity gratis. Frequently, there is no need for special provisions, since those services already exist in the lobby.

To the extent that it can be provided with little cost or disruption, concierge service can be of real value to employees. It represents the type of employee-oriented services that companies will use to attract and hold quality employees.

Some Final Words on Outsourcing

Administrative services should be considered for outsourcing, because the result is a more technically competent level of service. The facility manager retains control and ensures customer service. There may be some temporary initial savings if the company has substandard personnel or high company benefits, but the long-term savings are in operational efficiency, ease of human resources management, and the ability to stay up-to-date technologically.

Outsourcing is with us ($23 billion in services will be outsourced by the year 2001).[8] Facility managers need to develop their skills as outsourcing managers as much as they need to develop any technical skill. As our favorite consultant, Stormy Friday says, "We need to view outsourcing as a tool, not a weapon."[9]

Notes

1. *Facility Management Practices* (Houston, IFMA, 1996), p. 14.
2. John Soat, "The Ins and Outs of Contract Services," *Administrative Management* (February 1986): 59.
3. Lee Yeaton, "It's Past Time," *Today's Facility Manager* (March 1995).
4. Philip Binkow, "Control Delivery Service Charges and You'll Save," *Office* (December 1989): 56.
5. David O. Stephens, "What's Ahead for Records Management in the 90's?" *Office* (January 1990): 135–136.
6. "Telecom Management: The Key Issues" *Office* (February 1990). 17.
7. Cheri L. Sheridan, "Child Care: The Issue of the 80's," *Business Properties Magazine* (November 1988): 39.
8. Paul Tarricone, "Outsourcing Turns to Smart Sourcing," *Facilities Design & Management* (February 1997): 40–43.
9. Ibid.

Facility Management Practice

In this section we discuss a variety of topics under the umbrella of facility management practice. In some ways, these chapters are the most important in our book because, as we look at others in the field, they all stress the technical aspects of the profession, and there are many. However, unless you can apply them effectively and efficiently, you will never be successful. This is particularly important to remember because most of us come from a technical background. So, emphasis here is on management and business rather than the technical aspects of the facility management mission. We begin by discussing our interface and involvement with both procurement and personnel, then move on to outsourcing, partnering, and benchmarking. We close Chapter 28 with a discussion of work process loops, which each facility manager should ensure are working correctly within the department (that 95 percent of the effort which should flow almost automatically). Chapter 29 then discusses the premier role of quality in providing facility management services, a topic which, in our efforts to be leaner, we have somewhat neglected.

Chapter 30 explores the management aspects of the department's budget recognizing that 1) facility managers will be measured in the same manner as other managers in the organization but also 2) the budget can be your principal information management tool.

Chapter 31 emphasizes the need for facility managers to be skilled communicators, internally and externally . . . increasingly even to a contract staff. Chapter 32 delves into the rapidly changing (and somewhat unsettled) area of FM information technology management.

Finally, Chapter 33 pulls together our collective knowledge and that of our colleagues for a look at what major problems are on the horizon for facility managers, what are the current trends, and what is in the future for the profession and its professionals.

28

Administering the Department

Pulse Points

- *The facility manager must build solid, trusting relationships with the procurement staff.*
- *Contractor evaluation criteria should reflect what is truly important to the facility staff and their customers.*
- *Outsourcing is a staffing, not an organizational, issue. Get your organization right first.*
- *Partnering requires a well-developed system and procedures to be successful. Above all, it takes a commitment to make it work.*
- *Measure everything that is important to you. Set standards and measure performance against them. Establish an information system to calculate results automatically and transparently.*
- *Set up automated systems to manage the facility management "loops."*
- *In benchmarking, get beyond the metrics.*
- *The facility department normally faces a broader range of issues than most human resources departments are used to handling.*

A number of overall administrative functions are essential to the proper functioning of the department. We discussed the various kinds of planning in Section II. In addition, as part of the design-build cycle we covered the managerial duties of developing programs.

In this chapter, we discuss procurement, a major responsibility of facility managers, yet one where responsibility is often shared outside the department. We examine outsourcing, partnering, benchmarking, and evaluation. We close with a systems approach—a look at a number of management loops that the facility manager should ensure are alive and well within his department.

Procurement

A centralized procurement system can present challenges for the facility manager. The operational elements (of which the facility manager is one) generally function from one set of priorities, while procurement officers* frequently operate from another. Thus, an effective procurement operation depends largely on the successful integration of these two sets of priorities.

For the most part, the user is chiefly concerned with quality of goods and services, response time, and reduced paperwork. Users may not always give primary consideration to price. Depending on the urgency of a request and the tradeoffs among speed, quality of service, and cost, facility department users may sometimes wish to forgo competitive bidding and specify a preferred vendor.

The procurement officer, on the other hand, must follow procurement procedures, particularly in the public sector. These procedures include open competition, fair and equal treatment of all bidders, and cost-effectiveness. The procurement officer must be concerned principally with the cost-effectiveness of the procurement function, since he is judged primarily on his success in controlling costs. Fortunately, most procurement departments have become more service oriented than they were a decade ago. However, a natural tension will always exist.

If you understand these different priorities and are willing to negotiate, explore alternatives, and compromise, you'll ensure a procurement system that meets both your and organization objectives.

Reduced to its basics, the procurement process is a response to the need for goods or services. Goods are normally obtained through agreements called *purchase orders,* either for a one-time purchase (PO) or for a period of time (blanket purchase order, or BPO). During the term of a BPO, orders can be placed against the BPO and are limited only by a cumulative dollar figure.

Services are normally obtained through agreements whose contents vary widely but at a minimum spell out the scope of services to be provided, the term of the agreement, and the basis for compensation. The term may be fixed or may set a certain total dollar value. The price may be stated as a fixed amount or may be an estimate that cannot be exceeded without a formal change to the agreement.

All such contractual documents should contain a time frame for performance, a basis for costing, specifications describing the goods or services being acquired, and the general and special conditions. *General conditions* set the legal framework for the relationship between the company and the vendor. The agreements are prepared by

---

*We use the terms *purchasing department* and *procurement department* and *procurement officer* and *purchasing officer* interchangeably, since these terms vary widely from organization to organization.

the purchasing department and reviewed by the legal department, as necessary. The terms and conditions of a purchase order are preestablished and incorporated into the PO. For the most part, these conditions do not change; that is what makes them general. *Special conditions* are those that relate to a specific procurement and contain specially written paragraphs that define such items as working hours, security requirements, and special access. These provisions are prepared by the purchasing department staff, based on specific requirements the facility manager identifies. For simple contracts, the general and special conditions are often encapsulated in the agreement part of the contract; for complex procurements, the special conditions may be incorporated in the performance work statement.

More contracts today are focused on results and with the growth and sophistication of service providers, it is often better to look for performance-based contracts than prescriptive ones. Prescriptive contracts outline the exact specification expected or detail acceptable ranges. Our experience has been, where possible, to allow some flexibility; too prescriptive a contract leads to lack of innovation and reduced motivation on the part of the vendor. Facility managers need to clearly describe the results expected but leave room for the vendor to create new and better ways of providing service. This often provides for unanticipated improvements, increased pride from the vendors and staff, as well as potential improvements in the contractual relationship. How much flexibility to allow your contractor is a difficult decision for the facility managers and is best determined through experience. Performance-based contracting is sometimes counterintuitive, particularly for those who have been used to traditional low-bid contracting. Procurement specialists also should be familiar with performance-based contracts. We suggest that, prior to changing to performance-based contracting, both the facility manager and his procurement specialist (and others if you can afford it) attend a seminar at the Performance Based Studies Research Group (PBSRG) at Arizona State University. Dr. Dean Kashiwagi, the PBSRG head, speaks at most of the major FM conferences nationwide and annually so it is possible to be introduced to the subject. If interested, it might be worthwhile to invite Dr. Kashiwagi to address all service contract managers and procurement personnel in your organization on performance-based contracting.

Successful procurements do not just happen. They require technical input, managerial supervision, and cooperation between the facility and procurement staffs. The facility manager has a responsibility to manage the technical part of the procurement process as carefully as the procurement officer manages the form and process. While the purchasing and legal staffs may offer assistance, the facility manager is responsible for accurately defining the requirements.

In some cases, primarily in service contracts, the facility manager may be designated as the contracting officer's representative (COR) during contract execution.

The COR represents the contracting officer in day-to-day relations with the contractor. The COR is usually empowered to enforce the contract but is not permitted to change the scope or terms of it. Changes can be made only by the contracts office and must be in writing.

The Procurement Process

Current business literature is full of references to a major realignment of how companies will operate in the near future, i.e. non-core functions will be contracted out with the broadest possible definition of what is a non-core function. Another theory envisions companies composed only of core functions with all support functions gathered under a "headquarters management" function that could itself be outsourced. There are probably other theories but, regardless, the facility manager 1) must establish the *management* of facilities as a core function and 2) needs to be a skilled procurer and manager of outsourced services. Outsourcing is here to stay and that means that we need to have a well-developed relationship with the purchasing department.

Purchasing departments normally are organized according to functional responsibility. It is extremely important that the facility manager become familiar with the procurement officers who handle each type of request. Units having direct impact on procurement are the purchasing and contract sections, although organizations may vary in what they call them. The *purchasing section* is responsible for acquiring goods or services via standard purchase orders or preestablished terms and conditions, such as the federal General Services Administration Schedule. The *contracts management section* is responsible for acquiring goods and services that, because of their nature, performance period, or other criteria, require specific terms and conditions. Construction, consulting services, and multiyear buying arrangements generally fall into this category.

Despite what has developed historically in some organizations, budgetary control is not a function of procurement. Facility managers certify that funds are available for a requested procurement, since they control their budgets.

Exhibit 28-1 is a flowchart depicting the various stages of procurement. Listed below are three variations on these procedures and several cautions:

1. When a procurement request is received by the purchasing department, it is entered into the system and assigned to a procurement officer according to the nature of the request. Even on contract renewals, the procurement clock does not start until the properly completed request is received.
2. Any directed (sole-source) procurement must be justified even if there is only one local source of the goods or service. It is the facility manager's responsibility to justify a directed procurement.

- For utilities, for example, a sole-source procurement is commonly agreed on between the facility manager and the purchasing department.
- For a unique item (replacement part for an existing system) for which only one local vendor exists, a brief memo of justification should suffice.

3. An item ordered by phone directly to a vendor without a PO or before a PO is cut makes a contract with that vendor. The person placing the order could be held liable for payment to the vendor.

Evaluation criteria must be established in order to differentiate among bidders. This should be done jointly by the facility and procurement staffs. Selection criteria can include:

- *Lowest responsive bid.* Procurement staff is solely responsible for this type of evaluation, which is used only for the most straightforward bids. These procurements typically involve reorders, routine and well-defined user requirements, or name-brand purchases. When this evaluation criterion is selected, the award is made to the bidder submitting the lowest prices.
- *Lowest evaluated bid.* The facility and procurement staffs agree on the technical criteria for evaluation. The internal procedures of the unit determine who should approve the selections criteria developed by the facility manager in consultation with staff. All vendors are rated, and a floor (minimum passing technical score) is set. The vendor with the lowest bid that passes the technical floor is selected.
- *Highest evaluated bid.* The facility manager and the procurement officer agree on the technical criteria for evaluation. All vendors are rated, and those falling below the floor are eliminated. Those above the floor are reevaluated, perhaps by interview, with price being one evaluation criterion (25 to 40 percent). This is an elaborate process but has proved an excellent way to select the best all-around contractor.
- *Unique service.* For the procurement of unique consulting services, including architectural-engineering (A-E), the contractor is usually selected on the basis of technical merit rather than price. Final price is usually negotiated with the most technically qualified firm.

Procurement takes time. Further, larger procurements tend to take more time; that is, the larger the bid, the more formal the process and thus the more time it takes. The following time periods indicate average number of business days from receipt of request until the order is placed or an agreement is transmitted to the vendor. (Dollar values in this table and subsequent tables are representative only. In general, procurement restrictions are loosening and dollar restrictions are loosening giving the facility manager both more flexibility and more responsibility):

Exhibit 28-1. Procurement process flowchart.

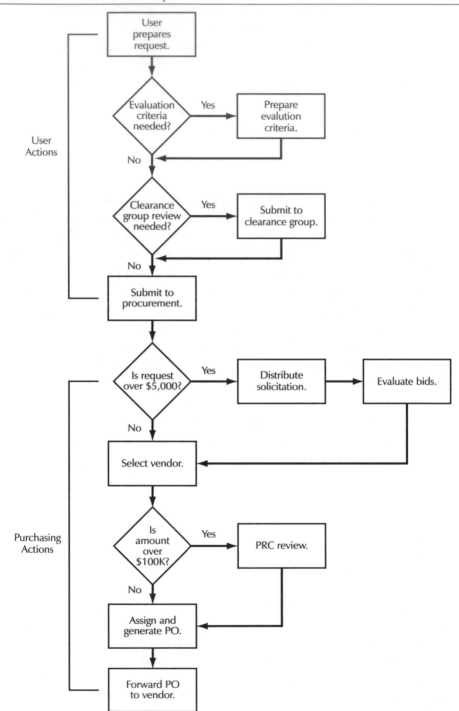

Procurements valued at less than $5,000:	5 days
Procurements valued at $5,000–$10,000:	10 days
Procurements valued at $10,000 to $50,000 involving a short list of vendors with a subsequent technical evaluation:	20–30 days
Procurements valued above $50,000:	30–45 days
Procurements subject to public bidding:	50–75 days

There is a tendency to underestimate the complexity, requirements, and time needed for procurements. Also, the purchasing department is probably not staffed to handle every procurement on an exceptional basis. For sure success, start early. Remember that on top of this processing time, there may be a two-week to six-month delivery period.

By and large, a company that ends up with an unacceptable contractor probably did not do the procurement process well. Here are some helpful points:

1. Develop, with the procurement department, a vendor questionnaire for use in evaluating bidders. Do not hesitate to request modifications if needed.
2. Provide a chairperson for any evaluation committee. He, in turn, recruits members for the committee. The committee should be composed of three to five members, in addition to the contracts officer, each of whom possesses expertise, interest, and commitment. Consider using in-house consultants as advisers, but be aware of their client base in order to avoid conflict of interest.
3. Keep on track during committee deliberations and interviews. Be democratic, but keep questions and comments focused on the needs of the procurement. Set the ground rules in the opening remarks and stick to them.
4. Finalize the evaluation criteria. The procurement staff will not open vendor submissions until the criteria have been finalized. Get agreement on the type of evaluation (one-step, two-step) and evaluation criteria before starting. Decide how scoring totals will be determined (for example, throw out high and low and average the rest).
5. Make sure the committee has had an opportunity to do its homework and has read the technical proposals before the first meeting.
6. Ensure that each committee member performs an independent rating of each vendor submission.
7. Have the procurement officer schedule formal interviews with bidders following their team members' area of interest.
8. Make sure the facility manager concurs with how the contracts officer converts bids to scores.

A procurement review committee (PRC) often reviews awards of $100,000 or more, although management may review a proposed procurement regardless of the dollar value. The PRC might be composed of representatives from the legal department, the planning and budget department, and two operational managers. Following the evaluation and prior to the award, the facility manager should expect to appear before the PRC with the supporting procurement officer, who will present the proposed procurement in a prescribed manner. The facility manager may then be asked to supplement this presentation with additional technical information. In most cases, the results of the PRC are announced the day following. A PRC usually meets monthly; supplemental meetings or informal reviews may be scheduled to consider time-sensitive procurements by discussing the matter with the appointed procurement officer. The procurement officer will most likely arrange for the special PRC review.

E-commerce in facility management has had mixed success according to IFMA Foundation research. According to its study, E-commerce was used most often to buy supplies and material from a specific vendor over the internet. The greatest perceived advantage of E-commerce has been to save time and keep projects on schedule but the study found little belief that E-commerce reduced cost.[1]

As we mentioned above, our organizations, recognizing the increased importance of procurement and outsourcing, have given us greater flexibility in contracting. While this is perhaps long overdue, it is also important that we impress our entire department with the importance of absolute integrity. Large organizational funds pass through our hands; use them wisely and for their intended purposes with not even a whiff of scandal in the contracting process.

Disposal

Every piece of equipment and furniture, every major assembly, and many building components become obsolete, or they are replaced by a newer item or a standardized one. For these reasons, every organization should have the capability of disposing of equipment or furniture.

Before an item can be offered for disposal, two determinations need to be made: (1) that the item is in excess of the organization's needs, and (2) that it has a residual value. Those determinations are the province of the facility manager, often with the help of the controller for determining residual value. The actual disposal is normally done by a disposal officer. The best system is one in which the disposal officer for a commodity (furniture, for example) is the purchasing officer for that same commodity; some procurement departments have individuals who handle only disposals.

A critical issue always is whether to trash an item or to put it up for disposal. Often that decision is best made by a knowledgeable individual using an on-site assessment. However, if an economic analysis is made, the costs of transporting, storing, and conducting walk-through inspections by potential purchasers must also be considered. Again, this is an issue that defies exact analysis. A spare executive chair, though it may have no depreciated value, could be more valuable than when it was purchased. Also, if it is the only spare for the set of boardroom chairs, its value is inestimable.

A good disposal program, if properly executed, can return funds to be used for facility programs. Often funds recovered through disposal go into a general fund, and this is a disincentive to prompt disposal. Other options are sale to company employees or transfers to local schools or charities.

Some Tips

Listed below are some additional tips and suggestions to help ensure success in procurement:

1. Do not expect a requirement to be treated as an exception. Handle 99 percent of business by the book, so that when an exception is really needed, it will generate a sympathetic response from the purchasing officer.
2. Include the purchasing and contracts managers in your major project planning.
3. Identify procurement policy exceptions early in the process so they can be addressed by the purchasing staff before the last minute.
4. Submit BPO and service contract renewals three months before the end of the fiscal year. This enables the procurement staff to program this workload for completion, on a routine basis, prior to the start of the new fiscal year.
5. Track procurement actions the same way operational projects are tracked. Include procurement actions as key project milestones in facility projects.
6. Process payments quickly. This fosters faster vendor response time and can result in prompt payment discounts.
7. Report outstanding or unsatisfactory vendor performance, in writing, to the purchasing department.
8. Be prepared to answer all technical questions in any prebid conference and, if appropriate, conduct a site tour. Bidders should not contact you directly prior to submitting a bid. After the procurement staff has released a solicitation and prior to the contract award, all communications with a potential vendor must be conducted through the appointed procurement officer.

Human Resources Management

Perhaps more than any other manager, facility managers find themselves managing a mixed blue-collar-white-collar, and now green-collar workforce in a company environment that is often oriented toward white-collar professionals. This is only complicated by the fact that many of "our staff" are now contractors, under a variety of contract vehicles, or consultants. This can result in our organizational staff being under-appreciated in both grade-level and for promotion. One of the real challenges many facility managers face is getting the human resources department to understand the department's employee needs and the management environment in which a facility manager works. The HR staff typically understands the core business skills, but may not be familiar with the facility management skill sets. You need to help the HR group understand the unique and diverse needs within facility management and provide resources to support them in properly setting grades and promotions for facility management functions. IFMA research, and this book, may be helpful for you in this task.

Because of the diversity of the staff (employee, contractor, consultant), the facility manager becomes, in fact, his own human resources manager for at least a part of his staff. Personally, we have always liked this situation because, with contractors and consultants, we had the flexibility to adjust the staffing to meet the workload and to eliminate non-producers with minimal effort.

Regarding organizational staff, unfortunately employment law has become so complex that its managerial manifestations can seem overwhelming. At times it is so intimidating that some managers shrink from actions that they should take for good morale and discipline. One of your authors worked for an organization that simply transferred underperformers instead of firing them. Managers who have a unionized workforce have an additional level of complexity to deal with. Training in human resources management by the professional associations would be helpful. One of the problems for such training mirrors the problem in the workplace; there are few experts. Managers nevertheless need the training and FM's should seek out professional development in this area even if it is non-specific to facility management.

Training has, for too long, been either downplayed or totally ignored, particularly in this era of cost-cutting and tight budgets. However, for both technical and managerial personnel, this issue is coming home to roost. As discussed elsewhere in this chapter, that is one of the main drivers toward outsourcing; we can't hire competent staff. One of our expert advisors, Dr. Bill Badger, who served on the panel which defined core competencies for federal facilities asset management (their new term for facility management) through 2020 states that, to overcome this problem, we should be devoting 2 percent of our personnel costs to the education and training of our workforce.[2]

Outsourcing

One of the hottest topics of the past ten years within facility management has been outsourcing. When companies are willing to contract out their accounting department, for example, it is not surprising that the facility department is a candidate for outsourcing. If you are not core business, you had better perform your own analysis of the costs and benefits of contracting out, because, if you don't, someone else will do it for you.

We are unabashed advocates of outsourcing to the maximum and have done so in our own practice. The reasons most often given for outsourcing are:

- Outsourcing saves money, particularly if in-house staff have high benefits.
- A contracted workforce can better adjust to fluctuations in work.
- Contractor personnel provide better access to higher-quality skills.
- Large contractors can use their size to get price breaks on supplies and services.
- Outsourcing allows the company to concentrate on its core business.
- The number of employees is greatly reduced.
- Particularly in the public sector, you save authorized personnel spaces.
- With outsourcing, the company can provide services or a level of service that in-house personnel cannot.

Having said that, we should add that there are good reasons *not* to outsource some functions. For instance, no contractor can do strategic facility business planning. Also, many companies have facilities whose operations are so sensitive that facility staff serving them need to be company employees (although that type of facility does not occur as often as you might think). Most of the objections to outsourcing are concerned with loss of control or that the workforce will be less loyal to management if contracted. Certainly, a judgment needs to be made by every organization when considering outsourcing, but our observation is that facility managers tend to be too conservative when outsourcing. Pressed to cut costs and personnel spaces, we would use our limited resources for top-flight contract managers and planners while outsourcing the technical work and supervision.

In almost all of the services offered by the facility department (discussed in Chapter 27) contracting to a third party is a viable option. The trend, in fact, is to contract out more. Outsourcing, which really started to accelerate in the mid-90s, has progressed to the point that functions which never would have even been considered for outsourcing in the past have been outsourced. Facility management, always a candidate for outsourcing, has reached the point that FM outsourcing has become common, even predominant, in organizations. Two of your authors have extensively outsourced and agree that in a large, complex organization, some outsourcing is absolutely necessary. Three of the benefits of contracting services are the ability to meet fluctuating workloads, the ability to obtain highly-specialized and/or certified technicians who are not needed full-time, and the ability to quickly get rid of workers who perform poorly. Some of the largest FM contracts are for U.S. military installations and FM contractors are performing in war zones. Frankly, it is a little breathtaking until you understand that, in some private companies, they are considering outsourcing all functions not directly related to the principal products or services of the organization.

Most companies end up doing what they feel comfortable with, and that's fine. The company must decide three issues: (1) what level of control is desired, (2) what level of service is required, and (3) what response level is required. If these can be met by a contract, the company is probably better off contracting out as long as specifications ensure the services. In most cases, three- to five-year service contracts are best. Contracting annually to exclusively low bidders tends, over several rebids, to rachet quality down to an unacceptable point.

Cost savings from contracting out can be illusory. Make sure the contracts maximize use of limited management time, allow for more flexibility in matching resources and workload, and produce the efficiencies and economies of scale on large contracts.

According to the Outsourcing Institute, the following are the most important factors in contracting out:

- Reduce and control operating costs
- Improve organizational focus
- Gain access to world-class capabilities
- Free internal resources for other purposes
- Resources are not available internally
- Accelerate re-engineering benefits
- Current function is difficult to manage/out of control
- Make capital funds available
- Share risks
- Provide a cash infusion[3]

Each of those factors has its own applicability to a particular situation, but we would like to mention several key aspects. Traditional low-bid, adversarial contracting will not work. Perhaps formal partnering is not necessary, but when you are widely outsourced, your contractor is now your staff. We are convinced that a facility manager can get as much loyalty from a contract staff as from in-house staff.

In North America, we find that the move to outsourcing is being accelerated by the lack of in-house technical skills in areas such as mechanical and electrical. This may provide just a temporary reprieve, however, since the failure of our training system to produce technicians will hamper contractors' abilities to hire also.

Facility managers should go slow in outsourcing, and use fact-based decision making. They must know their costs of doing business, including distributed overheads, before making the cost comparisons necessary for good decision making on outsourcing. That sounds elemental, but too many outsourcing decisions have not been made when they should have or have failed to produce promised savings solely because the cost figures for current operations were fallacious.

Once the decision is made to outsource, the facility manager should work with the procurement staff to outsource one function at a time rather than the whole department at once. One of the most important things to do, and one of the most difficult, is to be honest with staff and to keep them informed as the outsourcing analysis proceeds. No facility manager should ever get in the position of promising staff continued employment, but he should be sensitive to their concerns.

Just as you wouldn't send your child to a school without first checking its credentials and talking with the teachers, don't pick a service provider out of the phone book. Do some research, talk to management, and get a list of previous customers from the potential contractors. And check out their employees, who may be working for you soon.

Interestingly, the Outsourcing Institute lists "references/reputation" as only the fourth of five criteria for choosing an outsourcing partner. Not surprisingly, price is first.[4] While we are more than willing to understand the reality of that ranking, we have great concern about "bottom fishing" for a contractor that will be critical to your organization's ability to perform its mission. We also want to emphasize the importance of having a contract that is well-defined yet flexible enough to accommodate situations outside the scope or on the margins of your contract which are bound to arise, particularly if you are outsourcing for the first time. We suggest borrowing a sample contract for outsourcing the same service from several members of your local professional association to develop your own contract. Your human resources department may be able to help you also.

Methods of Contracting Services

If the facility manager decides to contract for services, there are multiple ways to do it. One is to contract for a specific project based on a given set of specifications. As an alternative, the contractor could be selected to provide a general service (electrical, for example) based on a listing of unit costs for those services. During contract execution, individual tasks are then approved for execution based on an expedited approval process. As an alternative, two to five contractors for each service can be prequalified for capability. For a specific task, the work can be assigned on a rotation basis or to the low bidder in an expedited bidding process.

Our personal preference is to gather functions into broad groups like custodial services or building maintenance. These services are then bid on an hourly basis by skill. The contractor provides an on-site superintendent and all first-line supervision, but the facility management staff assumes responsibility for work assignments, quality control, and, therefore, cost control.

One note of caution for those who employ contractors. The Internal Revenue Service is increasingly investigating cases in which companies convert staff into contract positions or hire new staff as private contractors to avoid paying social security taxes. Be careful to observe the "duck rule": "If it looks like a duck and quacks like a duck, then it's probably a duck." Contract employees normally (1) work for a contractor's supervisor, and (2) are subject to be moved to other job sites. If the only reason to convert a staff position is to avoid taxation and the personnel continue to function like staff, the company could be liable.

It is worthwhile to discuss the need for the facility manager to define both his requirements and the quality of the contractor needed to meet those requirements. Often when there is unhappiness with the procurement process or with a contractor's performance, the root problem is in inadequate specification or selection criteria.

The evaluation criteria and their comparative weights must reflect what is truly important to the facility manager (references, bonding capability, financial stability, stability of the workforce, ability to perform a specialized task), particularly if prequalification is used. Then the facility manager must set the cutoff score low enough so he will retain competition high enough to eliminate those with whom he cannot live. This sensitive process, of which the facility manager is only one participant, explains why procurement is an art, not a science. Time spent on properly defining a requirement and on properly stating and weighting selection criteria will not only lead to a much smoother bidder evaluation process, but will probably secure a better contractor.

Some purchasing departments and facility managers burden themselves with one-year term service contracts. Our experience is that a three-year term contract with two one-year options and pricing tied to a local pricing index is almost ideal because it provides continuity of service, yet ensures the continuation of competitive pricing.

Too many facility managers abrogate their responsibilities and rights in service contracting. Like all other functions, service contracting needs to be managed, and the facility manager must understand clearly and exercise his responsibilities.

Contractor and Consultant Evaluation

Service contractors and consultants should be competitively evaluated as part of the procurement process. When negotiation or directed procurement (sole sourcing) is not allowed, use a two-step procedure when the dollar cost of the procurement (say, $250,000) justifies it. The first step is an evaluation of technical ability, references, insurability, and financial capability. The second step is to evaluate four to six short-list contractors using the results of an interview, previously submitted material, and costing information.

How are these evaluations to be scored? Many public agencies unfortunately are tied to selecting the contractor or consultant submitting the lowest bid. Except for the most simple tasks, it is preferable to use the "most qualified" method and allocate 30 to 45 percent of the total score to price. In this way, the number of points allocated to the pricing of each contractor is calculated as follows:

Score of contractor (points)

$$= \text{Max score (points)} - \text{max score} \times \frac{(.5)(TS\text{–}LC)}{LC}$$

where:

TS = Price of contractor being evaluated
LC = Price of lowest contractor

Partnering

A facility manager who tries to manage a fully contracted department through a low-bid contract that emphasizes the adversarial relationship with the contractor is doomed to fail. We encourage facility managers in this situation to think of contract personnel, at least from an operational point of view, as being their employees. The facility manager works with the management of the contractor to provide customers seamless, customer-oriented service. Anything in the contract or his relationship with the contractor that gets in the way of serving customers has to be changed. Mutual focus on customers is the essence of partnering.

That philosophy deemphasizes the importance of the form of the contract and emphasizes results. Initially, this will be difficult. First, if the company has a centralized procurement function, the contact there may be reluctant to deviate from the exact wording of the contract. Second, no contract is perfect the first time. The facility manager needs to understand that and act accordingly, working with the contractor to create win-win situations. Regularly scheduled operational reviews with the contractor are very helpful in this regard. In some cases, the facility manager must be willing to give, expecting the contractor to do so in the future. If that doesn't occur, this may be the wrong contractor.

For every major contract we have, we specify that the contractor have a manager or senior supervisor on site (we pay). That individual must have the ability to speak for the contractor on all operational matters. After about six months, the contractor's front office becomes not much more than a pay and personnel office for our contract. We meet with the contractor's front office personnel only when we have a problem, or quarterly, to ensure they understand where we are going as a department and how it affects their contract.

The facility manager must be confident in his ability to administer contracts so that he can manage the fine line between cooperation with the contractor and keeping that contractor at arm's length. When faced with a conflict (and they will come up), he can resolve it by determining what is best for his customers.

This concept works as well for supplies as it does for services. One very large facility management organization turned all of its supply activities over to a local supply house. After a few initial problems, they were amazed to find that they got their materials faster, with less paperwork, and at a lower price because of the contractor's muscle in the local marketplace and expertise.

Some organizations like to have formal partnering agreements with their contractors. Often these agreements address open and effective communications, how problems and disagreements will be resolved, use of the team approach, trust in both the experience and commitment of all team members, and the goal to which all are committed.

Successful partnering is dependent on a team approach to common goals, with both partners able to talk frankly and as equals. One of your authors has always been the most successful by motivating the contractor toward exceptional behavior and performance. To most contractors, the greatest incentive is a contract extension with a suitable price adjustment. For a contractor who is performing exceptionally, that is a slight price to pay. Employment stability is a major payoff.

On the other side of the ledger, not all contractors are capable of being good partners. In one of your author's experience, one very fine company had to be dropped because its president would not let go and let his on-site supervisor meet our customers' needs. There are as many challenges for the contractor as there are for the facility manager.

Outsourcing and partnering are inextricably tied to one another. The modern facility manager needs to be a contract manager extraordinaire; in all but the exceptional case, his success will depend on how well he orchestrates a primarily outsourced workforce to meet organizational goals. It is a different management model, but one that can work exceptionally well as long as the transition to it is slow, thoughtful, and uses facts, not opinion.

Departmental Evaluations

The idea of evaluation often makes a facility manager nervous. The truth is that all organizations need to undergo self-examination from time to time to maintain their own health.[4] Unfortunately, evaluation is often linked to punishment. If that is the ultimate purpose of evaluation, subordinate managers will resist being evaluated, and the staff will sabotage the effort, making the validity of results doubtful.

Approximately every ten years, conduct a departmental evaluation. For unsophisticated facility departments, this may be no more than a hard look at functional responsibilities.

Most large organizations have internal organizational review methods. If not, you can either compare your department with others (i.e., benchmark), rate the department in its company context, or—most likely—use a combination of those two methods.

Comparators

One of the most frustrating situations for a facility manager is the almost inevitable desire by management to match certain facility costs and outputs against outside comparators. In fact, the Building Owners and Managers Association (BOMA) annually produces the *BOMA Experience Exchange Report,* an inch-thick document of facility costs for the United States and Canada, considering the following variables:

- Geographic location
- Size of facility
- Age of facility
- Type of occupancy
- Public or private sector
- Program costs (lease costs, operating costs)

These comparators are the best of their kind within the industry but are inadequate for the following reasons:

1. They are based predominantly on a property management rather than a facility management philosophy of management.
2. Though BOMA attempts to collect data in a uniform manner, it is extremely doubtful that reported operating costs, particularly unit costs, are calculated

consistently by everyone who contributed to the database. Unfortunately it is impossible to capture costs in the BOMA format from many facility budgets.

3. Despite a heroic effort by BOMA, its excellent system to classify and measure space is not used by a high percentage of facility managers. This has a major effect on unit costs and lease costs calculated on a square-footage basis.

4. BOMA cannot account for the quality expectations of various organizations. What is an acceptable level of facility operations to Acme, Inc., would get the facility manager at the Gotrox Corp. fired.

Other common comparators are those from similar organizations (bank vs. bank), sector (state government vs. state government), or facility type (laboratory vs. laboratory). However, it is extremely difficult for an individual organization to gather comparative data from other organizations, particularly if the organization is a competitor. And once comparator data are gathered, the same problems exist as with BOMA data.

If comparators are to be used to measure departmental efficiency and cost-effectiveness, the best comparison is against historical data within the organization. Then the facility manager can use other means (inspections, questionnaires) to evaluate the effectiveness and quality of the service.

If you insist on comparing yourself to others, then benchmarking is the choice. Benchmarking is at the heart of total quality programs.

Ken Burkhalter, a facility manager at the Rand Corporation, spells out the important distinction between data, information, and the Key Performance Indicator (KPI) that we want to use in managing our facilities. As we have stressed often, we believe that it is important to manage by the use of metrics; to manage by KPIs and to hold ourselves and those who work for us accountable by those metrics. Burkhalter offers the following best practices in gathering and using metrics:

- Internal benchmarking is more important than external benchmarking.
- Identify sources of differences and devise ways to measure them meaningfully.
- Best measurements look at cost drivers (but should omit allocated costs).
- Metrics should be detailed enough to spot efficiency problems and broad enough to compare across operating units.
- Automating data collection improves quality, timeliness, and accountability.
- Periodic review by the executive manager is essential to maintaining a continuous improvement culture.
- Compensation should be tied to KPIs.[5]

Annual Facilities Report

It is our experience and observation that facility managers are not good at relations within the organization. There are several theories why, but it is undeniable that all of us could do better in this area. One of the routes to a better image is to tell your story, and one of the very best vehicles for this is the annual facilities (or state of the facilities) report.

There is no set format for such a report, but Exhibit 28-2 is an example. Another approach is to prepare a facilities annex to the company's annual report. Either way, the annual report can serve as both an evaluation tool and a public relations device.

By performing an Internet search for "Annual facilities report," you can see a number of such reports and one may be to your liking. After reviewing them, one criticism is that they do not stress how important facilities are to the accomplishment of the organizational mission, a theme which cannot be repeated too often.

With environmental concerns and to reduce costs, many facility annual reports or similar information are now placed on intranet pages or facility department home pages on the Internet providing similar information, usually in more graphic, more

Exhibit 28-2. Annual facilities report.

   I. Executive Summary ("bullet" style)

  II. Introduction
     A. Environment
     B. Objectives
     C. Major challenges going into the year

 III. Resources
     A. Financial display by program
     B. Human resources display by program

 IV. Accomplishments
     A. Narrative by program
     B. Statistical data
        1. Energy consumption and savings
        2. Space trends
        3. Lease trends
        4. Projects
        5. Service orders
        6. Preventive maintenance

  V. Problems and Recommended Solutions

interesting formats. Even some building property managers with multiple small tenants provide similar information to the user groups at their homepage sites. Frequent updates are critical for any web-based information of this kind.

The Facility Management Loops

There is always a tendency to present an instant solution—a panacea—to every management problem. Facility management does not lend itself to simplistic approaches or simple solutions. The function is highly integrative, and facility managers must have their fingers on the pulse of each subfunction, while also tending to the external relations of the department.

One model that we have found successful to ensure integrated problem solving pays particular attention to groupings of related activities that feed one another in loops. While it would be simplistic to say that managing these loops will solve all problems, we do believe that every facility manager should understand completely these work processes and ensure that they are managed well. If this is done, many of the integration problems that plague so many facility managers will be eliminated.

Planning, Programming, Budgeting, Execution, Evaluation

Particularly in large organizations, the staff inevitably gets divided between those who are planners, programmers, and budgeters, and those who are operators and responsible for execution. This separation can lead to damaging discontinuities and major misalignments between available resources and operational requirements.

In a format that is organized by a facility program, the long-range plan should feed the midterm plan. The annual work plan then flows from the midterm plan. Once approved, that annual work plan is bumped against reality and is presented as a budget for execution.

Evaluation, however, is often the missing link. The execution of the budget must be evaluated for quality and quantity, effectiveness, and efficiency. This evaluation will uncover shortfalls that must be fed back into the system as work plan corrections. Budgetary weaknesses and factors requiring adjustments in both the current midrange and long-range plans will appear during execution of the annual work plan. The plans should be adjusted accordingly, at least annually. This process, though it is described here as consecutive, is actually both concurrent and ongoing. It constantly carries today's success and the corrective actions of yesterday's failures into the future and determines the ability of the facility department to:

1. Learn from its mistakes.
2. Capitalize on its successes.
3. Change with the changing environment of its company.
4. Survive.

The competent facility manager must control the planning, budgeting, execution, and evaluation loop for each program.

Budgeting, Accounting, Work Planning, Enterprise Systems Integration

Rather than a loop, these functions are a series of tasks that, despite having a high degree of overlap, are too often treated separately within facility management departments. The successful facility manager recognizes the commonality in these functions, particularly as they are being automated, and can reduce automating costs greatly while increasing the department's reporting accuracy.

At the core of these processes is a definition of facility programs—those building blocks of facility management. If a facility manager is on the right track, he will plan by program, budget by program, account by program, and report by program. Programs are the crosswalk from what he does to what he pays for.

All too frequently, the budgeting and accounting are automated under a set of accounts established outside the facility department. The work of the department typically is tracked by a work management system, which is heavily weighted toward project management. Enterprise systems are typically administratively-oriented but use one accounting system in all databases for easier integration with facility management and other enterprise-wide systems such as human resources and security. This automatic consolidation of data input and tracking avoids significant problems in cost accounting and errors in reporting, as well as saving employee productivity, while maximizing accuracy. While this type of system solves one of our problems by tying us to organizational accounting, it does not solve the management information problems if our budget is not properly constructed (See chapters 4, 5, and 30). An improperly structured budget tracked with an enterprise system ensures that we properly account for costs, for example, that mean little.

The major problem with such a mode of operation is that any typical question (for example: "How much facility support have we given to the marketing department at 625 High Street, floors 4 and 5, this fiscal year?") is likely to have three answers rather than one. That ensures organizational bickering and chaos. The facility manager's contribution in these areas should be to force programmatic planning, budgeting, and reporting.

The facility manager should be able to track a request for supplies or services from inception to delivery. He should know what part purchasing, receiving, accounts payable, and the cashier play in this process, how transactions flow through these staff elements, as well as understanding what type of procurement document (purchase order, blanket purchase order, or contract) the department has with each vendor. Having this knowledge not only makes the facility manager less vulnerable to bureaucratic excuses for why something does not get done, why the order hasn't arrived, or why the vendor hasn't been paid, but also makes him more sensitive to the complexities of ordering and receiving goods and services—one of the keys to his success.

The facility manager who properly manages budgeting, accounting, work planning, and reporting not only minimizes the effort expended on these functions, but will find the management information available will be more correct and more consistent.

Capital and Annual Budgeting

Too few facility managers examine and act on the relationship between the capital and annual budgets. There appear to be several reasons for this:

1. The organization's unwillingness to provide adequate capital funding to design maintainability, life-cycle savings, energy management, sustainability factors, and value engineering into major projects
2. The facility department's inability to analyze and quantify life-cycle costs
3. The lack of understanding of new facility technologies that truly can reduce operating and maintenance costs

If your organization is actively engaged in a capital improvement program, this relationship should be examined carefully. Start by examining the new materials, service delivery systems, and technologies that offer a possibility of personnel, operational, or maintenance savings. In general, the facility manager probably needs the assistance of vendors and consultants to do this. We prefer not to do it under the pressure of a specific project, but sometimes that is the best time to get the necessary focus. A five-year horizon for technology improvements is probably appropriate.

There are several areas that might be questioned at this point in history—for example:

- Should fiberoptics be pulled to individual workstations?
- Should large manual mailrooms be installed in organizations even while e-mail has become ubiquitous (and in some companies mail is screened remotely)?[6]

- What new cleaning technologies should we install in buildings?
- Should we sponsor cogeneration? Should we install thermal storage?
- How can sustainability features be introduced into design of our capital projects which will reduce operating costs?

Capital expenditures now, in some of these areas, could substantially reduce operating costs in the future.

Once the facility manager has decided what technological and sustainable features are affordable in new capital improvements, the entire design should be scrubbed for maintenance and operational savings that can be realized. This process can be started by ensuring that the architect assigns personnel who understand operational efficiency and maintainability, but it is best ensured by having operators and maintainers review the design at concept, at 30 percent, and at 80 percent completion.

All of this will be for naught if company management views these capital improvements to achieve technological, operational, and maintenance reductions in life-cycle costs as either goldplating or other suspect requirements. The facility manager must be capable of computing the life-cycle cost reductions from these measures and defending them through project reviews. This is often the means for justifying sustainable projects and moving toward a longer-range view of the facility and its value.

The capital costs of a new building are small compared to the life-cycle costs. Well-spent capital funds and a good understanding and management of the interdependence between the capital and annual budget can aid significantly in good facility management.

Condition Assessment, Maintenance, and Annual Level of Funding for Maintenance and Repair

Properly maintained facilities normally are well-documented facilities. Too often the facilities inventory has been inadequately maintained for so long that no one in the department knows the exact state of the facilities or the cost to bring those facilities to the desired state of repair. At this juncture, it is often necessary to conduct a condition assessment. Another scenario for a condition assessment (particularly by outside experts) is when the board of directors or legislative body has indicated that the facility department's estimate of the maintenance backlog is not credible. This seems to happen frequently in public-sector situations.

Condition assessments can be bought into at many levels. At any level, however, they are costly.[6] Also, money spent on assessing the facilities, though necessary, normally is money diverted from maintaining facilities. If 2 to 4 percent of the replacement value of facilities is invested annually in normal maintenance and repair (not backlog reduction), condition assessment should be required infrequently and only for highly specialized needs.[7]

The interrelationship of documentation, adequate resources for maintenance and repair, and a properly managed maintenance program cannot be overemphasized. Good maintenance and repair need to be managed just as competently as any capital project. Whenever one of those factors is absent, the program will be suboptimal, and eventually a condition assessment will be required to fill the void. If that occurs, the information in the condition assessment should be acted on and the facilities returned to their normal state of repair as soon as possible.

Work Management

Another important loop is work management: work standards, staffing, work reporting, and outputs. It is a loop that has been emphasized too much. Too often the approach to improving efficiency in the facility department has been to increase the work standards or to reduce the staffing. Both of those measures may be laudatory and necessary, but they often result in reduced quality of work or cheating in time reporting.

We are not committed to work standards because they are too easily corrupted. (The ultimate example is paying for standard tasks in auto repair facilities, none of which requires the effort for which the customer pays. Both the dealer and the customer know that, yet the charade continues.) Work standards complicate union relations. Unions and management can cast positions etched in stone based on work standards, even if they are outmoded, based on old technology, or incorrectly measured. However, in certain situations the facility manager is forced to use work standards.

If used, work standards should be simple, clearly stated, and agreed to by both management and the applicable trades. The standard should be in enough detail so that if technology later changes (switching from incandescent bulbs to fluorescent tubes, for instance), it is evident that the standard should be adjusted.

Time accounting becomes a critical component of this loop. Is each employee required to account for eight hours each shift? If so, to which job is travel time charged? Is it realistic to require all technicians to account for 100 percent of their hours on the job? What are the rules for allocating overhead hours? Unless the facility manager carefully manages the time accounting system, he will find these rules driving operations. Time allocation rules, like work standards, can become locked in concrete despite the fact that conditions and technology have changed. In fact, time accounting rules established merely for administrative convenience can become work standards if not used carefully.

The facility manager who wants to manage the work output of the department needs to put particular emphasis on work management. Too often a push for new levels of productivity falls solely upon the workforce. The facility manager must avoid that situation because it invariably leads solely to confrontation, and improvement is seldom primarily within the power of the workforce. Both work standards and time allocation rules must be necessary, but they should be managed well and capable of being changed.

Notes

1. *The Impact of E-Commerce on Facility Management Practices:* (Houston, TX; IFMA Foundation; 2002).
2. Personal communication from Dr. William Badger, Arizona State University, March 4, 2008.
3. "Top Ten Outsourcing Survey," *Executive Survey: The Outsourcing Institute's Annual Survey of Outsourcing End Users,* www.outsourcing.com, July 13, 2008, p. 1.
4. "Key Factors for Successful Outsourcing," The Outsourcing Institute, www.outsourcinginstitute.com, July 13, 2008.
5. Ken Burkhalter, "Aha . . . Unlocking Hidden Wisdom Through a Good Metrics Program," *FMJ* July/August 2007, pp. 52–53.
6. L. Terry Suber, "Evaluating Plant Management," *Facilities Management* (Washington, DC: APPA, 1984), pp. vi 5.
7. Building Research Board, *Committing to the Cost of Ownership* (Washington, D.C.: National Academy Press, 1990), p. 21.

29

Managing Quality Facilities

- *The customer, and the customer alone, defines the quality of the product or service provided.*
- *The facility manager must use every means available to measure his customers' perception of services.*
- *No one system of gathering opinions of your services will work forever.*
- *Do it right the first time!*
- *The facility manager must set quality goals and track them over time.*
- *Measure efficiency, effectiveness, and response.*
- *Empower employees, but empowerment without training is chaos. Make everyone in the department feel responsible for the total facilities mission.*
- *Use every means available to publicize services and successes. The facility manager needs to be the chief publicist for the department.*
- *Develop a profile on each customer.*

It is our sincere hope that many of the lessons of the total quality management (TQM) movement of the eighties have become standard operating procedure, literally a part of our management DNA. At the same time, we are disappointed that there is little in the FM dialogue about TQM because, to us, TQM focuses us totally on our customer where we believe it belongs. At the same time we have some difficulty separating discussing the data collection for benchmarking and data collection for TQM (they are in separate chapters) because we feel they are brought together through the concept of Key Performance Indicators (KPIs). Our KPI should be determined by what our stakeholders feel is important and that is what we should be measuring. In this chapter we hope to re-activate the importance of TQM in your practice.

Note: For a detailed discussion of TQM in a facility management context see Payant and Lewis' *The Facility Manager's Maintenance Handbook, 2nd Edition,* Chapter 8 or *Quality Facility Management* by Friday and Cotts.

TQM made an irrevocable imprint on businesses in the early 1990s. While they may no longer call it TQM, facility managers now manage in ways that are a result of the emphasis on quality. This chapter is organized around the characteristics of TQM that a successful facility manager must understand and incorporate into his business practices.

Some facility managers both recognize TQM and integrate it into their practice. In *Quality Facility Management,* Stormy Friday and Dave Cotts address in detail very practical examples of integrating facility and quality management for the betterment of both the facility department and the supported business. Essential to that process are what we call the Five Pillars of Quality.[1]

The Five Pillars of Quality

1. Quality services start with customer service. Only the customer will define whether you are performing the right service and how well you are doing it.
2. You must be committed to continuous improvement.
3. You must be willing and able to measure and be measured.
4. Employees must be empowered, must be held responsible, and must view themselves and their jobs within the broader context.
5. Quality service should be both recognized and marketed inside and outside the company.

In addition, Friday and Cotts observed three conditions within outstanding service organizations. First, employees in quality service organizations view themselves as totally responsible for the entire facility and feel that "it's *my* job!" Second, in great organizations, employees do things right the first time. Finally, outstanding organizations are totally focussed on meeting the service needs of their customers.[2]

Customer Service

Basic to the practice of TQM is customer service, and the bedrock of customer service is the fact that the customer, and the customer alone, defines the quality of the service or product provided. As APPA's former executive director Wayne LeRoy has put it so well, we must respect *customer sovereignty,* we must provide *customer service,* and we must ensure *customer satisfaction.* Many facility managers have difficulty understanding this customer-centered principle. Even more refuse to let it guide their practice. At its most basic level, this principle holds that it really does not matter what our education or experience tells us; we have to do what the customer says. That is difficult for a facility manager, particularly a strong and experienced one. Facility managers tend to feel that as facilities experts, they know what is best for facilities—and that normally is true. What they sometimes fail to understand is what is best for the business as expressed by their customer, the business unit.

One of the easiest ways to understand this concept is when a full, well-administered chargeback system is in place. The business manager is going to insist on preeminence even in facility decisions as long as he is paying for them. As long as what he desires is not illegal, unsafe, insecure, or harmful, the facility manager's job is to use his facility expertise to help that business manager carry out the facilities aspects of his business decisions as efficiently and effectively as possible.

For this reason, managing customer service is really managing expectations. In order to do that, facility managers need to measure those expectations in a uniform and impartial way. In this regard, they and their employees must be willing to be measured. If that concept is not understood and supported by employees—down to the last tradesman—they will sabotage the system. The facility manager needs to do the internal sales job to convince employees that the long-term success of the organization depends on having accurate customer service data. But he must avoid telling them that their performance will not be tied to their ability to serve customers properly. Exactly what he is trying to do is constantly improve the organization through goal setting, measurement, and adjustments. Ultimately, he may even tie compensation, at least in part, to employees' ability to meet customer needs and to work as members of participatory teams.[3]

Two of the first questions to ask in customer sampling are, "How often am I going to sample?" and "What do we measure?" Appropriate statistical sampling is the topic of entire books. Let us give some basic guidelines. Sample customer opinion of every major event, such as the relocation of a department or the construction of a new facility. For normal work orders, we prefer to sample every one for a set period—say, one month each quarter—rather than a percentage throughout the entire year. There are advantages and disadvantages to that approach, but when sampling customer response to every single service order during a fixed time period, we pay particular attention to the geographic distribution (building/location) and organizational distribution of the sample.

Surveying in depth is increasingly difficult to do. One of your authors used an extensive mail customer survey which provided a great deal of information about his customers' perceptions of the department's services. He was among the first to sample customer opinion within his organization. As more and more service providers in the organization turned to surveying for customer service, customers got "surveyed out" and the response rate fell to almost zero. This phenomenon has only

Customer Service Truths

1. Poor service is the number-one reason companies lose business. A full 68 percent of customers stop doing business with a company because of poor service.
2. Ninety percent of the customers that stopped doing business with a company made no attempt to tell the firm why.
3. Seventy percent of dissatisfied customers never complain because it is not worth their time; they think company personnel won't listen if the customer does complain, or they think the customer won't do anything about their complaint.
4. The average dissatisfied customer tells nine or ten others of their dissatisfaction.
5. Conversely, the average satisfied customer tells only five people.
6. It takes ten dollars in new business to replace one dollar of lost business.
7. It costs between five and ten times as much to attract a new customer as it does to keep an old one.
8. Quality service is the main thing that differentiates one business from another.
9. The first sixty seconds establishes the tone and first impression of a meeting.
10. Each time a customer comes in contact with a company employee for the first time, it is a new first impression.
11. The same attitudes that lead to increased customer satisfaction can lead to increased employee performance.
12. Customers pay more for better service.
13. Ninety-five percent of dissatisfied customers would do business again with that same company if their problem were solved quickly and satisfactorily.
14. The company person, no matter what rung on the ladder, should always ask himself or herself, "What can I do to satisfy the customer?"
15. Every company employee is involved in sales.
16. Excellent service leads to increased sales.
17. Companies should pay attention to how they spend money. It's unwise to overspend in some areas and underspend in others.
18. Customers will tell a company where it needs improvement. We need to ask customers how we can make our business more pleasurable, convenient, and suitable for them.

Source: Richard Tyler of Richard Tyler International, as quoted in *Modern Office Technology*, February 1993.

accelerated with the use of e-mail for customer surveying. The facility manager must be constantly changing the method of gathering customer input; every system has a shelf life. Unfortunately, this makes the gathering of consistent data difficult. While maintaining the survey format for major projects (which impacted any one customer infrequently), we switched to a response card for service orders which only required the customer to rate five things:

1. Did we do what you wanted us to do?
2. Did we do it well?
3. Did we do it in a timely manner that was acceptable to you?
4. Did we look good and clean up after ourselves?
5. Did we check with you to ensure that you were happy?

Each question had a place for comment, and there were three lines at the bottom for general comments.

Many companies are using their intranets to automate customer service sampling. All of the techniques that we already noted can be fed over the company network to the appropriate customer, who, with a few keystrokes and an emphatic touch of the Enter key, can send a service response reply to the facility manager's database, to be screened and compiled for statistical analysis. One enterprising facility manager conducts a random drawing for prizes such as a bottle of good wine or a floral bouquet to encourage customers to respond to service inquiries.[4]

Eventually, though, the customers rebelled against *any* written surveys, so we turned to running focus groups of a diverse profile of customers on each of our services. Initially we had service providers in each focus group. That was a mistake because they immediately became defensive, and that attitude stifled our customers' saying what they really thought. After that, our focus groups were customers only. If you have never done this, we suggest that you do so as a best practice. Repeat using focus groups about every three years or examine one-third of your services every year.

Despite the difficulties, it is important to track customer response over time. For an item that needs improvement—timeliness for instance—the facility manager must set goals, improve staffing or procedures, and then measure again. He will not always succeed, but often the analyses with employees will (1) uncover problems that he did not even know existed, (2) give employees buy-in to the process, and (3) confirm to all the seriousness with which he treats customer service.

Let us make one last point on sampling customer service: Facility managers must make every effort, by every means, to talk to customers and obtain their ratings in a meaningful way. The greatest challenge is to keep the medium fresh and to gather data consistently over time so that meaningful analysis is possible.

Assessing Customer Expectations of Service Quality

1. Excellent facility departments will have modern-looking equipment.
2. The physical facilities of excellent facility departments will be visually appealing.
3. Employees at excellent facility departments will be neat.
4. Materials issued such as pamphlets or statements will be visually appealing in an excellent facility department.
5. When excellent facility departments promise to do something by a certain time, they do it.
6. When a customer has a problem, excellent facility departments will show a sincere interest in solving it.
7. Excellent facility departments will perform their service right the first time.
8. Excellent facility departments will provide their services at the time they promise to do so.
9. Excellent facility departments will insist on error-free records.
10. Employees in excellent facility departments will tell customers exactly when services will be performed.
11. Employees in excellent facility departments will give prompt service to customers.
12. Employees in excellent facility departments will always be willing to help customers.
13. Employees in excellent facility departments will never be too busy to respond to customers' requests.
14. The behavior of employees in excellent facility departments will instill confidence in customers.
15. Customers of excellent facility departments will feel safe in their transactions.
16. Employees in excellent facility departments will be consistently courteous to customers.
17. Employees in excellent facility departments will have the knowledge to answer customer questions.
18. Excellent facility departments will give customers individual attention.
19. Excellent facility departments will have operating hours that are convenient to their customers.
20. Excellent facility departments will have employees who give customers personal attention.
21. Excellent facility departments will have the customers' best interests at heart.
22. The employees of excellent facility departments will understand the specific needs of their customers.

Source: Adapted by *Facilities Manager* from Zeithami, Parasuraman and Berry, *Delivering Quality Service* (The Free Press, 1990).

Closely aligned with talking to customers is the need to ensure that services are readily accessible to customers. We are amazed by the bureaucracy that still exists, particularly in government, to request services ("Submit Form 211-7-8 in four copies"). Modern facility departments are geared to accept customer requests by multiple modes and, through the use of automated forms or checklists, format the needed information in a way that is usable.

Finally, to satisfy customers, the facility department must produce. Services need to be delivered within an acceptable time (agreed to with the customer) by service providers who are neat, clean, well uniformed, and technically competent. They should be able to verify the customers' needs, get the work done, and ensure customer satisfaction before leaving the site. That takes intensive customer service training of all workers, even contractors, an area that most facility managers neglect.

Continuous Improvement

At the heart of quality facility management is the concept of continuous improvement. Unfortunately, in practice, continuous improvement is the antithesis of the way many of us manage. By our nature and training, we are interested in creating the big, perfect organizational machine and then stepping back and watching it run. Unfortunately, in the changing governmental and business climates in which we manage, the external environment is changing rapidly. Similarly, both our use of and response to technology demands change. In that type of environment, if we aren't continuously improving, we are going backward. That is why continuous improvement is so important. In fact, it must be a major business objective of every facility department: Goals need to be set, results measured (see Measure! Measure! Measure! below), improvements assimilated into the service delivery system, and incentives and disincentives tied to constant improvement right to the worker/technician level.

Perhaps the easiest way to understand constant improvement is to discuss the Shewhart cycle: Plan, do, check, act, try again with new information, and then repeat the process. One way to look at this is as shown in Exhibit 29-1. This process is simple to draw and comprehend but difficult to implement over a long period of time. Two human reactions enter the equation. First, people get bored, and instead of seeking meaningful improvement, they bureaucratize the process. Also, unless service workers and supervisors have truly bought in to continuous improvement, they will manipulate the system and the data so that improvement appears to be happening but really isn't. Those kinds of attitudes and actions will disappear only if there are total buy-in throughout the workforce, in-depth quality service training, and adequate incentives and disincentives tied to superior quality management. The challenge is to keep the process fresh after the first year.

Exhibit 29-1. Shewhart cycle.

Plan	Plan
Do	Do
Check	Check
Act	Act
Repeat with new information	Repeat with new information

The WRC should be the center of sampling and collecting data regarding continuous improvement. Because it receives, tasks, coordinates, and accounts for work already, it is the ideal vehicle to manage continuous improvement for the facility manager. He should use this vehicle to provide the metrics on quality management for the facility management information system.

Measure! Measure! Measure!

No one aspect of TQM can be separated from the others. We always are concerned whenever, for some reason, we break quality management into its components. For instance, constant improvement requires that we measure ourselves consistently and constantly and set goals that we try to achieve and against which we are measured.

The measurement aspect of quality management is the toughest part for which to get buy-in at all levels. We intellectualize the need for measurement, but none of us likes to be measured, because our experience shows that there is always some sort of punishment for failing to measure up. But how will we ever know if we are meeting objectives and customers' expectations unless there is a dispassionate, consistent way to measure progress—or failure? How do we know that we are achieving constant improvement if we are not measuring against some baseline? How do we know after the Plan and Do phases of the Shewhart cycle that we are proceeding in a way that justifies the resources committed to improving a process? Measurement—consistent measurement over time—is fundamental to good-quality facility management.

As instructors and observers of other facility managers, it is apparent that we have part of the measurement equation, efficiency, well in hand. Due perhaps to the emphasis on benchmarking, more and more departments have developed metrics to measure their costs (e.g., total facility costs per square foot, utility costs per square foot, total costs per occupant). We remain highly critical of the quality of the data used; however, that is the subject of another book. Overall, facility managers are moving rapidly to measure how efficiently they manage.

Some facility managers are doing a good job of measuring response. How long does it take the WRC to answer trouble calls? How long does it take the engineering force to answer a hot-cold call once tasked? By category of project, what is the cycle time? Response is a major factor in customer service and quality management (one of the factors where customers are most dissatisfied with their facility department). The facility manager should install systems and procedures to monitor response by type of work and track it over time.

Measuring effectiveness seems to be the Achilles' heel of most facility quality management efforts. It is ironic because it does not matter how efficient or responsive the facility department thinks it is. Effectiveness is solely determined by customers, and the biggest challenge is to figure out how to measure their opinions. No one way will work. In fact, every vehicle for measuring customer perception of facility department effectiveness seems to have a declining life, which makes it very difficult to compare results over time. That is one of the biggest challenges of managing quality facilities. We know of no perfect solution, but the facility manager must use every avenue available—written, electronic, focus groups, and others—to stay in touch with the perceptions of customers.

Facility managers need to become familiar with the techniques of sampling and the practical applications of statistics. Terms such as *median, mean, standard deviation,* and *normal distribution* should be as familiar as *HVAC, leasing,* and *churn rate.* Once statistics are gathered, facility managers should be able to display and analyze data using such methods as histograms, scatter diagrams, Pareto charts, and trend charts. We suggest a basic college statistics course to any facility manager who has not had one.

We have been torn whether a discussion of data gathering is more appropriately discussed under quality management or benchmarking so we do want to discuss it here. There are two aspects to this subject. George Lohnes of UNICCO, one of the major FM outsourcing providers, says that it is important 1) to have "actionable" data and 2) that Integrated Workplace Management Systems now give us the ability not just to collect a large volume of data, but to slice it and dice it so that it aids in both better management decisions and better service to our customers.[5] Leah Garris takes this discussion one step further by discussing "measuring what matters" in a specific framework. In addition, she discusses Six Sigma, a methodology to make business processes better by eliminating the variations in them.

Six Sigma, along with lean processes, are the latest quality tools used in many organizations. Based on manufacturing attempts to remove defects and errors, and reduce unneeded layers of management and process, many tools and concepts of Six Sigma management are easily adaptable to facility management practices. The American Society for Quality provides the popular color belts in Six Sigma training (www.asq.org/six-sigma/index.html)) and the American Management Association provides books and courses on the subject (www.amanet.org). In the never-ending quest to do more with less, these quality improvement tools are useful for streamlining and strengthening facility management processes. Six Sigma has become a requirement for facility departments in some organizations since the mid-1990s. Some facility managers have introduced the method into their departments based on presentations they heard at their professional associations. Eastman Kodak, for example, claims to have saved $8–10 million in operating expenses in facilities in just two years using Six Sigma. Iowa State University's Facilities Planning and Management Department used Six Sigma to make a good department great.[6] It is a methodology which has survived through the years and one that we recommend as a best practice.

One of the reasons that we like to set standards and measure is to use the normal competitive nature of human beings. We want to be the best and will strive to excel in those items we are measured on. That is why it is important to choose standards in the areas that are truly important to you and your customers. However, it is just as important to ensure that you have "controlled competitiveness" so that benchmarks are being achieved honestly and in a way that serves the customer. We also believe that it is important to re-examine the procedures and methods where standards are not met so that, rather than punish those who do not meet targets, the organization inspects itself and improves.

Benchmarking

We sense that the profession's interest in benchmarking has declined and think that is a shame.

Every facility manager should have a working knowledge of benchmarking as part of his managerial tool bag. Benchmarking has become a part of the language of our profession, if not the practice.

Key to good benchmarking is having accurate data, particularly cost data. Consistent programmatic budgeting makes that so much easier. Second, we need to know what the true costs of each service is, including overheads. Whether we benchmark externally or not, we need to know our *true cost of doing business*. Unfortunately, budget formats and accounting systems often are so convoluted that true costs are difficult to calculate without excessive manipulation. Producing accurate unit costs should be a priority of the financial management system.

Do not confine benchmarking to costs. For instance, it can be important to you as a manager that 96 percent of service orders in one geographic area are closed out within three days, while only 67 percent of them are closed in a similar facility in another area. That discrepancy should cause you to question why. Neither number is "right"; they are different. Operational improvements will be possible as we examine why they are different.

Beware of numbers that represent a broad universe when you are benchmarking. Experienced benchmarkers realize that there are so many reasons that the measurement of benchmarks is not consistent that you would like the two organizations or functions being benchmarked to be as similar as possible. For example, comparing your cost of carpet cleaning to a national average is of very limited value. However, there are several national companies that maintain large databases of facility management cost data. Some of the International Facility Management Association (IFMA) councils have active ongoing benchmarking groups for certain industry groups. Often, however, a facility manager can do benchmarking locally just by making some phone calls to other similar organizations.

Benchmarking partners may vary. We like to benchmark against an organization that is as close to our own business organization, even that of a competitor, as possible. Then we like to benchmark against a facility department that is as similar to ours as possible. Finally, we like to benchmark against the organization that is considered best in class in the function being benchmarked. For instance, if we were benchmarking the response time of our services reception desk, we might use the local electric or telephone company as our benchmarking partner.

Remember to get beyond the metrics in benchmarking. The reason there is a difference is the important factor. You might find out that the electric company gets 10 percent better response time than you do in services reception, but they have two additional staff in this area. You then have the information necessary to make a decision on staffing.

Benchmarking is a concept from total quality management (TQM). Applying good TQM principles, we measure (benchmark), then make necessary changes, implement, and measure again. This internal benchmarking is a valuable tool for plotting the success of management changes over time.

Googling "facility management benchmarks" can introduce you to benchmarking partners and sources locally, nationally, and internationally.

Evaluation of Routine Work

The first line of effective qualitative control in the FM realm is effective supervision. When dealing with contractors, for instance, effective supervision has two components: (1) by the contractor or consultant, and (2) by the owner or user. When hiring contractors or consultants, ask about their quality assurance policy and procedures, and emphasize the importance you place on quality work.

The facility manager has three responsibilities that help ensure quality control:

1. Setting the standards

2. Determining what testing is desired
3. Inspection! Inspection! Inspection!

For small organizations, effective supervision of project work can be handled by the architect or design firm, or by companies that specialize in inspection and testing services. In larger organizations, in-house staff may perform some quality control functions, but outsiders are likely to be hired.

For preventive maintenance, service orders, small projects, and ongoing services like custodial, sample customers monthly, using questionnaires. The work reception center can send, receive, and analyze these questionnaires. (Our experience is that to get a 10 percent sample returned, 30 percent of each service should be sampled, with questionnaires equally distributed for buildings and organizations.) For services like janitorial, concentrate questionnaires on one to two buildings each month but ensure that all facilities are surveyed twice annually.

Once the questionnaires are returned, the facility manager can evaluate small projects on a quarterly basis as to the following:

1. Number scheduled vs. number completed
2. Number completed within or over budget
3. Number completed on or over schedule

For preventive maintenance, analyze adherence to schedule and qualitative results of the questionnaires. For ongoing services such as custodial, look monthly for trends of satisfaction or dissatisfaction by building or by area, since that is how such services are normally delivered. Analyze service orders monthly, by trade, in the following ways:

1. Number outstanding
2. Cost per service order vs. historical average
3. Numbers completed within established time criteria
4. Satisfaction or dissatisfaction of customers with the service

Reengineering

Often we see facility manages tinkering with their organization, policies, and procedures to try to achieve major improvements. In fact, what is actually needed is an entirely new approach. One of your authors once participated in a well-led participatory management process, an excellent reengineering initiative. As the process unfolded and the final product became evident, it was obvious that the organizational shakedown was basically rearranging the deck chairs on the *Titanic*. The organization suffered mostly from outdated skills, unusually restrictive union conditions, and a less than fully productive work environment. Managers were spending an inordinate amount of their time solving human resources' problems. The situation was a prime example of one where outsourcing would help, yet the manager bristled when it was suggested because his management had arbitrarily said that no outsourcing would be considered. The point here is that, for true improvement, management needs to remove preconditions and let facility managers be limited only by the resources available and their imaginations. One of your authors has considerable experience as a consultant and has always been amazed by the client's failure to act on the recommendations that that same client sought and paid for.

For a formalized approach to reengineering, read Champy and Hammer's *Reengineering the Corporation*. Innovation in processes (reengineering) is as applicable to the public sector as to the private, though sometimes more difficult to implement. *Banishing Bureaucracy* by David Osborne and Peter Plastrik specifically addresses reengineering the public sector.

The top four reasons that reengineering efforts fail are:

1. Resistance to change (60 percent)
2. Limitations of the existing systems (40 percent)
3. Lack of executive consensus (40 percent)
4. Lack of a senior executive champion (40 percent)

Three of them reflect on management.[7] Don't enter into a reengineering effort just because it is the flavor of the day. It is hard, foot-slogging work, and requires high energy and great tenacity. Implementation of reengineering is fully as important as design. The most common errors that contribute to the failure of reengineering are trying to fix a process instead of changing it, not focusing on the business process, ignoring everything except the process design, neglecting people's values and beliefs, being willing to settle for minor results, and quitting too early.[8]

The facility manager's attitude is critical. He must indicate full support for reengineering (even if some of his pet oxen get gored), see that training is provided to all who need it, and be unmerciful in ensuring that things like compensation are tied to full implementation of reengineering.

Empowerment

Frontline workers need to have the flexibility to handle almost any situation they are sent to correct. Anyone who does not believe that as a management technique should conduct a detailed analysis of callbacks for one month and find out the reason why workers had to return to correct a situation that they had previously been sent to solve. We have observed a number of FM organizations over the years and it appears that callbacks range from 10–30 percent of total service calls—a terrible waste of human resources, particularly considering attendant travel time and customer dissatisfaction. Fully half of all callbacks could have been solved during the initial visit had workers been trained and permitted to do multitrade work or had they been allowed to task the correct colleague in the organization to perform the work. Too often workers act like automatons ("I'm sorry, ma'am, but I can't do this job because it is not part of my job, but someone will be here to fix it sometime") because managers do not give them the authority to solve problems ("Ma'am, this problem is beyond my ability, but I have called the master electrician, and she will be here at 2:00 this afternoon to fix this problem for you. If she does not show up by 2:15, please call me at this number."). If everyone tries to do the right thing the first time and all technicians view themselves as customer problem solvers, efficiency and effectiveness will rise substantially. Here are three rules in this area:

1. If a worker can fix something, he should do it right the first time.
2. If health, safety, or operations is involved, make sure that the worker is empowered to take responsibility for seeing that it is reported immediately to the right person and that he follows up until the problem is solved.
3. A worker should fix anything that he can. If he can't fix it, he should take responsibility for reporting it properly and by following up to see that it does get fixed.[9]

Nothing facilitates empowerment in an organization as much as staff reductions. Most facility departments cannot afford to have checkers checking checkers and the organizational sclerosis that vertical decision making causes. Everyone needs to share in decision making and accountability to a greater extent than ever before—daunting to some and even job threatening to others. It is our experience, for example, that some of the very best supervisors have the biggest problem with the concept of empowered teams.

One quick word about empowered teams: We strongly believe in them to solve individual problems and for a limited duration. It makes good sense that those closest to the problem probably have the best solutions to it. Choose leaders carefully; our personal bias is to appoint the leader rather than to have him elected. Ensure that there is representation on the team from all interested and affected parties. Then once the team arrives at a solution and the facility manager blesses it and provides the resources, there is more likely to be complete acceptance.

Empowerment without training is chaos. Front-line mechanics and workers must not only be multiskilled, but also must be able to talk to customers. They must be customer oriented, and they must understand how the entire department works so that they can tap the right resource if the problem is beyond their ability to solve. That approach is very different from the way craftspeople have traditionally been taught to act and react. The facility manager will obtain excellent results only after solid commitment to empowerment and reasonably intensive training. If both are not present, forget empowering teams. Empowerment without training will only complicate the problems.

Quality in facility management is imperative. The use of quality management tools along with good communications (See Chapter 31) are keys to making the facility management function known to and respected by our customers and management.[10] Without tools to measure and report improving quality of our operations, the facility management function will be overlooked and the true value of facility management underappreciated.

Exhibit 29-2. Three 5's Test.

---

1. Select five individuals at random while walking through the facility, and ask them the following questions:
   - Do you know who I am?
   - Describe five services provided by the facility department.
   - Describe the last five services provided to your department by the facility department.

This can be humbling. If four out of five individuals don't know you or the services you provide, you need to be concerned about how your value to the company is perceived.

2. Maintain a log of phone calls over a five-week period that you personally answer. Track the following:
   - Who the calls come from
   - The nature of the call

If more than half of the calls are not from senior managers or if more than half are complaints, you are in trouble because you have failed to gauge properly your customers' perceptions of your services and do not have sufficient visibility with top management.

3. Review the agendas for executive staff meetings that you have attended over a five-month period. If you have not made a major presentation or contribution in 80 percent of the meetings, you have failed to project the value-added worth of your department and are not being heard adequately by top management.

Source: Stormy Friday and David G. Cotts, *Quality Facility Management* (New York: Wiley, 1995), p. 135.

Facility managers in the 1960s and 1970s tended to view their mission as creating big, service-providing machines that could be turned on and then watched as they would hum efficiently. Customers were not the primary focus of facility organizations (they always complain or want something that we can't give them) because *we* know what is better for them and for the facilities. Because they held those attitudes, one of their greatest failings was that they did not sell their departments and services well.

Notes

1. Stormy Friday and David G. Cotts, *Quality Facility Management* (New York: Wiley, 1994), pp. 3–4. Copyright 1994 John Wiley & Sons, Inc. Reprinted by permission of John Wiley & Sons, Inc.
2. Ibid., p. 3.
3. For an excellent discussion of tying compensation to quality service, read Laura J. Davis and Michael L. Hagler, "Quality Service Through Employee-Defined Performance Management" *Facilities Manager* (Summer 1994): 48–59.
4. For an excellent discussion of what can be done with e-mail, see Donna Schliewe, "The Role of Electronic Mail in Customer Communication," *Facilities Manager* (Summer 1994): 44–47.
5. George Lohnes, "Transformative Data into Actionable Information," *FMJ* July/August 2007, p. 16.
6. Leah B. Garris, "Measuring What Matters," *Building*, August 2004, p. 28–32.
7. Compiled by Organizational Universe Systems, P.O. Box 38, Valley Center, Calif. 92082, http://www.improve.org/reengfl.html.
8. Ibid.
9. Friday and Cotts, *Quality Facility Management*, pp. 92–94.
10. Ibid., pp. 96–98.

Managing the Budget

Pulse Points

- *Facility managers should view themselves as businesspeople.*
- *The facility manager should structure the budget to be his principal management information system tool.*
- *Capital projects have annual cost implications (depreciation and operational costs).*
- *The facility manager should plan for 5 to 15 percent more discretionary work than budgeted.*
- *The facility manager should understand and manage his annual expenditure profile.*
- *If chargebacks are used, expend the effort to make them meaningful. The concept of a fixed package of services for a realistic internal rent (with services outside the package provided on a fee-for-service basis) is a best practice.*
- *Programmatic budgeting is a best practice.*
- *For a major project, the facility manager should invest early in a good project accounting system and accountant.*
- *The facility manager should know the true cost of providing major services and should benchmark those cost metrics with competitors, similar organizations, and best in class.*
- *Better facility business planning and the reduction in churn offer the two best opportunities for facility cost reduction.*

Financial management remains one of the weak links of facility management. Since facilities are second only to human resources among corporate expenditures, financial management is an area with great potential for improvement. Facility managers, viewing themselves as businesspeople, are key to this improvement.

We find public sector facility managers to be much more in tune with good programmatic financial management. On the other hand, in too many private organizations, the facility managers treat the budget and the accounting system as a *fait d'ac-*

compli, thrust upon them by "corporate" and, therefore, lose the ability to use the budget as their principal management information system tool. IFMA has begun to offer courses, *The Business of FM* and *Financial Competency,* BOMI offers a variety of webcasts in financial management oriented toward property management, and APPA has a specialized course on facility finances oriented principally toward capital budgeting or major project financing. We cannot be familiar with the content of all these seminars, but we hope that they contain some of our Pulse Points because they truly address the major issues regarding facility financial management.

When we ask facility managers to think of themselves as businesspeople, we mean six things.

Business Issues for Facility Managers

1. Know your business.
2. Know the language of business.
3. Understand, in detail, how you affect your company's business.
4. Be able to use capital budget evaluation tools.
5. Institute good financial controls.
6. Implement cost reduction and containment.

Most facility managers are knowledgeable about the technical aspects of their business but less skilled in understanding how they affect their company's bottom line. For instance, a facility manager must understand that, as a major cost center, the facility department will be constantly scrutinized. Also, facility managers tend to talk to upper management and business colleagues in "FMspeak" rather than in the language of business. (Chapter 5 gives some of the tools to do this.) They need to understand concepts like the net present value of money, life-cycle costing, and the cost of capital and then make their business arguments in those terms. Similarly, they need to build partnerships within the company based on their ability to help colleagues achieve their business goals (which are often defined as a financial ratio, the numerator or denominator of which they influence).

But although they need to think and speak like businesspeople, only in the rarest of cases should they advertise themselves as a profit center. Several facility managers have spun off the in-house department in their companies as an FM service firm serving other companies as well, but that is the exceptional case. In general, facility management is, and is viewed as, a cost center. Nevertheless, the successful facility manager will be as good a businessperson as the owner of a private FM service company because, in the current environment, the in-house department will have to be cost competitive or it will be outsourced.

Good financial management is based on good facility business planning, a subject covered in Chapter 4. The best practice here is programmatic planning and budgeting, which allows tracking the operations and maintenance (O&M) program, for example, from the long-range plan, through the annual work plan, and into the current annual budget. Unless the facility manager is a player in company business planning, he will always be short of resources and at a distinct disadvantage in financial management.

Key to good management is knowing the actual costs of doing business, yet too few facility managers have ever calculated the costs of each of their services. It is not uncommon for large facility departments to be offering sixty to seventy services, each with a direct labor cost, a cost of material, a direct overhead cost, and some allocated overhead cost. Facility managers need to know what those costs are and how they change over time for three reasons. First, there is so much emphasis now on cost control that managers who do not know their actual costs will fail. Second, many departments use chargebacks or allocations to charge customers for services. Facility managers who don't know their true costs will be in a constant battle with customers over the appropriateness of chargebacks. Third, once costs for all services are correctly calculated and tracked over time, the facility manager will note that five or six of those costs are the real drivers. These then become the cost categories that the facility manager will concentrate on and are the categories that will be used to benchmark with others.

Key to being able to track costs accurately and over time is a good budget format, which allows costs to be identified easily. (Our recommended planning and budget format is in Exhibit 4-2.) The budget should be the main facility management information tool, and programmatic budgeting allows this. That is why it is a best practice. We cannot emphasize this point too strongly.

To be successful, the facility manager should have the ability to:

- Develop and execute facility business plans.
- Develop, execute, and evaluate budgets.
- Administrate chargeback and allocations.
- Understand depreciation.
- Develop appropriate benchmarks and cost comparators.
- Calculate life-cycle costs.
- Calculate cost justification and project prioritization values.
- Understand pertinent ratio analysis.

At the center of these financial management skills is the ability to format, develop, and manage an annual budget. The remainder of this chapter focuses on those skills.

In 1994, FMLink, the preeminent Internet resource for FM surveyed facility managers on their short-term outlook for FM finances and it was evident that facility managers saw some "belt-tightening" coming. While there was a slight trend toward increased budgets, facility managers surveyed viewed balancing the facility budget as their greatest challenge and finding funding for deferred maintenance was their next biggest challenge.[1] If anything, FM budget concerns were understated. In the next four years, outsourcing, globalization, and constant executive oversight of administrative costs will put tremendous pressure on FM annual budgets and no relief appears in sight and this trend has heightened here in the last five years.

Almost concurrently 252 business managers were asked by the International Facility Management Association (IFMA) about their perception of facilities. Cost information was the information that they most wanted from their facility department, and they perceived facilities as follows:

A liability or cash drain:	3 percent
A cost of doing business:	60 percent
A resource that can provide a competitive edge:	37 percent

Ninety-six percent of those same executives said that for the profession to thrive in the future, facility management must demonstrate positive financial impacts.[2] The message here is that facility managers are not meeting the business expectations of upper management (or don't understand those expectations). The pressure to meet management's goals has not lessened and so it has become even more important for the facility manager to view himself as a business manager and to be competent in managing finances. It is encouraging that executive management views facility management as a resource that can provide a competitive edge so facility managers should never miss an opportunity to show how the organization's facilities are or could be such a business asset. (Frankly, our personal experiences and observations have not been so encouraging, hence Chapter 31.) Facility managers who are likely to succeed are those who are meeting their company's business expectations; those who don't will continue to fight the cycle of constantly diminishing resources until they are doomed to failure and outsourced. One way to success in facility financial management is through proper budget management. In the remainder of this chapter, we will concentrate on the annual budget.

Budgets are the *lingua franca* of an organization, particularly in the public sector. In any organization they show who's in and who's out, and they directly reflect the organization's priorities. Budgets need to be structured, should reflect the information needs of management, and should parallel the planning format so that work can be tracked from one year to the next. Finally, budgets should flow from the planning process of the company.

Programs, Planning, and Budgeting

In the current management environment, form does not have a high priority. However, we cannot emphasize too strongly how important it is to organize a budget by program so that the programs can be tracked, from plan to budget and over time within the budget. Second, the budget should be formatted so that the key indicators used for financial management, particularly benchmarks, can be easily calculated. Finally, the budget format should facilitate financial accountability so that department managers are held accountable for funds assigned to them. Unfortunately, the statements of accounts in most companies meet none of those criteria, and not enough facility managers fight to get their budget formatted in such a way that it is truly the chief financial information management tool.

Proposed or ongoing programs are the building blocks of the department's budget. A program—leasing or maintenance and repair, for instance—is what facility managers plan and budget for. Thus planning new programs is crucial to effective budgeting. A facility manager who is not actively engaged in planning is doomed to a reactive mode (back to the boiler room!). There is no major company initiative that does not require major facility planning, and the facility manager must be positioned to ensure that that happens. Failure to use programmatic planning and budgeting remains the single greatest deficiency in FM financial management.

The budget is important in all facility departments; in the public sector it is absolutely essential. In a government agency, the budget is the essence of the organization. It is the benchmark against which the facility manager will be judged, since there is no profit or loss statement for an agency. The importance of formulating, executing, and evaluating the budget, particularly to the public-sector facility manager, cannot be overstated.

For the budgeting process to work, it is essential that: all costs are planned and budgeted as part of some program, and programs are stabilized year to year so that the budget can be a management information system and costs can be compared.

Some facility managers don't know how to budget and account properly for the funds entrusted to them. Although the facility manager is not an accountant, it is difficult to see how he can be a good manager without understanding the details of money flow: how goods and services are procured, how vendor accounts are set up in the controller's department, and how invoices flow from submittal through issuance of payment.

A facility manager should be capable of setting up a management information system to monitor the department's budget for the fiscal year. He should be able to determine whether funds can be shifted between accounts and to what extent individual accounts and the total budget can be exceeded or underspent without drawing corporate sanction. Likewise, the facility manager should be able to determine who can or should commit funds and at what level. He should set up approval procedures so as to monitor spending. Without this knowledge, he cannot hope to control the administrative processes both internal and external to the department. In this chapter we discuss these various elements of budget management, beginning with the types of budgets a facility manager will deal with.

Jeff Crane, one of our favorite FM commentators and a practitioner, provides an excellent listing of tools that he has found helpful in preparing and reviewing his annual budget in his monthly column in the November 2007 *Today's Facility Manager*.[3] Crane, for instance, emphasized the problems that can occur merely because the facility manager does not understand whether his organization uses accrual or cash-based accounting and the importance of finding budget deviations quickly and acting on them.

Types of Budgets

There are three basic types of budgets: administrative, operational, and capital.

Administrative Budget

In many organizations, the facility department budget is part of the company's administrative budget. As we use the term, however, the administrative budget refers to those items of overhead that the facility department shares with other departments in the company. Exhibit 30-1 is an example of an administrative budget.

Often the administrative budget controls not only the funds for human resources but also the number of positions. That makes hiring a greater number of less expensive (and therefore less qualified) employees difficult. Also, normally the entire administrative budget is not *fungible*—that is, the manager may not transfer funds from this budget to another, or vice versa. Often within this budget, personnel costs are *fenced,* meaning they are not fungible even within the budget.

We also have included the amortization of capital projects in the administrative budget. If that figure reaches 8 percent of the annual budget in any one year while the total budget remains relatively fixed, the facility manager must control future capital expenditures better because payback is having a deleterious effect on the annual budget.

Exhibit 30-1. Administrative budget.

I. Personnel
   A. Salaries
      1. Fulltime
      2. Temporary
      3. Overtime
   B. Staff supplements
      1. Consultants
      2. Contract
   C. Benefits
      1. Regular leave
      2. Sick leave
      3. Group life insurance
      4. Health insurance
      5. Retirement
   D. Training, memberships, and conferences (travel and fees)
      1. Internal
      2. External

II. Office Expenses
   A. Supplies
   B. Rental
   C. Utilities and fuel
   D. Clothing and uniforms
   E. Office automation
   F. Voice and data access
   G. Automotive
      1. Fuel and oil
      2. Maintenance and repair
      3. Rental
   H. Reproduction
   I. Advertising

III. Depreciation of Capital Accounts

Operational Budget

The operational budget covers funds that the company gives to the facility manager to perform his mission. Exhibit 30-2 represents an operational budget.

Exhibit 30-2. Operational budget.

  I. Utilities
    A. Electric
    B. Water
    C. Heating
       1. Gas
       2. Fuel Oil
    D. Energy savings

  II. Rentals
    A. Land
    B. Operational facilities
    C. Other
    D. Lease income

  III. Planning and Design
    A. CADD development and maintenance
    B. Consultant fees
       1. Planning
       2. Design
       3. Furniture
       4. Audiovisual
       5. Kitchen
       6. Art
       7. Signage
       8. Life safety
       9. Energy management
       10. Other
    C. Photography and renderings
    D. Reproduction and printing
    E. To plan and design capital programs
    F. To support capital projects

  IV. Maintenance and repair
    A. Preventive maintenance
       1. Grounds
       2. Exteriors and roofs
       3. Interiors
       4. Electrical

(continued)

Exhibit 30-2. (continued)

        5. Plant and HVAC systems
        6. Security and life-safety systems
        7. Furniture
        8. Kitchen equipment
        9. Other
    B. Custodial
        1. Janitorial
        2. Trash removal
        3. Window cleaning
        4. Carpet cleaning
        5. Insect/rodent control
        6. Blinds and drapes
    C. Maintenance and repair
        1. Grounds
        2. Exteriors and roofs
        3. Interiors
        4. Plant and HVAC system
        5. Telecommunications
        6. Office technology
        7. Elevators
        8. Security and life-safety systems
        9. Furniture
       10. Electrical systems
       11. Kitchen equipment
       12. Signage
       13. Other

  V. New Work
    A. Alterations
    B. Construction
    C. Noncapital equipment
        1. Direct operational support
        2. Other
    D. Grounds improvement

 VI. Moving
    A. Direct support
    B. Other

Note: All budget categories in programs III through VI could have both material and labor sub-categories.

The level of detail in the budget is a matter of choice, negotiated with the boss and the chief budget officer. Since we favor bubble-up budgeting (aggregating budget figuring from the responsible work units that will execute the work plan), we also favor detailed budgets, since each item must be estimated anyway. The only question is how many subelements must be rolled up and how many can be displayed. In most cases, each line in the operational budget can also be divided into labor and materials, if desired. An item like preventive maintenance of interiors is likely to be a single line and a single cost, extrapolated from historical data. Conversely, alterations will have a separate listing of all recommended projects.

Many facility managers cringe at the detail shown in these example budgets; however, some facility managers consistently fail to provide comparative data. The degree of detail is determined by management information needs. If you are frequently asked how much it costs on a square-footage basis to remove trash (or the annual reproduction and printing costs for building drawings), then show that item clearly.

From this point forward, when we say "annual budget," we mean one containing both the administrative and operational aspects.

Capital Budget

The capital budget is a multiyear presentation. It provides information on the major buildings, furniture, furnishings, and equipment that the company needs to perform its mission. What may be capitalized is determined by both tax law and company policy. Often that policy sets a floor (for example, $50,000) under which certain purchases (furniture, for instance) cannot be capitalized for any one purchase. Each line in the capital budget is a separately justified project. The justification and costing sheets become a part of the capital budget.

Many organizations repay themselves by charging against the annual facilities budget the amortization cost of the outstanding capital account. When that depreciation approaches 8 percent of the annual budget, it starts seriously to affect annual operations, and future capital expenditures should be rigorously controlled.

Major capital projects have annual budget implications. For example, the construction of a new building could reduce lease costs and perhaps reduce alteration costs temporarily. However, there will be corresponding increases in administrative costs, utilities, and maintenance. During a major capital project, the annual budget normally increases, at least to the extent of funding the project team, unless its expenses are capitalized.

The facility manager should use the capital budget to solve the major long-term construction and replacement requirements uncovered in the strategic planning. In capital budgeting, it is very important to play by the rules for two reasons:

1. Most companies make the facility department pay back or depreciate its capital investments. Depreciation should be kept in the 6 to 8 percent range of the annual budget. When it exceeds that limit, it becomes a burden.
2. The facility manager loses credibility with the controller if he breaks the rules.

For more on the capital budget, particularly tools to prioritize or make decisions between projects, see Chapter 5.

Chargebacks

A device for controlling facility costs that has gained currency is the chargeback, a means by which the company's divisions are charged for facility services according to their use. The theory is that business managers will be more cost conscious if they have to pay for facility services.

Chargebacks have become predominant in facility management as both business and government have moved to business unit accountability. Chargebacks depend on the facility manager, as a monopoly provider, setting his own rates. The advantages of chargebacks are that they promote cost consciousness, facility costs become more apparent to line managers, and costs can be more readily tied to a product.

Opposition to allocated facility costs comes in primarily two forms. First, allocation rules tend to be arbitrary, difficult to calculate and justify, and therefore there is a significant administrative burden and an opportunity for conflict with line management. Second, some items are best funded by the company, and upper management must realize that the facility manager needs some discretionary budget not available under pure chargeback.

To administer chargebacks accurately, the facility manager must first accurately account for his cost. Most facility budget formats make accurate cost accounting difficult, a problem compounded by other factors. Consider the difficulty of fixing rates between two sets of space. The first is a loft converted to office space that has inadequate HVAC in the hottest and coldest months. The second space is a leased manufacturing facility where electrical distribution is a constant problem and part of the manufacturing floor has been converted to administrative space. Should each manager be charged the same amount for space? How should the qualitative differences be handled?

Chargebacks are most successful where the service or product cost can be directly and easily measured. Also, it is relatively easy to charge back for services or products that are above a norm or standard. Finally, chargebacks are effective when costs must be allocated to a company product. For that reason, our observation is that manufacturing companies often have the best handle on their facility costs.

As the process of allocating facility costs has become more widespread (it is now the norm, not the exception), facility managers have lost faith in this technique or largely ignore it. They view allocating facility costs as an administrative burden or a source of constant friction with line managers. In an informal survey, about a quarter of the facility managers say they have had to devote a person to administering chargebacks because of the complexity of setting rules and the constant complaints from line managers about allocations. Facility managers seem about evenly split on whether chargebacks really do cause line managers to alter their behavior.

Few advocates of allocating facility costs implement total chargeback, recognizing that some facility costs are best managed centrally and that facility managers need discretionary funds to meet the reactive part of their mission.

Managing an effective chargeback system emphasizes the need for facility managers to be able to calculate the true cost of each product and service, including overheads. The most effective chargebacks charge a "rent" for space based on gross square foot occupied and for which the line unit gets a bundle of services spelled out in an internal "lease." Services over and above the standard are also charged back. Automation allows us to calculate allocations properly and to administer a flexible chargeback system. If your company determines that chargebacks should be used, it is worth the effort to put a business-like system in place and to make it truly effective as a management technique. For a best practice in this area, see Alan D. Wilson's "Distribution and Measurement of Laboratory and Office Space Costs in *1995 Winter Best Practices Forum on Facility Management* (Houston: International Facility Management Association, 1995), pp. 193–211. While from its publication data, this material might seem dated, this article remains the outstanding example of the thinking and effort that should go into developing a proper chargeback system.

Budget Formulation

One of the problems that facility managers have traditionally had with finance departments is that the facility budget has some unique characteristics. That often complicates budget preparation, makes it difficult to explain and defend, and ensures it will be viewed as a source of cuts when funds are needed elsewhere in the company.

First, the FM department budget is large—normally the second largest expense budget in the company. That means it will draw attention.

Second, it is diverse, covering accounts such as space planning, reprographics, rent, security, utilities, mail distribution, and waste management. Each of those categories requires a different method of budget projection and justification, which complicates budget preparation.

A large part of the facility budget is driven by government regulation. Often these regulations have been written in such a way that the cost for compliance is difficult to determine (the Americans with Disabilities Act, for example). Trying to project regulatory compliance costs is often like trying to hit a moving target while blindfolded.

Facility managers need funds to react because theirs is a business where reaction is a fact of life. The facility budget must allow the facility manager to react to disasters. Even a new boiler can break down, and, when it does, there must be funds to fix it. We make our best guesses about the need for heating in the winter and cooling in the summer, but if our estimates were too low, the utility companies are still going to send a bill that has to be paid.

Utilities represent the best example of yet another characteristic of facility budgets. A large portion of a facility budget is not discretionary. If we have an active lease, we are going to pay the rent whether we have people or activities in the leased space or not.

That leads us to the final unique feature of facility budgets: they have both long and short-term aspects to them. For example, it is easy to slight the maintenance accounts in the near term, but you then compound the major repair and capital improvement accounts in subsequent years.

In the ideal system, the annual budget derives about 70 percent from the midrange work plan if the company has a sophisticated planning system. If it does not, formulating the budget is an exercise in gathering requirements, extrapolating historical data, and guesstimating. (See Section II on planning.) Either way, the question often is what the proper base should be for projections. Exhibit 30-3 is a suggested matrix for extrapolating budget data into the future. All data are ordinarily displayed in constant-year dollars. Normally the budget year is the base year, although some companies prefer to use the previous year so that comparisons can be drawn.

In large organizations, the facility department budget is often assigned to a budget analyst because it is so large. In smaller organizations, an analyst from the budget department or the controller may have the responsibility, along with responsibility for several other budgets. In very small organizations, the facility manager's supervisor may be the only analyst. The job of the budget analyst is (1) to ensure the budget is in compliance with budget guidelines, (2) to see that the budget interfaces with other department budgets and that there is no duplication, and (3) to be a liaison between senior management and the department.

There are several ways to approach the budget analyst. The best is to be cooperative, using the analyst as a sounding board for each new budget and obtaining

Exhibit 30-3. Projecting budget data.

Category	How Projected	Source
Capital	Gather discrete projects annually	Call for projects; estimate concepts
Utilities	Estimate discrete new requirements	In-house records
	Project annual growth from 3- to 5-year curve	Utility companies
Operations	Arithmetic projection	Unit cost indicators
Nondiscretionary maintenance and repair	Arithmetic projection (projects can be gathered discretely)	Unit cost indicators (estimate projects from concept design)
Custodial	Arithmetic projection	Unit cost indicators
Nonproject moving	Arithmetic projection	Unit cost indicators
Discretionary projects	Gather discrete projects annually	Call for projects; estimate concept
Lease costs and income	Review leases	Leases
Personnel costs	Arithmetic projections	Use actual salaries and benefits or standard salaries and benefits
Training and travel costs	Gather requirements	Actual costs for training and standard costs for travel
Office equipment and vehicles	Gather requirements for purchases; arithmetic calculation of operational costs	Call for requirements; cost data on vehicles/equipment
Nonprojects design and engineering	Guesstimate	Historical data

information on new initiatives. The two of you will never agree on all issues, but you can ensure that there are no surprises in the relationship.

Traditional Problem Areas in Annual Budgeting

Our observation of many annual facility budgets in both the public and private sectors indicates that the greatest problem is the lack of a useful budget format. Most facility department budget formats are poorly done and need to be put into a program format. That point cannot be overemphasized. Programmatic budgeting and a consistent budget format are key to budget estimating, formulation, tracking, analysis, evaluation, accountability, and benchmarking.

Hand in hand with the necessity for an appropriate format is the need to have valid budget data. Because budget formats are poor, costs are not transparent and cannot be tracked over time, so at budget time, good, valid data are available for future projection.

Another issue that has been magnified in the past several years is the under-funding of facilities and the reduction of facility staff. Some of this is caused by facility managers' failure to justify budgets and human resources needs in business terms, failure to communicate well with upper management, and failure to docu-ment well the actual costs of doing business. Having said that, the fact remains that facility departments are traditionally underfunded and understaffed. How many companies, for example, reinvest 2 to 4 percent of the replacement value of their building stock in annual maintenance and repair? Securing adequate resources remains perhaps the greatest challenge to the facility manager. The answer to this problem lies more in the business and communications skills of the facility manager than in just better data, but better data are essential also. Facility managers need to look to outsourcing creatively to solve their staffing problems.

Closely aligned with the fact of underfunding is that companies have traditional-ly taken a short-term view of their facilities. There is intense pressure on private-sec-tor managers to increase shareholder value, and that translates to cost cutting and a short-term perspective on their facilities. In some cases, that may even be the correct economic decision if the facilities are leased or likely to be sold or abandoned. However, in owned government facilities, the old adage, "You can pay me now or pay me later," is true. Maintenance deferred means costly breakdowns, possible loss of productivity, and higher repair bills down the road.

Note: It is the opinion of your authors that, if you can solve the problems spelled out in the last two paragraphs, a high percentage of your problems will be solved. Underfunding and the lack of management understanding of the importance of facil-ities are problems of such importance that strategies to address both should be high on the priority list of every facility manager. One of your authors suggests that these issues need "to be hammered" home to facility professionals and upper management alike. Consider yourself hammered! Now go get your upper management!

Others With an Interest

The budget is not formulated in a vacuum. Others in the organization have a legiti-mate interest in the budget. The controller obviously has an interest in faulty accounts; his automation system may limit the number of accounts displayed, for example. Also, he needs to maintain some semblance of order and format among all budget units to make the whole budget understandable. This insistence on uniformity can be a problem when the work of the company is vastly different from the work of the facility manager.

As you develop the budget, keep others informed; bring them along as budget decisions are made and priorities shift. For example, the human resources department chief or budget analyst will exhibit interest in the human resources section of the budget. Line managers with major annual or capital projects have an interest in seeing at least that portion of the budget approved. Since they probably assisted in justifying the project, they should be informed if the project is reprioritized, reduced in scope, or downgraded.

Last but not least, your manager will want to review the budget even if he does not have to approve it. Keep the boss informed of the general level of requests by program, obtaining guidance on all new initiatives and any major problems before actually formulating the budget. As the budget takes shape, inform your boss of major changes or problems. He can help with the problems, and needs to know the changes so that he does not get blindsided in the board room. "No surprises" is the best policy.

Budgeting Details and Characteristics

There are two kinds of budget increases. The first recognizes program growth; the second acknowledges inflation, rate increases (utilities, for example), or increases beyond the influence of the facility manager (personnel raises, for instance). Normally it is the responsibility of the facility manager to quantify and justify all growth in a program. Increases in rates or inflation ordinarily are granted automatically by the budget department or controller, to the extent that they can be quantified. Often this latter type of increase is awarded after all budget deliberations are completed, so that the proposed budget can be compared to the previous year's in constant-year uninflated dollars.

Many programs lend themselves to accurate budgeting—utilities, for example. On the other hand, discretionary annual projects should be planned at a level to 15 percent over budget guidance. Some projects drop out during the year, so there should be well-developed projects ready to substitute rather than go for something momentarily convenient or easy.

Often, in the final stages of budget formulation, the facility manager will receive instructions to submit requirements listed by priority or to group existing requirements in a band in case a last-minute decrement occurs or a cut is necessary.

Grouping is done only for discretionary programs. Common bands are 3, 5, or 10 percent of the program, starting from the bottom of the priority list. Building and decrementing a budget by bands is far superior to a random or across-the-board method, but it works better for project-related work than for something like utilities.

A good budget has the following characteristics:

1. It contains categories the manager and others feel need to be managed.
2. It is work-plan driven and reflects programs being managed.
3. It is structured the way the facility manager operates and ties together resource management and responsibility.
4. It provides management information on total costs, comparative costs, and easy-to-compute unit costs.
5. It identifies subunit manager responsibilities.

Communications and Security

A facility manager should expect the same level of savings from proper planning, design, and operation of the communications, security, and safety systems that he achieves from facilities. Exhibit 30-4 assumes that the planning and design savings and avoidance have already been credited. Good management and new technology can actually save both capital and annual costs. Cost avoidances occur because proper security, safety, and communication systems avoid insurance costs. They also avoid human resources costs by increasing productivity.

Areas for Cost Savings

An emerging theme among facility managers is that the facility department should be viewed as a profit center. We share their enthusiasm for good facility management, but we are concerned about overselling ourselves and the profession. It is our experience that profitability comes from extensive leasing and/or real estate development, which are more closely aligned with property management than with facility management as we define it.

There are, however, many areas for cost savings, particularly of life-cycle costs. Often facility departments have the reputation of devouring too large a share of the administrative budget without tangible results for the company. The facility manager should publicize the economic contributions of this department.

In this chapter we review, by major department functions, where cost savings opportunities exist. We have not included generalities like "manage better here" and instead confine ourselves to traditional management functions. A summary matrix of

Exhibit 30-4. Opportunities for cost savings and avoidances.

	Cost Savings (%)[1]			
Function	Capital	Annual	Avoidances[2]	Areas Affected
Facility planning and forecasting strategic and mid-term planning	5–15	10–20	15–25	Construction costs, O&M cost, leasing costs, financing costs
Lease administration	–	5–10	5–10	Utility costs, build-out costs, shared costs, property management costs
Space planning, allocation, and management	–	3–5	–	Rents and space-related costs
Architectural-engineering planning and design	8–12	10–30	20–30	Maintenance costs, energy costs, operating costs, construction costs, sustainable benefits to occupants
Workplace planning, design, and specification	–	–	3–7	Employee efficiency
Budgeting, accounting, and economic justification	1–2	2–3	–	Accuracy of accounts, better budget utilization
Real estate acquisition and disposal	2–5	2–5	5–7	Operational costs, acquisition costs, disposal price
Construction project management	7–10	7–10	10–15	Construction and alteration costs
Alterations, renovations, and workplace installation	–	2–3	7–10	Project costs, staff disruption costs
Operations, maintenance, and repair	–	7–10	15–20	Energy costs, maintenance costs, capital costs, insurance costs, and major repairs
Communications and security	2–3	2–3	7–10	Avoid insurance costs and increase productivity, save communications costs

1. Percentage of funds in current-year program.
2. Average mutual percentage over lifetime—capital and annual.

cost savings and cost avoidances is shown in Exhibit 30-4. The magnitude of these savings is purely experiential; we have done no research in this area.

Facility Planning and Forecasting

Good planning can conservatively save 5 to 10 percent of the typical costs on a capital project by permitting the design-construct cycle to proceed on a schedule that precludes costly crashing. This does not rule out fast-tracking, which in some industries is the most economical way to manage a capital project. But good long-term planning has payoffs in all facilities programs, even annual ones. For example, accurately predicting when a facility will open or close can avoid penalties to service contractors.

A good annual work plan can favorably affect the quality, quantity, and cost of work accomplished with an annual budget. Most obvious, however, the plan better uses existing funds and achieves higher-quality work because the work will have been designed, planned, and executed at a normal pace.

It is difficult to isolate the savings achieved with good capital planning apart from long- and midrange planning. For sure, rational capital planning that borrows and pays back on most favorable terms will offer welcomed savings.

Lease Administration

For a landlord, good lease administration can be critical to the margin of profitability. Proper metering of facilities, a good tenant workletter, a well-developed lease, and proper allocation of shared costs alone can save 5 to 10 percent of costs without diminishing the facility manager's reputation as a quality lessor. As the lessee, proper lease negotiation, particularly in a soft market, can help avoid at least 5 to 10 percent of the costs of a medium-term lease.

Lease management is no game for amateurs. Some organizations may have an assigned real estate expert. If not, you can have a leasing expert on retainer if you have enough leases to justify one. The bible in this area is *Facility Management, Second Edition,* by Rondeau, Brown and Lapides.

Space Planning, Allocation, and Management

One of your authors regularly moved thousands of employees within his former organization. For many reasons, there is great potential to reduce "churn" and there are great savings to be garnered by doing so. Among IFMA members, the mean number of annual moves in 2006 was 507, at a mean cost of construction of almost $3,606 per move[4] Interestingly, through good facility management policies and procedures, the number of moves have continued to decline (down 27 percent in ten years) but, during the same period we have only been able to reduce the costs per move by 14 percent. With the escalating costs of construction materials, this disparity is likely to continue so savings in this area are most likely to occur by limiting the number of moves to the absolute minimum. Fortunately, technology assists us in this goal. There is a potential savings of billions of dollars by reducing this churn by one-third. Why, in this era of advanced tele- and datacommunications, the intranet, and e-mail, must every worker in an organization be located contiguously? We do that at a tremendous cost, yet are in one of the most cost-conscious eras in history.

Microlevel forecasting, planning, and design are major items of interest in every organization; however, sometimes management emphasis is not in the right place. For example, one organization estimated that it was losing 6 percent of its net usable space each year to the increased storage of paper, two-thirds of which was duplicative. Analyses of space utilization trends by category and user assisted the facility manager in maximizing use of space. Since most facility costs are directly related to space, every square foot saved or better utilized produces savings. If space is not managed well at the microlevel, eventually there are capital or lease costs to produce more space.

Architectural-Engineering Planning and Design

Value engineering, life-cycle costing of new building technologies and equipment, designing for energy efficiency, sustainability, and designing to maintain are interrelated, highly effective ways to reduce and avoid costs. On large projects, value engineering alone can probably save 5 percent of capital costs and avoid 10 percent of operating expenses. In many organizations, life-cycle improvements must save approximately 10 percent to be adopted. The basis for any solid energy management program is good design. Good design for energy management should be expected to reduce annual energy costs by at least 10 percent and to avoid at least that much in the future.

The price increases in fuel oil, natural gas, and electricity in 2008 absolutely dictate increased efforts in energy management. This trend is in synch with the current emphasis on sustainability. Organizations, realizing that higher utility costs are probably here to stay, are developing projects for replacing inefficient or older systems, sometimes with incentives from the government or utility providers. This is one excellent area for the facility manager to prove to upper management that good facility management can be a major benefit to the overall financial health of the organization.

Some facility organizations have so convinced their management of the long-term financial benefits of sustainability efforts that projects are being launched simply for that purpose. Many organizations have adopted sustainability principles into all future design which should reduce, or at least limit, the growth of operating costs.

Workplace Planning, Design, and Specification

The percentage of employee productivity that can be assigned to facilities is very ambiguous, because employee productivity measures have many influences and typically are self-reported. Since, in almost all organizations, staff costs are the largest costs, there is a major interest in optimizing staff efficiency. As we scan the applicable references, this subject appears to be of particular interest in Great Britain where the Office Productivity Network (OPN) was formed. Having said this, more success in defining what staff productivity should be is the norm, not actually measuring it. Interestingly, many firms actually advertise that, through better design, they can improve productivity. This seems intuitive yet one of the authors always laughs when he relates that, in one of the most productive workplaces he ever worked in, a colleague had to move every time he wanted to enter or exit his desk because space was so cramped. Production there was high because of the commitment of the workers and the importance of the work.

In the OPN survey of office productivity, facility items noted are:

- Infrastructure and support
- Environmental conditions
- Design and layout
- Facilities and amenities
- Location and access

Using OPN's survey, the most highly productive organizations (offices) tended to score approximately 90 out of 100 with the lowest scorers 20 points lower.[5] This indicates that there is room for facility improvement in increasing productivity. Of course this is hard to quantify, but the payoff is advantageous because the base (staff costs) is so great.

Other examples from the U.S. Green Building Council support increased test scores in daylit schools, higher retail sales in stores with more daylight, and shorter recovery periods for patients in sustainable healthcare facilities. These somewhat anecdotal increases support increases in productivity for knowledge workers in comfortable environments as well.[6]

Budgeting, Accounting, and Economic Justification

In many ways, this category is the key to cost savings and avoidances. Unless funds can be accounted for properly, savings or cost avoidances cannot be documented. Unless you can utilize the economic justification tools, you do not truly know what the savings or avoidances mean.

When project accounting, budget accounting, and financial accounting are conducted under separate systems, as they often are, facility managers sometimes misspend their budget. Often they actually have more funds available than their budget accounts say. This excess is either lost or misspent on projects requiring little design or management in the final days of a fiscal year. Our experience is that loss can amount to 1 to 3 percent of the annual or capital budget. Programmatic budgeting tracked on one system can reduce that loss to zero.

Real Estate Acquisition and Disposal

It is difficult to separate the benefits of long-range planning of space, real estate planning, and real estate operations. In fact, they work together and are highly interdependent; but because we truly believe in the benefits of planning, we have weighted the savings from planning more heavily in our matrix.

Proper site selection can produce significant cost avoidances. One convincing example is moving all possible industrial activities and storage of an organization out of costly urban space and serving the downtown facility remotely. Transportation-related facilities are particularly sensitive to proper site selection.

The marketing and timing of property for disposal can produce significant savings. A discreet broker who knows the local market well can be a substantial help in disposing of excess real estate.

Construction Project Management

The savings shown in construction project management for savings and cost avoidance are those that can be achieved by a superior project manager over one who is merely good and those who recognize the planning and design savings discussed previously. A major factor in selecting a project management firm and/or builder is their track record on cost savings and how such savings will be shared.

Construction management has become extremely sophisticated, and there are many competent construction managers. Can, however, the construction manager harness the decision-making apparatus of the company so that timely decisions are made? When that occurs, the initial costs and the cost of changes for both major and minor construction can be reduced 7 to 10 percent. Constructing to maintain good turnover procedures and the preparation of good as-built documentation should conservatively avoid 10 to 15 percent in future alteration, renovation, and operational expenses.

Making appropriate use of commissioning reports on newly constructed facilities is another potential for cost savings. The efficient integration of all building systems, working as designed, can produce enormous savings over the life cycle and ensure systems maximization.

Alterations, Renovation, and Workplace Installation

Perhaps the numbers shown for this category give a false impression because they assume that the savings/avoidance from good planning, designing, and specifying have already been taken. So, in percentage terms, these numbers may seem small. However, these percentages are applied to a base that is often 30 to 40 percent of the facilities budget, so the actual savings are great.

Also, in this area, good on-site management will minimize the disruption to company employees before, during, and after the project starts. For organizations that churn at 30 percent, this cost avoidance is significant. Also, proper installation for the more sophisticated communication, fire, and life-safety systems probably generates 2 to 3 percent cost avoidance.

Operations, Maintenance, and Repair

This is the category where costs are principally avoided by good prior planning, design, project management, and operation. Good management in this area reaps real savings and avoids substantial costs because this category can account for 40 to 50 percent of the facilities annual budget.

The principal savings in the annual budget are through energy management and good inventory control. However, the major impacts here are in cost avoidance. Good maintenance will ensure the availability of key facility systems and reduce the lost time caused by system failure. Good cyclical and preventive maintenance programs can substantially reduce the need for major repair. Correction of hazards and a well-maintained facility reduce both insurance premiums and the funds paid out for liability and personal injury. A good O&M response is the basis for a disaster recovery program, the ultimate in avoiding costs.

All of us need to reenergize our energy management efforts, which we have let slide from the last North American energy crunch in the early 1970s. Another energy crunch is upon us just as the sensibility of sustainability is becoming apparent.

More efficient equipment alone can reduce energy consumption by 10 to 30 percent and therefore has an acceptable internal rate of return (IRR) for capital replacement. Software available from the Environmental Protection Agency's Energy Star Building Real Estate Management Program allows users to analyze the cost of building upgrades to include tenant recovery options, future occupancy impacts of the upgrade, financing alternatives and produced savings, net present value, IRR, payback, net operating increases, and asset value changes.[7]

Finally, in the area of O&M, many facility managers have outsourced extensively. One top area for additional cost savings is to explore shared savings with the contractors. Rewarding the contractor for being cost conscious can create a win-win situation while ensuring that the savings are documented and good for the long-term viability of the department and facilities.

Budget Completion

When the budget is assembled, the facility manager should conduct several analyses, including historical comparisons, unit-cost comparisons, detailed comparisons to the current year's budget, and trend analyses. Variances then become a principal part of the narrative, along with discussion of new issues. If the funding guidance is lower than the stated requirements, describe the impact that funding constraints, by category, will have on the department. It is important to view the annual budget as a tool to help manage and monitor the department's work while also meeting the reporting requirements of the accounting department and the boss.

Budget Execution

In many organizations, so much effort goes into formulating and defending the budget that executing it is almost an afterthought. In actuality, executing the budget largely determines how successful the budget is. Because organizations are dynamic, budgets must be also. Some projects suddenly drop by the wayside and completely new projects come along necessitating new, unplanned actions. Executing the budget means accommodating these changes.

Expenditure Levels

A variety of fiscal years are possible:

- Coincident with the calendar year
- July through June
- October through September

Ordinarily, annual budgets do not allow funds to be carried over from one fiscal year to the next. This means that the fourth quarter is a hectic one. Everyone is scrambling to execute the remaining portion of the annual work plan, and at the same time end-of-year funds become available from other programs. Particularly in the public sector, there is a reluctance to commit funds in an orderly flow. After an almost inevitable peak of expenditure at the start of each fiscal year, everyone wants to save for a rainy day. There is, however, a risk in doing that. If the mid-year review shows that the commitment rate is not at or near target, the department could have its funds withdrawn and given to some other department.

Exhibit 30-5 depicts the traditional and desirable expenditure profiles for an annual budget. Traditionally, at the start of a fiscal year there is pent-up demand for services. Concerned that he will not have funds for an emergency, the facility manager puts on the fiscal brakes until past midyear review, when he begins an end-of-the-year spending binge. Thus, the peaks and valleys make workload management in the facility and purchasing departments difficult. Also, because so much of the work plan is executed in the final quarter, the projects that are done tend to be those that can be pushed out the door easily, rather than those of greatest benefit to the company.

The more desirable expenditure profile also shows an early hump caused by the inevitable buildup of demand from the last fiscal year. But that hump is flatter, and the spending soon levels out until midyear. After the midyear review, expenditure activity increases slightly but not dramatically. The small hump at year's end reflects a minor increase in year-end funding for well-developed projects. This profile greatly reduces the demands on design, project management, and procurement resources,

Exhibit 30.5. Typical annual expense profile.

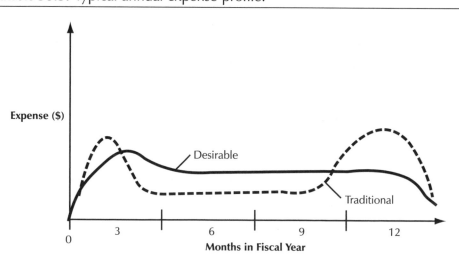

and at the end of a budget year, the facility manager should be able to close out his budget within ±0.5 percent.

With a normal work backlog, it is best to exceed the budget by 0.3 to 0.5 percent. There are no medals given for being closer than that, and your department can use that bonus to reduce its backlog.

Control of Spending

Much managerial effort goes into establishing and maintaining control of the budget. In many organizations, funds are allocated on a periodic basis for one purpose. For example, from a facilities annual alteration budget of $1 million, a company might allocate $300,000 for first-quarter projects. That ensures that the entire alterations budget will not be spent in the first quarter; allocated funds cannot be committed or expensed without an additional transaction.

Funds are committed through legal documents like contracts. Once the funds are committed, to decrease the obligation the facility manager has to resort to negotiation, arbitration, or the legal system. For instance, when five chairs are ordered at $1,535, those funds are committed and are not available for another use. Once the funds are spent, an expense is incurred—for example, paying $1,507 plus $26 shipping for the five chairs once received. When the check for $1,533 is sent out, the department incurs that expense. The $2 that was overcommitted, for whatever reason, is lost. It is very important to understand whether your budget report reflects funds allocated, funds committed, or actual expenses, since each category leads to much different conclusions. We strongly recommend tracking expenses.

Periodic reviews are a major control mechanism, so hold budget execution reviews with subordinate managers. For capital projects, conduct formal reviews monthly. For the annual budget, conduct informal reviews at midyear and three-quarters of the way through the year. If funds can be reprogrammed and effectively used, also conduct reviews monthly in the last quarter, weekly in the last month, and daily in the last week.

As another control method, use a double-signature authorization system for requirements and payment. It is helpful to require a technical manager to sell you the need for a new requirement before you approve it. Similarly, it is responsible to have two managers validate all expenses before they are sent for payment.

Because of human nature, people are uncomfortable with change. However, most of us realize that we work in a management function that is highly reactive. Change is almost inevitable, and we need to develop skills and procedures that permit us to manage change effectively. This is particularly true in executing the budget.

Budget changes have many sources: management decisions, shifts in priorities, new initiatives or opportunities, unforeseen cost increases, or an inability to execute planned work. Regardless of the source of a change, a facility manager needs to have procedures that minimize its impact. Failure to do so can have a serious impact on funding personnel and work effort, particularly design.

Budget reports during the year should provide essential information quickly and easily. With no more than one simple division, the facility manager should be able to answer such questions as:

- What are our unit custodial costs at 1325 Neptune Street vs. 1603 Mars Avenue?
- What percentage of our new work (alterations, minor construction) budget has been expensed as of July 31?
- What are our lease costs at the end of the fiscal year? Compared to last month? Last year?
- What percentage of our total facilities budget is spent on maintenance and repair?
- How does our unit cost for maintenance and repair compare to the General Services Administration standard for this city? To the Building Owners and Managers Association Experience Report for our category? To the International Facility Management Association benchmark?

Since the budget should reflect priorities, if preventive maintenance is a priority, do the expenditures reflect that? Also, how does the department's actual expenditure profile fit the intended profile? Budget reports should be structured in a way to provide such information almost instantaneously.

A facility manager will never truly control his budget unless he understands how transactions flow through the organization. Exhibit 30-6 is a depiction of such flow. The stations may vary, but the principle remains the same; for example, some companies may have a receiving section that verifies receipt of goods and validates the invoice for payment. Note that this system is reasonably complex, involves a substantial paper flow, and is operated by low-paid personnel. Therefore, if the budget is to be properly debited, it is necessary to monitor the transaction flow reasonably closely. Knowledge of this system also makes it possible to pinpoint anomalies that appear in budget reports.

Budget Closeout and Evaluation

The end of the annual budget year can be hectic. Often there are funds available, but they are lost if they cannot be committed by the end of the fiscal year and expensed by the end of the accrual period. In many companies, managers are required to make

Exhibit 30-6. Transaction flow through the organization.

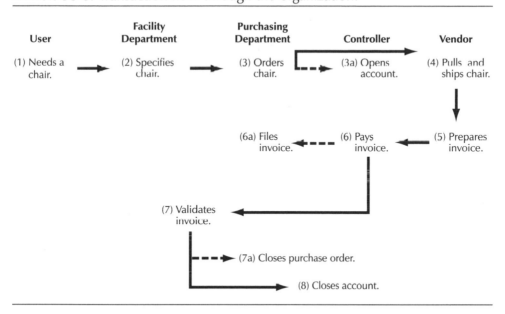

their best guess of the funds they will commit in that final sixty days before the end of the fiscal year. Those funds are then accrued (saved), but they must be expensed before another arbitrary date, often sixty to ninety days after the end of the fiscal year, when that year's budget is put to bed. Accruals not expensed then must be charged against the following year's budget, a double hit to be avoided at all costs.

Budget closeout can be both much smoother and much more effective if there is a backlog of projects on the shelf for year-end funding or for execution immediately in the new fiscal year. Work out the expedited procedures in advance with the purchasing department.

Since the final quarter of a fiscal year and the start of a new fiscal year are periods of such intense activity, there is little time for a rational evaluation of annual budget performance. That is counterproductive, since budget management needs as much scrutiny as the management of technical functions.

The budget postmortem need not be formal, but it should involve the departmental accountant and all department managers. In this review, focus on four issues:

1. Did we do what we said we were going to do?
2. Did we do it effectively, given the resources we were given?
3. What lessons were learned, and how can we apply them to the current budget?
4. Are our budgets in balance and supportive?

These reviews should look at the budget format and process as well as the execution. It is a good time to ask such questions as:

- Do we have more capital assets than we are willing to maintain?
- Do our standards need adjustment? Can we meet those standards with our current budget?
- Is the amortization of previous capital projects having a serious effect on our annual budget?
- What did our expenditure profile look like? Was it what we wanted it to be?
- What percentage of our total budget is administrative? New work? Maintenance and repair? Is that good or bad? What are the trends?
- Was the fact that we were on or off target good or bad? Could we have influenced it more?
- Is our budget structure conducive to good management? If not, how should we change?

Project Accounting

Project accounting is a topic that should be covered in an entire chapter in a book devoted only to project management. We touch only the highlights here. If the facility manager is asked to manage a major (multimillion dollar) project, he needs to be supported by a separate project accounting system and project accountant. Company accountants and most facility management accountants do not understand project accounting, which has its own set of accounts based on project work items. There certainly can be a feeder from the project accounting system into the company accounting system, but the importance of the project manager's having separate project accounting cannot be overemphasized.

A common practice is to organize project accounts to coincide with the sections of the specifications dealing with different work items (with perhaps several lines for "soft costs," which are outside the scope of the project contract). In most cases, these accounts are numbered in accordance with either the Construction Specification Institute's MasterFormat or Hanscomb Associate's UNIFORMAT. Both can be easily adapted for use with the common project management software so that project management and accounting go hand in hand and are mutually supportive.

Desired budget and accounting reports are as numerous as project managers, but the following are what we consider the minimum for good project management and accounting:

- *Estimate of probable cost.* Breaks out the latest construction estimate by work item and provides a cost, a percentage of the total work, and a unit cost for work item in the project (actually subitems in most cases). The recap should break out the work by estimated site work, building cost, soft costs, and total cost.

- *Master project budget.* Breaks out the original budget among all work items and subitems that the project manager wants to track.
- Lists approved changes with their effect on the budget and expected changes with their anticipated effect on the budget. As backup, each item has a listing by vendor of invoices, changes approved, and the remaining budget for that item.
- *Budget/cost comparison,* organized by item and subitem. Lists the current budget, the current contract amount, the budget variance, the amount billed to date, and the amount yet to be billed for each line item and subitem.

Most good project software permits one entry of any figure, and all affected project accounts will be adjusted accordingly.

Proper accounting for project funds supports the essence of good project management. The facility manager must not only account for current change and overruns, but must be able to project the cost of changes that have not yet been approved. No company accounting system can provide the response that the project manager needs on a major project. Invest effort early on in a good accounting system and project accountant.

Cost Comparators and Benchmarks

At the start of this chapter, we mentioned the need for facility managers to know the costs of their services and then to select those costs that are drivers of the department, to attempt to influence them positively, and to monitor them closely. In addition, those key unit costs should be the basis for benchmarking.

Costs, a measure of efficiency, should not be the only category that a facility manager benchmarks. He should benchmark effectiveness (as perceived by customers) and response as well.

The bible for benchmarking is Robert Camp's 1989 classic, *Benchmarking,* which should be in every facility manager's tool kit. After using Camp's methodology and ensuring that he understands the components of his costs, the facility manager should benchmark with competitors, with similar companies, and with best in class. In its initial stages, benchmarking will concentrate on the metrics. However, the real value, once the metrics of both partners is understood, is in exchanging information as to how the "better" value was achieved.

Remember two things when benchmarking. First, the law of diminishing returns applies. It requires much more effort and funding to squeeze out the last five percent of improvement. Is it worth it? Second, your management does not necessarily want you to be best in class in every category of your service since there is a cost in doing so. The lobby of a manufacturing facility need not have the visitor appeal of a top hotel, for example.

Benchmarking, if properly used, is a valuable tool for implementing and monitoring continuous improvement. Good cost accounting is the basis for good benchmarking, and a good budget format makes the computation of unit costs both accurate and easy.

Notes

1. "Facilities Industry Trends-Survey Results," *FMLink*, www.fmlink.com, June 2004, pp. 1–3.
2. *Views from the Top . . . Executives Evaluate the Facility Management Function*, (Houston: IFMA, 1997), pp. 1–3.
3. Jeff Crane, "Rolling With the Facilities Budget, *Today's Facility Manager*, November 2007, p. 10.
4. *Space and Project Management Benchmarks*, (Houston: IFMA, 2007), pp. 40–41.
5. Paul Bartlett, "Defining, measuring and benchmarking productivity," Office Productivity Network Power Point presentation, date unknown.
6. "EPA Software Rates Upgrade Cost Viability," *Facilities Design and Management*, November 1997, p. 13.
7. *Green Building Research*, U.S. Green Building Council, www.usgbc.org/DisplayPage.aspx?CMSPageUD=1718, August 2008.

31

Communications

Pulse Points

- *Work constantly to get the attention of upper management.*
- *The facility manager is the public relations officer for his organization.*
- *Drop "FM speak;" use the language of business.*
- *Prepare and submit an annual report.*
- *Manage by walking around and carry on meaningful conversations with employees of the organization, with your staff, and with contractors.*
- *Regularly meet with colleagues and operating managers to find out how you might help each other.*
- *Have an annual meeting for your entire organization and stress just how well you did.*

Public Relations

Often we don't market our services and department because we think that it is self-evident that everyone appreciates the wonderful services that we provide. Unfortunately, quite the opposite is true. Facility managers are almost universally viewed as naysayers, non-team players, and noncontributors to overall corporate goals.

For all of those reasons, facility managers need to be much more conscious of public relations in general and marketing their services and department in particular. This has been a particular theme of Stormy Friday in her consulting practice and is one of the base themes of Friday and Cotts' *Quality Facility Management*. It is not simply good enough to do a great job; your customers and bosses (and professional colleagues) need to know it too. You need to search out venues and means to promote your department. (The remainder of this section is heavily influenced by Stormy's ideas which, frankly, have become so intertwined with Cotts' that we no longer can separate them.)

Particularly in this era of downsizing, there will not be a position on an FM organization chart marked "Public Relations." In fact, the main public relations person for the facility manager needs to be the facility manager himself. Much of the public relations and marketing work is external to the department. Only the facility manager has the prestige and the access to the target groups who need to be reached.

If there is still doubt that marketing and public relations is needed, perform the Three 5's Test in Exhibit 29-2. From our considerable experience, we believe that most facility managers will fail the Three 5's Test, and that underscores the need for better marketing of facility departments and services. The key to marketing is setting realistic objectives:

1. Increase the awareness of facility services.
2. Decrease the resistance to a particular service or set of policies and procedures.
3. Improve the image of the facility organization as a service provider.
4. Enhance customers' knowledge about facility services.
5. Disclose specific qualifications about facility services.

The purpose of marketing is to increase service awareness, knowledge, and qualifications while decreasing resistance to the facility department's policies and procedures.

The development of a marketing strategy is an excellent area for participative management. Use the five objectives as a format to elicit suggestions for specific strategies to implement each.

Some tools can make public relations and marketing efforts more effective. We strongly suggest that facility managers develop an annual public relations plan. Keep it simple. Initially, it should define the target groups to reach in priority order (top management, visitors, specific employee departments—whatever fits the company) and then design one or two simple actions to be implemented to achieve the marketing objectives. For instance, there might be a major effort to improve the department's image with visitors through better custodial maintenance of lobbies and better visitor reception training for the security staff.

Second, develop a customer profile for each of the department's client groups and its leader. Again, this is information that should be gathered over a period of time (and it will change). The WRC can be particularly helpful in providing information regarding problem areas in departments and buildings. A suggested format for a customer profile is contained in Friday and Cotts, *Quality Facility Management,* but the format is really not important. The facility manager should review the pertinent customer profile before every meeting with a department head or upper management. The review might also indicate a need to provide service of a different quality or response time to individual customers.

Finally, determine the actual costs of doing business and whether the department is cost competitive in the market. Clients are actually challenging facility managers that they can obtain FM services outside the organization, using chargeback funds, and that the services would be more responsive and less costly. Eventually all facility managers will face that same challenge. Ordinarily there is a bias toward using in-house services, but that bias disappears when the cost is more than 10 to 15 percent over market or when the service cannot be obtained responsively.

Facility managers who cannot speak and write well do their department a great disservice. Most of our education and training has not stressed effective communication, the downfall of many technically competent facility managers. We keep a dictionary, a college-level style manual, and a freshman English book near our desks at all times and never send a message without spellcheck turned on. A facility manager who does not write and speak well will not have the confidence to be the type of leader that the department deserves. It should be a goal of each facility manager to make a presentation of a best practice at a local or national facility management meeting.

We address the physical aspects of communications (wiring, WiFi, etc.) in Chapter 32 but in this chapter we want to emphasize the necessity for the facility manager to be able to communicate to all of his stakeholders. Throughout the book, we have alluded to the importance of communication but want, in one chapter, to reiterate the importance of having good communications skills because *we find it one of the major weaknesses of facility managers* and one that has not really improved much over the years. Unfortunately, one of the prime educational trends, online education, while strengthening the technical knowledge of us FMs, downplays the practice of communicating effectively face-to-face and in small groups where FMs tend to be the most deficient.

All three of your authors are FM practitioners, not communications or public relations experts. So we do not intend to outdo the wealth of management, communications, and public relations experts, authors and consultants. You probably have been exposed or easily can find your own experts, in-house or for hire. However, there are specific communications issues that apply to facility management.

The FM Environment

In one way, the environment has never been better for the facility manager to communicate effectively to upper management. Rising energy costs and rising construction costs need to be quantified and their impact projected to the CFO and CEO. They probably have some knowledge of the issues, but lack understanding of how these issues affect their organization. The reduction in office space and the closing of factories are strong indicators that upper management does, in fact, realize the impact of facilities on the bottom line. Are there leases which we could negotiate our way out of? We have found that government agencies, in particular, often have excess leased space. Could an inefficient facility be replaced by leasing or building a new one that would lower operating costs? Did we shed or more efficiently use space after the last downsizing? If we use hoteling, could we shed some space? Could a condition assessment and some master planning which you have been trying to promote for years now seem more in line with organizational efforts to efficiently utilize resources? There has never been more pressure on management to control costs and so facility managers should present and advocate every way possible, with emphasis on the short-term, but also promoting long-term, sustainable savings. *Management needs to know we are here*; we are not just guys and gals in the boiler room but we are working hard, in our area of management to help them meet corporate goals. (This is more easily accomplished from the vice president-level which implies that we manage the total FM portfolio, including real estate).

Another communication factor that needs to be stressed is that, in every external communication, we must be customer-oriented. This is daunting, particularly when managing an organization that is substantially contractors. It means that you need to spend some of your time seeking out organizational colleagues, asking them how you can help them meet their business goals. It means, in particular, that your staff, particularly the WRC, are trained to treat every customer as an important customer and to be capable of handling every difficult situation on their own in a way that you would if you were present. It means that your workers need to approach, work with, and depart worksites where organizational employees are present in a way that convinces those employees that your workers will do everything possible to solve their problem. You need to train, measure customer satisfaction, correct customer service boo-boos, and reward good customer service.

It is our experience that, the more organized (or larger) an FM department becomes, the more bureaucratic it becomes . . . *and that the customer service orientation gets lost*. We know that has been true in our experience. When our departments are really humming there is a natural tendency to sit back, put a smile on your face and enjoy the hum. A corollary to this has been mentioned several times earlier. You cannot rest on your laurels in measuring customer service. No single measurement system has a shelf-life of much over six months. The bottom line is that customer service needs to permeate every attitude and action of a successful facility management organization. It is like our DNA. Customer service defines our every communication.

Gaining Attention

When facility managers are asked why they do not receive the support that they feel they should, the answer is often that upper management is not concerned about facilities. So . . . somehow we must gain their attention. The exact situation which any single facility manager might find himself in is too varied to define so we will present two cases, both from our experience. In the first case, one of your authors was involved in literally founding a FM department where only an unorganized contract O&M crew existed before. FM problems were legion. Phase I consisted of convincing upper management that their facilities were important, that someone did care about their facility requirements and complaints, and that, in fact, a simple service order could be accomplished in less than a month. The pain level from complaints to upper management, particularly the operational vice presidents during the previous lack of organization, made Phase I an easy sell. Phase II consisted of a complete building condition assessment, energy study, a series of customer service focus groups, an organizational study, and evaluation of all contractors. Though this project took slightly longer than expected, we took interim results to upper management as soon as we had vetted them (and knew we could live with them). This actually worked to our advantage by keeping FM on the agenda of upper management and giving us a chance to lay the groundwork for the roll-out of the final recommendations, which were the basis for a top-notch facility management department.

In the second situation, at the early stages of the IT revolution, one of your authors found herself trying to retrofit computers into facilities that were constructed in the mid-1930s. Concurrent with this was the awakening concerning the office environment, particularly demountable partitions. With training from IFMA and a helpful consultant, we were able to eventually (it was not easy) convince management that the IT revolution was here (a fireball IT director helped here as did complaints from operational vice presidents) and that it could best be met by 1) leasing new space in IT-friendly buildings built-out for us, 2) building a centrally-located, owned building which we had designed, and 3) completely renovating our old buildings as we could free up space using the previous two initiatives. This was an enormous effort and involved us soliciting help from organizational operating elements who convinced they needed the capabilities of new information technology to sell this multi-million dollar, multi-year effort to the CFO, CEO, and Board.

Communications Vehicles

There is almost a never-ending combination of message, vehicles, and targets if you were to plot the communication pattern of a facility manager. We will only cover several, but first a short sermon. It is our experience, having taught and associated with literally hundreds of facility managers that many, too many, facility managers lack good written and oral communications skills. When tested in the classroom, at least, this deficiency stands out starkly. If you cannot write and speak articulately, persuasively, and correctly, no IT gadget or PowerPoint presentation is going to save you. Managers must be able to communicate effectively. As a general admonition we recommend that facility managers join Toastmasters, or similar organization, and take a written and spoken English course at a local junior college. Amen!

Whether writing a paper, giving a presentation, or casually discussing a FM issue with upper management, we must drop the "FM speak" and speak the language of business, principally we must state how the action we desire is cost effective. If we are writing a paper or making a presentation, we can present the economic justification. In casual conversation we must simply state the bottom line and promise to follow up with the justification. State the problem simply in language familiar to your target audience, then explain your recommended solution. If you have time, present the advantages of your solution, address any concerns, and *then ask for approval*. Check for understanding by asking for feedback, or have your audience tell you in their own words what they understand. The old adage to "tell 'em what you're going to tell them, tell them, and tell them what you told 'em" is a good one.

It is also important to consider your target audience for each communication. We would not present the same information in the same way to the senior management team as we would to a mass Email distribution to all employees. Customize each communication to fit the need of the audience.

When you have a message to get out, put yourself in your audience's shoes. Consider what you would want to know, what you already know or think you know, and what concerns you might have about the subject. Address each of these topics in a customized presentation and you will be well ahead of any rumors, hearsay, or the organization's grapevine.

Always be truthful, but be careful not to promise too much, too soon. Never give a guesstimate budget figure off the cuff, for example. Once customers hear a number, they remember it and, no matter the intervening events, they will be dissatisfied if you miss that number. The best way to deal with these situations is to provide a wide range, if pressed for an estimate, and to research and provide a more accurate estimate within a reasonable time.

Never miss a chance to promote your organization; you are the FM public relations officer. Make sure that upper management is aware of honors that you, your organization, or individuals in your organization achieve, particularly in the FM area (such as achieving the CFM or FMP designation or a building achieving designation as a green building). Then, at the end of the fiscal year, prepare an annual report and submit it to upper management pointing out highlights of the year and your plans for the upcoming year. We find that a brief summary highlighting the truly extraordinary is likely to be read.

We have always been advocates of "management by walking around" so that you learn your personnel (including your contractors) and they know you and also that you verify the work reports crossing your desk. Facility managers get so busy that they often forget internal communications other than to chew someone out when something goes wrong. You will be surprised by the reaction of one of your painters if, for instance, you ask him how he paints so well or what's the secret to using the right kind of paint. **The questions need not be profound, but they need to be sincere.** We also are great believers in socializing with our foremen, superintendents, and managers at lunch, parties, and special occasions. Once a year at the end of the fiscal year, one of the author's organizations knocked off work an hour early and gathered everyone, staff and contractors, in an auditorium and reminded them of both the resources that they were given by the organization and what they accomplished with those resources. Since they generally performed well, they were thanked for a great job. The off-site management team from each contractor was often invited to these sessions. Rewards, even modest recognitions, go a long way toward motivating staff and building teams.

Colleagues and Operating Managers

There is another group with whom we need to communicate, our colleagues and the operational managers who are the key to the organization's success. We advocate quarterly, semi-annual, or annual meetings with each manager at your level plus the key operational managers. The subject is an easy one, "How can our department help you?" They are as knowledgeable as you are of fiscal restraints so, if their issue (Example: We need more space) needs financing to solve it, then ask them to support you and you will take the lead in making the appeal to upper management. This is a powerful technique and helps overcome the general impression of the facility department as a bunch of nay-sayers. The bottom line is learn how to COMMUNICATE, COMMUNICATE, COMMUNICATE!

Senior Management

Effective communication with senior management, the "C Suite" of CEO, COO, and CFO, and other senior operational managers is the ultimate key to facility management success. First, remember that these are busy people, that they deal with a different realm of issues than you do (and so have a different comfort zone), and that they expect you to be the expert in facility management. To communicate effectively with them, you need confidence, knowledge, an ability to speak in terms that they understand, and a few presentation skills.

Facility managers are in a unique position to see, talk with, and work with every level and function within the organization. If we are doing our job well, we get to know the specialized business and viewpoint of each business unit within the organization. We should easily be able to differentiate the needs of the Sales Department from those of Research and Development, for example. We need to know not only the type of space and equipment each department needs, but also the business drivers they experience. Only when we have this thorough understanding of the organization can we be considered "Board-worthy" advisors to the business organization not simply a service provider. Our department has the potential to help guide the business with our expertise on real estate, operations and maintenance needs, and occupancy issues. If we don't provide this level of advice, those executives will seek it elsewhere which can create a very difficult situation. One of your authors experienced this at a time when space and funds were tight and a disgruntled vice president, because of a social contact on the golf course, became convinced that he needed to move into a new building where the advertised amenities were great. Fortunately this time the CFO came to the rescue and declared any such move simply financially impossible.

After employee costs, facility costs are the largest "spend" in most organizations. We support the organization and make it possible for each employee to have the appropriate workspace for accomplishing maximum productivity. When we communicate these facts clearly, specifically, and in the business language that senior management uses, we are increasing our chances for a favorable appreciation of the FM organization. Good communications skills—listening, clarifying, probing, speaking, summarizing, and an ability to articulate succinctly in the appropriate media—are every bit as important to facility management success as is technical expertise.

32

Information Systems and Other Technology

Pulse Points

- Do not try to develop and automate data and procedures simultaneously.
- When estimating automation needs, do not underestimate the effort needed for data entry or overestimate what building data are truly needed for good management.
- FM automation can increase departmental efficiency and effectiveness; it should be justified within the company as a tool necessary for good business practice.
- Don't automate bad policies and procedures.
- An omnibus integrated workplace management system (IWMS) is now available to integrate the major FM functions. Facility managers of large companies should consider a system linking computer-aided design and drawing (CADD) and a geographic information system through a relational database.
- Research indicates that it is as important to be able to communicate data from FM technology tools as to possess the tools themselves.
- Facility managers should be using the Internet and intranet to communicate better, for training, to gather information and advice, and to review products and services.
- New communications technologies should be exploited to increase departmental efficiency.
- When purchasing an IWMS, develop an implementation plan consisting of a needs analysis, a budget, and an implementation schedule.
- Don't tie IWMS procurement to another big project.
- Ensure that the IWMS will mesh with company business systems.

• *Training on the Internet represents a paradigm shift: Training is no longer a one-time event; with the Internet we can train when and where we want. In addition, access to training materials via the Internet allows us to integrate training into problem solving at work.*

NOTE: In the remainder of this chapter and throughout the book we will refer to IWMS, an integrated workplace management system. This is not an endorsement of any manufacturer's product and is a theoretical but practical web-based platform. It could be fielded with current technology to do real estate management, lease administration, planning, design, work management, operations and maintenance management, move management, asset management, space management, project management, the physical aspects of communications management, regulatory compliance management, procurement and budget management while interfacing with the organization's enterprise technology such as finance, management reporting, and security as depicted in Chapter 22. One aspect of IWMS as we visualize it is the web-based virtual emergency operations center which allows all organizational functions having a call center, primarily facilities and security, to operate on a day-to-day basis as they would operate in an emergency. It specifically does not have the capabilities of BIM, building information modeling as currently conceptualized. Slowly but surely integrated systems are being fielded but

- No one is likely to completely switch over all organizational systems to one new system, and
- In the FM area, there are unique systems not easily integrated with the web-based systems which have great appeal for applications like facility work management and security management where there is a need for communication with the entire organization, and
- The developers of business software have been late to the party in fielding specific FM software.

A web-based Virtual Emergency Operations Center (VEOC) is in the field as one of the early efforts in a new generation of automation. The VEOC will incorporate not only the facility WRC but will be integrated with the security and public safety, information technology, and whatever other functions have either a 24/7 aspect or are needed in an emergency. One of your authors sees round-the-clock operations necessary in more and more organizations due to globalization and increased emphasis on emergency management. The VEOC will keep executives, managers, and selected workers in communication and able to access necessary information whenever and wherever it is needed.

We define IWMS as a consolidated approach to technology solutions that brings together the benefits of multiple systems in one software package.[1]

A detailed discussion of FM information systems and other FM technology would require a small book in and of itself. The problem is that, like all technology, FM technology is always being replaced by the improved model or by the integration of a new technology, like GIS for example, as an improving application. The best over-all summary that we have found is Eric Teicholz' "Technology" section of his *Facility Design and Management Handbook,* though it is now seven years old. Eric is a pioneer in the field who has always stayed on the cutting edge and someone whom we admire and trust. He presents both theory and practical examples of fielded technology and even highlights the one major attempt to put FM education onto the Internet.

The widespread use of the term *facility management* occurred simultaneously with the proliferation of business office automation. Interestingly, it also coincided with the early careers in FM of your authors and so we have seen, first hand, the challenge presented by a concept and devices that totally changed the workspace, particularly in the office environment. One of the greatest challenges was in this situation accommodating one personal computer per employee into buildings that were 1) fifty years old, 2) under construction and 3) on short-term leases with no advance warning. The challenge was cranked up a notch when shortly thereafter, organizations decided to network their office automation. We were often flying blind and our architect-engineer partners were not much better prepared.

Compounding the situation was the fact that automation to assist us was still in the R&D stage and was being fielded (amid great hoopla and promises) piecemeal and with no standards or interoperability (and with no realistic projections of what it would cost to gather and enter your organizational data into the system before you could ever use it). The lack of interoperability impairs us even today. Many small companies realized the need for good FM IT and tried to enter the marketplace. One of your authors actually purchased his first computer-assisted facility management system (CAFM) from two ex-Navy personnel who made their presentation in a partitioned-off leased space in a law library. The market, at that time, was not quite the Wild West, but close.

Three issues soon emerged. Because there were no standards, interfacing with other organizational systems, like the accounting system, or new FM systems, and computer-assisted design (CAD) were impossible or extremely expensive and notoriously unreliable. Consultants proliferated and, while they tried to make fixes, sometimes there just were none to be made.

Second, as mentioned earlier, data had to be gathered, arranged in a manner that fit your CAFM, and then entered. This not only was costly and took a long, long time but tied you to that system forever. Finally, as CAFM systems improved, the "early adapters" found themselves plodding along with systems based on COBOL and FORTRAN while those who waited were the beneficiaries of new systems, some of whom also benefitted from the development of the enterprise systems in the rest of the organization. One of your authors invested in the technology of a small, very entrepreneurial company which was cutting edge when his FM organization bought its CAFM system. Ten years later, the system was very difficult to maintain and almost impossible to update but the cost to go to a new system was huge. Finally the old system had to be junked and a new system purchased. None of the data in the old system was easily transferable to the new CAFM systems which had integrated CAD and had developed strong CMMS (Computerized Maintenance Management System) modules. So it was throw out the old and bring in the new (highly duplicative) and keep the department running smoothly as you do it. It was both a traumatic and costly experience.

In the interim, companies offering IWMS (the study still calls it CAFM) have shaken out (as has the list of FM automation consultants) and there has been a movement (though not perfect) toward standardization. The Open Standards Consortium for Real Estate (OSCRE) promises to "Deliver global standards for exchanging electronic real property information and drive their adoption."[2] The interoperability and standardization of these systems is gradually coming to fruition.

Occasionally, one of the major IT business consulting firms decides to advertise that they have a FM module (they do have the benefit of meshing better with the enterprise systems of the organization) but the applications are so limited (and some don't include CAD, for instance,) that they are not a serious application for full-service facility management organizations. Interestingly, the use of IWMS only increased 3 percent to 43 percent between 2002 and 2007 though some type of computerized facility management is practiced by 100 percent of those surveyed, principally in North America. Of those who had IWMS, 63 percent came off the shelf, 23 percent is web-based, and 9 percent of the FMs used an in-house developed system.[3]

It is not too much of a stretch to say that business automation has increased the visibility of the facility manager. Now FM automation technology offers the facility manager the opportunity for better management of the buildings and services than could be imagined twenty years ago. Effective fielding of facilities automation has a spotty history. It is widely accepted that more than half of the software, bought to make facility management more effective ends up as "shelfware,"[4] a disturbing fact given the current state of facility management, which sorely needs analytical and communication tools. We sense that this situation is becoming less prevalent as facility managers become more knowledgeable buyers and users.

E-mail, groupware, and the use of the Internet and intranet are so widespread in most businesses that we will refer to them only as they affect a specific FM automation application. A British study found that 87 percent of calls to the WRC could be processed on an organization's intranet without human intervention.[5] A brief explanation of how to establish facilities management on the organizational intranet is contained in Mick Dalton's and Case Runolfson's presentation to World Workplace 2005.[6] Bruce Cox has written an excellent discussion of integrating the Internet into facility management to include an extensive listing of applicable FM e-mail addresses.[7] E-mail, texting, and the cell phone give the facility manager ways to communicate effectively that were virtually unavailable when this book was first written.

The search for an acceptable IWMS has not been an easy one, nor have the solutions been neat. For example, in 1981–1982, the company one of your authors worked for wrote a specification for an omnibus FMIS that would allow them to manage each FM function well and provide the department the ability to share information within and without. They were unable to acquire such a system at that time—the technology was not there—so they automated each function independently but had no ability to share the information outside the department or feed information from one functional system or another. Finally, departmental management made the decision to junk the "stovepiped" functional systems and buy a single, omnibus system.

If it is still not clear to you what an Integrated Workplace Management System (IWMS) is, read Moussa Chaer's description in "CAFM Solutions" at the 2005 World Workplace.[8]

The most common building-related FM functions that have been automated are:

1. Drafting and design, commonly designated as CADD
2. Space planning and management, normally inherent in CADD systems
3. Project, construction, and move management
4. Work order and maintenance management
5. Building operations and energy management
6. Lease management
7. Asset (inventory and allocation) management
8. Telecommunications and data communications management
9. Regulatory compliance management
10. FM financial and procurement management to include chargeback administration
11. Security and emergency management

Every function mentioned above has been automated by multiple vendors and can be installed normally on a desktop computer, which leads us to ask how best to automate and what automation system is best for a particular company. We really have gone beyond deciding whether to automate FM functions. The issue is how best to do so.[9]

The facility manager has two options when seeking an IWMS or automating his department. The first is to automate each of the listed functions individually. This used to be the only option because no companies offered truly omnibus systems. Often this approach also ensures that you obtain an excellent solution to your problem—lease management, for example. Some facility managers of primarily leased facilities need only a few functions automated. In addition, the facility manager can often do a better job of automating by focusing intently on one function and ensuring that it works well before moving on to the next.

If the IWMS is built function by function, it may be possible to find a system integrator who can connect all of the functional subsystems into an integrated system. Normally, however, that is prohibitively costly or technically unfeasible.

The second option is to buy an omnibus system, with separate modules for all (or most) of the functions and the capability for data to be exchanged and used between the modules. There are at least four North American companies offering such omnibus systems and the international competition is growing.

Need is one of the factors that determines the way to automate. If the department's work is 90 percent project management, then the chosen system must do that function very, very well. Besides need, size and complexity of facilities are the major determinants of what type of IWMS is most appropriate. Those relationships are depicted in Exhibit 32-1.

The interesting thing about Exhibit 32-1, which is now over twenty-years old, is the genius of Jeff Hamer. As systems have developed, the spacing between the systems on this exhibit have varied, but the basic concept remains. We guess one could wonder if any current IWMS has reached the level of "The Ideal System?" We doubt it. Another extremely interesting point is that it seems like we will always need consultants to help us integrate off-the-shelf hardware and software with organizational hardware and software.

Trends

The most pervasive trend in FM is undoubtedly the opportunities available through web-based FM. Facility managers continue to use the Internet to meet the needs of their customers, as a source of information, and for better communication. The professional associations have developed web-based courses for both general education

Exhibit 32-1. Facility management information system.

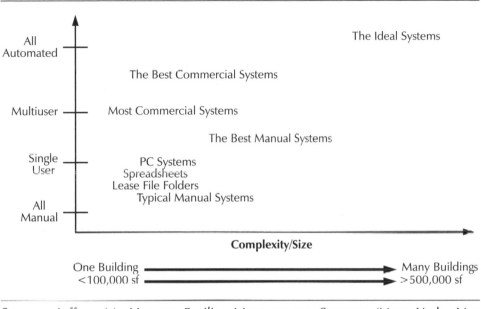

Source: Jeffrey M. Hamer, *Facility Management Systems* (New York: Van Nostrand Reinhold, 1988), p. 17.

and to work toward professional recognition. At least one firm, Meridian Knowledge Solutions of Chantilly, VA has developed "learning centers" for both facility management and occupational health, where it provides, on the Internet, not only training, but self-testing, and a library of applicable regulations and other FM related material.

A second important trend is the flexibility contained in new FMIS systems that link CADD systems with a geographic information system (GIS) through a relational database. Particularly for managers of large, geographically dispersed facilities, the ability to link graphics to data and then to ask the questions that are pertinent to facility management rather than what has been preprogrammed into the computer is exciting.

Communications technologies and handheld computers combined with software assessment tools offer outstanding opportunities to revolutionize the way facility managers collect information about the status of buildings, conduct building assessments, and manage work in facilities. Imagine a maintenance technician conducting an off-hours inspection of a manufacturing facility. During his inspection, he discovers a major operational problem. He calls it in on his cellular phone so that correction can immediately commence. He enters routine problems into his computer using deficiency and location codes. If there is a problem with a particular piece of equipment, the technician can go to a central location and log on to access automated maintenance instructions, maintenance history, and warranty information (including pictures and operational diagrams) about that piece of equipment. At the end of his shift, he can download his handheld computer into the work management system, which issues work orders for all deficiencies noted. Once those deficiencies are corrected, the workers (who might be contractors) enter time and materials into their handheld computers under the work order code and number. Then they download the data into the work management system at the end of their shift. The work orders are not only closed out, but the time and material are transferred to payroll or to vendor accounts for payment at month's end. At the same time, the assessment data gathered, combined with other assessment data, will provide management with funding profiles for maintenance, repair, and capital replacement.

The obvious difficulty in discussing trends is that there are many opportunities to be wrong. Technologies change; some even fail. New technologies will provide opportunities that we have not even thought about. However, we are reasonably sure that in the short term, the Internet, the linking of CADD with GIS, and the development of new assessment tools will be among the technologies offering facility managers the opportunity to work smarter and be more responsive to the business needs of their companies.

Choosing a System

From this point on, we will discuss only an omnibus IWMS, one that manages the functions set out in the first section of this chapter. The considerations discussed can be applied to choosing an individual work management system or asset management system. We will discuss how to select a system, justify it, and manage a successful installation. Successful management of this process is essential if we are substantially to decrease the amount of "shelfware" that represents both wasted funds and lost opportunities.

Three issues are present in every IWMS procurement; success will depend on the ability to manage them.

First, vendors are infamous for overstating their systems' capabilities—but facility managers are equally infamous for failing to understand what their automation needs really are. For instance, there will be a tendency on the facility manager's part to want to manage far more data than are necessary. At least initially, automate only those subfunctions that need to be managed intensely.

Second, there is a chicken-or-egg dilemma here. Prior to automating any single function, the facility manager will not know how best to do it. There is a synergy in automation that will not be recognized until the project is well under way.

The vendor's experience can be helpful here, as is focusing clearly on the automation task at hand, but the facility manager needs to realize that as he automates, he will see opportunities for change and need to be prepared to capitalize on them.

Finally, always balance the urgency of need for an integrated system with slow, methodical implementation steps. Never throw out a critical manual system until the automated system has been installed and a successful test of the system has been made. Keep the long-range goal of complete integration in view, but do not expect it to happen overnight.

In order best to manage those three issues, Jeff Hamer has developed the following list of do's and don'ts:[10]

Do
- Postpone automation until processes are redesigned.
- Ask stupid questions about how things are done.
- Try out rough prototypes for early feedback from the people who will use them.
- Agree on goals, after first hashing out a model of how the problem works.
- Start by fixing a small but annoying problem to win friends.
- Structure big projects so that there are payoffs along the way.
- Select your best employees for the teams even if it means disrupting day-to-day operations.
- Settle for the 80 percent solutions.

Don't
- Try to use a big job to cover the costs.
- Set vague objectives such as "improving productivity."
- Design your project to minimize conflict within the organization.
- Assign project implementation to a technically proficient person unskilled in negotiation.
- Assume that interviewing users reveals exactly what they need.
- Start by looking for places to apply the hottest new technologies.
- Leave technology for last, or you'll overlook opportunities for using it.
- Emphasize incremental improvement if what you really need is fundamental change.

Another important issue is to bring management along throughout the automation process. When there is a good business case, this is much easier to do than ten years ago when management tended to view technology, particularly in a noncore function, as a "nice-to-have" rather than a necessity. The pervasiveness of technology throughout the company has helped here also. Management is likely to ask the following kinds of questions:

- What was the current system meant to accomplish?
- What new tasks need to be accomplished that the current system cannot handle?
- What tasks are currently performed that are no longer necessary?
- What alternatives are available to handle both the old and new requirements?
- What characteristics of each alternative fit well or badly with what needs to be accomplished?
- Last, and perhaps most important, what is best for and what will be accepted by the users?

An additional question that will be asked is, How much does it cost? Facility managers should be able to answer by calculating an internal rate of return, a net present value, or a return on investment. At least one of those figures should already be available since they were used to choose among competing technologies. Costs include hardware and software, conversion of existing systems, training, maintenance and operations, and one-time costs for data input. On the other hand, savings result from any reduced operational costs and from reductions in relocation costs, direct labor, and any savings in space.

One of the simplest but most complete approaches to selecting and implementing an IWMS system has been developed by the Logistics Management Institute, a federally funded nonprofit research organization that excels in FM consulting (see Exhibit 32-2). This approach may be more elaborate than necessary in every case, but the point is to get a plan. To quote Jeff Hamer again, "No action steps equals no action" and "Even a bad plan is much better than no plan."[11] Another statement that is relevant to purchasing an IWMS by David Weisberg of Technology Automation Services in the December 1997 *A/E/C Systems:* "In general, I strongly believe that architecture and engineering firms should buy the best hardware and software products that they can afford at any given point in time."

Two substantive documents are critical to the chances of a successful IWMS procurement and implementation once management has bought in. First, there must be a detailed needs analysis for each function that is a candidate for automation. It should consider not only specific problems to be solved by automation, but the need to integrate functions and share information between organizational units and possibly contractors. During the needs analysis, a manager needs to be particularly mindful of company initiatives that might affect his IWMS during or shortly after implementation. For example, designing a system to operate independently, only to have the company become completely networked shortly after IWMS implementation, could render the entire system obsolescent, if not obsolete.

Automation needs to be a major issue when outsourcing. We have observed an organization, which had one type of IWMS, hire a contractor for operations which

Exhibit 32-2. Approach to IWMS selection and implementation.

Facilities Capabilities Overview

- Provide an overview of IWMS software products on the market.
- Describe IWMS applications.
- Discuss typical training requirements.
- Discuss the general price range of IWMS packages.

Functional Requirement Determination/Needs Analysis

- Review existing LAN/WAN, server, and hardware configurations.
- Develop inventory legacy systems.
- Interview functional/divisional offices; help desk staff and customers; determine needs and expectations.
- Determine business processes for work orders and preventive maintenance, major capital project planning and tracking, space analysis, lease administration, materials management, budgeting, and asset management.
- If requested, recommend business process improvements that could be made prior to implementing an IWMS.
- Develop functional requirements.
- Develop functional requirement priorities for organizational needs and management objectives.
- Brief the staff on prioritized functional requirements for an IWMS.

IWMS Product Analysis and Recommendations

- Survey market literature and associations.
- Develop a Request for Information tailored to the organization's functional requirements.
- Review updated product demonstrations.
- Interview IWMS vendors.
- Document product features.
- Develop a matrix comparing selection criteria to product and vendor features using weighted values.
- Perform a customer satisfaction survey and site visits to organizations that have bought the top-rated product.
- Brief the staff on the results of the matrix.
- For the leading products, coordinate on-site IWMS demonstrations.
- Recommend the IWMS.

(continued)

Exhibit 32-2. (continued)

Conceptual Design and Implementation Plan

- Develop a conceptual design to include:
  1. Hardware requirements for the selected IWMS
  2. Planned interfaces with legacy systems
  3. System administration issues such as database administration, server operations, backup and storage procedures, training, and contingency planning
- Develop a generalized implementation plan and schedule for the IWMS applications the organization will purchase and use.
- Produce a report on the selection process, conceptual design, and implementation plan.

Implementation Support

- Purchase IWMS software and supporting hardware.
- Ensure proper installation of client server hardware.
- Conduct vendor training.
- Develop a detailed implementation plan.
- Conduct regular implementation team meetings.
- Supervise data entry and drawing development/updating.
- Conduct initial and full product rollout.
- Conduct training of all users and customers, if needed.
- Supervise integration with legacy systems.
- Develop and publish instructions and procedures.

Source: Modified from a copyrighted (1977) procedure of the Logistics Management Institute.

used another IWMS but the topic had not been the subject of the outsourcing contract bidding or award. The conflict was eventually worked out but should not have been overlooked in the first place.

The needs analysis provides the framework for the installation plan. Actually the plan cannot be completed until basic decisions are made on what system will be procured. Do not forget the plan for postinstallation activities, such as system and data update, controls, access procedures, and training.

Once the facility manager has completed the needs analysis and installation plan, he can start to form a detailed budget, the implementation team, and a project schedule. Managing this process is much like managing any other complex project. One word of advice: Assign a budget to each line item of the implementation plan, and make conscious budget reallocation decisions each time a change is necessary (and there will be changes). Ensure that perhaps up to 10 percent of the implementation cost is retained for contingencies. Even if the process is managed well, costs appear during implementation that could not be anticipated in the planning phase. Be cautious, however, because automation projects have a history of cost overruns. The battlefield is littered with the bodies of FM warriors who allowed their implementation budget to grow unchecked until management stepped in, stopping the project and firing the responsible manager.

Here are some guidelines that have proved successful in evaluating and selecting software and will lead to better integration of the total system. The system should:

- Be an enterprise system that contains all the software functionality supporting facility and real estate management functions.
- Be modular by allowing use of one or more applications through multiple business units and have the ability to add applications as required.
- Be an off-the-shelf solution, since it offers quicker implementation and better technical support so time and effort can be spent on data standards and input.
- Tie functional and business areas into a singular database and graphics environment.
- Integrate with the organization's standard database, operating system, and networking environments.
- Be able to integrate with the corporate financial and human resources systems.
- Integrate with the CADD system.
- Be easy to use and therefore increase productivity due to shorter ramp-up time with decreased training and support costs.[12]

FM systems tend to be unique, and this can be a problem. Many of these systems—project management and financial management, for example—need to mesh with the organization's enterprise system. For that reason, an automation system needs to be particularly sensitive to the compatibility issue. For example, you might prefer to adopt Microsoft Project as your project management system rather than to buy a unique construction project management system. Do not be so self-centered in the automation effort that you forget that you must support the organization's enterprise system.

Selecting a specific system to meet the department's needs is the bottom line of the FM automation process. Actually, good general procurement procedures should ensure the acquisition of the appropriate system, but certain aspects need emphasis. First, we strongly suggest that unless your company has specialized internal expertise (most information systems departments do not have a clue about FM systems), a specialized consultant should be hired to help write specifications and select a vendor. Most major metropolitan areas have consultants who specialize in advising on procuring FM systems.

Second, reduce the possible vendors to a short list of two to three, and if possible, visit not fewer than two organizations that have each system being considered. Take a small but representative group to visit, but maximize the visit by deciding, with the help of a consultant, what to look for and what questions to ask. A predetermined scorecard of weighted criteria is often helpful to ensure that all systems are analyzed uniformly. Do not forget to inquire about technical support, data upgrade issues, training, and both successes and problems encountered during installation and operation. Compose the team, and visit so that technicians talk to technicians, finance people talk to their counterparts, and the facilities manager speaks to his counterpart. Two questions that we always ask are where the system has exceeded or failed expectations and if he would buy the system again knowing what he now knows.

Third, after reducing the potential vendors to a short list, ask the vendor to prepare a demonstration in the company's facility, using its data and hardware, if possible. Try to demonstrate an activity that is representative of the facility department and important to its success.

Finally, in your contract, give the vendor incentives to make suggestions during the implementation phase that will save money or make the system and the department more effective. Suggestions considered for incentives need to offer truly unexpected opportunities for savings. For an incentive program to be successful, allow the vendor to share in the savings.

Just one note to dampen undue enthusiasm: In a study of the impact of CADD on architectural-engineering firms, automation was found not to be the effective multiplier that it was predicted to be. Productivity gains of 50 to 70 percent were achieved, but it often took a decade to do so. How CADD was used appeared to be a bigger factor than what system was purchased and used. The most productive firms were those that automated most broadly, emphasized training, had the best internal electronic communication to share data, had specific automation managers, and whose basic administrative procedures were better defined prior to automation.[13] While CADD cannot be exactly equated to IWMS, there is a message here for us, and we ignore it at our own peril. Managing the implementation of an IWMS will probably be the single most important event in the tenure of a facility manager. Do it right![14]

Other Technologies

It is difficult to provide a comprehensive overview of technologies that are being used to manage facilities better. The field is very broad, and new technologies enter the market weekly. Following is a list of technologies that we have seen used with a few brief comments where appropriate. We have emphasized those that help to operate and manage better:

- *Bar coding*—to code fixed assets so that they can be uniquely identified and/or their location fixed. Although it can be very effective, it is relatively costly to implement and difficult to sustain.
- *Cellular communications*—the principal communications means for work crews.
- *Rugged laptop computers, PDAs and hand-hold devices*—to record building deficiencies or assessments and download into the work management system to generate work orders.
- *Regulatory compliance software*—to analyze and document compliance with federal regulations.
- *Analytical software*—to analyze the effects of changes prior to actual installation. One example is an EPA-developed tool to analyze lighting upgrades. ProjectKalc can be downloaded from http://www.epa.gov/docs/gdcoar/download.html. Other EPA tools are available for analyzing the cost-effectiveness of upgrading variable air volume systems, energy efficiency, and indoor air quality.
- *Environmental and energy management assessment software*—to provide technical and financial assessments of energy management efforts and environmental improvements.
- *Engineered management systems*—decision support tools that permit managers to decide when, where, and how best to maintain facilities.
- *Groupware*—for sharing information within the department or company, or among geographically dispersed groups.
- *Predictive maintenance technology and procedures*—to predict failure of critical equipment prior to failure.

In addition, there is a vast array of automation tools available to managers within the organizations to help them operate more effectively and efficiently.

Building Information Modeling (BIM)

Building Information Modeling (BIM) is a digital representation of the building process (and the building) which facilitates an exchange and interoperability of the building process in the digital format. Using BIM, we can see the mockup of an entire building (from structural elements to ductwork to the wiring) even as it is being built, and we can give managers and users a visual tour of the building as it is being built. It also permits architects and engineers to work out conflict problems before conflicting elements are installed. Used properly, BIM can help ensure that everyone is on board at every step of the process by creating a conflict-free mockup far superior to floor plans, as-builts, and other forms of project documentation.[15] BIM also will provide expedited procurement through automated estimating and specification and documents the building equipment, finishes, and specifications for reference post occupancy. That is an extremely helpful feature for facility managers who need to replace or reference original building specifications long after occupancy. Furthermore, BIM can be used to assist the O&M staff, especially during emergencies. (See Chapter 19 for more discussion.)

The consensus is that BIM is not cost-effective for general use at this time. Also it is undergoing a standardization effort which hopefully will avoid some of the problems of other FM automation innovations. Those who have used BIM are excited about its potential and hopefully we will be able to add it to the IWMS in the near future.

The Bottom Line

Despite the problems and issues that we have examined in this chapter, the bottom line is that the facility manager needs the Integrated Workplace Management System. While the numbers are all over the place, it appears that we should plan to average about $0.50 per rentable square feet annually to procure and run our IWMS (not including initial data entry).[16] The secret is to get the system which works best for the facility manager, the department and customers, *and allows him to work more effectively and efficiently with documented results of the department's work*. Too many facility departments seem driven by their IWMS rather than using it for a competitive advantage. If this is your situation, we hope this chapter has been helpful and will cause you to take action to correct the situation. If you desire a rapid introduction to FM technology, IFMA offers a seminar, *The Technology Competency Course*, to assist facility managers in their certification in this vital competency.

Notes

1. Rowley, Kristian, "Why Do Leading Organizations Implement IWMS?" White paper by Tririga Research, June 2007.
2. Open Standards Consortium for Real Estate (OSCRE) website, accessed 08/04/08 at www.oscre.org.
3. *Benchmarks, Report #28* (Houston, TX; IFMA, 2007), p. 47.

4. Eric Teicholz, "Technologies for Effective Facility Management" in *Federal Facilities Beyond the 1990's* (Washington, D.C.: National Academy Press, 1997), p. 55.

5. Emily Harup, "FM and the Internet," Bartlett Research, www.bartlett.ucl.ac.uk/graduate/program/msc_be/FEM_X_internet.doc

6. Mick Dalton and Case Runolfson, "Corporate Intranets and FM," FM Technology Users Forum, World Workplace, October 24, 2005.

7. Bruce Cox, "Integrating the Internet into FM," *Facility Design and Management Handbook,* Eric Teicholz, ed. (New York; McGraw-Hill; 2001), pp. 26-1 thru 38.

8. Moussa Chaer, "CAFM Solutions," FM Technology Users Forum, World Workplace, October 24, 2005.

9. George Laszlo, quoted in *Managing Facility Technology* (Arnold, Md.: BOMI Institute, 1989), pp. 12–17. Reprinted by permission of the BOMI Institute.

10. Jeffrey Hamer, "Best Practices in Technology Management" in *Conference Proceedings, World Workplace '95* (Houston: International Facility Management Association, 1995), pp. 961–972.

11. Ibid., p. 966.

12. Robb Dods and Rein Vares, "Strategic Asset Management Systems for Facility and Real Estate Management," *Facility Management Journal* (November–December 1997): 16.

13. George B. Korte, "CADD and A/E Firms: 10 Years Later," *The Military Engineer* (April–May 1996): 27–28. By permission of The Society of American Military Engineers (SAME).

14. Five excellent references on implementing an FMIS follow. Jeffrey Hamer, "Best Practices in Technology Management," in *Conference Proceedings, World Workplace '95,* (Houston: International Facility Management Association, 1995), pp. 961–972; Peter S. Kimmel, "Critical Ingredients for a Successful CAFM Installation," in *Conference Proceedings, World Workplace '95* (Houston, International Facility Management Association, 1995), pp. 913–925; Eric Teicholz, "The Business Side of Technology," in *Conference Proceedings, World Workplace '94* (Houston: International Facility Management Association, 1994), pp. 99–108; Eric Teicholz, "Cost/Benefit Analysis Justifies CAFM Investment," *Facilities Design and Management* (August 1990); and Eric Teicholz, *Computer-Aided Facility Management* (New York: McGraw-Hill, 1992), which is out of print but available through amazon.com. This classic of the field is worth hunting for.

15. Heidi Schwartz, "Decoding the Acronym Puzzle," *Today's Facility Manager,* June 2008, p. 2.

16. *Benchmarks V, Annual Facility Costs, Research Report #30,* (Houston; IFMA: 2008), p. 44.

33

Problem Solvers
Look at the
Current State and the
Future of Facility
Management

Pulse Points

- *Facility management needs to be treated as a business; facility managers need to have financial skills.*
- *A workable IWMS is possible to manage all FM functions along with associated functions such as security and to connect with organizational financial and management reporting.*
- *Workplace management is changing driven by demographics, technology, and the need to reduce costs.*
- *The facility manager must be involved in security and emergency management.*
- *The emphasis on cost reduction can present opportunities to demonstrate to upper management that we are effective financial managers.*
- *Most facility managers will find it necessary to cope with some aspect of globalization if it is no more than the changing nature of their contract workforce.*
- *Our aging building stock can provide a business opportunity through a well-justified recapitalization plan.*
- *Many, if not most, facility managers need to reassess their organizations. Many FM organizations operate 24/7 and this trend will increase over time.*
- *The facility manager should manage real estate.*

- *The facility manager needs to be at the same organizational level as the managers of human resources and information technology.*
- *The profession needs more consolidation of/cooperation by the various professional and trade organizations.*
- *Facility management needs to be taught to business leaders at our business schools as well as developed more completely through more and better degree programs.*
- *We need to re-emphasize both quality management and customer orientation.*

There has been no lack of introspection by the FM profession concerning either the current state or prognosis of the future for facility management. In fact, we have identified eight major documents examining FM since 2002, with several other minor efforts, and feel sure that we have missed others. In fact, one of the authors has tried to resist the tendency to feel that examining FM's current state and predicting its future was his "Groundhog Day." There is a tendency to say that the more things change (or at least the longer we stay in the profession), the more they stay the same.

Having said that, it is interesting to note which

- Issues were seen as current challenges at the time each study was done,
- What were current best practices,
- What mistakes facility managers seemed to be making, and
- What challenges were likely in the next five to ten years?

We could write another volume if we chose to analyze the data completely but there are interesting insights which are of interest and we share them with you here.

Perennial challenges

Five items stand out as appearing in almost all of the studies. The first is the need of the facility manager to have financial skills and to treat FM as a business. Second, these studies say that we need to cope with organizational technology as the physical implementer and to use FM technology to manage better.

The third challenge is that we feel we have already inadequate budgets yet must constantly reduce costs to make the organization's bottom line look better. The fourth of these challenges has taken on different aspects over the past eight years. The nature of our workspaces is changing driven both by economic factors, demographics, and the realization that work can be performed better in a variety of new and different workspaces. The final challenge is the realization of something that most people probably thought self-evident; that the facility manager, whether he was the officially designated head of security, was involved up to his eyeballs in emergency management and security.

The professional associations have stepped up on the first challenge by providing training in business skills. Other opportunities, not necessarily FM-oriented, present themselves for the facility manager to demonstrate business acumen. Two of these are justifying and presenting a sustainability plan's financials (See Chapter 11) and presenting the financial analysis for a recapitalization plan as part of your master plan. One company, Sightlines, www.sightlines.com realizes the need for this. They will analyze your facilities and calculate a ROPA (Return on Physical Assets) for you from four perspectives which connect finances and operations; asset reinvestment, asset consumption rate, operations effectiveness, and service. We should promote more of this approach. We can build confidence and trust in upper management by speaking to them in the language they understand, the language of business, and using business justifications for our initiatives.

Many of us only see the downside of management's aggressive emphasis on cutting costs. But we must realize that, if we can help achieve our goals while showing that we are on board with cost reduction through well-developed life-cycle costing, we can use this fiscal atmosphere to our advantage. Again, here is where the cost savings of sustainability, for example, can help us. We will not always win on every initiative, even with well-developed financial arguments, but we will no longer be viewed as "simply the guy who keeps the lights on" but as a management professional essential to the organization's successful mission and goals. (We have always been struck by the clearer realization by organizational management in the manufacturing sector of the relationship of facility management to organizational success because the mission-essential connection is more visible. If the power goes down, no widgets get made.) All facility managers need to make that connection to organizational management through business skills in all of the sectors in which we operate.

Technology remains a challenge also. While facility managers have become much more adept at accommodating organizational technology into their buildings than we were in the 90s, we tend to remain at the end of the organizational decision chain to accommodate new technology. Fortunately, most of us have coped with new information and communications technology long enough that we have built extra wiring or cabling and HVAC capacities into our buildings to accommodate most changes. The secret, however, is to work hand-in-hand with the IT manager and his consultants as they develop their plans so that there are no surprises.

Regarding our own technology, a web-based Integrated Workplace Management System is possible to 1) assist in the management of all FM functions, 2) tie your department into the organizational financial and management reporting systems, and 3) link with other technology systems, for example the security system. There is no one best system for everyone, but with the assistance of a good consultant and vendor, an IWMS can be fielded and can assist you in more efficiently and effectively managing your department. Anyone installing technology should be aware of the Work Request and Work Fulfillment (WRWOF) Standard Version 1.0 designed to automate service requests, work order management, and report generation between stakeholders with a shared business process.[1] (Unfortunately and to the detriment of everyone, IWMS standards have been too slow in developing, which means that systems which need to "talk" to one another often cannot. This has been good business for FM IT consultants and vendors, but not good for their customers.)

As two of our panel of experts highlight, however, it is important to train everyone to maximize the full capabilities of each installed IWMS. That can be a problem because it involves "standing down" critical staff and contractors for training while they are needed to repair and service equipment and perform our other daily tasks which never go away. One other commonly reported problem is the resistance of our staff to new equipment, methods, and procedures which can suboptimize the best technology. We have experienced this also and it can become a leadership issue. Initial installation of FM IT systems or switching to an IWMS system needs to be planned and implemented with great care so that 1) the customer does not suffer, 2) we are sure of the way we want to operate post installation and everyone is on board, 3) we do not lose all of our historical data during conversion, 4) we are in synch with the business systems of the organization, 5) we have provided adequately for training and 6) we have enough resources to do this installation properly. The landscape is littered with examples where installing or switching to a new FM IT system has been disastrous.

There are so many possibilities in BIM, Building Information Modeling, particularly in planning, design, operations and maintenance that it definitely is "the next Big Thing" in FM technology. We are encouraged that there is a concerted effort to adopt standards for BIM but early adapters face the same issues as with all new technology, being the training platform and losing the advantage of probable cost reduction as the technology matures.

Tight budgets and management scrutiny of non-core functions will be matters of business (and FM) life in the future. In the private sector, management, particularly in an economic downturn, must control costs. In the public sector, the revolt against more taxation while revenues are down is causing managers there to tighten their belts also. Facility organizations that have been downsized experience degradation in the services they provide, thereby lowering employee morale and crating a general feeling of apathy throughout the organization. Because the budget has been reduced while code and regulatory requirements remain, these organizations often exceed their allocated budgets. Since a major proportion of the facility budget is labor, there is a tendency to then reduce that cost compounding an already bad situation and sending it into a vicious downward spiral that impacts the organization's mission.

Traffic jams, the cost of transportation, and a re-look at functions like marketing have raised the issue of whether our organizations really need all of the space they have in existing facilities. Maybe John Brown's primary "office" should be his car; while Mary Jones will work from her home. Who would have thought that we would be considering how we should outfit a home office and what responsibilities we, as facility managers, have to home office users and how to provide a home base or other distributed work solution for John Brown when he is off the road?

The events of September 11, 2001 and the subsequent anthrax scare have had a profound effect on facility managers and facilities. It is interesting that the codeword, 9/11, needs absolutely no explanation. Since that date, facility managers, whether they are their organization's primary security manager or not, have rekindled their interest and responsibilities in the areas of emergency management and security, duties that they cannot ignore.

As we have stated, this can be a time of opportunity for facility managers with business skills who can show savings through properly documented financials for sustainability efforts and can show the economic advantages of, for example, recapitalization of aged and inefficient systems.

So, we predict with little fear of being wrong, that technology, tight budgets, security, an ever-changing workplace, and business issues will be challenges tomorrow, a year from now, and ten years from now though in probably different forms.

Two other trends permeated the studies but with different complexions in the different reports. There has been a general sense that the business world is changing, most often attributed to globalization. For many of us this has been dramatic as we find ourselves building in China, supporting a call center in Bangladesh, and using a European firm to keep our elevators working. While some of this effect has been buffered by the fact that we can deal with a U.S. surrogate that has international staffing and experience, many facility managers find themselves dealing with geographic, cultural, and business issues that they never anticipated. This can be seized upon as an opportunity because, in many countries, facility management is in its infancy, if known at all. Thus, we can start with a clean slate.

There has been a realization back to the turn of the century that the retirement of the baby boomers is going to have a major effect on facility management. We are seeing it as some of our senior management, supervisors, and talented senior technicians retire. Often there is an inadequate pool to replace these lost skills and even our contractors are having a similar problem. At the same time, the changing demographics in our organizations (accommodating Gen X'ers and Y'ers plus baby boomers who decided not to retire) are calling into question just what our work-spaces should look like, what functions they should fulfill, and where they should be located as remote officing, home officing, hoteling, and other distributed work arrangements become more and more prevalent. This has been exacerbated by the fuel crunch of 2007–2008. Businesses, for instance, are taking less office space which may, in fact, be another trend driven both by businesses shedding personnel, the changing nature of work, the fuel crunch, and the slowdown in the world's economy.[2] The trends and challenges are often intertwined.

Current Mistakes

We asked our panel of experts to augment our thoughts about current mistakes being made by the profession. Surprisingly, the response was tepid, less than we expected and many tended to be offshoots of one of the perennial challenges mentioned above so we will not repeat them here. Not wanting to look a gift horse in the mouth, we took this as a good sign but we still present (not in any particular order) a number of issues that we expect the profession and professionals need to correct.

Without a doubt, we feel that the biggest mistake facility managers make is complacency or, in some cases, stoically "playing the hand (a bad one) they have been dealt." We have long puzzled why, for instance, facility managers made no attempt to correct a budget format which yielded no usable management information or lived with an organizational structure which actually worked against effective and efficient management. Facility managers must realize that there are undoubtedly better organizational structures, policies, procedures, contracts, budget formats, etc. if they will just attempt to find best practices which we promote in this book and, in the case of IFMA, are regularly presented in a seminar. Innovation and improvement are a primary characteristic of good leaders and managers.

Several experts felt that we are still not good listeners. In one case, we are not listening to our customers and providing them with the services and service levels they need. This is the result of our failure to continually get fresh feedback, particularly in face-to-face contact with our organizational colleagues. Another aspect of this issue is that, even if all the feedback is good, we cannot be complacent. We need to get our head out of the sand and realize that, in the business world, everything is expressed in money as we have mentioned above. The key word here is that you can never, ever be complacent.

Two other panelists feel that we fail to keep up to date in our professional development and *bona fides*. We need to stay educated and should build education and training into the work schedule of our department so that we are a knowledge organization. This is a challenge too to the professional organizations and certificate and degree granting organizations to provide education, training, and certification methods that keep the profession up to date.

Overcapitalization, or at the least failure to take care of infrastructure we have already built, is another problem as evidenced by the collapse of the I-35 bridge in Minnesota. Several of us have concerns that we are building ourselves into a huge hole by continuing to construct facilities while ignoring the backlog of maintenance and repair on the current inventory. It is similar to the spiral of a tornado . . . winds at the top are a little less than the winds at the bottom. High winds at the bottom are destructive. As our facilities and infrastructure age, the "winds of the backlog of maintenance" grow exponentially, to the point that it will be cost prohibitive to correct and it may take decades to do so. Two factors may help here. One, the National Research Council has gone on record as saying that we should be investing 2–4 percent of the replacement value of our facilities into maintenance and repair annually[3] and this has been validated by one of your authors. This needs to be brought to the attention of management and is particularly important in organizations where most facilities are owned. Second, this issue can be raised with a discussion of recapitalization and revitalization discussed above. The important issue is to do so in business terms and with financial analyses as discussed earlier.

Several of our experts felt that facility managers and the profession are making mistakes because we tend to hunker down in our bunkers. Specifically, we do not get out of our comfort zone and talk to our organizational colleagues and others in the business world so that we can bring their perspectives into facility management. IFMA has been a trendsetter in trying to correct this mistake by always having business-oriented speakers at World Workplace, its international conference. One expert pointed out that our tendency to be introspective serves us ill with new staff, particularly young ones, and customers with new ideas and expectations.

The experts felt we were continuing to make mistakes by not having formalized succession planning and, as we mentioned earlier, not devoting enough attention to training. Here too are areas that we can treat as problems but, if we work at solving them, they pull us out of our comfort zone and cause us to have contact with folks who will help us in our organizational management also.

One final mistake that we find endemic, and which has been mentioned earlier, is the failure of facility managers to communicate effectively orally and in writing. There really is no excuse for this because if you cannot communicate effectively within your organization, you will not be heard, much less listened to.

In most of these mistakes, we see a silver lining because the solution to many require us to sell our good ideas and communicate effectively with colleagues and upper management of our organizations. We will not always be successful but being a player alone will elevate the importance of facility management and the status of the facility manager.

Trends for the Future

Exhibit 33-1 lists the trends discovered in the latest IFMA survey of a primarily U.S. group of FM practitioners to include contractors:

Exhibit 33-1. Facility Management Trends Forecast, 2007

- Linking facility management to strategy
- Emergency preparedness
- Change management
- Sustainability
- Emerging technology
- Globalization
- Broadening diversity in the workforce
- Aging buildings

Facility Management Forecast 2007 (Houston, TX: IFMA; 2007).

We concur with this list, in general, and have addressed it in this book and in this chapter. However, as we close we offer, one last time, the improvements that we feel are needed in 1) the profession and 2) facility manager's practice.

Needed Improvements in Facility Management as a Profession

We are gratified to see improvements that the profession has made since the Second Edition. Facility management is now the commonly-accepted term for those functions spelled out in Chapter 1 and it is growing in acceptance internationally. Certifications, particularly the Certified Facility Manager designation, are being sought by facility managers, are being recognized by FMs and their employers and are paying off in terms of better salaries and better job opportunities.

A second improvement, in FM technology, seems to be on the cusp of a major information management improvement for facility managers. An Integrated Workplace Management System (IWMS) capable of managing all FM functions, featuring web-based WRC functions, and adaptable to the organization's financial and reporting systems seems within reach if properly managed.

Research remains high on the priority list for improvement, with APPAs among the best as far as content and IFMAs perhaps best in defining the profession and where it is going. There has been increased cooperation on research, in appearances at each other's conferences, and in talk among the professional associations. In fact, IFMA, and the Society of American Military Engineers whose members have extensive interest in the construction and management of huge facilities, have gone so far as to have representation on each other's Boards of Directors.

Organization, particularly management of real estate- However, more needs to be done. Even given the fact that different organizations have different needs, there is not enough agreement on how facility departments should be organized. This book is, to our knowledge, the one book that really addresses this important issue. This is particularly true concerning how real estate will be handled. The management of real estate is a FM function and, if there is a separate Vice President of Real Estate, facility management will be suboptimized. We hold to our feeling that the facility manager in a large organization needs to be not more than two levels removed from the CEO and that he should be at the same organizational level as the managers of Human Resources and Information Technology. This is often not the case.

*Professional and trade organizations-*We reluctantly concede that a rational case can be made for the existence of BOMA (Building Owners and Managers Association) and one organization representing facility management by owners but that should represent the field of professional organizations. There is a need for both professional and trade associations which provide facility managers the ability to network with those providing services to our profession. We would hope, though we understand all of the challenges involved, that the profession would move in the direction of more co-operation and slowly consolidate the number of professional and trade organizations representing the workplace environment. Right now we speak with too many voices in the marketplace and there is not a unified message.

*FM degree programs-*It has been somewhat exasperating over the years to watch degree-granting programs come and go. It reflects the difficulty of "selling," on campus and to prospective students, the relatively new profession of facility management which requires multi-disciplinary faculty co-operation, not always popular on all campuses. APPA could be a major force here and, with the cooperation of IFMA and its local chapters, we can develop and teach the degree-level facility management curriculum that our young professionals deserve and expect.

*FM in the business schools-*Your authors all have been involved in the training and education of facility managers and we see progress being made in these areas though the number of long-standing degree and certificate programs continues to vary from year to year. However, facility management needs to be taught to budding CEOs, COOs, and CFOs in business schools before facility management will ever assume its rightful import in the business community. This can only be done by a coordinated push from the professional organizations, probably in the form of developing two or three high level courses on the business aspects of facilities and why they are necessary for successful organizations and presenting them to the business schools.

Public relations-There needs to be a broad-based improvement in the public understanding of facility management. Several target constituencies are vital. We have mentioned the business schools above. Another target should be the business press. There are enough exciting and controversial FM topics to have one covered in each of the major business journals, the major metropolitan business newspapers, and *The Wall Street Journal* once a quarter. Everyone agrees that this is needed, yet there is no organized effort by the professional associations to see that this happens. Facility managers should be anxious to tell their story, locally and nationally, and need to be involved in a variety of organizations to do so. Don't be afraid to promote yourself regionally, nationally, or even internationally. Finally, we should be targeting the management gurus with information on trends and issues in facility management so that the Center for Creative Leadership, for example, has a case study that emphasizes successful facility management.

Research-Facility management is applied science but still has room for improvement in its research. Due to its nature, the research that is most helpful is research into best practices. What is the best way to organize facility management in the manufacturing sector? What is the proper ratio of staff to contractors for effectiveness and efficiency? What lessons can be learned in implementation of an IWMS? What lessons are to be learned from installing wireless information systems? What sustainability initiatives have the highest payoff in older facilities? What are the key technical and cultural issues to be dealt with in establishing facility management in China? How cost effective are best value contracts? It is helpful to take a look at ourselves and our profession and how it is trending every five years or so, but the majority of our research effort should be aimed at improving how we practice.

Strides have been made in improving the profession, spearheaded by the professional associations, but we hope that the next ten years will find this improvement accelerating. In many ways, there must be continued improvement in the profession so that improvement in the practice of facility management can advance.

Needed Improvement in the Practice of Facility Management

Outsourcing has become so universal that the only concerns are that facility managers use the most advanced contracting methods and truly optimize our outsource contractor. Both sustainability and security/emergency management have such an organizational tailwind that, if managed properly, they will be at the forefront of all facility managers' practices. Of the remainder of the practices needing improvement in the Second Edition, we have already mentioned the need to promote our department as a business function: to realize that, particularly in officing, we are moving toward new work methods which must be accommodated; to understand that we need to get much, much more concerned about how we align facility management with organizational goals and structure; to re-examine how our departments are organized; and finally to ensure that facility management is on the same level as HR and IT on the organization chart.

*Quality management and customer orientation-*Unfortunately, in an effort to meet organizational business goals there is a tendency to forget our customers and to de-emphasize quality management. This easily is compounded unless we are on absolutely the same wavelength as our outsource contractor. Their local management must understand the importance of our customers and that they will be judged in customer service. They must buy into customer service goals and ensure that they are met. *Your department is being rated on their performance.* Many things change over time; customer service does not!

*Seek a differentiator-*In order to be recognized and to have credibility within the organization, the facility manager needs to stand out. He has unique skills and is positioned to do just that. Perhaps the difference-maker is a well-developed and justified sustainability plan. Perhaps the facility manager comes forward with an emergency management plan. Volunteering for additional responsibilities offers little risk in things that the facility manager would be a major contributor to anyway, such as emergency management. The upside is that the facility manager will be noted as both a business manager and a team player, both valued roles.

*Public relations-*No one can represent his department better than the facility manager. He owes it to his department to promote it and to represent it well. Unfortunately, most of us, by education and personality type, would rather retreat to our offices and ensure that our departments run well. Because facility management is not viewed as a core competency, the facility department starts out at a disadvantage within the organization. The facility manager must work hard to level the playing field. We recommend a simple annual public relations plan for the department that outlines one or two specific actions to promote the department to all of its constituencies: company employees, management, visitors, department employees, contractors, and others. Two specific examples that have proven track records are a FM Annual Report and a simple monthly or quarterly newsletter. The annual report summarizes everything the department has accomplished and funded throughout the year. One form of the newsletter is written for FM employees but also sent to targeted organization leaders. This also can be accomplished on the web and gets information out to the right target audiences but in a subtle way. Both of these examples are inexpensive but can generate large public relations dividends. At the same time, the facility manager needs to be active in professional activities at the local level and regionally and nationally, if possible.

The future

We tend to be optimistic so we believe that both the profession and practice of facility management will progress as much over the next ten years as it has in the past ten. Some are suggesting that facility management will disappear in one of two ways:

- The federal government in the U.S. is promoting the term "asset management" which they feel is more descriptive but does not really amount to any diminution of duties for the facility manager even under his new name.
- Some, primarily in the private sector, feel that facility management will be subsumed into a group of functions (human resources, information technology, etc.) which are not core to the organization and may, in fact, be contracted out individually or in a single, large package.

We doubt that either of these will occur because we know how hard it has been to change business history and traditions to get facility management established over the past twenty-five years. However, if either or both does occur, we would change little in this book. The bottom line is that we are the stewards of one of the most valued assets of the organization, its facilities. It is important that we keep reminding current management of the fact that we are as important to mission accomplishment as human resources and information technology. We have not done a good job of doing that and it shows.

We do believe that the trend toward outsourcing will continue and so it is important that the facility manager be a nimble and knowledgeable procurer of facility services. As more and more services are contracted, the size of these contracts will increase so it is important that facility managers are scrupulously honest in their contracting role. Equally important is that they use the right method to get the right contractor and then demand performance to their expectations while allowing the contractor to excel.

Sustainability will become an integral part of our operations both because of the cost reduction implications and because it is desired by our employees and customers. We anticipate more prescriptive regulations in this area but the real progress will be where it just makes good common sense to be sustainable.

Emergency planning should become a second nature for us if for no other reason than to ensure continuity in either a man-made or natural disaster. Whether we are the primary manager or not, we must be actively involved in emergency planning/implementation and in security. Web-based software exists which allows us to tie together, among other functions, the WRC of facilities, security operations, and our customers and management. Since we become accustomed to using this system in our daily business, it is not a new experience when needed in an emergency situation.

In order to reduce costs, some of our organizations are operating extended hours to maximize the use of the existing facilities rather than building or leasing new ones. In some cases, that could actually mean 24/7 operations in the facilities. At the same time, some of our company's major functions may have been outsourced to a provider that is a dozen time zones away and this may require extended hours in portions of the home operation for continuity. This can reduce the time that these facilities are available for operations and maintenance which may, in fact, require you to adjust your entire operations and maintenance schedules to accommodate your customers.

In closing, we paraphrase a set of skills for facility managers spelled out in the Second Edition but which we feel will carry us just as well into the future:

- Be a change agent.
- Be a decision maker.
- Be a people leader.
- Be an entrepreneur.
- Set and follow through on priorities.
- Develop and maintain a network.
- Be visible, be open to criticism, and manage by walking around.
- Be the type of person whom other people trust.
- Be flexible.[4]

Notes

1. *OSCRE's Work Request & Work Order Fulfillment Standard is Published,"* (Washington, DC: OSCRE Americas; July 2008), p. 1.
2. "Businesses Take Less Office Space Nationwide," *The Wall Street Journal,* July 3, 2008, p. A-2.
3. *Committing to the Cost of Ownership,* (Washington, DC: National Research Council; 1990), p. ix.
4. Anthony G. Zulkeski, "The FM as Change Agent," *Facilities Design and Management,* 15th Anniversary Special Advertising Section, 1997, p. 64.

APPENDIX

A

The Facility Manager's Tool Kit of References

The practice of facility management is an extremely complex one and requires knowledge in a broad range of disciplines. No one can be an expert in all areas and even experienced authors frequently head for the computer, a book, or a periodical for information for our practices and for teaching and writing. FM tool kit contents are highly personalized and contain those references that we have personally used or are promoted by one of the professional organizations; you probably have your own. We hope our suggestions are of value. Except for the first section below, we have included only books that have a direct connection with facility management since most have their own favorite authors and books on management, communications, etc.

Appendix B contains some of the Web sites and Internet addresses that we use frequently; Appendix C lists education programs. All of the professional organizations produce useful material, but of special mention is the annual *BOMA Experience Report* for comparator data, particularly for the office environment.

Special note. We want to make special reference to four publications from the Board of Infrastructure and the Constructed Environment, National Resource Council because they address the very essence of this book, the importance of and undercapitalization of facilities and facility management. *Get these books and share their recommendations with your management!* While their study model is the federal government, their recommendations are generally applicable to owned facilities of any kind, anywhere in the world.

- *Committing to the Cost of Ownership; Maintenance and Repair of Public Buildings,* 1990.
- *Pay Now or Pay Later: Controlling Cost of Ownership from Design Throughout the Service Life of Public Buildings,* 1991.
- *Investments in Federal Facilities; Asset Management Strategies for the 21st Century* 2004.
- *Core Competencies for Federal Facilities Asset Management through 2020,* 2008.

The importance of good facility management and good facility managers has been well documented. Now, we need to get on with the implementation!

Books

General References

A college or publisher's style manual
A college English text
A college basic statistics text
A college text on management theory and behavior
A college text on human resources management

General Facility Management

Facility Management, Second Edition, by Edmond P. Rondeau, Robert Kevin Brown, and Paul Lapides
Facility Design and Management Handbook, Eric Teicholz, editor
Facilities Management; a Manual for Plant Administrators, Third Edition, APPA edited
Facilities Management, by Frank Booty

Building Commissioning

The Building Commissioning Handbook, Second Edition, by John Heinz and Rick Casault

Disaster and Recovery Planning

Disaster and Recovery Planning; a Guide for Facility Managers, by Joseph F. Gustin
Disaster Planning and Recovery; a Guide for Facility Professionals, by Alan M. Levitt
Before Disaster Strikes; Developing an Emergency Procedures Manual (Third Edition), published by IREM

Emergency Planning

Facility Manager's Emergency Preparedness Handbook, by Bernard T. Lewis and Richard Payant

Environmental Safety

Environmental and Workplace Safety, by James T. O'Reilly, Phillip Hagen, and Peter de la Cruz

Facility Audit

The Facilities Audit and The Facilities Audit Workbook, by Harvey Kaiser

Facility Benchmarking

Benchmarking and Organizational Change, by Mohamad H. Qayoumi

Facility Management Finance

The Facility Manager's Guide to Finance and Budgeting, by David Cotts and Edmond P. Rondeau
Buildings . . . The Gifts That Keep on Taking, by Rodney Rose
Basics of Budgeting, by Terry Dickey

Facility Management Human Resource Management

Workplace Strategies and Facilities Management, by Rick Best, Gerard de Valence, and Craig Langston

Facility Management Leadership

Perspectives on Leadership in Facilities Management, Charles W. Jenkins, editor

Facility Management Organizations

Designing Facility Management Organizations by IFMA
Organization Development for Facility Managers, by Stormy Friday

Facility Management Planning and Design

Innovations in Office Design, by Diane Stegmeier

Facility Management Procurement

Best Value Procurement, by Dr. Dean Kashiwagi

Facility Management Quality and Customer Service

Quality Facility Management: A Marketing and Customer Service Approach, by Stormy Friday and David Cotts
Beyond Customer Service, by Richard F. Gerson

Facility Management Technology

Facility Management Technology, by Eric Teichholz and Takehiko Ikeda

Operations and Maintenance

Information and Communications Management

The Irwin Handbook of Telecommunications Management, by James Henry Green
Communications Systems Handbook, Sixth Edition, Anura Guruge and Lisa Gaetta, editors

Facilities Inspection Field Manual, by Bernard Lewis and Richard Payant
Facility Manager's Maintenance Handbook, by Bernard T. Lewis and Richard Payant

Project Management

The AMA Handbook of Project Management, by Paul C. Dinsmore and Jeannette Cabanis-Brewin

Real Estate and Lease Management

Managing Corporate Real Estate, by Kevin Brown, Alvin Arnold, Paul Lapides, and Edmond P. Rondeau

Security

Spotlight on Security for Real Estate Managers, by Lawrence J. Fennelly

Sustainability

Sustainable Federal Facilities, by Federal Facilities Council

Work Reception Center

Call Center Success, by Lloyd C. Finch

Proceedings

Annual Proceedings of the Annual Meeting, APPA
Annual Proceedings of World Workplace, IFMA

Magazines

Professional Journals

Facilities Engineering Journal, AFE
Facilities Manager, APPA
FMJ, IFMA
International Journal of Facility Management (new online journal that goes online in fall 2009)
Journal of Property Management, IREM
Military Engineer, SAME

Trade Publications

Building Operating Management
Buildings
Canadian Facility Management & Design
Contingency Planning & Management
Disaster Recovery Journal
Engineering News Record
McMorrow Report
Security
TFM

Academic (peer-reviewed) Journals

Behavior and Environment, published by Sage Publications
Building and Environment, published by Elsevier, Ltd.

Building Research and Information, published by Routledge Press
Facilities, published by Emerald Group Publishing
Maintenance Management, published by Aspen Publishers
Property Management, published by Emerald Group Publishing
Purchasing, published by Reed Elsevier, Ltd.
The Journal of Corporate Real Estate, published by Emerald Group Publishing
The Journal of Facilities Management, published by Emerald Group Publishing
The Journal of Green Building, published by College Publishing

APPENDIX

Web Sites and Internet Addresses

The Internet is an unbelievable aid when researching solutions for a problem and will only continue to grow and expand in the future. In fact, this appendix could have become so voluminous that we feared it would become unusable. The sites listed are those of specific value to facility managers plus some that we thought you might not immediately think of. Because security, emergency management, and sustainability are major new themes in this edition, we have tended to emphasize sites in those topic areas.

(Precede Internet addresses with www. unless otherwise indicated.)

Cost Data

Building Owners and Managers Association *Experience Report*—boma.org
R.S. Means—rsmeans.com
Whitestone Research—whitestoneresearch.com

Emergency Preparedness and Recovery

American Red Cross—redcross.org
American Society for Microbiology (bioterrorism)—
    asmusa.org/pcsrc/bioprep.htm
American Society for Public Administiation—aspanet.org
Association of Contingency Planners—acp-international.com
Business Continuity Institute—thebci.org
Centers for Disease Control—bt.cdc.gov
Center for Earthquake Research and Information—ceri.memphis.edu

Central Earthquake Consortium—cusec.org
Contingency Planning and Management Group—contingencyplanning.com
Cooperative Extension Disaster Resources—ag.uiuc.edu/hazards
Department of Homeland Security—ready.gov
Disaster Recovery Institute, International—dr.org
Disaster Report Archive—eqe.com/publications
Disaster Plan—disasterplan.com
Emergency Email network—emergencyemailnetwork.com
Emergency Preparedness Canada—epc-pcc.gc.ca
Federal Emergency Management Agency—fema.gov
Floodplain Management Resource Center—colorado.edu/hazards
HazardNet—oshweb.com/owd/owd01.nsf/s/58-01
Hazard Reduction and Recovery Center—hrrc.tamu.edu
Homeland 1—homeland1.com
International City/County Management Association—icma.org
International Drought Information Center—enso.unl.edu/ndmc
Multihazard Mitigation Council, National Institute of Building Science—
     nibs.org/MMC/mmchome.html
National Association of Counties—naco.org
National Domestic Preparedness Office—ndpo.gov
National Emergency Management Association—nemaweb.org
National Institute for Urban Search and Rescue—niusr.org
National Weather Service—nws.noaa.gov
Protection Knowledge Concepts—rjagroup.com
Small Business Administration Disaster Assistance—
     sba.gov/DISASTER/Survive-survive.com
Terrorism Research Center—terrorism.com
The Tornado Project—tornadoproject.com

Energy Conservation and Efficiency

American Council for Energy-Efficient Economy—aceee.org
Building Owners and Managers Association—boma.org/AboutBOMA/BEEP
National Sustainable Energy Association—nesea.org
U.S. Department of Energy—eere.energy.gov
World Energy Efficiency Association—weea.org
Center for Renewable Energy and Sustainable Technology—
     thinkenergy.com/assn/rs194877.html
Yahoo reference site—
     http://dl.dir.ac2.yahoo.com/Science/Energy/Conservation_and_Efficiency

Environmental Management

Environmental Information Association—eia-usa.org

Environmental Protection Agency—epa.gov

National Center of Excellence for Environmental Management—nceem.org

Facility Management Events Information

American Public Works Association—apwa.org

Association for Facilities Engineering—afe.org

Building Owners and Managers Association—boma.org

Facilities Network—facilitiesnet.com

FMLink—fmlink.com

International Facility Management Association—ifma.org

McMorrow Report—mcmorrowreport.com

National Facilities Management & Technology Conference—nfmt.com

TFM—todaysfacilitymanager.com

Tradeline—tradelineinc.com

Job Mart

Association for Facilities Engineering—afe.org

APPA—appa.org

American Public Works Association—apwa.org

Career Builder—careerbuilder.com

CoreNet Global—corenetglobal.com

FMLink—fmlink.com

International Facility Management Association—ifma.org

Monster—jobsearch.monster.com/Facilities-Manager/get-jobs-5.aspx

MySpace—jobs.myspace.com/ams-jobs/list/q-Facilities-Manager

Newsgroups and Forums

FMLink—fmlink.com

Forum Events—foramevents.co.uk

Outsourcing

APPA—appa.org

International Association of Outsourcing Professionals—
    outsourcingprofessionals.org

International Facility Management Association—ifma.org

Outsourcing Institute—outsourcing.com

Performance Improvement and Benchmarking—fmbenchmarking.com

Professional Associations

American Institute of Architects—aia.org

American National Standards Institute—ansi.org

American Planning Association—planning.org

American Public Works Association—apwa.org

American Society of Civil Engineers—asce.org

American Society of Heating, Refrigerating and Air-Conditioning Engineers—
ashrae.org

American Society of Interior Designers—asid.org

American Society of Mechanical Engineers—asme.org

American Society for Quality—asqc.org

APPA, the Association of Higher Education Facilities Officer—appa.org

Association of Energy Engineers—aeecenter.org

Association for Facilities Engineering—afe.org

British Institute of Facilities Management—bifm.org.uk

Building Owners and Managers Association—boma.org

Building Owners and Managers Institute—bomi-edu.org

Construction Specification Institute—csinet.org

CoreNet Global—corenetglobal.org

European Facility Management Network—eurofm.org

Facility Management Association of Australia—fma.com.au

Global Facility Management Association—globalfm.org

Institute of Electrical and Electronic Engineers, Inc.—ieee.org

Institute of Real Estate Management—irem.org

International Association of Assembly Managers—iaam.org

International Association of Emergency Managers—iaem.org

International Association of Professional Security Consultants, Inc.—iapsc.org

International Facility Management Association—ifma.org

International Interior Design Association—iida.org

International Society of Facilities Executives—isfe.org

National Association of College and University Business Officers—nacubo.org

National Fire Protection Association—nfpa.org

Project Management Institute—pmi.org

Society of American Military Engineers—same.org

Professional Journals

Note: Professional journals can normally be accessed at their professional
organization' web site and generally are a benefit of membership only.

Facilities Engineering Journal—afe.org
Facilities Manager—appa.org
FMJ—ifma.org
Homeland Defense Journal—homelanddefensejournal.com
Journal of Homeland Security and Emergency Management—bepress.com/jhsem/
Journal of Property Management—irem.org
Maintenance Technology—mt-online.com
The Military Engineer—same.org

Regulatory Information

Note: All states will have regulatory agencies in areas affecting facility
    management under the address of state.gov.

Environmental Protection Agency—epa.gov
Hazardous waste-radwaste.org—epa.gov/osw/hazwaste.org
National Institute for Occupational Safety and Health—cdc.gov/NIOSH
Occupational Safety and Health Agency—osha.gov
U.S. Army Corps of Engineers—usace.army.mil
U.S. General Services Administration—gsa.gov

Reliability Information for Operations and Maintenance

Maintenance and Reliability Center—engr.utk.edu/mrc
NASA Reliability-Centered Maintenance—http://nodis3.gsfc.nasa.gov/
    displayDir.cfm?Internal_ID=N_PR_8831_002D_&page_name
National Information Center for Reliability Engineering—enre.umd.edu
Quality and Reliability Engineering Center—rutgers.edu/~ie/qre
Reliability Analysis Center—src.alionscience.com
Society of Reliability Engineers—sre.org

Research and General Information

American Management Association—amanet.org
APPA—appa.org
American Planning Association—planning.org
American Productivity and Quality Center (now called APQC)—apqc.org
American Public Works Association—apwa.org
American Society for Testing and Materials—astm.org
American Society of Heating, Refrigeration and Air-Conditioning Engineers—
    ashrae.org
American Society for Quality—asq.org

Army Environmental Center—aec.army.mil/usaec

Buildings.com—buildings.com

Building and Fire Research Laboratory—bfrl.nist.gov

Center for Building Performance and Diagnostics—arc.cmu.edu/cbpd

Center for Job Order Contracting Excellence—eas.asu.edu.joc

Construction Business Review—
    constructionchannel.net/channel/construction/publication

CRS Center (Research in design and construction)—crscenter.tamu.edu

Construction Engineering Research Laboratory—cecer.army.mil

Facility Performance Group, Inc.—
    deskspaceanyplace.com/facility-performance-group.html

Federal Facilities Council—nas.edu/ffc

International Centre for Facilities—icf-cebe.com

International Customer Management Institute—icmi.com

International Council for Building Research Studies and Documentation—
    bcn.ufl/cib.html

International Facility Management Association—ifma.org

Maintenance Solutions—facilitiesnet.com/MS

National Fire Protection Association—nfpa.org

U.S. Air Force Civil Engineer Support Agency—afcesa.af.mil

U.S. Navy Facilities Engineering Command—navfac.navy.mil

Security

American Society for Industrial Security—asisonline.org

Building Security Council—buildingsecuritycouncil.org

The National Security Institute—nsi.org

Canadian Association of Chiefs of Police—cacp.org

International Association of Chiefs of Police—theiacp.org

Standardization Associations

American National Standards Institute—ansi.org

American Society for Testing and Materials—astm.org

American Society of Heating, Refrigerating, and Air Conditioning Engineers—
    ashrae.org

Business and Institutional Furniture Manufacturers Association—bifma.org

Construction Specifications Institute—csinet.org

Institute of Electrical and Electronic Engineers, Inc.—ieee.org

International Organization for Standardization—iso.org

National Fire Protection Association—nfpa.org

Open Standards Consortium for Real Estate—oscre.org

Sustainability

Alliance for Sustainable Built Environments—greenerfacilities.org

Association for Advancement of Sustainability in Higher Education—AASHE.org

Building Research Environment's Environmental Assessment Method—bre.co.uk

Construction Materials Recycling Association—cdrecycling.org

Environmental Design Research Association—edra.org

Environmental Energy Technologies Division—eetd.lbl.gov

Global Green USA—globalgreen.org/gbrc/

Green Building Initiative—thegbi.org

Green Globes—greenglobes.com

Healthy Building Network—healthybuilding.net

International Initiative for Sustainable Built Environment—IISBE.org

> *(This site also includes the SB Tool for downloading to assess the sustainability of your buildings.)*

Sustainable Buildings Industry Council—sbicouncil.org

Sustainable Design Update Blog—sustainabledesign.com

Sustainable Tracking and Rating System—STARS.org

The Inspired Economist—inspiredeconomist.com

U.S. Green Building Council—usgbc.org

Whole Building Design Guide—wbdg.org

Wiser Earth Coalition—wiserearth.org

World Green Building Council—worldgbc.org

> *(Country-specific green sites are now available in many countries as well as some U.S. States. A web search will provide the latest sites for each country, as developing guidelines are published and updated on a frequent basis.)*

Trade Associations

Association of Energy Services Professionals—aesp.org

Business and Institutional Furniture Manufacturers Association—bifma.com

Business Products Industry Association—bpia.org

Carpet and Rug Institute—carpet-rug.com

International Foundation for Protection Officers—ifpo.com

Mechanical Contractors Association of America—mcaa.org

Trade Journals

Green Building Press—newbuilder.co.uk
Green Building Product Dealer—gbproductnews.com
GreenSource—greensource.construction.com
TFM—todaysfacilitymanager.com

Training

American Public Works Association—apwa.org
American Society of Civil Engineers—asce.org
APPA—appa.org
Association for Facilities Engineering—afe.org
BOMI Institute—bomi-edu.org
Construction Specification Institute—csinet.org
FEMA National Emergency Training Center—fema.gov/emi
International Facility Management Association—ifma.org
Project Management Institute—pmi.org
U.S. Green Building Council/LEED—usgbc.gov

C

Facility Management Education Programs

In Appendix C, we list many organizations that provide facility management training. Here we emphasize programs that provide in-depth education for facility managers. Many of these programs are degree granting.

In 1980, there was one educational program in facility management—the B.S. and M.S. program at Cornell University. Professor Bill Sims, Ph.D., CFM, IFMA Fellow, deserves special recognition not only for helping found this program but for nurturing it for over twenty years. Many programs have come (and some have gone) during this period, but Cornell has continued to produce graduates who are highly sought within the profession.

Now colleges around the world are offering a variety of educational programs. So many colleges and universities are offering such a variety of courses that it is hard to track them—or to even find them all. We thank IFMA for its assistance in compiling the following list. The first thirteen colleges are IFMA Foundation Accredited Programs; they have first-professional degree programs specifically in facility management and have submitted a self-study application that was reviewed and approved by a committee of peers.

Unless otherwise noted, the programs are located in the United States. Each entry lists a contact person at the institution. All phone numbers listed are those used when calling from the United States.

This Accreditation is now managed by the IFMA Foundation and the contact is the Director of Academic Affairs at www.ifmafoundation.org

IFMA Foundation Accredited Programs

North America

Brigham Young University, Provo, Utah offers a B.S. degree in Facilities Management with a Business Management Minor, http://www.byu.edu/webapp/home/index.jsp, Contact: Dr. Jeffrey Campbell, Chair, Facilities Management, (801) 422-8758, jcambell@byu.edu

Conestoga College Institute of Technology and Advanced Learning, Kitchener, Ontario, Canada offers a Bachelors degree in Project and Facility Management. http://www.conestogac.on.ca. Contact James Bechard at +1.519.748.5220 x2778, 299 Doon Valley Drive, Kitchener, Ontario, N2G 4M4, Canada. jbechard@conestogac.on.ca.

Cornell University, Ithaca, New York offers a B.S. and M.S. degree in Facility Management, http://www.cornell.edu/, Contact: Ying Hua, Assistant Professor, (607) 255-1950, yh294@cornell.edu.

Ferris State University, Big Rapids, Michigan offers a Bachelor of Science degree program in Facilities Management, http://www.ferris.edu/homepage.htm, Contact: Joe Samson, CFM, (231) 591-2517, samsonj@ferris.edu.

Georgia Institute of Technology (Georgia Tech), Atlanta, Georgia, offers a Master of Science in Building Construction and Integrated Facility Management, http://www.gatech.edu/, Contact: Kathy Roper, CFM, CFMJ, IFMA Fellow, MCR, LEED AP, Associate Professor at (404)385-4139, kathy.roper@coa.gatech.edu

Pratt Institute, Manhattan, New York, New York offers a Master of Science Degree in Facilities Management, http://www.pratt.edu, Contact: Professor Harriet Markis, PE, Chair, at (212)647-7524, hmarkis@pratt.edu.

Wentworth Institute of Technology, Boston, Massachusetts, offers a B.S. in Facilities Planning & Management, http://www.wit.edu/index.php, Contact: Suzanne Kennedy, CFM, CFMJ, Department Head, Associate Professor at (617)989-4050, kennedys@wit.edu.

Europe

FHS, KufsteinTirol, Austria offers a Magister (FH) for Facility Management., http://www.fh-kufstein.ac.at/wi/jluethi/research_e.html, Contact: Ing. Mag. (FH) Thomas Madritsch, FHS Kufstein BildungsGmbH, +43 5372 71819, Thomas.madritsch@fh-kufstein.ac.at

Hanze University, Groningen, The Netherlands offers a Bachelor degree program in Facilities Management http://www.hanze.nl/home/International, Contact: Jaap Wijnja, +31 5059 52605, j.g.wijnja@pl.hanze.nl

Leeds Metropolitan University, Leeds, UK offers a web-based distance learning MSC in Facilities Management, http://www.lmu.ac.uk/, Contact: Chris Garbett MSc, BSc(Hons), FRICS, FHEA, +46 113 283 2600, C.Garbett@leedsmet.ac.uk.

NHTV Breda University of Applied Science offers a degree in Facility Management. http://www.nhtv.nl/default.aspx2?themaset=c910a88f-0245-4d9e-b847-4dd2ebc0e2a7 Contact: Rene J.F.M. Hermans, + 31 7653 02780, hermans.r@nhtv.nl.

Saxion Universities of Applied Sciences, Deventer, The Netherlands offers a Bachelors degree in Facility Management. http://www.saxion.nl. Contact: Dr. Brenda Groen, at +31.57.060.3153, Handelskade 75, Deventer, Postbus 51, 7400 AM Deventer, The Netherlands. b.h.groen@saxion.nl.

Asia

The Hong Kong Polytechnic University, Hung Hom, Kowloon, Hong Kong offers a Graduate Program in Facility Management. http://www.polyu.edu.hk/epa/polyu/main/main_e.php Contact: Dr Danny Shiem-Shin Then, (852) 2766 4558, bessthen@polyu.edu.hk

IFMA formerly recognized certificate programs in facility management. However, this process is in transition. These certificate programs are:

George Mason University, Fairfax, Virginia, offers the Professional Certificate in Facility Management. Contact: Kirt Miller, Acting Program Manager, Facility Management Program or Carol Stockman at (703) 993-8335, www.ocpe.gmu.edu.

Portobello School, Dublin, Ireland, Offers the Facilities Management Professional certificate. Contact: Rebekah Lyons, +01 872-1277, rlyonsl@ireland.com.

University of California, Berkeley Extension, Berkeley, California, offers the Certificate in Facilities. Contact: Ann Godfrey, Facilities Management Program Director, (415) 284-1050, Agodfrey@unex.berkeley.edu.

University of California, Irvine, Irvine, California, offers the Facilities Management Certificate. Contact: Rogelio C. Rodriguez, Director of Engineering and Science Programs at (949) 824-5380, rcrodrig@uci.edu

University of California Riverside, Extension, Riverside, California, offers the Certificate in Facilities Management Contact: Kathy Craig at (951)827-1600, or email kcraig@ucx.ucr.edu

University of Washington, Seattle, Washington, offers two online certificate programs, Certificate Program in Facility Management: Principles and Certificate Program in Facility Management: Practices. Contact: Trisha Dvorak, PhD, (202) 685-6443, Tdvorak@extn.Washington.edu

Other Degree Programs

Arizona State University, Tempe, Arizona, offers an MS in design with a facility management concentration. Contact: Bob Wolf or Lorri Cutler, (602) 965-8685

Birmingham City University, Birmingham, UK, offers MSc in Facilities Management. Contact: Dr. Ghasson Shabha, ghasson,shabha@uce.ac.uk

Canadian School of Management, Toronto, Ontario, Canada, offers a certificate program, diploma, and fellow in facility management, Contact: Yvonne Bogorya, (416) 327-0309

College of Dupage, Glen Ellyn, Illinois, offers an associate's degree in facility management, Contact: Steve Mansfield, (630) 942-3046

Delaware County Community College, Media, Pennsylvania, offers an associate's degree in facility management technology, Contact: Larry Woodward, (610) 359-5027

DePaul University, Chicago, Illinois, offers a BA and MA with individually designed areas related to facility management. Contact: Douglas Murphy, (312) 362-8001, ext. 5756

Heriot-Watt University, Edinburgh, Scotland, offers a postgraduate diploma and an MSC in facilities management and asset maintenance, Contact: William Wallace, 011-44-131-444-9511, ext. 4647

Indiana State University, Terre Haute, Indiana, offers a BS and a specialized MS in interior design and facility management, James Landa, (812) 237-3303

London South Bank University, London, UK, offers undergraduate and graduate studies in Building Services Engineering, Contact: Graduate Clerk, 44 020 7815 7815

Michigan State University, East Lansing, Michigan offers an MA and a PhD in human environment with a concentration on facility design and management, Contact: Dana Stewart, (517) 355-7712

Mount Ida College, Newton Centre, Massachusetts offers an associate's degree in facility management, Contact: John E. Williams, (617) 928-4565

Mount Saint Vincent University, Halifax, Nova Scotia, Canada offers a bachelor of home economics with a major in housing and facility management, Contact: Margaret Ellison, (902) 443-4450

Napier University, Edinburgh, Scotland offers a MSc in facilities management, Contact: 44 13108452 60 60 40

Ngee Ann Polytechnic University, Singapore, Malaysia, offers an undergraduate diploma in Leisure and Business Facilities Management, Contact: 65 6466 6555

North Carolina A&T University, Greensboro, North Carolina offers an MS in facility management, Contact: Ronald L. Helms, (910) 334-7575

North Dakota State University, Fargo, North Dakota, offers a BS in facility management, Contact: Shauna Corry, (710) 231-8604

Polytechnic of North London, London, England offers an MA in health and facility planning, Contact: 011 44 607 2798

Rochester Institute of Technology, Rochester, New York offers an MS in facility management in distance format. Contact Dr. Abi Aghayere, Acting Department Chair, (484) 475-6664.

Royal Melbourne Institute of Technology, Melbourne, Australia offers a Masters of Project Management with a Facilities Management certificate, Contact: Ian McBean, Program Director, 613 9925 2230, ian.mcbean@rmit.edu.au

Salford University, Manchester, UK offers an MSc in facilities management, Contact: Professor Phil Roberts, Programme Director, 44 0161 295 4600, philnroberts@btinternet.com

Sheffield Hallam University, Sheffield, UK offers an MBA/PgDip/PgCert in Facilities Management, Contact: 44 0114 225 2820, ominfor@shu.ac.uk

Singapore Polytechnic, Singapore, Malaysia offers an undergraduate degree in Property and Facilities Management, Contact: C. Pannirselvam, Directr, 65 6772 1725

Texas A&M University, College Station, Texas offers an MS in facility management, Contact: David Bilbo, (409) 845-7003

University College London, London, UK offers an MSc in Facility and Environment Management, Contact: Graduate Clerk, 44 020 7679 1738, bartlett.pgclerk@ucl.ac.uk

University of Brighton, Brighton, UK offers an MSc in Facilities Management, Contact: Dr. Kassim Gidado, 44 0127 364 2394

University of Florida, Gainesville, Florida offers a BS and a MS in facility management, Contact: Felix Uhlick, (352) 392-7288

University of Greenwich, Greenwich, UK offers an MSc in Faciities Management, Contact: 44 020 8331 8000

University of Manchester, Manchester, UK offers an MA in health facilities management, Contact: Cliff Price, 011 44 061 275 2908

University of Manitoba, Winnipeg, Manitoba, Canada offers an MS in facility management through distance learning on the Internet, Contact: Christine Adams, (204) 474-7488

University of Reading, Berkshire, England offers an MS in facilities management, Contact: Admissions assistant, 011 44 073 487 5123

University of the West of England, Bristol, UK offers an MS in facility management, Contact: A.H. Spedding, Oil 44 117 965 6261

APPENDIX D

Life-Cycle
Cost Example

Life-cycle costing is a best practice that is not yet widely used in facility management. The reasons usually given are that management is only interested in first cost (a dubious excuse, if you really think about it) and that facility managers are either ill prepared or too busy to do the calculations.

Actually the calculations are relatively simple, especially when using automated spreadsheets. The more difficult task is to obtain adequate projections of the savings and costs. A facility manager with a sophisticated department is likely to be able to project into the future fairly accurately. However, often facility managers have to depend on vendors or contractors to predict costs and savings in the future for new initiatives. Even that can work well provided that the facility manager views those predictions skeptically through the prism of experience.

The example that follows was developed by Professor John Preston when he was teaching facility management at Eastern Michigan University (and for which we thank him and IFMA).[1] It is an excellent example because it develops the concept of life-cycle costing and in a facility management environment. This is an example of a fairly simple application of life-cycle costing but, in its simplicity, it should give anyone confidence that they can perform life-cycle costing. For a discussion of using automated spreadsheets for life-cycle costing, see Professor Mike Hoots's excellent article, "Dr. Spreadsheet or How I Learned to Stop Worrying and Love Financial Analysis," in the January–February 1998 issue of *FMJ, the Facility Management Journal*.

In this problem, we are faced with a decision of whether to buy more expensive but longer-lasting carpet. (Ignore the fact that in most organizations carpet is replaced after about six years because it has been cut, penetrated, and pieced during moves or has "uglied out.") We will do the same analysis twice to show the advantages and disadvantages of each. In most cases, the simple life-cycle and net present value analyses will be merely steps toward computing the average annual cost of whatever we are analyzing.

The simple life-cycle analysis table in Exhibit E-1 shows that high-quality carpet for our project costs $8,000 to purchase and $2,000 to install. Based on our records, our staff have told us that the life of that carpet is ten years, and it will cost us $1,000 ($800 labor and $200 materials) annually to maintain it to our high standards. Therefore, the total simple life-cycle cost of the high-quality carpet is $20,000 ($8,000 installation labor plus $2,000 initial carpet cost plus ten years of maintenance cost at $1,000 per year).

The same simple life-cycle analysis for regular carpet is shown in Exhibit E-2. Not unexpectedly, initial costs for regular carpet are lower, but the annual maintenance costs are higher. Intuitively, as shown here, we note that the useful life of the regular carpet is seven versus ten years for the high-quality carpet.

Based on this simple analysis, it would appear that we would recommend to management the purchase of the regular carpet. However, this simple life-cycle analysis has two major deficiencies. First, it doesn't take into account the time value of money. Second, it is not valid for comparisons of projects, or options of the same project, that have different lifetimes. These analytical deficiencies lead us to take the comparison two steps further—the first of these is to do a net present value analysis based on the simple life-cycle cost figures.

Exhibit E-1. Simple life-cycle cost for high-quality carpet (in dollars).

	Initial costs	Annual costs	Year									
			1	2	3	4	5	6	7	8	9	10
Purchase	8,000	Labor	800	800	800	800	800	800	800	800	800	800
Installation	2,000	Materials	200	200	200	200	200	200	200	200	200	200
Other	—	None	—	—	—	—	—	—	—	—	—	—
Subtotal	10,000		1,000	1,000	1,000	1,000	1,000	1,000	1,000	1,000	1,000	1,000
Total cost:	$20,000											

Exhibit E-2. Simple life-cycle cost for regular carpet (in dollars).

	Initial costs	Annual costs	Year						
			1	2	3	4	5	6	7
Purchase	6,000	Labor	1,000	1,000	1,000	1,000	1,000	1,000	1,000
Installation	2,000	Materials	250	250	250	250	250	250	250
Other	—	None	—	—	—	—	—	—	—
Subtotal	8,000		1,250	1,250	1,250	1,250	1,250	1,250	1,250
Total cost:	$16,750								

The basis for conducting a net present value analysis is the old question, "Would you prefer to have $100 now or a year from now?" Although there are several practical reasons for answering, "Today!," the economic reason is that cash in hand today can earn income for us in that interim period. Therefore, we lay out the cash flows (savings or costs) from our options under consideration and then compute their present value using an appropriate discount (interest) rate (for example, the present value of $1 after one year is $0.935, after two years is $0.873, after three years is $0.816 when the discount rate is 7 percent). We then total those discounted cash flows. The option having the highest total will have the greatest net present value. We do not discount initial costs, of course, because they occur at a time when the present value of $1 is $1.

What discount rate to use is a valid question. In larger organizations, the chief financial officer will dictate that discount rate. Absent guidance, add 2 to 3 percent for administration to the rate at which the company borrows funds for capital projects on the open market. The present values for each discount rate are available in a book of discount tables or are resident in financial calculators.

Exhibit E-3. Net present value for high-quality carpet (in dollars).

	Initial costs	Annual costs	Year 1	2	3	4	5	6	7	8	9	10
Purchase	8,000	Labor	800	800	800	800	800	800	800	800	800	800
Installation	2,000	Materials	200	200	200	200	200	200	200	200	200	200
Other	—	None	—	—	—	—	—	—	—	—	—	—
Subtotal	10,000		1,000	1,000	1,000	1,000	1,000	1,000	1,000	1,000	1,000	1,000
Annual Present Value	10,000		935	873	816	763	713	666	623	582	544	508

Exhibit E-4. Net present value for regular carpet (in dollars).

	Initial costs	Annual costs	Year 1	2	3	4	5	6	7
Purchase	6,000	Labor	1,000	1,000	1,000	1,000	1,000	1,000	1,000
Installation	2,000	Materials	250	250	250	250	250	250	250
Other	—	None	—	—	—	—	—	—	—
Subtotal	8,000		1,250	1,250	1,250	1,250	1,250	1,250	1,250
Annual Present Value	8,000		1,168	1,092	1,020	954	891	833	778

Net present value: $14,737

The two analyses for computing the net present value of the life cycles of costs for the high-quality and regular carpets are shown in Exhibits E-3 and E-4.

Since we are comparing options with two different life cycles, however, we need to take one more step. We create an equivalent average annual cost. In the case of the high-quality carpet, we divide the net present value of its costs by 10; for the regular carpet, we divide by the service life of 7 years:

$17,024/10 = $1,702.40 average annual cost for the high-quality carpet
$14,737/7 = $2,105.28 average annual cost for the regular carpet

Using this analysis, we can recommend to management that we install the high-quality carpet.

If this carpet project had to compete with others for limited funds, we would take one additional step and compute the internal rate of return to determine which among competing projects gives our company the "greatest bang for the buck" or which should be rejected because it does not generate a high enough return on our investment.

Note

1. John Preston, "Life Cycle Cost Analysis for the Beginner," in *Proceedings of the Fourteenth Annual Conference of the International Facility Management Association* (Houston: IFMA, 1993), pp. 115–124.

APPENDIX E

Synopses of Economic Studies on Sustainability

A number of studies have been completed providing overviews of costs related to sustainable buildings. The findings overall indicate that sustainable building provides economic savings, especially when considered over the full life of a building. Some premium costs have been found for design and construction of new sustainable buildings; however, those costs are lower today, now that more green products are in the marketplace, and architects, engineers, constructors, and facility managers understand the value of including all team members in the initial design phase, understanding that a sustainable building is the ultimate objective.

This list is not all inclusive but does provide sources for additional details on the economic and financial analysis of sustainability if you need further information, comparisons and ammunition to defend green building design, construction, operation, and disposal. Web links are provided where known.

Doing Well by Doing Good? An Analysis of the Financial Performance of Green Office Buildings in the U.S.A., a RICS Research Report, March 2009, by Paul Eicholz and Nils Kok, Maastricht University, Netherlands and John Quigley, University of California Berkeley, U.S.A., http://www.rics.org/NR/rdonlyres/44F67595-7989-45C7-B489-7E2B84F9DA76/0/DoingWellbyDoingGood.pdf

Energy Performance of LEED® for New Construction Buildings, FINAL REPORT, Prepared for the U.S. Green Building Council by: Cathy Turner and Mark Frankel, March 2008. https://www.usgbc.org/ShowFile.aspx?DocumentID=3930

Cost of Green Revisited: Reexamining the Feasibility and Cost Impact of Sustainable Design in the Light of Increased Market Adoption, by Lisa Fay Matthiessen and Peter Morris, July 2007. http://www.davislangdon.com/upload/images/publications/USA/The%20Cost%20of%20Green%20Revisited.pdf

National Review of Green Schools: Costs, Benefits, and Implications for Massachusetts A Report for the Massachusetts Technology Collaborative by Greg Kats, Jeff Perlman, and Sachin Jamadagni, December 2005. http://www.cap-e.com/ewebeditpro/items/O59F7707.pdf

GSA LEED® Cost Study Final Report, A Report to the U.S. General Services Administration, by Steven Winter Associates, Inc., October 2004 http://www.wbdg.org/ccb/GSAMAN/gsaleed.pdf

The Costs and Financial Benefits of Green Buildings: A Report to California's Sustainable Building Task Force, A Report to California's Sustainable Building Task Force, by Greg Kats, Leon Alevantis, Adam Berman, Evan Mills, and Jeff Perlman, October 2003. http://www.ciwmb.ca.gov/greenbuilding/Design/CostBenefit/Report.pdf

Building Better Buildings An Update on State Sustainable Building Initiatives, by the Building Sustainable Task Force and Consumer Services Agency, State of California, 2003. http://www.ciwmb.ca.gov/GreenBuilding/blueprint/2003/FullReport.pdf

The dollars and sense of green retrofits, A joint study by Deloitte and Charles Lockwood, 2008. http://www.usgbc.org/ShowFile.aspx?DocumentID=4391

Sustainable Building Fiscal/Economic Analysis, State of California, Department of Finance and Department of General Services Scope of Work to specify, design, deliver, maintain, and operate integrated sustainable buildings, 2001. http://www.ciwmb.ca.gov/greenbuilding/taskforce/Blueprint/LCCSOW.doc

"Health and Productivity Gains from Better Indoor Environments and Their Relationship with Building Energy Efficiency," by William Fisk, Lawrence Berkley National Laboratory, in *Indoor Environments,* 2000. https://www.usgbc.org/Docs/Resources/Fisk%28LBNL%29HealthandProductivityEE2000.pdf

Greening the Building and the Bottom Line: Increasing Productivity Through Energy-Efficient Design, by Joseph Romm and William Browning, Rocky Mountain Institute, 1998. http://www.rmi.org/sitepages/pid174.php

APPENDIX F

Facility Security and Emergency Best Practices

In the FM business, *Best Practice* could be interpreted as the activity identified as the most effective method of accomplishing some aspect of the mission. It is often associated with efficiency and effective cost savings. It's a target to shoot for and compare against because it minimizes problems and maximizes results. Below are a few emergency and security practices which will help you be the *best* at what you do.

1. Design chemical and biological (CB) defense systems into new buildings' construction.
2. Hold regularly scheduled physical security meetings. These meetings help keep security elevated in everyone's mind.
3. Use intelligent video, as a technical surveillance tool, which will help make preemptive decisions.
4. Information technology groups are now involved with examining how various technologies can be integrated. The demand from field representatives is to be able to link access control monitoring and visitor management control with other organization networks. The Honeywell Corporation is focused on developing a comprehensive security system that seamlessly links physical and technological security. For example, electrified locking systems are being used to lock specific access doors from one central location. This allows for immediate lockdown capability of any facility in a matter of seconds. Schools systems and higher education institutions are

looking at this technology to lockdown buildings and separate classrooms to protect against an intruder.[1]

5. Implement a Building Security Council (BSC) to promote building security. In November 2005 a group of professionals concerned about physical security established the BSC. The purpose of this council is to promote building security. Currently, the BSC is developing and "deploying a Building Security Rating System and a Building Security Certified Professional credential."[2]

6. Conduct a physical security survey of the facility. Use this survey to develop present and future facility costs for physical security implementation plans.

7. Closed circuit television cameras (CCTV) now have wireless capabilities and are connected to the organization's server. These cameras are no longer physically limited on where they can be placed.

8. Text messaging is now available wherein during a security or emergency situation a text message can be sent out to thousands of individuals in a matter of minutes. Messages can be predetermined and provide instructions on what to do and general information concerning the situation.

9. Magnetic stripe and proximity cards are currently used extensively for access. The future is the *smart card* because it contains a personal information computer chip and can be used for multiple applications. Some organizations are exploring the use of *smart cards* coupled with a biometric thumb or eye scan.

10. Use Geographic Information technology to identify key security features, property, and equipment. For example, identify all fire hydrants, shut off valves, barricades, bollards, emergency phones, gate access locations, etc. on a campus by their geographic digital locations so that information can be generated immediately through the computer.

11. Budget security for the long term. It is best to project 3 – 5 years out.

12. Video surveillance allows the facility manager to tour and operate the facility remotely.

13. Develop scenarios and constantly drill and exercise emergency plans. Conducting drills and exercises can also help reduce insurance costs.[3]

14. Ensure your insurance provider has a copy of your emergency plan. It can lower the cost of your business insurance.

15. A significant finding from the 1993 bombing of New York City's World Trade Center buildings which helped save lives during the 9/11 attack was stairwells lighted for emergency egress. Install photo-luminescent tape and lights in stairwells and ensure the smoke exhaust operates.[4]

16. Plan for long distance, out of region, logistical support during the recovery period following an emergency situation. This must be included in the organization's emergency plan.

17. Cross train all facility personnel to enable them to provide critical services.
18. Have multiple means of communicating. Remember: what can go wrong, will go wrong. Have a backup plan to the FM radio and cellular systems. Satellite phones and amateur ham radios are very dependable.
19. Facility emergency plans should include facility intelligence. This information can be documented or in an easily retrievable database. It can be as extensive and as detailed as you are willing to invest time, effort, and funding. But in an emergency it will *pay for itself!*[5]
20. Building HVAC systems are vulnerable to foreign substances being introduced, especially where outside air intakes are located close to ground level. Sensors can be installed at strategic locations in HVAC systems to monitor the air for chemical or hazardous gases. If the sensor identifies a threat, gas or chemical, it informs a central control station. The control station evaluates and measures the concentration to determine if it exceeds established limits. If it does then an alarm is triggered and the HVAC system immediately shuts down.
21. Window film made specifically for safety purposes can be applied to the interior of glass and keeps the glass contained if an explosion occurs. The pieces and shards of glass are held in place instead of being dispersed as shrapnel.[6]

Notes

1. Honeywell Corporation, *Protecting Your Campus with Integrated Security Solutions,* June 2006. See www.security.honeywell.com/hsc/documents/CampusSafety_060206.pdf
2. Building Security Council. See www.buildingsecuritycouncil.org/home.html
3. Lewis, B. T., & Payant, R. P., *The Facility Manager's Emergency Preparedness Handbook,* New York: AMACOM, 2003, p.29 & 56.
4. Building Owners and Managers Association (BOMA). Kingsley Report. *Practical Industry Intelligence for Commercial Real Estate Emergency Preparedness.* Fall 2007, p. 9.
5. Lewis, B. T., & Payant, R. P., *The Facility Manager's Emergency Preparedness Handbook,* New York: AMACOM, 2003, p. 55.
6. American Society of Testing and Materials, International (ASTM), Google: ASTM Standard E 1996-05b.

APPENDIX

Backup Documents

G-1

The Facility Plan

This is a sample mid-range facility plan for a large law firm that has two office buildings (one owned, one leased) in one city. The firm plans continued growth through the period and desires to be in all owned buildings by year 5. Note: All material in brackets is editorial. Estimate approximately twelve hours to compile such a first-ever plan.

ANNEX G

June 4, 2009
Rev 1

Facility Plan
Mid-Range Business Plan (2010–2012)
Smith, Miller, Allen, Richardson and Tucker (SMART)

Approved By

Reviewed By

_____

Sandra J. Lloyd
Facility Manager

_____

Gerald S. Gruen
Controller and Planning Director

I. Introduction
   A. Introduction—The purpose of this plan is to present the impact of the SMART business plan (2010–2012) on facilities and the facilities department. In addition, the plan will highlight significant facility issues for SMART management.

   This plan considers the work plan currently in execution for 2009 and under consideration for 2010. In turn, it is the basis for the strategic facility plan 2013–2017.

II. Environment
   1. The business environment is appropriate for SMART to continue to grow during the period. [From business plan.]
   2. SMART, during the period, will phase out its tax practice, reduce its criminal practice substantially, but expand rapidly its international practice. [From the business plan.]
   3. The local environment is mixed. The manufacturing sector continues to decline, but internationally-oriented firms are the most rapidly expanding part of the economy. [From business plan.]
   4. SMART is viewed locally as highly competent but somewhat overly bureaucratic. Clients seek us for our name but not for our creativity. [From business plan.]
   5. SMART is committed to owning its operating space to control its image and the quality of its surroundings.
   6. The facilities department, during the period, must move from caretaker approach and organization to a full-service department.

III. Assumptions
   1. SMART will continue to grow during the period at a rate of 10 percent annually. [From business plan.]
   2. Space and furnishing standards will be approved, as written, by the end of this year.
   3. All staff will be in owned space by 2012, i.e., the newly planned headquarters will be ready for occupancy by November 2011. [From business plan.]
   4. New leased costs will be constant through 2010 but will increase $2/gsf in 2011. All new lease costs will absorb the cost of tenant build-out.
   5. No "rent" is charged for owned space.
   6. Av Tech Inc., will sublease space (approx. 8,000 gsf) for 2009–2010.

IV. Constraints

1. Administrative expenses [less capital] will be constrained at 5 percent growth throughout the term. [From business plan.]
2. There will be resistance to increasing staff size; consultants and contractors must be maximized.

V. Discussion

A. Presentation of Scenarios

1. Most Probable—In this scenario, the business will continue to grow throughout the period. Staff will increase at approximately 10 percent per year.

   Initially these staff increases will have to be met by leasing space near headquarters. Current leasing rates average $22/gsf until 2011, when the current overbuilt condition should dry up. Commencing in 2009 the company will be capable and desirous of subletting some space.

   During the period, the department will attempt to impose a 280 gsf/ person space standard for all space, owned or leased.

   The new building will be available for occupancy late in 2011. Some lease space will be available for release or sublet late in 2011, but it is assumed to be a trade-off for leases which will extend 1–2 months into 2012 as the new building is occupied.

   Maintenance in existing owned space will be reduced to minimum essential, commencing with 2011.

   Moves and alteration projects will be limited to those 1) needed to accommodate acknowledged growth and 2) those necessary to occupy the new building.

   Utility costs during the period are extremely difficult to predict. The Public Service Commission is likely to approve a moderate (3–4 percent) increase in the electric rate January 1, 2009. Energy management initiatives will continue to dampen the upward pressure on utility costs. The thermal storage built into the new building should reduce the utility costs approximately 8 percent.

2. Best Case (from a facilities viewpoint)—In this case, SMART will construct two new buildings: the new headquarters plus an approximate 150,000 gsf building contiguous to it, to be complete for occupancy in 1995. This smaller building will be used for two purposes 1) gradually absorbing the long-term growth of the firm and 2) generating income through leases.

While it is estimated that this scenario will require two additional staff, this building should pay for itself in four years (occupancy rate = 85 percent) and assist in paying for the new headquarters.

3. Worst Case (from a facilities viewpoint)—The worst case (which is still credible) would be a failure to get management agreement on imposing a space standard, a corporate headquarters growth rate of 15 percent, and slippage of the completion of the headquarters for one year. Each or any of these situations, while not probable, is possible.

B. Impacts on/of Programs for Each Scenario

1. Most Probable Case

    a. Financial display at attached Financial Display, Most Probable Scenario.

    b. Implementation of this scenario will have several very *positive impacts* upon SMART and the facilities department.

        1) Implementation of space standards

        2) Elimination of leasing

        3) Provision of adequate space plus room for growth

        4) Ability to provide workplace standards to increase productivity

        5) Ability to eliminate asbestos and radon concerns

        6) Ability to better accommodate office technology

        7) Continuing to implement energy management, particularly thermal storage

        8) Reduction in long-range churn

C. Negative Impacts

        1) Capital expenditure

        2) Higher than average short-term churn

1. Best Case

    a. Positive Impacts

        1) Same as Most Probable Case

        2) Capital costs will be offset by lease income

        3) Long-term space needs met

    b. Negative Impacts

        1) Slight increase in staff

        2) Company is into the landlord business

2. Worst Case

    a. Positive Impacts—None

    b. Negative Impacts

        1) Lease costs will be both higher and longer lasting

        2) Capital costs likely to be higher

      3) Space will continue to be inconsistently assigned

      4) Expansion space, built into the new headquarters, will disappear 50 percent faster than planned

      5) Possible difficulties in getting current leases extended without paying a penalty

VI. Conclusion—Despite the advantages of the Best Case Scenario, there is a strong sense within the corporation 1) to stop any growth in non-legal staff and 2) not to become a major landlord.

VII. Recommendation—Implement the Most Probable Scenario.

Facility Plan, 1992–1994

Financial Display
Most Probable Scenario

		2010	2011	2012
a.	Capital ($K)	15,000	12,000	——
b.	Annually Funded Nondiscretionary ($K)	767	791	3,455
c.	Annually Funded Discretionary ($K)	850	975	350
d.	Lease Costs ($K)	3,934	4,740	——
e.	Lease Income ($K)	(56)	——	——
f.	Overhead Costs ($K)	1,600	1,700	1,900
g.	Space Needs (GSF)	388,800	422,400	408,800

G-2
Capital Budget Request

FUND: NAME & CODE	CAPITAL (300)	AGENCY: NAME & CODE		PROJECT JUSTIFICATION & SCOPE OF WORK
				RECREATION (HA)

PROJECT NAME	PROJECT NUMBER
Outdoor Lighting Improvements	RIG

PROJECT LOCATION
Various Locations

PROJECT JUSTIFICATION

The Department of Recreation is requesting $600,000 in additional authority to renovate and replace outdoor lighting at its recreation centers. This project will continue work started in fiscal year 2010. Some of the department's most popular evening activities are severely handicapped because outdoor lighting systems are obsolete and in some cases inoperative for long periods of time. The lack of adequate outdoor lighting because of deteriorating fixtures and breakage causes many evening activities to be cancelled. When play is attempted on badly lighted fields, players are in danger of injury. The department's lighting system includes a great variety of types and sizes of lighting fixtures, making standardization of purchase of parts and repairs impossible.

A survey of the lighting system undertaken in 2010 has revealed that previous estimates of renovation and replacement costs are too low. This project will supplement the FY 2010 authorization for field lights and permit its extension to security and playcourt lights, as well.

OPERATING BUDGET IMPACT

This project will result in operating budget savings as more energy-efficient fixtures are installed and as maintenance and replacement procedures can be standardized.

IMPACT ON THE COMMUNITY

This project will not displace homes or businesses. Benefits to the community will be increased safety and security at recreation centers by having better lighting for evening activities. Redesign of lighting fixtures will also, in some cases, reduce the impact of field lights on adjacent residential areas by directing light away from residences

more efficiently. The project is consistent with two goals of the 1981 Comprehensive Recreation Plan: "to provide the highest level of service for the least possible cost" and "to achieve and maintain efficient use of energy. . . ."

SOURCES OP REVENUE FOR THE REQUESTED PROJECT

The project will be funded by general obligation bonds to be issued by the City government.

SCOPE OP WORK

This project will allow the continuation of the installation of a fully efficient and standardized system of outdoor lighting at all Recreation Department properties. Based on the survey and lighting plan being prepared in FY 2010, field, playcourt, and security lights will be renovated or replaced with the most effective and cost-effective lighting available. Whenever possible, existing wiring systems and light standards will be used. Highest priority will be given to sites with the highest level of activity and the highest potential for continued or increased activity.

CAPITAL PROJECT SCHEDULE—REVENUE & EXPENDITURE SUMMARY 3 CAP

FUND:	CAPITAL (300)	AGENCY:	RECREATION (HA)		
NAME & CODE		NAME & CODE			

PROJECT NAME	PROJECT NUMBER	WORD(S)	PROJECT IS:		
Outdoor Lighting Improvements	RIG	DW	☐ NEW CONSTRUCTION ☒ RENOVATION ☐ REPAIRS		

PROJECT LOCATION		ESTIMATED COMPLETION DATE	NUMBER OF SQUARE FEET	USEFUL LIFE (YEARS)
Various Locations		2016	NA	15

PROJECT BUDGET AUTHORITY

PHASE	FY 2011 City Request	FY 2011 Federal Grant(s)	Prior City Authority	Prior Federal Grant(s)	Future City Request	Future Federal Grant(s)	Total City Authority	Total Federal Grants	Estimated Total Authority (City + Federal)
Site	---						---		---
Design	72						72		72
Project Management	48						48		48
Construction	480						480		480
Equipment	---						---		---
TOTAL AUTHORITY	600						600		600

Allocations of Expenditures Based on FY 2011 Total Capital Authority

FISCAL YEAR	GENERAL FUND	BONDS/LOANS	GRANTS	TOTAL
FY 2011		100		100
FY 2012		100		100
FY 2013		100		100
FY 2014		100		100
FY 2015		100		100
FY 2016		100		100
FY 2017		---		---
FY 2018		---		---
FY 2019		---		---
TOTAL		600		600

Supplementary Project Information

If grant funded, name the grantor:

Project is related to:	Objective of project is to:	Land ownership:
☐ Infrastructure	☐ Restore Service	☐ Private
☒ Public Facilities	☐ Expand Service	☐ Federal
☐ Institutions	☒ Enhance Service	☒ City
☐ Land Acquisition	☐ Comply with Court Order or Statute	☐ Not Applicable
☐ Major Equipment	☐ Stimulate Economic Development	
	☐ Other	

Will the project cause the relocation of individuals or businesses?

☐ Yes
☒ No

Number: _____

See CAP 4 for further information

G-3

Comparison of Outcomes Using Different Capital Project Analysis Alternatives

The type of capital project analysis used will influence the outcome. Here are the different project rankings possible using various analysis tools. The cases are hypothetical alternative uses of an enterprise's capital.

Example Projects for Comparison of Analysis Alternatives

Net investment	Project A $120,000		Project B $75,000		Project C $75,000	
Year	Profit	Cash Flow	Profit	Cash Flow	Profit	Cash Flow
1	$ 20,000	$ 44,000	$ 30,000	$ 45,000	$ 10,000	$ 25,000
2	30,000	54,000	30,000	45,000	20,000	35,000
3	70,000	94,000	30,000	45,000	40,000	55,000
4	100,000	124,000	30,000	45,000	60,000	75,000
5	100,000	124,000	30,000	45,000	85,000	100,000
Totals	$ 320,000	$ 440,000	$ 150,000	$ 225,000	$ 215,000	$ 290,000
Averages	$ 64,000	$ 88,000	$ 30,000	$ 45,000	$ 43,000	$ 58,000

The following summary of various analysis alternatives applied to the three projects shown above illustrate the sometimes conflicting results you might obtain:

	Project		
	A	B	C
Net investment	$120,000	$75,000	$75,000
Average annual:			
Profit	64,000	30,000	43,000
Cash flow	88,000	45,000	58,000
Project total:			
Profit	320,000	150,000	215,000
Cash flow	440,000	225,000	290,000

Analysis alternatives (ranking shown in parentheses):

	Project					
	A		B		C	
Average rate of return	107%	(2)	80%	(3)	115%	(1)
Average payback period	1.36 yrs	(2)	1.67 yrs	(3)	1.29 yrs	(1)
Actual payback period	2.23 yrs	(2)	1.67 yrs	(1)	2.27 yrs	(3)
Net present value with:						
Cost of capital 15%	$153,446	(1)	$75,847	(3)	$101,967	(2)
Cost of capital 20%	$118,197	(1)	$59,578	(3)	$78,324	(2)
Internal rate of return	50.9%	(3)	52.8%	(1)	51.0%	(2)

If your criteria are:

	Select		
	A	B	C
(1) Getting invested cash back as quickly as possible	Second	First	Third
(2) Containing the highest net present value of future cash flows	First	Third	Second
(3) Getting invested cash back within 1.5 years	(No project meets criteria)		

As the examples illustrate, the criteria used dictate the selection and the analysis technique. In most companies, both the method of analysis and the time period (three, five, ten years) is set by the CFO or controller.

G-4

Moving Instructions for Staff

I. Preface

The following information and instructions have been prepared to assist staff members in preparation for their move to new offices.

II. General Information
A. Cartons—Packing cartons may be obtained through the Move Management Office by submitting Form 17 a week prior to the move.
B. Moving Labels—Labels for tagging cartons, office machines, and all loose items to be moved may also be secured by telephoning the Move Management Office, ext. 72346, or by requesting them on Form 17 a week prior to the move.
C. Office Layout Drawing—It would be most helpful to the facilities staff and moving contractor if staff members would complete a rough sketch of their new office layouts and affix it to their office door in the new office area prior to the move. Please note layouts must adhere to existing room conditions in regard to telephone and electrical outlets. If in doubt, contact your Facilities Project Manager. The drawing need not be exact. Movers will be available on the first workday after the move to rearrange furniture as directed by staff members.
D. Packing and Unpacking Services—It is the responsibility of staff members being relocated to pack and unpack their offices and work stations. Moving services will provide movers to assist with packing and unpacking services only in special instances where approval is obtained from the Move Manager. Examples are information centers, etc.

III. Packing Instructions
A. Personal Items—Neither Moving Services nor our moving contractor will assume responsibility for personal items.

B. Cartons—Be sure each carton is assembled properly. The carton supplied
    does not require sealing tape.

    A two-inch space left at the top of the box is required in order to close the
    inter-locking flap properly. Cartons should be tagged or marked in space
    provided on each end of box.

    If instruction in assembling or marking cartons is needed, contact your
    Move Coordinator.

C. Contents (All Items)—Pack all contents from drawers and top of desk.
    Small items—pens, paper clips, pencils, and rubber bands are best placed
    in envelopes, and packed in the box.

    All items should be in boxes. Any items which will not be in boxes but must
    be moved should be reported to the Move Coordinator before the move.

D. File Cabinets, Uprights—These types of files DO NOT have to be emptied.
    (Remove all breakables from drawers). The drawer "backup plate" should
    be pulled forward in order to compress contents and hold in place. Cabinets
    will be moved in an upright position. Lock cabinets if possible and remove
    key. Cabinets should be locked or the drawer taped.

E. Lateral File Cabinets—This type of cabinet must be emptied of all contents.
    (Cabinet construction—false bottom, sliding tracks, thin metal fronts and
    sides, etc., do not permit moving contents intact).

F. Bookcase—Pack all contents, drop shelves to bottom of bookcase, and
    remove pegs or clips. (Pack in envelopes and place in carton).

G. Storage or Supply Cabinets—Pack all contents in cartons. Cabinet doors
    should be locked or taped closed.

H. Coat Racks—Remove hangers and pack in carton.

I. Office Machines—Do not pack typewriters, desk-size adding machines,
    and calculators. Remove cover and pads and pack these in carton.
    Unplug and center carriage. Wrap cord around carriage. Tag machines
    on front surface. Small calculators and dictating machines should be
    packed carefully in carton.

J. Pictures, Maps, Chalk or Bulletin Boards—Wherever possible pack pic-
    tures in cartons back to back and on end (do not lay flat in cartons). Each
    item should be tagged. Consolidation of pictures within an office is
    encouraged. Leave carton opened. Bank maintenance staff will be avail-
    able the day following the move to rehang pictures and maps.

    Large items—tag and leave in place. Movers will handle as is. Tag plastic
    chair mats. (These items should be reported to the Move Coordinator
    prior to the move).

K. Map or Plan or Special File Cabinets—Contact the Move Management
    Office (ext. 72346) for special instructions.

L. Office Technology Equipment—It is the responsibility of all staff to transfer files to a CD prior to the move. In general this equipment can be moved without further servicing. If you have a question contact User Services at 32121. Contact Copying Services, ext. 73738, to move all copiers.

Notify Moving Services for advice on making appropriate arrangements for all special equipment (CPUs, printing equipment, etc.).

M. Plants (live or artificial)—Moving contractors are not responsible for transporting staff members' personal plants.

Plants for common areas will, in general, remain there. If they are to be moved, the Project Manager will make the arrangements.

IV. Tagging and Marking

Your Move Coordinator has layouts of the assigned new office space—names, floors, room numbers, etc. Check drawings for your room or area.

Each item to be moved must be tagged with a properly color-coded tag. A crayon or magic marker should be used for marking on the tags. Do not type or use ballpoint pen or pencil in marking tags. Print clearly and as large as possible.

All items of furniture, equipment, and cartons should be marked with the same information. Show name, letter prefix followed by room number for the principal room in which items are to be placed (i.e., A-800). The prefix "O" will designate the area outside the principal office, such as the administrative assistant or reception area (i.e., O/A-800).

A. Location of Tags—A uniform tagging systems is most important to the movers locating various offices and placing items in them.

B. Please refer to attachment "A," where to place tags on furniture, boxes, and equipment.

C. Certain items, such as metal shelving, conference tables, "L" units from administrative assistant desks, need to be dismantled for moving. Be sure to tag each piece. For shelving, tag at least 10 pieces of shelving and all uprights, ends, or posts.

V. After the Move

Packing boxes should be broken down flat, and stacked in central locations (near elevators, if possible) for removal from the floors by the movers. Please note that these cartons are re-usable, and should not be taken from premises for personal use.

VI. Information or Advice

All requests for information or advice regarding moving procedures should be addressed through your Move Coordinator to the Moving Management Office.

G-5

A Maintenance and Repair Program

Management Function	Maintenance and Repair (M&R) Element
Planning and Programming	• Inventory of facilities (input)
	—By category
	—By condition
	—Highlight critical deficiencies
	—Pickup "new finds"
	• Categorization of work (input)
	• Standards (input)
	—Timeliness
	—Quality
	—Work
	• Condition assessment (input)
	—Trends
	—Critical deficiency trends
	—Adverse impacts
	• Priorities (input)
	—By activity
	—By class
	—By critical deficiency
	• Annual work plan (product)
	• Mid-term plan (product)
Budgeting	• Budget guidance sets the tone
	• Flows from the work plan
	• Budget process
	• Cost accounting must initially be considered

Management Function	*Maintenance and Repair (M&R) Element*
	• Impact of capital budget —Design to maintain —Life-cycle costs to be optimized; not simply capital costs • Comparison to target range of percentage of current replacement value (CRV) • Historical trend comparison • Comparison to current budget year • Impact statements if inadequate • Definition of requirements —By activity —By criticality • Eliminate leakage of funds —By definition —By migration • Submission often "banded" to meet multiple funding scenarios
Organizing	• Organizational models are available • Lines of responsibility must be clear • Placement of program is important • Material management has an impact • Analysis capability needed in large organizations • "Submeter" facilities for comparison
Staffing	• Quality, technical competence • Quantity • Contract vs. in-house mix • Training • Leadership • Inspection
Directing	• Priorities set in budget cycle • Work management and coordination (the key) • Appropriate level of design needed • Rapid response to crises • Some provision for necessity to react • Allocation of budgets to subactivities —Ability to execute

Management Function	*Maintenance and Repair (M&R) Element*
	—Criticality
	—Provide specific guidance
	• Contracting strategy
	• Condition assessment
	• Commissioning periods/procedures for new buildings to reduce maintenance
	• Automate diagnostics
Controlling	• Approval levels
	• Control of budget
	• Control of finances
	• Management information systems (MIS)
	• Accountability
	• Ability to react to crises, new priorities, or end-of-year windfalls
	• Documentation
Evaluating	• Comparators
	• Condition assessment
	—Critical deficiency trends
	—Total deficiency trends
	• Work management system
	• Comparison with historical data
	• Field assessment
	• Customer feedback

G-6

Maintenance Schedule

Interior PM

	Inspection	Repair	Comments
Cafeterias/Dining Rooms	Weekly	IROAN*	
President's Dining Room	Weekly	IROAN	Major cleaning done annually in coordination with his office.
Carpet	Quarterly	IROAN	Cleaning done by custodial services; carpet in common areas inspected weekly.
Major Conference Rooms/ Auditoriums	Weekly	IROAN	
Elevator Interiors	Weekly	IROAN	Replace carpet annually.
Exterior of Building	Annually	IROAN	Clean building every five years; plan to recaulk every 10 years.
Floors	Quarterly	IROAN	
Hallways and Stairs	Weekly	IROAN	
Lobbies	Weekly	IROAN	
Occupied Areas (3)	Quarterly	IROAN	Priority to owned space.
Restrooms	Weekly	IROAN	
Roofs, Patios, Sidewalks, Garages, Exteriors	Semi-Annually	IROAN	Plan roof replacement every 15 years.
Venetian Blinds	Quarterly	IROAN	

*Note: IROAN = Inspect repair only as necessary.

591

Fire/Life Safety PM

	Inspection	*Repair*	*Comments*
Aiphone System	Annually	IROAN	
Fire Alarm System	Quarterly	IROAN	
Smoke Detectors	Semi-Annually	IROAN	
Pull Stations/Bells	Annually	IROAN	
P.A. System	Semi-Annually	IROAN	
Access Control	Semi-Annually	IROAN	
Door Guard	Semi-Annually	IROAN	There is also a weekly check by security.
Duress Alarm	Monthly	IROAN	
Laser System	Semi-Annually	IROAN	
Security Video Equipment	Semi-Annually	IROAN	
Surveillance Cameras	Semi-Annually	IROAN	
Transponder Cabinet	Semi-Annually	IROAN	
Autoterms	Semi-Annually	IROAN	
Motion Detectors	Quarterly	IROAN	
Temperature Sensors	Quarterly	IROAN	

Furniture PM

	Inspection	*Cleaned*	*Repair*	*Comments*
Lobbies	Weekly	Quarterly	IROAN	
Cafeterias/Dining Rooms	Weekly	Monthly	IROAN	Cleaned daily by food service contractor.
Board Room	Weekly	Quarterly	IROAN	
Executive Directors' Offices	Quarterly	Quarterly	IROAN	
Office and Systems	Quarterly	Quarterly	IROAN	

Note: All furniture is replaced only as necessary.

Electrical PM

	Inspection	*Repair*	*Comments*
Disconnects	Annually	IROAN	Thermograph.
Floor Panels	Annually	IROAN	Thermograph.
Main Panels	Annually	IROAN	Thermograph.
Service Units	Annually	IROAN	This includes copy rooms, print shop, computer rooms, etc.
Switchboards	Three Years	IROAN	Thermograph, cleaning, testing.
Transformers	Quarterly	IROAN	Thermograph, grounding, ventilation cleaning.

G-7

Space Forecasting
Survey Form

Senior Management Overview
(To be completed prior to the interview)

I. Business Plan

   A. Is the organization likely to grow?

      1. Five-year percentage   _____

      2. Ten-year percentage   _____

      3. By year 2000   _____

      4. Comments   _____

   B. What services or markets will be added?

   C. What are the market forces that will:

      1. Encourage growth?

      2. Limit growth?

II. Organization Structure

   A. What new organizational units will be needed?

   B. What current organizational units:

      1. Will grow?

      2. Will become less important?

   C. What new types of personnel will be required?

   D. Will the current personnel skills, mix change substantially?

   E. Comments.

III. Strategic Facility Outlook

   A. Describe what image our facilities should project.

     1. To outsiders, particularly our client.

     2. To our staff.

   B. How comfortable are you with the image of our current facilities, particularly your own?

   C. As we grow, ownership of our facilities is an option that we must consider. On a rating of 0 (do not favor ownership) to 7 (strongly favor ownership), where do you rate us? _____ Comments: _____

IV. Special Facilities. On a rating of 0 (oppose) to 7 (strongly favor), how do you rate the importance and desirability of the following commonly desired corporate special facilities?

   A. Auditorium _____

   B. Training facilities _____

   C. Medical facility _____

   D. Newstand or bookstore _____

   E. Coffee stations _____

   F. Take-out food facilities _____

   G. Employee cafeterias _____

   H. Employee dining rooms with table service _____

   I. Reserved dining rooms for client business _____

   J. Lounges _____

   K. Fitness center with shower facilities _____

   L. Swimming pool _____

   M. Jogging or walking track _____

   N. Library _____

   O. Free parking _____

   P. Guaranteed parking on a pay deduction or commercial basis _____

   Q. High-tech conference room(s) _____

   R. A main lobby that "makes a statement" _____

   S. An art program _____

   T. Other (Specify) _____

   U. Other (Specify) _____

   V. Other (Specify) _____

   W. Comments: _____

V. Location

    A. Should we remain in the metro area?

    B. Will regionalization occur?

    C. Must some element of the headquarters remain in a downtown location? If so, what and where?

    D. If we moved totally, or in part to a suburban location, rank-order (0—not important; 7—extremely important) the following factors concerning location:

        Current employee home locations _____

        Closeness to mass transportation system (bus or rail) _____

        Rental/construction site _____

        Parking _____

        Local amenities _____

        Other (Specify) _____

        Other (Specify) _____

        Which of these factors do you consider the most important?

    E. If we relocate, what will be the triggering event? When do you feel it will occur?

    F. Do you favor relocation in the near future? Ever?

    G. Comments:

G-8

Real Estate Tracking System

Owned Property—Pages 1–2
Leased Property—Pages 3–6

This form was developed by Edmond P. Rondeau and is representative of the type of automated real estate tracking systems available.

OWNED PROPERTY INPUT SHEET

R.E. FILE NO: PAGE 1

SECTOR --------|__|
COMPANY NO. ------------|__|__|__| IS THIS A
STATE ----------|__|__| PERMANENT
EXCHANGE NO. -----------|__|__|__|__| DATE SUBMITTED: SURPLUS APPROVAL: EASEMENT?
BLDG. NO. ---|__|__|__|__|
PARCEL NO. ----------------|__|__| |__|__|/|__|__|/|__|__| (Y/N) |__| (Y/N) |__|

• •

PROPERTY INFORMATION

LOCATION
NAME: |__|__|__|__|__|__|__|__|__|__|__|__|__|__|__|__|__|__|__|__|__|__|__|__|__|__|__|__|__|__|__|__|__|__|__|__|__|__|__|
SECTOR/
DIVISION: |__|__|__|__|__|__|__|__|__|__|__|__|__|__|__|__|__|__|__|__|__|__|__|__|__|__|__|__|__|__|__|__|__|__|__|
PROPERTY
ADDRESS: |__|__|__|__|__|__|__|__|__|__|__|__|__|__|__|__|__|__|__|__|__|__|__|__|__|__|__|__|__|__|__|__|__|__|__|

           |__|__|__|__|__|__|__|__|__|__|__|__|__|__|__|__|__|__|__|__|__|__|__|__|__|__|__|__|__|__|__|__|__|__|__|

CITY: |__|__|__|__|__|__|__|__|__|__|__|__|__|__|__|__|__|__|__|__|__|__|__| STATE: |__|__| ZIP: |__|__|__|__|__|

COUNTY: |__|__|__|__|__|__|__|__|__|__|__|__|__|__|__|__|__|__|__|__|__|__| COUNTRY: |U|S|A|__|__|__|__|__|__|__|

NUMBER OF FLOORS: |__|__| (COUNTRY DEFAULT IS <u>USA</u>)

LOCATION MANAGER: |__|__|__|__|__|__|__|__|__|__|__|__|__|__|__|__|__|__|__|__|__|__|__|__|__|__|__|__|__|__|__|__|__|

              AREA CODE: | | | | TELEPHONE: | | | |-| | | | | EXTENSION: |__|__|__|__|__|

LEGAL REVIEW BY: |__|__|__|__|__|__|__|__|__|__|__|__|__|__|__|__|__|__|__|__|__|__|__| DATE: |__|__|/|__|__|/|__|__|

FINANCIAL REVIEW BY: |__|__|__|__|__|__|__|__|__|__|__|__|__|__|__|__|__|__|__|__|__|__|__| DATE: |__|__|/|__|__|/|__|__|

A/R REQUIRED (Y/N) |__|;   A/R APPROVED (Y/N) |__|;   IL ONLY (Y/N) |__|;   IF Y, DATE: |__|__|/|__|__|/|__|__|
TOTAL ACREAGE:
LAND: |__|__|__|__|__|__|__|__|__| · |__|__| BUILDING: |__|__|__|__|__|__|__|__||SQ. FT.   OTHER: |__|__|__|__|__|__|__|

TYPE OF FACILITY: |__|__|__|__|__|__|__|__|__|__|__|__|__|__|__|__|__|__|__|__|__|__|__|__|__|__|__|__|__|__|__|__|
                                                             SURVEY/PLOT
TOPO AVAILABLE (Y/N) |__| DATE: |__|__|/|__|__|/|__|__| PLAN AVAILABLE (Y/N) |__| DATE: |__|__|/|__|__|/|__|__|

APPRAISED VALUE: $ |__|__|__|__|__|__|__|__|__|__|__| · |__|__| APPRAISAL DATE: |__|__|/|__|__|/|__|__|
PICTURES   ZONING
AVAILABLE (Y/N) |__| JURISDICTION: |__|__|__|__|__|__|__|__|__|__|__|__|__| ZONED: |__|__|__|__|__|__|__|__|__|

INSURANCE COVERAGE: |__|__|__|__|__|__|__|__|__|__|__|__|__|__|__|__|__|__|__|__|__|__|__|__|__|__|__|__|__|__|__|__|__|__|

              |__|__|__|__|__|__|__|__|__|__|__|__|__|__|__|__|__|__|__|__|__|__|__|__|__|__|__|__|__|__|__|__|__|__|

PROPERTY TAXES: LAST YEAR |__|__|/|__|__|/|__|__| $ |__|__|__|__|__|__|__| · |__|__|

              LAST YEAR |__|__|/|__|__|/|__|__| $ |__|__|__|__|__|__|__| · |__|__|

              LAST YEAR |__|__|/|__|__|/|__|__| $ |__|__|__|__|__|__|__| · |__|__|

continued . . .

R.E. FILE NO: **OWNED PROPERTY INPUT SHEET**   PAGE 2

|_| · |_|_|_| · |_|_| · |_|_|_|_| · |_|_|_|_| · |_|_|

• •

TITLE INFORMATION

DEED   DEED BOOK
DATED: |_|_|/|_|_|/|_|_| RECORDED: |_|_|/|_|_|/|_|_| VOLUME: |_|_|/|_|_|/|_|_| PAGE: |_|_|_|_|

TOTAL PURCHASE PRICE: $ |_|_|_|_|_|_|_|_|_|_| · |_|_| PURCHASE DATE: |_|_|/|_|_|/|_|_|

BOOK VALUE: LAND: $ |_|_|_|_|_|_|_|_|_| · |_|_|

      IMPROVEMENTS: $ |_|_|_|_|_|_|_|_|_| · |_|_| DATE: |_|_|/|_|_|/|_|_|

GENERAL WARRANTY: (Y/N) |_|;   SPECIAL WARRANTY: (Y/N) |_|;   QUITCLAIM: (Y/N) |_|;   GRANT: (Y/N) |_|

TITLE INSURANCE: (Y/N) |_| AMOUNT: $ |_|_|_|_|_|_|_|_|_|_| · |_|_|

PURCHASER: |_|_|_|_|_|_|_|_|_|_|_|_|_|_|_|_|_|_|_|_|_|_|_|_|_|_|_|_|_|_|_|_|_|_|_|_|_|_|_|_|_|

              |_|_|_|_|_|_|_|_|_|_|_|_|_|_|_|_|_|_|_|_|_|_|_|_|_|_|_|_|_|_|_|_|_|_|_|_|_|_|_|_|_|

SELLER: |_|_|_|_|_|_|_|_|_|_|_|_|_|_|_|_|_|_|_|_|_|_|_|_|_|_|_|_|_|_|_|_|_|_|_|_|_|_|_|_|_|

              |_|_|_|_|_|_|_|_|_|_|_|_|_|_|_|_|_|_|_|_|_|_|_|_|_|_|_|_|_|_|_|_|_|_|_|_|_|_|_|_|_|

        EASEMENT(S) AT PURCH. (Y/N) |_| IF YES, SEE DEED;   EASEMENTS AFTER PURCH. (Y/N) |_| IF YES, SEE FILE.

• •

GENERAL INFORMATION

GENERAL
COMMENTS: |_|_|_|_|_|_|_|_|_|_|_|_|_|_|_|_|_|_|_|_|_|_|_|_|_|_|_|_|_|_|_|_|_|_|_|_|_|_|_|_|_|

             |_|_|_|_|_|_|_|_|_|_|_|_|_|_|_|_|_|_|_|_|_|_|_|_|_|_|_|_|_|_|_|_|_|_|_|_|_|_|_|_|_|

             |_|_|_|_|_|_|_|_|_|_|_|_|_|_|_|_|_|_|_|_|_|_|_|_|_|_|_|_|_|_|_|_|_|_|_|_|_|_|_|_|_|

             |_|_|_|_|_|_|_|_|_|_|_|_|_|_|_|_|_|_|_|_|_|_|_|_|_|_|_|_|_|_|_|_|_|_|_|_|_|_|_|_|_|

             |_|_|_|_|_|_|_|_|_|_|_|_|_|_|_|_|_|_|_|_|_|_|_|_|_|_|_|_|_|_|_|_|_|_|_|_|_|_|_|_|_|

             |_|_|_|_|_|_|_|_|_|_|_|_|_|_|_|_|_|_|_|_|_|_|_|_|_|_|_|_|_|_|_|_|_|_|_|_|_|_|_|_|_|

             |_|_|_|_|_|_|_|_|_|_|_|_|_|_|_|_|_|_|_|_|_|_|_|_|_|_|_|_|_|_|_|_|_|_|_|_|_|_|_|_|_|

             |_|_|_|_|_|_|_|_|_|_|_|_|_|_|_|_|_|_|_|_|_|_|_|_|_|_|_|_|_|_|_|_|_|_|_|_|_|_|_|_|_|

• •

DIV. APPROV/DATE: |_|_|_|_|_|_|_|_|_|_|_|_|_|_|_|_|_|_|_|_|_|_|_|_|_|_|_| , |_|_|/|_|_|/|_|_|;

SECT. APPROV/DATE: |_|_|_|_|_|_|_|_|_|_|_|_|_|_|_|_|_|_|_|_|_|_|_|_|_|_|_| , |_|_|/|_|_|/|_|_|;

CORP. APPROV/DATE: |_|_|_|_|_|_|_|_|_|_|_|_|_|_|_|_|_|_|_|_|_|_|_|_|_|_|_| , |_|_|/|_|_|/|_|_|.

• •

USER DEFINED INFORMATION

(ONE HUNDRED TEN USER DEFINED FIELDS FOR USER CODES AND USER DEFINED INFORMATION HAVE BEEN PROVIDED)

R.E. FILE NO: **LEASED PROPERTY INPUT SHEET**   PAGE 3

SECTOR------|__|
COMPANY NO.------------|__|__|__|
STATE NO.-----|__|__|
EXCHANGE NO.------|__|__|__|__| DATE SUBMITTED:
BLDG. NO.----|__|__|__|__|
PARCEL NO.------------------|__|__| |__|__|/|__|__|/|__|__|

LEASE/
GROUND LEASE/
EASEMENT:
(L/G/E) |__|

NEW LEASE/
EXTENSION/
RENEWAL:
(L/E/R) |__|

VACANCY
APPROV.:
(Y/N) |__|

SUBLESSORS:

(Y/N) |__|

• •

PROPERTY INFORMATION

LOCATION
NAME: |__|__|__|__|__|__|__|__|__|__|__|__|__|__|__|__|__|__|__|__|__|__|__|__|__|__|__|__|__|__|__|__|__|__|__|__|__|__|__|__|__|

SECTOR/
DIVISION
(LESSEE): |__|__|__|__|__|__|__|__|__|__|__|__|__|__|__|__|__|__|__|__|__|__|__|__|__|__|__|__|__|__|__|__|__|__|__|__|__|__|

PROPERTY
ADDRESS: |__|__|__|__|__|__|__|__|__|__| | | |__|__|__|__|__|__|__|__|__|__|__|__| NUMBER OF FLOORS: |__|__|

|__|__|__|__|__|__|__|__|__|__|__|__|__|__|__|__|__|__|__|__|__|__|__|__|__|__|__|__|__|__|__|__|__|__|

CITY: |__|__|__|__|__|__|__|__|__|__|__| | | |__|__|__|__|__|__|__|__|__| STATE: |__|__| ZIP: |__|__|__|__|__|

COUNTY: |__|__|__|__|__|__|__|__|__|__|__|__|__|__|__|__| COUNTRY (DEFAULT IS): |U|S|A|__|__|__|__|__|__|__|__|

LOCATION MANAGER: |__|__|__|__|__|__|__|__|__|__|__|__|__|__|__|__|__|__|__|__|__|__|__|__|__|__|__|__|__|__|__|__|

AREA CODE: |__|__|__| TELEPHONE: |__|__|__| - |__|__|__|__| EXTENSION: |__|__|__|__|

LANDLORD
(LESSOR): |__|__|__|__|__|__|__|__|__|__|__|__|__|__|__|__|__|__|__|__|__|__|__|__|__|__|__|__|__|__|__|__|__|__|__|__|

|__|__|__|__|__|__|__|__|__|__|__|__|__|__|__|__|__|__|__|__|__|__|__|__|__|__|__| | | | | |__|__|

ADDRESS: |__|__|__|__|__|__|__|__|__|__|__|__|__|__|__|__|__|__|__|__|__|__|__|__|__|__|__|__|__|__|__|__|__|

|__|__|__|__|__|__|__|__|__|__|__|__|__|__|__|__|__|__|__|__|__|__|__|__|__|__|__|__|__|__|__|__|__|

|__|__|__| | |__|__|__|__|__|__|__|__|__|__|__|__|__|__|__|__|__|__|__|__|__|__|__|__|__|__|__|

CITY: |__|__|__|__|__|__|__|__|__|__|__|__|__|__|__|__|__|__|__|__| STATE: |__|__| ZIP: |__|__|__|__|__|

AREA CODE: |__|__|__| TELEPHONE: |__|__|__| - |__|__|__|__| EXTENSION: |__|__|__|__|

TYPE OF FACILITY: |__|__|__|__|__|__|__|__|__|__|__|__|__|__|__|__|__|__|__|__|__|__|__|__|__|__|__|__|__|

LEGAL REVIEW BY: |__|__|__|__|__|__|__|__|__|__|__|__|__|__|__|__|__|__|__|__|__| DATE: |__|__|/|__|__|/|__|__|

FINANCIAL REVIEW BY: |__|__|__|__|__|__|__|__|__|__|__|__|__|__|__|__|__|__|__|__| DATE: |__|__|/|__|__|/|__|__|

A/R REQUIRED (Y/N) |__|;   A/R APPROVED (Y/N) |__|;   IL ONLY (Y/N) |__|;   IF Y, DATE: |__|__|/|__|__|/|__|__|

OWNERS REPRESENTATIVE: |__|__|__|__|__|__|__|__|__|__|__|__|__|__|__|__|__|__|__|__|__|__|__|__|__|__|__|__|__|

AREA CODE: |__|__|__| TELEPHONE: |__|__|__| - |__|__|__|__| EXTENSION: |__|__|__|__|

LEASING AGENT: |__|__|__|__|__|__|__|__|__|__|__|__|__|__|__|__|__|__|__|__|__|__|__|__|__|__|__|

AGENT'S REPRESENTATIVE: |__|__|__|__|__|__|__|__|__|__|__|__|__|__|__|__|__|__|__|__|__|__|__|__|__|__|__|__|

AREA CODE: |__|__|__| TELEPHONE: |__|__|__| - |__|__|__|__| EXTENSION: |__|__|__|__|

R.E. FILE NO: **LEASED PROPERTY INPUT SHEET**   PAGE 4

|__| - |__|__|__| - |__|__| - |__|__|__|__| - |__|__|__|__| - |__|__|

• •

RENT
PAYMENT
PAYABLE TO: |__|__|__|__|__|__|__|__|__|__|__|__|__|__|__|__|__|__|__|__|__|__|__|__|__|__|__|__|__|__|__|__|__|__|__|__|__|__|__|__|__|

          |__|__|__|__|__|__|__|__|__|__|__|__|__|__|__|__|__|__|__|__|__|__|__|__|__|__|__|__|__|__|__|__|__|__|__|__|__|__|__|__|__|

RENT |__|__|__|__|__|__|__|__|__|__|__|__|__|__|__|__|__|__|__|__|__|__|__|__|__|__|__|__|__|__|__|__|__|__|__|__|__|__|__|__|__|
PAYMENT
ADDRESS: |__|__|__|__|__|__|__|__|__|__|__|__|__|__|__|__|__|__|__|__|__|__|__|__|__|__|__|__|__|__|__|__|__|__|__|__|__|__|__|__|__|

          |__|__|__|__|__|__|__|__|__|__|__|__|__|__|__|__|__|__|__|__|__|__|__|__|__|__|__|__|__|__|__|__|__|__|__|__|__|__|__|__|__|

          |__|__|__|__|__|__|__|__|__|__|__|__|__|__|__|__|__|__|__|__|__|__|__|__|__|__|__|__|__|__|__|__|__|__|__|__|__|__|__|__|__|

CITY: |__|__|__|__|__|__|__|__|__|__|__|__|__|__|__|__|__|__|__|__|__|__|__| STATE: |__|__| ZIP: |__|__|__|__|__|
CORRESPONDENCE
NOTIFICATION
ADDRESS: |__|__|__|__|__|__|__|__|__|__|__|__|__|__|__|__|__|__|__|__|__|__|__|__|__|__|__|__|__|__|__|__|__|__|__|__|__|__|__|__|__|

          |__|__|__|__|__|__|__|__|__|__|__|__|__|__|__|__|__|__|__|__|__|__|__|__|__|__|__|__|__|__|__|__|__|__|__|__|__|__|__|__|__|

          |__|__|__|__|__|__|__|__|__|__|__|__|__|__|__|__|__|__|__|__|__|__|__|__|__|__|__|__|__|__|__|__|__|__|__|__|__|__|__|__|__|

CITY: |__|__|__|__|__|__|__|__|__|__|__|__|__|__|__|__|__|__|__|__|__|__|__| STATE: |__|__| ZIP: |__|__|__|__|__|

• •

LEASE TERMS

LEASE DATES
EFFECTIVE: |__|__|/|__|__|/|__|__| **OCCUPANCY:** |__|__|/|__|__|/|__|__| **TERMINATION:** |__|__|/|__|__|/|__|__|
TOTAL
INITIAL TERM: **YEARS:** |__|__| **MONTHS:** |__|__|__|__| **DAYS:** |__|__|__|__| **HOLDOVER:** |__|__|__|__|__|__|__|__|

OPTIONS? (Y/N) |__|;   **IF YES, NUMBER OF OPTION PERIODS:** |__|__| **FOR YEARS PER OPTION:** |__|__|
 # OF DAYS NOTICE   **PURCHASE**
REQUIRED: |__|__|__|__|;   **OPTION FOR OTHER SPACE? (Y/N)** |__| **IF Y, SEE LEASE;**   **OPTION? (Y/N)** |__|

       OPTION BEGINS: **OPTION ENDS:**   **OPTION EXERCISE NOTIFICATION SENT TO LANDLORD:**

1. |__|__|/|__|__|/|__|__| |__|__|/|__|__|/|__|__| **(Y/N) ?** |__|;   **IF YES, DATE:** |__|__|/|__|__|/|__|__|

2. |__|__|/|__|__|/|__|__| |__|__|/|__|__|/|__|__| **(Y/N) ?** |__|;   **IF YES, DATE:** |__|__|/|__|__|/|__|__|

3. |__|__|/|__|__|/|__|__| |__|__|/|__|__|/|__|__| **(Y/N) ?** |__|;   **IF YES, DATE:** |__|__|/|__|__|/|__|__|

4. |__|__|/|__|__|/|__|__| |__|__|/|__|__|/|__|__| **(Y/N) ?** |__|;   **IF YES, DATE:** |__|__|/|__|__|/|__|__|

OPTION INFORMATION: |__|__|__|__|__|__|__|__|__|__|__|__|__|__|__|__|__|__|__|__|__|__|__|__|__|__|__|__|__|__|__|__|__|

                        |__|__|__|__|__|__|__|__|__|__|__|__|__|__|__|__|__|__|__|__|__|__|__|__|__|__|__|__|__|__|__|__|__|

                        |__|__|__|__|__|__|__|__|__|__|__|__|__|__|__|__|__|__|__|__|__|__|__|__|__|__|__|__|__|__|__|__|__|

                        |__|__|__|__|__|__|__|__|__|__|__|__|__|__|__|__|__|__|__|__|__|__|__|__|__|__|__|__|__|__|__|__|__|

                        |__|__|__|__|__|__|__|__|__|__|__|__|__|__|__|__|__|__|__|__|__|__|__|__|__|__|__|__|__|__|__|__|__|

                        |__|__|__|__|__|__|__|__|__|__|__|__|__|__|__|__|__|__|__|__|__|__|__|__|__|__|__|__|__|__|__|__|__|

                        |__|__|__|__|__|__|__|__|__|__|__|__|__|__|__|__|__|__|__|__|__|__|__|__|__|__|__|__|__|__|__|__|__|

R.E. FILE NO: **LEASED PROPERTY INPUT SHEET** PAGE 5

|_| · |_|_|_| · |_|_| · |_|_|_|_| · |_|_|_|_| · |_|_|

• •

RENT/PENALTY: |_|_|_|_|_|_|_|_|_|_|_|_|_|_|_|_|_|_|_|_|_|_|_|_|_|_|_|_|_|_|_|_|_|_|_|_|

CANCELLATION

PENALTY: |_|_|_|_|_|_|_|_|_|_|_|_|_|_|_|_|_|_|_|_|_|_|_|_|_|_|_|_|_|_|_|_|_|_|_|

DEPOSIT ? (Y/N) |_|, IF YES, AMOUNT $ |_|_|_|_|_|_|_| · |_|_| PARKING PER 1000 SQ.FT. |_|_| · |_|_|

UPFIT ALLOWANCE ? (Y/N) |_|, IF YES, AMOUNT $ |_|_|_|_|_|_|_|_|_|

FLOORS LEASED: |_|_|_|_|_|_|_|_|_|_|_|_|_|_|_|_|_| DATE OF AGREEMENT: |_|_|/|_|_|/|_|_|_|_|

• •

RENTAL INFORMATION

TOTAL

LEASE COMMITMENT: $ |_|_|_|_|_|_|_|_|_|_|_| · |_|_| RATE PER RENTABLE SQ.FT./YR: $ |_|_|_| · |_|_|

BASE RENT

PAYMENT PER MO.: $ |_|_|_|_|_|_|_|_|_|_| · |_|_| OPERATING EXPENSE PER MO.: $ |_|_|_|_|_|_|_| · |_|_|

COMMON AREA

MAINT. PER MO.: $ |_|_|_|_|_|_| · |_|_| OPTION PERIOD COST: $ |_|_|_|_|_|_|_|_|_|_| · |_|_|

OPTION PERIOD COST INFO.: |_|_|_|_|_|_|_|_|_|_|_|_|_|_|_|_|_|_|_|_|_|_|_|_|_|_|_|_|_|_|_|_|_|

AREAS (SQ.FT.)

TOTAL: |_|_|_|_|_|_|_|_|_| OFFICE: |_|_|_|_|_|_|_|_|_| WAREHOUSE: |_|_|_|_|_|_|_|_|_|

PRODUCTION: |_|_|_|_|_|_|_|_|_| NET RENTABLE: |_|_|_|_|_|_|_|_|_| NET USABLE: |_|_|_|_|_|_|_|_|_|

COMMON

AREA FACTOR: |_|_|% PROPERTY AREA: |_|_|_|_|_|_|_|_|_|_| SQ. FT. OR |_|_|_|_|_|_|_|_| ACRES

ADDITIONAL AREA AFFECTED BY: OPTION: |_|_|_|_|_|_|_|_|_|_| SQ. FT.; LAND: |_|_|_|_|_|_|_|_|_| ACRES

ESCALATION CLAUSE ? (Y/N) |_|

ESCALATION TERMS: |_|_|_|_|_|_|_|_|_|_|_|_|_|_|_|_|_|_|_|_|_|_|_|_|_|_|_|_|_|_|_|_|

|_|_|_|_|_|_|_|_|_|_|_|_|_|_|_|_|_|_|_|_|_|_|_|_|_|_|_|_|_|_|_|_|

|_|_|_|_|_|_|_|_|_|_|_|_|_|_|_|_|_|_|_|_|_|_|_|_|_|_|_|_|_|_|_|_|

|_|_|_|_|_|_|_|_|_|_|_|_|_|_|_|_|_|_|_|_|_|_|_|_|_|_|_|_|_|_|_|_|

|_|_|_|_|_|_|_|_|_|_|_|_|_|_|_|_|_|_|_|_|_|_|_|_|_|_|_|_|_|_|_|_|

|_|_|_|_|_|_|_|_|_|_|_|_|_|_|_|_|_|_|_|_|_|_|_|_|_|_|_|_|_|_|_|_|

|_|_|_|_|_|_|_|_|_|_|_|_|_|_|_|_|_|_|_|_|_|_|_|_|_|_|_|_|_|_|_|_|

ESCALATION PERIODS:

BEGINS: 1. |_|_|/|_|_|/|_|_| ENDS: |_|_|/|_|_|/|_|_| RENT PER MO.: $ |_|_|_|_|_|_|_|_| · |_|_|

2. |_|_|/|_|_|/|_|_| |_|_|/|_|_|/|_|_| $ |_|_|_|_|_|_|_|_| · |_|_|

3. |_|_|/|_|_|/|_|_| |_|_|/|_|_|/|_|_| $ |_|_|_|_|_|_|_|_| · |_|_|

4. |_|_|/|_|_|/|_|_| |_|_|/|_|_|/|_|_| $ |_|_|_|_|_|_|_|_| · |_|_|

continued . . .

R.E. FILE NO: **LEASED PROPERTY INPUT SHEET**   PAGE 6

|_|-|_|_|_|-|_|_|-|_|_|_|_|-|_|_|_|_|-|_|_|

• •

BEGINS: 5. |_|_|/|_|_|/|_|_| ENDS: |_|_|/|_|_|/|_|_| RENT $ |_|_|_|_|_|_|_|_|·|_|_|
                                                               PER MO.

         6. |_|_|/|_|_|/|_|_| |_|_|/|_|_|/|_|_| $ |_|_|_|_|_|_|_|_|·|_|_|

         7. |_|_|/|_|_|/|_|_| |_|_|/|_|_|/|_|_| $ |_|_|_|_|_|_|_|_|·|_|_|

         8. |_|_|/|_|_|/|_|_| |_|_|/|_|_|/|_|_| $ |_|_|_|_|_|_|_|_|·|_|_|

         9. |_|_|/|_|_|/|_|_| |_|_|/|_|_|/|_|_| $ |_|_|_|_|_|_|_|_|·|_|_|

        10. |_|_|/|_|_|/|_|_| |_|_|/|_|_|/|_|_| $ |_|_|_|_|_|_|_|_|·|_|_|

• •

LESSEE RESPONSIBILITIES

PROPERTY TAXES BY LESSEE ? (Y/N) |_| INSURANCE BY LESSEE ? (Y/N) |_|

IF YES: LAST YEAR |_|_|/|_|_|/|_|_| $ |_|_|_|_|_|_|·|_|_| IF YES, COVERAGE: |_|_|_|_|_|_|_|_|

            THIS YEAR |_|_|/|_|_|/|_|_| $ |_|_|_|_|_|_|·|_|_| |_|_|_|_|_|_|_|_|_|_|_|_|

            NEXT YEAR |_|_|/|_|_|/|_|_| $ |_|_|_|_|_|_|·|_|_| UTILITIES BY LESSEE ? (Y/N): |_|

SERVICES INCLUDED IN LEASE: |_| |_| |_| |_| |_| |_| |_| |_| |_| |_| IF YES: |_|_|_|_|_|_|_|_|_|_|
SERVICE CODES:

            0 - NO SERVICES INCLUDED   4 - PLUMBING   7 - SIGNAGE |_|_|_|_|_|_|_|_|_|_|_|_|_|
            1 - JANITORIAL   5 - GROUNDS/C.A.M. 8 - LIGHTING
            2 - HVAC   6 - ROOFING   9 - EXTERIOR
            3 - ELECTRICAL

GENERAL |_|_|_|_|_|_|_|_|_|_|_|_|_|_|_|_|_|_|_|_|_|_|_|_|_|_|_|_|_|_|_|_|_|_|_|_|_|_|_|_|
COMMENTS:
             |_|_|_|_|_|_|_|_|_|_|_|_|_|_|_|_|_|_|_|_|_|_|_|_|_|_|_|_|_|_|_|_|_|_|_|_|_|_|_|_|

             |_|_|_|_|_|_|_|_|_|_|_|_|_|_|_|_|_|_|_|_|_|_|_|_|_|_|_|_|_|_|_|_|_|_|_|_|_|_|_|_|

             |_|_|_|_|_|_|_|_|_|_|_|_|_|_|_|_|_|_|_|_|_|_|_|_|_|_|_|_|_|_|_|_|_|_|_|_|_|_|_|_|

             |_|_|_|_|_|_|_|_|_|_|_|_|_|_|_|_|_|_|_|_|_|_|_|_|_|_|_|_|_|_|_|_|_|_|_|_|_|_|_|_|

             |_|_|_|_|_|_|_|_|_|_|_|_|_|_|_|_|_|_|_|_|_|_|_|_|_|_|_|_|_|_|_|_|_|_|_|_|_|_|_|_|

             |_|_|_|_|_|_|_|_|_|_|_|_|_|_|_|_|_|_|_|_|_|_|_|_|_|_|_|_|_|_|_|_|_|_|_|_|_|_|_|_|

             |_|_|_|_|_|_|_|_|_|_|_|_|_|_|_|_|_|_|_|_|_|_|_|_|_|_|_|_|_|_|_|_|_|_|_|_|_|_|_|_|

• •

DIV. APPROV/DATE: |_|_|_|_|_|_|_|_|_|_|_|_|_|_|_|_|_|_|_|_|_|_|_|_|_|_|_| , |_|_|/|_|_|/|_|_|;

SECT. APPROV/DATE: |_|_|_|_|_|_|_|_|_|_|_|_|_|_|_|_|_|_|_|_|_|_|_|_|_|_|_| , |_|_|/|_|_|/|_|_|;

CORP. APPROV/DATE: |_|_|_|_|_|_|_|_|_|_|_|_|_|_|_|_|_|_|_|_|_|_|_|_|_|_|_| , |_|_|/|_|_|/|_|_|.

• •

USER DEFINED INFORMATION

(ONE HUNDRED TEN USER DEFINED FIELDS FOR USER CODES AND USER DEFINED INFORMATION HAVE BEEN PROVIDED)

G-9

Service Evaluation Questionnaire

In order to improve the quality of our service, we would appreciate you spending a few minutes completing this form.

1. Our record shows that you requested service on ___/___/___ at _____:_____
   Date   Time

2. The service or repair was completed on ___/___/___ at _____:_____
   Date   Time

3. Was the repair time acceptable to you?
   a) Extremely b) Very c) Satisfied d) Somewhat e) Not
      satisfied   satisfied   satisfied   satisfied

4. Was the response time acceptable to you?
   a) Extremely b) Very c) Satisfied d) Somewhat e) Not
      satisfied   satisfied   satisfied   satisfied

5. Did the technician fix the problem to your satisfaction?
   a) Extremely b) Very c) Satisfied d) Somewhat e) Not
      satisfied   satisfied   satisfied   satisfied

6. Did the technician leave the working area neat and clean?
   Yes _____ No _____ Explain _____

7. Did the technician answer your questions satisfactorily?
   a) Extremely b) Very c) Satisfied d) Somewhat e) Not
      satisfied   satisfied   satisfied   satisfied

8. If not, did the technician refer you to another person?
   Yes _____ No _____ Explain _____

9. Which of the following best describes the technician's performance?
   a) Excellent b) Very good c) Good d) Poor e) Unacceptable

10. Are there any suggestions for improving our services?

Name: _____ Ext.: _____ Service Order Number: _____
Please return to Service Evaluation, Room _____

(This form can easily be automated to evaluate overall shop or individual qualitative performance.)

G-10

Bidder Qualification Questionnaire

Bidder: _____

By: _____

1. What year was your company incorporated? _____
   In what state or country is your company incorporated? _____
   What were your (year) _____ annual Sales? $_____
   What were your _____ annual Sales? $_____
   Is your company publicly held? Yes _____ No _____
   (If publicly held, attach your (year) _____ annual report. If privately held, attach your (year) _____ audited financial statements.)
   Has your company ever filed or petitioned for bankrutpcy? Yes _____ No _____. If yes, explain in detail the reasons why, filing date, and current status.

2. Provide the number of *full-time* employees, by category, from your local office. If no local office, list the office that would support this requirement. Enclose a work résumé of your proposed superintendent and other key personnel.

3. If your employees are represented by a collective bargaining unit, list the name of the unit and expiration date of the current agreement, and give a brief explanation of past labor problems, if any.

4. What is the average length of service your *full-time* managers have within the industry? _____ years; in your company? _____ years

5. What is the average length of service your *full-time* carpenters have within the industry? _____ years; in your company? _____ years

6. Provide three major (over $2 million annual) projects of a same or similar nature you are currently engaged in or will be by (year) _____, including project description, location, client, contact, phone number, and dollar amount.

7. Provide the two largest projects of a same or similar nature that you have accomplished in the last five years, including project description, location, client, contact, phone number, and dollar amount.

8. Provide any and all exceptions and/or variances to the specifications that your firm requests and/or is restricted from complying with.

9. Do you currently have any contracts or agreements for building supplies? Yes _____ No _____. If yes, list manufacturers and expiration dates.

10. Describe *in detail* what training you currently have in-house or under contract for your employees.

11. Describe *in detail* what experience your company had or has with _____ and include any reason(s) for termination.

12. Have you ever been terminated on a contract? Yes _____ No _____. If yes, describe *in detail*.

13. Do you currently, or within the last two years, have any staff on-site at a customer's facility performing similar services? Yes _____ No _____. If yes, list the number of personnel, company, services performed, and annual dollar scope of each.

14. Does your company have 24-hour emergency service? Yes _____ No _____. If yes, describe what services are provided.

15. Provide all current (last three years) customer references with contact and phone number, noting contracts of a same or similar nature.

16. Provide your financial reference with contact and phone number.

17. Provide your insurance reference with contact and phone number.

18. Provide your bonding reference with contact and phone number. What is your maximum bonding limit and your current available amount?

19. Describe *in detail* what your company's greatest strength is.

G-11

Contractor/Consultant Evaluation (Two-Step; Most Qualified Accepted)

Typical Phase I (Written Material) Evaluation of Contractor/Consultant[1]

		Points
1.0	Project Manager Evaluation	<u>20</u>
	1.1 Experience in project management and construction industry	10
	1.2 Size, scope, and complexity of previous projects assigned	7
	1.3 Experience in local area	3
2.0	Key Staff Qualifications	<u>10</u>
	2.1 Qualifications of key staff	6
	2.2 Stability of key staff	4
3.0	Project Experience	<u>20</u>
	3.1 Current workload	5
	3.2 Size of recent projects	5
	3.3 Customer references	5
	3.4 Similar types of projects	5
4.0	Experience and Technical Capabilities	<u>20</u>
	4.1 Stability and breadth of company	6
	4.2 Ability to perform requirements	10
	4.3 Relevant experience	4
5.0	Approach of Terms of Reference	<u>15</u>
	5.1 Anticipated approach	10
	5.2 Proposed schedule and team	5
6.0	Financial and Insurance Capabilities	<u>15</u>[2]
	6.1 Sales history	7

6.2 Financial reference	4
6.3 Insurance reference	<u>4</u>
Total	<u>100</u>

Notes: 1. Items evaluated and weights vary from bid to bid.
        2. Normally done by procurement specialist.

Typical Phase II (Short-List)
Evaluation (Written Material, Price, and Presentation)[1]

Points

1.0 Project Manager Evaluation <u>10</u>
    1.1 Experience in project management and construction industry   5
    1.2 Size, scope, and complexity of previous projects assigned   4
    1.3 Experience in local area   1

2.0 Project Experience <u>15</u>
    2.1 Project similar to this type of project in scope and size   5
    2.2 Phased projects   5
    2.3 Minimizing staff disturbance   5

3.0 Experience and Technical Capabilities <u>10</u>
    3.1 Stability and breadth of firm   5
    3.2 Customer references   3
    3.3 Relevant experience   2

4.0 Approach of Terms and Reference <u>10</u>
    4.1 Anticipated approach   5
    4.2 Proposed schedule and team   5

5.0 Presentation <u>20</u>
    5.1 Cohesiveness of firm   5
    5.2 Commitment   5
    5.3 Understanding of complex organization   5
    5.4 Understanding of role   5

6.0 Price <u>35[2]</u>
    Total <u>100</u>

Notes: 1. Items evaluated and weights vary from bid to bid.
      2. Points are calculated, normally by the procurement specialist, according to the following formula (low bidder gets 35 points):

$$\text{Contractor score (points)} = \text{Max score (points)} - \text{max score} \times \frac{(.5)(TS - LC)}{LC}$$

where:
TS = Price of contractor being evaluated
LC = Price of lowest contractor

G-12

Checklist for Rating Your Facility Management Department

The checklist has eight principal facility management activities. Beneath each is a breakdown of specific functions. According to the following definitions, place check marks in the appropriate columns to indicate where the responsibility for that function falls:

1 = **Facility Management Department**
2 = **Sister Department**—reporting to the same senior executive as does the facility management department.
3 = **Remote Department**—not reporting to the same senior executive
4 = **No Department**—no provision is made for specific functions

	1	2	3	4
A. Real Property Management				
1. Maintenance long-term property acquisition/lease program.				
2. Purchase of buildings and land.				
3. Leasing of non-owned premises for corporate use.				
4. Marketing and leasing of corporate owned or leased premises to others.				
5. Lease management.				
6. Service and management for tenants of the corporation.				
7. Cost control and financial reports.				

	1	2	3	4
B. Building Design and Construction				
1. General contracting.				
2. Construction management.				
3. Project management (for all new construction and all renovation of leasehold improvements).				
4. Architectural design.				
5. Landscape and site design.				
6. Specification of building operating systems.				
7. Upgrade programs.				
8. Engineering design.				
9. Estimating.				
10. Preparation of contract drawings and specifications.				
11. Preparation of bid packages.				
12. Bid supervision and contract award.				
13. Code compliance and contract supervision.				
14. Field supervision.				
15. Cost control and financial reports.				
C. Building Operations				
1. Operation of building operations systems.				
2. Building maintenance and repairs.				
3. Carpentry and minor renovation.				
4. Grounds maintenance.				
5. Cleaning, housekeeping, porter service.				
6. Inspection of premises.				
7. OSHA compliance.				
8. Maintaining files (plans, licenses, inspections).				
9. Security systems.				
10. Security staff.				
11. Life safety systems.				
12. Cost control and financial reports.				
D. Office Facility Planning				
1. Determining work place area standards.				

	1	2	3	4
2. Determining work place furniture and equipment standards.				
3. Specifying the common facilities.				
4. Programming long-term office space needs (2 years or longer).				
5. Programming short-term office space needs (less than 2 years).				
6. Programming future office furniture and equipment needs.				
7. Maintain office space inventory.				
8. Monitor quality of workplace environment.				
9. Space allocation to user groups and to individuals.				
10. Project management for interior layout and design.				
11. Project management for interior furniture and layout changes (non-leasehold improvements).				
12. Planning moves.				
13. Supervising moves.				
E. Interior Layout and Design				
1. Stacking and blocking plans.				
2. Layout plans.				
3. Furniture and furnishings specifications.				
4. Art program.				
5. Determine decorative standards (colors, materials, finishes).				
6. Interior design (color, finish, graphics, signage, flooring, furniture selection, fabrics, accessories).				
F. Interior Architecture and Construction				
1. Interior architecture (leasehold improvements).				
2. Estimating.				
3. Preparation of contract drawings and specifications.				
4. Preparation of bid packages and purchase orders.				
5. Bid supervision, contract award, contract supervision.				

	1	2	3	4
6. Field supervision.				
7. Cost control and financial reports.				
8. Updating of building plans following construction / renovation				
G. Office Furniture and Furnishings				
1. Purchasing.				
2. Expediting.				
3. Installation of workstations, furniture, equipment.				
4. Furniture storage.				
5. Furniture repair and maintenance.				
6. Maintaining furniture inventory records.				
7. Cost control and financial reports.				
H. Telecommunications Planning & Control				
1. Plan individual user needs and features for telephones, data terminals, other information devices.				
2. Coordinate installation.				
3. Order required electrical or other leasehold work.				
4. Maintain telephone / terminal location plans.				
5. Cost control and financial reports.				

Source: "Checklist for Rating Your Facilities Management Department," *Facilities Design & Management*, November / December 1984, pp. 114–115.

G-13

The Facility Management Checklist

Themes

Because we think they're so important, themes that seem to be essential to public or private sector facility management in organizations—small or large—bear repeating.

Recurring Themes

- *Business issues.* We must understand not only our business, but, in detail, how we affect the company/agency that we support. We must know the language of business and be able to use capital budget evaluation tools.
- *The cost of ownership.* There are initial and ongoing costs of the ownership of facilities. Management must understand and provide for those costs from planning through disposal.
- *Life-cycle costing.* As a general rule, all economic analyses and comparisons should be based on life-cycle costs. Comparisons leading to bad decisions are often made by considering capital or initial costs only.
- *Integration of services.* Consider one example: Interior illumination design may be based solely on appearance and violate the principles of a good energy management program simply because no one bothered to integrate the two services of design and operations.
- *Design for operations and maintenance.* Operators and maintainers, even if they are contractors, must be actively involved in the design review process.
- *Responsibility.* Facility management functions should be grouped into budget programs, with a manager responsible and accountable for each.
- *Cost-effectiveness.* The key is to properly identify and compare costs; comparison must be made over time.
- *Constant efficiency improvement.* Efficiency should be judged through comparators, through user feedback, and through MBWA (management by walking around).

• *In-house vs. contracting out.* There is, and will continue to be, strong support for contracting out facility management services. Each facility manager should have clearly defined in his or her own mind what functions must be controlled in-house. The manager must be willing to fight for the resources to perform those functions. Those functions are generally managerial, not technical, in nature.

• *Quality of life.* The facility manager must actively promote and protect the quality of life of the company's employees. A safe and healthful workplace is the minimum; a workplace where the facility promotes individual and group productivity should be the goal.

Philosophy

We present here a list of short themes that are particularly applicable to facility management.

- Safety is always the first concern; legality is a close second.
- Someone should be directly responsible for every physical asset and function.
- Service, service, service!
- Quality, quality, quality!
- There is a cost of ownership of facilities; it is your task to ensure that your management understands that cost in its entirety.
- Your responsibility to management is well known; concentrate on your responsibility to the employees.
- Be cost-effective in everything you do, but capture all costs in your analyses.
- If something looks like a good idea, use it on a trial basis. If it doesn't work out, change it.
- No one is right 100 percent of the time. A good, commonsense decision beats paralysis by analysis every time. Excessive dependence on quantitative measurement can be the downfall of a facility department.
- A budget is a management tool. Put personal effort into its preparation and format; monitor its execution.
- Don't mind being compared, but insist upon true comparators (quantity, quality, time).
- Every physical asset should be under life-cycle maintenance.
- When an outside consultant is used, you must define the requirement or you have lost control.
- As the design-construct cycle proceeds, changes become costlier and less effective. Contractors and consultants bring special talents to the facility department, but the facility manager must retain control.
- In the planning of major projects, engineering requirements are nearly always

understated. They are also the most costly to meet through changes at a later date. Plan for flexibility and redundancy.
- Plan with care, but always retain the capability to react.
- Cultivate lasting and long-term relationships. Develop them carefully. Any successful facility management organization is a team (staff, suppliers, contractors, consultants) and needs stronger bonding than what is provided in a least-cost contract.

FM Checklist

By now you know that we are great believers in evaluation. We evaluate constantly and expect to be evaluated. Fair, accurate, and continuous evaluation is the basis for improvement.

We provide you with a checklist that we have found valuable when giving a department an initial evaluation or the 30,000 mile checkup. Use it in good health—for yourself and for your department.

- Is there a clearly defined (regardless of name) facilities department?
- Is the department manager no further than two echelons from the CEO/agency head?
- Does the department (manager) have sufficient control over the fourteen functions of facility management?
- Is there a facilities plan to support all long- and short-range business plans? Is there an annual facilities work plan?
- Is at least one person focused on strategic facilities planning?
- Does a *knowledgeable* person make buy/lease decisions?
- Is work centrally received, coordinated, and controlled?
- Is there a preventive maintenance program in place that extends beyond the physical plant?
- Is there any energy management program in place?
- Is there a close tie among the information management, communications, and facilities departments?
- Is there good asset accountability?
- Does the department's organization reflect the need for both planning and design (proactive) and operations and maintenance (reactive)?
- Can someone in the department perform the economic analyses necessary to "sell" capital projects within the organization?
- Is there a close working relationship with the purchasing department?
- Do design, space, and engineering standards exist?
- Does the facilities budget format support good management information?

Glossary

Attempting to provide a glossary for a profession is a daunting task, particularly for facility management, with its many dimensions. We have limited this Glossary to the building functions and the financial aspects of facility management. The terms listed here have been drawn from many sources, and most are defined as commonly used in practice. For terms not listed here, try IFMA Foundation's FMpedia, http://gsishare.com/ifma/FMpedia/index.html

above building standard   Services and materials provided by a landlord that exceed those provided under the base rent and are therefore reimbursable to the landlord.

acceleration   The situation in which a contractor is forced to increase his work effort and speed in order to meet the contract completion date and avoid the assessment of liquidated damages.

access control   Physical security protective standard procedures and devices such as barriers and light used to control access to a facility.

access floor   A floor structure, normally raised over the floor slab, that allows almost unlimited access for below-floor cabling.

accessibility   A determination of the capability of a facility to permit disabled people to enter and use the room or building.

adapt   In building, to make suitable for a particular purpose by means of change or structure.

add   In building, to extend by means of new construction or by enclosing an existing structure.

adjacency diagram   A diagram documenting critical physical proximities or organizational groups, equipment, or support functions.

administrative approval   Approval that a work request has been processed correctly and that funding or level-of-effort floors or ceilings have been met.

administrative services   In facility management, services that are not building related (e.g., transportation, food service, security, reprographics).

A-E   Architectural-engineering firm. Such firms traditionally have enough in-house design capability to be the principal designers of major facilities.

AIA   American Institute of Architects

allocate   To set aside funds for a purpose.

allocations   *See* Chargeback System

allowance items   Items of materials and/or labor that the owner has the option to delete from the contract and procure directly, or allow to remain in the contract to be provided by the contractor. Alternatively, an item for which a budget amount only is specified.

alterations   Work required to change the interior arrangements or other physical characteristics of an existing facility or installed equipment, so that it may be more effectively used for its currently designed purpose, or adapted to a changed use as a result of a programmatic requirement. May include work referred to as improvements, conversion, rehabilitation, remodeling, and modernization.

ambient lighting   Surrounding light, such as that reaching an object in a room from all light sources in the room.

amortization of tenant allowances   The return to the landlord over the term of the lease of those costs included in the landlord's building standard work letter and any other costs that the landlord has agreed to assume or amortize.

amortization of tenant improvements   An agreement by the landlord to pay for above-building-standard improvements and amortize those improvements as a defined interest rate over a fixed term as additional rent.

annual plan   A plan that projects programs for twelve to eighteen months. Normally, at any one time, a facility manager will be gaining approval of next year's plan and formulating one for the out-years.

APPA   Association of Higher Education Facilities Officers

approved vendor list   A current list of vendors providing the owner with goods and services.

APWA   American Public Works Association.

arbitration   The settlement of a contract dispute by selecting an impartial third party to hear both sides and reach a decision.

area   *See* Building Area.

as-built drawing   Construction drawing revised to show changes made during the construction process, usually based on marked-up prints, drawings, and other data furnished by the contractor.

ASCE   American Society of Civil Engineers.

ASHRAE   American Society of Heating, Refrigeration and Air-Conditioning.

ASID   American Society of Interior Designers.

asset   Something, such as a building or piece of equipment, that retains value for a period of time after it is purchased and, therefore, has both an economic life and a residual value.

asset management   (1) The process of maximizing value to a property or portfolio of properties from acquisition to disposition within the objectives defined by the owner. (2) Management of real property, installed equipment, and furniture, furnishings, and equipment using automated and inventory techniques.

ASTM   American Society for Testing and Materials.

authority having jurisdiction (AHJ)   Federal, state and local agencies are responsible for protecting the public. When they arrive on site, they are in charge of operations unless other arrangements have been agreed to.

background noise   Noise in a work environment at a level low enough not to interfere with the normal conduct of business and conversation.

balance sheet   An accounting statement listing a company's total assets, total liabilities, and net worth. Capital assets are included, but operating expenses are not.

ballasts   The common term for the starting and regulating mechanism in a fluorescent light fixture.

base building   The basic building structure, including roof and exterior walls, basic mechanical and electrical systems, and the service core.

base-level services   In facilities operations, those services required to support occupancy of a facility.

baseline   A compilation of metrics to establish a starting point or current state which is used for comparison with future improvements for savings. Time forms and units of measure must be identified as valid measurement prior to gathering the metrics.

base power feeds   Electricity supplied via junction boxes in the floor of a building.

base rental   The initial rental rate, normally identified as the annual rent in a gross lease.

base year   The year of building operation, normally a calendar year, in which the landlord fixes or identifies the operating costs included in a gross or semi-net lease. Any increase in operating expenses over the base year is "passed through" to the tenant on a pro rata share of rentable area.

benchmaking   The management practice of comparison to industry best practices to improve performace and quality.

benefit-cost ratio   Benefits divided by costs, where both are discounted to a present value or equivalent uniform annual value.

best value procurement   A procurement that provides best value to the procurer by minimizing risk, that emphasizes cost, time and customer satisfaction proportionately to the desires of the procurer, and that emphasizes co-operation to meet customer needs between the procurer and the contractor.

bid   A written response to an invitation for bid.

BIM   *See* Building Information Modeling.

biometrics   Technology that stores individual information in digital form used to make comparisons. Some better known forms include fingerprint and eye scans.

blanket purchase order (BPO)   An agreement, normally for a fixed time, for a purchase of low-dollar-value goods and services from a single vendor. BPOs are designed to fill anticipated repetitive needs for small quantities of goods and/or services.

block allocation plan   A drawing showing the location of each employee group relative to other groups and the associated support areas. The block plan should be approved primarily for group locations on the floor.

BOMA   Building Owners and Managers Association.

BOMA standard measurement   A defined way of measuring space by the Building Owners and Managers Association (BOMA). Landlords may choose their own method to measure space, normally by increasing the amount of common areas added to the usable area.

BOMI Institute   A nonprofit organization devoted to providing education for property professionals.

book value   The value of an asset at a given point in its economic life based on its value on the date when first placed into service, minus any accumulated depreciation since that date.

break-even analysis   A technique for determining the value of a variable that results in savings just even to the costs.

bubble diagram   *See* Adjacency Diagram

budget   A financial plan for allocating funds during a specific time period.

building   A shelter comprising a partially or totally enclosed space, erected by means of a planned process of forming and combining materials.

building area (floor area)   A generic term referring to some aspect of the size measurement of a building. One method to characterize the subdivisions of this area is as follows:

amenity area   Any area in a facility used by employees for nonwork activity, such as dining rooms, vending areas, lounges, day care centers, and fitness and health centers.

area of penetration   The sum of the area of those physical objects that vertically penetrate the space serving more than one floor (e.g., elevator shafts).

assignable area   Floor areas of a facility designed to or available for assignment to occupant groups of functions, including interior walls, building columns, and building projections and excluding circulation.

circulation area   That portion of the gross area of a building required for physical access to various divisions and subdivisions of space.

common area   That area with common access to all users within a gross space (e.g. public corridors). Common area = Rentable area – usable area.

core and service area   Floor area of a facility necessary for the general operation that is not available for general occupancy, including primary circulation areas; mechanical, electrical, telephone, and custodial rooms serving individual floors; toilet rooms; building lobbies and atriums, stairways, elevators, vertical shafts, and chases; loading docks; and also central, mechanical, electrical, telephone, and custodial spaces and penthouses, but excluding the interstitial area.

gross area   The sum of floor areas within the outside faces of the exterior walls for all building levels that have floor surfaces.

leased rentable area   That area to which the base lease rate applies.

mechanical area   That portion of the gross area of a building designated to house mechanical equipment and utility services.

net assignable area   The sum of the floor areas available for assignment to a program occupant. By definition this excludes custodial, circulation, core, and mechanical areas.

net floor area   That part of the gross floor area located within occupiable space.

open space   The floor space inside a workstation for furniture, equipment, and internal circulation.

primary circulation area   That portion of a building that is a public corridor, lobby, or atrium; or is required for access by all occupants on a floor to stairs, elevators, toilet room, or building entrances.

secondary circulation area   That portion of a building required for access to some subdivisions of space, whether bounded by walls or not, that does not serve all occupants on a floor and is not defined as primary circulation area.

support space   Part of the usable area not assigned or dedicated to a specific task or function (e.g., meeting rooms, waiting areas, storage, lounges, computer rooms, copy areas, libraries).

usable area   The floor area of a facility assigned to, or available for assignment to, occupant groups or functions, including the interior walls, building columns and projections, and secondary circulation.

workplace   Part of the usable area intended for the individual or group to work in.

workspace   Part of the usable area intended for a specific function or type of work.

workstation   All or part of a workplace, suitable for carrying out one function or type of work.

building component   A building element using industrial products that are manufactured as independent units capable of being joined with other elements.

building construction   (1) The act or process of making or forming a building by assembly or combining elements, components, or systems. (2) The structure or part thereof so formed.

building economics   The application of economic analysis to the design, financing, engineering, construction, management, operation, or ownership of buildings.

building efficiency rate   The usable area divided by the rentable area multiplied by 100.

building envelope   Perimeter elements of a building, both above and below ground, that divide the external from the internal environment.

building information modeling (BIM)   A digital three-dimensional design and simulation model which has great potential to improve the planning and design process and to capture and provide material which will be invaluable for subsequent operations and maintenance.

building maintenance   *See* Maintenance.

building module   Standard dimensions within the usable area dictated by window mullion or column spacing (e.g., a five-foot module dictates spaces dimensioned in multiples of five feet).

building operating expense (BOE)   Expenses incident to occupying buildings and grounds that are not repair, improvement, or maintenance. Includes rent payments under leases of less than ten years; custodial services; the salaries of building operating staff; service contracts; fuel and utilities; taxes; and fire and comprehensive insurance.

building performance   The behavior in service of a building as a whole or of the building components. Often measured in terms of durability and serviceability.

building permit   A permit issued by the local government authorizing construction of a project according to plans found to comply with that government's codes.

building projection   Pilaster, convector, baseboard heating unit, radiator, or other building element located in the interior of a building wall that prevents the use of that space for furniture, equipment, circulation, or other functions.

building renewal   A term referring to the complete reworking of an entire building or of a major, discrete portion to develop a facility equivalent to a new one. It involves the complete upgrading of systems, such as heating and ventilating; it usually includes element replacement, such as a new roof or new sashes; and it may involve program and occupancy changes. At the completion of a building renewal project, the expected useful life of the building should approximate that of an entirely new facility.

Building Research Establishment's Environmental Assessment Method (BREEAM)   Sustainable guidelines for designs construction and operations of buildings used primarily in the United Kingdom and countries of the former British Empire.

building services   Services provided to ensure that the building is operable, such as heating, cooling and ventilation, and elevator services.

building standard Standard building materials and quantities provided by the landlord at no cost to the tenant to improve tenant premises.

building standard work letter A document that delineates the type and quality of materials and quantities to be furnished by the landlord as building standard.

building subsystem Complete, integrated set of parts that function as a unit within the finished building.

building system Collection of equipment, facilities, and software designated to perform a specific function.

building team The group of managers and professionals responsible for developing a broad project definition of owner's criteria and conceptual design and implementing it into a completed structure. Such teams necessarily include the owner, in varying degrees of involvement depending on his own expertise: the architect-engineer, which may be made up of one or more design consultants; and a builder, who may be a general contractor or a construction manager. The team may also include one or more construction consultants. Building teams vary in makeup principally because of variation in the required services in that portion of the project that are overlapped by the design and construction phases.

build-to-suit An approach to real estate development that enables a corporation to assume ownership by having a developer hold ownership until the project is complete and ready for occupancy. It is a form of delayed ownership.

built-up roof A roof constructed of successive layers of waterproof material sealed with a sealer such as bitumen.

business continuity plans Plans providing policies and procedures for alternative site operations or that recovery term personnel can follow to enable the restoration of vital and critical business services within the predetermined recovery time objectives.

CADD Computer-assisted design and drawing.

CAFM Computer-assisted facility management. Integrated facility management hardware and software to manage diverse facility management functions—most commonly space management, design, inventory management, work management, building operations, lease management, and financial management.

capital costs *See* Cost.

carbon footprint The total measurement of emissions or greenhouse gases caused by human processes. Typically, carbon footprint implies choices that could be made to reduce these emissions.

cash flow The stream of dollar values, costs, and savings resulting from an investment decision.

CBX A telephone switchboard that switches data and voice.

ceiling (financial) A level of funding that must not be exceeded.

ceiling plenum The space between the suspended ceiling and the floor slab above.

centrex A centralized switch controlled by the local phone company.

CERCLA Comprehensive Environmental Response, Compensation and Liability Act.

certificate of occupancy A certificate issued by a local government authorizing occupancy of a space that has been found to meet building code requirements and is considered safe for the function for which it was designed.

Certified Facility Manager (CFM) The professional designation of someone who has passed a comprehensive exam administered by the International Facility Management Association.

change order A written order from the contracting officer to the contractor modifying the quantity, quality, or method of work required in the contract.

charge A financial obligation incurred pursuant to a valid contract.

chargeback system A system of cost control that requires the requesting business unit to pay for work done in its area or for work done over and above a standard.

churn The ratio of the number of employees moved annually compared to the total employees of the organization.

CIFM (computer integrated facility management) *See* CAFM.

classes of buildings Buildings categorized by selected attributes concerning facility serviceability and performance.

clean circuit A circuit that has only one technology device connected.

clerestory A window in a wall, often extending from door top to the ceiling to allow light into the interior of a space.

closed plan An approach to designing workspace with a predominance of full-height walls and few or no panels or modular furniture.

code compliance trigger Events that necessitate the compliance of a building to current codes.

code requirements Building code requirements that must be satisfied by the tenant or the landlord in preparing space or a building for tenant occupancy. Examples are seismic, life safety, energy, hazardous/toxic materials, and handicapped code requirements.

command operations center A central location where various organizational representatives are stationed 24/7 during an emergency.

commissioning The orderly turnover of a building or major project from the contractor to the owner. Involves completing the operating tests on all major systems, the passing of all user manuals, material safety data sheets, and warranties, the passing of the as-built drawings, training for all operational personnel, agreeing on the satisfaction of all punch list items, and, in some cases, clearing the building of off-gases and ensuring initial air quality.

common area factor (rentable/usable ratio) The factor used to determine a tenant's pro rata share of the common area. CAF = rentable area/usable area.

compartmentalization A code requirement to divide large floor plates into smaller units to meet fire code requirements.

competitive range In procurement, the range of proposal bids that will be considered responsive so that other factors of the bid will be considered.

complex An organized group of two or more facilities designed to operate as a unit to achieve some programmatic end (e.g., a laboratory and a hospital).

computer-assisted drawing and drafting (CADD) system An automated drawing system that can manage space, furniture, and equipment as well as produce drawings.

computer-assisted facility management (CAFM) system A system that automates facility management functions. It commonly contains a computer-assisted drawing and drafting system, a work management system, a project management system, and an asset management system.

concessions Those inducements offered by a landlord to a tenant to sign a lease. Common concessions are free rent, extra tenant improvement allowances, payment of moving costs, and lease pickups.

concurrent delay   A delay attributable to the actions of both the contractor and the owner. Because there is joint responsibility for a concurrent delay, the contractor is generally not entitled to recover damages for the delay, and the owner is not entitled to assess liquidated damages for delayed completion of the project.

constant dollars   Dollars of uniform purchasing power exclusive of general inflation or deflation.

construction   The erection, installation, or assembly of a new facility; the addition, expansion, alteration, conversion, or replacement of an existing facility; or the relocation of a facility from one installation to another. Includes equipment installed and made a part of such facilities, and related site preparation, excavation, filling, landscaping, or other land improvements.

construction consultant   One who provides specialized professional services to the owner, architect-engineer, or general contractor. Consultant services include such broad areas as budget costing, cost estimating, major purchasing, and scheduling control or more specialized services relating to particular project needs, such as architectural concrete design, foundation construction techniques, and curtain wall specifications.

construction documents (CDs)   Drawings and specifications for a building project, along with the applicable bid and administrative documents.

construction management (CM)   The process of applying management techniques to the design and construction of a project. Generally involves coordinating the overlap of the project's design and construction phases and the activities of multiple prime building contractors.

construction manager   One who furnishes all the services of a general contracting organization, as well as all the construction consulting services necessary from the inception of project planning. As such, the construction manager has a professional services contract with the owner and provides consulting and managerial functions. He is the construction professional of the building team and is responsible for design liaison, the proper selection of materials and methods of construction, and cost and scheduling information and control. In managing the construction activities, he contracts with subcontractors and suppliers on behalf of the owner.

contingency funds   Funds allotted to cover unexpected costs that may be incurred throughout the term of a project.

contract   A consensual relationship based on the willingness of the parties (owner and vendor) to be bound by its terms. It is a promise or a set of promises, the breach of which the law gives a remedy, or the performances of which the law recognizes as a duty. An annual contract is for a twelve-month period, normally one calendar or fiscal year.

cooling load   The amount of heat that must be removed to maintain a structure at a given temperature during cooling.

contract architect   The outside design professional retained by the owner to prepare a project design—normally an architectural-engineering firm for major projects.

contract change proposal   An offer by the contractor to perform work different in quantity, quality, or method from that required by the contract. Typically includes the price of the changed work and an estimate of the time necessary to complete it.

contractor   A vendor who has entered into a contract with the owner for the construction, modification, or rehabilitation of a project.

contracts officer   A staff member of the owner's purchasing department legally responsible for the contracting of services.

contracts officer's representative (COR)   Facility staff member appointed in writing as responsible for monitoring completion of contracts according to the terms and conditions stated therein.

corporate real estate   The owned or leased real property used by a corporation in support of its business mission.

cost

> **capital costs**   The costs of acquiring, substantially improving, expanding, changing the functional use of, or replacing a building or building system. Capitalization rules are driven by tax laws, so they vary according to location.
>
> **operations costs**   Total costs associated with the day-to-day operation of a facility. Includes all maintenance and repair (both fixed and variable); administrative costs; labor costs; janitorial, housekeeping, and other cleaning costs; all utility costs; management fees; and all costs associated with roadways and grounds.
>
> **ownership costs**   The cost to the owner to own the building, service existing debt, or receive a return on equity. Also includes costs of capital improvements, repair, and upkeep, which would not be considered standard operating costs.

cost avoidances   Projected or actual costs avoided by an initiative.

cost center   An organizational unit in which budgetary funding is used to sustain operations.

cost-effectiveness   Getting best value for funds expended, not necessarily lowest cost.

cost savings   Money saved by a proposed or actual initiative that can be used for other business purposes.

costs of providing the fixed asset   Capital costs, mortgage costs, capital improvements, taxes, insurance, and depreciation charges. Does not include lease costs, security costs, or relocation or rearrangement costs.

critical path method (CPM)   A project management method using a chart that shows the minimum amount of time required to complete a project and which tasks must be completed before subsequent ones can commence (the critical path).

crossover floor   A floor in which one bank of elevators connects to another bank of elevators, allowing tenants to have access to floors in other elevator banks without returning to the lobby of the building.

CSI   Construction Specification Institute.

current dollars   Dollars of purchasing power in which actual prices are stated, including inflation or deflation.

custodial services   Commonly used to mean janitorial services, window cleaning, rodent and pest control, and waste management.

custody   Condition of items procured in connection with or for use on a project, which are stored at the site or, if stored off-site, marked in such a manner as to indicate their intended use on the project.

customer satisfaction index (CSI)   An index whereby a service organization's customer service performance is measured against an established baseline.

customer service agreements   Informal minicontracts between the facility department and its customers.

damage assessment   The evaluation of buildings, grounds, and utilities to determine whether the organization's mission will be imputed and safety jeopardized if conducted in those facilities.

day porter services   Miscellaneous services, normally custodial in nature, provided during hours that the facility is occupied (e.g., cleaning up spills, light moving, setting up meeting spaces, lobby tidying).

delegated contracting authority   The act of a contracting officer's giving limited contracting authority (e.g., a $5,000 limit) to an authorized line manager.

demising walls   The walls between one tenant's area and another, as well as walls between tenant areas and public corridors.

demolition plan   A construction drawing that delineates all demolition for an alteration project.

demountable partition   A prefabricated modular wall assembly that can be installed, removed, and reinstalled.

depreciation   The loss in value of a capital asset over its economic life.

design-build   A construction approach in which the owner buys both design and construction services from the same provider.

design development   The phase of a project consisting of preparing the drawings and specifications to fix and describe the size and character of the building systems, materials, and elements.

design program   Document specifying what facilities will be provided to the occupants and confirming to the owner the requirements of the facility.

direct charge of operating expenses   On a gross or seminet lease where the tenant does not pay costs directly, the pro rata share of occupancy costs that the landlord directly bills tenants. In most instances, this will be done on a good-faith, best-estimate, advanced-payment basis, whereby the landlord bills the tenant for estimated operating expense costs during the lease term.

discount rate   That rate of interest reflecting the investor's time value of money; used to determine discount factors for converting benefits and costs occurring at different times to a base time.

discounting   A technique for converting cash flows that occur over time to equivalent amounts at a common time.

distributed workplace arrangements   Various work places and arrangements enabled via remote technology such as virtual work, telecommuting, satellite offices, and other mobile possibilities, which enable workers to work in their most effective manner at any time.

drawings   *See* Plans.

due diligence survey   A facility survey taken before a major acquisition to validate building condition, regulatory compliance, the presence or absence of environment hazards, financial value, and other risks.

durability   The capability of a building, assembly, component, product, or construction to maintain serviceability for at least a specified period of time.

dwelling   Building designed or occupied as the living quarters for one or more families or households.

economic life   That period of time over which an investment is considered to be the least-cost alternative for meeting a particular objective.

efficiency   The percentage of rentable area that is usable area.

efficient rent   The dollar amount per square foot per year that the tenant pays on an average over the term of the lease. This would be the average of specified rents in a stair-stepped lease, as well as the average of a lease with substantial free rent period. *Example:* A five-year lease with six months' free rent offers a 10 percent discount from the face rate.

emergency management   The managerial function charged with creating the framework within which communities reduce vulnerability to hazards and cope with the disasters.

enclosed space   The floor area inside the enclosed space, measured to the inside surface of walls, major protrusions, or other surfaces that define the limit of functionally usable floor surface. Does not include the area of freestanding columns that inhibit functional use of the space or include circulation area outside the space.

engineering economics   Application of engineering, mathematical, and economic techniques to the economic evaluation of engineering alternatives.

EPA   Environmental Protection Agency.

equity   An owner's right in a property after all claims against the property have been settled.

ergonomics   Applying biologic and engineering data and techniques to solve the problems of the interface of the worker and his workplace.

errors and omissions insurance   Insurance taken by design professionals to protect themselves from liability claims arising from mistakes made in design and construction documents.

estimate   Short-form proposal from a prospective vendor for the provision of certain services.

estimating   The process of determining the cost and/or duration of an item of work. Also refers to quantity determination for materials.

evaluate   To assess the capability of a facility to perform the function(s) for which it is designed, used, or required to be used.

excess currency contract   A contract in connection with which payments are to be made solely in excess of local currency held by the government.

excusable delay   An unforeseeable delay that results from one of a number of causes specified in the contract. Since an excusable delay is not considered to be the fault of the contractor, he is entitled to a time extension for the period of the excusable delay.

expense stop   An identified dollar amount, on either a dollar per square foot per year basis or a pro rata share basis of the total operating expense cost, that the landlord is responsible to pay. Any increase over the expense stop will be allocated to the tenant.

extension of time   A period of time that extends the contractor's performance period beyond the contract completion date specified in the contract. Time extensions are granted by the contracting officer upon written request by the contractor when he has experienced an excusable delay.

fabric of a building   All the elements, components, parts, and materials of a building, at any scale and of any age.

face rate   The identified rental rate in a lease that is subsequently discounted by concessions offered by the landlord. Also called the *contract rate*.

facility   Something that is built, installed, or established to serve a purpose.

facility audit (building audit)   Identifying the physical condition, functional performance, and maintenance deficiencies of a facility to assist in long-term capital renewal and maintenance and operations planning.

facility emergency operations center (FEOC)   The facility manager's central location where the facility portion of emergency operations are coordinated 24/7.

facility evaluation   Comparison of the qualitative and quantitative results of judgment, observations, measurements, analyses, or other tests against performance criteria established for a specified purpose and to a specified precision and reliability.

facility-in-service   Facility as completed and operational.

facility intelligence   Specific emergency procedures for each individual facility. This information is collected and assembled in one location. The information contains all critical data concerning the operation of the facility (alarm systems, utilities, life safety systems, valves, electrical disconnects, etc.).

facility management (FM)   A profession that encompasses multiple disciplines to ensure functionality of the built environment by integrating people, place, process, and technology.

Facility Management Administrator (FMA)   The professional designation conferred by the BOMI Institute for those who have successfully completed the FMA curriculum.

Facility Management Professional (FMP)   A knowledge-based credential for newer facility management professionals administered by the International Facility Management Association.

facility operator   Organization or agency having a contract with the owner or investor to operate a facility.

facility performance   Behavior in the service of a facility for a specified use; for example, how effectively could an architectural firm use a renovated warehouse as a principal office?

fair market value   The rental value of space similar to the leased premises for comparison purpose in rental adjustments.

fast track   Overlapping the phases of a project to save as much time as possible.

feasibility study   Study of a planned scheme or development, the practicality of its achievement, and its projected financial outcome.

feature of a facility   A building, building element, building component, or aspects of design, arrangement, form, or color that help or hinder the satisfaction of a requirement for serviceability.

FFE   Furniture, furnishings, and equipment.

finish plan   A construction drawing that shows all new finishes keyed to the applicable specifications.

final acceptance date   The date, as determined by the project manager, in writing, and confirmed by the contracting officer, on which all items of work required by the contract have been satisfactorily completed.

final inspection date   The date on which the project manager makes a detailed inspection of the contractor's work to determine if it complies with contract requirements. During this inspection, the project manager compiles a punch list of incomplete or unsatisfactory items, which is transmitted to the contractor. This date normally coincides with the substantial completion date.

fire corridors   Special corridors with partitioning designed to create escape routes in time of fire.

fire rated   A designation for special building materials such as partitioning and doors that have been manufactured and tested to provide greater fire resistance than normal building-standard material.

first cost   Costs incurred in placing a building or system in place.

fiscal approval   The approval that verifies funds are available to complete the project.

fit-up (or fitout)   Alterations and improvements to the base building and to the building systems, including demolition, where required, to prepare the accommodation for occupancy.

flat cable   Cable designed to be used under carpet.

floor   A level of funding that must be exceeded.

floor area   *See* Building Area.

floor plate   A common term for floor size.

formal competitive bidding   A written solicitation in the form of an invitation for bid or request for proposal for procurements that are other than a telephonic solicitation or sole-source solicitation.

footprint   The working square footage required to support a particular function; often includes space for furniture as well as chair movement and circulation.

force majeure   The so-called "act of God." For example, particularly violent weather or unpredictable events such as war.

free rent   Period of time in which the tenant occupies the premises under the lease but does not pay rent.

functional program   The document that specifies functional facility serviceability requirements of the occupants and owner.

fungible   The ability to move funds from one account to another with no restrictions.

future value   The value of a benefit or a cost at some point in the future considering the time value of money.

Gantt chart   A form of bar chart used extensively to show schedules, time frames, and time sequences.

general contractor   The traditional builder who engages in the complete on-site management of the actual construction project. He performs the work by contracting on his own behalf with subcontractors and suppliers.

Global FM   The worldwide network of facility management associations.

gross lease rate   A rental rate that includes normal building standard services as provided by the landlord within the base-year rental.

guarantee (warranty) period   A period of time from the date of acceptance of goods or services in which the contractor or supplier is obligated to repair or replace goods or work done by him that proves unsatisfactory because of defective material or workmanship.

Guaranteed Maximum Price (GM4X or GMP)   A contractor's price that will not be exceeded before all contract documents, including drawings and specifications are completed.

handicapped requirement   Code-required features designed to accommodate those with disabilities. Typical areas affected are rest rooms, signage, hardware, stairs, and doors.

hard costs   In a project, the costs associated directly with construction.

hardwiring   Physically connecting using cable or wire.

heat load   The amount of heat that must be added to a structure to bring it to a certain temperature during heating.

high performance building   In the context of sustainability, an efficient, sustainable building built and/or operated to reduce energy consumption while maximizing building quality, occupant comfort, and cost-effectiveness. The U.S. Energy Department has a specific high performance building initiative with goals, objectives, and performance materials.

hours of operation

> **active hours**   Times when a facility is normally fully occupied and operational.

> **silent hours**   Period when a facility is essentially unoccupied and only security and building operations staff are present.

> **transitional hours**   Times in the morning after the first workers normally arrive, until a facility is fully operational and, in the evening, from the end of the normal workday until the occupants have left.

HVAC   Heating, ventilating, and air-conditioning systems. Those systems that control and maintain the temperature, humidity, and air quality.

IDSA   Industrial Designers Society of America.

IFMA   International Facility Management Association.

improvement   A valuable or useful addition or alteration that increases the value or changes the use of a building or property; something more than mere maintenance, repair, or restoration to the original condition.

improvement allowance   The estimated or dollar value of the building-standard work letter being offered by the landlord.

individual job order (IJO)   A category of work that is more than a work order but less than a project.

indoor air quality (IAQ)   The state of air pollutants (presence or absence) within a building.

Information and Communication Technology (ICT)   All the data and voice technologies that enable advanced computing and Internet access, as well as telephone services.

infrastructure   The basic framework for building—for example, utilities, roads, and access.

installed equipment   Equipment affixed to the owner's buildings, the maintenance of which is the responsibility of the facility manager, not a business unit manager.

integrated workplace management system (IWMS)   A theoretical but practical web-based system which could be fielded with current technology to do real estate management, lease administration, planning, design, work management, project management, procurement, and budget management while interfacing with the organization's enterprise technology such as finance, management reporting, and security. It specifically does not have the capabilities of BIM, building information modeling, as currently conceptualized.

intelligent video   Sensors and television monitors programmed to trigger an alarm to a computer when activity falls outside pre-established parameters.

internal rate of return (IRR)   The compound rate of interest that, when used to discount the terminal values of costs and benefits of a project over a given period, will make the costs equal the benefits when cash flows are reinvested at a specific rate.

intraoffice   The common area between departments and sections used for corridors, aisles, or walkways.

invitation for bid (IFB)   A written solicitation for bids normally used when the requirement is clearly and completely specified and the basis for award is principally price.

IREM   Institute of Real Estate Management.

job order contracting   Contracting for the reception, prioritization, and execution of work orders and small alteration projects.

key plan   Small-scale floor plans designed to show room locations, occupant room numbers, and occasionally telephone numbers.

land use control measures   In real estate management, plans and capital improvement budgets, zoning ordinances and master land use plans, subdivision regulations, mandatory dedications, development or impact fees, and construction codes.

landlord   One who leases rights of use of real property to a tenant.

layout   A space plan showing the locations of tenant improvements and the utilization of space by the tenant.

layout efficiency   Efficiency of the usable area to meet the tenant's work requirements, office design, employees, and so forth. Efficiency of usable area is dictated by building shape, core location, floor size, corridors, and other similar factors.

Leadership in Energy and Environmental Design (LEED)   The designation of buildings or systems which meet the U.S. Green Building Council's guidelines for sustainable design, construction, and operations.

lease   A contract between the owner of real property (lessor) and another party (lessee) for the possession and use of the property for a specified term in return for rent or other income.

>   **net lease**   Base rent plus tenant pays directly a share of real estate taxes.

>   **triple net lease**   Base rent plus tenant pays directly a share of real estate taxes, insurance, maintenance, repair, and operating costs.

>   **gross lease**   One payment in which the owner has included estimated costs of operations.

>   **long-term lease**   A lease of real property of not less than ten years.

lease buyout   A cash inducement offered by a landlord to a tenant's previous landlord or by the tenant to the current landlord to cancel the remaining term of the tenant's lease.

lease pickup   The landlord's commitment to assume the costs associated with paying a tenant's rent in premises to be vacated that are still under lease.

license agreement   A means of legalizing and formalizing the terms of a temporary occupancy of property without creating a leasehold right to occupy property for a specified period of time.

life-cycle assessment/analysis   The analysis of total cost over all phases of a building's or project's life, including design, contruction, operations, maintenance, and disposition. It encompasses the full life of the property or project and appends costs over the entire lifespan.

life-cycle costing   Process of determining (in present-value terms) all costs incident to the planning, design, construction, operation, and maintenance of a structure over time.

life safety regulations   Regulation and code requirements for buildings relative to seismic, fire, and handicapped requirements.

liquidated damages   An amount of damages on a daily basis specified in the contract. This amount will be assessed against the contractor for each day beyond the contract completion date that the project remains uncompleted.

load factor   A method of allocating common areas among tenants. That percentage of the building in which common area is allocated to tenants to increase their usable area to rentable area.

local area network (LAN)   Assemblages of cable and switches that provide an interconnecting path for the flow of information among computer, terminals, word processors, facsimile, and other office machines within a building office complex.

lump-sum contract   A contract under which the contractor agrees to do the specified work for a single, fixed price.

maintainability   Capability of a system or facility to be maintained to a specified level of reliability at a specified measure of cost or economy.

maintenance   Work necessary to maintain the original, anticipated useful life of a fixed asset. It is the upkeep of property and equipment. Includes periodic or occasional inspection, adjustment, lubrication, cleaning (nonjanitorial), painting, replacement of parts, minor repairs, and other actions to prolong service and prevent unscheduled breakdown. Does not prolong the life of the property or equipment or add to its value.

> **corrective maintenance**   Maintenance activities performed because of equipment or system failure. Activities are directed toward the restoration of an item to a specified level of performance. Sometimes called *breakdown maintenance.*

> **cyclical maintenance**   Maintenance that can be predicted and scheduled on a regular basis (cycle).

> **deferrable maintenance**   A formal or informal listing of unaccomplished maintenance tasks. Such situations arise because of shortages of funds, personnel, or specific management practices.

> **emergency maintenance**   Corrective maintenance that requires immediate action because of impending danger to the occupants, the building, or a building system.

> **normal maintenance**   Maintenance activities that occur on a reasonably regular basis.

> **predictive maintenance**   Maintenance performed as a result of testing, such as oil or vibration analysis. Partially replaces preventive maintenance for some equipment.

> **preventive maintenance (PM)**   Planned actions undertaken to retain an item at a specified level of performance by providing repetitive scheduled tasks that prolong system operation and useful life: inspection, cleaning, lubrication, and part replacement.

> **special maintenance**   Maintenance activities that, because of cost, size, and/or infrequency of occurrence, tend to fall outside the normal frame of reference.

management of real property   Space allocation that is in the best interest of the owner with regard to representation, function, and economy; the economic organization of building operation and protection services; and control of property condition through timely maintenance and repair.

master plan   A technical plan showing the proposed development of a particular piece of real property for a specific period of time, often twenty years.

midrange plan   A facility business plan that projects programs three to five years into the future.

millwork   Special architectural construction (e.g., cupboards, shelving, special wood trim).

mitigation   The reduction of potential emergency situations; a review process to determine what actions can be taken beforehand to minimize the chances of emergencies occurring.

modernize   In building, to adapt to current needs, tastes, or usage by remodeling or repair.
modular furniture   Furniture designed as a set of dimensionally standardized components. May be free-standing or systems furniture.
moves
   to existing workspace (box move)   No furniture is moved, and no wiring or new telecommunications systems are required. Files and supplies are moved.
   furniture/workstation move   Existing furniture is reconfigured and/or furniture is moved or purchased; no major new wiring or telecommunications installation is required.
   moves requiring construction   New walls, new or additional wiring or telecommunications system are required, or other construction is needed to complete the move.
moving allowance   An offer by a landlord to pay all or part of a tenant's moving costs.
MSDS (material safety data sheet)   A document required by the Occupational Safety and Health Administration to be included with certain chemicals or products that could adversely affect the environment or human health or safety.
mullion   The vertical member of a window frame. The mullion often determines the placement of full-height interior partitions that connect to the outside wall of a building.
multiyear agreements   Agreements made with vendors for goods or services for a period exceeding one year (often three years) in order to obtain favorable pricing.

NFPA   National Fire Protection Association.
notice to proceed   A written notice from the contracting officer to the contractor that authorizes the contractor to incur obligations and proceed with work on the project.
noise reduction coefficient (NRC)   The average of sound absorption coefficients for a material tested at 250, 500, 1,000, and 2,000 cycles per second; this average gives the general effectiveness of a material as a sound absorber and is expressed as a decimal. Example: A .95 NRC indicates that about 95 percent of the average sound energy striking a tested material is absorbed.

occupancy cost   The total cost incurred by a company or organization to provide space for operations. Includes all costs of operating the facility, plus the costs of providing the fixed asset.
occupancy permit   The permit that allows a facility to be used for the designed purpose.
occupant   The department, agency, corporation, or a part thereof that is or will be occupying space. An occupant has certain rights to, possession of, or control over the premises occupied.
office plans
   private offices   Offices enclosed by floor-to-ceiling walls.
   open-plan offices   Offices divided by movable partitions.
   bullpen-style offices   Offices are open with no partitions.
office space utilization rate   The number of office workers divided by the facility's total number of work spaces and multiplied by 100.
operating costs (expenses)   *See* Cost.
operating drawings   Information drawings for use in the operation of erected and installed equipment.

operational test A test designed by the owner or representative to test major mechanical or electrical items.

operations Work to keep the facility performing the function for which it is currently classified. Commonly includes the cost of utilities; heating, ventilation, and air-conditioning; work reception and coordination; moving; and work associated with building systems.

OSHA Occupational Safety and Health Administration of the U.S. Department of Labor.

outsourcing The provision of a bundle or a full range of services by a single contractor so that the facilities staff is responsible only for managing the contractor relationship and monitoring its performance.

outtasking The provision of individual services by a service provider.

overhead Administrative and indirect costs for both job site and home office incurred by the contractor in connection with work on a project. Does not include the cost of direct labor and materials.

ownership costs *See* Cost.

panels Modular furniture sections used to define the limits of a workstation. Panels do not extend floor to ceiling.

partitions Inside floor-to-ceiling structures not otherwise meeting the criteria of walls. Partitions are movable and removable.

partnering An outsourcing technique in which the owner establishes a long-term relationship with a single or small group of high-performance contractors.

pass-through costs Costs that can be directly associated with a particular project, program, or cost center.

pay request The contractor's periodic request for payment that covers work completed and materials stored at the site during the pay period.

payback method A technique of economic evaluation that determines the time required for the cumulative benefits from an investment to recover the investment cost and other accrued costs.

payback period The length of time it takes an investor to recoup the costs of a capital investment.

PBX A voice telephone switch.

performance criterion A quantitative statement of the level of performance needed to satisfy a serviceability requirement.

performance specification A document in which results are described precisely but methods to achieve them are left to the discretion of the contractor.

PERT chart *See* Gantt Chart.

physical protection Barriers that will delay or deter someone attempting unauthorized physical access to assets at a specific location.

plans (drawings/construction drawings)
>   **architectural: finish, millwork, partition**
>   **datacommunications**
>   **demolition**
>   **electrical: lighting, power**
>   **furniture**

    mechanical
    reflected ceiling plan
    telecommunications

POE (postoccupancy evaluation)   A survey taken after project completion to assess end users' level of satisfaction with the various aspects of the new working environment, as well as to check on the performance against specifications of the major systems.

portfolio   Group of securities, buildings, or other properties held by an individual or institutional investor.

power poles   Poles suspended from a ceiling or extended to the ceiling that supply electricity or communications via internal cabling.

raised flooring   A flooring system with removable panels supported by pedestals to enable cabling and air circulation beneath the usable floor. Raised flooring is frequently used in data centers, computer rooms, or other areas requiring highly reconfigurable wiring and extensive cabling.

Real Properly Administrator (RPA)   A professional designation conferred by the BOMI Institute for those who successfully complete an RPA curriculum.

rebuild   An alteration to return a building to its previous state or condition.

recapture   The billing to tenants of their pro rata share of increased operating expenses after those expenses have been incurred and paid for by the landlord.

recovery   The final phase of emergency preparedness. It starts when the emergency is under control and stabilized.

reliability   The probability of performing without failure a specified function under normal conditions for a specified period of time.

remodel   An alteration to return a building to its previous state or condition.

rent   The cost charged per rentable square foot on a monthly or annual basis for a leased area.

repair   Work to restore damaged or worn-out property to a normal operating condition. As a basic distinction, repairs are curative, and maintenance is preventive. Repair can be classified as minor or major. Major repair commonly exceeds one to two man-days of effort or exceeds the in-house capability to perform.

replacement   Work to replace an item of equipment or a building component. It is the exchange or substitution of one fixed asset for another having the capacity to perform the same function. The replacement may arise from obsolescence, wear and tear, or destruction of the item to be replaced. In general, as distinguished from repair, replacement involves a complete, identifiable item.

replacement cost   Building component replacement and related costs, included in the capital budget, that are expected to be incurred during the period studied.

request for proposal (RFP)   A written solicitation used when the owner wants the option of making an award on initial proposals or conducting discussions with the offerors.

responsive bid   A bid that meets all the terms and conditions of a solicitation.

retrofit   In building, alterations to add new materials or equipment not provided at the time of original construction.

ROA (return on assets)   The net profit after taxes divided by the total value of assets employed to generate income.

ROE (return on equity)   The net profit after taxes divided by the net worth yielding the total percentage of equity gained through an investment.

ROI (return on investment)   The total profit divided by the total amount originally invested to gain a profit.

sale-leaseback   A combination ownership-lease development method in which a company develops and completes a project and then sells it to a third party, usually a developer or property manager. The developer then executes a lease with the same company that it purchased the building from. The company, now the developer's tenant, rents and occupies the facility for the lease term.

schematic plans (schematics)   Drawings to scale that show all basic design features of a space or building but no construction details or dimensions.

serviceability   The capability of a building, assembly, component, product, or construction to perform the function(s) for which it is designed or used, or both.

service contract   Agreement for the performance of various labor-oriented services, funded on a fiscal-year basis.

service evaluation   An evaluation of service to include customer service (effectiveness and responsiveness) and efficiency.

service order   The work category of the smallest category of work. Normally no design is required.

serviceability requirement   A qualitative statement of the serviceability required from a facility.

serviceability requirements profile (SRP)   A listing of the levels of serviceability required in a facility.

shared tenant services   Services provided by a building to allow tenants to share the costs and benefits of sophisticated telecommunication and other technical services.

shelter in place   Selecting a small interior room, with few or no windows, and taking refuge there because of a hazardous materials release in the atmosphere.

shop drawings   Drawings prepared by the contractor and/or subcontractors that show the proposed method for fabricating and erecting in order to achieve the result outlined in the contract drawings.

short-term lease   A lease with a basic term of less than ten years.

short list   A list of vendors selected for further consideration following initial review of all bids.

simple payback period   The time required for the cumulative benefits from an investment to pay back the investment cost and other accrued costs, not considering the time value of money.

six sigma   A quality assessment methodology which analyzes progress in order to eliminate rework and reduce errors to a minute minimum.

smart building   A building that has additional technical capabilities to provide enhanced building management and operating efficiency.

soft costs   Costs related to the management of a project (e.g., overhead, fees, management time).

sole-source procurement   A procurement awarded to a single vendor without competition.

solicitation   A formal competitive procurement package consisting of applicable documents to obtain bids and proposals.

sound transmission class (STC)   A single-number rating determined by comparing the measured transmission loss in decibels through a partition against a standard STC contour. Denotes the reduction of intensity that occurs when sound energy passes through a barrier such as a partition (e.g., STC 40 indicates that about 40 decibels of energy are lost when a sound passes through the tested barrier).

source selection   Selecting a contractor or vendor through negotiations.

space   The generic definition of a particular enclosed area. May be a building, floor, or any other defined area. As a practical matter, a space is the area defined by the drawing for that area.

space allocation   Assigning space, normally by rank or by function.

space limits   A limit, normally physical, that defines a space (e.g., walls, partitions, panels).

space planner   The individual responsible for planning, managing, and documenting the space holdings of an agency or company.

specification   A precise statement of a set of requirements to be satisfied by a material, product, system, or service.

sprinklers   A fire-suppression system, usually water, designed into many buildings to reduce compartmentalization of space and provide additional fire protection.

stacking plans   Plans showing multiple floors of the same building, the departments occupying space, and the spaces they occupy.

staging area   Space for uncrating, assembly, and temporary storage during a project.

stair-stepped rent   A rental rate that increases by fixed amounts during the period of the lease term.

standards   The level of service or product that management is willing to fund and expects to be provided as basic.

statement of work   A document describing services to be provided by the design consultant (architect, engineer, or interior designer) for a facility in detail sufficient for the design to proceed.

stop-work order   A written order issued by the contracting officer to direct the contractor to suspend all or any part of the work.

strategic plan   The facility business plan that projects programs five to ten years for most businesses. Some facility strategic plans project three to five years.

subcontractor   A firm that enters into an agreement with the contractor to assume responsibility for a portion of the work covered by the contract.

sublease   Leasing of premises by the current tenant to another party for the remaining balance of an existing lease term.

submittal   An item that the contractor is required by the contract to submit to the project manager.

substantial completion date   The date, as determined by the project manager and confirmed by the contracting officer, on which the project is suitable for the use for which it was intended. Normally coincides with the final inspection date.

substitution and credits   The ability to substitute nonstandard or nonspecified materials as specified in a work letter or contract, or to receive dollar credits for the differential cost versus the standard or specified materials.

supplier   A firm that enters into an agreement with the department, the contractor, or a subcontractor to provide materials and/or equipment for use on a project.

support equipment environment (SEE)   The support surroundings to meet the specific needs of the operation for equipment (e.g., printers, modems, controllers).

support services   A generic term for services structured to support facility management as well as the rest of the organization such as procurement, human resources, and information technology. In very large and very small organizations, these units often report to a common manager.

suspension of work   A temporary work stoppage ordered by the contracting officer for the convenience of the owner.

sustainability   The capability to meet the demands of current users without compromising the ability of future generations to meet their needs.

swing space   Space in which occupants of space under construction can temporarily reside.

task lighting   A localized light or light system to accommodate the specific visual task or work area needs.

technical approval   Approval that a work request has received the appropriate technical review and design.

technical evaluation team   A team that includes a procurement officer, the contract officer's representative (COR), and other knowledgeable staff as may be determined by the COR and the purchasing department. This team is responsible for establishing the technical evaluation weights and criteria included in a solicitation, and reviews and evaluates the technical proposals of each fully responsive bidder in accordance with preestablished evaluation criteria.

technical operation   The operations that support the design and construction process (e.g., scheduling, cost engineering, value engineering).

technology unit   The organization that supports electronically augmented office work, terminals, modems, controllers, and so forth.

tenant   An organization that has rights and obligations of occupancy in a facility as specified in a lease or occupancy agreement.

tenant improvements   Construction alterations made to make a space suitable for occupancy by a specific tenant.

tender   Primarily a term used in the U.K. More familiar in the U.S. as a bid on an offer in response to a request for offers.

terminal use environment (TUE)   The support surrounding of a terminal designed to meet a specific purpose and function.

> **cluster**   A terminal within arm's reach of two users.
>
> **dedicated**   A terminal within arm's reach of one user.
>
> **regional**   A self-contained room with four terminals servicing an average of seven intermittent users.
>
> **satellite**   Two terminals within close proximity to four users for quick and sporadic access of information.

threat assessment   An assessment by competent authority which provides the leadership of the organization with a tool to assess probable threats, the weaknesses of the organization, and more specifically, the facility.

time and materials method   A retroactive method of change order pricing based on the contractor's verified accounting of direct costs collected as the work is actually being done.

time value of money   The time-dependent value of money stemming from both changes in the purchasing power of money (inflation/deflation) and the real earning potential of alternative investments over time.

TQM (total quality management)   Meeting or exceeding customer expectations and the system to measure performance toward that goal.

triple bottom line (TBL)   An accounting method which considers not only financial impacts but also includes environmental and social responsibility impacts. Also called people, plant, profit reporting.

turnkey   (1) A complete build-out of tenant's premises to the tenant's specifications. (2) A project totally managed outside the owner or occupant's organization but to meet their program.

two-step bidding   A variation on formal bidding used most often when price is the dominant but not the only award factor. The first step is to establish technical acceptability. In the second step, bids reveal the lowest-priced, technically acceptable offer.

underfloor ducts   A system of ducts permanently located within the floor structure to assist in the installation of telephone, datacommunications, and electrical wiring.

unit price (unit cost)   The contractor's bid or proposal price for performing a specified quantity or unit of work. Normally includes the cost of labor, material, and equipment, plus an amount of overhead and profit.

unprogrammed costs   Costs not anticipated or included in a budget but incurred, such as for an emergency repair.

useful life   The period of time over which an investment is considered to meet its original objective.

user   The generic definition of the occupant of a space. May be a tenant or a company department or an owner.

U.S. Green Building Council   A nonprofit consensus coalition of the building industry promoting the understanding of, development, and accelerated implementation of environmentally efficient buildings.

utilization rate   Net assignable area/gross area.

vacancy rate   The current vacant square footage in a facility divided by the total usable area.

value analysis   The procedure for developing and evaluating alternatives to a proposed economical design that best fulfills the needs and requirements of the owner/user of a building.

value engineering   Evaluation of construction methods and/or materials to determine which have the net result of reducing cost, consistent with specified performance, reliability, maintainability, aesthetic, safety, and security criteria.

VAV system   Variable air volume system. A system that allows great flexibility for controlling how air is distributed within a building.

vendor evaluation report   A written document for a specific vendor detailing the satisfactory or unsatisfactory performance area ratings calculated in the vendor evaluation system.

vendor evaluation system   A system that evaluates vendor performance in the areas of delivery, quality, and compliance with contract provisions.

video display terminal (VDT)   The screen and keyboard, often detachable, of a computer.

virtual emergency operations center (VEOC)   A web-based application which links the normal facility work reception center, security operations, and other emergency service providers with their customers, organizational management, and responders. The VEOC, can be accessed globally, but is simply the activation of normal operations during an emergency which precludes the necessity to have unfamiliar channels and procedures during an operation because the responders and their management use it daily.

visitor   A person present who is not an occupant of a facility.

Volatile organic compounds (VOC)   Gases emitted from certain solids and liquids that have negative impacts to health.

white noise   Background, random-frequency noise used to mask high-frequency sounds, such as the consonants in human speech.

work   The completed construction required by the contract. In a multiple prime contractor situation, the work will not be synonymous with the project.

work letter   A written attachment to the lease that specifies the types, quantities, and qualities of fixtures and finishes that will be provided as standard by the landlord.

work order   *See* service order.

workplace (office) solutions

    flexspace   A combination of dedicated offices and shared team space. The offices are laid out to stress privacy or openness and flexible work arrangements.

    floating office   An office whose location is determined by the changing location of its occupant. A floating office is the antithesis of assigned office space.

    free address   Offices exist but are available on a first-come-first-served basis. Communications are wireless, and storage is mobile and limited.

    name-based and shared offices   Offices are reduced in size, and more space is devoted to team space.

    just-in-time space   Shared office or group space whose use must be scheduled.

    shared/assigned space   Office and group space is assigned but its use is unscheduled. Lack of scheduling allows conflicts over space to occur.

work reception center   The facilities department unit responsible for receiving, organizing, and prioritizing work requests. It is the place that customers call for facility services. Should also be the center of customer service evaluation.

zero-based budgeting   A budgeting approach whereby each budget is prepared as if the current year were the first year such a budget was prepared. Each line and requirement must be justified from a zero base.

zones   The identified portions of a building served by the heating, ventilation, and air-conditioning system that have separate controls.

Index